PROCEDURAL ENVIRONMENTAL RIGHTS:
PRINCIPLE X IN THEORY AND PRACTICE

European Environmental Law Forum Series, Volume 4

PROCEDURAL ENVIRONMENTAL RIGHTS: PRINCIPLE X IN THEORY AND PRACTICE

Edited by

Jerzy Jendrośka
Magdalena Bar

intersentia
Cambridge – Antwerp – Portland

Intersentia Ltd
Sheraton House | Castle Park
Cambridge | CB3 0AX | United Kingdom
Tel.: +44 1223 370 170 | Fax: +44 1223 370 169
Email: mail@intersentia.co.uk
www.intersentia.com | www.intersentia.co.uk

Distribution for the UK and Ireland:
NBN International
Airport Business Centre, 10 Thornbury Road
Plymouth, PL6 7 PP
United Kingdom
Tel.: +44 1752 202 301 | Fax: +44 1752 202 331
Email: orders@nbninternational.com

Distribution for Europe and all other countries:
Intersentia Publishing nv
Groenstraat 31
2640 Mortsel
Belgium
Tel.: +32 3 680 15 50 | Fax: +32 3 658 71 21
Email: mail@intersentia.be

Distribution for the USA and Canada:
International Specialized Book Services
920 NE 58th Ave. Suite 300
Portland, OR 97213
USA
Tel.: +1 800 944 6190 (toll free) | Fax: +1 503 280 8832
Email: info@isbs.com

Procedural Environmental Rights: Principle X in Theory and Practice

Cover image: Joseph Sohm – Shutterstock

ISBN 978-1-78068-610-3
D/2017/7849/39
NUR 823

British Library Cataloguing in Publication Data. A catalogue record for this book is available from the British Library.

CONTENTS

INTRODUCTION

PROCEDURAL ENVIRONMENTAL RIGHTS IN THEORY AND PRACTICE

Jerzy JENDROŚKA

The importance of procedural environmental rights is currently widely recognised. They serve not only as a guarantee of the right to environment and a tool to increase participatory democracy and active involvement of the public in environmental protection but also as an effective instrument of monitoring compliance with – and enforcement of – environmental law. Following recognition of their importance, procedural environmental rights have increasingly been acknowledged in legal frameworks at the national, supranational and international level. The first comprehensive approach to procedural environmental rights at the international level was undertaken when access to information, public participation in decision making and access to justice in environmental matters were codified in Principle X of the Rio Declaration. Although the Rio Declaration belongs to the instruments of so called 'soft law' (i.e. having not binding legal nature but only a form of recommendations or political declarations) Principle X is commonly considered to be significant as a clear global expression of the developing concepts of the role of the public in relation to the environment. It was soon after its adoption acknowledged as an international benchmark against which the compatibility of national standards could be compared and as a forecast of the creation of new procedural rights which could be granted to individuals through international law and exercised at the national and possibly international level.[1]

The binding international standard in relation to procedural environmental rights was set with the adoption in 1998 in the Danish city of Aarhus of the UNECE Convention on access to information, public participation in decision making and access to justice in environmental matters (Aarhus Convention). Since then a number of legal instruments regulating procedural environmental rights have been developed or are in the process of development at the national, supranational (regional) and international level.

1 *P. Sands*, Principles of International Environmental Law, Manchester University Press, Manchester/ New York, 1995, p 99.

The role of the Aarhus Convention for the development of procedural environmental rights is well acknowledged in the academic literature, It is described as "the first multinational environmental agreement that focuses exclusively on obligations of the nations to their citizens and nongovernmental organizations"[2], and the first binding international instrument attempting to comprehensively and exclusively address issues of citizens' environmental rights.[3] Furthermore, it is considered to be a "driving force for environmental democracy" in Europe[4], and "at the forefront" of developing the legal framework in this respect worldwide.[5]

A number of academic studies have been already devoted to the Aarhus Convention. There were special issues of academic journals devoted to the Aarhus Convention[6] and also monographic books covering the Convention and its role in a very comprehensive manner – like the seminal collection of extensive essays issued to mark the 10th anniversary of the adoption of the Convention.[7]

The current book is about procedural environmental rights but it is not focused on the Aarhus Convention. It presents a monographic collection of contributions, each subject to double peer review process, selected with a view to provide in a structured manner the overview of the current research regarding the experience gained with the adoption and implementation of the procedural environmental rights under the various legal instruments. Following this aim the book provides an insight into the various aspects of procedural environmental rights ranging from theoretical issues of global application to practical problems at local level, from comprehensive analysis of particular legal instruments to commenting line of developments of jurisprudence or specific findings in particular judgements.

The concept of this book assumes going far beyond presenting merely the issues related to environmental procedural rights in Europe – as the issue has also been already well covered in the literature. There have been academic articles attempting to provide a stock-taking of the situation with procedural environmental rights in

2 *S. Kravchenko*, The Aarhus Convention and Innovations in Compliance with Multilateral Environmental Agreements Compliance Mechanisms, in Yearbook of European Environmental Law, Cambridge U. Press, volume 7, 2007, see also *S. Kravchenko and J. Bonine*, Human Rights and the Environment: Cases, Law, and Policy, Carolina Academic Press, 2008, p. 220.

3 See *J. Jendroska and S. Stec*, The Aarhus Convention: Towards a New Era in Environmental Democracy, Environmental Liability, Vol 9 Issue 3, June 2001, p. 148.

4 *J. Wates*, The Aarhus Convention: a Driving Force for Environmental Democracy, JEEPL Vol 2, Number 1.

5 *J. Ebbeson*, Public participation, (in) The Oxford Handbook of International Environmental Law, D. Bodansky, J. Brunnee and E. Hey, Oxford University Press, 2007, p 686.

6 Like for example a special 'Aarhus issue" – JEEPL Volume 2 Number 1 – JEEPL 1/2005.

7 The Aarhus Convention at Ten. Interactions and Tensions between Conventional International Law and EU Environmental Law, ed. M. Pallemarts, Europa Law Publishing, Groningen 2011.

Europe[8], and recently the entire monograph was published about the role of the Aarhus Convention in making "the new European legal culture".[9]

The book *Procedural Environmental Rights: Principle X in Theory and Practice* is a joint effort of scholars representing different legal cultures from different continents to collect and compare the experience gained with the adoption and implementation of the procedural environmental rights in different jurisdictions and under the various legal instruments.

The contributions to this monograph are clustered under the 7 headings presenting various aspects of the current status, development and practice of rights of access to information, public participation in decision making and access to justice in environmental matters following their codification as non-binding principles in Principle X of the Rio Declaration.

The first heading is devoted to presenting the status and some of the current developments related to procedural environmental rights. Stephen Stec in his chapter (Developing Standards for Procedural Environmental Rights Through Practice: The Changing Character of Rio Principle 10) presents the role of the two leading instruments in this sphere (Aarhus Convention in the region of UNECE and Bali Guidelines globally) in the context of Sustainable Development Goals and emerging challenges like climate change and rise of populism and the backlash against public participation in decision-making in general.

Also the next chapter (The Evolution of Participatory Rights in the Era of Fiscal Austerity and Reduced Administrative Burden by Jukka Similä) presents the developments of procedural environmental rights in the context of yet another challenges: those resulting from horizontal policies aiming at reducing administrative burden by deregulation.

Finally, the third contribution under this heading (Definitions of the Aarhus Convention v. the proposal for a new Latin America and the Caribbean instrument: mapping the differences in the material scope of procedural environmental rights in international law by Juliana Zuluaga Madrid) is devoted to the draft Regional Agreement on Access to Information, Participation and Justice in Environmental Matters in Latin America and the Caribbean (so called Regional LAC Agreement on Principle X). It presents the origins of the negotiation process and compares the definitions of key terms such as 'public authorities', 'environmental information' and 'public concerned' in the Aarhus Convention with the proposed respective definitions in the preliminary document on the regional instrument prepared

8 For example *J. Jendrośka*, Citizen's Rights in European Environmental Law: Stock-Taking of Key Challenges and Current Developments in Relation to Public Access to Information, Participation and Access to Justice, JEEPL Vol. 9 No. 1 (2012) pp 71–90.

9 The Making of a New European Legal Culture: The Aarhus Convention. Roberto Caranta, Anna Gerbrandy & Bilun Müller (eds), Europe Law Publishing, 2018.

by the Economic Commission for Latin America and the Caribbean (ECLAC). The article dealing with definitions is expected to be finalised only at the very last negotiating session to be held in March 2018 and it is already obvious that its final version would differ significantly from the version proposed in the preliminary document but this does not diminish the value of the observations in this contribution.[10]

The second heading comprises of three chapters attempting to look at the practical implementation of procedural environmental rights. Robert Esser in his contribution (Procedural Environmental Rights in the Jurisprudence of the European Court of Human Rights and their impact on Criminal Procedure Law) presents an insight into the development of the respective case law under the European Convention on Human Rights and examines if procedural environmental rights originating from the Convention do also exist in the area of criminal procedure law.

Next chapter (Ilva: an environmental case by Nicola Lugaresi) presents the story of the steel plant Ilva in Italy where insufficient implementation of environmental procedural rights, in particular lack of reliable and coherent information and problematic public participation for years prevented a solution to ecological problems.

Finally, the third contribution under this heading (The Improvement of Article 37 of the EU Charter of Fundamental Rights: a Choice Between an Empty Shell and a Test Tube? By Marco Túlio Reis Magalhães) provides a critical analysis of the current wording of article 37 of the Charter in the context of the catalogue of fundamental rights and discussions regarding substantive right to clean environment. Against this background some radical proposals *de lege ferenda* are formulated to design this provision not as a mere policy principle but as a solid legal basis for environmental procedural rights.

The third heading is focused on public participation. It consists of five contributions devoted to specific issues. Ludwig Krämer in his contribution (The EU and public participation in environmental decision-making) presents the legal framework created in the EU to implement the relevant provisions of the Aarhus Convention and provide legal basis for public participation at the EU level and, via secondary EU law, at the level of its Member States. The discussion is based on the short description of the respective obligations under the Aarhus Convention which indicates that the rights under the public participation pillar are granted to the public concerned. Worth noting in this context is the fact that the issue is far more complicated and some of the rights under the participation pillar are granted to "the public" which is a term much broader than the term

10 The value of the observations in this contribution is also not affected by the fact that the author of this Introduction does not necessarily share all the views expressed in this contribution.

"public concerned". Furthermore, the respective secondary EU law also does not seem to recognize this distinction, which affects the scope of the rights granted by the Convention.[11] As far as the secondary EU law is concerned, the contribution provides a critical analysis of some of the areas of EU policy lacking sufficient framework for public participation. The observations of the author, in particular in relation to so called "Trans-European projects", can be complemented by a reference to the fact that these deficiencies have been subject to number of cases under the Aarhus Compliance Committee.[12]

The second chapter under this heading (Public Participation in Rulemaking and Decision-Making in Environmental Matters: Legal Framework and Jurisprudence in Spain and the Basque Country by María del Carmen Bolaño Piñeiro and Iñaki Lasagabaster Herrarte) provides an overview of the respective legal framework in Spain and the Basque Country and against this background examines the legal consequences of failing to provide an effective public participation in rulemaking and administrative decision-making processes on environmental matters.

The contribution of Margherita Paola Poto (Legal Instruments to Protect Indigenous Peoples' Participation in Europe and in the Arctic Region) describes the participatory mechanisms to protect and safeguard the status and the participatory rights of minorities and indigenous groups at international, regional and national level. The basic assumption of the study is that traditional legal instruments designed to facilitate a broader participation of the public in the environmental decision-making (such as the Arhus Convention) have not been sufficient to offer an adequate level of protection to the effective participation of specific target groups. Worth noting in this context is that this assumption seems to be confirmed by the fact that during the already mentioned above current negotiations regarding Regional LAC Agreement on Principle X it was found useful to grant special procedural environmental rights to minorities and indigenous groups commonly coined as "persons or groups in vulnerable situations". The role of granting rights to the specific target groups is also underlined in another contribution to this book which presents crucial role of local communities for the long-term success of cross-border conservation of Transfrontier Conservation Areas (TFCAs) in Africa.[13]

11 For more about the subjects of rights under the participation pillar and the approach in the respective EU secondary law see *J. Jendrośka*, Public Participation in Environmental Decision-Making. Interactions Between the Convention and EU Law and Other Key Legal Issues in its Implementation in the Light of the Opinions of the Aarhus convention Compliance Committee (w:) The Aarhus convention at Ten. Interactions and Tensions between Conventional International Law and EU Environmental Law, ed. M. Pallemaerts, Europa Law Publishing, Groningen 2001.

12 See cases ACC/C/54 and ACC/C/68 where the EU was found to be not in compliance with article 7 of the Convention, see also case ACC/C/96 (pending).

13 See chapter Strengthening Conservation through Participation: Procedural Environmental Rights of Local Communities in Transboundary Protected Areas by Emma Mitrotta.

Viktoria Rachynska in her contribution (Notifying the Public as a Part of Public Participation Procedure in EU, Polish and Ukrainian Law) provides a comparative analysis of the implementation of the requirements of the Aarhus Convention regarding notification of the public during public participation procedure in the EU, Polish, and Ukrainian legislations. Contribution of Kamila Sobieraj (Public Participation Rights Enhancement within the Wind Power Plants Location in Poland in the context of EU Renewable Energy Requirements) provides an analysis of the recently adopted new Polish legal framework regarding location of wind farms from the point of view of assuring effective procedural environmental rights of the public on the one hand and achieving the goals and targets concerning renewable energy stemming from the EU legislation.

The fourth heading is devoted to access to environmental justice. Contribution of Gitanjali Nain Gill (Access to Environmental Justice in India: Innovation and Change) presents an overview of the key features of environmental justice in India. The analysis is focused on the role of judiciary (Supreme Court of India and the National Green Tribunal) in contributing to the development of this probably one of the most progressive and developed system of environmental justice in the world. The progressive approach of Indian judiciary is particularly interesting when compared with rather restrictive approach to providing access to environmental justice in many countries in Europe and at the EU level.

Vicky Karageorgou in her contribution (The Scope of the Review in Environment-related Disputes in the light of the Aarhus Convention and the EU Law-Tensions between Effective Judicial Protection and National Procedural Autonomy) provides an extensive analysis of the approaches to the scope of the judicial review of the environment-related decisions, acts or omissions falling in the scope of Article 9.2 of the Aarhus Convention and the relevant provisions of the EU Directives. She presents how the scope of the review is determined by different systems of judicial review, analyses the respective jurisprudence of the Aarhus Compliance Committee and the CJEU and concludes with some proposals *de lege ferenda*.

The contribution of Žaneta Mikosa (Implementation of the Aarhus Convention through *actio popularis*) presents the most extensive approach to regulate legal standing (often referred to as an *actio popularis* or open standing) under Article 9(3) of the Aarhus Convention. Both pros and cons of this approach are discussed in the light of different approaches to legal standing in Europe and respective views presented in the academic literature. The discussion is illustrated by the examples of the court practice, mostly from Latvia, which arguably is the country with the most extensive experience in Europe with *actio popularis* due to the peculiar features of the development of its legislation and court practice in this respect.

The fifth heading is the first one out of three headings presenting procedural environmental rights in the context of some specific areas of environmental law. This heading comprises of three chapters focused on procedural environmental rights in the context of nature protection.

First is the extremely interesting and innovative contribution of Hendrik Schoukens (Towards a legally enforceable duty to restore endangered species under EU nature conservation law: on wild hamsters, the rule of law and species extinction) where a case is made for a legally enforceable restoration duty for strictly protected species,.

Taking into account recent case law developments before the Court of Justice of the EU (CJEU) it is argued that environmental NGOs might step in as effective guardians of endangered species that are in dire need of additional recovery measures in order to avoid the imminent extinction. The author claims that the combination of Article 9(3) of the Aarhus Convention and the general principles of EU is capable of overcoming the traditional procedural obstacles to environmental litigation.

Also the next contribution under this heading (Recognition of rights of Nature, as a subject of law, in the International Environmental Law Framework by Santiago Vallejo Galárraga) offers an innovative approach to procedural environmental rights. It calls for the recognition of Nature, as a subject of international law and a holder of rights, as a legitimate, independent, representative and effective mechanism to stop the environmental depletion.

Finally, Emma Mitrota in her contribution (Strengthening Conservation through Participation: Procedural Environmental Rights of Local Communities in Transboundary Protected Areas) describes how procedural environmental rights can be applied across state borders by way of the non-discrimination principle within the framework of regional organizations, such as the European Union and the Southern African Development Community (SADC), that can facilitate the emergence of higher participatory standards and, based on those standards, foster legislative harmonisation among the member states. As an example the rights of local communities are presented within the cross-border conservation initiatives, like transboundary protected areas (TBPAs) and the Kavango Zambezi Transfrontier Conservation Area is used to exemplify the extraterritorial dimension of procedural environmental rights of local communities in the context of TBPAs.

The next of the headings presenting procedural environmental rights in the context of some specific areas of environmental law is devoted to procedural environmental rights in the context of environmental impact assessment. In many countries (and also in the EU legislation) legal instruments related to environmental assessment are the key legal acts within which procedural environmental rights are being regulated, and environmental impact assessment plays an important role in particular in facilitating the effectiveness of public participation.[14]

First contribution under this heading (Public participation and EIA in the multi-stage decision making process: the Czech example by Petra Humlíčková and Vojtěch Vomáčka) presents the legal framework for public participation and access to justice within the multiple-stage (tiered) decision making process in the Czech Republic in the light of the respective judgements of the EUCJ and Aarhus Compliance Committee. The authors claim that hugely diversified scope of procedural rights granted at various stages of the multi-stage decision making process significantly affects effectiveness of public involvement and has cost implications for all stake-holders. While the above observation is made in relation to the Czech legal system, it applies also to many other jurisdictions. On the other hand the overall conclusion blaming the very existence of the multiple-stage (tiered) decision making process for the problems stemming from granting different procedural rights to the public at the various stages of the procedure seems to be misguided as it mixes the causes with the results. The lack of effectiveness of public involvement seems to be resulting first and foremost from the restrictive procedural rights granted to the public in the stages of the decision-making which follow the EIA decision stage. Of key importance in this context seems to be the fact that rights of access to justice come either too late or too early in order to sufficiently support the scheme for public participation.[15]

The next contribution under this heading (Use of bounding conditions envelope concept in the Polish system of environmental impact assessments by Mariusz Wójcik, Paweł Grabowski, Maciej Stryjecki, Dominik Gajewski) provides an analysis of legal and procedural conditions for the use of the concept of Bounding Conditions Envelope ("BCE") in the system of environmental impact assessments ("EIA") of projects in Poland. The contribution presents some methodological principles of BCE and discusses the impact of using this method on the effectiveness of public participation. While the discussion is based on the practice with using this method in Poland it might be worthwhile to mention that this method is commonly applied worldwide in case of EIA procedures related to nuclear power plants and its consequences for the public participation remain not quite certain. Paradoxically, in this context the fact that the contribution is focused on technical aspects and not purely legal makes it very useful for those involved in practical legal disputes regarding public participation in nuclear decision-making procedures.[16]

---

14 *J. Ebbesson, H. Gaugitsch, J. Jendroska, S. Stec and F. Marshall*, Aarhus Convention Implementation Guide, second edition, United Nations 2013, p 123.

15 *J. Jendrośka*, Public Participation under Article 6 of the Aarhus Convention. Role in Tiered Decision-making and Scope of Application (w:) Environmental Democracy and Law, G. Bandi (red.) Europa Law Publishing, Groningen/Amsterdam, 2014, p 123.

16 For example – the issue of using this method (so-called "envelope approach") in the context of Article 6.6 of the Convention was one of the key issues to be decided by the Aarhus Compliance

The third contribution under this heading (Special provisions on the issuance of environmental decisions in sectoral legislation in Poland by Sergiusz Urban) is focused on analysing the special arrangements regarding EIA procedure for some specific types of projects in Poland. These arrangements provide certain deviations from generally applicable rules, in particular in relation to challenging the respective decisions which in turn has negative consequences for the environment.

Last but not least the seventh heading in the book consists of three contributions dealing with procedural environmental rights in the context of climate change.

Esmeralda Colombo in her contribution (Uncomfortably Numb: The Role of National Courts for Access to Justice in Climate Matters) argues that right to access to justice – while absent from the international climate change treaty regime – appears to be emerging in national climate change cases. On the basis of the analysis of the two cases at the national courts (Urgenda in the Netherlands and Leghari in Pakistan) she claims that the judgments of national courts may boost the enforcement of international law and its legitimacy in relations to global issues.

The second contribution related to procedural environmental rights in the context of climate change (Access to information, the Hidden Human Rights Touch of the Paris Agreement? by Delphine Misonne) provides an analysis of the Article 12 of the Paris Agreement in the context of the features and goals of the Paris agreement and also in comparison to similar provisions in previous climate change instruments. She concludes that Article 12 could provide the impetus that the international community still needs to consolidate that right to know, in relation with the achievement of the global objectives the Agreement.

Finally, the contribution by Samvel Varvaštian (Access to justice in climate change litigation from transnational perspective: private party standing in recent climate cases) provides an overview of the current trends in private party standing in the US, Australian and European climate cases. Despite all the differences between the respective legal system, he offers some observations regarding broader picture of the relevant issues.

Committee in its findings regarding Czech Nuclear Plant Temelin (Case ACCC/C/2012/71-available at https://www.unece.org/envenv/pp/compliancecommittee/71tablecz.html.

PROCEDURAL ENVIRONMENTAL RIGHTS: STATUS AND DEVELOPMENTS

DEVELOPING STANDARDS FOR PROCEDURAL ENVIRONMENTAL RIGHTS THROUGH PRACTICE

The Changing Character of Rio Principle 10*

Stephen STEC**

1. PRINCIPLE 10 AND THE COMPLEXITY OF SUSTAINABILITY TRANSITION

THE STANDARD NOTION OF PRINCIPLE 10'S INDISPENSABILITY TO SUSTAINABILITY

In 1992, advanced Western democracies celebrated the adoption of the Rio Declaration[1] and Agenda 21[2] as a blueprint for a more sustainable world. One of the 27 principles in the Declaration recognized the implementation challenges

---

* This paper builds upon my remarks entitled "Developing Standards for Procedural Environmental Rights Through Practice: The Guide to the Bali Guidelines on Rio Principle 10," delivered at the 2016 EELF Conference on Procedural Environmental Rights: Principle X in Theory and Practice, Wroclaw, 14 September 2016, and draws upon my further talks: "Application of International Best Practice Related to SDG16: the UNEP Bali Guidelines on Rio Principle 10," delivered at Osaka University International Symposium on Public Participation and Access to Justice in Environmental Matters, 3 November 2016; "Is the Rule of Law an Endangered Species?" delivered at the World Congress on Environment, Delhi, India, 25 March 2017; and "Participatory Mechanisms in the Context of the Energy Transition: Application of Rio Principle 10," delivered at the workshop, An Inclusive Energy Transition? Global Low-carbon Strategies and Their Discontents, University of Cambridge, 21 June 2017. Portions are adapted from Stec, Stephen; translated by Jinen Kita (2017). "Application of International Best Practice Related to SDG16: The UNEP Bali Guidelines on Rio Principle 10" [Japanese]. *Review of administrative law [Gyoseiho-kenkyu]* 18, pp. 21–44.

** Adjunct Professor, Department of Environmental Sciences and Policy, Central European University.

1 Report on the United Nations Convention on Environment and Development, UN Doc. A/CONF.151/26/Vol. I (12 Aug 1992).

2 United Nations, Agenda 21 Earth Summit: United Nations Program of Action from Rio (April 1992).

arising from the fundamental restructuring of the global economy and the need to engage and mobilize the global population. Rio Principle 10 had its roots in the following statement in *Our Common Future (The Brundtland Report)*:

> "The law alone cannot enforce the common interest. It principally needs community knowledge and support, which entails greater public participation in the decisions that affect the environment."[3]

This notion of the common interest, which requires community knowledge and support to be realized, extends even further into the past, to Principle 1 of the Stockholm Declaration of the UN Conference on the Human Environment (1972), the clearest statement in any global legal or political instrument on the fundamental relationship between humans and their environment. Public participation is indispensable to the sentiment in Stockholm Principle 1 that "[humankind] bears a solemn responsibility to protect and improve the environment for present and future generations."[4] Rio Principle 10 is an expression of the operative principle that through the exercise of civil, political and procedural rights individuals and associations can influence civic space in order to promote policymaking and decision-making that will protect and improve the environment and ensure sustainability.

Application of Principle 10 goes hand-in-hand with the increasing realization of the potential for global harm arising from pollution in its various forms. International law has responded through the progressive development of concepts related to the principle of harm prevention, as elaborated in cases such as the *Gabcikovo-Nagymaros Case (Hungary v. Slovakia)*[5] and the *Pulp Mills on the River Uruguay case (Argentina v. Uruguay)*[6], which present a logical framework that can lead towards the gradual acceptance of public participation in environmental decision-making as a necessary component of the international community's due diligence in preventing harm to the global commons.

Principle 10 is undoubtedly the single most empowering global policy statement on the role of the public in the transition to sustainability. With its pillars on access to information, public participation in decision-making, and access to justice in environmental matters, it took its shape from lessons learned during a generation of coping with acute industrial pollution in the developed world. It takes therefore a rights-based approach – based on civil, political and procedural rights such as the right to receive and impart information, the right of association, the right of assembly, and the right to petition governments.

---

3 Bruntland Commission, Our Common Future (Oxford U. Press, 1987).

4 Report of the United Nations Conference on the Human Environment, UN Doc. A/CONF.48/14/Rev.1.

5 Case concerning the Gabcikovo-Nagymaros Project (Hungary-Slovakia), Judgment of 25 Sep 1997, 37 I.L.M. 162 (1998).

6 Case concerning pulp mills on the River Uruguay (Argentina-Uruguay), Order, Provisional Measures, ICJ GL No 135, [2006] ICJ Rep 113, (2006) 45 ILM 1025, ICGJ 2 (ICJ 2006), 13th July 2006.

Rio Principle 10 carried with it certain assumptions about how societies could or should be organized, and became associated with notions of "environmental democracy."[7] This is as valid today as it was then, but the assumption that the West would not face too many challenges in applying Principle 10, while the developing world and countries in transition would benefit greatly due to their comparative democratic deficit has been belied by many years of implementing the most elaborate instrument based on Principle 10, the Aarhus Convention.[8] In fact, based upon the record of compliance cases brought under the Convention, the obstacles faced in implementing Principle 10 are practically universal.

For the rest of the world outside the pan-European region, the adoption in 2010 in Bali, Indonesia by the United Nations Environment Program Governing Council, Global Ministerial Environment Forum, of the "Guidelines for the Development of National Legislation on Access to Information, Public Participation in Decision-making and Access to Justice in Environmental Matters"[9] (Bali Guidelines) marked an important milestone in international standard-setting and the establishment of good practices related to application of Principle 10. The Bali Guidelines represent a major building block in the edifice of norms and laws leading towards sustainability. Similar to the experience under the Aarhus Convention, the development of a Guide to the Bali Guidelines[10] collecting cases from the developing as well as the developed world shows that good practice on Principle 10 is not the monopoly of the advanced Western democracies, nor even of those countries with experience under the Aarhus Convention.

Subsequent to the adoption of the Bali Guidelines, the international consensus on sustainable development advanced on several fronts, particularly with the adoption in 2015 of the Sustainable Development Goals (SDGs).[11] Under SDG 16 the international community pledges to "promote peaceful and inclusive societies for sustainable development, provide access to justice for all, and build effective, accountable and inclusive institutions at all levels." While SDG 16 applies throughout societies, without specific attention to or an explicit connection with environmental protection, its aims, including several of the targets adopted under the SDG, correspond to the three pillars of Rio Principle 10. For example:

---

7 As stated by UN Secretary Generals Kofi Annan and Ban Ki-Moon. See the Forewords to United Nations, "The Aarhus Convention: An Implementation Guide," 1st (2000) and 2nd (2013) editions; and UNEP, Putting Rio Principle 10 Into Action: An Implementation Guide for the UNEP Bali Guidelines for the Development of National Legislation on Access to Information, Public Participation and Access to Justice in Environmental Matters (2015, English) (2016, Spanish).

8 Convention on Access to Information, Public Participation in Decision-Making and Access to Justice in Environmental Matters (Aarhus, 1998), 2161 UNTS 447; 38 ILM 517 (1999).

9 Adopted by the Governing Council of the United Nations Environment Programme in decision SS.XI/5, part A of 26 February 2010.

10 UNEP, Putting Rio Principle 10 Into Action: An Implementation Guide (2015, English) (2016, Spanish).

11 UNGA Res. 70/1, 25 Sep 2015.

16.3 Promote the rule of law at the national and international levels, and ensure equal access to justice for all

16.7 Ensure responsive, inclusive, participatory and representative decision-making at all levels

16.10 Ensure public access to information and protect fundamental freedoms, in accordance with national legislation and international agreements

16.b Promote and enforce non-discriminatory laws and policies for sustainable development

The four targets above are fully aligned with Rio Principle 10, while the title of SDG 16 links these elements with social justice and accountability in government. These linkages are analogous to the linkage made between Rio Principle 10 and the notion of "environmental democracy."

THE POLITICAL RESPONSE TO THE SECURITIZATION OF ENVIRONMENTAL DEMOCRACY NORMS

Principle 10 has now been with us for a quarter century. But during this time the world has changed. Further in this article, below, I discuss a case that raises questions about the place that the kind of free, open and transparent determination of the common interest based on Rio Principle 10 should occupy in an increasingly polarized world. In so doing I would like to raise a warning flag about the tactics that existing power structures based upon unsustainable practices could use to undermine public participation and to politicize debate to the detriment of civic discourse.

Just as the realization becomes more widespread that Rio Principle 10 represents an emerging global norm, we are seeing an increase in attacks on civic discourse in the so-called "advanced" democracies. The form so far has been mostly in legal attacks and intimidation through media, but a trend towards more violent confrontation is worrying. Even more worrying is the signal that is being sent to environmental defenders in the "front-line" states. We may be used to attacks on those who would exercise their rights in the developing world and in bureaucratically centralized regimes, but until now there has been a solid consensus in favour of participation in the Euro-Atlantic region. That consensus is beginning to crack, and the true defenders of Mother Earth in the most vulnerable regions have fewer and fewer examples to inspire them to take action and to risk everything to protect our precious natural resources.

In recent years, public awareness of the contradictions between the continued, existing course of development and the changes needed to address fundamental challenges such as climate change has grown. The immense and daunting scale of the transition to sustainability is becoming better understood. A few simple facts bear mentioning:

1) Urbanization – at the beginning of this century, for the first time more than half the world's population was living in cities, expected to rise to 60% by 2020. In 2050 there will be as many people living in cities as the entire population of the world in 2002 (6.3 billion).[12]
2) Global energy demand will double by 2050 and continue to rise through the end of the century.[13] Meanwhile, the transition to renewables needs to increase sixfold to meet international policy goals, and the Paris Agreement is estimated to meet only 1/3 of the needs.[14]
3) For a large and influential part of society, providing energy access and opportunities for connection to global society to 1.5 billion people is a matter of human dignity.[15]
4) $20 trillion – the current value on the books of known fossil fuel reserves that would need to remain in the ground in order to meet current internationally-agreed policy goals on climate change. There is a factor of 2.8 between existing reserves and what is permitted to be emitted under international law. These stranded assets are not yet devalued.[16]

These facts present an emerging challenge to the application of Principle 10. Deliberative processes involving transparency and accountability can be shoved aside where issues are clothed in the trappings of security considerations. The existential threat to elites is easily characterized as such.

It seems that we are seeing the phenomenon of opportunism in the securitization of transition, particularly with respect to energy. Some bold actions – the Crimea example comes to mind – seem to be aimed at leveraging depreciating resources – that is, profiting from a crisis. Territorial ambitions therefore become much more of a threat, especially where the ambitions are held by advanced industrially developed, fossil-fuel dependent economies. While the transition to sustainability requires common security thinking, the present reality is the precise opposite. In a world where many regimes have retrenched towards stronger states and more traditional forms of sovereignty, where do the seemingly chaotic responses of "environmental democracy" fall?

---

12 *Stephen Stec*, "What the World Could Say About Future Energy in 2017," Bureau International des Expositions (ed.), Energie du Futur (2013) 95, 101 (citing UN sources).

13 *Gerd Leipold*, "Expo 2017: Future Energy," Bureau International des Expositions (ed.), Energie du Futur (2013) 53, 58.

14 *Christoph Frei*, World Energy Council, presentation at workshop "An Inclusive Energy Transition? Global Low-carbon Strategies and their Discontents," University of Cambridge, 22 Jun 2017.

15 *Leipold*, op cit., 59.

16 *Stec*, op cit., 99; *Frei*, op cit.

The complex tradeoffs necessary to address climate change and other challenges raise the stakes for society's winners and losers, and raise the spectre of political decision-making. Thus, the usual calculus for public participation changes. The basic rights that underlie Principle 10 are, after all, civil and *political* rights. It was to be expected that the "political content" of climate change decision-making could result in modification of the public participation model, but what was not expected was the backlash against public participation in decision-making in general – i.e., the questioning of the values of public participation based upon decades of experience – coming from certain quarters. In other words, the combination of climate change with the explosive issues related to migration has politicized certain decision-making processes, threatening to carry over into environmental decision-making as a whole. At the same time, the emerging understanding of climate change justice, in particular the influence of environmental degradation on refugees, confirms the relationship between human rights and the environment.

Another political question going forward is the extent to which society as a whole should work towards addressing the interests of elites to assist them towards a post-carbon transition, that is, to soften the blow, or whether on the other hand a revolutionary transition that involves a fundamental shift in power is needed, in which "loser" fossil fuel elites may be driven to fight to the last drop of oil. In the former case, it is possible to hammer away in the court of public opinion and demonstrate the positive attributes of Principle 10. In the latter case, affected groups view Principle 10 only from the point of view of whether it supports or threatens the elites remaining in power. The key factor in the path to be taken is the extent to which the public considers this transition to be a matter of urgency and basic security.

The Bali Guidelines stand as a political declaration that is the culmination of the kind of traditional, "enlightened" approach to participatory democracy in the environmental field that is based upon civic discourse within societies. With their emphasis on access to justice, the Guidelines address the most pressing obstacles to application of Principle 10 in many parts of the world. They implicitly recognize the environmental justice elements arising from some of the most difficult and challenging questions facing societies today – those kinds of questions that cannot be resolved without the engagement and fair treatment of the widest possible range of society, groups and peoples. Opportunities for access to justice before a fair and impartial tribunal are fundamental attributes of the balance of powers. This is the essence – not of democracy – but of civilization. From the Homer-Dixon environment and security perspective, moreover, the balance of powers is among the most important ideational factors that lead societies towards innovation in the face of governance challenges.[17]

[17] *Thomas F. Homer-Dixon*, Environment, Scarcity and Violence (Princeton U. Press, 1999).

While the challenges are great, the answers do not lie in the past. The rise of populism and nativism may be an appropriate defensive response of weak and vulnerable societies that seek to ride out the storm while other, more resourceful societies bear the burden of innovation, but it is an abdication of responsibility for those societies that have the available resources to respond to such challenges. It is a failure of leadership in those societies to cling to power by raw appeal to outmoded traditions, to divide the world into good and bad according to arbitrary distinctions, to set up rivalries for dwindling resources. Only if one accepts that a no-holds-barred free-for-all is what is needed to restore balance to the world does it make sense to follow a path based on polarization, vilification and obfuscation. The question is, can we afford the time to fight such a battle.

2. THE OKINAWA DUGONG CASES

PROCEEDINGS IN THE CASE

Let us now turn to the Okinawa dugong, a subspecies of an aquatic mammal related to the manatee and the elephant, consisting of a few distended and endangered populations in the islands around Okinawa, Japan. A series of cases involving the protection of the Okinawa dugong have taken an alarming turn recently in which a certain form of judicial activism (or inactivism) has reared its head that could lead to a sharp retraction of the area where the rule of law, and therefore access to justice based upon Principle 10, may reach. In a decision of the U.S. District Court for the Northern District of California, a judge in a case that had been going on for several years concerning public participation aimed at protecting an endangered species introduced *sua sponte* an analysis of the political question doctrine to dismiss the case with prejudice on justiciability grounds.[18]

The series of cases involves an agreement between the governments of Japan and the United States about the relocation of Futenma Air Base from the city of Naha, Okinawa to a less inhabited area. The new military installation is known as the Futenma Replacement Facility (FRF). The FRF is being built partly adjacent to an existing facility called Camp Schwab in an area that includes sensitive habitat of the critically endangered Okinawa dugong, which is declared a "national monument" under Japanese law. According to the agreement, the United States is responsible for the design and operation of the FRF, while Japan is responsible for its construction.

For strategic reasons, plaintiffs brought a claim against the U.S. Government based upon the application of the National Historic Preservation Act (NHPA)[19],

---

18 *Center for Biological Diversity v. Hagel*, No. C-03-4350 EMC (N.D. Cal., 13 Feb 2015) (amended order granting defendants' motion to dismiss) [*Okinawa Dugong III*].

19 16 U.S.C. §470.

domestic legislation that had been amended in 1980 to implement the U.S.'s obligations as a Party to the UNESCO Convention Concerning Protection of World Cultural and National Heritage (the "World Heritage Convention" or "WHC").[20] Section 402 of the NHPA states:

> Prior to the approval of any Federal undertaking outside the United States which may directly or adversely affect a property which is on the World Heritage List or on the applicable country's equivalent of the National Register, the head of a Federal Agency having direct or indirect jurisdiction over such undertaking shall take into account the effect of the undertaking on such property for the purposes of avoiding or mitigating any adverse effects.[21]

In 2005, the plaintiffs prevailed on the issue of the applicability of the NHPA, the court holding that the Okinawa dugong was "property" protected under Japan's equivalent of the National Register.[22] Three years later, the same court held that the relevant federal agency – the Department of Defense – had not taken into account the effect of its actions on the Okinawa dugong in violation of the NHPA.[23] The Department of Defense subsequently completed an NHPA assessment in April 2014, without notification to plaintiffs and without public participation. Plaintiffs then challenged the procedural adequacy of the assessment.

In the interim the original judge in the case, Judge Patel, had died and been replaced by Judge Chen, who took a completely different approach to the case. Even though the United States had not brought up the issue in its own defence, in a surprise move, Judge Chen brought up the political question doctrine *sua sponte* from the bench at oral argument. He subsequently dismissed the case with prejudice for lack of subject matter jurisdiction. In interpreting the applicability of the political question doctrine, the court stated that it is ill-equipped to balance the "serious harm construction of the FRF will likely cause to the dugong (including ***possible extinction***) against claimed benefits of the FRF."[24] In the balancing of interests, Judge Chen listed the following benefits:

> e.g., maintaining the United States' "deterrence capability" in Asia, "sustaining public support on Okinawa" for the United States military presence, addressing the "threat posed by a nuclear-armed North Korea" or defusing "tensions over competing territorial and maritime claims in the East China Sea and South China Sea." Evaluating these types of harm is an exercise "for which the Judiciary has neither aptitude, facilities nor responsibility," and thus they "have long been held to belong in the domain of political power not subject to judicial intrusion or inquiry."[25]

---

20 1037 **UNTS** 151; 27 UST 37; 11 ILM 1358 (1972).

21 16 U.S.C. §470a-2.

22 *Dugong v. Rumsfeld*, 2005 WL 522106 (N.D. Cal. March 2, 2005) [*Okinawa Dugong I*].

23 *Okinawa Dugong v. Gates*, 543 F.Supp. 1082 (N.D. Cal. 2008) [*Okinawa Dugong II*].

24 *Okinawa Dugong III* (emphasis supplied).

25 Ibid. (references and citations omitted).

Note how this approach contrasts with other recent legal developments that grant legal personality to rivers and otherwise acknowledge rights of nature. Judge Chen's position places rights of nature into a political balancing act.

APPLICATION OF THE POLITICAL QUESTION DOCTRINE

The court applied the U.S. Supreme Court's so-called *Baker* test[26] to the plaintiffs' claims. *Baker* is generally held up as the decision in which the Supreme Court most clearly elaborated the political question doctrine, setting out six sets of considerations a court should apply in determining whether a case is justiciable. In first applying *Baker* to plaintiffs' claims for declaratory relief, Judge Chen found they were not barred by the political question doctrine. He then moved on to the request for an injunction and found that the political question doctrine prevented the court from issuing an injunction since the court could not order the United States to abrogate a treaty with Japan. Put simply, according to the decision, "this Court lacks the power or necessary competence to enjoin or otherwise interfere with the construction of a U.S. military facility overseas that is being built consistent with American treaty obligations and in cooperation with the Japanese Government."[27] Without the possibility of injunctive relief, according to the court, declaratory relief alone would be "meaningless," and therefore the case should be dismissed for lack of standing due to the requirement that the plaintiffs' claims should be capable of redress.

The decision in *Okinawa Dugong III* is currently (as of July 2017) the subject of an appeal to the Ninth Circuit Court of Appeals.[28] During the hearing on appeal in March 2017, at least one of the appellate judges expressed a great deal of scepticism about the lower court's decision and the government's position. Nevertheless, a statement by counsel for US government in the *Dugong III* appeal hearing is telling as to the analysis applied by the lower court:

> "[T]he court is not well-equipped to determine what is in the public interest when the government of Japan is deciding what's in its interest for a project on its sovereign territory, and which it is paying for itself pursuant to a treaty."[29]

The vague imprecision of the *Baker* test has provided fodder for scholars studying the judiciary's approach to political questions. For example, recent scholarship

---

26 *Baker v. Carr*, 369 U.S. 186 (1962).

27 *Okinawa Dugong III*.

28 After the article was written, but before it went to press, the 9th Circuit Court of Appeals issued its decision in *Center for Biological Diversity v. Mattis*, No. 15–15695, decided 21 August 2017, in which it reversed the District Court's decision that the political question doctrine barred the plaintiffs' claims, and remanded the case to the District Court for further proceedings.

29 *Helen Christophi*, "Court Signals Bend of U.S. Marine Base for Okinawa Dugong," *Courthouse News Service*, 16 Mar 2017.

by Zachary Baron Shemtob examines the approaches taken by the U.S. Supreme Court when considering the political question doctrine by showing that the Court has applied up to four competing conceptions of the doctrine, despite the tendency for lower courts to consider the *Baker* decision binding.[30] Shemtob gives particular attention to the distinction between textual and prudential considerations related to justiciability and concludes that the core of federal court decisions on the political question doctrine evinces a prudential approach to justiciability, with generally three considerations:

(1) Courts should stay out of matters where they cannot exercise enough expertise, that is, which are incapable of *judicial* resolution. Judicial overreaching in such cases could undermine other branches of government, and in some cases negatively influence delicate foreign relations. But this limitation ought not apply in a case involving matters that can normally be dealt with by courts in a domestic setting, and which only differs from such typical cases insofar as there are national security ramifications.[31] That is, the fact that national security is implicated is insufficient alone to render a case non-justiciable.

(2) Courts should stay out of matters of "great political momentousness" where judicial balance could be (unconsciously) affected. This prudential concern evinces respect for the political branches of government, which are better equipped to manage the necessarily complex political balancing to come to a resolution of such matters. Nevertheless, the judiciary may need to play a role in such cases to help shape or form questions in the most legally significant way.

(3) Courts should stay out of matters when "resolution would threaten the courts' credibility in the eyes of the public or the executive or legislative powers."

Shemtob's analysis also comes to terms with the confusion over the political question doctrine engendered by cases such as *Zivitofsky v. Clinton*[32] that apply a simple textualist view of pure constitutional interpretation. Even this case, however, included examination of mixed textualist-prudential factors about whether standards of review are available and capable of determination.

There are substantial grounds for expecting the Ninth Circuit to vacate the decision in *Okinawa Dugong III* and remand for further proceedings, purely on the basis of domestic law. In the first place, while deferring to the Executive Branch on political grounds, the lower court seems to have disregarded another co-equal branch – the Congress. Under *Chevron U.S.A. Inc. v. Natural Resources Defense Council, Inc.*, if Congress has directly spoken to the precise issue in question and

30 *Zachary Baron Shemtob*, "The Political Question Doctrines: *Zivotofsky v. Clinton* and Getting Beyond the Textual-Prudential Paradigm," 104 *Georgetown L. J.* 1001 (2016).

31 See *Japanese Whaling Ass'n v. Am. Cetacean Soc'y*, 478 U.S. 221 (1986).

32 132 S. Ct. 1421 (2012). In *Zivotofsky*, the Court found that the question whether the parents of a child born in Jerusalem could challenge the government's refusal to identify his birthplace as Israel was justiciable.

the intent of Congress is clear, "that is the end of the matter."[33] The language of the NHPA clearly applies to U.S. government action overseas. The Judicial Branch has the power and the authority to hold the Executive Branch to a legal standard, even outside U.S. territory. Otherwise, the Executive would be able to frustrate Congressional intent anywhere outside U.S. territory simply by acting within the sphere of international relations – essentially a veto power.

Assuming that the *Baker* test still has legal validity, Judge Chen, who has relied upon it, seems to have misapplied it. Justice Brennan's majority opinion in *Baker* makes it clear that a federal court cannot escape its obligation to decide cases and controversies properly presented to it on political question grounds unless the political question is "inextricable" from the matter in dispute. A court therefore should make every effort to extricate the case from any supposed political question. Judge Chen in *Okinawa Dugong III* held that the political question is inextricable from the matter because granting relief would require the court to order the United States to abrogate a treaty. However, this conclusion ignores the vast range of actions that could be taken by the Department of Defense to limit or mitigate damage to the Okinawa dugong short of abandoning the project. There is nothing in the record to support the conclusion that the only way the Department of Defense could comply with the NHPA would be to abrogate the treaty. Moreover, Japan and the U.S. did not negotiate their agreement in a legal vacuum – presumably both parties to the international agreement expected the other to comply with various corollary legal requirements outside the four corners of the agreement while fulfilling their obligations under the treaty.

Furthermore, the court had another means of extricating the political question in its hands but chose to ignore it. It expressly determined that the plaintiffs' *request for declaratory relief* did not entail a political question. Under the Administrative Procedure Act, declaratory relief to "hold unlawful and set aside agency action... found to be... arbitrary, capricious, an abuse of discretion, or otherwise not in accordance with law" is a goal of the statute in and of itself, as the Supreme Court has noted in *Japanese Whaling*.[34] This type of relief clearly does not require the court to compel action through injunctive relief. The court could have extricated the political question from the case simply by determining that declaratory relief was a viable remedy. Another way in which the court could have extricated the political question from the case would have been to use its discretion to fashion an equitable remedy even beyond that requested by the plaintiffs. The NHPA does not limit available remedies.[35]

Finally, the court takes an extreme position as to what it is being asked to do. For example, it claims that it is ill-equipped to balance the "serious harm construction of the FRF will likely cause to the dugong (including possible

---

33 467 U.S. 837, 467 U.S. 843 (1984).

34 5 USC §706(2). *Japanese Whaling*, at 230 n. 4.

35 See *Weinberger v. Romero-Barcelo*, 456 U.S. 305 (1982).

extinction) against claimed benefits of the FRF." However, merely requiring the Department of Defense to apply duly enacted legislation by conducting an assessment according to legal standards does not entail any balancing of such interests by the court itself.

APPLICATION OF INTERNATIONAL LAW TO THE CASE

If Rio Principle 10 and other sustainable development principles had been applied by the U.S. and Japanese governments, legislatures and courts, a different result might have been reached long before now. In the first place, the court could have given weight to the international legal obligations found in the World Heritage Convention. There are few treaties as universally accepted as the WHC, which had 192 Parties as of 9 June 2016. The U.S. and Japan are presumed to have negotiated their agreement on the FRF in good faith in contemplation of their obligations under the WHC. A court is eminently equipped to reconcile legal obligations from various sources in a manner that gives maximum effect to them all, and it would do no harm to a co-equal branch of government for it to do so. It could hardly be said that the requirement to do a proper dugong assessment pursuant to a treaty to which both countries are a Party could be an "affront" to Japan. It should not come as a surprise to either party that the other has to respect certain legal requirements. Japan has been going through its own domestic legal processes and there is no evidence that the U.S. was affronted.

The court could have interpreted the FRF agreement in a manner that would enable the implementation of the joint project to take into account new knowledge and developments in the interests of protecting and improving the environment for present and future generations. The court could have solved the dispute in the same way that the International Court of Justice did in the *Gabcikovo-Nagymaros* case, by holding that the regime for the joint project was flexible enough to take into account such developments as a matter of the adjustment of technical specifications. If the court wanted to go even further it could adopt Judge Weeramantry's reasoning in the same case by requiring the application of a customary norm of continuing environmental impact assessment in order to prevent imminent harm. Naturally, the harm would be defined according to the terms of the WHC regime.

The Bali Guidelines include no restrictions on grounds of national security in public participation. The Aarhus Convention, however, does include a national defence exception under Article 6, paragraph 1(c). The use of this exception requires a determination that application of Article 6 in a case or class of cases would have an adverse effect on "national defence purposes." If a state would want to make case-by-case determinations, such would have to be provided under national law. Use of this exception should be limited in accordance with the Preamble, Objective (Art. 1) and General Provisions (Art. 3). In practical terms, other provisions of the Convention already allow certain information to be protected from public disclosure in appropriate circumstances. There have been no Compliance Committee cases yet about this paragraph.

If the Aarhus Convention were applied prior to the negotiation of the FRF agreement, the two countries might have taken into account Article 3.7 of the Convention, which provides:

> Each Party shall promote the application of the principles of this Convention in international environmental decision-making processes and within the framework of international organizations in matters relating to the environment.

The application of this paragraph might have resulted in the inclusion of negotiated text in the US-Japan agreement, recognizing that decisions related to the design, construction and operation of the FRF may fall under the definition of environmental decision-making processes. Consequently the two countries might have promoted the application of the principles by ensuring that public participation in relevant decision-making would be carried out in accordance with the provisions of the Convention.

As the question of remedies played such an important role in the decision in *Okinawa Dugong III,* Bali Guideline 21 should be examined. It reads:

> States should provide a framework for prompt, adequate and effective remedies in cases relating to the environment, such as interim and final injunctive relief. States should also consider the use of compensation and restitution and other appropriate measures.

The adequacy of remedies is an important consideration in the operation of Rio Principle 10. Damage to the environment is often irreversible, and in appropriate cases appeal bodies must have sufficient powers to act urgently to avoid such damage. The Guideline brings specific attention to the remedies of interim and final injunctive relief. These key remedies have been essential to protecting the environment in cases reliant upon the concepts at the root of Rio Principle 10.

Application of the Guideline in a transboundary context could influence legislation with extraterritorial effect, such as the NHPA, to include provisions that guarantee the availability of adequate remedies, including injunctive relief in appropriate cases. If the legislature would choose to do so, it would be much more difficult for a government party (or court) to invoke the political question doctrine.

If the plaintiffs prevail on appeal the next step in the litigation will be to require the Department of Defense to meet the standards for taking into account public comments. The court (Judge Patel) in *Okinawa Dugong II* already examined the issue and concluded that the "take into account" process must minimally include: (1) identification of protected property, (2) generation, collection, consideration, and weighing of information pertaining to how the undertaking will affect the historic property, (3) a determination as to whether there will be adverse effects or no adverse effects, and (4) if necessary, development and evaluation of alternatives or modifications to the undertaking that could avoid or mitigate the adverse effects.[36] Again, in an international context the Bali Guidelines and Aarhus Convention would be relevant in determining the applicable standards.

JUDICIAL SKEPTICISM OF POLITICAL ARGUMENTS

The amount of deference granted to the Executive Branch in *Okinawa Dugong III* stands in sharp contrast with a polar opposite approach to deference currently playing out in U.S. courts in another arena, which arguably is linked to global environmental change. Yishai Schwartz in *Foreign Policy* recently examined U.S. immigration cases where judges have viewed evidence of executive intent and expressed scepticism of and a lack of deference to Executive Branch pronouncements.[37] In these cases, courts have not taken statements of the political justification of certain measures at face value, but have looked at the totality of the circumstances to determine whether the true intent behind the executive actions renders them legally or constitutionally permissible.

Schwartz thinks these cases may show a shift in the standard of review. He refers to the fact that bipartisan "national security professionals" do not support the President's view. This is told to buttress his argument that courts are responding to current circumstances by exercising their functions to assess credibility and to weigh the evidence in new and unusual ways. In the unusual situation (at least in recent times) that the President lacks credibility, the usual deference accorded to the declared rationale of the Executive branch will not be maintained. Furthermore, the Judiciary will require the Executive to meet a higher standard to show that its policies are based on permissible grounds.

In other countries with a similar legal tradition to the US, including the UK, India and British Commonwealth states, the judiciary shows little restraint in wading into areas wherever it sees fit. This role is unquestioned as it has been vindicated many times over. The US system perhaps has diverged from this more traditional view, as judicial appointments have become politicized to a certain extent through the application of litmus tests, resulting in a rather great disparity in judicial philosophy within the judiciary itself. Whereas we hear about the judiciary in many countries finding a way to play an important societal role in dealing with new challenges such as climate change, in the US for a long time there has been a "civil war" across judicial philosophies of expansionism and

---

36 *Okinawa Dugong II*, at 1104.

37 *Yishai Schwartz*, "This Is What It Looks Like When Courts Don't Trust the Commander in Chief," Foreign Policy, 21 Mar 2017.

retractionism that has had a self-cancelling effect. This phenomenon may be limited to the US system. But as the US has stood as one of the beacons of the rule of law globally it would be very important whether the country can work its way through these challenges without a major upheaval of constitutional order. If US courts begin to apply a similar approach to areas other than immigration, they may reaffirm an important role of the judiciary, that is, acting in order to fill a vacuum, i.e., the dysfunction of the other branches. This might be what Shemtob means when he talks about the Supreme Court sometimes shifting its approach to the political question doctrine among the four variations he identifies because its specific usage sometimes has political overtones.[38]

3. CONCLUSION

This paper began with a description of how Rio Principle 10 has been applied in practice to develop a body of standards for the ways and means by which individuals and associations can carry out their duty to protect and improve the environment for present and future generations. It has also placed Rio Principle 10 and the Bali Guidelines in the context of the gradual development of a cluster of customary norms connected through a notion of prevention of harm.

Practical studies have shown that the challenge in implementing Principle 10 is universal. A moral crisis in the West has raised new challenges to instruments such as Principle 10 that promote transparency, plurality of opinion, the rights-based approach, and fair and open access to justice. Much of the world is undergoing a process of polarization, where opponents are viewed as undeserving of the normal respect accorded to those with differing viewpoints in a civil society. The polarization of societies, including in the Euro-Atlantic region, over the effects of the transition towards sustainability has exacerbated tensions with the result that entrenched elites have begun to undermine notions of civic discourse and the role of public participation in achieving sustainability. One of the main fault lines for social divisions has emerged around the issue of energy strategy, particularly the future of fossil fuel energy. While judicial mechanisms can help fill gaps where co-equal branches of government fail, the fragmentation of judicial philosophies results in widely varying approaches to drawing the line between proper judicial consideration and deference to the political branches. In an increasingly polarized world, where civic space is shrinking, the fragmentation of the judiciary's own approach to sustainability is in danger of undermining the traditional role of the Judiciary Branch.

A recent case has been examined in order to illustrate that the appreciation of sustainability principles and norms does not always enable states, individuals, associations, public authorities, judges and courts to carry out their responsibility

38 *Shemtob*, at 1027–28.

to protect and improve the environment for present and future generations in individual cases. *Okinawa Dugong III* is significant for several reasons. For one thing, it demonstrates the extent of polarization in outlook as to the rule of law and the role of courts in deciding cases. Allowing the decision to stand on appeal would signal a retreat from the important role that an independent judiciary has played in American government throughout its history. Furthermore, the subject of this case has drawn out the polarization in a special way. The balance of interests might be seen to lean very far towards upholding regional security concerns, at the "acceptable" price of extinction of an endangered population. A judge predisposed to this outcome but hampered by the rule of law might seek an outlet in the political question doctrine allowing avoidance of his/her judicial responsibilities. If successful, this kind of argument can be used in other cases where judges are uncomfortable with outcomes mandated by the law.

Following the court's reasoning, the mere invocation of a national security interest involving international relations could deprive U.S. courts of subject matter jurisdiction. This would be significant where parties would be asking the courts to hold U.S. government action to agreed environmental standards or to protect the environment in furtherance of existing U.S. legal commitments, *even where Congress has specifically expressed that those standards should be applied by the US administration globally.*

The danger that the mere mention of a national security interest involving international relations could be taken to deprive a U.S. court of subject matter jurisdiction on the grounds that the court would be powerless to fashion an effective remedy has to be doubly concerning in today's political climate. The current state of political tension in the US and other countries should give cause for concern as to whether the political arena is extending into the judicial one. The long saga of the legal efforts to save the Okinawa dugong stands as a beacon of things to come. We are seeing unprecedented attacks on the notion of judicial independence as well as arguments about separation of powers that would seek to unacceptably limit the scope of power of the judicial branch of government.

Over the last several years the population of the Okinawa dugong has dwindled. The delay in applying legal standards to decision-making concerning the FRF has certainly played a role. Let us hope that the Okinawa dugong will not become a victim of the civil war between judicial philosophies, and that the rule of law will help protect it. There is no better model for developing healthy institutions globally than Rio Principle 10 and the massive body of work involving application of this principle in policymaking and decision-making, as a means of increasing resilience and driving innovation.

THE EVOLUTION OF PARTICIPATORY RIGHTS IN THE ERA OF FISCAL AUSTERITY AND REDUCED ADMINISTRATIVE BURDEN*

Jukka Similä**

1. INTRODUCTION

Recent decades have seen a robust improvement in participatory rights in environmental decision-making in Europe. While participatory rights, transparency and accountability have increased in national law since the Stockholm Conference[1] in 1972, it was not until the Rio de Janeiro Summit[2] in 1992 that a similar development started internationally. Prior to Rio, organising participation was considered a matter of national sovereignty and hence there were only few references to these rights in environmental treaties.[3] Principle 10 of the Rio Declaration defines basic categories of participatory rights, namely, access to information, the right to participate and access to justice, which have dominated the debate ever since. Furthermore, the Rio Declaration pointed out the importance of enhancing participation for women (Principle 20) and indigenous people (Principle 22). Recently, human rights and environmental participatory rights have evolved together.[4] For Europe the adoption of the

---

* The research has been funded from the Academy of Finland project (nr 283116) 'Governing adaptive change towards sustainable economy in the Arctic'.

** Research Professor in Natural Resources Law, University of Lapland, Finland.

1 United Nations Conference on the Human Environment. For the Declaration of the Conference, see www.unep.org/documents.multilingual/default.asp?documentid=97&articleid=1503.

2 For the Rio Declaration on Environment and Development see: www.unep.org/documents.multilingual/default.asp?documentid=78&articleid=1163.

3 *J Ebbesson*, The Notion of Public Participation in International Environmental Law, Yearbook of International Environmental Law, 1998 (8) pp.51–97.

4 *E Secker*, Expanding the concept of participatory rights, The International Journal of Human Rights, 2009 (13) pp. 697–715; *J Steele*, Participation and Deliberation in Environmental Law: Exploring a Problem-solving Approach, OJLS 2001 (21) pp. 415–442, *J Dryzek*, Strategies of Ecological Democratization, in W Lafferty and J Meadowcroft (eds.), Democracy and the Environment, 1998, p. 108 et seq.; *John Knox*, Report of the Special Rapporteur on the issue

Aarhus Convention[5] was crucial, whereas the EU has taken even somewhat more developed steps in its own implementation of the Convention.[6] As a result of this development and long national traditions in administrative law, the law on participatory rights is quite well developed in many European countries[7], one example being Finland. Current national law in Finland provides for all basic categories of participatory rights, with a number of features that exceed the level set in international and European law.

Fiscal austerity is a policy widely used in Europe, not without the influence of the European Union. Fiscal austerity aims to reduce public spending through structural changes. In the eyes of those implementing the policy, environmental issues are not an exception. Cutting administrative burden – a key tool to achieve the goals of better regulation policy – aims to improve the competiveness of regulated industries. This is based on the assumption that excessive and rigid regulation causes unnecessary costs – administrative burden – for regulated industries, which reduces competitiveness in relation to foreign competitors that manage to avoid such costs. Administrative burden is strongly affected by the procedural requirements of regulation.

In political rhetoric, participatory rights tend to be promoted, not discouraged. Most politicians keep claiming that changes in regulation will affect neither the level of environmental protection nor opportunities for the public to participate. Simultaneously, interest groups and some politicians frequently present critical arguments against public participation. The critics' main argument is that the negative side effects of public participation outweigh its benefits. Participatory processes are complicated, expensive and time consuming and delay investment.[8] On the other hand, arguments in favour of public participation include incorporation of public values into decisions, greater acceptability of decisions, improving the substantive quality of decisions, lessened conflict, better policy

---

of human rights obligations relating to the enjoyment of a safe, clean, healthy and sustainable environment. A/HRC/34/49, 19 Jan. 2017. www.ohchr.org/EN/Issues/Environment/SREnvironment/Pages/Annualreports.aspx.

5 The Convention on Access to Information, Public Participation in Decision-making and Access to Justice in Environmental Matters was signed on 25 June 1998 and entered into force 30 October 2001. The Convention is open to all member states of the UN Economic Committee for Europe (UNECE); these include the USA and Canada, which, however, have not signed the Convention.

6 The newest draft report from the European Commission on the Implementation of Aarhus Convention describes legislative and other acts adopted for implementation in the EU. http://ec.europa.eu/environment/aarhus/pdf/EU_aarhus_implementation_report_2017.pdf.

7 *J Steele supra* note 5; *M Lee and C Abbot*, The Usual Suspects? Public Participation Under the Aarhus Convention, MLR, 2003 (66) pp. 80–108; *B Richardson and J Razzaque*, Public Participation in Environmental Decision-making, in B Richardson and S Wood (eds), Environmental Law for Sustainability 2006, pp. 165–194.

8 *W Filho*, Getting People Involved, in S Buckingham-Hatfield and S Percy (eds), Constructing Local Environmental Agendas: People, Places and Participation, 1999, pp. 31–41.

implementation and educating and informing the public.[9] Regardless of the political rhetoric, horizontal policies are likely to affect the evolution of all basic categories of participatory rights in environmental matters. This does not necessarily mean that the impact will always be negative or that there are no forces working in the opposite direction. However, the influence of horizontal policies might be stronger than any effort which openly and explicitly favours public participation.

In this article, I will discuss how horizontal policies may affect the evolution of participatory rights and whether a structural reform could provide a win-win-win situation in which horizontal policies achieve their goals yet opportunities for public participation remain the same or even improve. While the article is addressed to a broad international audience, it uses examples from one EU member state, Finland, as an illustration of development assumed to be typical in other countries as well. Furthermore, few references to other European countries are made to give a broader picture. The hypotheses of implications of fiscal austerity for environmental policy developed by a group of American researchers are used as a source of inspiration. Their theoretical arguments, although not directly concerning public participation, give a basis for the discussion how fiscal austerity policy may affect public participation in environmental matters. Still no substantial comparison between the U.S. and Finland is made.

The rest of this article is divided into four sections. First, I will say a few words about the history of fiscal austerity policies and reduction of administrative burden, and then discuss whether the policies are shaping environmental regulation in Finland. Thereafter I undertake to identify hypothetical implications of the horizontal policies on the realisation and design of participatory rights. Next I move on to discuss whether the great promise of structural reform can be realised. Finally I will put forward a number of conclusions.

2. HORIZONTAL POLICIES AND REGULATION

Fiscal austerity policy aims to reduce budget deficits and control the rise of debt. The policy is supported by the Maastricht criteria, which were convergence criteria that the EU member states were required to meet in order to adopt the euro as their currency. The most relevant Maastricht criteria for fiscal austerity are the

9 *S Arnstei*, A Ladder of Citizen Participation, Journal of the American Institute of Planners, 1969 (35) pp. 216–224; *M Appelstrand*, Participation and Societal Values: The Challenge for Lawmakers and Policy Practitioners. Forest Policy and Economics, 2002 (4) pp. 281–290; *G Cowie and L O'Toole*, Linking Stakeholder Participation and Environmental Decision-Making: Assessing Decision Quality for Interstate River Basin Management, in F Coenen, D Huitema and L O'Toole (eds.), Participation and the Quality of Environmental Decision Making, 1998, pp. 61–72. T.C. Beierle, Using Social Goals to Evaluate Public Participation in Environmental Decisions, Policy Studies Review, 1999 (16) pp. 75–103.

government budget deficit and the government debt-to-GDP ratio. The former criterion forbids EU member states to have a budget deficit that exceeds 3 per cent of their gross domestic product, and the latter a national debt that exceeds 60 per cent of GDP.[10] This applies only to those member states that belong to the Eurozone. However, austerity policies have also been adopted by member states outside the Eurozone and non-member states in and outside Europe. The economic crisis that started in 2007 intensified fiscal austerity policy world-wide. Ageing populations will significantly increase public spending in all developed countries. In environmental policy, fiscal transfers are employed only to a minimal extent and the size of environmental budgets in relation to other sectors of government is small. Nevertheless, fiscal austerity policy may affect environmental policy and regulation through the reduction of resources for environmental administration.

Reducing the administrative burden of regulated industries is a desired outcome of better regulation policy. Administrative burden refers to the costs imposed on regulated industries in complying with the procedural and information requirements of regulation. Hence, environmental protection measures required by regulation are not measures that increase administrative burden, although they may be very costly. Better regulation policy already has a history of its own in Europe, although its roots are in the US.[11] Such policy undertakes to ensure that "legislation must continue to keep pace with evolving political, societal and technological developments."[12] Regulation is seen as a dynamic phenomenon, one which needs to be continuously changed. Changes in the technologies or raw materials that regulated activities employ may limit harmful environmental impacts of regulated activity to a minimal level, which then calls for a change in regulation. This should not necessarily be considered problematic from the point of view of public participation. The need for regulation may have disappeared at that point.[13]

The balanced goals of better regulation policy distinguish between better regulation and the earlier deregulation policy. Deregulation policy in the 1980s aimed to remove or reduce regulation in a rather straightforward way. However, the economic research[14] done in the 1970s, which strongly influenced the

10 The Maastricht Treaty, which entered into force in November 1993, outlined five convergence criteria for those EU member states that would like to adopt the new currency, the euro. The criteria pertain to inflation, the government budget deficit, government debt-to-GDP ratio, exchange rate stability, long-term interest rates.

11 *JB Wiener*, Better Regulation in Europe, 59 Current Legal Problems, 2006 (59), p. 447–518. Available at: http://scholarship.law.duke.edu/faculty_scholarship/1586.

12 Commission staff working document, Better Regulation Guidelines, COM (2015) 215 final, p. 4.

13 There is no doubt that development can also go in the other direction. New technologies and production methods or a new market situation can create a need for new regulation with public participation mechanisms.

14 *S Peltzman*, The economic theory of regulation after a decade of deregulation. Brookings Papers on Economic Activity. Microeconomics (1989) p. 1–59.

deregulation policy in 1980s, is still informing better regulation policy. Although better regulation policy is sensitive to a broad set of public values, both better regulation and deregulation policies are, after all, motivated by similar criticisms against excessive regulation, administrative overload and the inefficiency of command-and-control regulation.[15] When it comes to the means for reducing administrative burden, there is no difference, practically speaking, between deregulation and better regulation. However, the approaches as a whole differ.

Cutting red tape, simplifying the regulatory environment and striking the right balance between the costs and benefits of regulation to make industries competitive are seen as core elements of better regulation policy.[16] The tools of better regulation policy are impact assessment of proposed legislation, simplification of existing legislation (through codification, recasting and repeal), consultation procedures on drafting proposals, screening and withdrawal of pending proposals and monitoring and reducing administrative burdens.[17] Despite the existence of explicit means, the concept of better regulation policy is "an umbrella term" which may refer to serious attempts to mediate deregulation and re-regulation – or may only be an empty political catch phrase.[18] Currently one the key tools of better regulation policy at the EU level is the REFIT Programme.[19] REFIT does not explicitly aim to deregulate, but rather supports the design of smart regulation. Smart regulation is seen as combining effective achievement of public policy goals with cutting unnecessary administrative burden.[20] While the EU has developed its own better regulation policy, member states have adopted their own policies covering national regulation. Interestingly, many countries having a reputation for being forerunners in environmental matters – like the Netherlands and Denmark[21] – have also taken an active role in pushing forward better regulation agendas.

Do the policies of fiscal austerity and reducing administrative burden affect environmental regulation in Finland? This issue can be examined by taking a look first at the strategic programme of Prime Minister Juha Sipilä's Government Programme and then at the legislative programme of the Ministry of the

15 *U Collier*, The Environmental Dimensions of Deregulation, An Introduction, in U Collier (ed.), Deregulation in the European Union: Environmental Perspectives, 1998. p. 3 et seq.

16 *A Alemanno*, The Better Regulation Initiative at the Judicial Gate: A Trojan Horse within the Commission's Walls or the Way Forward? European Law Journal 2009, (15), p. 383.

17 Id. p. 383.

18 *C Radaelli and A Meuwese*, Better Regulation in Europe: Between Public Management and Regulatory Reform. Public Administration 2009, Vol. 87, No. 3, p. 639.

19 Https://ec.europa.eu/info/law/law-making-process/overview-law-making-process/evaluating-and-improving-existing-laws_en (accessed Feb. 9th, 2017).

20 Communication from the Commission to the European Parliament, the Council, the European Economic and Social Committee and the Committee of the Regions, Smart regulation – Responding to the needs of small and medium – sized enterprises. COM/2013/0122 final.

21 *A Ekroos & M Warsta*, Ympäristölupajärjestelmän keventämishankkeista eräissä maissa. Oikeusvertaileva katsaus, 2014. Available at: https://ek.fi/wp-content/uploads/Ymparistolupajarjestelman-keventamishankkeita-eraissa-maissa.pdf.

Environment.[22] The strategic programme is the main political document adopted when a new government is formed and outlines its key political ambitions. In the legislative programme, the ministry lists all ongoing legal drafting processes for which it is responsible. The key responsibilities of the ministry are pollution control, nature conservation, land use planning and housing. The EU dominates policy-making in the first of these two policy sectors, whereas regulation in the last two is mainly of national origin.

Not surprisingly, improving the competitiveness of Finnish industry and preventing the increase of debt are major goals of the current government. The government estimates that there is a sustainability gap of 10 billion euros in public finances, which it aims to close by cutting expenditures and introducing structural reforms. This has direct implications for environmental expenditures and structural reforms of regional administration, which fundamentally affect how environmental administration works. According to the government, excessive regulation is among the key reasons why Finland has lost its agility and competitiveness. As a response, the government aims to deregulate[23] and reduce administrative burden. There is no specific section in the strategic programme for environmental protection; rather, most environmentally relevant issues are located under the heading 'The bioeconomy and clean solutions' and the rest in other parts of the programme. Hence, the visibility of the government's environmental protection policy goals is weak. Deregulation is explicitly claimed to be needed to promote the bioeconomy.[24] While bioeconomy, should, according to its definition given in a major Finnish policy document[25], provide environmental benefits, also the reverse is possible. The definition is a political concept without any legal implications. What direction the bioeconomy takes will depend on regulation and the way how strategy will be implemented. For

---

22 Strategic Programme of Prime Minister Juha Sipilä's Government – Finland, a land of solutions (29 May 2015), Government Publications, 12/2015. http://valtioneuvosto.fi/documents/10184/1427398/Ratkaisujen+Suomi_EN_YHDISTETTY_netti.pdf/8d2e1a66-e24a-4073–8303-ee3127fbfcac. The legislative programme of the Ministry of the Environment, August 2016. The programme is updated twice a year and the most recent version (only in Finnish) is available at: www.ym.fi/fi-FI/Lainsaadanto.

23 The Ministry of the Environment currently has a webpage with the heading "Deregulation" (norminpurku), although only in Finnish www.ym.fi/fi-FI/Lainsaadanto/Norminpurku.

24 Strategic Programme of the Government *supra* note 23, p. 12.

25 The Finnish Bioeconomy Strategy defines bioeconomy as follows: "Bioeconomy refers to an economy that relies on renewable natural resources to produce food, energy, products and services. The bioeconomy will reduce our dependence on fossil natural resources, prevent biodiversity loss and create new economic growth and jobs in line with the principles of sustainable development." http://biotalous.fi/wp-content/uploads/2014/08/The_Finnish_Bioeconomy_Strategy_110620141.pdf. This definition of bioeconomy differ from definitions used in other context, see for OECD definition. The Bioeconomy to 2030: designing a policy agenda. OECD 2009. Both EU and many of its member states have adopted bioeconomy strategies, where the definition of bioeconomy may to some extent vary. For EU, see Communication from the Commission to the European Parliament, the Council, the European Economic and Social Committee and the Committee of the Regions, Innovating for sustainable growth: A bioeconomy for Europe. COM (2012) 60 final.

example, the aim of the Finnish government to increase the logging of forests in combination with its decision to reduce funding for nature conservation, may have detrimental impact on biodiversity. In Finland, forest habitats are by far the most important habitats for biodiversity. Still the increase industrial use of forest resources is seen to promote bioeconomy.

The current government (in power since June 2015) is not the first Finnish government, which has cut environmental expenditures. To understand this, we need to take a look at the development of personnel available for environmental matters at fifteen Centres for Economic Development, Transport and the Environment (hereinafter the ELY Centres).[26] The ELY Centres (environment) are responsible for the implementation of environmental policy, including reporting and monitoring the state of the environment, nature conservation and landscape protection and environmental protection. While six regional state administrative agencies grants the environmental and water permits, their staff is much lower than that of the ELY Centres (environment). Municipalities have also environmental responsibilities, but in minor issues apart from land use planning. The Ministry of the Environment is focusing on legislative drafting and policy strategies. Most of the environmental staff is located in the ELY Centres (environment).

Between years 2010 and 2016 the amount of person years made for the ELY Centres (environment) has drop from 1343 person years to 819 person years. The total amount of person years was reduced by 39% in seven years. These figures includes both direct budget funding and external funding. Particularly external funding, like state aid for subsidised employment or EU project funding, was reduced (from 416 person years to 127 person years, 69%). Person years funded directly from budget was reduced by 25%. As a part of this development, environmental restoration projects were closed down and laboratory services and sampling were outsources. Some specialisation between the Centres has also occurred, meaning that a Centre may have a national responsibility with respect to a specific task.[27]

The legislative programme of the Ministry of the Environment dated August 2016 contains 19 legislative proposals for Parliament, not counting housing-related proposals.[28] Eight of the proposals are for measures that implement EU directives. Only three of the eight undertake to improve the level of environmental protection. The rest involve correction of previously insufficient implementation

---

26 ELY Centres are major regional state authorities, which are responsible for the implementation and development of state policies. They have three areas of responsibility: business and industry, labour force, competence and cultural activities; transport and infrastructure; and environment and natural resources. All figures given in this article concern only the responsibility area of environment and natural resources. For more information about the authority: https://www.ely-keskus.fi/en/web/ely-en/environment.

27 This information is based on interview with Jukka Rusanen 23 March 2017, and the statistics and explanation given by him. Rusanen is the administrative director of three ELY Centres. The figures are national covering all ELY Centres.

28 These proposals are mainly irrelevant for environmental protection point of view.

of EU law. Previously, legislative proposals implementing an EU directive would contain additional national elements to make the regulation somehow stricter or broader than required by the EU. The present government has decided that this will not be the case anymore. Legislative proposals implementing a directive should not contain any additional features of national origin, but only implement what the EU requires.

The remaining eleven proposals are of national origin and show what the government wishes to do should it have free reign without international commitments. I have classified them into three categories according to their main objective: (1) increasing the level of environmental protection in some way; (2) deregulation or streamlining; (3) neutral. The last category includes proposals that do not aim to change the behaviour of regulatees in any particular direction or are corrections of previously insufficient implementations of EU directives. Only three of the eleven aim to improve environmental protection, whereas four seek to deregulate or streamline environmental decision-making. The rest are neutral. The proposals aiming to improve the level of environmental protection related to establishment of a national park, exceptional circumstances of waste management and secondary responsibility for environmental damage. The two largest legislative proposals by far are the reform of the Environmental Protection Act and the reform of the Land Use and Planning Act. The former aims to streamline decision-making and the latter plainly focuses on deregulation.[29]

In sum, reducing public spending and strengthening the competiveness of industries are among the key goals of the government of Finland, and deregulation and streamlining regulation are the tools chosen to achieve those goals. The largest legal reforms that the current government seeks to carry out in the environmental field pertain to deregulation and streamlining. The government has adopted a policy geared to ensuring that the EU directives will be implemented at a minimal level. While it would not be fair to claim that the Finnish government does not intend to improve the level of environmental protection in any way, it must be pointed out that the main political emphasis and the resources needed for legislative drafting are being directed to deregulation and streamlining. One can conclude that the policies of fiscal austerity and reducing administrative burden are extensively affecting the evolution of environmental regulation in the country.

3. PUBLIC PARTICIPATION AND FISCAL AUSTERITY

Fiscal austerity policy is affecting public budgets everywhere in the western world and this is supported by international institutions, among them the European Union. Expenditures on the environment in state budgets are small in relative

29 Legislative Programme, *supra*, note 23.

terms, but fiscal austerity has nevertheless affected environmental budgets as well. James Salzman, J.B. Ruhl, and Jonathan Remy Nash[30] have written an interesting paper about the potential implications of fiscal austerity for the Environmental Protection Agency (EPA) in the US. They analyse these for four different categories of regulatory activities, namely, enforcement, compliance monitoring, permitting and regulations, and outline a set of possible alternative responses that might enable a regulatory agency to tackle the problem of dwindling financial resources.

Before going to their analysis, it is important to point out that the division of powers in the EU and its member states is different from that in the US. In Europe, there are no regulatory agencies comparable to the EPA. The European Environmental Agency (EEA) only gathers, analyses and publishes environmental information. In Europe, rule-making powers tend to belong exclusively to political bodies such as parliaments and ministries, whereas in the US many environmental laws empower the EPA to impose regulation of its own. Furthermore, enforcement, compliance monitoring, and permitting are functions which belong to member states, not to the EU. Despite these differences, public bodies in the US and Europe face similar kinds of challenges in the face of fiscal austerity.

Broadly speaking, Salzman, Ruhl and Nash identify three major alternative developments: doing more with less, doing less with less, or perhaps doing different with less.[31] As they still lack empirical evidence, they do not give a definite answer as to how austerity has affected the behaviour of the EPA, but put forward a number of assumptions (hypotheses) on how a public authority like the EPA could respond to a reduced budget. They point out that fiscal austerity is not a new thing in the US; it has in fact been shaping the EPA for long time over the course of several presidential administrations.[32] One could add here that with the Trump administration now in power, it seems highly unlikely that pressures for fiscal austerity will lessen in the coming years.

With regard to enforcement, two alternatives responses are identified; higher authorities may rely more on others – that is, lower-level public authorities or greater use of citizen suits – and/or the emphasis in enforcement may shift from specific to general deterrence.[33] In regard to compliance monitoring, increasing use of smart technologies and/or shifting more and more costs onto the regulated parties would reduce the costs of running the agency. Furthermore,

30 *J Salzman, JB Ruhl, and JR Nash*, Environmental Law in Austerity, Pace Environmental Law Review, 2015 (32) p. 481 et seq., Available at: http://digitalcommons.pace.edu/pelr/vol32/iss2/6.

31 Id. pp 483–486. They, however, point out that it is not their position that the EPA should be reduced; rather, they state that their purpose is to analyse implications in a neutral way, Id. p. 491.

32 Id. p. 483.

33 For factors affecting compliance behaviour, see *J Similä, I Pölönen, J Fredrikson, E Primmer, and P Horne*, Biodiversity Protection in Private Forests: an analysis of compliance. J of Environmental Law, 2014 (26), pp. 90–97.

new monitoring technologies – including drones and biomarkers – may provide real-time and reliable information at low cost and the use of big data could make enforcement activities more efficient.[34] In addition to the delegation of responsibilities to lower levels, the two key options for permitting are letting the processes become longer and increasing the use of general permits.[35] Finally, the authors assume that fiscal austerity would reduce both the rate at which new regulation is developed and old regulation is revised. As a consequence, private regulation could have a more important role than it has traditionally had.[36]

Salzman, Ruhl, and Nash do not directly discuss possible implications of fiscal austerity for public participation. However, some of their assumptions are directly relevant to the issue. Clearly, any prolonging of processes will also affect those participating; they will have to wait longer for the final decision. One could also assume that fiscal austerity will see agencies dispense with all participation activities that go beyond the minimum legal requirements. In addition, while public authorities may never avoid trying to follow the requirements of administrative law, such as responding to all comments and arguments, they might use less time to do so. This would reduce the quality of decisions and, in the longer term, the legitimacy of the decision-making. Public authorities may also shift the costs of a permit to the applicant. This could mean relying more on information gathered by the applicant and less on investigation by the authorities. However, there are also possibilities for doing more with less. Digitalisation – or eGovernment – provides new opportunities to improve public services and increase democratic participation while at the same time reducing the cost of government and encouraging citizens and businesses to interact with public authorities.[37] New digital monitoring techniques combined with eGovernment efforts may also provide a better information base at low cost.

Rule-makers have options other than the enforcing authority to manage in the face of shrinking budgets. Enforcing agencies are not empowered to make rules governing participation process or to decide on their own budgets. While much of environmental law is of European origin in the EU member states, apart from the treaties and the EU legislation referred to in the introduction, the principle of national procedural autonomy leaves it to a large extent up to the member states to decide on procedural rules. A rule-maker may reduce the number of regulated activities, reformulate information requirements, move responsibilities from a

---

34 *Supra*, note 31, pp. 487–488.

35 *Supra*, note 31, pp 488–489. E Biber and JB Ruhl have claimed that expanded use of general permits creates opportunities for adaptive management and can significantly streamline costs. *E Biber and JB Ruhl*, The Permit Power Revisited: The Theory and Practice of Permitting in the Regulatory State, Duke Law Journal 2014 (64) Num. 2, p. 133 et seq. Available at: http://scholarship.law.berkeley.edu/facpubs/2439.

36 *Supra*, note 31, pp. 489–490.

37 *R Davies*, eGovernment – Using technology to improve public services and democratic participation, European Parliamentary Research Service, In-depth analysis,2015 www.europarl.europa.eu/RegData/etudes/IDAN/2015/565890/EPRS_IDA(2015)565890_EN.pdf.

public body to a regulated industry, streamline administrative processes and even limit access to justice.

Furthermore, political bodies may merge two or more administrative bodies into one as apart of larger reform. The explicit reason for such metamorphoses is typically making administration more efficient. Having one process instead of many tends to reduce costs – if not immediately then at least in the longer run. Although a merge of two or more administrative bodies into one would make the administration more efficient, it may has detrimental impacts on the management of environmental matters as a side-effect. Let's take an example. If nature conservation authority is merged with an agricultural authority, the outcome may be that the promotion of agricultural production becomes dominant and nature conservation subordinate interest of the new authority. While both high-level political bodies and enforcing authorities have opportunities to respond independently to fiscal austerity, action from both levels of government is often required. A case in point is eGovernment. While building up efficient eGovernment calls for new behavioural models, this might not be possible without changes in the rules.

4. PUBLIC PARTICIPATION AND REDUCTION OF ADMINISTRATIVE BURDEN

Reduction of administrative burden for regulated industries may take many forms. All of them should reduce the costs of doing business when a company is complying with the procedural and information requirements of regulation. The basic types of measures are the following:

- releasing an activity from administrative control
- changing of the form of control to a lighter one
- lightening information gathering and delivery requirements
- speeding up the decision-making process

An extreme form would be a full release of administrative control on activities potentially harmful to the environment, but the prospect of this is considered very remote.[38] Instead, raising the threshold size of activities requiring an environmental permit[39] can be used to cut the number of activities falling under the most resource-intensive control mechanism, namely, environmental permitting. This often means a change of the form of control from a permitting

[38] *E Rehbinder*, States between Economic Deregulation and Environmental Responsibility, in: K Bosselmann & B Richardson (eds.), Environmental Justice and Market Mechanisms: Key Challenges for Environmental Law and Policy, 1999, p. 96.

[39] The term 'permit' is used here to refer to all supervisory mechanisms which require an administrative authorisation before an activity can be started.

regime (with a participatory mechanism) to direct regulation (without a participatory mechanism). While this change keeps the most risky businesses still under the strict control of a permitting regime, the change can significantly reduce the number of regulated activities.

Rehbinder considers all instruments that provide an alternative to command-and-control regulation to be deregulation. According to this idea, various kinds of market instruments (tradable permits, environmental charges and taxes), flexible instruments (environmental agreements, regulatory agreements), informative instruments (environmental management systems eco-auditing, information delivery requirements), as well as privatisation of environmental services, are seen deregulation.[40] Incorporating full-blown public participation mechanisms in these instruments is, if not impossible, challenging. However, the adoption of these instruments can be seen as deregulation – or an attempt to reduce administrative burden – only when they replace previous regulation. To date, most of these alternatives to command-and-control regulation have supplemented existing regulation than rather replaced it.

Various types of information obligations[41] may also cause significant costs to industries, although sound information is the basis for effective participation. The information obligation does not necessarily mean that information has to be supplied to the public authority or private persons; it may only include a duty to make information available. For polluting industries, information gathering is a continuous activity, one starting from the preparation of the permit application and ending, perhaps, only years after the commercial activity has been discontinued.

Making information obligations lighter may not only reduce the costs of gathering information, but also speed up the administrative process. Other means to speed up the process include time-limits for decision-making, and limitations on appeal rights as regards who can file an appeal, on what grounds and whether leave to appeal is required to have a case heard by the Supreme (Administrative) Court.

How should we judge measures aiming to reduce administrative burden from the point of view of public participation? The first type of measures, namely, full release of an activity from administrative control, would have fatal consequences for public participation. Fortunately, this seldom occurs and I am unable to provide any relevant Finnish example. The lighter form of this same approach is to raise the threshold size of activities requiring an environmental permit, and

40 *Supra*, note 39, pp. 97–108.

41 There are at least the following types of information obligations: notification of activities or events; submission of reports; information labelling for third parties; non labelling information for third parties; registration; inspection on behalf of public authorities; certification of products or processes; cooperation with audits and inspection. Sometimes an application for authorisation or an exemption is also considered as an information obligation. However, here these are not included in this category.

this has taken place several times in Finland since the year 2010. It is estimated that new Environmental Protection Act (27.6.2014/527), along with its recent amendments (Act 10.4.2015/423), will reduce the number of environmental permit applications by 20 per cent.[42]

It is obvious that increasing the threshold size of activities requiring an environmental permit reduces opportunities to participate. However, it is important to put this in broader perspective. Activities released from permit regimes are small in scale and tend not to cause significant environmental harm. Some comparative background information might be illuminating on this point. A recent report[43] suggests that in Finland public participation is incorporated into the governance of much smaller activities than in some other EU member states. For example, there are countries where public consultation is limited mainly to activities governed by the Industrial Emissions Directive (2010/75/EU). Denmark, which has a population similar in size to Finland, has only 6500 regulated installations, whereas in Finland the number is threefold. Furthermore, most of the regulated installations in Denmark are governed by a lighter procedure that does not exist in Finland. The public consultation procedure is applied only to activities governed by the IE directive. Previously, the number of installations requiring a permit or notification in Denmark was much higher (13,000), but nowadays most installations are governed by direct regulation.[44] Furthermore, it is generally believed that the permitting authority tends to use standard permit conditions for small activities, which means that direct regulation contains similar requirements that do not differ significantly from those in permits. Hence, the changes in the law seem to have borne out the hypothesis that participation does not make a difference, or at least not a significant one. Sound empirical research, however, could shed some light on whether this is a valid assumption.

EU law impose limits for replacement of permitting by direct regulation. Both the IE Directive and the Directive (2011/92/EU) on the Assessment of the Effects of Certain Public and Private Projects on the Environment make public enquires obligatory with respect to installations listed in their annexes. While the EU member states may choose – subject to other EU law – otherwise with regard to non-listed installation, it is important to stress that the EU law set only minimum requirements. The benefits on public enquiries are well-documented in research[45], and the added value of public participation may override the efficiency gains of direct application of environmental standards in many other cases as well.

---

42 *L Tarasti, R Rönn, M Pantsar, K Kuusiniemi and T Kähö*, Ympäristömenettelyjen sujuvoittaminen ja tehostaminen. Arvio toteuttamisvaihtoehdoista, 2015.

43 *A Ekroos & M Warsta*, Ympäristölupajärjestelmän keventämishankkeista eräissä maissa. Oikeusvertaileva katsaus, 2014. Available at: https://ek.fi/wp-content/uploads/Ymparistolupajarjestelman-keventamishankkeita-eraissa-maissa.pdf.

44 Id.

45 *Supra*, note 10.

The Arhus Convention on Access to Information, Public Participation in Decision-Making and Access to Justice in Environmental Matters, brings some additional limitation to the parties, like Finland, to weaken participatory rights. The Convention requires each party to provide opportunities to participate in decision-making regarding not only those activities, which are listed in the annex of the Convention, but also to other activities, which may have a significant effect on the environment. This applies also to activities, which are excluded from the scope of the IE Directive, but may have significant effect on the environment. Furthermore, the Convention require that public participation procedures must be effective, and, for example, include reasonable time-frames.

Making changes in information obligations – what information is needed, how it should be delivered and updated – may significantly affect the effectiveness of participatory rights. Hence, potential changes in information obligations are relevant indeed for public participation. However, digitalisation, as well as cutting duplicated or reducing excessive information gathering obligations, may provide opportunities to make information gathering less burdensome.

Time-limits for decision-making do not necessary undermine effective use of participatory rights, assuming that those affected have a long enough time to investigate and assess the information made available to them. How much time is long enough time depends so much on the particular situation that it is not possible to draw any general lines on this issue. While it is undeniable that the use of rights of appeal postpones commencement of activities, research suggests that it is rare for these rights to be used to delay developments. In fact, the substantive content of administrative decisions changes fairly often, which shows that the original decisions were (partly) illegal. The changes take place clearly more often in favour of the environment and those opposed to the project.[46] The assertion that appeal rights are insignificant for those affected is unjustified. Reducing appeal rights (access to courts), if done in an uncompromising way, would seriously undermine participatory rights. Instead, a system of leave of appeal would allow courts to allocate their limited resources to cases in which the legal issues are most challenging.

In sum, it is obvious that recent evolution has reduced opportunities for public participation. However, without detailed, case-specific information and empirical, research-based evidence. it is hard to draw clear conclusions as to whether the benefits of reducing opportunities override the benefits of cutting administrative burden (and improving the competiveness of industries). While research-based evidence is important for public discussion, the choice between the two values is a political one. In any case, it needs to be acknowledged that governance architectures have indeed evolved into very complicated systems[47]

---

46 *J Similä, A Inkinen and J Tritter,* Public Participation by Appeal – Insights from Empirical Evaluation in Finland, Journal of Environmental Law 2008 (20), pp. 391–416.

47 *Radaelli and Meuwese supra,* note 19, p. 651.

and the complexities may hamper the full realisation of the benefits of public participation. It would be too categorical to deem fiscal austerity or reduction of administrative burden to be something that is always negative from the point of view of public participation. It is also important to ask whether the choice between well-developed participatory rights and efficiency of decision-making is a zero-sum game. If it is, the intention of governments to maintain the current participatory rights in reforms designed to promote fiscal austerity or better regulation policies is really only rhetoric, words without content. A truly innovative reform would mean a move from a zero-sum game to a win-win-win situation. Is this possible?

5. STRUCTURAL REFORM – A WIN-WIN-WIN SITUATION?

Could a structural reform of environmental permitting (creation of a one-stop shop) produce a win-win-win situation, where administrative burden of industries is reduced, public costs are cut and opportunities for public participation are improved? The promise of a one-stop shop reforms is high. For example, the letter setting up a high-level expert group to prepare a model for a one-stop shop in Finland states that regulated industries, those affected by the proposed installations, the general public and the authorities will all benefit from the adoption of one-stop shop.[48] It is assumed that this will be the case, although the idea is to keep the level of environmental protection the same as it used to be. The common enemy for all is the fragmented regulation and dispersed decision-making structures that have emerged as environmental regulation has gradually evolved. In a one-stop shop, there would be less need to gather and deliver information, organise participatory events and investigate issues.

The scope and depth of structural reforms can vary significantly, and naturally this affects the nature of the risks.[49] At one end is the full-blown one-stop model,

48 Ympäristöllisen menettelyjen yhdentämisen lainsäädäntöhanke (ns. yhden luukun lainsäädäntöhanke). Asettamiskirje 14.10.2016. www.ym.fi/download/noname/%7BF119B923-F491-4729-80D2-0E633DEF0E74%7D/121949.

49 The EU's energy infrastructure Regulation (No. 347/2013) gives a good illustration of alternatives for a one-stop shop and how one form of one-stop shop can take integration farther than another. The regulation requires member states to organise the permitting based on one comprehensive decision made by the competent authority responsible for facilitating and coordinating the permitting. The comprehensive decision must be made according to one of the following schemes: integrated scheme, coordinated scheme, or collaborative scheme. In the integrated scheme, the comprehensive decision must be the sole legally binding decision resulting from the statutory permit-granting procedure. Other authorities may give an opinion as input. In the coordinated scheme, the comprehensive decision comprises multiple individual legally binding decisions issued by several authorities; the decisions must be coordinated by the competent authority. In the collaborative scheme, the comprehensive

in which several environmentally relevant procedures are metamorphosed into one in terms of procedure, substantive rules and administrative structures. At the other end is integration of some procedures, with substantive rules and administrative structures remaining essentially unchanged. In real life, the process may be gradual. The first step might be procedural integration, which would then be followed by integration of substantive requirements. This is the envisaged course of the reform in Finland. At present, legislation is being drafted to achieve procedural integration, part of a major reform of administration with cross-sectoral goals beyond environmental administration. According to a government policy outline, a nationwide environmental authority with local offices will be created.[50] This is a unique possibility to give authority to a single public body to fully govern or coordinate several permit procedures that are currently governed by different public bodies.

While the promise of a one-stop shop is great, it is far from certain that the goals of the reform will be achieved. There are at least three major risks. The first is political, the second the unavoidable need to make choices based on values, and the third the complexity of environmental problems as well as legal regulation. The political risk stems from the fact that the principal motive for creating a one-stop model is to increase efficiency and streamline regulation, as stated in the letter setting up the expert group. The hidden agenda of such a reform, as Wilkinson and others suspect[51], may be different than is explicitly stated in policy documents. If so, then the goals of fiscal austerity and reduction of administrative burden may dominate the preparation of the one-stop shop model. Kirk and Blackstock indicate that this might have happened in the evolution of the British environmental permitting regimes.[52] Whether this will happen in Finland is too early to judge.

The second challenge relates to the idea of an 'environmentally neutral' reform, which is an assumption behind the preparatory work on the Finnish one-stop shop. There is no intention to upgrade or downgrade the level of environmental protection and hence there is no need to make value choices, for example, between environmental protection and competitiveness of industries. In the first phase of the reform, achieving this goal look easier, because the idea is to integrate procedures, not substantive rules. Where substantive rules continue to differ, this may make decision-making and the outcome – the permit

---

decision must be coordinated by the competent authority, but each authority makes its legally binding decision within prescribed time limits set by the competent authority.

50 Government policy outline of 5 April 2016, http://alueuudistus.fi/en/reform-of-regional-administration.

51 *D Wilkinson, C Monkhouse, M Herodes, A Farmer,* For Better or Worse? The EU's "Better Regulation" Agenda and the Environment, Institute for European Environmental Policy, 2005. www.ieeplondon.org.uk/assets/476/FinalReport_pdf10.pdf.

52 *EA Kirk and KL Blackstock*, Enhanced Decision Making: Balancing Public Participation against 'Better Regulation' in British Environmental Permitting Regimes, Journal of Environmental Law, 2011 (23) pp. 97–116.

– complicated and difficult to understand, but at least the rules would remain the same and familiar. When the time comes to merge rules that were originally set out in a variety of laws into one coherent set, it is hard to avoid making value choices. The legislator might be forced to choose either a higher or lower level of environmental protection, or a more or less inclusive participatory approach.

The integrated pollution control system created in Finland in 2000 serves as an illustrative example of this approach at work. The reform merged four different pollution control permit mechanisms into one. Although there was no stated aim to improve the level of environmental protection, the point of departure was that the level would not be downgraded in any respect either. Ultimately, it was in fact upgraded. Prior to the reform, a sectoral system prevailed in which the scope of regulated activities differed from one law to another. After the reform, all activities that were regulated by any one of the four laws were – with minor exceptions – included in the integrated permit mechanism. The outcome was that all activities were governed by substantive rules covering the whole spectrum of pollution control issues. This was good news for the environment and those affected, but things could also have gone in the opposite direction. Participatory rights and substantive rules are inseparable.[53]

The third risk is that the prospect of achieving all three benefits through a one-stop shop may, after all, be no more than a nice theory despite the good will of those drafting the new law. The complexities of environmental problems[54] and the legal system itself[55] may be too great for a win-win-win situation to ever materialise on the ground. Whether this is the case can be assessed only in retrospect. However, one can draw attention to earlier experiences. In the evaluation of the Finnish integrated pollution control system, no reduction in costs for the regulated industries was found, although this had been presented as a goal of the reform.[56] While the result of the evaluation might be undermined by the fact that the evaluation was carried out a mere two years after the reform[57] and achieving cost reductions might require more time, there is no research-based evidence indicating later cost reductions. If the threat is taken seriously that achieving a win-win-win situation is by no means certain in the real world, the legislator might be prompted to make choices that ensure that the ultimate goal of the reform is achieved, that is, making decision-making more efficient.

---

53 *J Similä*, Onko YSL -uudistus tehostanut ympäristönsuojelua? Ympäristöjuridiikka 2003 (1) pp. 121–136. *M Hildén, P Mickwitz, A Mulders, J Similä, S Sjöblom and E Vedung*, Evaluation of Environmental Policy Instruments – a case study of the Finnish paper & pulp and chemical industries. Monographs of the Boreal Environment Research No 21, 2002.

54 *N de Sadeleer*, EU Environmental Law and the Internal Market, OUP, 2014, p. 178–186.

55 *JB Ruhl*, Law's Complexity: A Primer, Georgia State University Law Review: Vol. 24, 2007, p. 885–911. Available at: http://readingroom.law.gsu.edu/gsulr/vol24/iss4/9.

56 *M Hildén, P Mickwitz, A Mulders, J Similä, S Sjöblom and E Vedung*, Id.

57 On the challenges of evaluating recently introduced policy instruments and possibilities to overcome the challenges, see *P Kautto and J Similä*, Recently Introduced Policy Instruments and Intervention Theories, Evaluation 2005 (11) pp. 55–68.

Complexities may also affect whether the assumed benefit of a one-stop shop for participatory rights is realised. A one-stop shop contains a large number of issues that need to be taken into account in decision-making, meaning that citizens must comment on all of them in a short period of time. The amount of information a citizen needs to absorb in a short period of time is significantly higher in integrated decision-making than in a fragmented system. In such a situation, too many things may go unnoticed. The risk is even higher if time limits for the procedure are tight.

6. CONCLUSIONS

The development of participatory rights in environmental decision-making has already been – and will continued to be – affected by horizontal policies. Policies that seek fiscal austerity and reduction of administrative burden call for changes in administrative procedures and the rights to appeal administrative decisions. Environmental budgets are shrinking and this cannot happen without indirect implications for participatory rights, even though the letter of the law remains untouched. While the policies of fiscal austerity and reduced administrative burden for industries need to be separated conceptually, they are partly interlinked and may also conflict with each other. Transferring responsibilities from public administration to regulated industries decreases costs for the former and increases costs for the latter. However, smart use of resources and design of law can avert negative consequences. The notion that to date real deregulation has been essentially confined to small-scale (although numerous) activities with lesser environmental impacts and almost standard permit conditions indicates that no striking changes have occurred as yet. Full use of the opportunities provided by digitalisation may even result in a situation where it is possible to do more with fewer resources.

The promise of a structural reform of the law, a one-stop shop, is great. Potentially, such a reform might create a win-win-win situation, where the administrative burden of industries is reduced, public costs are cut and opportunities for public participation are improved. However, reformers face a situation where they are forced to make value choices. An assumption that a large, environmentally neutral structural reform is possible is an illusion. There are two additional risks which might undermine the great promise of structural reform. The first is political. The key motive for such a reform is neither to improve environmental protection nor to strengthen participatory rights; it is to increase efficiency and streamline regulation. Do these motives create a hidden agenda that will dominate legal drafting at the cost of the environment and participatory rights? The other risk is technical. A structural reform involving many laws and procedures designed to govern different challenges is an extremely complex undertaking. Despite the good will of the legislator, the final outcome may not necessarily reduce administrative burden, cut public costs and improve the position of those affected by the regulated activity. Whether this occurs can only be assessed in a retrospective evaluation of the reform.

The gradual development of a full-blown one-stop shop with integrated substantive norms will take its time; nevertheless, there is an acute need to assess the risk and potential of alternative ways of effecting structural reforms and to seek new legal solutions for effective public participation. Sharing experiences from other countries would contribute to that goal. Furthermore, retrospective evaluation of the gradually developing reform would reveal whether there are differences between the desired and actual outcomes.

Public participation is a deeply rooted facet of environmental decision-making and is an essential part of environmental law throughout the world, and no less so in Finland. Law provides for participatory rights that serve many goals, such as incorporating public values into decisions, improving the substantive quality of decisions, resolving conflict among competing interests, building trust in institutions and educating and informing the public. While it seems unlikely that this overall picture would change dramatically anytime soon, the possibility that important conditions for effective public participation might be deteriorating should be taken seriously.

DEFINITIONS OF THE AARHUS CONVENTION v. THE PROPOSAL FOR A NEW LATIN AMERICA AND THE CARIBBEAN INSTRUMENT

Mapping the Differences in the Material Scope of Procedural Environmental Rights in International Law

Juliana Zuluaga Madrid*

ABSTRACT

The negotiations for the adoption of an international instrument to implement Principle X of the Rio Declaration in Latin America and the Caribbean are currently taking place and expected to finish in 2017. Notwithstanding the premature state of the new instrument, the present study takes an exploratory approach to compare the material scope of the rights to access information, participate in decision-making and access justice under the current Draft and the Aarhus Convention, as the main international reference, by analysing the definitions of key terms such as 'public authorities', 'environmental information' and 'public concerned' in both texts.

KEYWORDS

Aarhus Convention; LAC Regional Instrument; Private entities; Procedural environmental rights; Public participation; Rio Declaration.

* Juliana Zuluaga Madrid is a PhD candidate at KU Leuven, Belgium. Her research focuses on the right of access to environmental information from the private sector under international, European and comparative law. She obtained her LLM in Energy and Environmental Law from the same university in 2011.

1. INTRODUCTION

In June 2012, at the Rio+20 UN Conference on Sustainable Development,[1] several Latin-American governments put forward a proposal which led to the adoption of the 'Declaration on the application of Principle 10 of the Rio Declaration on Environment and Development' in Latin American and the Caribbean ('The Declaration').[2]

As of April 2017, this agreement has been signed by twenty three States in the region[3] and has given place to the negotiating process for an international instrument to ensure the application of the rights of access to information, public participation in decision-making and access to justice in environmental matters, as envisioned in Principle 10 of the Rio Declaration (the 'Regional Instrument'). Whilst the precise 'nature' of the Regional Instrument is still to be defined, since the Parties have left to the end of the process the discussion on whether or not it will be legally binding,[4] and a comparison between the working draft and the Aarhus Convention may thus be premature, the definitions contained in the current working text[5] on terms like 'environmental information', 'competent authority' and 'directly affected public' provide a glimpse into what the material scope of the new instrument will look like and how it would compare to Aarhus'.

The present study takes an exploratory approach to compare the definitions in the current version of the working draft for the Regional Instrument to the definitions of the Aarhus Convention in order to assess if, under the actual conditions, the material scope of procedural environmental rights in the new instrument would be broader, comparable or more limited than that of the Aarhus Convention, particularly in key aspects like the potential application of the instrument to private entities, the recognition of the right to environmental

---

1 United Nations Conference on Sustainable Development Rio+20, Rio de Janeiro, Brazil, 20–22 June 2012.

2 Declaration on the application of Principle 10 of the Rio Declaration on Environment and Development, adopted at Rio de Janeiro, 25 July 2012. UN Doc. A/CONF.216 (2013). The declaration was initially subscribed by the governments of Chile, Costa Rica, Ecuador, Jamaica, Mexico, Panama, Paraguay, Peru, Dominican Republic and Uruguay.

3 The list is available at www.cepal.org/sites/default/files/pages/files/tabla_incorporacion_paises_web_es_1.pdf. Last accessed 22 December 2016. As of October 2017 there are 24 Parties to the Declaration, Santa Lucía joined at the Seventh Meeting of the Negotiating Committee.

4 UN ECLAC, 'Report of the First Meeting of the Negotiating Committee of the Regional Agreement on Access to Information, Participation and Justice in Environmental Matters in Latin America and the Caribbean', (7 May 2015), Par. 53. Found at: http://repositorio.cepal.org/bitstream/handle/11362/38885/S1500706_en.pdf?sequence=1&isAllowed=y.

5 As of 5 April 2017, the latest available text is the fifth version of the UN ECLAC, 'Text Compiled by the Presiding Officers Incorporating the Language Proposals Received from the Countries on the Preamble and Articles 1 to 10 of the Preliminary Document on the Regional Agreement on Access to Information, Participation and Justice in Environmental Matters in Latin America and the Caribbean', Fifth Version (27 December 2016), [the Draft]. Found at: <http://repositorio.cepal.org/bitstream/handle/11362/39051/S1601326_en.pdf>. The study is based in this text.

participation for the general public and the extent of environmental information covered, considering the importance of these issues for the efficacy of the procedural environmental rights and the possible influence of the Aarhus Convention in their implementation process in Latin America and the Caribbean (LAC).

This study is, however, limited by a (mostly) textual analysis of the definitions and does not consider other provisions of both instruments that directly affect their operating scope, such as the exceptions to the general right of access to environmental information and the compliance mechanisms. Some of the reasons for this 'limited approach' are the early state of the negotiations of the Regional Instrument on these particular aspects and other practical and methodological reasons. At this point, the Regional Instrument leaves the bulk of the regulation of the exceptions to national legislations,[6] and there are no specific provisions on compliance mechanisms.

2. PRECEDENTS AND METHODOLOGY

In the Declaration, the Parties expressed the need for the LAC region to work cooperatively taking proactive action for the adequate implementation of Principle 10 of the Rio Declaration. To this end, they committed to establish an action plan 2012–2014 for the adoption of a regional instrument, which could be a binding treaty or other kind of legal instrument, to ensure the effective implementation of the rights of access to information, participation in decision-making and access to justice in environmental matters. The UN Economic Commission for Latin America and the Caribbean (ECLAC) would serve as a technical secretariat in this process.

Between 2012 and 2014, fourteen meetings of the working groups and four meetings of the focal points appointed by the signatory countries took place. In November 2014, the negotiating phase was launched, with the view of concluding the negotiating process in December 2017.[7]

As of April 2017, six negotiating meetings have taken place between the representatives of the signatory parties with the participation of stakeholders, and there is a fifth version of the compiled text and comments under review of the Parties.[8]

The sixth meeting of the negotiating committee was held in Brasilia, Brazil, between 20 and 24 March 2017, and the seventh meeting is forthcoming in July 2017, and will take place in Argentina.

---

6 Ibid, Article 6 (5).

7 ECLAC, Principle 10 website: www.cepal.org/en/topics/principle-10.

8 Minutes to the meetings and reports are available at www.cepal.org/en/comite-de-negociacion-principio-10.

2.1. THE DRAFT OF THE REGIONAL AGREEMENT ON ACCESS TO INFORMATION, PARTICIPATION AND JUSTICE IN ENVIRONMENTAL MATTERS IN LATIN AMERICA AND THE CARIBBEAN

Building on the consensus reached in the Declaration, the signatory Parties issued additional documents setting grounds for the negotiation process. One of the most important is the 'Lima Vision', adopted on October 2013, a brief document about the benefits of the regional agreement for the application of Principle 10 and the values and principles that should guide the regional instrument. These are:

- Equality (no discrimination)
- Inclusion (specially women and vulnerable groups)
- Transparency
- Proactivity (governments must take initiative)
- Collaboration
- Progressive realization (gradual implementation)
- Non-regression (from the existing international instruments and national laws).[9]

The focal points of the signatory parties also adopted the 'San Jose Content', a commented outline on the subjects to be included in the negotiation of the Regional Instrument.[10] This document references existing international instruments and guidelines on access rights, including the Bali Guidelines,[11] the Aarhus Convention[12] and the Kiev Protocol,[13] and reaffirms the basic principles

---

9 Lima Vision for a Regional Instrument on Access Rights Relating to the Environment. Adopted at the third meeting of the focal points appointed by the Governments of the signatory countries of the Declaration on the application of Principle 10 of the Rio Declaration on Environment and Development in Latin America and the Caribbean. Lima, 30–31 October 2013. UN Doc. LC/L.3780 (2014).

10 San Jose Content for the Regional Instrument, approved in the Santiago Decision, *infra,* note 14 at 22 Annex B. Available (in English) at: www.cepal.org/sites/default/files/pages/files/san_jose_content.pdf. Last accessed on 6 September 2016.

11 United Nations Environment Programme – UNEP, Guidelines for the Development of National Legislation on Access to Information, Public Participation and Access to Justice in Environmental Matters, Adopted by the Governing Council of UNEP, UNEP/GCSS. XI/11, Decision SS.XI/5, pt A, 26 February 2010. Available at: www.unep.org/civil-society/Portals/24105/documents/Guidelines/GUIDELINES_TO_ACCESS_TO_ENV_INFO_2.pdf. Last accessed on 28 August 2016.

12 UNECE, Convention on Access to Information, Public Participation in Decision-making and Access to Justice in Environmental Matters, 25 June 1998 (entered into force 30 October 2001) [Aarhus Convention]. The Convention text and related documents can be found at www.unece.org/env/pp/introduction.html. Last visited on 14 March 2016.

13 Protocol on Pollutant Release and Transfer Registers to the UNECE Convention on Access to Information, Public Participation in Decision-making and Access to Justice in Environmental Matters, Doc. MP.PP/2003/1 (2003) (entered into force on 9 October 2009) ['Kiev Protocol'].

of the process: a rights-based approach and capacity-building and cooperation for the effective implementation of Principle 10 of the Rio Declaration. The San Jose Content was approved by the parties to the negotiation in the Santiago Decision, which officially declared the beginning of the negotiation phase.[14]

For the construction of the text of the Regional Instrument, the negotiating committee worked on a preliminary document developed by the ECLAC taking into account the principles already agreed on by the parties and other sources.[15] The first version of the compiled text with the proposals of the parties was published on 22 October 2015. The second version of the text, with the output of the first and second meetings of the negotiating committee,[16] was issued on 3 December 2015; a third version of the document was made available on 3 May 2016 following the third meeting of the negotiating Committee, which was held in Montevideo, Uruguay, in April 2016; the fourth version dated 16 September 2016 was made available for the fifth negotiating meeting held in Chile, and, finally, a fifth version of the document was published on 26 December 2016.

The fifth version of the 'Text compiled by the Presiding Officers incorporating the language proposals received from the countries on the preamble and Articles 1 to 10 of the preliminary document on the Regional Agreement on access to information, participation and justice in environmental matters in Latin America and the Caribbean' [the Draft][17] will be the main input for the present analysis of the definitions in the regional agreement, which aims to assess the material scope of the future instrument employing the definitions in the Aarhus Convention as an international reference.

It is important to note, however, that the negotiation phase is still undergoing and is expected to end in 2017. The current version of the proposed text will be entirely subject to review, and many of the actual contents, including the definitions, could be supressed or modified. Nevertheless, the present analysis may help in the construction of a framework for the discussions around the scope

---

14 Santiago Decision, adopted at the fourth meeting of the focal points appointed by the Governments of the signatory countries of the Declaration on the application of Principle 10 of the Rio Declaration on Environment and Development in Latin America and the Caribbean. Santiago de Chile, 4–6 November 2014. Available at http://repositorio.cepal.org/bitstream/handle/11362/37213/S1420708_es.pdf?sequence=1&isAllowed=y. Last accessed 22 December 2016.

15 The report commissioned to ECLAC [Access to Information, Participation and Justice in Environmental Matters in Latin America and the Caribbean: Situation, Outlook and Examples of Good Practice (Guadalajara: United Nations, 2013)], and the current national laws of the signatory parties. See Santiago Decision, *supra*, note 14. The preliminary document is available at: http://repositorio.cepal.org/bitstream/handle/11362/37953/S1500260_en.pdf?sequence=1. Last accessed on 6 September 2016.

16 The first meeting of the Negotiating Committee of the Regional Agreement on Access to Information, Public Participation and Access to Justice in Environmental Matters in Latin America and the Caribbean was held in Santiago de Chile, between 5 and 7 May 2015; the second meeting was held in Panama City between 27 and 29 October 2015.

17 Draft, *supra*, note 5.

of the Regional Instrument in light of the progress made at the international level in the application of access rights.

3. MAPPING THE DIFFERENCES OF THE MATERIAL SCOPE OF PROCEDURAL ENVIRONMENTAL RIGHTS IN INTERNATIONAL LAW

3.1. 'COMPETENT AUTHORITIES' v. 'PUBLIC AUTHORITIES'

The concept of 'competent authorities' is employed in the Draft of the Regional Instrument to generally indicate a certain authority or entity which is in charge of exercising functions related to environmental access rights. The more specific part of the definition establishes which entities are obliged under Article 6 of the Draft to provide access to environmental information. With this reservation, it would be comparable to the definition on Article 2(2) of the Aarhus Convention of 'public authorities'.

The definition of the Draft reads:

> "Competent authority" means any public body that, by legal mandate, exercises the powers, authority and functions for the application of access rights. In the right of access to information provisions set out under Article 6 the present Agreement, a competent authority shall mean any public authority in any branch of the State (executive, legislative and judicial) and at any level of the internal government structure (central or federal, regional, provincial or municipal); it also applies to independent and autonomous bodies, organizations and entities owned or controlled by the government, whether by virtue of powers granted by the Constitution or other laws, as well as to private organizations that receive substantial[18] public funds or benefits (directly or indirectly) or that perform public functions and services, but only with respect to the public funds or benefits received or to the public functions and services performed.[19]

Firstly, it is not without meaning that the Draft defines the term 'competent authority', as opposed to 'public authority' like the Aarhus Convention does for

[18] The word 'substantial' is found in the English version of the text but it is omitted in the Spanish version. Arguably this could have some impact in the final application of the Instrument. See Spanish version of the Draft at http://repositorio.cepal.org/bitstream/handle/11362/39050/LCL4059Rev4_es.pdf?sequence=20&isAllowed=y. Last accessed on 2 April 2017.

[19] Mexico and Colombia have proposed to leave the definition of the actual authorities and entities that would be responsible for the application of access rights to national law. Draft, *supra*, note 5 at p. 12.

the same purpose, suggesting a more comprehensive definition and setting apart from the connotation given by the term 'public'.

The definition is broader than that of the Aarhus Convention as it includes:
- Authorities acting in a legislative and judicial capacity.
- Entities owned or controlled by the government, regardless of whether they perform public authorities or services related to the environment.
- Private entities that receive public funds or benefits, directly or indirectly.
- Entities performing public functions and services, without conditioning the definition to national law.[20]

The definition is equal to that of 'public authorities' in the Aarhus Convention by including government entities at the federal, regional, provincial or municipal level and certain private entities when they are State-owned or controlled by a government agency and perform public functions or provide public services in relation with the environment.

The definition of the Draft is more restricted as it does not extend to the institutions of regional integration organisations which are a party to the agreement, though the practical effects of this omission are doubtful.

The Aarhus Convention's definition of 'public authorities' extends to entities which, even if not performing public administrative functions by virtue of a statute, have responsibilities or provide public services in relation with the environment, when they do so under the control of the government or agencies performing public administrative functions under national law.[21] This shows an intention to ensure the public's access rights even against private entities when the performance of their environment-related activities can be subject to public control, which is usually the case for public interest activities.

The definition of the Draft accomplishes this through different and perhaps more straight-forward channels: it does not limit to the concept of 'under the control' used in the Aarhus Convention but employs different criteria to ensure that private entities performing public functions related or not to the environment, are subject to the access provisions of the Regional Instrument. These include the case of entities performing public functions and entities receiving public funds or benefits, which may cover an extensive array of different organisations such as NGOs, public utility services providers, public transport operators, universities,

---

20 Unlike the Aarhus Convention which conditions this definition to national law: 'Natural or legal persons performing public administrative functions under national law, including specific duties, activities or services in relation to the environment' (emphasis added), *supra*, note 12, Article 2 (2) (b).

21 Aarhus Convention, *supra*, note 12 at Article 2(2)(c). The European Court of Justice (ECJ) has confirmed the need to examine the national law of Member States to determine when a certain entity can be considered to be performing 'public functions' and should be subject to the access provisions of Directive 2013/04, whose definition mirrors Aarhus'. See ECJ, case C-279/12, *Fish Legal & Emily Shirley v. The Information Commissioner United Utilities, Yorkshire Water and Southern Water* [2013] ECR.

political parties and any State-owned enterprises. The 'public funds' criterion clearly moves the Regional Instrument's access to information scope beyond Aarhus and closer to the recommendations for transparency legislation at the international level.[22]

Current international standards suggest increasing transparency obligations of private entities, especially if related to information deemed to be of 'public interest', such as emissions into the environment and the industries' environmental performance. The Model Law on Access to Information for Africa, prepared by the African Commission on Human and Peoples' Rights, goes even further by stating that every person has the right to access information of private entities when the information may assist in the exercise or protection of any right.[23]

In a general context, transparency obligations are being placed upon private entities when they perform public functions, exercise public authority or receive public monies. This practice mainly responds to the privatisation of what used to be public services and the need to increase accountability and legitimacy of government activities, which may be carried out through private operators.[24]

From this viewpoint, the explicit inclusion of private entities, not only when they perform public functions but when they are State-owned or even partially funded by public monies can be considered a step forward.

The Aarhus Convention's definition of 'public authorities' has been interpreted broadly to include private entities that supply public utility services and other

22 Some examples of non-binding instruments suggesting more openness are: *Article 19*, The Public's Right to Know: Principles on Freedom of Information Legislation, 1999. Available at: www.article19.org/pdfs/standards/righttoknow.pdf. Last visited on 5 March 2016. Article 19 advocate for an extended understanding of the concept of public authority containing 'all branches and levels of government including local government, elected bodies, bodies which operate under a statutory mandate, nationalised industries and public corporations, non-departmental bodies or quangos (quasi non- governmental organisations), judicial bodies, and private bodies which carry out public functions (such as maintaining roads or operating rail lines). Private bodies themselves should also be included if they hold information whose disclosure is likely to diminish the risk of harm to key public interests, such as the environment and health. Inter-governmental organisations should also be subject to freedom of information regimes'; Right2Info, similarly argue that 'It is important that bodies that rely significantly on public funds to perform public functions should be covered by ATI legislation in order to address the specific problem of State functions being devolved to private bodies, sometimes precisely to avoid transparency and accountability requirements'. ATI laws should apply to 'natural or legal persons insofar as they perform public functions, exercise administrative authority or are substantially financed by public funds'. Right2Info.org, available at: www.right2info.org/scope-of-bodies-covered-by-access-to-information/private-bodies-and-public-corporations.

23 African Commission on Human and Peoples' Rights, Model Law on Access to Information for Africa. Available online at: www.achpr.org/files/news/2013/04/d84/model_law.pdf. Last visited on 22 February 2016.

24 *D. Bünger & T. Schomerus*, Private Bodies as Public Authorities under International, European, English and German Environmental Information Laws, JEEPL 2011(8) p. 62, 64 et seq.; *J. Ebbesson*, Public Participation and Privatisation in Environmental Matters: An Assessment of the Aarhus Convention, Erasmus Law Review 2011 (4), p. 71.

entities which perform environment-related activities 'under the control' of a governmental authority,[25] but it has yet to develop further to prevent important public interest environmental information held by private entities to remain hidden from the public eye. This would be the case, for instance, of private State contractors performing environment-related activities such as monitoring air quality standards, cleaning up water sources or performing waste collection and disposal when their functions are not considered 'public' under national law nor do they operate 'under the control' of a public authority. Arguably, private entities in general were never expected to fall within the 'public authorities' definition of the Convention, which is probably why Article 5(6) provides for Parties to encourage operators of high-impact activities to regularly inform the public about their products and performance, where appropriate within the framework of voluntary eco-labelling or eco-auditing schemes or by other means.[26]

The intention to include private entities in the scope of the LAC instrument is more clearly appreciated. The definition of the Draft must be read in light of other provisions addressing private entities specifically. Article 7(12) states that Parties shall take the necessary measures to promote access to environmental information generated by private entities, through legal and administrative frameworks. Additionally, Article 7(13) provides that Parties shall encourage public and private companies to prepare sustainability reports that reflect their social and environmental performance. While these provisions share the soft language of unbinding dispositions, they reflect the unmistakable intention of reconsidering the role and obligations of private actors about the not-so-private environmental information they hold.

In conclusion, the textual analysis of the definition of the Draft suggests that it is more comprehensive than Aarhus's regarding the inclusion of private entities in certain cases, clearly embodying recent international transparency standards and recommendations, although the differences in practice may not be as significant. The case-law of the Aarhus Convention Compliance Committee, for instance, points to a flexible application of the Convention definitions in light of its objectives and principles, leaning towards the inclusion of private entities in a variety of situations not explicitly included in the text of the Convention.[27]

---

25 *United Nations Economic Commission for Europe - UNECE*, The Aarhus Convention: An Implementation Guide, 2nd, 2014, p. 37. ECJ, *supra*, note 21, par. 68.

26 Aarhus Convention, *supra*, note 12 at Article 5 (6).

27 See Aarhus Compliance Committee (ACCC) in Belarus, Case ACCC/C/2009/37, ECE/MP.PP/2011/11/Add.2, April 2011, paras. 67–68: 'The Committee considers that it is not conflicting with the Convention when national legislation delegates some functions related to maintenance and distribution of environmental information to private entities. Such private entities, depending on the particular arrangements adopted in the national law, should be treated for the purpose of access to information as falling under the definition of a "public authority", in the meaning of article 2, paragraph 2 (b) or (c) of the Convention. (...) Therefore, for the purpose of access to information issues, which are the subject of the present communication, the developer should be treated as a public authority under the obligation to

3.2. 'ENVIRONMENTAL INFORMATION'

The Draft proposes the following:

> 'Environmental information' means any information that is written, visual, audio, electronic or recorded in any other form, concerning the state of the environment and natural resources, including information on possible adverse impacts associated with the environment and human health:
> (a) the state of the biotic and abiotic elements of the environment, such as the air and atmosphere, water, earth, landscapes, protected areas, biological diversity and its components, including genetically modified organisms; and the interaction between these elements;
> (b) factors, such as substances, energy, noise, radiation and waste, including radioactive waste, emissions, spills and other releases into the environment, that affect or could affect elements of the environment;
> (c) legislation, administrative acts related to environmental matters or that affect or could affect the elements and factors cited in subparagraphs (a) and (b), and the measures, policies, rules, plans, programmes that support them;
> (d) reports and administrative acts on compliance with environmental legislation;
> (e) economic and social analyses, as well as other studies used to make decisions related to the legislation, administrative acts and supporting mechanisms referred to in subparagraph (c);
> (f) the state of the health and safety of individuals, living conditions, cultural assets, when these are or could be affected by the state of the elements of the environment cited in subparagraph (a) or any of the factors or measures indicated in subparagraphs (b) and (c);
> (g) acts, resolutions, and decisions on matters related to the environment that are issued by the national judicial and/or administrative bodies; and
> (h) any other information on the environment or on elements, components or concepts related thereto.

The term 'environmental information' is employed throughout the text of the Draft in reference to the information which should be available to the public by request or through active dissemination by the authorities, in a similar fashion as the definition of the same term in Article 2(3) of the Aarhus Convention.

The analysis of the definition in the Regional Instrument must be made in light of Article 6(1) of the Draft, which states:

> The Parties shall guarantee that all environmental information in possession of, under the control of, or in the custody of competent authorities is public and presumed to be relevant regardless of format, medium, support, date of creation, origin, classification or processing, except as established in the present agreement.

---

provide access to environmental information in compliance with the requirements of article 4 of the Convention'.

First it should be noted that all information in possession of a competent authority, whether directly held by it or by a third party under its control, should be accessible under the instrument's provisions. The Aarhus Convention only provides for access to information which is held by the 'public authorities', thus, if the information is not held by the authority, the request may be refused (without prejudice to the duty to inform the applicant which authority may hold it or transfer the request).[28] The restrictive effect of this provision is somewhat counteracted by Article 5 of the Convention which provides that each Party shall ensure that public authorities possess and update environmental information relevant to their functions. Secondly, the Article of the Draft provides for the information complying with these conditions that it should be public and presumed to be relevant regardless of format, date of creation, origin or processing. The relevancy of this provision is not clear from the text, but it could imply that no information can be denied on the basis of not being finalised or for having its origin in a non-obliged entity.

The Draft foresees that Parties shall *endeavour to ensure, to the extent possible,* that environmental information is reusable, processable and available in accessible formats.[29]

The definition is broader that that in the Aarhus Convention by including:

- Reports and administrative acts related to compliance with environmental legislation.
- Acts from judicial and administrative authorities, in addition to legislation.
- Any other activities or elements related to the information categories set above (residual clause).

The definition is equivalent to that of Aarhus' as it equally covers:

- The state of the elements of the environment such as air, water, soil, landscape, genetically modified organisms and the interaction among them.
- Factors, such as substances and activities that may affect the aforementioned elements of the environment.
- Administrative acts, measures, activities and legislation affecting the elements or factors of the environment.
- Information on the state of human health and safety, cultural sites and living conditions inasmuch as they can be affected by the factors, elements and measures referred to before.

The definition doesn't appear to be more restrictive in any way, taking into account the residual clause and the inclusive, general language employed.

The formal differences between the definitions suggesting a broader material scope of the Regional Instrument may only be an appearance, however. The

28 Aarhus Convention, *supra*, note 12 at Article 4(3)(a) and Article 4(5).
29 Draft, *supra*, note 5 at Article 7(2).

definition of the Aarhus Convention is drafted in very broad, non-exhaustive terms, and the intention of the Parties should be taken into consideration in its interpretation.[30] It is difficult to picture a case in which administrative reports on compliance with environmental legislation would be withheld by a public authority under the argument that this sort of information is not included in the definition of 'environmental information' of the Convention. Decisions of judicial authorities are usually public in any democracy, regardless of whether they are related to the environment, and the exclusion from the Aarhus definition may be based on reasons of consistency with the definition of 'public authorities', which explicitly excludes judicial authorities. The Bali Guidelines, however, recommend that States ensure that decisions relating to the environment taken by a judicial authority are publicly available (as appropriate and in accordance with national law).[31]

It is worth noting, however, that there are currently several proposals by the negotiating Parties to the Regional Instrument to include additional elements, such as traditional knowledge of indigenous people and information on the income that States receive from the exploitation of their national resources which, in case of being adopted, would enlarge the material scope of this instrument comparing to Aarhus, at least theoretically.[32] The inclusion of traditional knowledge as an element of the environment under literal (a) of the definition in Aarhus is not clear, nor is it as a form of 'cultural site' or 'built structure' under literal (c) due to its immaterial nature. The information about the income of the State for the exploitation of its natural resources is more likely to be included in the definition of the Aarhus Convention, specifically under 'cost-benefit and other economic analysis and assumptions used in environmental decision-making',[33] but there is room for interpretation, nevertheless.

The actual differences between the instruments as regards the right of access to information could possibly be better appreciated when the transcribed Article 6(1) of the Draft is put into practice, which would still be subject to the binding nature of the final agreement and the compliance mechanisms put into place to ensure its effectiveness. The Draft does, however, provide guidelines to implement mechanisms for access to justice in case of the violation of the participatory rights afforded in the instrument. It will probably be left to these authorities to ultimately determine the scope and limits of the definition of 'environmental information' for the purposes of public access.

In summary, the formal definitions of 'environmental information' in both instruments are fairly the same, but other provisions in the Draft suggest a wider material scope of the Regional Instrument, like Article 6(1) establishing the public (*ergo* accessible) status of all environmental information *in the possession, under*

30 Aarhus Convention Implementation Guide, *supra,* note 25 at p. 50.

31 Bali Guidelines, *supra*, note 11 at Guideline 24.

32 Draft, *supra*, note 5 at p. 14. Proposals by Peru and Antigua and Barbuda.

33 Aarhus Convention, *supra,* note 12 at Article 2(3)(b).

the control or in the custody of the competent authorities, regardless of format, date of creation, origin, classification or processing.

3.3. 'PUBLIC' AND 'PUBLIC CONCERNED'

The definitions of 'public' in the Draft and in the Aarhus Convention are practically the same. According to the Draft, 'public' means one or more natural or legal persons and, their associations, organizations or groups. There is a clear division among signatory parties with a group backing the inclusion of the words 'in accordance with national legislation or practice', as in the Aarhus Convention, and the rest opposing to this inclusion.[34]

This term is used throughout the Regional Instrument to refer to the people who are entitled to the access rights in general and it should be applied taking into account the provisions banning any form of discrimination and prescribing the most favourable interpretation in order to guarantee the effectiveness of access rights and environmental protection.[35]

In the Regional Instrument, the most qualified definition of 'Directly affected public' means public affected or potentially affected by decisions with environmental impacts. This definition is wide enough to encompass the categories set out in the definition of 'the public concerned' in the Aarhus Convention, except for the case of environmental non-governmental organisations (meeting the requirements of national law), which, under the Aarhus Convention, are always deemed to have an interest, hence are considered 'public concerned', but in the Draft are not even mentioned.[36]

This definition is relevant regarding public participation in decision-making in specific projects or activities. Under Article 8(16) of the Draft, competent authorities shall make efforts to identify and promote the participation of the 'directly affected public' in the decision-making processes, including by providing financial and technical assistance. When the directly affected public speaks primarily languages other than the official language, measures shall be taken to facilitate their understanding and participation.[37]

Notably, under the current Draft and opposed to the Aarhus Convention, access to justice is not conditioned to the demonstration of any particular interest. On the contrary, Article 9(2) prevents that the Parties shall ensure, under national legislation, that any person is entitled to have access to a judicial (or other autonomous) authority to challenge the legality of any action or omission related

34 Draft, *supra*, note 5 at p. 14.

35 Draft, *supra*, note 5 at Article 5(12)(13).

36 Jamaica, Saint Vincent and the Grenadines and Chile have put forward a proposal to include environmental NGOs in the definition as in the Aarhus Convention. See Draft, *supra*, note 5 at p. 15.

37 Draft, *supra*, note 5 at Article 8(10).

to environmental access rights or any other action or omission that may affect the environment or contravene environmental laws, either by private or public persons.

To sum up, when and if the Draft conditions access rights to the 'directly affected public', these rights could not be exercised by environmental NGOs (complying with the requirements of national law), whereas under the Aarhus Convention they are considered 'public concerned' and enjoy all the prerogatives granted in the Convention to this particular category of public.

However, the definition of 'directly affected public' is significantly less employed in the Draft of the Regional Instrument than the definition of 'public concerned' in the Aarhus Convention, meaning that, in practice, the inclusion of environmental NGOs within the definition of 'directly affected public' is not a determining factor of their ability to participate effectively in the terms of the Regional Instrument. The following table explains the point:

Access Rights	**Draft of the Regional Instrument**		**Aarhus Convention**	
	Public	**Directly Affected Public (excluding Environmental NGOs)**	**Public**	**Public Concerned (including environmental NGOs)**
Participation in decision-making in specific projects and activities	✓	✓	✓ (with lesser prerogatives than the Public Concerned)[38]	✓
Additional measures to facilitate participation in decision-making when primarily language is not the official language.	X	✓	-	-
Access to a review procedure for violation of the right to participation in decision-making on specific activities	✓	✓	X	✓
Direct access to courts (or equivalent) for the violation of environmental legislation	✓	✓	Subject to conditions of national law	

38 Aarhus Convention, *supra*, note 12 at Article 6. The 'public concerned' has privileged access, early in the decision-making process, to relevant information indispensable for effective decision-making. Applicants are also encouraged to enter into discussions with the public concerned prior to the application for a permit.

In this comparison it can be observed that the exclusion of environmental NGOs from the Draft's definition of 'directly affected public' does not affect significantly their rights of access as it would if they were excluded from the definition of 'public concerned' in the framework of the Aarhus Convention. This could also mean that the definitions of 'directly affected public' and 'public concerned', despite their semantic affinity, are just not comparable, as they are used differently in the proposal for the Regional Instrument and in the Aarhus Convention.

3.4. OTHER DEFINITIONS AFFECTING THE SCOPE OF THE REGIONAL INSTRUMENT v. THE AARHUS CONVENTION

There are other definitions that are not found in the Aarhus Convention but may have an impact in the material scope of the Regional Instrument. These are the definitions of 'persons in vulnerable situations', which to the point is still much controverted, the definition of 'decision-making in environmental matters', and 'public participation'.

'Persons in vulnerable situations' means

> Those persons who, because of their age, gender, physical or mental condition, or social, economic, ethnic and/or cultural circumstances, face particular difficulties in fully exercising the access rights recognized in this Agreement. The causes of vulnerability may include, age, disability, belonging to indigenous communities or minority groups, victimization, migration and internal displacement, poverty, gender and deprivation of liberty. The determination of persons in vulnerable situations in each country shall depend on its specific characteristics, including its level of social and economic development.

The Draft prevents that Parties shall facilitate access to information for persons in vulnerable situations by providing assistance from the formulation of requests through to the delivery of the information.[39] Additionally, each Party shall endeavour to ensure that competent authorities prepare environmental information to be disseminated in various languages and through alternative formats comprehensible to these individuals and groups.[40] Persons in vulnerable situations shall also be exempted from delivery and reproduction costs that could be charged to the general public for accessing information,[41] and special measures shall be taken to ensure their access to justice including by providing free technical and legal assistance and enabling *linguistically, culturally, economically, spatially and temporally appropriate* access channels.[42]

---

39 Draft, *supra*, note 5 at Article 6(3).
40 Draft, *supra*, note 5 at Article 7(6).
41 Draft, *supra*, note 5 at Article 6(16).
42 Draft, *supra*, note 5 at Article 9(6).

These provisions are consistent with State policies of several Parties, they constitute a clear application of the principle of inclusion established in the 'Lima Vision', and are based in the same principles as other international instruments such as ILO Covenant 169 on Indigenous and Tribal Peoples, which has been ratified by most of the negotiating Parties.[43]

Although provisions to guarantee equalitarian access to environmental participatory rights to vulnerable groups should not limit the scope of the instrument *vis-à-vis* the general public, it would, necessarily, imply different categories of participation that may result, from comparison, in 'diminished' access prerogatives for the general public than those afforded to the these groups and individuals. Special attention should be paid in the implementation to avoid negative effects of this 'positive discrimination' measure to ensure equal access in practice.

Another definition which is not found in the Aarhus Convention is 'decision-making in environmental matters'. According to the Draft, this means:

> the development, implementation, compliance, and evaluation of laws and regulations, policies, plans, strategies, programmes, projects whether public or private liable to affect the environment or the use, exploitation or conservation of natural resources at all levels of the internal government structure (central or federal, regional, provincial or municipal).

The definition should be read in accordance with another definition proposed in the Draft of the term 'Public Participation', which means

> the process by which natural or legal persons, individually or collectively, contribute to decision-making on environmental matters through different modalities of participation that are institutionalized or otherwise established in accordance with national legislation or practice.

This definition does not appear to improve the clarity of the instrument, and could even lead to confusion since the term is generally employed in reference to environmental access rights (access to information, participation in decision-making processes and access to justice) and not only to participation in decision-making. Within the instrument, it is not used consistently; the term 'environmental decision-making' is found instead.[44]

---

43 Argentina, Bolivia, Brazil, Chile, Colombia, Costa Rica, Ecuador, Guatemala, Honduras, Mexico, Paraguay, and Peru have ratified the ILO Covenant 169 and are parties in the negotiation. See www.ilo.org/dyn/normlex/en/f?p=NORMLEXPUB:11300:0::NO::P11300_INSTRUMENT_ID:312314.

44 See Draft, *supra*, note 5 at Preamble, Recital 16; Article 5(4); 9(2)(c) and the title of Article 8. In the current Draft, there is a comment by Brazil suggesting that 'environmental decision-making is replaced with 'decision-making in environmental matters' throughout the text.

The term 'decision-making in environmental matters' (or environmental decision-making) is employed throughout the text to determine the material scope of the right of public participation in the deliberative processes undertaken prior to the adoption of a measure that may affect the environment. The Aarhus Convention does not establish any explicit definition of such processes, but rather builds the concept on the basis of the rights conferred to the public in the context of environmental decision-making.

Arguably, the definition in the Draft is bound to limit the material scope of the Regional Instrument, mainly because, even if the intent is to make it very comprehensive, it is very difficult to foresee all possible scenarios of decision-making related to the environment in which the public should be entitled to consultation and active participation according to Principle 10 of the Rio Declaration.

If the definition is to be included in the final agreement, measures should be taken to ensure a flexible interpretation taking into account the principles and objectives of the Regional Instrument and Principle 10 of the Rio Declaration. A provision to this effect is already included in Article 5 (13) of the Draft, which mandates that Parties adopt the most favourable interpretation in order to guarantee the fullest effectiveness of access rights and the protection of the environment.

4. CONCLUSIONS

The Aarhus Convention was adopted in 1998 with the objective of ensuring the application of Principle 10 of the Rio Declaration under minimum standards among different countries. The Regional Instrument currently under discussion in Latin America and the Caribbean also aims to guarantee the implementation of Principle 10 in the region, almost twenty years later, with the similar aim of establishing a floor, not a ceiling, for environmental access rights.[45]

The Aarhus process provides valuable lessons to be considered in the adoption of the LAC instrument to better ensure the effectiveness of its aims, including information about the negotiation process at the international level, the difficulties during implementation, and possible mechanisms for compliance, among others. There is also important 'case-law' on the application of Aarhus provisions, for example from the European Court of Justice and the Aarhus Convention Compliance Committee, which provides invaluable insight of the aspects which are more likely to raise difficulties for the application of the instrument by the Parties and the public.

This exploratory analysis reviewed the current version of the text under discussion for the Regional Instrument and compared the definitions therein

[45] Draft, *supra*, note 5 at Preamble, Recital 18; Article 5(9).

(to the extent logically possible and with the reservations expressed throughout the analysis) with those found in the Aarhus Convention, in order to assess the material scope of the instrument in light of the international standards.

Generally speaking, the material scope of the Regional Instrument broadens in comparison to Aarhus by including crucial elements in its definitions such as private entities receiving public funds directly or indirectly and also authorities acting in a judicial or legislative capacity for the purposes of access to information, though a more detailed analysis of the exemptions to disclosure in both texts would be necessary to fully assess the impact of these inclusions (e.g. business confidentiality).

Although the definition of 'environmental information' is fairly the same in both texts, the draft of the Regional Instrument provides additional criteria to ensure the broad interpretation of this concept, in the form of a residual clause covering all matters related to previously listed elements of the definition and an explicit provision ordering the adoption of the most favourable interpretation to maximise the effectiveness of access rights.

The proposed definitions of 'public' and 'directly affected public' in the Draft are used throughout the text in a way that supports the effective exercise of access rights for the general public without having to prove any particular interest, but granting special conditions to facilitate public participation when there is actually such an interest. In contrast, environmental non-governmental organisations are not presumed to have any particular interest for these purposes, like they are under the Aarhus Convention, but this hardly restricts their ability to participate effectively considering how the term 'directly affected public' is employed in the Regional Instrument.

However, the additional definition of 'decision-making in environmental matters' is likely to restrict rather than to amplify the scope of the right of public participation in decision-making, by introducing additional criteria to determine when a decision falls within the scope of the instrument, whilst the definition of 'public participation' does not seem to make any appreciable contribution.

The definitions of the Regional Instrument are still under discussion, but the overall impression based on the previous analysis suggests a detailed approach that, to this point, would make the material scope of the rights to information, participation and justice in environmental matters more extensively applicable in Latin America than they are under the Aarhus Convention provisions. This of course would still be subject to other crucial aspects, for instance: that the Regional Instrument adopts a binding nature, the definition of exceptions to the right of access to information, the adequate implementation by the Parties and the possibility to establish effective compliance mechanisms to enforce its provisions.

Unlike Aarhus, the LAC Instrument still lacks the clarity provided by the experience of the Parties, courts and public decisively committed to the materialisation of Principle X of the Rio Declaration, which have offset some of the textual shortcomings of the Convention, like the understanding of the definition of 'public authorities' by the ECJ and the guidelines for the application of the term 'environmental information' contained in the Aarhus Convention Implementation Guide.[46]

In this sense, the lessons learned from the Aarhus Process and current international guidelines may still be more readily implemented, contributing to the consistence, coherence and, ultimately, to the effectiveness of the Regional Instrument once it enters into force.[47]

---

46 UNECE, *supra*, note 25; ECJ, *supra*, note 21.

47 As of October 2017, there is a seventh version of the Draft. The main change regarding the topic of the article is the replacement of the term 'competent authorities' with 'public authorities' throughout the text of the instrument, although the definition has not been modified yet.

PROCEDURAL ENVIRONMENTAL RIGHTS IN PRACTICE

PROCEDURAL ENVIRONMENTAL RIGHTS IN THE JURISPRUDENCE OF THE EUROPEAN COURT OF HUMAN RIGHTS AND THEIR IMPACT ON CRIMINAL PROCEDURE LAW

Robert Esser*

ABSTRACT

This article will mainly focus on the question as to what degree human rights standards require an effective criminal investigation of environmental law cases and where the interests of potential suspects pose limitations to such investigations. It will mainly deal with the provisions of the European Convention on Human Rights (ECHR), particularly emphasizing the case-law of the European Court of Human Rights (ECtHR) in Strasbourg. The ECtHR has stressed many times the necessity of transparency and the possibility of people concerned to participate effectively in judicial proceedings as regards the compliance of a national decision-making process with the procedural impact of Article 8 ECHR in relation to environmental issues. It will be examined if *procedural environmental rights* originating from the Convention do also exist in the area of *criminal procedure law*. Finally, it will also be analysed whether the legal institute of "private accessory prosecution", known to German Criminal Procedure Law, corresponds with the procedural requirements set forth by the ECtHR concerning Article 6 §1 ECHR.

KEYWORDS

Article 8 ECHR; Article 2 ECHR; Article 1 of Protocol No. 1; Article 6 § 1 ECHR; criminal procedure law; effective criminal investigation; environmental law cases;

* Prof. Dr. Robert Esser, University of Passau (Germany), Chair of German, European and International Criminal law, Criminal Procedure and White-Collar Crime / Research Centre Human Rights in Criminal Proceedings (HRCP).

human rights standards; involvement of the public concerning environmental decision-making processes; private accessory prosecution (*Nebenklage*).

1. INTRODUCTION – ENVIRONMENTAL LAW CASES AND THEIR CONNOTATION TO CRIMINAL LAW

Situations that are dangerous for the environment often pose a risk to people directly affected. Linking those dangers to criminal law can be done relatively easily. In case damages could be caused because of a threat to life or bodily integrity (both being legally protected values), the question arises whether the State is obliged to take concrete preventive measures or (if necessary) authorize specific countermeasures. This question can be examined on the basis of (non-) constitutional provisions of the national law. However, the following analysis will focus on human rights standards derived from the European Convention on Human Rights (ECHR).

As regards the compliance of a domestic decision-making process with the procedural impact of Article 8 ECHR (and also of Article 2 ECHR) in relation to environmental issues *in general*, the ECtHR stresses the necessity of transparency and the possibility of people concerned to participate effectively, i.e. in the early stages of the decision-making process, as well as the right to seek judicial review.[1]

Based on this case-law analysis the next step will be to decide if *procedural environmental rights* – as derived from the Convention, in other words, from a human rights perspective – do also exist in the sphere of *criminal procedure law*, in the early stages of criminal investigations of environmental crimes as well as during the main trial.

The final part will concentrate on the legal institute of "private accessory prosecution", known for example to German Criminal Procedure Law (Section 395 et seq. German Code of Criminal Procedure – *Strafprozessordnung*), by analysing if these law provisions fit in the "procedural framework" of the ECtHR`s jurisprudence concerning Article 6 § 1 ECHR.

---

1 *Robert Esser* holds the Chair for German, European and International Criminal Law, Criminal Procedure and Economic Criminal Law at the University of Passau (Germany). Since 2010 he leads the Research Centre Human Rights in Criminal Proceedings (HRCP).
See for Human Rights Challenges after a nuclear accident: *Esser*, Nuclear Accidents: Human Rights Challenges in Criminal Proceedings, European Energy and Environmental Law Review (EEELR) 2013, pp. 86–100.

2. OBLIGATION OF THE STATE TO PROTECT PEOPLE'S LIFE AND THE DUTY TO CONDUCT AN EFFECTIVE INVESTIGATION (Article 2 ECHR)

Article 2 ECHR obliges the Contracting States to respect the right to life by taking protective measures in order to defend it from risks including private interventions. The provision does not only cover situations where a certain action or omission on the part of the State led to a death complained of, but also situations where there clearly existed a risk to an individual`s life who survived.[2]

The ECtHR has constructed a positive duty of the Contracting States to set up a *legal framework* penalising at least acts of intentional infringements of the right to life ("*wilful homicide*"). So far, however, no general duty exists to provide criminal law provisions and an "effective judicial system" for all cases in which the infringement of the right to life or to physical integrity is caused unintentionally, i.e. by negligence ("*involuntary manslaughter*"); in some cases the access to (effective) civil proceedings may also provide adequate protection[3], as well as administrative measures or disciplinary sanctions.[4] However, in the particular context of "dangerous activities", an official criminal investigation is indispensable because public authorities are often the only entities to have sufficient relevant knowledge to identify and establish the complex phenomena that might have caused an incident.[5]

The positive obligation to take all appropriate steps to safeguard life for the purposes of Article 2 ECHR entails above all a primary duty on the State to put in place a legislative and administrative framework designed to provide effective deterrence against threats to the right to life.[6] The ECtHR`s guiding line is that in cases of involuntary manslaughter "an effective independent judicial system *[needs]* to be set up so as to secure legal means capable of establishing the facts,

---

2 ECtHR, *Kolyadenko and Others v. Russia*, 28.02.2012, nos. 17423/05, 20534/05, 20678/05, 23263/05, 24283/05 and 35673/05, §151; ECtHR (GC), *Makaratzis v. Greece*, 20.12.2004, no. 50385/99, §§49–55.

3 ECtHR, *Byrzykowski v. Poland*, 27.06.2006, no. 11562/05, §105.

4 ECtHR, *Kolyadenko and Others v. Russia*, 28.2.2012, nos. 17423/05, 20534/05, 20678/05, 23263/05, 24283/05 and 35673/05, §189 (discharge of large quantities of water from a water reservoir into a river which had not been kept in a proper condition; triggering of a flash flood); ECtHR, *Öneryildiz v. Turkey*, 30.11.2004, no. 48939/99, ECHR 2004-XII, §92 (fatal methane gas explosion on a dump the city was responsible for); ECtHR, *Calvelli and Ciglio v. Italy*, 17.01.2002, no. 32967/96, §51.

5 ECtHR, *Kolyadenko and Others v. Russia*, 28.02.2012, nos. 17423/05, 20534/05, 20678/05, 23263/05, 24283/05 and 35673/05, 190.

6 ECtHR, *Kolyadenko and Others v. Russia*, 28.02.2012, nos. 17423/05, 20534/05, 20678/05, 23263/05, 24283/05 and 35673/05, §157; ECtHR, *Öneryildiz v. Turkey*, 30.11.2004, no. 48939/99, ECHR 2004-XII, §89; ECtHR, *Budayeva and Others v. Russia*, 20.03.2008, nos. 15339/02, 21166/02, 20058/02, 11673/02 and 15343/02, §129.

holding accountable those at fault and providing appropriate redress to the victim."[7]

In addition to building up a legal framework for the protection of human rights guarantees the ECtHR has stressed that Article 2 § 1 ECHR enjoins the State not only to refrain from the intentional and unlawful taking of life but also to take (concrete) appropriate (preventive) *steps to safeguard* the lives of those within its jurisdiction.[8] The scope of any such positive obligation in a concrete case should not impose an impossible or disproportionate burden on the authorities, i.e. not every claimed risk to life may force the public authorities to take operational measures to prevent that risk from materialising. It also depends on the circumstances if the authorities knew or ought to have known at the time of the existence of a real and immediate risk to the life of an identified individual (so-called "*Osman-Test*").[9]

Whenever a company is subject to public supervision or there is private-public joint ownership, a State's direct responsibility under Article 1 ECHR is obvious. In cases of environmental dangers or accidents, the risk for life of the people affected is normally attributed to private companies and persons operating hazardous facilities for instance. In these cases it needs to be determined whether there is a State's responsibility to protect human rights infringements, meaning to investigate dangerous situations and to intervene in order to remedy/avoid potential shortcomings of private parties (see Article 1 ECHR: "*The High Contracting Parties shall secure to everyone within their jurisdiction the rights and freedoms defined in Section 1 of this Convention*").

Furthermore, a positive duty of the State to protect certain human right guarantees – including and especially the right to life (Article 2 ECHR) – goes hand in hand with procedural elements of an effective (retrospective) investigation if a danger has already caused damage. Generally speaking, the right to life (Article 2 ECHR) requires a State to provide an effective system of regulation, supervision and control[10] where a risk to life results from risky, even lawful, both public and private engagements. As the ECtHR pointed out in *Yasa v. Turkey* this obligation

---

7 ECtHR, *Kemaloglu v. Turkey*, 10.04.2012, no. 19986/06, §38; see also ECtHR, *Ciechonska v. Poland*, 14.06.2011, no. 19776/04, §66; compare *Esser*, EEELR 2013, 86 f. with further references.

8 ECtHR, *van Colle v. United Kingdom*, 13.11.2012, no. 7678/09, §88; ECtHR, *L.C.B. v. United Kingdom*, 09.06.1998, Reports 1998-III, no. 23413/94, §36. Leading Case: ECtHR, *Osman v. United Kingdom*, 28.10.1998, Reports 1998-VIII, no. 23452/94, §115 (preventive operational measures to protect an individual whose life is at risk from the criminal acts of another individual).

9 ECtHR, *Osman v. United Kingdom*, 28.10.1998, Reports 1998-VIII, no. 23452/94, §116; see also: ECtHR, *van Colle v. United Kingdom*,13.11.2012, no. 7678/09, §§88–91. Compare with further references: *Esser*, EEELR 2013, p. 86, 87.

10 Rainey/Wicks/Ovey in Jacobs/White/Ovey, *The European Convention on Human Rights* (6th ed., 2014), p. 158 ff.

is not limited to the death of people being attributed to a state official`s conduct or where relatives formally request public investigations.[11]

The ECtHR has also specified how and to which extent these investigations must be realised: They should be carried out by an independent and public body[12], of the states` own motion, immediately after the knowledge of a forceful cause of death[13] and *"be capable of leading to the identification and punishment of those responsible"*.[14] They must include the actual circumstances of the case as well as the persons possibly involved, irrespective of the existence of a private criminal complaint.[15]

In recent years the ECtHR has taken the opportunity to apply and to develop his idea of a *"system of effective control"* derived from Article 2 ECHR on cases concerning environmental matters. In *Smaltini v. Italy*, the Court noted that, as far as matters are in question, which concern the exercise of industrially hazardous activities, *"the judicial system required by Article 2 [ECHR] must contain an official investigation mechanism that is independent and impartial and effective"*.[16] More precisely the Court observed that *Smaltini*'s complaint consisted in alleging not that the domestic authorities had omitted to take legislative or administrative measures to protect her right to life, but that they had not established the existence of a causal link between the polluting emissions from the industrial plant and her illness.[17] It also comes quite clear from *Smaltini* that a responsibility of the State to *investigate deaths* caused through private enterprises may derive from the government's administrative decision to grant a permit for its operation and from the public supervision thereof.

---

11 ECtHR, *Yasa v. Turkey*, 02.09.1998, no. 22495/93.

12 ECtHR, *Finucane v. United Kingdom*, 01.07.2003, no. 29178/95, ECHR 2003-VIII, §§68 f.; ECtHR (GC), *Ramsahai et al. v. The Netherlands*, 15.05.2007, no. 52391/99, ECHR 2007-II, §§333 ff.; ECtHR, *Brecknell v. United Kingdom*, 27.11.2007, no. 32457/04, §72.

13 ECtHR, *Yasa v. Turkey*, 02.09.1998, no. 22495/93, §100; ECtHR, *Güngör v. Turkey*, 22.05.2005, no. 28290/95, §67.

14 ECtHR, *Grams v. Germany* (dec.), 05.10.1999, no. 33677/96, Reports 1999-VII; ECtHR (GC), *Oğur v. Turkey*, 20.05.1999, no. 21594/93, ECHR 1999-III, §88; ECtHR, *Kaya v. Turkey*, 19.02.1998, no. 22729/93, Reports 1998-I, §86; ECtHR, *Ceyhan Demir et al. v. Turkey*, 13.01.2005, no. 34491/97, §107.

15 ECtHR, *Hugh Jordan v. United Kingdom*, 04.05.2001, no. 24746/94, ECHR 2001-III, §105; ECtHR, *Ceyhan Demir et al. v. Turkey*, 13.01.2005, no. 34491/97, §§106 ff.; ECtHR, *Paul and Audrey Edwards v. the United Kingdom*, 14.03.2002, no. 46477/99, ECHR 2002-II, §§69–73; ECtHR, *Öneryildiz v. Turkey*, 30.11.2004, no. 48939/99 §94; ECtHR (GC), *Šilih v. Slovenia*, 09.04.2009, no. 71463/01, §§153–154 (medical mistreatment); ECtHR (GC), *Jaloud v. the Netherlands*, 20.11.2014, no. 47708/08, §186; ECtHR (GC), *Armani Da Silva v. the United Kingdom*, 30.03.2016, no. 5878/08, §231 (Shooting a person by police officer in subway); see also *R. Esser, Auf dem Weg zu einem europäischen Strafverfahrensrecht* (2002; thereafter: Esser), p. 105 with further references.

16 See ECtHR, *Smaltini v. Italy*, 24.03.2015, no. 43961/09, §53; see also ECtHR (GC), *Öneryıldız v. Turkey*, 30.11.2004, no. 48939/99, ECHR 2004-XII.

17 See ECtHR, *Smaltini v. Italy*, 24.03.2015, no. 43961/09, §40.

3. ENVIRONMENTAL DANGERS AND THE RIGHT TO PRIVATE LIFE, ARTICLE 8 ECHR

3.1. ECTHR'S JURISDICTION ON ENVIRONMENTAL PROTECTION

According to Article 8 § 1 ECHR everyone enjoys the right to respect, i.e. protection of his private life including his physical and psychological integrity.[18] Apart from its obligation under Article 2 ECHR, the State has also a corresponding positive obligation to protect the private life of people.[19]

Therefore, where *environmental pollution*, such as noise or odour emissions, reaches a degree as to prevent a claimant from permanently residing at his domicile, it may impose a violation of Article 8 ECHR. In *López Ostra v. Spain* the Court declared admissible the applicant's complaint about the local authorities' inactivity in dealing with the nuisance caused by a waste-treatment plant situated a few metres away from her home. It assessed that whether the question is analysed in terms of a positive duty on the State to take reasonable and appropriate measures to secure the applicant's rights under Article 8 § 1 ECHR or in terms of an "interference by a public authority" justified in accordance with Article 8 § 2 ECHR, the applicable principles would be quite similar. In both contexts regard must be had to the fair balance that has to be struck between the competing interests of the individual and of the community as a whole, and that either way the State is given a certain margin of appreciation.[20]

The Court has also reiterated its jurisdiction multiple times in the recent past – and has extended the protection from private life additionally to the home, which is equally protected by Article 8 § 1 ECHR. In *Udovičić v. Croatia* the Court stressed that the individual has a right to respect for his home, meaning not just the right to the actual physical area, but also to the quiet enjoyment of that area. Breaches of the right to respect for the home are not limited to concrete or physical breaches, but also include noise, emissions, smells or other forms of interference.[21] The Court reiterated that although no explicit right in the Convention to a clean and quiet environment exists, environmental protection or nature conservation, in a situation where an individual, its home, family or private life is directly and

---

18 See also *Esser* in: Löwe/Rosenberg, Die Strafprozessordnung und das Gerichtsverfassungsgesetz: StPO, Band 11: EMRK/IPBPR (26th ed., 2012; thereafter: LR/*Esser*), Art. 8 ECHR, §67; *P. Leach*, Taking a case to the European Court of Human Rights, 3rd ed. 2011, §6 p. 353.

19 ECtHR (GC), *Janković v. Croatia*, 05.03.2009, no. 38478/05, §45; ECtHR, *Bensaid v. United Kingdom*, 06.02.2001, no. 44599/98, §47; ECtHR, *Guerra v. Italy*, 19.02.1998, no. 14967/89, Rep. 1998-I, §58; see also LR/*Esser* (Fn. 18), Art. 8 ECHR, §24.

20 ECtHR, *López Ostra v. Spain*, 09.12.1994, no. 16798/90, Series A No. 303-C, §51; *Esser*, EEELR 2013, p. 86, 90.

21 ECtHR, *Udovičić v. Croatia*, 24.04.2014, no. 27310/09, §136; see also ECtHR, *Moreno Gómez v. Spain*, 16.11.2004, no. 4143/02, ECHR 2004-X, §53; ECtHR, *Luginbühl v. Switzerland* (Dec.), 17.01.2006, no. 42756/02; ECtHR, *Ruano Morcuende v. Spain* (Dec.), 06.09.2005, no. 75287/01.

seriously affected by noise or other pollution an issue may arise under Article 8 of the Convention.[22]

In the contexts of paragraph 1 and paragraph 2 of Article 8 ECHR, the State must take regard to the fair balance that has to be struck between the competing interests of the individual and of the community as a whole.[23]

Since the Court perceives even minor forms of damage to the health as an infringement of private life, a breach of Article 8 ECHR is always conceivable where emissions of any kind damage the physical and/or psychological integrity.[24]

3.2. CONTENT OF THE STATE'S POSITIVE DUTY

The positive obligation "*inherent*"[25] in Article 8 ECHR also calls for intervention by public authorities where the rights guaranteed to the individual are violated or endangered by another private party.

Firstly, there are those cases in the Court`s case law dealing with planning decisions concerning environmental issues arising in connection with certain structural works.

Reasonable and adequate provisions for the protection of the rights guaranteed by Article 8 § 1 ECHR imply the access to effective proceedings suitable to safeguard the interests and legally protected rights of the victim. Where legal provisions unfold their effects only in a compensatory way but fail to protect legally protected interests from infringements in the first place, they will not fulfil the requirements under Article 8 § 1 ECHR.[26]

Health hazards can, under certain circumstances, also impose an obligation on the State to take action resulting from his protective duties under Article 8 ECHR. E.g., this positive duty also contains the distribution of information about health hazards, which can result in a State's obligation to grant access to governmental information and case files.

Additionally, the State has to take reasonable and adequate precautions to secure the rights granted by Article 8 § 1 ECHR in a concrete case.[27] In the context of dangerous activities the scope of the positive obligations under Article 2 and Article 8 ECHR largely overlap as the Court noted in *Kolyadenko v. Russia*: "*Indeed, the positive obligation under Article 8 and Article 1 of Protocol No. 1 required the national authorities to take the same practical measures as*

22 ECtHR, *Udovičić v. Croatia*, 24.04.2014, no. 27310/09, §137; similar ECtHR, *Fadeyeva v. Russia*, 09.06.2005, no. 55723/00, ECHR 2005-IV, §68.
23 ECtHR, *Udovičić v. Croatia*, 24.04.2014, no. 27310/09, §138.
24 ECtHR, *Storck v. Germany*, 16.06.2005, no. 61603/00, ECHR 2005-V, §143; concerning nuclear accidents: *Esser*, EEELR 2013, p. 86.
25 See ECtHR, *Cossey v. United Kingdom*, 27.09.1990, no. 10843/84, §37.
26 ECtHR, *Tysiac v. Poland*, 20.03.2007, no. 5410/03, ECHR 2007-IV, §§126 f.
27 ECtHR (GC), *Evans v. United Kingdom*, 10.04.2007, no. 6339/05, ECHR 2007-I, §75; ECtHR (GC), *Hatton et al. v. United Kingdom*, 08.07.2003, no. 36022/97, ECHR 2003-VIII, §§98, 119.

those expected of them in the context of their positive obligation under Article 2 of the Convention [...]. Since it is clear that no such measures were taken, the Court concludes that the Russian authorities failed in their positive obligation to protect the applicants' homes and property".[28]

3.3. INTERFERENCE BY A PUBLIC AUTHORITY ACCORDING TO ARTICLE 8 § 2 ECHR

Article 8 § 2 ECHR provides that

> "there shall be no interference by a public authority with the exercise of this right except such as is in accordance with the law and is necessary in a democratic society in the interests of national security, public safety or the economic well-being of the country, for the prevention of disorder or crime, for the protection of health or morals, or for the protection of the rights and freedoms of others".

A case, where the Court interpreted the interference by a public authority in accordance with the national law, was *Eckenbrecht and Ruhmer v. Germany*. The ECtHR reiterated that according to Article 8 § 2 ECHR, restrictions are permitted in the interests of the economic well-being of the country and for the protection of the rights and freedoms of others (like the turning of an airport into an international hub for air freight, particularly for express freight). It is therefore legitimate for the State to have taken the economic interests into consideration for the shaping of its policy.[29] In the concrete case the economic aims pursued by the reconstruction of the airport were legitimate and followed sound policy reasons for the development of a whole geographic region.

It can be described as settled case-law that, whilst Article 8 ECHR contains no explicit procedural requirements, the decision-making process leading to measures of interference must be fair and such as to afford due respect to the interests safeguarded to the individual by Article 8 ECHR.[30] It is therefore necessary to consider all the procedural aspects, including the type of policy or decision making process involved, the extent to which the views of individuals were taken into account throughout the decision-making process and the procedural safeguards available. *"A governmental decision-making process concerning complex issues of environmental and economic policy must in the first place involve appropriate investigations and studies so that the effects of activities that might damage the environment and infringe individuals' rights may be*

---

28 ECtHR, *Kolyadenko and Others v. Russia*, 28.2.2012, nos. 17423/05, 20534/05, 20678/05, 23263/05, 24283/05 and 35673/05, §216; ECtHR, *Budayeva and Others v. Russia*, 20.3.2008, no. 15339/02, 21166/02, 20058/02, 11673/02 and 15343/02, §133.

29 ECtHR, *Eckenbrecht and Ruhmer v. Germany*, 10.06.2014, no. 25330/10, §34.

30 ECtHR, *Eckenbrecht and Ruhmer v. Germany*, 10.06.2014, no. 25330/10, §36.

anticipated and evaluated in advance and a fair balance may accordingly be struck between the various conflicting interests at stake."[31]

In *Eckenbrecht and Ruhmer v. Germany*, the German courts took into account all decisive factors and balanced them in a reasonable way, so the ECtHR came to the conclusion that the impugned decisions cannot be said to have overstepped the margin of appreciation as regards Article 8 ECHR.

3.4. INVOLVEMENT OF THE PUBLIC IN THE DECISION-MAKING PROCESS, MARGIN OF APPRECIATION OF THE STATE AND ACCESS TO JUDICIAL REVIEW COMPLYING WITH ARTICLE 8 § 2 ECHR

In a decision-making process, the State must not only fairly balance the colliding interests of the private parties, but also assure compliance with general interests of the community.[32] In this respect generally the same principles as for the justification of public infringements apply.[33]

Whether the State lived up to this positive duty can be determined by a comparison with the boundaries set out in Article 8 § 2 ECHR, which can be applied to Article 8 § 1 ECHR correspondingly.[34]

In *Eckenbrecht and Ruhmer* the Court was, after having regarded the planning process in particular, of the opinion that the residents affected by the planning had the right to participate actively in the proceedings by advancing their views. The expert reports on noise impacts were rendered public as were the planning materials. The planning authority defined areas where owners had to be compensated as the premises were considered to have become unhealthy for habitation, and areas where passive noise protection was provided for. There was access to judicial review, too.[35] The authority, for example, imposed a supervisory duty on the airport for the future to ensure that the major part of night goods would consist of express goods, and not of express freights. The Court said, that it is "not in a position to substitute the authority's balancing decision with its own".[36]

Another case affecting environmental matters in a decision-making process, dealing with the establishment of a nuclear waste repository, was *Traube v. Germany*, which the ECtHR had to decide in 2014. The Court recalled the

31 ECtHR, *Eckenbrecht and Ruhmer v. Germany*, 10.06.2014, no. 25330/10, §36.

32 ECtHR, *Gaskin v. United Kingdom*, 07.07.1989, no. 10454/83, Series A no. 160, §42; ECtHR, *Petrenco v. Moldova*, 30.03.2010, no. 20928/05, §52.

33 ECtHR (GC), *Dickson v. United Kingdom*, 04.12.2007, no. 44362/04, §70; ECtHR (GC), *Hatton et al. v. United Kingdom*, 08.07.2003, no. 36022/97, ECHR 2003-VIII, §98; ECtHR, *Ciubotaru v. Moldova*, 27.04.2010, no. 27138/04, §50.

34 ECtHR, *López Ostra v. Spain*, 09.12.1994, no. 16798/90, Series A No. 303-C, §51.

35 ECtHR, *Eckenbrecht and Ruhmer v. Germany*, 10.06.2014, no. 25330/10, §42.

36 ECtHR, *Eckenbrecht and Ruhmer v. Germany*, 10.06.2014, no. 25330/10, §44.

necessity of transparency and the possibility for the public to participate in the decision-making process as well as the right to seek judicial review as regards the compliance of the domestic decision-making process with the procedural aspect of Article 8 ECHR. The Court also noted that the public was indeed involved in the plan-approval procedure at an early stage of the decision-making process. The planning permission was publicised and the objections had been the subject of discussion in public hearings lasting over a total of 75 days. In the planning decision the objections were regrouped and dealt with by subject matter and with respect to each category the licencing authority provided reasons for its finding that the objections were ill-founded.[37] So the applicant had the benefit of adversarial proceedings before administrative bodies and the domestic courts in three instances which took into consideration his submissions. The domestic courts examined the applicant's offers of proof and gave reasons why they decided not to take the requested evidence. There was no violation of the procedural aspect of Article 8 ECHR.[38]

Especially important to the Court is the decision-making process in cases like *Koceniak v. Poland*, where the local authorities had to deal with the lawful operation of a meat factory site. The ECtHR wants to ensure that due weight is accorded to the interests of the individual in the decision-making process.[39] On a number of occasions, the Court has held that in cases involving environmental issues the State must be allowed a wide margin of appreciation (see *Eckenbrecht and Ruhmer v. Germany* above).[40] The national authorities are in principle in a better position than an international court to assess the requirements relating to the treatment of industrial waste in a particular local context and to determine the most appropriate environmental policies and individual measures while taking into account the needs of the local community.[41]

It was also the case *Koceniak v. Poland*, where the ECtHR repeated that it consistently held that although Article 8 ECHR contains no explicit procedural requirements, the process must be fair and afford due respect to the interests of the individual safeguarded by Article 8 ECHR.[42] *"In particular, the individuals concerned must also be able to appeal to the courts against any decision, act or omission where they consider that their interests or their comments have not been given sufficient weight in the decision-making process."*[43]

---

37 ECtHR, *Traube v. Germany*, 09.09.2014, no. 28711/10, §32.
38 ECtHR, *Traube v. Germany*, 09.09.2014, no. 28711/10, §33.
39 ECtHR, *Koceniak v. Poland*, 17.06.2014, no. 1733/06, §59; see also ECtHR, *Taşkın and Others v. Turkey*, 10.11.2004, no. 46117/99, §115, ECHR 2004-X.
40 ECtHR, *Koceniak v. Poland*, 17.06.2014, no. 1733/06, §59.
41 Ibid.
42 ECtHR, *McMichael v. UK*, 24.02.1995, no. 16424/90, Series A no. 307-B, §87.
43 ECtHR, *Koceniak v. Poland*, 17.06.2014, no. 1733/06, §59.

4. DO PROCEDURAL REQUIREMENTS DERIVED FROM ARTICLE 8 ECHR DEMAND CRIMINAL INVESTIGATIONS IN ENVIRONMENTAL CASES?

The positive duties resulting from the right to private life (Article 8 ECHR) may, under specific circumstances, even require a State to provide *criminal law provisions* for the general protection of the rights granted under Article 8 §1 ECHR.[44] This approach naturally requires the creation of respective mandatory provisions in criminal law and explains at the same time the extensive legislative initiatives in the area of environmental criminal law brought forward in Germany and several other states in Europe in the 1990s.[45] Even though abstract material criminal law provisions do exist, national procedural law must not fail to provide a way of finding the perpetrator and holding him responsible in a concrete case.

This basic rule alone does not, however, state in which cases the State is not only obliged to take administrative measures, but has to apply abstract criminal law in the concrete situation, too.[46] At least in cases of serious environmental burdens and (presumable) dangers resulting thereof to the legally protected interests life and/or bodily integrity, the ECtHR might request the initiation of criminal investigations.[47]

On the other hand, there exists up until now not a single case in the context of environmental protection in the jurisdiction of the ECtHR in which the Court would have *clearly requested* the retrospective application of criminal law as a characteristic of the State's duty to protect deriving from Article 8 ECHR or from Article 2 ECHR, in order to investigate/solve matters of environmental law. Cases

44 ECtHR, *Janković v. Croatia*, 05.03.2009, no. 38478/05, §47.

45 Since 1980 the most important environmental criminal law provisions are listed in Sections 324–330d of the German Criminal Code (*Strafgesetzbuch* – StGB). Those were modified by the 31st Criminal Code Amendment Act (*Strafrechtsänderungsgesetz*) of 27.06.1994. With the 6th Law Reforming German Criminal Law (*Gesetz zur Reform des Strafrechts*) from April 1998, the criminal penalties contemplated in Sections 330 and 330a StGB were increased. There was also a Convention of the Council of Europe on the Protection of the Environment through Criminal Law of 4.11.1998. In the beginning of the 1990s, the German Regional Courts started installing special chambers for environmental crimes, see *Minoggio*, in: "Umweltschutz im Baubetrieb" loose-leaf, as of 10/2001, "*Umweltstraf- und -ordnungswidrigkeitenrecht*", §2.4.5; Concerning the hole branch of environmental criminal law in Germany: *Michalke, Umweltstrafsachen*, 2nd ed. 2000; *Saliger, Umweltstrafrecht* (2012); Klöpfer, *Umweltrecht*, 4 ed. 2016.

46 Compare for medical crimes: ECtHR, *V.V.G. v. former Yugoslav Republic of Macedonia* (Dec.), 20.1.2015, no. 55569/08, §§40 ff.: "*If the right to personal integrity has not been infringed intentionally, the positive obligation imposed under the Convention does not necessarily require the provision of a criminal-law remedy in every case. In the specific sphere of medical negligence, the positive obligation may be satisfied if the legal system affords victims a remedy in the civil courts, either alone or in conjunction with a remedy in the criminal courts, enabling any liability of the doctors concerned to be established and any appropriate civil redress, such as an order for damages and for the publication of the decision, to be obtained. Disciplinary measures may also be envisaged.*"

47 Compare: ECtHR, *K.U. v. Finland*, 02.12.2008, no. 2872/02, §47.

in the environmental sphere decided by the ECtHR concern without exception proceedings in which the environmental impacts in question and the dangers resulting thereof had to be assessed in an abstract manner or in which (provable) damages to legally protected values had not yet happened. In short, cases in which the preventive manifestation of the State's duty to protect was under debate (prevention of damage) but not the retrospective alternative (solving occurred damages).

5. ACCESS OF INJURED PERSONS AND RELATIVES TO CRIMINAL INVESTIGATION

Taking the assumption that the ECtHR calls for the initiation of criminal investigations in cases concerning dangers for the environment, the question arises, whenever a State carries out criminal investigations, whether victims (and their relatives, respectively) have to be given access to these investigations or at least (upon their completion) to the results.[48]

A right of the victim of an environmental accident to access public investigations might result from Article 6 § 1 ECHR. Special rights of victims and their relatives enabling an "effective" participation (ie. the right to access to the case file) as elements of the right to a fair trial (hearing) come into consideration. However, according to its wording, Article 6 § 1 ECHR exclusively guarantees the rights of the *accused* in criminal proceedings, not those of potential victims of a crime. Its guarantees therefore only apply to persons either subjected to *criminal charges* or seeking to enforce *civil rights* in court.[49]

Since the purpose of *private action* in criminal proceedings is usually not to achieve the compensatory enforcement of these rights, Article 6 ECHR is not applicable under the aspect of a trial concerning *civil rights*, with the consequence that neither the victim nor his relatives etc. can rely on procedural rights to participation under Article 6 ECHR.

The victim of environmental damages caused by a private company may however rely on the *civil rights* aspect of Article 6 § 1 ECHR – also in criminal proceedings – where national procedural law provides for a legal remedy to recover civil claims in such proceedings.

Sometimes national law allows the victim to seek the enforcement of compensation for damages caused by a criminal offence within criminal proceedings. However, in case the victim decides to launch a separate legal action

48 The following remarks have already been developed in relation to nuclear accidents, compare: *Esser*, EEELR 2013, p. 86, 91 ff.

49 For a different opinion see *S. Walther*, 'Zum Anspruch des Deliktsopfers auf rechtliches Gehör und auf ein faires Verfahren' [2007] Goltdammer's Archiv 615 (thereafter: Walther), p. 620 with reference to a decision of the German Federal Constitutional Court (*Entscheidungen des BVerfG – BVerfGE*, vol. 38, p. 102 [114 f.]).

for compensation in civil courts, its participation in the criminal proceedings (e.g. when pursuing accessory prosecution) is once again limited to a purely punitive one and therefore results in no "*civil rights*" in the sense of Article 6 § 1 ECHR being claimed.[50]

Close relatives of a deceased, and, in cases of attempted manslaughter, also the victim him- or herself, have to be involved *ex officio* and allowed adequate access to the case file (Article 2 ECHR).[51] Such involvement is condition to the exercise of the right to an *effective remedy* (Article 13 ECHR) in cases of manslaughter caused by (the violation of positive duties of) a State.[52] The victim's relatives must therefore have access to the investigations as to "*safeguard their legitimate interests*".[53]

The States also have to supply a legal framework providing effective remedies to live up to their positive duties under the protection of the right to private life, Article 8 ECHR, in relations between private parties.[54]

These remedies have to guarantee access to the courts at least in cases of grave breaches, be it by civil law remedies or through the initiation of criminal proceedings.[55]

Effective criminal proceedings do not necessarily have to be carried out by public authorities; granting victims access to private action can also be sufficient. Therefore no positive obligation of the State to introduce provisions for private action in criminal procedure law follows from Article 8 ECHR.

On the other hand, the ECtHR assumes that no support by public authorities is necessary for the prosecution of suspected violations of individual rights under Article 8 ECHR, where the remedies set up in national law provide for an effective enforcement of the individual interests.[56] Whenever a victim in court exercises these rights granted to him without being represented by a lawyer, no excessive requirements shall be put on its applications.[57]

---

50 LR/*Esser* (Fn. 18), Art. 6 ECHR, §62; ECtHR (GC), *Perez v. France*, 12.02.2004, no. 47287/99, §§70–71; ECtHR, *Mihova v. Italy* (dec.), 30.03.2010, no. 25000/07; *Garimpo v. Portugal*, see S. Trechsel, *Human Rights in Criminal Proceedings* (2006; thereafter: S. Trechsel), p. 36 ff. for a critical review of the ECtHR's approach in *Perez* and arguing for a limited application of Article 6 §1 ECHR to the victim.

51 ECtHR, *Slimani v. France*, 27.07.2004, no. 57671/00, §47; ECtHR (GC), *Oğur v. Turkey*, 20.05.1999, no. 21594/93, ECHR 1999-III, §92; ECtHR, *Wasilewska and Kalucka v. Poland*, 23.02.2010, no. 28975/04 and 33406/04, §59; *Esser* (Fn. 15), p. 106; *Meyer-Ladewig/Huber* in Meyer-Ladewig/Nettesheim/von Raumer, *Europäische Menschenrechtskonvention – EMRK: Handkommentar*, 4. ed., 2017, Art. 2 ECHR, §§24–25; see also Section 406e StPO (German Code of Criminal Procedure – Access to the case file for the victim).

52 See *Esser* (Fn. 15), p. 107; LR/*Esser* (Fn. 18), Art. 2 ECHR, §36.

53 ECtHR (GC), *Giuliani and Gaggio v. Italy*, 24.03.2011, no. 23458/02, §303.

54 ECtHR, *Airey v. Ireland*, 09.10.1979, no. 6289/73, §§32 f.; ECtHR, *Karakó v. Hungary*, 28.04.2009, no. 39311/05, §§17 ff. (conflict between Articles 8 and 10 ECHR).

55 ECtHR, *K.U. v. Finland*, 02.12.2008, no. 2872/02, §§43 ff.

56 See *LR*/Esser (Fn. 18), Art. 8 ECHR, §25; ECtHR, *Janković v. Croatia*, 05.03.2009, no. 38478/05, §50.

57 ECtHR, *Janković v. Croatia*, 05.03.2009, no. 38478/05, §§54 ff.; see also P. Leach (Fn. 18), §6, p. 382.

6. PRIVATE ACCESSORY PROSECUTION IN GERMAN CRIMINAL PROCEDURE LAW (*NEBENKLAGE*)

Whoever is aggrieved by an unlawful criminal act as enumerated in Section 395 § 1 German Code of Criminal Procedure (*Strafprozessordnung* – StPO) can join an ongoing public prosecution as a so-called private accessory prosecutor (*Nebenkläger*). The number of private accessory prosecutions (*Nebenklagen*) amounts to round about 12.000 cases per year (status: 2011).[58] Environmental crimes as such are not listed in Section 395 § 1 StPO; however, in case of (attempted) voluntary homicide or of a voluntary act causing bodily harm – both of which may actually occur in context with environmental crimes – the way would be paved for private accessory prosecution.[59]

Where the aggrieved person is actually killed by an unlawful act (which notably includes every kind of involuntary manslaughter which may occur in the context of environmental crimes) the right to join public prosecution as private accessory prosecutor is open to some close relatives (children, parents, (half-) siblings, spouses or life partners) as stated in Section 395 § 2 StPO.[60] Whilst a sufficient ground for suspicion is needed in order to prosecute, the possibility of the unlawful commission of the offence is sufficient for being entitled to join the trail as a private accessory prosecutor.[61]

In the abovementioned cases of §§ 1 and 2 of Section 395 StPO it is the victim's or the close relative's absolute right to join a public prosecution. Where there is a declaration of joinder the competent court will merely examine whether formal requirements are adequately fulfilled before allowing the private accessory prosecution (see Section 396 StPO).[62] However, we should note the most interesting redraft of Section 395 § 3 StPO, which took place in 2009.[63] This new piece of legislation contains an omnibus clause (*Auffangtatbestand*) which grants the victim the right to join public prosecution as a private accessory prosecutor if, for "*particular reasons*" (*besondere Gründe*), especially because of the serious consequences of the unlawful act, the victim's participation in the

---

58 *Höllinger/Duttge/Rössner*, Handkommentar, 4. ed., 2017, StPO, Section 395 §2.

59 Graf-StPO/*Weiner*, 2 ed., 2012 (thereafter: Graf-StPO/*Weiner*), Section 395 §13a; *Meyer-Goßner*/Schmitt, StPO, 60 ed., 2017 (thereafter: *Meyer-Goßner*), Section 395 §3; Radtke/Hohmann-StPO/*Merz*, 2011 (thereafter: RH/*Merz*), Section 395 §5; Karlsruher Kommentar-StPO/*Senge*, 7. ed., 2013 (thereafter: KK-StPO/*Senge*), StPO, Section 395 §2, 6.

60 SK-StPO/*Velten*, Vol. III, 4 ed., 2013 (thereafter: SK-StPO/*Velten*), Section 395 §21; *Meyer-Goßner*, Section 395 §§ 7 f.; KK-StPO/*Senge*, Section 395 §8.

61 BGH NStZ-RR 2002, p. 340; Beck'scher OnlineKommentar StPO/*Weiner*, 27. Ed. 1.1.2017 (thereafter: BeckOK/*Weiner*), Section 395 §23.

62 Graf-StPO/*Weiner*, Section 396 §§1–11; SK-StPO/*Velten*, Section 396 §§2–10; RH/*Merz*, Section 396 §§1 ff.

63 See BT-Drs. 16/12098, p. 49; Graf-StPO/*Weiner*, Section 395 §16; KK-StPO/*Senge*, Section 395 §11.

criminal proceedings as private accessory prosecutor appears to be necessary to safeguard his or her personal interests.[64] Whether such particular reasons exist is decided by the competent court based on dutiful discretion.[65] Although Section 395 § 3 StPO states a few examples of criminal offences this omnibus clause may, in theory, be applied to any criminal offence (before 2009 Section 395 § 3 StPO applied only in cases of bodily harm caused by negligence, Section 229 of the German Criminal Code [StGB][66]). The practical impact is of course limited as the right granted by this omnibus clause is a relative one; the court will accept the joinder only if it actually deems the requirements set forth in Section 395 §3 StPO to be fulfilled, and there is no legal remedy against the court's decision (Section 396 § 2 sentence 2 StPO).[67] It is, however, possible to file a renewed application for admission to private accessory prosecution in the appeal (instance).[68] The clause is still rather new and it appears that there is no practical case yet of private accessory prosecution related to environmental crimes.

Until recently the indefinite legal concept of the *"particular reasons"* mostly came into play when criminal traffic cases were concerned. Initially, the connecting factor is the extent of the caused injuries. In case of serious injuries, it is widely agreed that an access reason (*Anschlussgrund*) is given.[69] Fractures that need a long healing time or injuries that need stationary or surgical treatment come into consideration as serious injuries.[70] Minor injuries as for example slight bruises or sprains as well as mere pecuniary losses or material damages preclude from the permission to join the trial as a private accessory prosecutor.[71] Those criteria developed from Section 229 StGB also apply for the newly added criminal offences and are applicable for the assessment of psychological consequences of the unlawful act, too. Grave consequences are given if the injured party suffers from physical or psychological damages of a certain degree of relevance or is expected to suffer from those.[72] These can be for example health impairments, traumas or significant shocking experiences.[73]

The private accessory prosecutor (*Nebenkläger*) may avail himself of the assistance of an attorney (Section 397a StPO).[74] This attorney (and the victim or the victim's relative) may always be present at the main hearing where he has most

64 BeckOK/*Weiner*, Section 395 §§16 ff.; *Meyer-Goßner*, Section 395 §10 ff.; RH/*Merz*, Section 395 §2.
65 KK-StPO/*Senge*, Section 395 §11.
66 See BeckOK/*Weiner*, Section 395 §17; *Meyer-Goßner*, Section 395 §11.
67 Graf-StPO/*Weiner*, Section 396 §21; *Meyer-Goßner*, Section 395 §23.
68 Graf-StPO/*Weiner*, Section 396 §21; of the opposite opinion: *Meyer-Goßner*, Section 397 §23.
69 BeckOK/*Weiner*, Section 395 §18.
70 BeckOK/*Weiner*, Section 395 §18.
71 *Beulke* DAR (Deutsches Autorecht) 1988, p. 114 (116); BeckOK/*Weiner*, Section 395 §18.
72 KK-StPO/*Senge*, Section 395 §11; BeckOK/*Weiner*, Section 395 §19.
73 KK-StPO/*Senge*, Section 395 §11.
74 Graf-StPO/*Weiner*, Section 397a §1; SK-StPO/*Velten*, Section 397a §2 ff.; *Meyer-Goßner*, Section 397a §§1–4.

notably the right to ask questions and the right to request for measures of enquiry (Section 397 §§ 1, 2 StPO).[75] The (victim's) attorney also possesses a right of access to the trial files (Section 406e StPO).[76] The private accessory prosecution may join the public prosecution even as late as after a judgment has been delivered in order to appeal against the judgment (Section 395 § 4 StPO).[77]

If the accused is acquitted or if main proceedings are not opened or terminated the private accessory prosecutor may avail himself of legal remedies against such decision (Sections 400 § 2, 401 StPO).[78] However, if the accused is actually sentenced the private accessory prosecutor cannot appeal and aim at increasing the accused's sentence whereas the public prosecutor can do that (Sections 400 et seq. StPO, *argumentum e contrario* of Section 331 § 1 StPO).[79]

So all in all one comes to the conclusion that the private accessory prosecution (*Nebenklage*) in German Criminal Procedure Law (Sections 395 seq. StPO) fulfils all requirements of "*effectiveness*" the ECtHR sets in the procedural framework of Article 2 and Article 8 ECHR, in case criminal law proceedings have been opened by the public prosecution and the police. However, this legal instrument seems to be quite unknown or at least unusual to lawyers in Germany when dealing with environmental law matters. The reason for that might be that many environmental law cases start in the system of civil law (*Zivilrecht*) or in the sphere of ordinary public (administrative) law (*Verwaltungsrecht*) which both offer the "victim" special, quick and effective protective measures and procedures of preliminary nature. What`s more, many public prosecutors are still not "familiar" with complex issues of environmental protection – leaving the first step of investigation many often to specialized agencies.

7. CONCLUSION

The Jurisprudence of the ECtHR on "procedural environmental rights" sets specific standards for national criminal procedure law. However, taking into account the rule of law and the vulnerable position of the accused in criminal proceedings, the judicial framework of the ECtHR on "procedural environmental rights" needs to be adjusted to the special features of criminal procedure law, also from a human rights perspective (Article 6 § 1–3 ECHR).

---

75 SK-StPO/*Velten*, Section 397 §6, 8; *Meyer-Goßner*, Section 397 §§5, 11; RH/*Merz*, Section 397 §8.

76 SK-StPO/*Velten*, Section 397 §6; RH/*Merz*, Section 397 §7.

77 Graf-StPO/*Weiner*, Section 395 §§26 ff.; *Meyer-Goßner*, Section 395 §12; KK-StPO/*Senge*, Section 395 §14.

78 SK-StPO/*Velten*, Section 400 §§2–10; *Meyer-Goßner*, Section 401 §§1 ff.; RH/*Merz*, Section 401 §§2 ff.

79 SK-StPO/*Velten*, Section 400 §10; *Meyer-Goßner*, Section 400 §§3–3b.

"Procedural environmental rights" have to be interpreted as "victim rights" in criminal procedure law. Therefore investigating authorities have to balance the "procedural environmental rights" of the victim against the rights of the accused, always taking into account the presumption of innocence (Article 6 § 2 ECHR).

From a defendant's rights point of view, it is of utmost importance to treat criminal proceedings concerned with environmental accidents with the same due rule of law – avoiding any polemics or political controversies and accepting the paramount importance of the principles of a fair trial (Article 6 § 1 ECHR) – as any other criminal proceedings, even though the misconduct in question may have cost or endangered many lives.

In recent years the need for an Additional Protocol to the ECHR on "Victim Protection" has become obvious. "Victims' rights" play an increasingly important role in criminal proceedings. In the long run, it will become difficult to derive their human rights nucleus from the procedural elements of Articles 2 and 8 ECHR. The Council of Europe's political bodies should reflect on fixing the essential safeguards for victims of crime in an additional protocol to the Convention. The political will to manifest the human rights core elements of victim's procedural rights in criminal proceedings will probably never become higher than in times of terrorist threats.

ILVA: AN ENVIRONMENTAL CASE

Nicola Lugaresi*

ABSTRACT

A history of conflicts and failures: the Ilva case might be summarized like that. The Ilva steel plant, located just outside the city of Taranto, is a big polluter, but also a provider for thousands of jobs. In 2012 criminal judges seized core parts of the factory, in order to shut it down; the Italian Government intervened in order to overcome the seizure and its effects. The citizens of Taranto are torn between the anxiety for their health, jeopardized by the industrial activities, and the concern for their economic future, should the plant be closed. Failures are evident in the persisting unsustainability of the environmental, social and economic crises. In this context, lack of reliable and coherent information and problematic public participation has made things worse, delaying and altering the awareness of the local community and, in the end, procrastinating the adoption of incisive measures.

KEYWORDS

Environmental permit; Ilva; Information; Integrated pollution prevention and control; Participation; Pollution; Steel plant; Sustainable development.

1. INTRODUCTION: THE ISSUES

Ilva is the Latin name for *Isola d'Elba*, a beautiful island rich in iron off the coast of Tuscany. Ilva is also the name of the company (Ilva s.p.a.[1]) that owns, among others, the steel plant located just outside the city of Taranto[2], in the Southern Italy Region of Apulia. Its business is the production, processing and marketing

---

* Trento University Law School, Italy.

1 On Ilva s.p.a. and its data, see its own website [www.gruppoilva.com].

2 Ilva s.p.a. owns 16 production unit (13 in Italy, 3 in France) and employs around 15,000 workers; the Ilva factory in Taranto is responsible for over 60% of the base products of the group and employs almost 12,000 workers (source: Ilva website [www.gruppoilva.com]).

of steel products. The Ilva steel plant in Taranto has been operating, and polluting, for more than fifty years, but it is just in the last few years that it attracted a high level of legislative, administrative, judicial and mass media attention.

The basic and dramatic dilemma concerning the Ilva factory in Taranto is between shutting it down and letting it open. In the first case, social and economic measures would be needed in order to avoid a "welfare disaster", as thousands of people would lose their jobs or substantially reduce their income and their business chances. In the second case, environmental measures would be needed in order to avoid further deterioration of the quality of air, water and soil, which would put the health of the population under additional, intense, stress. Both solutions aim to protect some basic rights and interests: life and health, in the first case; work and private enterprise, in the second case. But, at the same time, they may compromise others.

Following complaints from citizens and reports from local NGOs, the heavy impact of the plant on the population and on the environment has been put under stricter judicial and political scrutiny over the last few years. In 2012 a criminal judge in Taranto[3] seized core parts of the plant, in order to close the factory, considering the continuation of the productive activity inconsistent with the right to life and the right to health of the local population. The Italian Government, considering the economic and social consequences of the closure, stepped in before the effects of the judicial order could be implemented, in order to keep the plant open. The conflict between the judiciary and the central Government did not stop there: more orders and seizures have been issued by the judges in Taranto, and more special legislation and administrative measures have been enacted. Since then, saving the Ilva plant from others judicial interventions and trying to strike a balance among public interests and private fundamental rights, were the declared goal of politics, while the judiciary, more simply, aimed at ending the industrial activity, and, consequently, the daily, deeply harmful, pollution. Waiting for a definitive way out, the plant still operating and impacting on the environment, people in Taranto are both worried for today's (and tomorrow's, and the day after tomorrow's) health and concerned for their jobs and welfare.

The Ilva company, including the factory in Taranto, was sold in June 2017 to a private consortium (AM InvestCo Italy) led by ArcelorMittal, the world's largest steel maker, with the participation of the Italian Marcegaglia group. The Ilva plant in Taranto, at that time, was losing money every day, as its production levels had been gradually reduced since 2012, which cut pollution levels too. In that period (2012-2017), management decisions and technical measures helped in improving the environmental situation, but the price to pay was high, as the competitiveness of Ilva decreased, and social conflicts were still there.

3 Judge for Preliminary Investigations, Court of Taranto, order 25 July 2012 (confirmed by order 10 August 2012). The order of 25 July 2012 was particularly complex and circumstantial (almost 300 pages).

The Ilva case, in other words, is about the core of sustainable development and its basic quest: how to harmonize social, economic and environmental issues, considering present and future generations. This quest faces an extremely serious situation, going far beyond general statements: it is about daily people's life, health and dignity. The main concern is focused on present generations, as they are dealing with serious, potentially lethal, health issues: long-term perspectives for the future generations are inevitably moved to the background.

The actors involved are many: the Taranto and Apulia population, trade unions, entrepreneurs, NGOs, central, regional and local governments, the judiciary, public administration, environmental agencies, public and private technical bodies. Their respective positions are not always neatly sketched within the fight between health and jobs, a fight that should not have gone that far and that deep. The interests involved in the Ilva case are many as well. Just to name the most relevant, the right to life, health and dignity of the people living close to the plant; the right to work and to fair working conditions of the people employed in the factory; the freedom to conduct a business and the right to property of the past and next owners of the industrial facility; the social development of Taranto and Apulia; the local, regional and national economy; the protection of the environment; the institutional balance among the public actors; the need of justice and the needs of justice.

It is evident that an effective solution for Ilva and Taranto, workers and population, economy and social justice, is not simple to be found and it will not come cheap. It is not an easy task even because, so far, access to complete and reliable information has not been guaranteed and public participation, hampered by that, has not been so effective and relevant as it could have been. If solid data bases lack, and public participation is not promoted and organized, political analyses and people's contributions to such a complex environmental case are compromised.

To make things harder, the crisis could not and cannot be faced just under a national framework. The European Union stepped in, adding even more issues, like the assumed violations of the EU environmental legislation on one side and the infringement of the EU state aid rules on the other side. The options at a national level are therefore less, as EU law does not allow some answers that the Italian government was trying to give. Moreover, the European Court for Human Rights has been involved. The Court, that in 2015 rejected a requested presented by a Taranto individual, declaring it not admissible, opened proceedings against Ilva in May 2016.

A number of factors are therefore progressively reducing the political and administrative leeway: time is running out.

2. ILVA: HISTORY AND DATA

Ilva has a long history behind it: more than a century, as for the company, more than fifty years, as for the plant in Taranto. It is a history of steel production and environmental pollution; a history of entrepreneurial successes and downfalls;

a history of relationships, often opaque, among managers, politicians, public servants; a history of battles and negotiations with trade unions; a history of civil, criminal and administrative trials.[4] It is not surprising that loads of data about the economic, social and environmental impact of Ilva on different local, regional and national contexts are available, even though often inconsistent and incomplete. Moreover, in the last few years both the company and the steel plant have been, almost daily, at the centre of mass media attention: it is a major environmental, social, economic, political, legislative and judicial case. It would be impossible to list all the data, administrative provisions and laws in a limited space, but some references are needed in order to understand the dynamics and what is really at stake.

The Ilva company, Ilva s.p.a., was founded in 1905. In 1934 it became public. The Ilva steel plant in Taranto was inaugurated in 1965. In 1995 the plant was privatized and sold to the Riva group. In 2013, following the judicial and legislative turmoil of 2012, the Italian Government designated a "Special Commissioner" for the Ilva plant: the property stayed private, but it was managed under public control. In 2015 Ilva s.p.a. was placed under "extraordinary administration", becoming, again, public. In 2016 Ilva was put up for sale[5] and then sold to AM InvestCo Italy in June 2017.

Taranto is not only Ilva, though. On one side, the industrial and productive sectors include other big actors: the ENI refinery, the Cementir cement and concrete plant, the Italcave mining site, the military base and arsenal, the harbour. On the other side, its economy is also based, or could have been based (and might still be based), on tourism, agriculture, livestock farming, fishing, mussels harvesting. Nevertheless, it looks like, in the collective consciousness, that Taranto "is" Ilva and that its economic, social and environmental issues start and finish with the steel plant.

What makes the Ilva plant so relevant is not only its dimension, but also its position. Ilva was built very close to the city, next to the Tamburi neighbourhood and few kilometres from the centre. Dust and emissions, depending on the direction of the wind, can easily infest Taranto, and often do.

The data about the Ilva steel plant clearly show the impact on the city of Taranto and its population.[6] The keyword, here, is "big".

---

4 On these aspects, see *C. Ruga Riva*, Il caso Ilva: profili penali-ambientali, 17 October 2014, pp. 1 et seq. [http://lexambiente.it/ambiente-in-genere/188-dottrina188/10999-ambiente-in-genereil-caso-ilva-profili-penali-ambientali.html].

5 See "*Call for expressions of interest in relation to the transfer of businesses owned by Ilva S.p.A. in Extraordinary Administration and other companies of the same group*" of 5 January 2016 [www.gruppoilva.com/items/571/allegati/1/Bandopermanifestazioneinteresse.pdf].

6 Data are extracted by many sources, not always congruent and not always updated. The difference among sources, though, is often not significant, as the issues and their relevance do not change. Other times the data inconsistencies make evaluations, at any level, harder. As for general data, on different profiles, see *A. Lucifora, F. Bianco & G.M. Vagliasindi*, Environmental and Corporate Mis-compliance: A Case Study on the Ilva Steel Plant in Italy.

The Ilva steel plant is big. It is the largest steel plant in the European Union, occupying a 15 square km area. It has 200 km of railways, 50 km of roads, 190 km of conveyor belts, a dedicated harbour with 6 docks.[7] Intervening on such a large and "structured" industrial zone is not easy. Closing the factory would create a large area to be cleaned up and to be used in a different way. What way, though, it is not clear.

The Ilva steel plant is a big employer and job provider. In a city, Taranto, with an unemployment rate of 15.5% (and in a Region, Apulia, with an unemployment rate of 19.8%), about 12,000 workers are directly employed at the plant, while about 8,000 additional people indirectly depend on it. Closing Ilva would be a social disaster, that public interventions supporting workers could mitigate and postpone, but not avoid.

The Ilva steel plant is a big economic actor. It has an annual production capacity of about 10 million tons (40% of Italian steel production), even though, as for now, it is producing about half of it. The steel is sent to factories in Northern Italy and exported, mainly within the EU. Closing Ilva would deeply impact on the regional and national productive system, but also on the European Union industrial policy.[8] The impact on the gross domestic product of Taranto and

---

Study in the Framework of the EFFACE Research Project, 2015 [http://efface.eu/sites/default/files/EFFACE_Environmental%20and%20corporate%20mis-compliance.pdf]; *F. Tonelli, S. W. Short, P. Taticchi*, Case Study of Ilva, Italy: The Impact of Failing to Consider Sustainability as a Driver of Business Model Evolution, in G. Seliger (ed.), Proceedings of the 11th Global Conference on Sustainable Manufacturing – Innovative Solutions, 2013, pp. 25 et seq. [www.gcsm.eu/Papers/33/1.2_7.pdf]; *G. M. Vagliasindi & C. Gerstetter*, The Ilva Industrial Site in Taranto, European Parliament – Directorate-General for Internal Policies, Policy Department A: Economic and Scientific Policy, 2015, pp. 5, 7 et seq. [www.europarl.europa.eu/RegData/etudes/IDAN/2015/563471/IPOL_IDA(2015)563471_EN.pdf]; see also the regional plan for improving the air quality in the Tamburi neighbourhood ("Piano contenente le prime misure di intervento per il risanamento della Qualità dell'Aria nel quartiere Tamburi per gli inquinanti Benzo(a)pirene e PM10"), July 2012; *A. Bonelli*, Good Morning Diossina, 2014 [www.verdi.it/taranto/GoodMorningDiossina.pdf]; see also the Ilva website [www.gruppoilva.com]; for environmental data, see the facility details at the European Pollutant Release and Transfer Register [http://prtr.ec.europa.eu/#/facilitylevels].

7 Source: Ilva (2012 website).

8 European Parliament, Resolution 13 December 2012 on a new sustainable and competitive steel industry, based on a petition received [2012/2905 (RSP)], (2015/C 434/16) [www.europarl.europa.eu/sides/getDoc.do?pubRef=-//EP//TEXT+TA+P7-TA-2012-0510+0+DOC+XML+V0//EN], para. E: "*in terms of EU industrial policy, it is strategically essential to prevent the further relocation of steel plants and production outside the European Union*"; European Commission, Press release, 20 January 2016, State aid: Commission opens in-depth investigation into Italian support for steel producer Ilva in Taranto, Italy [http://europa.eu/rapid/press-release_IP-16-115_en.htm], p. 2: "*The European steel industry has a turnover of around € 180 billion, with direct employment of about 360,000 people, producing around 170 million tons of steel per year in more than 500 production sites in 23 Member States. Effective overcapacity in the EU in 2015 has been estimated at c.a. 10–15% of total European capacity. European steel producers face global challenges, among which stiff competition from low cost countries which also experience major overcapacity, the decrease in global demand for steel, increasing energy costs, and a heavy reliance on imported raw materials*".

Apulia is huge, and essential for the local economy, but it comes with many drawbacks, unbalancing the economic framework of the city. While, on one side, the presence of Ilva has boosted industrial and commercial activities, on the other side it has adversely affected other economic sectors, like agriculture, livestock farming, mussels cultivation, and tourism. Closing Ilva would turn upside down local and regional economies, with unpredictable, but surely problematic, outcomes.

The Ilva steel plant is a big polluter. The emissions have always been very relevant in quantity and quality, affecting air, water and soil. Dangerous substances, such as dioxin, mineral dust, benzene, nitrogen dioxide, sulphur dioxide, hydrochloric acid, are emitted by the factory.[9] Besides, even though it is a profile less considered, Ilva is a big emitter of carbon dioxide and greenhouse gases. The pollution comes from both production (furnaces) and storage (mineral parks) activities, invading the territory and the city. Closing Ilva would radically diminish pollution, improving, immediately, the quality of air and, gradually, the quality of soil and waters.

The Ilva steel plant is a big danger for people's health.[10] Dioxin, polycyclic aromatic hydrocarbons, heavy metals, and other substances produced by the plant, can be carcinogenic. Particulate matter smaller than 10 micrometres (PM10) penetrates and damages lungs, causing respiratory diseases. Others serious diseases are deemed attributable to the Ilva activities. Children are, not surprisingly, the most affected. Closing Ilva would eliminate further pollution and reduce these consequences.

Beyond data, the impact of the Ilva steel plant on the population of Taranto can be visualized and perceived through administrative orders, that, in their cold bureaucratic language, show how Ilva presence has permeated population's daily life and, in the end, the city identity. In 2008 hundreds of sheep and goats were slaughtered after high quantities of dioxin were detected in their milk and meat. In 2010 children of the Tamburi neighbourhood were prohibited to play outside in the public gardens, as the soil contamination level was considered dangerous. In 2011 mussels harvesting was prohibited in a portion of Mar Piccolo (an inner semi-enclosed basin adjacent to the Ilva factory and the city of Taranto), as its waters were too polluted. In 2015 dozens of cows were shot down, due to the dioxin in their milk. Starting from 2015, when the wind comes from Northwest, and therefore the city of Taranto is downwind of the factory, not only ordinary traffic

---

9 See European Pollutant Release and Transfer Register [http://prtr.ec.europa.eu/#/facilitylevels].

10 As for health data, the starting source was the "Studio SENTIERI", Epidemiologia e Prevenzione (5–6) 2010 [www.epiprev.it/materiali/2010/EP5-6_2010_suppl3.pdf] and (6) 2011 [www.epiprev.it/pubblicazione/epidemiol-prev-2011-35-5-6-suppl-4]. See also *P. Comba et al.*, Ambiente e salute a Taranto: evidenze disponibili e indicazioni di sanità pubblica, Epidemiologia e Prevenzione (6) 2012, p. 305 et seq. [www.salute.gov.it/imgs/c_17_pubblicazioni_1833_allegato.pdf]; Ilva criticized the studies produced by the Apulia Region through a different study realized by its consultants (Boffetta, La Vecchia, Lotti, Moretto) on 27 June 2013. That study was, in turn, harshly criticized by other scientists and NGOs.

limitations are introduced, but residents of the neighbourhoods close to the plant are advised, between noon and 6 p.m., neither to do sports outside nor to open their windows. These days are called "wind days". In the administrative orders the expression used is, strangely enough, in English, as though a foreign (and therefore fancy), name could soften the constraints and the underlying situation. Wind is a relief in other cities or territories, allowing to lift environmental limitations. In Taranto wind, depending on its direction and strength, can be a serious environmental nuisance, carrying and spreading dust and pollution and imposing restrictions on ordinary activities and daily life.

It is easy to understand why the Ilva steel plant in Taranto is representing a very thorny political issue. Any decision, or lack of decision, might improve the situation on one side, but it would adversely affect some fundamental interests or rights (life, health, work, dignity, economy, private enterprise) on the other side. Unfortunately, and unforgivably, things have been so for decades, without anyone seriously facing the dramatic issues.

3. ILVA, THE LAW AND THE ENVIRONMENT

3.1. ITALY

Reading newspapers and reports, it looks like that Ilva became a relevant legal, environmental and political case just in the last few years. It is not so. The Government declared the area of Taranto as an "area of high risk of environmental crisis" in 1990[11], when the Ilva plant was public, confirming the declaration in 1997[12], after it was sold to a private company. Environmental agreements among Ilva, Apulia Region, local administrations and trade unions have been signed since 2003.[13] Criminal, administrative and civil trials started in the nineties and have never stopped.

But only the seizure of core parts of the Ilva plant by the judiciary in 2012 sped things up, hit the news and ignited the institutional and social conflicts. The Taranto judges have been criticized for going beyond their powers, for some excesses in their orders, for heavily antagonizing the Government. But without their interventions, it is unlikely that politics would have woken up, as it had not for decades. On 25 July 2012, the Judge for Preliminary Investigations of the Taranto Court seized the "hot working areas" of the plant, basing the order on

11 Council of Ministers, Decision 30 November 1990, that called for an environmental recovery plan. The reclamation plan was adopted with Decree of the President of the Republic 23 April 1998.

12 Council of Ministers, Decision 11 July 1997.

13 See agreements 8 January 2003, 27 February 2004, 15 December 2004, concerning the improvement of the environmental impact of the Ilva factory; agreement 23 October 2006, concerning dioxin pollution.

an epidemiological survey showing that Ilva activities were harming not only the environment but also the health of workers and citizens. The goal of the judicial order was the final closure, a very complex technical task for such a large steel plant. Closing the factory would have taken months, and restarting it would have been neither easy nor quick. Moreover, damages could have occurred in the process. Still, the order relied on two assumptions: the first was that the right to life (and health) had to absolutely prevail on other rights, including the right to work; the second, consequently, was that the "death vs jobs" assessments was a legal, unacceptable, absurdity.

The day after (26 July 2012) the judicial seizure order was issued, the Italian Government, the Apulia Region, the Taranto Province, the Taranto local administration and the Special Commissioner for the Taranto harbour signed an agreement for urgent environmental clean-up in Taranto. Just some days after, a Special Commissioner for the Taranto area[14] was designated by law.[15]

On 26 October 2012 the IPPC permit, granted only fifteen months earlier, was revised. When the judges ordered to stop the productive activity of the factory, due to its extremely dangerous activities, Ilva was operating on the basis of a permit issued just one year earlier.

The political and administrative response did not satisfy the Taranto judges. On 26 November 2012, a new order, concerning the products manufactured during the seizure of the plant, was issued. The seizure of the products meant that the factory could not sell them, causing an economic damage that put at risk the survival of the factory.

To avoid the closure of the plant, the Government enacted the Decree-Law 3 December 2012, no. 207[16], allowing the plant to keep working, notwithstanding the judiciary decisions.[17] The compliance with the revised IPPC permit allowed

---

14 "Commissario Straordinario per gli interventi urgenti di bonifica, ambientalizzazione e riqualificazione di Taranto" [www.commissariobonificataranto.it/sito_commissario_2015_-_19_gennaio_009.htm].

15 Decree-Law 7 August 2012, no. 129 converted with amendments into Law 4 October 2012, no. 171.

16 The Decree-Law no. 207/2012 was converted with amendments into Law 24 December 2012, no. 231.

17 On the Decree-Law no. 207/2012, *G. Arconzo*, Il decreto legge "ad Ilvam" approda alla Corte costituzionale: osservazioni preliminari al giudizio di costituzionalità, Diritto Penale Contemporaneo 2013 (1), pp. 28 et seq. [www.penalecontemporaneo.it/foto/37031.2013.pdf#page=33&view=Fit]; *G. Arconzo*, Note critiche sul "decreto legge ad Ilvam", tra legislazione provvedimentale, riserva di funzione giurisdizionale e dovere di repressione e prevenzione dei reati, Diritto Penale Contemporaneo 2013 (1), pp. 16 et seq. [www.penalecontemporaneo.it/foto/37031.2013.pdf#page=33&view=Fit]; *R. Bin*, L'Ilva e il soldato Baldini, Diritto Penale Contemporaneo 2013 (1), pp. 5 et seq. [www.penalecontemporaneo.it/foto/37031.2013.pdf#page=33&view=Fit]; *R. Bin*, Giurisdizione o amministrazione, chi deve prevenire i reati ambientali? Nota alla sentenza "Ilva", Giurisprudenza costituzionale 2013 (3), pp. 1505 et seq.; *petter*, Le politiche pubbliche dell'emergenza tra bilanciamento e "ragionevole" compressione dei diritti: brevi riflessioni a margine della sentenza della Corte costituzionale sul caso Ilva, Federalismi.it 2014 (3) [http://federalismi.it/nv14/articolo-documento.cfm?artid=24088]; *L.*

production even under judicial seizure. The Government, on the other side, established some other conditions, concerning the designation of an independent "Guardian" to monitor the implementation of the prescribed requirements; the obligation for Ilva to send an implementation report to the competent authority every three months; the direct access of the same authority to the emission monitoring system of Ilva; the publication of the monitoring results and of the permit requirements on the official website of the Ministry of Environment. The Decree-Law no. 207/2012, that had both general provisions that could apply to other companies and specific provisions that could be applied only to Ilva, was commonly known as the "Save-Ilva Decree".[18]

The Judge for Preliminary Investigations at the Court of Taranto and the Court of Taranto challenged the Decree-Law no. 207/2012 before the Constitutional Court, maintaining that some provisions of the decree violated several (seventeen) articles of the Italian Constitution.[19] The Constitutional Court, with the judgment no. 85/2013[20], did not agree, affirming that there was no violation of the Constitution and finding that the balance of the rights struck by the decree was reasonable. The Court, moreover, sustained that the fundamental rights recognized by the Constitution are to be mutually integrated, without a pre-determined hierarchy, and that the prerogatives of the judiciary had not been violated.[21]

Geninatti Satè, "Caso Ilva": la tutela dell'ambiente attraverso la rivalutazione del carattere formale del diritto (una prima lettura di Corte cost., sent. n. 85/2013), Quaderni Forum Costituzionale 2013 (5), [www.forumcostituzionale.it/wordpress/images/stories/pdf/documenti_forum/giurisprudenza/2013/0008_nota_85_2013_geninatti_sat.pdf]; *A. Morelli*, Il decreto Ilva: un drammatico bilanciamento tra principi costituzionali, Diritto Penale Contemporaneo 2013 (1), pp. 7 et seq. [www.penalecontemporaneo.it/foto/37031.2013.pdf#page=33&view=Fit]; *A. Muratori*, Decreto salva Ilva: scelte difficili, Ambiente & Sviluppo, 2013 (1), pp. 8 et seq. [www.giuristiambientali.it/documenti/280113_AM.pdf]; *D. Pulitanò*, Fra giustizia penale e gestione amministrativa: riflessioni a margine del caso Ilva, Diritto Penale Contemporaneo 2013 (1), pp. 44 et seq. [www.penalecontemporaneo.it/foto/37031.2013.pdf#page=33&view=Fit]; *A. Sperti*, Alcune riflessioni sui profili costituzionali del decreto Ilva, Diritto Penale Contemporaneo 2013 (1), pp. 12 et seq. [www.penalecontemporaneo.it/foto/37031.2013.pdf#page=33&view=Fit].

18 An unusual intervention of the President of the Italian Republic, who had to sign the Decree in order for it to be enacted, explained in a letter to the Taranto population why he had signed it.

19 The articles of the Italian Constitution that the Judge for Preliminary Investigations considered violated were: articles 2, 3, 9, 24, 25, 27, 32, 41, 101, 102, 103, 104, 107, 111, 112, 113 e 117.

20 Constitutional Court, judgment 9 May 2013, no. 85 [www.cortecostituzionale.it/actionSchedaPronuncia.do?anno=2013&numero=85].

21 On the judgment no. 85/2013 of the Constitutional Court, *C. Petteruti*, Country Report: Italy. Italian Environmental Law Development in 2013, IUCN eJournal 5, 2014, pp. 206 et seq. [www.iucnael.org/en/86-journal/issue/491-issue-20142]: "the judgment of the Constitutional Court acknowledged the capacity of an administrative act (the reassessed IEA) to stop the Criminal Courts in suppressing environmental crimes. These elements reveal an unequal approach of the Constitutional Judge to the different fundamental rights involved in the Ilva episode".

Some days after the Constitutional Court judgment, the Government, with the Decree-Law 4 June 2013, no. 61, instituted a Special Commissioner for the Ilva plant in Taranto. The Special Commissioner had to adopt an "industrial plan" and an "environmental plan"[22] designed to comply with the IPPC permit and to clean up the area. The company was still private, the owners unchanged, but its operations were under the control of public powers. That hybrid situation did not last much. By decree of the Minister of Economic Development of 21 January 2015, Ilva (subsequently declared insolvent by the Court of Milan) was admitted with immediate effect to the extraordinary administration procedure provided by Decree-Law 23 December 2003, no. 347[23] on industrial restructuring of large companies in a state of insolvency. Ilva met the criteria concerning the scale of the company (at least 500 employees) and the state of insolvency (at least 300 million euros of debts in the previous year). The goal was to let the company continue its business in view of a future transfer, saving the production and the jobs. The decree also appointed three "Special Commissioners" for the Ilva steel plant in Taranto.

Emergency became routine. To date, nine more "Save-Ilva Decrees" have been enacted in order to avoid the seizure and the closure of the steel plant, adopting new measures, postponing deadlines and, in the end, buying time while a definitive solution is being searched. The solution, as for now, relies on the sale of the plant to a private entity, scheduled for 2017. It remains to be seen if the property change will solve the environmental and health issues and what the legislative and administrative frameworks for the private new owner will be. Taranto cannot afford to face the same mistakes made in the past decades.

3.2. EUROPE

The European Union, exercising its control powers, and alerted by Taranto individuals[24], has challenged more than once the Italian institutional behaviours regarding the Ilva steel plant in Taranto.[25] The European Union interventions

[22] The environmental plan was approved by Decree of the President of the Council of Ministers on 14 March 2014.

[23] The Decree-Law no. 347/2003 was converted with amendments into Law 18 February 2004, no. 39.

[24] See European Parliament, Committee on Petitions, Notice to Members, 13 Dec 2016 [www.europarl.europa.eu/sides/getDoc.do?type=COMPARL&reference=PE-404.458&format=PDF&language=EN&secondRef=09], and the petitions reported: Petition 0760/2007 (Fracasso): "*The petitioner expresses alarm at the high dioxin content of the atmosphere caused by harmful emissions from an industrial plant in Taranto*"; Petition 2207/2013 (Sion): "*The petitioner expresses concern at the serious problem of pollution being caused by Ilva plant in Taranto and in particular the impact of toxic dust from the 70-hectare mineral parks*".

[25] See European Parliament, Committee on Petitions, Notice to Members, 13 Dec 2016 [www.europarl.europa.eu/sides/getDoc.do?type=COMPARL&reference=PE-404.458&format=PDF&language=EN&secondRef=09], reconstructing the difficult relationship between the Italian Government and the European Union Commission concerning Ilva.

have been related to many different concerns and interests: people's health; environmental quality; workers' employment; local economy; steel industry policies; EU market competition; state aids.

The steel industry is a very delicate sector, both for its economic crisis and for its impact on the environment.[26] The European Parliament, in a resolution dedicated to the steel industry as a whole, explicitly refers to Ilva, calling for the environmental reclamation of the site and the implementation of the polluter pays principle. The European Commission has sent Italy two letters of formal notice, in September 2013 and April 2014, urging Italian authorities to bring the Ilva steel plant into compliance with the Industrial Emissions Directive[27] and the Environmental Liability Directive.[28] Besides, the Commission opened an in-depth investigation about the violation of State aid rules through the financing support (€ 2 billion) of Ilva in Taranto.

The substantial environmental issues relate to the operating conditions of the plant and the level and quality of its polluting emissions (with special reference to dioxin and PM10), causing severe health and environmental problems. The formal legal issues involve, in a first stage, the violation of Directive 96/61/EC[29]

---

26 Communication from the Commission, Action Plan for a competitive and sustainable steel industry in Europe, 11 June 2013 [COM(2013) 407 final], para. 1: "*The ongoing economic crisis has led to a marked downturn in manufacturing activity and associated steel demand, which remains 27% below pre-crisis levels. As a result, several production sites have closed or reduced output with corresponding job losses, with up to 40 000 jobs lost in recent years. Consequently the pressure to restructure and reduce production capacity will remain one of the main challenges for this industry in the foreseeable future*"; see also Commission Staff Working Document, 24 June 2014, State of play on implementation of the Commission Communication Action Plan for a competitive and sustainable steel industry in Europe of 11 June 2013 [SWD(2014) 215 final]; Opinion of the European Economic and Social Committee on the Action Plan for the European Steel Industry, 11 December 2013 [http://eur-lex.europa.eu/legal-content/EN/TXT/PDF/?uri=CELEX:52013AE4522&from=EN].

27 European Commission, Press Release, 16 October 2014, Environment: European Commission urges Italy to address severe pollution issues at Europe's biggest steel plant [http://europa.eu/rapid/press-release_IP-14-1151_en.htm]: "*Although some shortcomings have been addressed, a number of breaches of the Industrial Emissions Directive remain. Today's action, a reasoned opinion, concerns deficiencies such as lack of compliance with the conditions set out in the permits, inadequate management of by-products and wastes, and insufficient protection and monitoring of soil and groundwater. The Commission is giving Italy two months to reply. Most of the problems stem from a failure to reduce the high level of uncontrolled emissions generated during the steel production process. Under the Industrial Emissions Directive, industrial activities with a high pollution potential must be licensed. Ilva does have a permit for its activities, but it is failing to adhere to the requirements in a number of areas. As a result, dense particulate fumes and industrial dust are escaping from the plant, giving rise to potentially serious negative impacts on the health of the local population and on the state of the surrounding environment. Tests have shown heavy pollution of the air, soil, surface and ground waters both at the Ilva site and in nearby areas of the city of Taranto. The contamination of the Tamburi quarter of the city in particular can be attributed to the emissions from the steel plant*".

28 European Commission, Press Release, 26 September 2013, Environment: European Commission urges Italy to bring a steel plant in Taranto up to environmental standards [http://europa.eu/rapid/press-release_IP-13-866_en.htm].

29 Council Directive 96/61/EC of 24 September 1996 concerning integrated pollution prevention and control.

and of Directive 2008/1/EC[30] (the "*IPPC Directives*"), concerning integrated pollution prevention and control, and, then, the violation of Directive 2010/75/EU[31] (the "*IED Directive*"), concerning industrial emissions, that replaced the IPPC Directives.[32] Ilva has fallen under the scope of all the mentioned Directives. Permits based on emission limit values and on best available techniques (BAT) are the core of the environmental legislation. The aim is to prevent or reduce the emissions to air, water and soil. Permits can be issued only in accordance with the rules enacted by the Directives, taking into account the BAT reference documents (BREFs) adopted by the European Commission. Moreover, in order to ensure better implementation, the Commission, under the IED Directive, adopts decisions on best available techniques for each industrial sector. For the iron and steel production sector, the Commission adopted the Implementing Decision of 28 February 2012.[33]

In a first stage, Italy simply kept delaying, and not only for the Ilva steel plant in Taranto, the issuance of the IPPC permits, postponing the deadlines set and therefore breaching Directive 96/61/EC and Directive 2008/1/EC. The infringement procedure, launched in 2008, led to the European Court of Justice judgment of 31 March 2011 (case C-50/10), that declared that Italy had failed to fulfil its obligations.[34]

The IPPC permit (AIA, "*autorizzazione integrata ambientale*", that is "environmental integrated authorisation") was granted, at last, in August 2011[35], and it was supposed to last six years, but just one year after, in October 2012[36], it was revised. Ilva sent, in both cases, a letter criticizing the permit, asking for

30 Directive 2008/1/EC of 15 January 2008 concerning integrated pollution prevention and control.

31 Directive 2010/75/EU of 24 November 2010 on industrial emissions (integrated pollution prevention and control); in Italy the IED Directive was implemented with the legislative decree 4 March 2014, no. 46.

32 Directive 2010/75/EU (IED) replaced Directive 2008/1/EC starting from 7 January 2014.

33 Commission Implementing Decision of 28 February 2012 establishing the best available techniques (BAT) conclusions under Directive 2010/75/EU of the European Parliament and of the Council on industrial emissions for iron and steel production (2012/135/EU). Full compliance was due within four years.

34 ECJ, Case C-50/10, *Commission v. Italy* [2011] ECR I-00045, para. 39: "*the Italian Republic has failed to fulfil its obligations under Article 5(1) of Directive 2008/1/EC of the European Parliament and of the Council of 15 January 2008 concerning integrated pollution prevention and control (codified version), by failing to take the necessary measures to ensure that the competent authorities see to it, by means of permits in accordance with Articles 6 and 8 of that directive or, as appropriate, by reconsidering and, where necessary, by updating the conditions, that all existing installations within the meaning of Article 2(4) of that directive operate in accordance with the requirements of Articles 3, 7, 9, 10, 13, 14(a) and (b) and 15(2) of that directive*".

35 The "Environmental Integrated Authorisation" was issued on 4 August 2011. It was constituted of 1162 pages (9 articles in 19 pages, and 1143 pages of procedural and technical attachments) [http://aia.minambiente.it/DettaglioAutorizzazionePub.aspx?id=4822].

36 The revision of the "Environmental Integrated Authorisation" was issued on 22 October 2012. It was constituted of 149 pages (4 articles in 23 pages, and 126 pages of procedural and technical attachments) [http://aia.minambiente.it/DettaglioAutorizzazionePub.aspx?id=5135].

changes and revealing in advance possible legal actions.[37] The revision was only partially due to the Commission Decision 2012/135/EU, implementing the IED Directive for the iron and steel sector, as the deadline for its implementation was still far away (2016). What really mattered was that the Taranto criminal judges intervened, seizing the plant in order to shut it down.

The European Court of Human Rights (ECtHR) has been involved as well.

A citizen of Taranto, who was diagnosed with leukaemia in 2006, brought a proceeding against Italy in 2009[38], alleging that the harmful emissions from the Ilva factory caused the development of her cancer and therefore violated Article 2 ("*Right to Life*") of the European Convention on Human Rights (ECHR). The complainant had previously sued the Ilva management before the national judges, but, after a scientific report ruled out, on the basis of the available scientific data, a causal link between the emissions from the factory and her illness, the proceedings were discontinued. The ECtHR unanimously declared the application inadmissible, as the complainant had not demonstrated that the Italian authorities had failed in their obligation to protect her right to life (Article 2, ECHR).[39]

In 2016 the ECtHR formally opened proceedings against Italy for having failed to protect life and health of 182 Taranto citizens from the polluting emissions caused by the Ilva factory. The applicants alleged that the Italian authorities did not take the necessary measures to safeguard the environment and the health of people. The Court deemed the evidence presented by the applicants (that applied in two stages, in 2013 and in 2015[40]) solid enough and referred to Article 2 (Right to Life), Article 8 (Right to Respect for Private Life) and Article 13 (Right to an Effective Remedy) of the Convention.

4. ILVA, (UN)SUSTAINABLE DEVELOPMENT, INFORMATION AND PARTICIPATION

There are two perspectives that may help to understand today's Ilva issues: the perspective from the past and the perspective for the future. The former is about

---

37 See letters from Ilva 31 August 2011 and 6 November 2012.

38 ECtHR, *Smaltini v. Italy*, application no. 43961/09, published on 16 April 2015. Ms. Smaltini died in 2012. Her husband and her two children continued the proceeding.

39 See ECtHR, *Smaltini v. Italy*, application no. 43961/09, para. 60 (available only in French): "*Compte tenu de ces circonstances, et sans préjudice des résultats des études scientifiques à venir, la Cour ne peut que constater que la requérante n'a pas prouvé qu'à la lumière des connaissances scientifiques disponibles à l'époque des faits de l'affaire, l'obligation imposée au Gouvernement de protéger sa vie, au sens de l'article 2 de la Convention, sous son volet procédural, a été méconnue*".

40 *Cordella and Others v. Italy* (application no. 54414/13) and *Ambrogi Melle and Others v. Italy* (application no. 54264/15) [http://hudoc.echr.coe.int/eng/?i=001-163116].

what has been done, the many mistakes and the contested liabilities. The latter is about what can be done, the suggested solutions and the necessary responsibilities.

What happened in the past is somehow clear, at least as for the basic dynamics.[41] The Ilva private owners' hunger for profit heavily affected their approach to environmental issues, postponing protection measures as long as possible. Their opaque closeness with politics and public officials favoured reprehensible business behaviours. The Government did not seriously intervene until the closure of the plant became a plausible option, due to the judicial orders of 2012. The implementation of European Union directives had to be forced through a decision of the European Court of Justice.[42] The IPPC permit was issued with a delay of years, but that did not mean that it was well thought and accurate: it was substantially revised just one year later. Monitoring and control of the productive and entrepreneurial activity lacked. The judiciary itself was not blameless. For years it had not intervened, even though the environmental situation has been compromised for decades. When the criminal judges stepped in, they sometimes pushed their own powers boundaries and the confrontation with the company and with the government was extremely harsh.

Besides, administrative judges have often decided in favour of Ilva s.p.a. when it challenged administrative orders or sanctions, saying that the company was respecting the legislative and administrative rules (starting from the IPPC permit). The administrative judges, on the other hand, underlined that administrative provisions were often inconsistent and flawed. That means that Ilva s.p.a. has had its faults, but it has not been alone: the legal and institutional framework contributed to the disaster.

Delay, opaqueness and lack of accountability are the keywords.

The result is today's situation. Ilva s.p.a. has been always considered strategic for local, regional and national economy, and too big to fail. The Ilva factory in Taranto is the heart of the Ilva company, that is the heart of the national steel production sector. The steel plant is still working, polluting less because of environmental measures, but also because is producing much less.[43] The employment level, though, has not substantially decreased, which means that the Ilva plant is daily losing money.[44] The cleaning up of the area has started but,

---

41 *J. Mackenzie*, Steel pollution case highlights Italy's slow decline, August 29, 2012, Reuters, United States Edition [www.reuters.com/article/us-italy-pollution-idUSBRE87S07B20120829] *"Behind the immediate health threat, Ilva is a stark example of the suffocating mix of short-term political expediency, poor oversight and endemic corruption that has given Italy the most sluggish economy of any euro zone country over the course of a decade, with average growth of less than one percent a year"*.

42 ECJ, Case C-50/10, *Commission v. Italy* [2011] ECR I-00045.

43 The Ilva Taranto factory produced more than 10 million tons before 2012, 8.3 million tons in 2012, 4.7 million tons in 2015. The "survival limit" for such a plant is estimated in 6.5 million tons.

44 See *M. Borrillo*, Ilva, effetto Cina sull'acciaio. Perdite record di 2,5 milioni al giorno, Corriere della Sera, 1 aprile 2016 [www.corriere.it/economia/16_aprile_02/ilva-effetto-cina-sull-

as the plant is still operating, it is slower and less effective than it could have been in case of closure. The European Union is calling Italy's responses to the crisis into question under two points of view: environmental law violations and state aid violations. The European Court of Human Rights is challenging Italy's behaviours as well. The economic and social situation is still hard and the future is uncertain.

Italy has not, in its Constitution, an article devoted to sustainable development. Though, the Legislative Decree 3 April 2006, no. 152 (so called "environmental code") has an article (article 4) that states that every legally relevant human activity must comply with sustainable development (para. 1), that public administration activity must aim at implementing sustainable development (para. 2) and that any controversy involving environmental aspects must be solved ensuring sustainable development (para. 4). Notwithstanding these principles, sustainable development is far from being respected in the Ilva case. At a national level it is often misunderstood, misused, "lost in translation", speciously declared with rhetoric and demagogy, without any real will to comprehend and substantially pursue it.

The lack of reliable data is one of the major issues, as it affects both institutional (political, economic, environmental, social) analyses and public awareness (information and participation). The availability of data has been irregular, and data themselves were often outdated and inconsistent. Data are often presented in an emotional way, and other times they are hardly comprehensible.

The Ilva plant is ISO 14001 certified, and it has been since 2004.[45] So, while the judiciary was saying that the Ilva factory was killing people and destroying the environment, technical bodies, accredited by national authorities and implementing international technical norms, were saying that the same factory was environmental friendly and virtuous above average.

In 2011 the European Environment Agency (EEA) released a report[46] assessing the damage costs to health and the environment caused by pollutants emitted from industrial facilities in 2009. Ilva was at the top neither in Italy (2nd[47]) nor in Europe (52nd[48]) and, as for steel plants, it was just at the 6th place. Reading the

acciaio-perdite-record-25-milioni-giorno-5be1d166-f850–11e5-b848–7bd2f7c41e07.shtml]: losses are estimated, for 2015, in 2.5 million daily, for a total amount of 918 million, to be summed to 641 million for 2014, 911 million for 2013 and 620 million for 2012 (that is an average daily loss of more than 2 million over a four-year period).

45 In 2002 a representative of a local NGO publicly challenged Ilva to get the ISO 14001 certification, considered a "truth test". Ilva got it in 2004, but, clearly, it was no silver bullet.

46 European Environment Agency, *Revealing the costs of air pollution from industrial facilities in Europe, Report 2011* [www.eea.europa.eu/publications/cost-of-air-pollution].

47 At the top in Italy (18th in Europe) was the thermal power station "Centrale termoelettrica Federico II" in Brindisi, located in the Apulia Region as well.

48 At the top, in Europe, was the thermal power station "PGE Elektrownia Bełchatów", located in Rogowiec, Poland.

report the first impression was that the Ilva situation was not that bad, as there were worse cases around Europe that had not sparked a similar interest.

In 2014 the EEA released an updated report[49], that considered the 2008–2012 period. This time Ilva was on the top in Italy, 29th in Europe and 3rd as for steel plants. The five-year term (2008–2012) included the single year (2009) analysed by the previous report. Besides, Ilva started to modify its productive behaviours at the end of 2012, so such a change in the ranking is hardly justifiable.

The point is that criteria and methodology changed. Moreover, as the 2011 Report explicitly states in its introduction, the reports do not assess the consistency of facilities' emissions with the national and EU requirements, nor they consider "diffuse" sources, such as transport. Furthermore the EEA reports evaluate neither the social (employment) and economic (production, tax revenues) benefits that they generate nor the efficiency of the facilities. The largest factories release more pollutants and impose the higher costs, but smaller facilities may be less efficient and pollute more if compared with the amount of goods and services provided to the market. The EEA analysis admits that there are uncertainties in assessing the damage costs, related to scientific knowledge about impacts, exposure methods applied and models used, inviting therefore to caution in interpreting the results.

The EEA, for these reports, drew the data from the European Pollutant Release and Transfer Register (E-PRTR)[50], the Europe-wide register, created by Regulation (EC) no. 166/2006, that provides environmental data from industrial facilities in Europe.[51] The E-PRTR is a transparency and public participation tool connected to the Aarhus Convention[52], but its data may be not totally reliable: the information concerning pollutants released and off-site transfers of waste are provided by the companies. In absence of effective control and monitoring mechanism, the risk that the companies alter the data cannot be excluded.

Available data at a national level suffer from the same limits. The first data on Taranto, collected since 2001 in the INES register[53], are extracted from the ILVA declarations. Monitoring occurs, but the company is informed beforehand about when it will take place. The scientific studies are often outdated and not

---

49 European Environment Agency, *Costs of air pollution from European industrial facilities 2008–2012 – an updated assessment*, Report 2014 [www.eea.europa.eu/publications/costs-of-air-pollution-2008–2012].

50 The E-PRTR, that replaced the European Pollutant Emission Register (EPER) contains data reported annually by more *than 30,000 industrial facilities* covering 65 economic activities across Europe (EU Member States and Iceland, Liechtenstein, Norway, Serbia and Switzerland). See the E-PRTR website for more data [http://prtr.ec.europa.eu/#/home].

51 Regulation (EC) no. 166/2006 of 18 January 2006, concerning the establishment of a European Pollutant Release and Transfer Register and amending Council Directives 91/689/EEC and 96/61/EC.

52 United Nations Economic Commission for Europe (UNECE) Convention on Access to Information, Public Participation in Decision-Making and Access to Justice in Environmental Matters, adopted on 25 June 1998 in Aarhus.

53 The INES register was established with Legislative Decree 4 August 1999, no. 372 and Ministerial Decree 23 November 2011.

unanimously accepted by the scientific community. Besides, the way they are presented are often misleading. A recent report from researchers of the Ministry of Health states on one side that Ilva is polluted like Rome and, on the other side, that there may be serious neurological consequences due to the pollution in Taranto that have not been considered so far.

The result of this uncertainties in data and in their interpretation affects public participation, especially if added to other factors. The IPPC permit procedure in 2011 and 2012 did not favour participation due to its extreme complexity. While the Save-Ilva decree was not deemed in violation of the Constitution, the fact that administrative provisions were adopted by law lowered (or cancelled) the chances to participate to the proceedings. The selling procedure, due to its confidentiality, is making public information and participation harder, both for citizens and for public authorities (like Region Apulia and the local administration of Taranto) other than the ones directly involved.

In other words, public opinion is kept in the dark as for what is really happening, limiting its chance to participate at the political debate on fundamental choices that are going to influence life, health, economy and employment in Taranto and Apulia.

That said, it came as a surprise the outcome of the advisory referendum of 14 April 2013 on Ilva, promoted by the "*Taranto futura*" committee. There were two questions for the Taranto population: the first concerning the total shutdown of the factory, the second concerning the shutdown of the main problematic areas (the "hot area" and the mineral parks). A large majority of the voters supported the shutdowns (respectively 81,29% and 92,62%), but the results were invalidated as only 19,5% of the population participated (the quorum was 50%). In the Tamburi neighbourhood the percentage of voters was even lower (14,57%). Considering the physiological rate of non-voters, people in Taranto that did not want Ilva to close decided to abstain. It is a legitimate choice. Still, seeing that, in Taranto, in 2013, less than one person out of five went to vote for a referendum concerning Ilva, was somehow unsettling.

5. CONCLUSIONS

There are four main, intertwined, factors that can help Ilva and Taranto: new legislation, better implementation, technical progress and the sale of the factory. The legislation should abandon the emergency approach, and adopt a long-lasting perspective, enacting coherent rules that clearly define policy objectives and actors' accountability. The application of the rules must avoid the mistakes and the drawbacks of the past, establishing reliable monitoring and control mechanisms. The advancement in technology, through new best available techniques, may help in reducing the emissions and their dangerousness. The sale procedure of Ilva was finally closed, finding a reliable buyer, in June 2017. One month after the new IPPC permit was requested by the new owner, and at the end of September the Italian government issued a decree that approved the environmental plan changes. Still, while waiting for the European Union anti-trust ruling, the social situation has gotten complicated one more time, when AM InvestCo Italy has revealed its labor strategy, that should lead to a gradual, but substantial, decrease in the employment level and to an immediate reduction of the wages and the guarantees of the remaining workers. The faraway deadline (23 August 2023) established for the completion of the environmental plan has been also criticized for its inadequateness, taking into account the health issues involved.

On the other hand, several issues will stay open. The Ilva plant is located in a polluted area, experiencing a difficult relationship with a city, Taranto, and its population. The area has to be cleaned up, and it will be very costly and controversial. The pollution in Taranto is not coming only from the Ilva plant, and the soil pollution layering derives also from thirty years of public ownership and management. It will not be easy to calculate the contribution of the different actors to the pollution occurred in Taranto over the years, and it would not be fair not to (try to) do it.

The sale should have occurred in 2016, but it was postponed, trying to find better offers. In the meantime, though, Ilva became less competitive and less attractive. The Italian economy is still struggling to exit the crisis and the political situation is not stable.

The new owner has to face several delicate issues: adopt and implement an environmental plan that will have to guarantee a dramatic change from the past; deal with the consequences of EU new legislation, policies and case law; resort to the best available techniques and respect the IPPC permit; take care of the social issues in Taranto.

Moreover, clear rules have to be enacted, in order to avoid EU infringement procedures, to strictly monitor the new owner's activities, to further improve the environmental legislative and administrative framework, to guarantee employment levels that can ensure a profit to the company without creating a social turmoil in Taranto. Public information and participation have to be promoted through the provision of clear, updated, coherent data.

After being a history of conflicts and failures, Ilva may turn out to be an example of economic resilience, environmental recovery, social justice: in two words, sustainable development. It is a strong hope. It will not be easy at all.

THE IMPROVEMENT OF ARTICLE 37 OF THE EU CHARTER OF FUNDAMENTAL RIGHTS

A Choice Between an Empty Shell and a Test Tube?

Marco Túlio Reis Magalhães*

ABSTRACT

This paper proposes an improvement to Article 37 of the Charter of Fundamental Rights of the European Union (CFREU) through the introduction of procedural environmental rights. It challenges the current legal provision, which takes into account solely a policy principle (interest-based approach). The presentation has a three-part structure: the first one analyses the development of European environmental law under different perspectives in order to ascertain the role of the CFREU regarding environmental protection. The second part investigates some aspects in the EU Charter, particularly the legal structure of Article 37, aiming to highlight some opposite ideas and problems concerning the so-called "rights of solidarity". The third part presents critical comments to the current policy principle approach in Article 37, proposing an alternative by the introduction of procedural environmental rights, according the framework of the Rio Declaration and the Aarhus Convention. The conclusion reaffirms the proposal initially presented, reviewing the main arguments and advantages of such an alternative, specially taking into account the role of individuals and non-institutional actors in the process.

KEYWORDS

Article 37; Charter of Fundamental Rights of the European Union; environmental protection; European environmental law; procedural environmental rights; right to environmental protection.

* PhD Candidate, Freie Universität Berlin and University of São Paulo.

1. INTRODUCTION

EU institutions solemnly proclaimed a Charter of Fundamental Rights of the European Union (CFREU) in 2000. It alludes to dignity, freedom, equality, solidarity, citizen's rights and justice – although it did not have a legally binding effect at that time.[1] Article 37 of the Charter specifically addresses environmental protection. Before reading the content of this Article, we should presume that such legal provision is a sort of right to environmental protection, considering that we are here under the scope of a Charter of Fundamental Rights.

Nevertheless, Article 37 has only prescribed a policy principle for environmental protection addressed only to EU institutions. In 2009, the Charter of Fundamental Rights of the European Union became a part of EU primary legislation with legally binding effect.[2] However, the wording of Article 37 remained the same, without any significant modification.

The question is if the perspective of a policy principle (interest-based approach) is coherent with a catalogue of fundamental rights. We should also ask about the compatibility of that approach with the development of European environmental law and the international environmental law, which includes a variety of instruments and legal tools for environmental protection. Finally, we can also inquire if there are alternatives for this sort of appraisal.

The present paper investigates those questions, proposing the improvement of Article 37 of the Charter of Fundamental Rights of the European Union through the introduction of procedural environmental rights, as a contribution to the development of European environmental law.

The main issue relates to the viable ways of improving the legal provision in order to promote an enforceable legal tool for the environmental protection with the individual's participation, coherently to the expectations of a catalogue of fundamental rights. In other words, what are the alternatives to a current approach that simply establish a policy principle (interest-based approach) for environmental protection, addressed only to EU Institutions and Member States?

To reach the proposed goal, this essay presents a three-part discussion. The first one is an overview of some aspects of the legal framework about environmental protection, considering the phases of development of European environmental law, the phases of development of international environmental law, and the current legislation tools of the European Union in this specific field.

The second part examines the meaning and the scope of a catalogue of fundamental rights, specifically the accomplishment of the Charter of Fundamental Rights of the European Union in this sense. The analysis takes into special account the example of the legal provision regarding the environmental protection – Article 37.

---

1 *J. Machado*, Direito da União Europeia, 2nd ed., 2014, p. 285 et seq.

2 *S. Pais*, Estudos de Direito da União Europeia, 3rd ed., 2014, p. 143.

The third part brings a criticism to the current policy principle approach, proposing an alternative based on ideas of experimentalism and the introduction of procedural environmental rights in the CFREU.

2. DEVELOPMENT OF EUROPEAN ENVIRONMENTAL LAW

The understanding of the current features of European environmental law is more complete from a wider perspective, which takes into account not only the legislation, but also European environmental policy and its administration. It is also interesting to analyse this development in comparison to the international environmental law. Therefore, an overview of the bigger framework intends to highlight some elements that might be helpful for a better analysis regarding the potential directions of Article 37 of the CFREU, as well as the comprehension of the full meaning and scope of such a catalogue of fundamental rights.

2.1. ENVIRONMENTAL PROTECTION AT EUROPEAN LEVEL

The initial course of the environmental policy at the EU level occurred without a firm and explicit legal basis due to political and economic reasons focused on the main goals of the "founding treaties" – the Treaty of Paris (establishing the Economic and Steel Community) and the two Treaties of Rome (one settling the European Economic Community and the other determining the European Atomic Energy Community – EURATOM).[3]

According to Christoph Knill and Duncan Liefferink, the environmental policy started its development in the 1970s as a part of the trade policy, mostly related to the Paris Summit meeting of heads of state and government under the European Economic Community (EEC) in 1972. The settlement of such a declaration on environmental and consumer policy aimed to grant to the European Commission a way to drawn up an action programme for environmental protection. It is possible to point as an important reason for that sort of approach – which we can also consider as a successful strategy at the time in the view of an absence of legal provisions for environmental protection in the Treaties the "fear that trade barriers and competitive distortions in the Common Market could emerge due to the different environmental standards."[4]

---

3 *A. Jordan & C. Adelle*, EU Environmental Policy – Contexts, Actors and Policy Dynamics, in: A. Jordan & C. Adelle, Environmental Policy in the EU, 3th ed., 2013, p. 1, 2.

4 *C. Knill & D. Liefferink*, The Establishment of EU Environmental Policy, in: A. Jordan & C. Adelle, Environmental Policy in the EU, 3rd ed., 2013, p. 13, 14 et seq.

In this sense, we can draw three different phases of European environmental policy. Within the first phase (1972–1987), the legal justification for environmental measures had a fundament on the trade police motives: harmonization and completion of the conditions of a Common Market; the improvement of living conditions in the EU; the increase of cross-border environmental problems[5]; the pioneering role of some individual states to implement environmental measures at the EU level – such as Germany, Netherlands and Denmark. The second phase (1987–1992) is the beginning of a formal recognition of legal and institutional consolidation and further development of a common environmental policy, recognized in the Single European Act (SEA) as an official field of activity (with the establishment of objectives, basic principles and decision-making procedures for EU environmental policy).[6] In the third phase (post 1992), two opposing trends deserve a mention: on the one hand, there is an accommodation of the legal and institutional basis of the environmental policy[7]; on the other, we identify a reduction of dynamics and impulses for new developments regarding environmental policy, due to economic issues and the prevalence of other policy areas in the European agenda.[8]

In a different but similar approach, Jan H. Jans and Ann-Katrin von der Heide emphasize five different phases of development of European environmental law. A first phase (1958–1972) presents no special environmental measures or rules, excepting some sparse environmental aspects (such as Directive 67/548 – related to classification, packing and description of hazardous materials) involving other policy areas. The second phase (1972–1987) is the start signal of an environmental policy, illustrated by the first environmental action programme aiming to achieve the goals established in the Treaties not only quantitatively, but also by a qualitative manner, even if the legal grounds had a relation to trade policy. A third phase (1987–1993) began with the introduction of environmental legal provisions at the EU level by the SEA, establishing competences for the environmental field. The forth phase (1993–1999) covered the period between the implementation of the Treaty of Maastricht and the Treaty of Amsterdam, by which the idea of sustainable economic growth became a part of the Community's goals. Also in this stage, the relevance of environmental action programmes had increased, reaching the daily work of European institutions (e.g. the European Parliament). A fifth phase (post 1999) consisted in some modifications that the Treaty of

5 E.g. the episode of the dieback of forests (*Waldsterben*).

6 The SEA established the Title XIX – "Environment" (ex Articles 174–176 TEC), with relevant interpretative connections with ex Articles 18 and 95 TEC, focused on the improvement of the Common Market. "The explicit establishment of environmental policy as an official domain of the EU occurred at a certain extent as a by-product of economically motivated reforms." *Knill & Liefferink, supra,* note 4 at p. 20.

7 Without any consistent or remarkable revision by the further Treaties of Maastricht and Amsterdam.

8 *Knill & Liefferink, supra,* note 4 at pp. 28–29.

Amsterdam and the Treaty of Nice presented, introducing the term "sustainable development" in the definition of the goals of the Community, and also enforcing the integration principle to environmental policy, with some changes related to decision-making procedures.[9]

One important achievement regarding decision-making procedures was the establishment of the Convention on Access to Information, Public Participation in Decision-Making and Access to Justice in Environmental Matters (Aarhus Convention), adopted on June 25, 1998 in the Danish city of Aarhus (Århus), which entered into force on the October 30, 2001.[10]

Another important aspect in the understanding of the institutional framework of the European Union in the field of environmental law consists in recognizing the role of some institutional actors – such as the Commission and the European Parliament, the Council and the European Council. Nevertheless, it is important to emphasize, there were always a sort of limited participation of individuals and environmental non-governmental organizations.[11]

Besides, since the beginning of the Economic European Community, Member States had different legal standards and engagements for environmental protection, which has certainly influenced the way national courts interpret and apply rules concerning environmental protection in the context of an interaction between national and supranational levels.[12]

2.2. A COMPARISON WITH THE DEVELOPMENT OF INTERNATIONAL ENVIRONMENTAL LAW

The impulses of international environmental law had also influenced relevantly the development of environmental law at the European level. As a brief comparison, we can point four phases on the development of international environmental law.[13] At first (between the end of the nineteenth and the early twentieth century), there was the implementation of international agreements and rules aiming a better use of natural resources under a merely utilitarian and anthropocentric approach. A second phase (post 1945 until the 1950s) marked the establishment

9 *J. Jans & A.-K. Heide*, Europäisches Umweltrecht, 2003, pp. 3–10.

10 For an overview and understanding of the Aarhus Convention, see: *J. Jendroska*, Accès à la Justice: Remarques sur le Statut Juridique et le Champ des Obligations de la Convention D'Aarhus dans le Contexte de L'Union Européenne, RJE, 2009 (No. special), pp. 31–48.

11 *L. Krämer*, Thirty Years of Environmental Governance in the European Union, in: R. Macrory, Reflections on 30 Years of EU Environmental Law, 2006, p. 553, 555 et seq.

12 For interesting investigations facing the extension to which national courts interpret and apply the EU Law and its doctrines – such as "direct effect", "consistent interpretation" and "state liability" –, normally designed to implement the EU Environmental Law, see: *J. Jans, R. Macrory & A.-M. Molina*, National Courts and EU Environmental Law, 2013 (chapters 9 to 21).

13 *G. Soares*, Direito Internacional do Meio Ambiente, 2nd ed., 2003, pp. 39–93; *P. Casella & H. Accioly*, Manual de Direito Internacional Público, 19th ed., 2011, pp. 681–703.

of international organizations, regional agreements and the beginning of an environmental approach.

The third phase (from 1960s on, but specially post the 1970s) has two main perspectives: on the one hand, the adoption of the Stockholm Declaration in the context of the United Nations Conference on the Human Environment (1972) and the publication of the Brundtland Report in 1987 (World Commission on Environment and Development: Our Common Future)[14]; on the other hand, the increasing awareness and recognition of the negative side effects of probable risks and dangerous activities, such as military tests, nuclear energy plants, oil exploration, and others as the industrial, space and navigation activities. At the third phase's end, the humanity had already been introduced to a wide range of ecological disasters at the regional and international levels.[15] The 1970s has as a main characteristic the growth of international bilateral and multilateral agreements, reports and other international documents regarding environmental protection[16], but not necessarily through a linear evolution in terms of hierarchical uniformity or legal effects.[17]

The transition to the forth phase (1992–1997 and post 1997) occurred on the scope of UN Conference on Environment and Development (1992), so-called Earth Summit (or Rio Summit), that established relevant international instruments and steps for future action.[18] Some highlights in this period are: an increase of multilateral international conventions and agreements, with participation of international organizations and governing bodies attached to environmental protection; more dynamic instruments for treaty-making (revision and control instruments), and the rising use of umbrella conventions and framework agreements; the strengthening of the ethical importance of environmental acts

14 Important outcomes were the establishment of the United Nations Environment Programme in 1972, a range of international agreements regarding environmental protection and an increased multilateralism trend.

15 Some relevant examples are: the negative effects of the nuclear bombs in Hiroshima and Nagasaki; methylmercury contamination at the Minamata Bay Incident (post 1950s); Trail Smelter Arbitration between United States and Canada and the trans-boundary pollution (1941); Lake Lanoux Arbitration on use of waters between France and Spain (1957); Torrey Canyon oil spill in the southwest coast of the United Kingdom (1967); the Seveso industrial accident with dangerous chemicals (1976), which prompted the adoption of the so-called Seveso-Directive (Directive 82/501/EEC); damages resulting from the disintegration of the Soviet satellite "Cosmos 954" over northwest Canada (1978); The Amoco Cadiz oil spill (1978); the Bhopal disaster from a gas leak incident in an industrial plant in India (1984); the Chernobyl nuclear disaster in a power plant in Ukraine (1986); the fire and chemical spill at Sandoz in the industrial area near Basel, Switzerland, leading to trans-boundary pollution problems in the river Rhine (1986). *Soares, supra*, note 13 at pp. 696–697 (translated from the original in Portuguese by the author).

16 *A. Trindade*, Direitos Humanos e Meio-Ambiente, 1993, p. 40.

17 *M. Varella*, O Surgimento e a Evolução do Direito Internacional do Meio Ambiente: da Proteção da Natureza ao Desenvolvimento Sustentável, in: M. Varella & A. Platiau (eds.), Proteção Internacional do Meio Ambiente, 2009, p. 6, 7.

18 *G. Silva*, Direito Ambiental Internacional, 2nd ed., 2002, pp. 33–41.

by governments, resolutions and soft law (specially declarations and charters); expanding international actors and their growing relevance (international organizations, companies, individuals, humanity, communities – not state entities – and, rather prominently, non-governmental organizations); establishment of new legal principles and flexible normative-regulatory instruments, as the recognition of the principle of Common But Differentiated Responsibilities.[19]

In the period from 1992 to 2012, the United Nations' Conferences and the environmental international law settled similar approaches, mainly in the field of sustainable development, concrete measures against climate change and acts implementing clean energy's methods, for example.[20]

Moreover, the United Nations Conference on Sustainable Development (or Rio+20), that took place in Rio de Janeiro in 2012, continued the discussion about the promotion of sustainable development and its economically, socially and environmentally dimensions (through the Declaration "The future we want"). However, it did not bring so many developments as expected, on account mainly to the pressure from the world economic crisis since 2008.[21]

2.3. PRIMARY AND SECONDARY EU LEGISLATION

European environmental law is supported by the legislative and administrative basis established by the Treaties, the CFREU and correlated documents. Articles 191 and 193 of the Treaty on the Functioning of the European Union (TFEU) are the main guidance provisions regarding the Union environmental policy and law, in coordination with other provisions, such as Article 11 TFEU.[22]

A summary of the current types of rules in European environmental law leads to a set of four major groups. The first group consists in general provisions (*allgemeine Regeln*), that comprises legal acts stated by Article 288 TFEU, procedural and structural rules, and important principles related to the environment (precaution, integrated environmental protection, transparency, involvement of the citizens). In this sense, we can name some instances as the Directive on environmental liability, the Directive on environmental impact assessment and the Directive on industrial emissions. The second group comprehends rules concerning the quality of the different elements in nature (*medienbezogenen Regelungen*) – e.g. air and water –, that are means for life on earth and, therefore, subject of legislation (e.g. EU Water Framework Directive). The third group comprises rules regarding specific activities and materials

---

19 *Soares*, *supra*, note 13 at pp. 407–437.

20 *A. Lago*, Conferências de desenvolvimento sustentável, 2013, p. 69 et seq.

21 *Id.* at p. 157 et seq.

22 Astrid Epiney quotes other relevant Articles of TFEU – Article 4(2)e; Article 13; Article 114 (1), (4), (5) and (6) – and Article 3(3), (5) 2nd sentence TEU. *A. Epiney*, Umweltrecht der Europäischen Union, 3rd ed., 2013, pp. 48–49.

(*Regeln, die einen Schutz vor bestimmten Tätigkeiten oder Stoffen verfolgen*), such as genetic engineering, chemicals, which is believably a great risk of danger, and hence should be controlled from the source. The forth group contains stipulations related to the rational use and protection of environmental resources (*Vorschriften, die der Bewirtschaftung und dem Schutz von Umweltressourcen dienen*), aiming to materialize the sustainability into the economic practices, allowing conservation and reutilization of environmental goods – as Directives regarding the climate, fauna and flora and all the procedures related to waste disposal.[23]

There are, at this point, two important remarks to highlight. First, the special role played by the directives concerning the environmental field, which shall be binding, as to the result achieved, upon each Member State to whom it is addressed, but shall leave to the national authorities the choice of form and applied methods. Moreover, Article 11 (TFEU) is of great importance, working as a cross-section clause, integrating environmental protection requirements to the definition and implementation of the EU policies, in accordance with a sustainable development's approach.

Furthermore, the case law also plays an essential role in the matter, taking into account not only decisions from the European Court of Human Rights, but also those from the Court of Justice of the European Union – specially due to the absence of legal provisions regarding environmental protection and human rights in the first phases of the European integration process.[24]

2.4. EVALUATING THE EUROPEAN ENVIRONMENTAL LAW

The present overview about the development of European environmental law, side by side with the development of international environmental law, had the purpose to highlight some important evidences. Both spheres have experienced a fast and consistent development since the 1960s, presenting many interconnected points and mutual influences. Moreover, European environmental law evinces a bigger flexibility and political potential to improve environmental protection measures through directives and other instruments, achieving a significant number of European states, and expressing the potential to be a global player in the field of environmental protection (acting as a mirror for the rest of the world).[25]

---

23 *C. Calliess & M. Ruffert*, EUV-AEUV Kommentar, 4th ed., 2011, pp.1943–1949.

24 "It was in the Maastricht Treaty on European Union 1992 that formal Treaty recognition was finally given to human rights as part of EU law." *G. de Búrca*, The Evolution of EU Human Rights Law, in: P. Craig & G. de Búrca, The Evolution of EU Law, 2nd ed., 2011, p. 465, 480. For an overview of the environmental case law (ECHR and CJEU), see: *R. Gordon & R. Moffatt*, EU Law in Judicial Review, 2nd ed., 2014, p. 447 et seq.

25 *Krämer*, *supra*, note 11 at pp. 575–576.

In this perspective, the dynamics of a multilevel system in the European Union also contributes to a wider establishment of environmental measures in a high level of protection – in terms of legislation, policies and administration.[26]

Nevertheless, one element is missing at this point. None of the brief summaries (bigger framework) aforementioned emphasizes the Charter of Fundamental Rights of the European Union as a significant legal tool for environmental protection, despite the explicit provision regarding environmental protection (Article 37) contained in the Title IV (Solidarity) of the Charter since 2000.

Therefore, it is imperative analysing the Charter of Fundamental Rights of the European Union (closer framework) in order to identify the linkage between Article 37 and its context.

3. EU CHARTER OF FUNDAMENTAL RIGHTS AND ENVIRONMENTAL PROTECTION

The proposed outlook of European environmental law receives, at this point, the complement of the investigation of a closer frame: the Charter of Fundamental Rights of the European Union, specifically by its Article 37. In addition, the question about what is expected from a catalogue of fundamental rights and what the EU Charter effectively delivers are objects of analysis here.

3.1. CONCEPT OF A CATALOGUE OF FUNDAMENTAL RIGHTS

The choice for a charter of fundamental rights usually involves the development of the humanity in a wider perspective, not only from the standpoint of law, but also taking under consideration historical connections to politics, society, economy, ethics and philosophy.[27] It means the adoption of some basic ideas, principles and values – as limitation of governing powers, establishment of instances to protect rights and receive claims against their violation, judicial guarantee of individual rights and freedoms. Such elements appear in some important historical references such as the *Magna Charta Libertatum* (1215); the Petition of Rights (1628); the *Habeas Corpus* Act (1679), and the Bill of Rights (1668), combined with a further development of the Virginia Bill of Rights (1776) and the French *Déclaration des Droits de l'Homme et du Citoyen* (1789).[28]

---

26 For an example of the complex dynamics of a multilevel system under the administrative perspective, see: *G. Winter*, Matching Tasks and Competences in the EC Multi-level Environmental Administration, in: R. Macrory, Reflections on 30 Years of EU Environmental Law, 2006, pp. 399–414.

27 *K. Stern*, Das Staatsrecht der Bundesrepublik, Band III/1, 1988, pp. 54–56.

28 *I. Münch & U. Mager*, Staatsrecht II, 6th ed., 2014, pp. 9–10.

It is worth mentioning that not only the increment of fundamental rights in the nineteenth century, including the recognition of different theoretical approaches, plays an important role regarding this subject.[29] The international and regional recognition of human rights in the twentieth century – Declarations, Conventions and regional systems of protection – also has a relevant place on the matter. Human dignity, freedoms and rights remain central goals. Fundamental rights are at the core of the rule of law, providing a significant contribution for the statement of freedom and democracy, particularly for those countries used to a constitutional tradition and written constitutions.[30]

Taking into account the characteristics of a traditional catalogue of fundamental rights, we present the question: does the Charter of Fundamental Rights of the European Union follow such a trend?

3.2. EU CHARTER OF FUNDAMENTAL RIGHTS

The Charter of Fundamental Rights of the European Union is composed by a preamble and seven chapters: (I) dignity, (II) freedom, (III) equality, (IV) solidarity, (V) citizenship, (VI) justice, and (VII) general provisions – the last is responsible for regulating the Charter's interpretation and application.[31] Similar to the German Basic Law, it presents first a provision of respect for the human dignity.[32]

The EU Charter of Fundamental Rights recognizes rights, freedoms and principles, reaffirms some universal values of human dignity, freedoms, equality and solidarity. It expresses also the intention of respect for the principles of democracy and the rule of law, emphasizing that individuals are important and must be considered by the EU. This way, it works in the direction of improving the citizenship in the Union and the development of a common area of justice, freedoms and security.[33]

---

29 Regarding the important contribution of german doctrine in this field, see: *F. Hufen*, Staatsrecht II, 4th ed., 2014, pp. 20–31. Böckenförde mentions five different theoretical perspectives of fundamental rights: the liberal, the institutional, the axiological, the democratic-functional, and the theory related to the welfare state. *E. W. Böckenförde*, Escritos sobre Derechos Fundamentales, Translated by Juan Luis Requejo Pagés e Ignacio Villaverde Menéndez, 1993, pp. 48–65.

30 *Münch & Mager*, *supra*, note 28 at pp. 1–2.

31 *A. Dashwood* et al., Wyatt and Dashwood's European Union Law, 6th ed., 2011, p. 361.

32 For a closer study about the textual relevance and the inherent meaning of the legal provision regarding human dignity in the German Basic Law, see: *K. Stern*, Menschenwürde als Wurzel der Menschen- und Grundrechte, in: A. Norbert, W. Krawietz & D. Wyduckel (eds.), Recht und Staat im sozialen Wandel, 1983, p. 627, 630 et seq.

33 "The Charter is narrower in scope than the general principles and it applies only to acts of the Union institutions and to the Member States when they implement Union law." *Dashwood* et al., *supra*, note 31 at p. 359.

Although the EU Charter of Fundamental Rights fulfilled the lack of a written catalogue within the primary legislation of the European Union, it did not necessarily meet the standards preconized by the rule of law – mostly because the Charter establishes matters beyond the competences of the European Union regarding legislation, a factor that disrespects the parallelism of competence and protection of fundamental rights.[34]

The preamble contains significant evidences about the Charter's origins and scope. Firstly, the EU increased government powers and the potential negative impacts of its acts on citizens of the Member States evidenced, through the years, the need for a consistent basis at the EU level for the protection of fundamental rights, which would not only prioritize economic values, but also establish a space of recognition for Member States' citizens. In this sense, the need of a Charter represents a counterpart for the development – mostly since 1995 – of the Union new competences regarding security, home affairs and justice, all elements that could threaten individuals rights and freedoms. That is a fundamental aspect to understand why the Charter was a result from a conference devoted to "Internal Affairs" and "Justice and Home Affairs".[35]

Secondly, it is important to mention that the initial idea was clearly reinforce common values and strengthen the protection of fundamental rights already recognized by the constitutional traditions and international obligations common to Member States, the Treaty on European Union, the Community Treaties, the European Convention for the Protection of Human Rights and Fundamental Freedoms, the Social Charters adopted by the Community and by the Council of Europe, and the case-law of the Court of Justice of the European Communities and the European Court of Human Rights.[36]

This was the mission of a group called "The Convention", in 1999, under the chair of Roman Herzog (former President of Germany and former judge of the Federal Constitutional Court of Germany): draw up the draft Charter of Fundamental Rights of the European Union, solemnly proclaimed by the European Parliament, the Council and the Commission at Nice (07.12.2000).[37]

Notwithstanding, due to economic and political disagreements between some Member States, the aforementioned Charter did not reach a formal binding legal effect in 2000, even if this was the intended goal as an impulse for the constitutional project for the European Union.[38] Therefore, the Charter remained

34 *C. Calliess*, The Charter of Fundamental Rights, in: D. Ehlers (ed.), European Fundamental Rights and Freedoms, 2007, p. 518, 526.

35 *I. Pernice*, The Treaty of Lisbon and Fundamental Rights, in: S. Griller & J. Ziller (eds.), The Lisbon Treaty. EU Contitutionalism without a Constitutional Treaty?, 2008, p. 235, 237.

36 In this sense, see: *K. Stern*, Die Charta der Grundrechte der Europäischen Union vor und nach Lissabon, in: M. Breuer et al., Der Staat im Recht, 2013, p. 669, 675 et seq.

37 Stern mentions the decisive influence of German representatives for a EU Charter of fundamental rights. *Id.* at pp. 675–676.

38 *A. Martins*, Manual de Direito da União Europeia, 2014, p. 147.

as an element of soft law in the European Union, what did not forbid its reference and volunteer compliance by institutional actors – such as the EU Commission.[39]

Only a few years later, and after the failure of the Constitutional Treaty, the EU institutions changed Article 6 TEU. This way, it adapted the original wording of the Charter of Fundamental Rights of the European Union (12.12.2007), which also acquired its legally binding effect, according to the Treaty of Lisbon entry into force (from 01.12.2009 on). In this sense, it acquired the same status of the Treaties, as a primary legislation in the European Union.

However, the Charter's new status had a need for the negotiation in order to settle certain political concessions. On the one hand, there was a sort of opt-out from some provisions of the Charter on behalf of a few Member States (United Kingdom and Poland)[40], described in Protocol No. 30 to the Lisbon Treaty. At that time, the then Labour UK Government was worried about the possible overturn that those provisions could have upon the national law.

On the other hand, there was an express and clearly message for a limitation on the legally binding effect's range, recognized by the legal provisions in the Treaty of Lisbon (Article 6(1) 2st sentence), by the legal provisions in the Charter (Articles 51 to 53 – regarding the interpretation and application of the Charter) and also in the contents of the further Declarations concerning provisions of the Treaties.[41]

The establishment of such provisions could lead to a deep concern – almost a phobia – from a group of Member States preoccupied in avoiding a wider approach regarding the competences of the European Union.[42]

About the matter, we consider appropriated to point out Articles 1 and 2 in the Protocol No. 30 in the Treaty of Lisbon about the application of the Charter of Fundamental Rights of the European Union in Poland and the United Kingdom:

> Article 1
>
> 1. The Charter does not extend the ability of the Court of Justice of the European Union, or any court or tribunal of Poland or of the United Kingdom, to find that the laws, regulations or administrative provisions, practices or action of Poland or

---

39 See the Commission Communication on the Compliance with the Charter of Fundamental Rights in Commission Legislative proposals – COM (2005) 172 final, Brussels, 27.4.2005.

40 "Regarding the Charter of Fundamental Rights representatives of UK and Poland have not only made all efforts to avoid the Charter or at least to limit its impact, but have finally achieved what is called an opt out from the Charter." *Pernice, supra*, note 35 at p. 244. In the case of Czech Republic, its "President *Vaclac Klaus* made a Protocol, allowing the "opt-out" of the Czech Republic to the same extent as granted to Poland and the UK, a precondition for him signing the Treaty of Lisbon." *C. Grabenwarter & K. Pabel*, Article 6 [Fundamental Rights – The Charter and the ECHR], in: H. Blanke & S. Mangiameli (eds.), The Treaty on European Union (TEU): a Commentary, 2013, p. 287, 340–341.

41 Article 51 (2) CFREU prescribes that the Charter doesn't extend the field of application of Union law beyond the powers of the Union or establish any new power or task for the Union, or modify powers and tasks as defined by the Treaties.

42 *Pernice, supra*, note 35 at p. 243. See also: *Dashwood* et al., *supra*, note 31 at p. 386–388.

of the United Kingdom are inconsistent with the fundamental rights, freedoms and principles that it reaffirms.
2. In particular, and for the avoidance of doubt, nothing in Title IV of the Charter creates justiciable rights applicable to Poland or the United Kingdom except in so far as Poland or the United Kingdom has provided for such rights in its national law.

Article 2
To the extent that a provision of the Charter refers to national laws and practices, it shall only apply to Poland or the United Kingdom to the extent that the rights or principles that it contains are recognised in the law or practices of Poland or of the United Kingdom.[43]

The mentioned provisions in the Protocol No. 30 in the Treaty of Lisbon contain interesting evidences. The Charter's main goal was to express the fundamental rights consolidated at the EU level; by doing that, it intended to make them more visible. Thereby, the referenced legislation should have been the European Convention for the Protection of Humans Rights and Fundamental Freedoms, the case law in the Court of Justice of the European Union and the common constitutional traditions from Member States.

However, there was evidence about how some of those references were not unanimous. In so far, the firm position of the United Kingdom and Poland in guaranteeing a total avoidance of justiciable rights derived from the Solidarity Chapter (Title IV), which contains provisions regarding social and economic rights and principles, is remarkable.

Such a scenario of restrictions, concerns and exemptions represents, at a point, an opposition to what one commonly expects in a Charter of Fundamental Rights, figuring as a counterpart of granting new competences to the governing powers. Furthermore, it certainly does not encourage advances towards social and economic rights and principles. Besides, the direct opposition against possible legal effects of Title IV in the Charter (Solidarity) certainly affected the legal provision of environmental protection (Article 37).

Nevertheless, in an analysis of a Charter of Fundamental Rights, what should we assume as the proper content? In which way should (or could) we establish the approach of environmental protection in a document of this nature? As a fundamental right, a duty, a principle or a freedom? Is it enforceable by the law? At last, what should be the adequate (or best) perspective for this purpose? The answer for those questions requires a closer view of Article 37 of the Charter of Fundamental Rights of the European Union.

---

43 *M. Wyrzykowski & G. Guliyeva*, Protocol (No 30) on the Application of the CFR to Poland and to the United Kingdom, in: H. Blanke & S. Mangiameli (eds.), The Treaty on European Union (TEU): a Commentary, 2013, p. 1737, 1738.

3.3. ENVIRONMENTAL PROTECTION IN THE TERMS OF ARTICLE 37

The chapter of Solidarity[44] (Title IV) presented in the EU Charter of Fundamental Rights approaches, among a diversity of social and economic rights (which also suffered restrictions in terms of justiciability)[45], other interests, such as environmental protection:

> Article 37
> Environmental protection
> A high level of environmental protection and the improvement of the quality of the environment must be integrated into the policies of the Union and ensured in accordance with the principle of sustainable development.[46]

First, the aforementioned legal provision has the same wording since the proclamation of the EU Charter of Fundamental Rights in 2000, meaning that there were no changes simultaneously to the Treaty of Lisbon establishment. This sort of absence indicates a lack of intent to change, improve or develop its wording until the moment.

Moreover, in opposition to many other legal provisions in the EU Charter of Fundamental Rights – whether it is within or out of the scope of Title IV – Article 37 does not use terms as "right of" or "right to". There is no element addressing individuals or groups in order to provide any kind of procedural or material rights and freedoms.

In this regard, neither a literal and grammatical interpretation nor a teleological, historical and systematic interpretation leads to the conclusion that the catalogue provides a right or freedom regarding environmental protection. Actually, the simple recognition of the relevance of environmental protection as part of the policies in the European Union obviously does not constitute a right to a clean environment.[47] Therefore, it establishes only a principle (*Grundsatz*), assuming its characteristic as a guide to the action of EU policies, without any kind of individual right.[48]

---

44 *C. Calliess*, Subsidiaritäts- und Solidaritätsprinzip in der Europäischen Union, 2nd ed., 1999, pp. 187–196.

45 For a critical approach of the different treatment given to the social and economic rights in comparison with the civil and political rights in the European Union, see: *B. Bercusson*, Social and Labour Rights under the EU Constitution, in: G. Búrca & B. Witte (eds.), Social Rights in Europe, 2005, pp. 169–197.

46 Charter of Fundamental Rights of the European Union, OJ C 326, 26.10.2012, p. 391–407, available at: http://eur-lex.europa.eu/legal-content/EN/TXT/?uri=CELEX:12012P/TXT [accessed 30 December 2016].

47 *F. Ermacora*, The Right of a Clean Environment in the Constitution of the European Union, in: J. Jans (ed.), The European Convention and the Future of European Environmental Law, 2003, p. 29, 29 et seq.

48 *H. Jarass*, Charta der Grundrechte der Europäischen Union, 2nd ed., 2013, p. 331. See also: *H.-W. Rengeling & P. Szczekalla*, Grundrechte in der Europäischen Union: Charta der Grundrechte und Allgemeine Rechtsgrundsätze, 2004, pp. 847–852.

Concerning the time of the discussions about the formulation of Article 37, it is important to mention that there were intensive debates about the meaning and the normative structure of a legal provision regarding environmental protection in the draft of the EU Charter of Fundamental Rights.[49] The legal doctrine refers to a wide range of approaches, such as the adoption of a right to environmental protection measures, the refusal of any kind of individual right, the formulation of a principle guiding the European Union and Member States. At the end, the scepticism prevailed against the idea of an individual right.[50] The legal provision's final draft remained in general terms, under the influence of the German comprehension of a State objective (*Staatszielbestimmung*) as presented in the German Basic Law.[51]

Therefore, it was a clear message: the prevalent choice was a normative structure of a principle, not a right to environmental protection.[52] Beyond that, there were other discussions regarding the strengths and weaknesses of the terms in the legal provision – such as "sustainable development" – or the application of the term "ensured" (*wird … sichergestellt*) instead of "contribution" or "promotion".[53]

However, what are the reasons for the Convention to give up a provision establishing a sort of environmental right? Moreover, what does a choice like that mean (and imply)? In this sense, it is also relevant to consider Article 37 in the field of the legal doctrine regarding fundamental rights.

4. IMPROVEMENT WITHOUT REINVENTION: A PLEA BASED ON EXISTING LEGAL TOOLS

After the understanding of the content and context of Article 37 in the Charter of Fundamental Rights of the European Union, we pass to the consideration of the many options, challenges and potentialities of other kinds of normative structures to be established, in a near future, as a legal provision for environmental protection in the EU Charter of Fundamental Rights. Hereupon, a further investigation about the notion of a right to environmental protection seems appropriate.

---

49 *E. Orth*, Grundrecht auf Umweltschutz in Europa?, 2007, pp. 108–113. See also: *E. Riedel*, Artikel 37 Umweltschutz, in: J. Meyer (ed.), Charta der Grundrechte der Europäischen Union, 3rd ed., 2011, p. 492, 494 et seq.

50 *Calliess & Ruffert*, *supra*, note 23 at pp. 2922–2923. See also: *S. Barriga*, Die Entstehung der Charta der Grundrechte der Europäischen Union, 2003, pp. 132–133.

51 *L. Krämer*, Direct Effect and Consistent Interpretation: Strenghts and Weakenesses of the Concepts, in: J. Jans, R. Macrory & A.-M. Molina, National Courts and EU Environmental Law, 2013, p. 53, 60.

52 *H.-W. Rengeling*, Umweltschutz in der Charta der Grundrechte der Europäischen Union, in: C. Franzius et al., Beharren. Bewegen: Festschrift für Michael Kloepfer zum 70. Geburtstag, 2013, p. 161, 163 et seq.

53 *N. Bernsdorff & M. Borowsky*, Die Charta der Grundrechte der Europäischen Union, 2002, pp. 341–343.

4.1. DOES A RIGHT TO ENVIRONMENTAL PROTECTION ENCOMPASS THE SCRUTINY OF FUNDAMENTAL RIGHTS?

First of all, neither the primary and the secondary legislation in the European Union nor the European Convention of Humans Rights contain an explicit substantive right to a clean environment – understood as a provision granting an individual right and the possibility of invocation before a court or national administration.[54] In general terms, we can issue the same logic at the level of international law, which does not have an explicit example of a directly justiciable and legally binding individual substantive right to environmental protection. The mention of provisions similar to a material environmental right in political international documents – mostly declarations – is usually comprised in the field of soft law.[55]

It is important mentioning that such evidence does not foreclose the possibility that the case law takes into account that environmental protection belongs to the concept of other rights (positive obligations) – as an example, the right to respect private and family life established in Article 8 of the ECHR and the decision ruled at ECHR case *López Ostra v. Spain*.[56]

Regarding the matter, the debate about duties of protection (*Schutzpflichten*) for state action against violations of individual fundamental rights – as the right to life, the right to the integrity of the person and the right to property – represents an important contribution.[57] Considering that environmental degradation has the potentiality for interfering negatively in the fruition of individual fundamental rights, the objective dimension of those rights determines a state duty protecting the environment in order to guarantee their fruition.[58]

In addition, there is no expressed refusal or prohibition towards adopting propositions that equal a right to a clean environment or a right to environmental protection. In political and normative terms, there is not an absolute impossibility

---

54 *Ermacora, supra*, note 47 at p. 30. For an overview of the ECHR case law about environmental protection and human rights, see: *K. Reid*, A Practitioner's Guide to the European Convention on Human Rights, 5th ed., 2015, p. 525 et seq.

55 "Soft law is by its nature the articulation of a 'norm' in a non-binding written form." *P. Birnie, A. Boyle & C. Redgwell*, International Law and the Environment. 3rd ed., 2009, p. 35. Ulrich Beyerlin affirms that "most principles of international environmental law actually still belong to the sphere of morals or policies ('soft law')." *U. Beyerlin*, Different Types of Norms in International Environmental Law: Policies, Principles, and Rules, in: D. Bodansky, J. Brunnée & E. Hey, The Oxford Handbook of International Environmental Law, 2007, p. 425, 438.

56 *Ermacora, supra*, note 47 at p. 32. See also: *F. Munari & L. Di Pepe*, Tutela transnazionale dell'ambiente, 2012, p. 119 et seq.

57 Hans-Werner Rengeling affirms that Articles 3 and 7 CFREU are relevant for the environmental protection, in a similar approach of the discussion concerning the duties of protection (*Schutzpflichten*). *Rengeling, supra*, note 52 at 170 et seq.

58 *P. Unruh*, Zur Dogmatik der grundrechtlichen Schutzpflichten, 1996, p. 89. See also: *J. Dietlein*, Die Lehre von den grundrechtlichen Schutzpflichten, 2nd ed., 2005.

to do so. Concrete examples refer mostly to cases at the national level, in which several constitutional traditions accept this kind of formulation. A reasonable number of countries – whether inside or outside the European Union – adopted the recognition of a right to environmental protection, some by constitutional provisions, some by other sorts of regulations.[59] Relevant cases in the European Union are the constitutions of Greece, Portugal, Spain, Belgium and France.[60] In addition, a not negligible number of countries worldwide chose to turn into this direction, with remarkable examples in Latin America (e.g. Brazil, Argentina, Chile, and Colombia).[61]

The question remains, though: does a substantive individual right to environmental protection belong in the pantheon of fundamental rights?[62]

The answer depends on different perspectives. From a political, ethical, historical or sociological standpoint, perhaps it would be easier to assume a positive reply. For example, the international environmental law usually refers to a right to environmental protection in the field of soft law – which means, in other words, no legally binding nature or enforceability.[63]

In addition, even if some countries recognize that kind of provision in their constitutional tradition, most of them, as a matter of fact, enforce it more as a legal objective duty pertaining to the governing powers than as an individual right.[64]

From a legal perspective, and considering the approach of those who do not recognize the right to environmental protection, the argument presented is that this sort of right does not belong in the traditional standards of individual fundamental rights – such as the right to life, the right of the integrity of the person and the right to liberty.

---

59 *J. May*, Constituting Fundamental Environmental Rights Worldwide, in: PELR 2006 (23), pp. 138–145.

60 For an overview of the norms established in the mentioned countries, see: *Orth*, *supra*, note 49 at pp. 108–113.

61 *May*, *supra*, note 59 at p. 131 et seq. Specifically about the brazilian case, see: *M. Magalhães*, Será o Direito ao Meio Ambiente Sadio e Equilibrado um Direito Fundamental? Em Busca da Nota de Fundamentalidade do Direito ao Meio Ambiente Ecologicamente Equilibrado, PRISMAS: Dir., Pol.Pub. e Mundial., 2006 (3), p. 288, 290 et seq.

62 That is one provocative question made by James May. *May*, *supra*, note 59 at p. 113.

63 Despite the general definition of soft law, Pierre-Marie Dupuy says that "It is thus generally understood that "soft" law creates and delineates goals to be achieved in the future rather than actual duties, programs rather than prescriptions, guidelines rather than strict obligations. It is true that in the majority of cases the "softness" of the instrument corresponds to the "softness" of its contents. After all, the very nature of "soft" law lies in the fact that it is not in itself legally binding. Although this assertion is generally correct, it remains necessary both from a conceptual and, in certain situations, a practical point of view to distinguish clearly between the substance and the instrument – they are not necessarily always in perfect accordance with one another." *P.-M. Dupuy*, Soft Law and the International Law of the Environment, Mich. J. Int'l L., 1990–1991 (12), p. 420, 428 et seq.

64 *Orth*, *supra*, note 49 at pp. 49–50.

Firstly, it would not be strictly an individual right, because it does not refer to individuals and their freedom's sphere, in terms of a subjective right against unauthorized interventions of the governing powers. In other words, it does not fit the classical provisions regarding typical liberal rights, that not only guarantee a duty of abstention (negative *Kompetenzbestimmung*) on behalf of the citizen against the action of the State – also referred as negative rights (*Abwehrrechte*)[65] –, but also provides enforceable positions under the law.

Still according this approach, a right to environmental protection also does not fit as a right concerned to social justice and equality, which usually demands an action from the governing powers to establish normative or material (factual) conditions in order to enable individuals the full exercise of their rights (*Leistungsrechte*).[66] In this sense, the usual reference is to subjective rights concerning the Welfare State, and their fruition depends on a state positive action to fulfil the preconditions that would allow materializing such rights.

Moreover, the right to environmental protection does not figure as a typical political right, in terms of a right concerned to citizen's action and participation in order to contribute to political decisions from the governing powers (*Teilhaberechte*).[67]

The aforementioned scepticism towards a rights-based approach also identifies critical points in the right to environmental protection as a substantive individual right – subjective and negative right (*Abwehrrecht*) –, concern that has reasonable arguments. On the one hand, there is the question of how one would be able to determine the extent of protection (*Schutzbereich*) of that fundamental right, to allow the comprehension of which legal authorization to grant to the individual person. It is an issue that points out to which extent could (or should) such an individual right grant natural resources such as water, air or landscape. On the other hand, how would it be possible to define who will be committed to this right, and also the adequate distinction between a legal interference and an illegal one?[68]

Furthermore, the notion of the right to environmental protection as substantive positive right (*Leistungsrecht*) also does not lead to a satisfactory result, as those positive rights aim goods that are sought by the individuals as private – or, at least, goods for individual fruition. Considering that environmental goods, even if facing a variety of limitations of use, usually still are free common goods, the problem concerns the definition of who is the legitimate subject of that right. At the end, with the exception of extreme cases, that kind of alternative would not

---

65 *Hufen, supra*, note 29 at pp. 50–51. See also: *R. Alexy*, Theorie der Grundrechte, 2nd ed., 1994, p. 174; *G. Mendes & P. Branco*, Curso de Direito Constitucional, 9th ed., 2014, pp. 157–159.

66 See: *Hufen, supra*, note 29 at p. 51; *Alexy, supra*, note 65 at p. 179, p. 395 et seq.; *Mendes & Branco, supra*, note 65 at pp. 159–166.

67 See: *Hufen, supra*, note 29 at p. 51; *Mendes & Branco, supra*, note 65 at p. 166.

68 *C. Calliess*, Ansätze zur Subjektivierung von Gemeinwohlbelangen im Völkerrecht – Das Beispiel des Umweltschutzes, ZUR 2000 (4), p. 246, 254.

only demand long-time efforts to provide the good (benefit), but it also would resemble a principle of state action.[69]

Until this point, the discussion around the outlook of a substantive individual right to environmental protection faces critical issues concerning legal requirements in terms of legal certainty and procedural rules, according the approach refusing it, grounded on a more liberal perspective of fundamental rights.

4.2. A PROCEDURAL FUNDAMENTAL RIGHT TO ENVIRONMENTAL PROTECTION: FROM AN EMPTY SHELL TOWARDS A TEST TUBE?

The intent of the EU Charter is to be a charter of fundamental rights. For that reason, it should contain rights and freedoms as its core. Despite this presumption, it does not establish a right in Article 37, but only a principle of action for the Union and Member States, which practically repeats the wording of what is already disposed in the EU Treaties. In this regard, it could be compared to an empty shell, one that contains an external structure of a shell (a charter of rights) without a pearl (the right regarding environmental protection) inside.

There are authors who criticize the maintenance by the European Union of such approach in a Charter of Fundamental Rights, which does not address any kind of right. They consider that the redundancy (also repetition) of legal provisions already established in the primary legislation seems superfluous, unsystematic and out of the scope of a catalogue of fundamental rights.[70]

At this point, does the European Union have other options to improve the legal provision in order to find a home for the right to environmental protection in the pantheon of fundamental rights in the EU Charter?

The answer is positive. However, it is still depending on European Union's will to embrace it as a new experiment (test tube), which overcomes the interest-based approach, not leading properly to controversial or miraculous solutions.

Besides the already mentioned refused alternatives in the Convention, some authors argue that instead of repeating the existing provisions (Articles 11 and 191 TFEU) in order to reaffirm a general principle in Article 37 of the EU Charter of Fundamental Rights, it would be better to establish a procedural fundamental right to environmental protection.[71] The argument considers that this solution

69 *Calliess*, *supra*, note 68 at p. 255.

70 *Calliess & Ruffert*, *supra*, note 23 at p. 2923. See also: *G. Bándi*, Enlargement and its Consequences for EU Environmental Law, in: J. Jans (ed.), The European Convention and the Future of European Environmental Law, 2003, p. 99, 113.

71 *Calliess & Ruffert*, *supra*, note 23 at p. 2924. Also recognizing the relevance and potential of procedural environmental rights at the EU level: *Ermacora*, *supra*, note 47 at pp. 37–42; *Rengeling*, *supra*, note 52 at p. 173.

is not a new discovery, being already recognized in the national level of Member States and at international and EU regional levels. That happens not only in the Rio Declaration on Environment and Development (Principle 10)[72], but also in the Aarhus Convention on access to information, public participation in decision-making and access to justice in environmental matters.[73]

Therefore, we can list three basic components of the aforementioned procedural right: a right to citizen participation in administrative decision-making regarding the environment; a right to access information concerning the environment, and a right to judicial review in order to enforce the former two.[74]

Another advantage in the proposition is that it allows derivation of concrete procedural provisions on behalf of individuals, to demand and to enforce their needs of environmental protection. It also reinforces the individual position related to administrative and legislative procedures. At last, it has the potential to avoid the critical problems and controversies appointed by some authors in the sense of what a substantive (material) individual right would face – as a negative or positive right –, at the same time that it equally preserves the requirements of a necessary "limited subjectification (*Subjektivierung*) of environmental protection as a common interest".[75]

Other advantages on this approach would be: the concentration and better comprehension of such elements in just one article, which could clarify the normative concept and provide legal certainty; the attention of the EU citizens to a right of this nature, transferring back to political actors and legislators the task to take it seriously instead of waiting a slowly development by the case law; the reinforcement of the measures against the deficit (lack) of implementation and monitoring of actions.[76]

It is a kind of approach that can lead to an advantage and a new experimentalism in the field of environmental protection, with potential positive side effects to other spheres and values within the European Union, such as the improvement of citizenship at EU level, the creation of improved interactive mechanisms that could bring more democratic legitimacy to the institutions and the reinforcement of values of transparency and democracy.

Beyond that, this approach certainly is fairer not only to the current phase of the development of European environmental law and policy, but also to the legal instruments of international environmental law recognized by the European Union.

---

72 For an overview and understanding of the field and context of the Principle 10, see: *J. Ebbesson*, Principle 10: Public Participation, in: J. Viñuales (ed.), The Rio Declaration on Environment and Development: a Commentary, 2015, pp. 288–309.

73 *Orth*, *supra*, note 49 at pp. 56–57.

74 *Calliess*, *supra*, note 34 at p. 528.

75 *Id.* at p. 529. And also: *Calliess*, *supra*, note 68 at pp. 255–257.

76 *Ermacora*, *supra*, note 47 at pp. 37–42.

5. CONCLUSION

The overview of the development of European environmental law, on the one hand, in comparison to the development of international environmental law, highlights a bigger framework of mutual influences and interconnections, and the significant increase of attention that they have achieved in the second half of the twentieth century. Thus, European environmental law clearly experiences a remarkable improvement as a result of big challenges, particularly when we consider that the mainstream founding Treaties were strictly economic.

On the other hand, it is also possible to point out that the effect of an action for environmental protection at EU level is potentially much faster and more dynamic than what we observe in international law. This impulse, however, is greatly dependent on EU institutions, and the pressure of economic and trade issues.

Nevertheless, the standpoint achieved – at least in institutional terms – demonstrates that EU primary legislation has important legal provisions to dispose of political and legal instruments for an integrative and cross-section environmental policy. The secondary legislation, notably the directives, has proved that a lot can be done in the field of EU policies – respecting the principle of subsidiarity – in order to equalize basic environmental standards, and stimulate a high level of environmental protection.[77] Thus, the European case law also plays an important role for the further discussion of environmental protection in connection to individual fundamental rights.

Furthermore, an overview of the European environmental law's development points out also a lack of expressive contribution – at least at the moment – from the EU Charter of Fundamental Rights in terms of environmental protection. History, though, can be rewritten in different perspectives, and openness to new experiments in the "laboratory" in the EU context probably will give hope for new scenarios.

Regarding this matter, a better understanding of what means the incorporation of a Charter of Fundamental Rights and what is expected from it are of great importance to apprehend the limits and potentials of a catalogue of fundamental rights in the EU as a supranational organization – which is neither an international organization nor a State.[78] Among a variety of issues, such as the referred fear and anxiety by some Member States regarding the extent of the application and interpretation of the Charter, the controversy concerning social and economic rights, the principles and the problem presented by the enforceable

77 About the strong influence of EU environmental law at national level, see: *L. Knopp & J. Hoffmann*, Progredientes Europäisierungsphänomen im Umweltrecht, 2010, pp. 27–42.

78 Calliess defines the EU as a *Staats- und Verfassungsverbund* – a sort of state and constitutional integration. For a better comprehension about this definition, see: *C. Calliess*, Staatsrecht III, 2014, p. 169 et seq.

notion inherent to those rights, it is possible to affirm that, perhaps from the start, the Charter figures more as a compensation of a deficit than an assertive approach.

The analysis of Article 37 of the EU Charter of Fundamental Rights brings the proper focus to a portion of the controversy and problems regarding the "rights" of solidarity. The false expectation for a catalogue of rights comes true, in part, with a catalogue of principles addressed only to the EU institutions.

In opposition to an unsystematic and conceptual displaced intention of a mere policy principle that does not fit the scope of a catalogue of fundamental rights, besides not addressing a tangible right to individuals, environmental organizations or other non-institutional actors – what allows the comparison, regarding the subject field, according to which the catalogue mirrors an empty shell –, there is the argument in favour of experimentalism as a fairer and more honest approach to the current stage of development of fundamental rights and European environmental law. This way, the introduction of a procedural fundamental right directed to environmental protection in the CFREU is a possible alternative.

The assumption of three basic components – right to access information, to public participation in decision-making and to access to justice in environmental matters (the last as much as necessary to enforce the two former rights), instead of the merely establishment of a principle within the scope of Article 37, can act as a test tube for an improvement of such a right at the EU level.

The procedural environmental right as a viable alternative presents a reasonable row of advantages, mostly because: it corresponds to a fundamental right; overcomes the barriers against material individual rights to environmental protection; allows individuals to demand and enforce those rights; improves legislation and administration in order to structurally consider individual requests; reinforces the proper meaning of the right; enables individuals to a closer participation in the institutions at the EU level; increases the compliance to international and regional conventions and declarations (Rio Declaration – Principle 10; Convention of Aarhus), and, at last, it does not constitute an innovative tool in legal and political terms. Therefore, it should not be considered a threat to the EU interests.

Through the proposal of choosing between an empty shell and a test tube, this paper has emphasized that the propositions here established potentially work as a sort of new experiment, in the context of experimentalism, with the introduction of procedural environmental rights in Article 37 of the CFREU. It is a suggestion that contains potential benefits in order to improve environmental protection, indicating a more coherent approach in the current phase of development of European environmental law, increasing, consequently, the role of individuals and non-institutional actors in the establishment of rights.

PUBLIC PARTICIPATION

THE EU AND PUBLIC PARTICIPATION IN ENVIRONMENTAL DECISION-MAKING

Ludwig KRÄMER*

ABSTRACT

The Lisbon Treaties constitute a new stage in the process of European integration. They promote an open society in which decisions are taken as openly as possible and as closely as possible to the citizen.[1] The functioning of the EU shall be founded on representative democracy, which includes that right of every citizen "to participate in the democratic life of the Union".[2]

This individual right to participate is further concretized by the right to participate in elections to the European Parliament (Articles 22(2) and 223 TFEU), the right to participate in a citizen initiative (Article 11(4) TEU), the right to submit petitions to the European Parliament (Articles (24(2) and 227 TFEU, the right to submit complaints to the European Ombudsman (Articles 24(2) and 228 TFEU), the right to have access to documents held by EU institutions (Article 15 TFEU) and the right to write to any EU institution or body and obtain an answer (Article 24(4) TFEU).

The present contribution will limit itself to examining how the right of participation of citizens in environmental decision-making was put into practice by EU institutions and bodies at EU level and, via secondary EU law, at the level of the Member States. After a description of the different provisions of primary law – the TEU and the TFEU – (1) and of secondary EU law (2), the application of the right to participate at EU level (3) and in EU legislation regarding the participation in environmental decision-making at national level will be examined (4). Some concluding remarks will round up the contribution (5).

---

* Derecho y Medio Ambiente, Madrid.

1 TEU, Article 1 and Recitals 1 and 13, Article 10(3).

2 TEU, Article 10(1) and (3).

1. PRIMARY EU LAW

The EU Treaties do not contain specific provisions as regards the rights of citizens to participate in environmental decision-making. As a general obligation, apart from the provisions mentioned above, Article 11(2) TEU is to be mentioned, which obliges the EU institutions to maintain an open, transparent and regular dialogue with representative associations and civil society. Article 11(3) TEU obliges the Commission to "carry out broad consultation with parties concerned in order to ensure that the Union's actions are coherent and transparent". The objective of the open and regular dialogue is clarified in Article 15(1) TFEU, which asks the Union institutions and bodies to conduct their work as openly as possible, "(I)n order to promote good governance and ensure the participation of civil society". This provision makes it clear that citizen participation is not possible without an open administration and a regular and transparent dialogue between the EU institutions and civil society.

The Commission is "only" asked to ensure broad consultation, not to ensure the participation of civil society (Article 11(3) TEU); this obligation is limited to the coherence and transparency of EU activities. In supplement, though, the Commission is, of course, as all other EU institutions and bodies, under the obligation to maintain a regular dialogue with civil society (Article 11(2)) and, furthermore, enable citizens and representative associations to make known their views and "exchange" their views.

The general obligation of Article 11(2) to maintain a "dialogue" with citizens is clearly broader than the obligation to consult citizens. In the consultation process, an EU institution or body – in Article 11(3) the Commission is named – issues a document and asks the addressees or the interested citizens or associations for comments. At what time this consultation takes place, is in the hands of the consulting institution. The opinions expressed by the consulted public are in no way binding for the consulting institution and no explanation needs to be given, why this or that option was finally chosen and if and to what extent the opinions of the consulted persons were taken into consideration. Consultation is thus essentially a unilateral process.

"Dialogue", in contrast, is a bilateral or multilateral process. It implies a discussion between the EU institution and the representatives of civil society, an exchange of views between the dialoguing bodies. Only in this way is a "participation" of citizens possible which goes beyond a mere "consultation". All provisions of the EU Treaties mentioned above clearly indicate that the dialogue, the exchange of views and the participation of citizens and civil society shall be the regular and normal form of cooperation between the EU institutions and civil society.[3]

---

3 In this sense also *R. Bieber*, in: Vonder Groeben/Schwarze/Hatje, Europäisches Unionsrecht, 7thed.2015, Art. 11 TEU. para. 12; *R. Bieber and F. Maiani*, Bringing the Union closer to its

2. SECONDARY EU LAW

While primary EU law is thus largely silent on the specific situation of participation in environmental decision-making, secondary EU law is all the more detailed in this regard. This comes as no surprise, as the environment is an interest without a social group behind it. Its protection is of general societal interest, not of individual persons or (vested) interest groups, but the environment has no voice. One cannot ask trees, the birds or the soil what they think of this or that measure which has the potential to affect the environment. This is fundamentally different to the interests of farmers, or transport organizations, of fishermen or of industrial operators, who defend their vested interests and are capable, either individually or via their representative associations, to voice their concerns. All the more is it important and even vital that participation of individual citizens and of environmental organizations – which defend, be it repeated, general and not vested interests – is organized in a structured dialogue which allows an appropriate participation of those who represent environmental interests. Their participation rights need all the care of public authorities, so that the authorities are not confronted with vested interest arguments alone. At international, EU and national level these considerations motivated a number of legal developments to promote public participation in environmental decision-making.

The Rio Declaration

In 1992, the United Nations Conference on Environment and Development which met in Rio de Janeiro, adopted the "Rio Declaration on Environment and Development", which laid down a number of environmental principles. These principles were subsequently outformed, specified, fine-tuned and further developed in international agreements, national legislation and academic specifications.

Article 10 of the Rio Declaration reads:

> "Environmental issues are best handled with participation of all concerned citizens, at the relevant level. At the national level, each individual shall have appropriate access to information concerning the environment that is held by public authorities, including information on hazardous materials and activities in their communities, and the opportunity to participate in decision-making processes. States shall facilitate and encourage public awareness and participation by making information widely available. Effective access to judicial and administrative proceeding, including redress and remedy, shall be provided".

---

citizens? "Participatory democracy" and the potential contributions of the Lisbon Treaty. Schweizerisches Jahrbuch für Europarecht 2009/2010, p. 229.

There is consensus that the principles laid down in the Rio Declaration are not part of customary international law and are thus not binding.[4] However, as the EU "shall contribute to … the strict observance and the development of international law"[5], Rio principle 10 constitutes a sort of orientation or guideline for action by the EU institutions. It has to be recognized, though, that principle 10 was never mentioned in EU legislative measures or in the jurisprudence by the European Court of Justice (ECJ) concerning public participation in decision-making.

The Aarhus Convention

Principle 10 of the Rio Declaration was mentioned in the Preamble of the Convention on access to information, public participation in decision-making and access to justice in environmental matters, which was signed in June 1998 in Aarhus (Denmark) (hereafter Aarhus Convention). The EU adhered to the Convention in 2005.[6] The Aarhus Convention became thus, in the words of the ECJ[7], integral part of the legal order of the EU. As its conclusion had the effect that it became binding on the EU Member States *and* the EU institutions (Article 216(2) TFEU), it ranked higher than other secondary EU legislation, such as regulations, directives and decisions.[8]

The Aarhus Convention provides in Article 1 rather far-reaching rights for citizens:

> "In order to contribute to the protection of the right of every person of present and future generations to live in an environment adequate to his or her health and well-being, each Party shall guarantee the rights of access to information, public participation in decision-making, and access to justice in environmental matters in accordance with the provisions of this Convention".

"Public participation in decision-making" is not defined in the Convention. It follows from Articles 6 to 8, which deal with participation, that the participation consists of several steps that affect the "public concerned" – a term that is defined as follows:

> "'The public concerned' means the public affected or likely to be affected by, or having an interest in, the environmental decision-making; for the purposes of this definition, non-governmental organisations promoting environmental protection and meeting any requirements under national law shall be deemed to have an interest" (Article 2(5)).

4 *Ph. Sands*, Principles of international environmental law, Cambridge 2003, p.118; *J. Ebbesson*, Participation, in D. Bodansky – J. Brunnée – E. Hey (eds), The Oxford Handbook of International Environmental Law, Oxford 2007, p.681.

5 TEU, Article 3(5).

6 Decision 2005/370, OJ 2005, L 124 p. 1. The Aarhus Convention is reproduced there on p. 3.

7 ECJ, case C-240/09, *Lesoochranárske zoskupenie*, ECLI:EU:C:2011:125, para 30.

8 ECJ, joined cases C-401/12P to 403/12P, *Council a.o. v. Vereniging Milieudefensie a.o.*, ECLI:EU:C:2015:4, para. 52.

When activities are concerned which are either listed in Annex I to the Convention or which are included in the relevant provisions of national law, the public concerned shall

- be informed, in an adequate, timely and effective manner, of the details of the proposed activity (Article 6(2));
- dispose of sufficient time to prepare and participate effectively during the environmental decision-making (Article 6(3));
- be able to participate "early" in the decision making process, "when all options are open and effective public participation can take place" (Article 6(4));
- be entitled to ask for information on "all information relevant to the decision-making" and at least information on the site and the physical and technical characteristics of the proposed activity, including an estimate of the expected residues and emissions, a description of the significant environmental effects of the activity, a description of the measures to prevent or reduce the effects, a non-technical summary, and an outline of the main alternatives studied by the applicant (Article 6(6));
- have the possibility to submit in writing or, as appropriate, at a public hearing or enquiry with the applicant, comments, information, analyses or opinions (Article 6(7)).

The administrative decision shall take due account of the outcome of the public participation. The public shall be informed of the decision and the text of the decision shall be made accessible, together with the reasons and considerations on which the decision was based (Article 6(8) and (9)).

When plans or programmes relating to the environment – this term is not defined in the Aarhus Convention – are being prepared, Article 7 provides that the public authorities shall ensure an appropriate framework for public participation and shall ensure that the public concerned has sufficient time for preparing its participation (Article 6(3)), is informed early when all options are open (Article 6(4)) and that due account is being taken of the outcome of the public participation (Article 6(8)).

The participation provisions of the Aarhus Convention thus go far beyond consultation requirements. Indeed, the public concerned shall also be informed of expected effects of an activity on the environment, including residues and emissions; the administration shall furthermore make available a description of the measures to mitigate negative environmental effects; and the public must obtain a non technical summary of the documentation concerning the activity, which is understandable if one realizes that an application may easily comprise 5000 or more pages and may be accompanied by highly technical, statistical, economic or ecological documents (Article 6(6)). All provisions aim at ensuring an *effective* participation of the public, which implies early and complete information and the possibility to submit comments in time. And the public authorities shall take "due account" of the comments and, once the decision is taken, give the reasons of the decision that was taken.

3. PUBLIC PARTICIPATION IN MEASURES AT EU LEVEL

The EU transposed the participation provisions of the Aarhus Convention together with those on access to information and access to justice in one single legislative act, Regulation 1367/2006.[9] Article 9 deals with the participation chapter of the Aarhus Convention. It is completed, though, by a definition on "plans and programmes relating to the environment" in Article 2(1)(e), which reads as follows:

> "'plans and programmes relating to the environment' means plans and programmes,
> (i) which are subject to preparation and, as appropriate, adoption by a Community institution or body;
> (ii) which are required under legislative, regulatory or administrative provisions; and
> (iii) which contribute to, or a likely to have significant effects on the achievement of the objectives of Community environmental policy, such as laid down in the Sixth Community Environment Action Programme, or in any subsequent general environmental action programme.
> General environmental action programmes shall also be considered as plans or programmes relating to the environment.
> This definition shall not include financial or budget plans and programmes, namely those laying down how particular projects or activities should be financed or those related to the proposed annual budgets, internal work programmes of a Community institution or body, or emergency plans and programmes designed for the sole purpose of civil protection;".

There is no provision on public participation in decisions concerning the authorization of certain activities or projects. Article 9 of Regulation 1367/2006 only provides for the participation in plans and programmes. It repeats the requirement of the Aarhus Convention on early and effective participation, when all options are still open. This participation shall take place when the plans or programmes are being prepared by the Commission, even when they are to be adopted by another institution. Article 9(3) provides for the information which is to be made available to the public concerned, as well as practical arrangements for the participation (time frame, responsible administrative unity etc.). The minimum time frame for receiving comments is eight weeks (Article 9(4)). The results of the participation shall be taken into account and information shall be conveyed to the public on the participation process and on the reasons and considerations on which the decision is based (Article 9(5)).

---

9 Regulation 1367/2006 on the application of the provisions of the Aarhus Convention on Access to Information, Public Participation in Decision-making and Access to Justice in Environmental Matters to Community institutions and bodies, OJ 2006, L 264 p. 13.

3.1. PUBLIC PARTICIPATION IN DECISIONS ON ACTIVITIES AND PROJECTS

Regulation 1367/2006 provides for a participation in the elaboration of EU plans and programmes, but not in other activities. With the progressive integration of the European Union, there are, however, decisions on substances or products that are taken at EU level. Examples are decisions on active substances which may be used in pesticides[10] or biocidal products[11] or restrictions of the use of chemical substances under the REACH Regulation 1907/2006.[12]

Active substances for pesticides are approved by Commission regulation. The application for an authorization of an active substance is sent by the producer to a Member State who acts as a rapporteur.[13] The Member State establishes a report and sends the application and the full dossier accompanying it to the European Food Safety Authority (EFSA) and establishes a draft assessment report. The EFSA makes a summary dossier and the draft assessment report available to the public, which may comment on it within sixty days. Then the EFSA concludes on the application and sends the dossier with its conclusion to the Commission, which adopts a regulation; that regulation may contain restrictions or other conditions of use of the substance. Pesticides may only contain active substances which are authorized by the above-mentioned procedure. Authorizations for pesticides are granted by Member States.

The approval procedure for active substances of biocidal products is organized in a similar way.[14] For the purposes of this presentation, though, the following differences are to be mentioned:

- the competent authority for assessing the active substance is the European Chemical Agency, set up under Regulation 1907/2006;
- since 2013, biocidal products may also be authorized by the Commission, where they have similar conditions of use across the EU (Article 42);
- no provisions are foreseen for the public or the public concerned being allowed to submit comments.

Neither for pesticides nor for biocidal products are there any participation provisions foreseen under EU law. This is all the more regrettable, as a producer or a user of a pesticide or a biocidal product may appeal to the EU Court of Justice against a Commission implementing decision which restricts or completely

10 Regulation 1107/2009 concerning the placing of plant protection products on the market, OJ 2009, L 309 p. 1.

11 Regulation 528/2012 concerning the making available on the market and use of biocidal products, OJ 2012, L 167 p. 1.

12 Regulation 1907/2006 concerning the registration, evaluation, authorisation and restrictions of chemicals (REACH), establishing a European Chemical Agency, OJ 2006, L 396 p. 1.

13 See for the procedure in detail Articles 7 to 13 of Regulation 1107/2009 (fn. 10, above).

14 See for the procedure in detail Articles 7 to 9 of Regulation 528/2012.

prohibits the use of the substance or product. In contrast, environmental organizations or citizens do not have this possibility when a substance is authorized or its conditions of use are not satisfactory, because they are not "directly" concerned by such a decision. And the internal review procedure under Article 10 of Regulation 1367/2006[15] is of no help either, because the Commission decision to authorize a substance or a product is of general nature and not an administrative act.

When the restriction of use of a chemical substance is in question, the EU Chemical Agency shall invite comments from interested parties to its draft opinion on such a restriction.[16] Committees for risk assessment and for socio-economic analysis shall give an opinion on the restriction, taking into account the views of interested parties. The final decision is taken by the Commission by way of comitology procedure. The whole procedure resembles much more a consultation procedure than a participation procedure, as no dialogue or other bilateral form of discussion is foreseen.

In 2005, the Aarhus Convention was amended in order to provide for a participation procedure in the permitting of genetically modified organisms (GMO). A new Article 6*bis* and an annex were introduced, which essentially repeated the participation provisions of Article 6, adapted to the permitting of releases of GMOs.[17]

The EU ratified the amendment, but did not amend its substantive law.[18] However, this appears not to be in compliance with the Convention. Indeed, Regulation 1829/2003 on genetically modified food and feed[19] provides that applications for the permitting of genetically food and feed are sent to the EFSA[20]; the EFSA shall make a summary of the application dossier available to the public and shall give an opinion to the Commission. This opinion shall again be made public and the public shall be entitled to send comments to the Commission within 30 days. The Commission decides on the application by way of comitology procedure.

These provisions do not specify that the application dossier shall be made available to the public in full and as early as possible, when all options are open. They do not either specify that the EFSA or the Commission shall take due account of the opinions of the public and give the reasons and considerations on which their final decision was based. There is not even an obligation to make available

15 Regulation 1367/2006 (fn. 9, above), Article 10: "Any non-governmental organization which meets the criteria set out in Article 11 is entitled to make a request for internal review to the Community institution or body that has adopted an administrative act under environmental law..."

16 See for details of the procedure, Articles 69–73 of Regulation 1907/2006 (fn. 12, above).

17 See text of the Aarhus Convention amendment, OJ 2006, L 386, p. 48.

18 Decision 2006/957, OJ 2006, L 386 p. 46.

19 Regulation 1829/2003 on genetically modified good and feed, OJ 2003, L 268 p. 1.

20 See for details of the procedure Articles 5 to 7 (food) and 17 to 19 (feed) of Regulation 1829/2003 (fn. 19, above).

to the public the environmental risk assessment, which, according to Annex I to the Convention, may in "no case" be kept confidential. And the possibility to send comments to the Commission does not constitute a participation procedure.

Directive 2001/18 on the deliberate release into the environment of GMOs[21] is of no help either. Article 9 of that Directive provides for a consultation of the public. Article 24 introduces the obligation to inform the public of the application and allow it to comment to the Commission. Nothing is said about any participation right of the public and about the subsequent treatment of comments made by the public.

3.2. PLANS AND PROGRAMMES ADOPTED AT EU LEVEL

The Aarhus Convention, as part of EU law, grants participation rights to citizens with regard to plans and programmes "relating to the environment". Regulation 1367/2006 considers plans or programmes relating to the environment which are prepared by an EU institution or body, which are required under legislative, regulatory or administrative provisions and which contribute to or are likely to have significant effects on the objectives of EU environmental policy.[22] Financial plans and programmes and those for civil protection purposes are excluded.

The EU institutions adopt quite frequently plans and programmes that relate to the environment. The first observation to be made is that the definition given in Regulation 1367/2006 is too narrow. The limitation to such plans and programmes which are *required* under legislative, regulatory or administrative provisions is not found in the Aarhus Convention.

In case C-567/10, the Court of Justice decided, as regards national law (Directive 2001/42), that a plan or programme is also "required" when it is regulated by legislative or regulatory provisions that determine the competent authority for adopting it and that contain provisions on the procedure for preparing the plan or programme.[23] Whether the EU institutions will follow this line, is not clear until now. When, for example, the Commission adopts a plan to promote alternative energies, co-finance model projects in coastal zones or finance measures for access to clean drinking water in rural areas, such plans or programmes are nowhere laid down in regulatory measures; the details of such plans are not determined beforehand and the way of elaborating them is at the discretion of the Commission. It is thus more than doubtful that such plans are *required*, though they undoubtedly relate to the environment.

The exclusion of financial plans or programmes or emergency plans is not in conformity with the provisions of the Aarhus Convention. There is no reason, for example, to exclude a financial plan to finance the underground storage of carbon

21 Directive 2001/18, OJ 2001, L 106 p. 1.
22 Regulation 1367/2006 (fn. 9, above), Article 2(1)(c).
23 Court of Justice, case C-567/10, *Inter-Environnement Bruxelles*, ECLI:EU:C:2012:159, para 31.

dioxide or a programme to finance the promotion of renewable energy sources. As regards emergency plans, it might be understandable to exclude civil protection plans in cases of an inundation or severe fires. However, where a plan is elaborated in order to reconstruct, after an inundation, a partly destroyed village, there is no reason whatsoever to have such a plan excluded from participation procedures, though such a plan might be classified as being part of "civil protection".

In practice, the EU institutions largely ignore the provisions of Regulation 1367/2006 and the Aarhus Convention. They rather follow the Commission's better regulation guidelines for the consultation of stakeholders.[24] In 2002 already, the Commission explicitly had rejected the idea of accepting a "right of participating" and pleaded for a non-binding commitment on consultation.[25] It saw no reason to change its position after the EU ratification of the Aarhus Convention, which does give such a "right to participate", though it is not clear whether it also gives the right to challenge the substantive and procedural legality of a decision on a plan or programme which does not respect the participation rights under Article 7. Indeed, Article 9(2) of the Convention gives such a right for omissions under Article 6, but not under Article 7. However, it would be contradictory to grant on the one hand a "right" of participation, but not allow for court action when this right is disregarded.[26]

In practice, the Commission sends out, at best, via internet a draft plan or programme and invites comments within a specific time-span. This consultation – rather than participation – procedure normally takes place in one language (English), though the European Parliament asked since long that no linguistic discrimination should take place[27] and though the European Ombudsman qualified this practice as an instance of maladministration.[28] Also the EU

---

24 Commission, Better Regulation Guidelines, COM(2015) 111, Chapter VII: Guidelines on stakeholder consultation.

25 Commission, Towards a reinforced culture of consultation and dialogue – proposal for general principles and minimum standards for consultation of interested parties by the Commission, COM(2002)704, p. 10: "A situation should be avoided in which a Commission proposal could be challenged in court on the grounds of alleged lack of consultation of interested parties. Such an over-legalistic approach would be incompatible with the need for timely delivery of policy, and with the expectations of the citizens that the European Institutions should deliver on substance rather than concentrating on procedures".

26 The Court of Justice did not yet decide on this question. Generally, it is very restrictive in recognizing a direct effect of provisions of the Aarhus Convention, see cases C-240/09 (fn. 7, above) (Article 9(3)) and C-612/13P *ClientEarth v. Commission*, ECLI:EU:C:2015:486 (Article 4).

27 European Parliament, Resolution of 14 June 2012 (2012/2676/RSP), P7_TA(2012)256: "The European Parliament ... urges the Commission to ensure that every EU citizen's right to address the EU institutions in any of the EU official languages is fully respected and implemented by ensuring that public consultations are available in all EU official languages, that all consultations are treated equally and that there is no language-based discrimination between consultations".

28 European Ombudsman, Decision of 4 December 2012 (640/2011/A): "public consultations should, as a matter of principle, be published in all official languages. Its failure to do so is an instance of maladministration".

recognized this by stating in Regulation 1367/2006: "As a general principle, the rights guaranteed by the three pillars of the Aarhus Convention are without discrimination as to citizenship, nationality or domicile".[29]

There are numerous plans and programmes relating to the environment which are elaborated at EU level. They cannot all be enumerated here. Some examples concern:

- an annual work programme for industrial standardization[30];
- a work plan for the eco-design of energy-related products[31];
- an action plan for the energy performance of buildings[32];
- an EU strategy on the adaptation to climate change[33];
- an EU forest strategy[34];
- an EU biodiversity strategy[35];
- a blueprint to safeguard Europe's water resources[36];
- a policy framework for sustainable production and consumption[37];
- multiannual plans for the conservation of marine resources[38];
- financial support programmes on climate change, nature and biodiversity, environmental governance and information and environmental and resource efficiency.[39]

With the exception of the Regulation on standardization[40], nowhere is any participation of the public foreseen in the form of Article 7 of the Aarhus Convention – participation when all options are open, taking due account of

---

29 Regulation 1367/2006 (fn. 9, above), Recital 6; see also Aarhus Convention (fn. 6, above), Article 3(9).

30 Based on Regulation 1025/2012 on European standardization, OJ 2012, L 316 p. 12, Article 8. For example, the annual programme for 2015 (COM(2015) 500) required, as a priority, the elaboration of standards, among others, for bio-based products, including fuels, ecodesign of energy-related products, waste recycling and air quality and industrial emissions; all these are clearly related to the environment.

31 Based on Directive 2009/125 establishing a framework for the setting of ecodesign requirements for energy-related products, OJ 2009, L 285 p. 10, Article 16.

32 Based on Directive 2010/31 on the energy performance of buildings, OJ 2010, L 153, p. 13, Article 9(5).

33 Based on Decision 1386/2013 on a general Union environment action programme to 2020: Living well, within the limits of our planet, OJ 2013, L 354 p.171, Annex, paras 28(iv) and 54(vi).

34 Based on Decision 1386/2013 (fn. 33, above), Annex, para 28(viii).

35 Based on Decision 1386/2013 (fn. 33, above), Annex, para 28(i).

36 Based on Decision 1386/2013 (fn. 33, above), Annex, para 28(ii).

37 Based on Decision 1386/2013 (fn. 33, above), Annex, para 43(v).

38 Based on Regulation 1380/2013 on the Common Fisheries Policy, OJ 2013, L 354 p. 22, Article 9.

39 Based on Regulation 1293/2013 on the establishment of a programme for the environment and climate change (LIFE), OJ 2013, l 347 p. 185, Article 24.

40 Regulation 1025/2012 (fn. 30, above), Article 5. The participation shall take place "in particular" with those organizations that are financially supported by the European Commission. Whether in practice there is "participation or "consultation", is not known.

the outcome of the participation. The procedures limit themselves to provide for public consultation.

Article 9(3) of Regulation 1367/2006 provides that the public be informed, among other things, of "the environmental … assessment relevant to the plan or programme under preparation, where available". The Commission normally prepares impact assessments of the decisions which it adopts, where the different options are discussed under economic, social and environmental aspects. However, these impact assessments are made available only once the Commission has taken its decision. This practice appears to have been approved by the General Court.[41] However, it bluntly contradicts the objective of public participation, which is to allow a discussion of possible options of plans or programmes as early as possible, when all options are still open.

4. EU LAW WITH REGARD TO PARTICIPATION RIGHTS AT NATIONAL LEVEL

EU law strongly influenced the law of the Member States. In particular, Directive 2011/92 on the environmental impact assessment of projects (EIA), which substituted Directive 85/337, Directive 2010/75 on industrial emissions and Directive 2001/42 on the environmental impact of plans and programmes had a far-reaching influence on the national legislation.

4.1. PARTICIPATION IN PROJECTS AND ACTIVITIES

Directive 2011/92[42] requires an environmental impact assessment for projects listed in two annexes, before development consent may be given. For projects of annex 1, an environmental impact assessment has always to be made, for projects in annex 2, when the project may have significant effects on the environment. Details of the participation process are regulated in Articles 6 to 9. The provisions are similar to those of the Aarhus Convention. This is no surprise, as Directive 85/337 served, during the negotiations on the Aarhus Convention, as a model, and numerous of its provisions were taken over by the Convention, including even large parts of the list of projects which had to undergo an EIA.

Directive 2011/92 provides for public participation in the elaboration of the environmental impact assessment report – which is to be prepared by the developer of the project –, though Article 1(2)(g) of the Directive qualifies the

41 General Court, joined cases T-424/14 and T-425/14, *ClientEarth v. Commission*, ECLI:EU:T:2015:848. The cases are under appeal (C-67/15).

42 Directive 2011/92 on the assessment of the effects of certain public and private projects on the environment OJ 2012, L 26 p. 1, as amended by Directive 2014/52, OJ 2014, L 124 p. 1.

process as "consultation" and Articles 6(2) and 11(1) as "participation". It is less satisfactory that the developer of a project may ask for an opinion of the competent authority on the scope and the level of detail of the information which is to be included in the environmental impact assessment report, such as for example the study of alternative options for the location. The public concerned does not participate in such "scoping meetings" between the developer and the authorities, though the opinion of the authority is largely decisive on the whole impact assessment process.

The main problem of the participation provisions is Article 7 of Directive 2011/92. This provision reads as follows: "Where a Member State is aware that a project is likely to have significant effects on the environment in another Member State or where a Member State likely to be significantly affected so requests, the Member State in whose territory the project is intended to be carried out shall send to the other Member State [EIA documentation] ...". It is then up to the other Member State to collect information from its public concerned and transmit it to the Member State of origin.

Article 7 thus formulates an intergovernmental consultation procedure. The public concerned in the Member State affected will only be able to participate in the EIA procedure of the Member State of origin through its own government. This is, however, incompatible with the provisions of the Aarhus Convention which give an individual right of participation to citizens, also when they live in a neighbouring State. Article 3(9) of the Convention explicitly prohibits any discrimination "as to citizenship, nationality or domicile". Therefore, Article 7 of Directive 2011/92 is not in conformity with the Aarhus Convention, insofar as it allows a participation in the EIA procedure only via the agreement of the neighbouring government, but not to citizens directly.[43] The fact that the EU adhered to the Espoo Convention on environmental impact assessment in a transboundary context is of no remedy, as the Espoo Convention also only provides for intergovernmental cooperation for projects[44] which might have transboundary effects; however, it does not give participation rights to citizens in a neighbouring country.

Another problem of Article 7 is that it limits the intergovernmental cooperation procedure to EU Member States. However, the Aarhus Convention was ratified by 47 States and its requirements would thus apply to any project within the EU with effects on any of the non-EU Parties to the Convention.

---

43 This constellation became practical in the procedure concerning the Hinkley nuclear power plant in the United Kingdom. The Austrian Government had asked to participate in the EIA procedure which was accepted, and Austrian citizens were allowed to make comments on the project. In contrast, the German Government had not asked to participate, and German citizens were denied participation in the EIA procedure for the plant. See for the facts Aarhus Convention Compliance Committee, ACCC/C/2013/91.

44 Decision to adhere to the Espoo Convention of 15 October 1996. The decision was not published. The Convention is published in OJ 1992, C 104 p. 7.

When the participation rights of the public concerned are disregarded, Article 11 of Directive 2011/92 gives a right to challenge the substantive and procedural aspects of the development consent decision. This is a clear recognition of a "right" to participate in the decision-making process.

A similar approach was adopted in Directive 2010/75[45] as regards public participation in the procedure for the permitting of larger industrial installations; these installations are enumerated in an annex to the Directive. The public concerned shall be informed of applications for a permit and has the right to participate in the decision-making procedure by making comments, opinions, statements etc.[46] Where this right is disregarded, it has the possibility to challenge the substantive or procedural legality of the permit in court (Article 25). When an industrial project may have significant effects on another Member State, the Directive again provides for intergovernmental procedures, not for the participation of citizens in the other Member State.

Directive 2010/75 also covers large combustion plants (50 MW or more). No participation requirements are foreseen for the permitting of medium power plants (between 1 and 50 MW).[47]

4.2. TRANS-EUROPEAN PROJECTS

Transport and energy infrastructure measures within the EU received a considerable support through the decision in the early 1990s to promote trans-European networks in these areas.[48] Permits for such projects continue to be issued by the Member States. The requirements of the EU environmental impact assessment legislation also apply in the context of the trans-European networks. Progressively, the EU considerably influenced the framework of the permitting process for such projects.

For energy projects, Regulation 347/2013 applies.[49] Though Article 171 TFEU only provided for the elaboration of guidelines – which are non-binding by nature –, Article 172 TFEU clarifies that they are to be adopted by way of (binding) legislation. Regulation 347/2013 establishes an EU list of energy projects of common interest, which is prepared by twelve regional groups and adopted by the Commission; the regional groups are composed of representatives of the Member States concerned, the Commission, the Agency for Cooperation

45 Directive 2010/75 on industrial emissions (integrated pollution prevention and control) OJ 2010, L 334 p. 17.

46 *Ibidem*, Article 24 and Annex IV. The annex again uses "participation" and "consultation" as synonyms.

47 Directive 2015/2193 on the limitation of emissions of certain pollutants into the air from medium combustion plants.

48 See now Articles 170 to 172 TFEU.

49 Regulation 347/2013 on guidelines for trans-European energy infrastructure, OJ 2013, L 115 p. 39.

of Energy Regulators and – without voting rights – professional organizations.[50] Environmental organizations are not members of these regional groups.

In 2013, the Commission adopted a first list of 242 energy projects of common interest.[51] Recital 4 mentioned: "In the context of Regional groups, organizations representing relevant stakeholders, including producers, distribution system operators, suppliers, consumers and organizations for environmental protection were consulted". No further information is given. Nothing is known on the procedure of the regional groups and, in particular, which environmental organizations from which Member States and neighbouring States were consulted, whether also citizens were heard, what their concerns had been, to what extent this concern had been taken into account by the regional group and why this or that project was suggested and, later on, selected.

The inclusion of the projects in the EU list establishes the necessity to realize the project, subject to its exact location, routing and used technology (Article 7). The project shall obtain the highest national priority and "shall be considered as being of public interest from an energy policy perspective and may be considered as being of overriding public interest, provided that all the conditions set in Directives 92/43 [conservation of natural habitats and of species] and 2000/60 [water protection] are fulfilled".

Regulation 1391/2013, together with Regulation 347/2013, must be seen as a plan to realize a number of energy infrastructure projects. It is obvious that these provisions on public participation in the decision-making process of the different regional groups do not comply with the most elementary requirements of such participation as laid down in Article 6 of the Aarhus Convention. Neither is there any participation foreseen as early as possible, when all options are open. Nor is there any information available, which public was informed on the intention to realize the project, what documentation was made available to the public, to what extent its comments were taken into consideration and what kind of explanation was there given, why the project in question was chosen.

The permit procedure, which is, as mentioned, a national one, is split into a "pre-application procedure" – which dates from the start of the permit procedure until the acceptance of the application by the competent authority – and a "statutory permit granting procedure", which dates from the acceptance of the application until the decision on it (Article 10). Before the beginning of the procedure, at least one public consultation on the project shall be organized, in particular in order to find the most suitable location and trajectory of the project. The consultation shall be preferably made by the developer of the project.

---

50 *Ibidem*, Article 3 and Annex III.

51 Delegated Regulation 1391/2013, OJ 2013, L 349 p. 28. The list contains, among others, liquid natural gas (LNG) and oil terminals, the construction and reinforcement of electricity and gas pipelines, interconnectors, internal lines, storage projects for electricity, for gas and for liquefied natural gas, air energy and hydro-pumped projects, and the construction and extension of transformers.

While not explicitly stated in Regulation 347/2013, it may be expected that the process of participation of the public will in the future be organized by the project developer and not by the competent public authority.[52] If this interpretation is correct, the public authorities will hear of the public concern only via the report which the developer has to submit on activities – not *his* activities! – concerning the project.

In the sector of trans-European transport networks, Regulation 1315/2013 provided guidelines for two networks, one for those transport projects that are of "highest strategic importance" and shall be realized until 2030, and another one that lists the projects that are to be realized until 2050.[53] The networks include projects for railways, inland waterways, road, maritime transport, motorways of the seas and airports. The projects are structured in nine European corridors, within which the projects shall be realized. For each corridor a European coordinator was appointed; he is to be assisted by a "Corridor Forum", whose composition is decided by the Member States concerned.[54] For projects in each corridor, a plan shall be elaborated, which shall be approved by all Member States concerned. The plans and projects are to respect existing EU environmental law.

Also Regulation 1315/2013 must be considered, in legal terms, as a plan adopted at EU level in order to realize, within a certain time-span, a number of transport infrastructure projects. Thus, the observations that were made on public participation in decision-making on EU plans and programmes – see section 3.2 above – also apply here.

It follows that for energy and for transport projects, decisions to realize them are taken already at EU level, with the explicit agreement of the different Member States concerned. Their realization cannot be questioned anymore in any participation procedure. At best, such a participation may reach a displacement of the project by some meters, or other details concerning the dimension of the project.

All this is a flagrant disregard of the participation provisions of EU law. Trans-European transport and energy networks more or less determine the different project, without any meaningful citizen participation. The delegation of such participation to regional groups or to corridor groups is no remedy, as the different projects are already specified and detailed in the two guideline Regulations. In other words, the EU infrastructure planning restricts the possibilities of the public concerned to participate in decision-making on projects or plans. The technocratic concern of accelerating and streamlining the permitting process for trans-European projects very largely prevailed over concerns to have a democratic decision-making process. It is not surprising that in such circumstances, citizens

52 This follows in particular from Article 9(4) of Regulation 347/2013 (fn. 49, above).

53 Regulation 1315/2013 on Union guidelines for the development of the trans-European transport network, OJ 2013, L 348 p. 1.

54 *Ibidem*, Articles 46 and 50.

at local level tend to adopt a NIMBY attitude: the project might be realized, but "Not In My Backyard".

To overcome these deficiencies, this author had proposed to accept environmental organizations and representatives of civil society groups as members of the twelve regional energy groups, to set up a specific advisory group of civil society representatives for each of the twelve regions, to appoint for each of the twelve regional energy groups as well as for the different transport corridor forums an environmental coordinator, whose tasks would be to bring the environmental concerns to the discussion and negotiation table and, at the same time, closely liaise with the public concerned, in order to ensure that due participation is possible.[55] Such an "Ombudsman for the environment" would be particularly necessary and welcome in the EU-wide, transnational planning of large infrastructure projects as foreseen in the trans-European networks. He could increase transparency, promote early and open discussion on projects and thus contribute, in the long term, to a much better acceptability of projects by citizens, citizen initiatives and environmental organizations. The examples of Stuttgart 21, where a trans-European railway line construction was held up for years due to citizens' objections to the planned project, of the railway line Lyon-Torino, where Italian citizens strongly and successfully protested against the plans, the objections in Germany against the electricity lining North-South, which led to the conclusion of placing the lines under ground, or the protests in the Rhine valley against excessive noise from freight trains should be sufficiently clear warnings for public authorities that an early participation of citizens is also necessary for trans-European projects.

The EU made considerable efforts to set up governance structures for producers, developers and operators of infrastructure projects. Next to the regional energy groups, the corridor groups and the EU coordinators, mentioned above, mention should be made of the European Agency for the cooperation of energy regulators[56], the European networks of transmission system operators for electricity (ENTSO-electricity)[57] and for gas (ENTSO-gas).[58] The EU should make comparable efforts to ensure the participation of the public in trans-European transport and energy projects. This is all the more necessary, as projects that come under Directive 2011/92 in their majority concern the local population, where citizen initiatives and environmental groups might ensure participation.

---

55 *L. Krämer*, The EU and the participation of civil society in large projects, in: B. Vanheusden – L. Squintani (eds): EU environmental and planning law aspects of large scale projects, Cambridge 2016, p. 45.

56 Regulation 713/2009 establishing an Agency for the cooperation of energy regulators, OJ 2009, L 211 p. 1.

57 Established by Regulation 714/2009 on conditions for access to the network of cross-border exchanges in electricity, OJ 2009, L 211 p. 15, Recital 7 and Articles 4 and 5.

58 Established by Regulation 715/2009 on conditions for access to the natural gas transmission network, OJ 2009, L 211 p. 36, Recital 16 and Articles 4 and 5.

The trans-European projects, in contrast, are typically transnational and neither environmental organizations nor citizen groups are at present organized at this level. The above-mentioned ENTSO-electricity and ENTSO-gas were also groupings which were established by EU decisions, not by the will of the different private members to cooperate.

It is thus submitted that the EU has an obligation to ensure appropriate participation of the public (citizens and environmental organizations) in the decision-making process on trans-European electricity and transport networks.

4.3. PARTICIPATION IN NATIONAL DECISIONS ON PLANS AND PROGRAMMES

For plans and programmes at national level, Article 7 of the Aarhus Convention applied, which provides for the public participation in the elaboration of plans and programmes "relating to the environment". The framework for such participation shall be transparent and fair. Reasonable time-frames for the different phases of the planning process shall be provided, allowing sufficient time for informing the public and for the public to prepare and participate effectively. The participation shall take place "early", when all options are open and effective public participation can take place. In the decisions on the plans or programmes, due account is taken of the outcome of the public participation.

The EU adopted Directive 2001/42.[59] That Directive applied to plans and programmes that were prepared by a public authority and were required[60] by legislative, regulatory or administrative provisions. An environmental impact assessment had to be made for such plans and programmes that "set the framework for future development consent of projects listed" in the annexes to Directive 2011/92 or that require an assessment under Articles 6 and 7 of Directive 92/43 (Article 3(2)). This requirement is narrower than the Aarhus Convention provisions, as not all plans relating to the environment are covered.

Though Directive 2001/42 also applies to all plans and programmes that the Member States elaborate in the context of the EU regional policy[61], the relevant EU regional policy Regulations do not mention anything on public participation, but limit themselves to the requirement that the financial support of the EU shall be in keeping with the applicable provisions of EU law.[62] In practice,

---

59 Directive 2001/42 on the assessment of the effects of certain plans and programmes on the environment, OJ 2001, L 197 p. 30.

60 As regards the term "required" see above, section III.b.

61 Argument from Directive 2001/42, Article 3(9), which only excludes the "current" plans and programmes of the European Structure and Investment Funds.

62 See Regulation 1303/2013 laying down common provisions on the European Structural and Investment Funds, OJ 2013, L 347 p. 320, Article 6. See also, for example, Regulation 1300/2013 on the Cohesion Fund, OJ 2013, L 347 p. 281.

the different plans and programmes that the Member States elaborate do not provide for any public participation, a clear case of non-compliance with the requirements of EU law.

For other plans and programmes, the "participation" of the public is dealt with in Article 6 of Directive 2001/42, which has the title "consultation". When an assessment is required, the competent authority shall establish an environmental report which identifies, describes and evaluates the likely effects of the plan or programme on the environment and also examines "reasonable alternatives" to the plan or programme (Article 5). The draft plan and the environmental report shall be made available to the public, which is affected or likely to be affected by the plan. The public shall have the opportunity to give an opinion on the plan and the report. The decision on the plan or programme shall take due account of the opinions expressed. Once the plan is adopted or submitted to the legislative procedure, the competent authorities shall make available to the public the plan and a statement how the environmental concerns and opinions expressed have been integrated into the plan or have otherwise been taken into consideration (Article 9).

For plans or programmes that might have an effect on the environment of another Member State, again an intergovernmental consultation is foreseen, but not a participation of the public affected (Article 7). The Espoo Convention also requires that in such a case, it must be examined whether the plan really needs to be realized at all ("zero alternative"), an issue which was not taken up by Directive 2001/42, but which applies, as the Espoo Convention prevails over secondary EU law.

No sanction is foreseen in Directive 2001/42 for cases where the participation obligations were disregarded. The Directive left this to national law. It is presumed that the majority of Member States did not foresee an effective sanction for such cases.

For plans and programmes that do not set the frame for a subsequent environmental impact assessment, the EU adopted Directive 2003/35.[63] This Directive does not concern all plans and programmes relating to the environment, but only applies to six plans and programmes elaborated in the area of waste management, nitrate pollution of waters and air quality.[64] Recital 10 of the Directive stated that "in future, public participation requirements in line with the Aarhus Convention will be incorporated into the relevant legislation from the outset". This, however, was a commitment that was not kept, as will be shown hereafter. In substance, the provisions of the Aarhus Convention concerning plans and programmes relating to the environment are correctly transposed, for

63 Directive 2003/35 providing for public participation in respect of the drawing up of certain plans and programmes relating to the environment, OJ 2003, L 156 p. 17.

64 *Ibidem*, Annex I.

the six plans and programmes covered, by the provisions of Article 2 of Directive 2003/35.

Numerous EU legislative acts did not provide for public participation in the elaboration and adoption of national plans relating to the environment.[65] Overall, the impression is given that public participation in decision-making in environmental matters is not taken seriously by the Commission and the other EU institutions.

5. RESUMING REMARKS

1. Existing EU law requires the adoption of provisions that allow public participation in environmental decision-making of projects, plans and programmes relating to the environment.

2. EU law does not differentiate clearly between "consultation" and "participation".

3. At EU level, participation in decision-making on plans and programmes relating to the environment is frequently not ensured. The participation of the public in permitting decisions on genetically modified organisms is insufficient.

---

[65] Only some acts can be mentioned here: Directive 2003/87 establishing a scheme for greenhouse gas emission trading within the Community, OJ 2003, L 275 p. 32, Article 10c (National allocation plans); Directive 2006/21 on the management of waste from extractive industries, OJ 2006, L 102 p. 15, Article 5 (management plans for extractive waste); Directive 2007/60 on the assessment and management of flood risks, OJ 2007, L288 p. 27, Article 7 (Flood risk management plans); Directive 2008/50 on ambient air quality and cleaner air for Europe, OJ 2008, L 152 p. 1, Article 23 (Air quality plans), Article 24 (Short term action plan); Directive 2008/56 Marine Strategy Framework Directive, OJ 2008, L 164 p. 19, Articles 5 and 13 (programme of measures), Article 11 (monitoring programme); Directive 2009/29, amending Directive 2003/87, OJ 2009, L140, p. 63, Article 10c (National plans on retrofitting and upgrading of infrastructure); Directive 2009/128 establishing a framework for Community action the achieve the sustainable use of pesticides, OJ 2009, L 309, p. 71, Article 5 (National action plans); Regulation 1380/2013 on the Common Fisheries Policy, OJ 2013, L 354 p. 22, Article 22 (Action plans to combat structural overcapacity); Directive 2002/49 relating to the assessment and management of environmental noise, OJ 2002, L 189 p. 12, Article 8 (Action plans on the management of noise issues); Directive 2010/31 on the energy performance of building, OJ 2010, L 153 p. 13, Article 9 (Plans for increasing the number of zero-energy buildings); Directive 2009/28 on the promotion of the use of energy from renewable energy sources, OJ 2009, L 140 p. 16, Article 4 (National renewable energy action plans); Directive 2012/27 on energy efficiency, OJ 2012, L 315 p.1, Article 12 (consumer information and empowering programmes), Article 14 (Plans for potential of high-efficient cogeneration); Directive 2013/30 on the safety of offshore oil and gas operations, OJ 2013, L 178 p. 66, Article 29 (external emergency plans).

4. EU law provides for participation provisions in decisions on permit procedures at national level that concern projects that undergo an environmental impact assessment and large industrial installations. No provision exists on other plans and programmes relating to the environment.

5. Participation in the decision-making for projects that have an effect in another State is not foreseen for citizens in that other State. This is replaced by an intergovernmental consultation, which is not in compliance with the provisions of the Aarhus Convention.

6. For trans-European projects, the participation provisions are very vague and do not comply with the provisions of the Aarhus and the Espoo Conventions.

7. Numerous EU legislative acts provide for the adoption of national plans or programmes without ensuring public participation.

PUBLIC PARTICIPATION IN RULEMAKING AND DECISION-MAKING IN ENVIRONMENTAL MATTERS

Legal Framework and Jurisprudence in Spain and the Basque Country*

María del Carmen Bolaño Piñeiro** and
Iñaki Lasagabaster Herrarte***

ABSTRACT

The aim of this paper is to examine the legal consequences of failing to provide an effective public participation in rulemaking and administrative decision-making processes on environmental matters in Spain and the Basque Country. This work provides an overview of the Spanish Supreme Court and other regional Court's jurisprudence on public participation. The particular moment in which citizens participate in a decision-making process is of major importance. For instance, it is not the same thing to participate at an early stage of the process (this is, when the administrative file is not complete) than to do it when the compulsory reports are issued or when the last draft of the decision is already made. As it is going to be examined in this paper, the law sets that if 'important amendments' are submitted to the regulations or decision during the approval procedure, public authorities are obliged to provide citizens with the opportunity of taking part again. What in reality happens and the legal consequences of it are analysed in this work.

* This project has received funding from the Spanish Ministry of Economy and Competitiveness [Research project: 'Las ordenanzas locales reguladoras del espacio público, derechos fundamentales y actividades económicas: propuesta de un protocolo de mejoras' (grant agreement no. DER2015-67181-R)].

** Lecturer in Administrative Law, University of the Basque Country, Faculty of Economics and Business.

*** Professor of Administrative Law, University of the Basque Country, Faculty of Economics and Business.

KEYWORDS

Decision-making process; European Union; Public participation; Rulemaking process; Spanish and Basque Environmental Law

1. INTRODUCTION

Public participation in environmental rulemaking and decision-making processes has been regulated over the last decades in almost every European country.[1] In some European countries, even when no regulation on the issue had been specifically passed, public participation was already a reality due to their democratic background.[2] However, other European countries needed a clear and specific regulation by Law on the right of citizens to participate in rulemaking and decision-making processes.[3] Countries with an advanced democracy may not need an express recognition of this right but, others, such as Spain, not only need an express recognition of public participation by law, but also the recognition of the right to challenge the authorities' decision or regulation adopted without participation.[4] This means that in the event of authorities' non-compliance with the law, citizens should be entitled to challenge the illegal decision. In such countries, Courts play a key role because they may have to oblige authorities to comply with the law and protect citizens' right to participate. In the latter countries, public participation in rulemaking and decision-making processes was formulated firstly as a legal principle and, afterwards, recognised as a subjective right. Both International and European Law have been part of the development of the right of citizens to participate within the European Union.[5] The Aarhus Convention in particular, along with a number of different European legislative instruments, has played a fundamental role in its development. As a result of this policy, every member state has incorporated the right to participate in rulemaking and decision-making processes to their legal system.[6]

Like any other right, the right of citizens to take part in environmental rulemaking and decision-making processes has to be appropriately enforced by

1 Most European countries have already ratified the Aarhus Convention. See www.unece.org/env/pp/aarhus/map.html.

2 Such was the case of the Scandinavian countries or Germany.

3 That was the case of Spain.

4 ECJ Judgment, Cases C-530/11, Commission v United Kingdom [2014]; C-72/12, Gemeinde Altrip and Others [2013].

5 *J.I. Cubero, M. Iturribarria, & I. Lasagabaster*, Acceso a la información, Participación y Acceso a la Justicia en materia de Medio Ambiente / Informazioa eskuratzea, parte-hartzea eta epaitegietara jotzea ingurumen arloan, Servicio Central de Publicaciones del Gobierno Vasco, Vitoria-Gasteiz, 2009, *in totum*.

6 *G.F. Cartei*, The Implementation of the European Landscape convention and Public Participation, European Public Law, 2012 (18.2), pp. 269–282.

public authorities and Courts. In practice, an adequate implementation of the right is what makes it a reality. Moreover, not only should the right be sufficiently implemented, but authorities should make it easy to exercise this right so as to turn it into a reality. Making the right efficient may lead to the adoption of more accurate public decisions. In turn, the right to participate will be more efficient if public authorities give citizens access to the whole final regulation or decision.

The right of citizens consists of two different – but connected – parts. On the one hand, the citizens' real possibility to exercise the right; on the other, the adequate materialization of citizens' participation right in rulemaking or decision-making processes by public authorities. In fact, if it was necessary to make the right efficient, public authorities should be obliged to do so by courts. When a right is expressly recognised in the law, the question that arises is how its real value can be determined. The theoretical recognition of a right does not imply *per se* its proper materialization. There must be legal consequences so that citizens' right is protected in the event of public authorities not applying the law properly. Therefore, people should have the possibility of exercising the right and the exercising of the right should also result in legal consequences for the right to become – as already stated – real and efficient.[7]

Authorities' double role in informing and giving citizens the chance to participate in rulemaking and decision-making processes has not been specifically considered by the legal doctrine and lawyers in Spain. The right to access information along with the right to participate have sometimes been categorised as subjective rights. However, those rights should be understood as part of public authorities' obligations. Public authorities are duty bound to act and provide citizens with information and means of participation.[8] Citizens should not have to ask authorities for information or participation as these are their rights and not their obligation. Information and participation are both public functions and as such, in a democratic state, they oblige authorities to act accordingly. Currently, those public duties are easier to implement than ever before thanks to the new technologies. Information and participation, as public functions, are democratic requirements and without them, citizens' cultural development becomes impossible. Public information and participation are the appropriate means to prevent knowledge from becoming something exclusive to the elites. Besides, they enable people to develop a free public opinion, what is of great relevance regarding environmental issues.[9]

---

7 *J.I. Cubero*, Proyectos y planes aprobados por Ley: contradicciones a la luz de la evaluación ambiental, el derecho de participación y el acceso a la justicia en materia ambiental, Revista Vasca de Administración Pública, 2014, 99/100, pp. 1007–1039.

8 For instance, Spanish Law number 42/2007 on Natural Heritage and Biodiversity, Articles 13(2), 22(2), 43(2), in relation with article 47(2) Spanish Law number 39/2015.

9 See: *K.-P. Sommermann*, La exigencia de una Administración transparente en la perspectiva de los principios de democracia y del Estado de Derecho, R.J. García Macho (Ed.), Derecho administrativo de la información y administración transparente, 2010, pp. 11–26; *C.O. Sanz Salla*, El derecho a

There have been a number of international efforts, especially with the adoption of the Aarhus Convention, that have led States to force their governments and authorities to inform citizens about the development of environmental policies, to promote participation in those issues and to encourage citizens to go to courts if their rights are not being respected. The Aarhus Convention, the importance of which must be highlighted, establishes the formal and material requirements that shall be met by public authorities in their provision of information and means of participation. One of the aims of the Convention is to make information about environmental policies accessible to everybody.[10] Likewise, the convention states the obligation to employ civil servants whose duties are to give and expand this information and help citizens understand it.[11] It is also vital to provide the information via the internet, so that it reaches citizens in a simple and convenient way, avoiding unnecessary displacements and other difficulties citizens may find. Authorities must provide citizens with IT resources to make information more accessible, in a continued way, 24 hours a day and 7 days a week. Those IT resources should speed up the formalities and facilitate participation in rulemaking and decision-making processes.

In practice, participation is often nothing more than empty rhetoric and its non-implementation does not have any legal consequences. However, the Aarhus Convention sets some requirements in order to make participation real. Specifically, it states that participation must ensure that citizens' opinions and ideas have some kind of impact on the rules or the decisions authorities are making.[12] This should in turn favour transparency and responsibility on the part of public authorities during the rule or decision-making process. This attitude towards participation would contribute to an increase of citizens' awareness on environmental issues.

la información administrativa en la era digital: una aproximación al derecho norteamericano, Ricardo Jesús García Macho (Ed.), Derecho administrativo de la información y administración transparente, 2010, pp. 203–230; *A. Nogueira López*, La participación en la evaluación de impacto ambiental, dogma y realidad, A. García Ureta (Ed.), La Directiva de la Unión Europea de Evaluación de Impacto Ambiental de proyectos: balance de 30 años, Marcial Pons, Madrid, 2016, pp. 117–156; *J.I. Cubero Marcos*, La transposición de la Directiva en el Estado español, A. García Ureta (Ed.), La Directiva de la Unión Europea de Evaluación de Impacto Ambiental de proyectos: balance de 30 años, Marcial Pons, Madrid, 2016, pp. 65–90; *I. Lasagabaster*, Notas sobre el derecho administrativo de la información, Ricardo Jesús García Macho (Ed.), Derecho administrativo de la información y administración transparente, 2010, pp. 103–120.

10 Articles 1, 3(1), 4 and 5 Aarhus Convention.

11 Articles 3(2) and 3(3) Aarhus Convention. ECJ Judgment, Cases C-612/13 P, *ClientEarth v Commission* [2015] and C-71/14, *East Sussex County Council* [2015].

12 *A. Aragao*, Los impactos ambientales transfronterizos, entre el hecho y el derecho, A. García Ureta (Edit.), La Directiva de la Unión Europea de Evaluación de Impacto Ambiental de proyectos: balance de 30 años, Marcial Pons, Madrid, 2016, pp. 157–172. *C.H. Born*, El juez europeo y la directiva de impacto ambiental: balance de treinta años, A. García Ureta (Edit.), La Directiva de la Unión Europea de Evaluación de Impacto Ambiental de proyectos: balance de 30 años, Marcial Pons, Madrid, 2016, pp. 9–28. *R.J. Santamaría*, Evaluando al evaluador: razones técnicas, jurídicas y políticas en la evaluación de impacto ambiental de proyectos, A. García Ureta (Edit.), La Directiva de la Unión Europea de Evaluación de Impacto Ambiental de proyectos: balance de 30 años, Marcial Pons, Madrid, 2016, pp. 29–63.

Citizens' different opinions have to be taken into account as much as possible and must be reflected in the rulemaking or decision-making process. This means that authorities have to provide the reasons as to why they do not admit citizens' claims. This approach to participation legitimates to public authorities' rules and decisions. How this issue has been ruled by courts is addressed below.

This paper examines both the Spanish and Basque legislation and jurisprudence. The aim of this work is to give an overview of the Spanish and Basque authorities' compliance with the law on the right to public participation.[13] Although courts' ruling does not cover the whole spectrum of the issue, the recognition of authorities' non-compliance with the law by courts is absolutely necessary so as to make the right to public participation real in Spain and the Basque Country. If public authorities do not enforce the law, courts have the duty to oblige them to comply with the legislation. Moreover, even when the law is clear and it protects the right properly, citizens still find other obstacles. The right of citizens to access justice always goes along with a number of added difficulties, mainly economic problems, but also the loss of time, among others.

2. LEGAL FRAMEWORK REGARDING PUBLIC PARTICIPATION IN ENVIRONMENTAL RULEMAKING AND DECISION-MAKING

There are a wide number of legal instruments on public information and citizens' participation in rulemaking and decision-making processes. All those instruments are different from each other, both in content and in nature. On the one hand, there are international legal instruments, especially the Aarhus Convention mentioned above. The Aarhus Convention has already been ratified by all the European Union Member States and by the European Union itself.[14]

---

13 *I. Urrutia*, La jurisprudencia del Tribunal Supremo en materia ambiental, Anuario de Derecho Ambiental - IeZ, 2016 (14), pp. 173–204; *Idem*, La jurisprudencia del Tribunal Supremo en materia ambiental, Anuario de Derecho Ambiental - IeZ, 2015 (13), pp.132–158; *Idem*, La jurisprudencia del Tribunal Supremo en materia ambiental, Anuario de Derecho Ambiental - IeZ, 2014 (12), pp. 218–249. *J.I. Cubero*, La jurisprudencia del Tribunal Superior de Justicia de la Comunidad Foral de Navarra", Anuario de Derecho Ambiental - IeZ, 2016 (14), pp.222–247; *Idem*, La jurisprudencia del Tribunal Superior de Justicia de la Comunidad Foral de Navarra, Anuario de Derecho Ambiental - IeZ, 2015 (13), pp. 176–205. *Idem*, La jurisprudencia del Tribunal Superior de Justicia de la Comunidad Foral de Navarra, Anuario de Derecho Ambiental - IeZ, 2014, 12, pp. 262–280. *M.N. Arrese & I. Lazkano*, La jurisprudencia del Tribunal Superior de Justicia del País Vasco en materia ambiental, Anuario de Derecho Ambiental - IeZ, 2016, 14, pp. 205–221. *Idem*, La jurisprudencia del Tribunal Superior de Justicia del País Vasco en materia ambiental, Anuario de Derecho Ambiental - IeZ, 2015, 13, pp. 159–175. *Idem*, La jurisprudencia del Tribunal Superior de Justicia del País Vasco en materia ambiental, Anuario de Derecho Ambiental - IeZ, 2014, 12, pp. 250–261.

14 The European Union passed a number of legal instruments to implement the Aarhus Convention. Mainly but not exclusively: the Decision on conclusion of the Aarhus Convention

Those legal instruments set a compulsory stage of public information and citizens' participation in the European Union rulemaking and decision-making processes.[15]

In Spain, constitutional rules set the right to information and participation and so do some parliamentary legal instruments. General regulations establish the right of citizens to participate in decision-making processes in every administrative procedure – this is the case of administrative procedure law (Spanish Law number 39/2015). Other rules set this right more specifically regarding some environmental matters. Such is the case of the Spanish Law number 42/2007 on SAC, SCI and SPAB.[16] Given the variety of instruments that rule the right to participate, it is necessary to take it into due consideration.

In accordance with Spanish constitutional law, international law prevails over domestic law.[17] This means that if the Aarhus Convention sets a clear obligation to give information to the public and open a citizens' participation stage during

by the EC was adopted on 17 February 2005 [Decision 2005/370/EC]; Directive 2003/4/EC of the European Parliament and of the Council of 28 January 2003 on public access to environmental information and repealing Council; Directive 90/313/EEC Directive 2003/35/EC of the European Parliament and of the Council of 26 May 2003 providing for public participation in respect of the drawing up of certain plans and programmes relating to the environment and amending with regard to public participation and access to justice Council Directives 85/337/EEC and 96/61/EC; Regulation (EC) No. 1367/2006 of the European Parliament and of the Council on the application of the provisions of the Aarhus Convention on Access to Information, Public Participation in Decision-making and Access to Justice in Environmental Matters to Community institutions and bodies (OJ L 264, 25.9.2006, p.13) entered into force on 28 September 2006 and into application on 17 July 2007. See: *J. Jendroska*, Public Participation in Environmental Decision-Making. Interactions between the Convention and EU Law and other Key Legal Issues in its Implementation in the Light of the Opinions of the Aarhus Convention Compliance Committee, M. Pallemaerts (Ed.), Interactions and Tensions between Conventional International Law and EU Environmental Law, Europe Law Publishing, 2011, pp. 105–12 and *J. Jendroska*, Aarhus Convention and Community Law: the Interplay, Journal for European Environmental & Planning Law, Volume 2, Issue 1, 2005, p. 8.

15 For further reading about the evolution of the interpretation of public participation: *Y. Jegouzo*, La Loi Grenelle II: La réforme des enquêtes publiques et la mise en œuvre du principe de participation, Actualité Juridique - Droit Administrative, 2010 (32), pp. 1812–1818. *O. Montouto & J. Lusi*, ¿Cómo participaron los ciudadanos de los municipios de Albacete en sus procesos de Agenda 21 local?, Ecosostenible, 2009 (56) pp. 19–33. *Ídem*, Aproximación al "empadronamiento" de los ciudadanos en la gestión local y su evaluación como herramienta de democracia participativa, Ecosostenible, 2009, 57, pp. 25–37. *F. Spagnuolo*, Beyond Participation: Administrative-Law Type Mechanisms in Global Environmental Governance. Toward a New Basis of Legitimacy?, Public Law, 2009, spring, pp. 49–61. *M. Iovane*, La participation de la société civile à l'élaboration et à l'application du droit international de l'environnement, Revue Générale de Droit International Public, 2008, 112.3, pp. 465–519. *B. Jadot*, Faire payer au public le "droit" de participation au processus de décisions en matière d'environnement?, Revue européenne de droit de l'environnement, 2007 (2), pp. 171–180. *A. Garcia*, Algunas cuestiones sobre la regulación del derecho de participación a la luz del Convenio de Aarhus de 1998, Revista Aranzadi de Derecho Ambiental, 2005 (7), pp. 43–70.

16 Special Protection Areas for Birds (SPAB), Sites of Community Importance (SCI) and Special Areas of Conservation (SAC). Wild fauna and flora, hydrocarbons, mines or environmental planning are other examples of matters in which the right of citizens to participate is protected.

17 Article 96 from the Spanish Constitution.

environmental decision-making processes, domestic law cannot contradict the convention. If it does, courts must apply the Aarhus Convention while taking its international nature into consideration. International Law also takes priority over the European Union Law, what can be easily derived from the fact that the European Union signed the Aarhus Convention and passed the Directive number 2003/35/CE to transpose it. It is common knowledge that European Law prevails over domestic Law regardless of the nature of the legal instrument. The Court of Justice of the European Union set its ruling on the issue decades ago – the well-known principle of primacy of the European Union Law. As a consequence, if the Spanish or the Basque Law does not comply with the European Law on participation, courts must apply European Law to the case.

The next question to analyse is the relationship between general and specific rules. In any case, the interpretation of the relationship between those different rules should be in favour of enforcing public participation and the right of access to information in environmental matters. This means that if a more specific regulation does not set the right to participate – for example, the Land Pollution Law – the more general regulation must be implemented – that is to say, the Law on Environmental Protection. The non-regulation of the right in the most specific legal instrument cannot be an excuse to avoid the general regulation's enforcement and vice versa. In other words, if the specific rule establishes the right to participate and the general regulation does not, the specific rule must be applied in order to protect the right of citizens to participate.[18]

Sectoral laws contain very limited rules regarding participation. In most cases, it is compulsory to apply the most general law on participation rather than the most specific ones. For instance, a glance at the sectoral laws –such as the law on water, noise pollution, soil pollution[19], atmosphere pollution, territory management and urbanism[20], biodiversity, waste, chemical products, biotechnology or environmental impact assessment, amongst others – shows that there are almost no rules that regulate participation in those very specific environmental areas. In all those cases, participation in rulemaking and decision-making processes has to comply with the requirements established in the general law, this is, the Spanish Law number 27/2006, the Basque Law number 8/2003, the

18 For instance, if the Law on EIA recognises the right to participate – and the general regulation does not, the specific rule must be applied in order to protect citizens' right.

19 *M.C. Bolaño*, El procedimiento de declaración de calidad del suelo en la Comunidad Autónoma del País Vasco, Revista Aranzadi de Derecho Ambiental, 2015 (30), pp. 259–294. *I. Lasagabaster & M.C. Bolaño*, Medio Ambiente y Obligación de Difusión, Ingurugiroa eta Zuzenbidea, 2009 (7), pp. 21–34.

20 *I. Lasagabaster & M.C. Bolaño*, Public Participation in Land Management Law-Making Process in the Basque Country: Effects on Soil and Other Natural Resources, *B. Vanheusden & L. Squintani (Eds.)*, EU Environmental and Planning Law. Aspects of Large-Scale Projects, Intersentia, 2016, pp. 367–384.

Provincial Laws number 6/2005 and 7/2007 and the different Council regulations on the issue.[21]

The law regulates more specifically participation in decision-making processes than in rulemaking processes. This difference lies in the fact that projects have a more direct impact on citizens' daily lives than regulations. Actually, the Environmental Impact Assessment Law expressly sets the need to open an information and participation stage during the plan or programme-making process.[22] This is also established in cases such as when highly contaminating activities as well as activities in the field of biotechnology or projects that affect public domain, amongst others, are permitted by license.[23]

Summing up, the sectoral law on public participation and access to information is very poor. This is why in almost every case authorities and courts have to apply the general law rather than the sectoral law and this is why it is of major importance that the more general laws on the environment set standards that public authorities are obliged to comply with, not only regarding decision-making processes but also rulemaking processes.

3. JURISPRUDENCE

3.1. DISTINCTION BETWEEN ADMINISTRATIVE REGULATION AND ADMINISTRATIVE DECISION

Citizens' participation in environmental matters is the bedrock of the international and European policy on environment. Two main legal instruments are testimony to this: The Aarhus Convention, which was ratified by Spain and published in the Official Journal of Spain on 16 February 2005, and Directive 2003/35/EC.[24] Participation, which is both a principle and a subjective right, was transposed into the Spanish legal system by the Spanish Law number 27/2006 on the right of access to information, public participation and justice in environmental matters. More specific laws on the environment, such as the ones that regulate Special Protection Areas for Birds (SPAB), Sites of Community Importance (SCI) and Special Areas of Conservation (SAC) set that the procedures they regulate must include public participation.[25]

---

21 In the Basque Country Provincial Laws are called *Normas Forales*.

22 Article 21 Spanish Law number 21/2013 on Environmental Impact Assesement.

23 *Nogueira, Cubero, Santamaría, supra* note 9 at page 117.

24 Directive 2003/35/EC of the European Parliament and of the Council of 26 May 2003, providing for public participation in respect of the drawing up of certain plans and programmes relating to the environment and amending with regard to public participation and access to justice Council Directives 85/337/EEC and 96/61/EC.

25 Spanish Law number 42/2007 – which, in turn, transposes Directives 79/409/CE and 92/43/CE. The Law number 42/2007 sets the procedures to designate an area as a SPAB, SCI or SAC,

The clarity of the Law does not go hand in hand with public authorities' decisions or courts' ruling. When public authorities designate SPAB and elaborate the proposal of SCI – in order to be included in Natura 2000 network – the Supreme Court has ruled that there is no obligation to open a public information stage because the resolution is an administrative decision and not a regulation. Supreme Court's ruling states that the law only obliges to open a public participation stage when the resolution is a regulation.[26]

The first issue that must be discussed is the reason why the Supreme Court differentiates between administrative decisions and regulations. There is a major debate around this issue in both the European Union and the member states' domestic legislation. However, in this particular case there is no need to determine whether the decision is administrative or regulatory because the Spanish Law on Birds, Sites of Community Importance and Special Areas of Conservation, establishes that a public information stage is compulsory in order to classify a natural area into one of the categories the law sets. It makes no mention as to whether that declaration is made by administrative decision or regulation. Nevertheless, the Spanish Supreme Court has ruled that if the designation of SCI or SPAB is administrative in nature, public authorities are not obliged to open a public information stage. In other words, the Supreme Court sets that public authorities must open such a stage only when the decision is regulatory in nature, and this is not what the law states.

The Supreme Court's jurisprudence is misguided and does not comply with the law for at least a couple of reasons. Firstly, the Supreme and Regional Courts have not set out a clear ruling on the nature of the resolution. In some cases, they have established that the designation of a SCI or SPAB is of administrative nature and, sometimes, of regulatory nature.[27] This evidences that there is no clarity on the legal nature of those resolutions. Secondly, the law in force – international, European and Spanish regulations – expressly sets the obligation of public authorities to open a participation stage. Actually, the Spanish Law number 42/2007 clearly defines the stage as compulsory regardless of the nature of the decision – Articles 43 and 45 Law number 42/2007. In this manner, we can draw the conclusion that the Supreme Court's ruling does not enforce the current legislation. Even more, instead of facilitating the exercising of the right, the Court interprets it restrictively.

Courts are also under the rule of international law and they must apply it to particular cases, which has not happened with regard to public participation in environmental issues so far. Specifically, the Aarhus Convention sets the right to public information and participation in connection not only with legislative

---

procedures which must include a public information stage – articles 43 and 45 Law number 42/2007.

26 Spanish Supreme Court's Judgments: 5 September 2013, 26 February 2010, 20 May 2008.

27 Spanish Supreme Court's Judgment 5 September 2013.

instruments but also with programmes and policies which can be understood as regulations. This means that neither public authorities nor courts comply with the legislation in Spain.[28]

3.2. 'SUBSTANTIVE AMENDMENT' AS A LEGAL CATEGORY

Public information in environmental plans frequently encounters problems which may be the result of two different reasons: the normal course of the plan in itself, or the consequence of public authorities' deliberate actions aimed at hiding parts of the project. The latter happens when authorities replace the initial another by another with very different provisions.

Some legal instruments deny the possibility of opening a second stage of public information when the amendments of the project are not substantive.[29] The question to be raised is what 'substantive amendment' means. As mentioned before, the authorities entitled to pass a project may introduce problematic clauses after the first public participation stage. In this manner, citizens and the people concerned cannot exercise their right to participate effectively, what makes the right a real fraud. Certainly, we may think that if the modifications are not relevant, a new public information stage becomes unnecessary because it would postpone the decision excessively.

In view of all of this, there is a need to define the legal meaning of 'substantive amendment', which can be done in an abstract or a specific way. Thus, Courts have defined this legal concept in very different manners. Recently, the Constitutional Court declared a law unconstitutional because it did not comply with the Parliament's legislative act-making process. Modifications were introduced by the Senate into the legislative act, some of which could not have been debated in the Parliament. If these situations occur in the Parliament, this is still more likely to happen when public authorities pass regulations.[30] In order to open a new participation stage, what should be taken into account is not the effect on some individuals but the changes in the previously adopted territorial model.[31] The Supreme Court understands that 'substantial amendments' occur when essential lines and criteria of the plan and its structure are changed in such a way that it looks like as if it was a new plan.[32]

---

[28] Although it is not that clearly stated in the Convention and there is an important debate on the issue. See *J. Jendroska*, Public participation in the preparation of plans and programs: some reflections on the scope of obligations under Article 7 of the Aarhus Convention, Journal for European Environmental and Planning Law, Volume 6, Issue 4, 2009, p. 496.

[29] Spanish Law number 27/2006, Article 18(3), 2nd indent.

[30] Whether they are passed by councils, autonomous communities or the state.

[31] This is, the territorial model set before the first public information stage.

[32] Spanish Supreme Court's Judgments 2 July 2014, 2 March 2004, 13 June 2001.

The Supreme Court's consideration is a major one. It can be inferred from it that public information is not a guarantee of the individuals but of the environment or the spatial planning. Either way, this ruling raises some questions. The right to property may be affected when some usages of the land are prohibited and these prohibitions are extended to other lands not included in the initial project. In such a case, the Supreme Court has stated that if some lands were not previously affected by the decision of the authorities but, as a consequence of the public information stage they became included in the project, it would not be necessary to open a new public information stage.[33] However, if other rights – different from property – are affected, such as health or equity in the distribution of benefits and burdens, this ruling hardly seems appropriate. In a particular case which reached the Supreme Court, the essence and purpose set in the initial project was not altered and only some minor measures were introduced to ensure further protection of the environment[34], which was the actual aim of the project.

A modification to be considered as a 'substantial amendment' has to affect the structure or the aim of the project. In the words of the Court, it has to affect 'structural elements such as surface or forestry'. For example, if the location of a motorway is changed and the last amendment is more disruptive than the previous one, a new public information stage has to be opened.

The principle of legal certainty implies that citizens should know, as precisely as possible, if a first public information stage can be followed by changes that would not be debated in a following public information stage. The Aarhus Convention and State's Law number 27/2006, clearly set the right to participate in the decision-making processes regarding plans, projects and policies – which includes regulations, but the regulation should specify the cases in which a project should undergo substantive modifications. If the law was clearer, it would guarantee the principle of legal certainty in the exercising of citizens' right to participate and would not be a fraud. It is not an easy job to define it but it is highly advisable in order to protect citizens' right.

3.3. IMPOSITION OF SPECIFIC OBLIGATIONS TO PUBLIC AUTHORITIES BY COURTS

The rights to information and participation ruled in the norms mentioned above, principally the Aarhus Convention, have had an important effect on environmental matters. These rights or the defective exercising of them can result in specific obligations for the authorities imposed by courts. In a particular case, the person concerned sent the Government of the Autonomous Community of Valencia to trial. He asked a Council for some information about a quarry, specifically about

33 Even if the protection of the area implied the prohibition of some usages not previously banned.

34 The new measures were aimed to protect the cork oak, a native tree species in the area.

the licence and inspections made in it, but the Council did not give a response. He requested an answer from the Government of the Autonomous Community[35] and asked for the opening of a sanction procedure against the company because it was operating with no license.

The fact that the people concerned may request public authorities to open a sanction procedure arises some questions from the point of view of Administrative Law's theory. We may ask whether the power to impose sanctions is a fully discretional competence of the authorities or whether authorities are obliged to initiate a procedure when the law is not being complied with, in this very case, by the company.[36]

We may also ask about the usefulness of the right of access to information if 1) the information is not given on time or 2) if it is not possible to make authorities take action to solve the problems evidenced by the information provided. Valencia's regional court set its ruling on the issue and obliged Authorities to start a sanction procedure. This showed that the right to participate is of major importance because, in cases like this, unless there were citizens' complaints, authorities would not take any action against the infringing company. The Court set the following ruling: 1) the appellant has the right to get public information and public authorities must provide him with the information about the quarry's licence, its characteristics and the inspections made in it; 2) from the information obtained, it can be easily deduced that the quarry does not have a licence; therefore, the applicant is entitled to ask public authorities to take some actions. In particular, the court sets that public authorities must inspect the quarry within one month and the Autonomous Community of Valencia must finalise the file against the company and issue the closure of the quarry; 3) finally, the court ordered the authorities to open a sanction procedure against the owner of the company for not having the compulsory licence to operate.

As a result of this judgement, it can be deduced that citizens asking for environmental information can derive in legal obligations towards public authorities, which was dubious up to now. This judgement represents a major step forward, although it has been established by a regional court and not by the Supreme Court, which would be best placed to provide ruling on this issue.

3.4. NULLITY

Some Regional Courts have annulled regulations and decisions due to the omission of any possibility of citizens to participate during the rulemaking and the decision-making process. In those cases, the authorities' obligation to provide means of participation was very clearly stated by law and it was evident

---

35 The law set that when a Council does not answer the Government can give answer on its behalf.

36 Judgment of the Regional Court of Valencia, 22 December 2008.

that they did not comply with the requirements. For instance, such were the following cases: 1) Judgement of the Regional Court of Valencia, April 8, 20. In this case, the Natural Resources' Management Plan's modifications had been passed without any public information and were declared annulled by court. The Court understood that the modifications made to the Plan had been 'substantive' because they consisted of leaving a previously protected natural area unprotected; and 2) Judgment of Regional Court of Catalonia, 3 December 2013. In this case, the content of the plan examined had not been completely published, what impeded citizens' participation.

4. CONCLUSIONS

Spanish jurisprudence is not clear in its ruling on the nature of the resolutions that designate SAC, SCI and SPAB. In some cases, the Supreme Court has set that such a resolution is administrative in nature, which means that a public participation stage is not necessary. However, in other cases in which public participation was not involved, the court set that they were of regulatory nature. Sometimes the court has set the resolution was an administrative decision in nature and established that a public participation stage was compulsory. However, in the particular case studied here, they decided it was not necessary because the resolution was only based on objective criteria.[37]

The distinction made by the court between regulations and administrative decisions – without observing the law– results in the breach of the obligation of public authorities to open a participation stage in every case. Another obstacle that citizens encounter to exercise public participation is when authorities modify an already adopted project. Quite frequently public authorities introduce a number of minor amendments in the initial project with the aim of avoiding a public information stage, so that citizens cannot ask for participation. In our view, every amendment should be accessible to public participation. In fact, the law only excludes organisational and procedure regulations from participation.

The regional court of Valencia's judgement is very positive since it clearly acknowledges the right of citizens to participate. The information provided during this stage may evidence the hazardous activity of a company which is operating without licence and in which no inspection is being carried out. In spite of the theoretical limits imposed by Administrative Law's theory, the regional court of Valencia obliged authorities to open a sanction procedure, along with the obligation to finish the company's closure.[38]

---

37 Although Article 44 Spanish Law number 42/2007 obliges public authorities to open it in any case.

38 We shall remember that they did not hold a licence to operate as a quarry and were not being properly inspected by public authorities.

Although this paper does not cover all the wealth of jurisprudence on the issue and the different areas of environmental law, we can conclude that the ruling of the courts is not clear enough. On the one hand, participation is protected by courts only when the decision is a regulation, but it is not when it is an administrative decision, although the law makes no difference between them. On the other, the refusal to open a second information stage is also an obstacle to the proper implementation of the right just because the modification of the project is not 'substantive', more so when 'substantive modification' has not been clearly defined.

Undoubtedly, the major step forward of this jurisprudence is the possibility of public authorities to be compelled by courts both to close a company and to impose a sanction for operating without licence. It is also remarkable that Courts have declared some decisions and regulations null for not having offered citizens the possibility to participate. Nevertheless, there still remains much to be done. Although the general law protects participation in quite wide terms, in line with the Aarhus Convention, public participation cannot be considered a real right until authorities and courts implement the law in force adequately. An 'adequate implementation' means not putting obstacles to public participation that are not set in the law, such as limiting the right's scope by denying participation when the resolution is an administrative decision or a regulation, or by restricting the right alleging that the modification has not been substantive. We shall bear in mind that authorities and Courts' attitude towards the right to participate in environmental matters also has to do with the strength or weakness of their democratic values.

5. BIBLIOGRAPHY

A. Aragao, Los impactos ambientales transfronterizos, entre el hecho y el derecho, A. García Ureta (Edit.), La Directiva de la Unión Europea de Evaluación de Impacto Ambiental de proyectos: balance de 30 años, Marcial Pons, Madrid, 2016, pp. 157–172.

M.N. Arrese & I. Lazkano, La jurisprudencia del Tribunal Superior de Justicia del País Vasco en materia ambiental, Anuario de Derecho Ambiental - IeZ, 2016, 14, pp. 205–221. *Idem*, La jurisprudencia del Tribunal Superior de Justicia del País Vasco en materia ambiental, Anuario de Derecho Ambiental - IeZ, 2015, 13, pp. 159–175. *Idem*, La jurisprudencia del Tribunal Superior de Justicia del País Vasco en materia ambiental, Anuario de Derecho Ambiental - IeZ, 2014, 12, pp. 250–261.

M.C. Bolaño, El procedimiento de declaración de calidad del suelo en la Comunidad Autónoma del País Vasco, Revista Aranzadi de Derecho Ambiental, 2015 (30), pp. 259–294.

G.F. Cartei, The Implementation of the European Landscape convention and Public Participation, European Public Law, 2012 (18.2), pp. 269–282.

C.H. Born, El juez europeo y la directiva de impacto ambiental: balance de treinta años, A. García Ureta (Edit.), La Directiva de la Unión Europea de Evaluación de Impacto Ambiental de proyectos: balance de 30 años, Marcial Pons, Madrid, 2016, pp. 9–28.

J.I. Cubero Marcos, La transposición de la Directiva en el Estado español, A. García Ureta (Edit.), La Directiva de la Unión Europea de Evaluación de Impacto Ambiental de proyectos: balance de 30 años, Marcial Pons, Madrid, 2016, pp. 65–90.

J.I. Cubero, La jurisprudencia del Tribunal Superior de Justicia de la Comunidad Foral de Navarra", Anuario de Derecho Ambiental - IeZ, 2016 (14), pp.222–247; *Idem*, La jurisprudencia del Tribunal Superior de Justicia de la Comunidad Foral de Navarra, Anuario de Derecho Ambiental - IeZ, 2015 (13), pp. 176–205. *Idem*, La jurisprudencia del Tribunal Superior de Justicia de la Comunidad Foral de Navarra, Anuario de Derecho Ambiental - IeZ, 2014, 12, pp. 262–280.

J.I. Cubero, Proyectos y planes aprobados por Ley: contradicciones a la luz de la evaluación ambiental, el derecho de participación y el acceso a la justicia en materia ambiental, Revista Vasca de Administración Pública, 2014, 99/100, pp. 1007–1039.

J.I. Cubero, M. Iturribarria, & I. Lasagabaster, Acceso a la información, Participación y Acceso a la Justicia en materia de Medio Ambiente / Informazioa eskuratzea, parte-hartzea eta epaitegietara jotzea ingurumen arloan, Servicio Central de Publicaciones del Gobierno Vasco, Vitoria-Gasteiz, 2009, *in totum*.

A. Garcia, Algunas cuestiones sobre la regulación del derecho de participación a la luz del Convenio de Aarhus de 1998, Revista Aranzadi de Derecho Ambiental, 2005 (7), pp. 43–70.

M. Iovane, La participation de la société civile à l'élaboration et à l'application du droit international de l'environnement, Revue Générale de Droit International Public, 2008, 112.3, pp. 465–519.

B. Jadot, Faire payer au public le "droit" de participation au processus de décisions en matière d'environnement?, Revue européenne de droit de l'environnement, 2007 (2), pp. 171–180.

Y. Jegouzo, La Loi Grenelle II: La réforme des enquêtes publiques et la mise en oeuvre du principe de participation, Actualité Juridique - Droit Administrative, 2010 (32), pp. 1812–1818.

J. Jendroska, Public Participation in Environmental Decision-Making. Interactions between the Convention and EU Law and other Key Legal Issues in its Implementation in the Light of the Opinions of the Aarhus Convention Compliance Committee, M. Pallemaerts (Edit.), Interactions and Tensions between Conventional International Law and EU Environmental Law, Europe Law Publishing, 2011, pp. 93–147.

J. Jendroska, Public participation in the preparation of plans and programs: some reflections on the scope of obligations under Article 7 of the Aarhus Convention, Journal for European Environmental and Planning Law, Volume 6, Issue 4, 2009, pp. 495–515.

J. Jendroska, Aarhus Convention and Community Law: the Interplay, Journal for European Environmental & Planning Law, Volume 2, Issue 1, 2005, pp. 12–21.

I. Lasagabaster & M.C. Bolaño, Public Participation in Land Management Law-Making Process in the Basque Country: Effects on Soil and Other Natural Resources, B. Vanheusden & L. Squintani (Eds.), EU Environmental and Planning Law. Aspects of Large-Scale Projects, Intersentia, 2016, pp. 367–384.

I. Lasagabaster, Notas sobre el derecho administrativo de la información, Ricardo Jesús García Macho (Edit.), Derecho administrativo de la información y administración transparente, 2010, pp. 103–120.

I. Lasagabaster & M.C. Bolaño, Medio Ambiente y Obligación de Difusión, Ingurugiroa eta Zuzenbidea, 2009 (7), pp. 21–34.

O. Montouto & J. Lusi, ¿Cómo participaron los ciudadanos de los municipios de Albacete en sus procesos de Agenda 21 local?, Ecosostenible, 2009 (56) pp. 19–33. *Ídem*, Aproximación al "empadronamiento" de los ciudadanos en la gestión local y su evaluación como herramienta de democracia participativa, Ecosostenible, 2009, 57, pp. 25–37.

A. Nogueira López, La participación en la evaluación de impacto ambiental, dogma y realidad, A. García Ureta (Edit.), La Directiva de la Unión Europea de Evaluación de Impacto Ambiental de proyectos: balance de 30 años, Marcial Pons, Madrid, 2016, pp. 117–156.

R.J. Santamaría, Evaluando al evaluador: razones técnicas, jurídicas y políticas en la evaluación de impacto ambiental de proyectos, A. García Ureta (Edit.), La Directiva de la Unión Europea de Evaluación de Impacto Ambiental de proyectos: balance de 30 años, Marcial Pons, Madrid, 2016, pp. 29–63.

C.O. Sanz Salla, El derecho a la información administrativa en la era digital: una aproximación al derecho norteamericano, Ricardo Jesús García Macho (Coord.),

Derecho administrativo de la información y administración transparente,, 2010, pp. 203–230.

K.P. Sommermann, La exigencia de una Administración transparente en la perspectiva de los principios de democracia y del Estado de Derecho, Ricardo Jesús García Macho (Edit.), Derecho administrativo de la información y administración transparente, 2010, pp. 11–26.

F. Spagnuolo, Beyond Participation: Administrative-Law Type Mechanisms in Global Environmental Governance. Toward a New Basis of Legitimacy?, Public Law, 2009, spring, pp. 49–61.

I. Urrutia, La jurisprudencia del Tribunal Supremo en materia ambiental, Anuario de Derecho Ambiental - IeZ, 2016 (14), pp. 173–204; *Idem*, La jurisprudencia del Tribunal Supremo en materia ambiental, Anuario de Derecho Ambiental - IeZ, 2015 (13), pp.132–158; *Idem*, La jurisprudencia del Tribunal Supremo en materia ambiental, Anuario de Derecho Ambiental - IeZ, 2014 (12), pp. 218–249.

6. JURISPRUDENCE

ECJ Judgment, Cases C-530/11, Commission v United Kingdom [2014]; C-72/12, Gemeinde Altrip and Others [2013]; C-612/13 P, ClientEarth v Commission [2015]; C-71/14, East Sussex County Council [2015].

Spanish Supreme Court's Judgments: 2 July 2014, 5 September 2013, 26 February 2010, 20 May 2008, 2 March 2004, 13 June 2001.

Judgment of the Regional Court of Valencia, 22 December 2008.

LEGAL INSTRUMENTS TO PROTECT INDIGENOUS PEOPLES' PARTICIPATION IN EUROPE AND IN THE ARCTIC REGION*

Margherita Paola Poto**

"I support the indigenous people anywhere in the planet."
Edward James Olmos

ABSTRACT

The paper describes the participatory mechanisms granted to minorities or indigenous groups in Europe and in the Arctic Region.

The first part analyses various legal instruments approved in Europe (and more specifically by the Council of Europe and by the Organization for Security and Cooperation in Europe) to protect and safeguard the status and the participatory rights of minorities and indigenous groups at international, regional and national level.

The second part explores the initiatives undertaken by the Arctic Council and then more specifically by Norway as an example of Arctic State, that grants to the Arctic indigenous peoples an active role as decision makers and participants in environmentally-related decisions.

---

* This contribution follows the logical development of the author's research project on the Arctic environmental governance and it is linked with previous works concerning: 1. The participation of the Indigenous Peoples in the Arctic Council's decisions; 2. The indigenous peoples engagement in actions aiming to protect biodiversity at national level. *M. Poto*, Participatory engagement and the empowerment of the Arctic indigenous peoples, *Environmental Law Review*, 2017, March, 30–47.; *I. Jakobsen, M. Poto*, Biodiversity conservation in the Arctic: the Norwegian Perspective, Environmental Liability: Law, Policy and Practice, 2016, f. 6; *M.P. Poto, L. Fornabaio*, Participation as the essence of good governance: some general reflections and a case study on the Arctic Council, forthcoming in Arctic Review on Law and Politics, vol. 8, 2017, pp. 137–157. The research is funded by the K.G. Jebsen Centre for the Law of the Sea, UiT, Tromsø, Norway.

** Postdoctoral Fellow at the K.G. Jebsen Centre for the Law of the Sea, UiT, Tromsø, Norway. For correspondence: margherita.p.poto@uit.no.

The scope of such a dual analysis is to show that only an inclusive approach can offer an effective restoration to the injustice of marginalisation. The inclusive stance has a dual meaning: first, it allows to apply legal restorative provisions to the widest extent of groups, no matter what formal category they fall into; second, it orientates such provisions to the common scope of fulfilling the substantive equality principle.

The inclusive approach does not foresee any contrast between the international instruments that provide restorative rights to minorities and indigenous groups and the regional provisions that grant an official status to the indigenous groups, as well as other effective mandatory tools to engage them in decision-making processes; it rather encourages the application of minimum standards for responding to the needs of vulnerable groups.

KEYWORDS

Arctic; Environmental decision making; Europe; Indigenous peoples; Minority groups; Participatory rights

1. INTRODUCTORY REMARKS

This work offers a dual analysis of different legal regimes that aim to restore and protect the indigenous peoples' substantive and procedural rights: a regional overview of the indigenous rights' protection in Europe (with a focus on the international conventions approved by the European Council and the Organization for Security and Cooperation in Europe, OSCE) and an analysis of the state-of-the-art of the indigenous peoples' protection in the Arctic Region (Arctic Council at regional level; Norway at national level). The scope is to show that only an inclusive approach can offer an effective restoration to the injustice of marginalisation. The inclusive stance allows to apply legal restorative provisions to the widest extent of groups, no matter what formal category they fall into; additionally, it orientates such provisions to the common scope of fulfilling the substantive equality principle.

The inclusive approach does not foresee any contrast between the international instruments that provide restorative rights to minorities and indigenous groups and the regional provisions that grant an official status to the indigenous groups[1], as well as other effective mandatory tools to engage them in decision-making processes.[2]

---

1 As in the case of the Arctic Council, where the indigenous peoples are established as Permanent Participants in a non-binding international forum.

2 As it happened respectively, in the Finnmark Act 2005 and in the Norwegian Nature Diversity Act 2009.

The extra emphasis given to the participatory guarantees for specific target groups, such as the indigenous peoples, speaks for itself: the international community, be it the European Union or the Arctic Council, had to restore an ancestral injustice related to an unfortunate long series of land expropriation, redistribution, marginalisation when not discrimination. The traditional legal instruments designed to facilitate a broader participation of the civil society in the environmental decisions (such as the Århus Convention[3]) have not been sufficient to offer an adequate level of protection to the effective participation of specific target groups. The process to grant them an effective engagement to environmental issues had to start early on and had to be developed on different forefronts: from the effective restitution of the lands they originally inhabited, to the recognition of the self-determination principle (as formulated in the ILO Convention n. 169[4]); to any substantial action preventing discrimination (such as the international instruments to protect regional or minority languages[5]); finally, to the recognition of procedural rights that could enable their voice to be effectively heard and their social and ecological interests to be taken in due consideration (examples in this regard are the legal provisions engaging the Sami peoples in the political and administrative life: the Finnmark Act 2005[6] and the Norwegian Nature Diversity Act, NDA, 2009[7]).

---

3 The United Nations Economic Commission for Europe (UNECE) Convention on Access to Information, Public Participation in Decision-Making and Access to Justice in Environmental Matters was adopted on 25 June 1998 in Århus at the Fourth Ministerial Conference as part of the "Environment for Europe" process. It entered into force on 30 October 2001. For recent up-dates and the follow-up process see the UNECE Convention website. More specifically, the Aarhus Convention has structured participation into three main pillars, dealing with: (1) the right of access to information; (2) the right to participate in decision-making, and (3) the right of access to justice in environmental matters. The pillars reflect the shift in mentality required to the Aarhus Convention parties in terms of opening up the doors of environmental decisions to good administration principles, such as transparency, participation, and judicial review.

4 Convention n. 169, International Labour Organization (27 June 1989), Art. 1(2). Available at: www.ilo.org/indigenous/Conventions/no169/lang–en/index.htm. See also The United Nations Declaration on the Rights of Indigenous Peoples: A Manual for National Human Rights Institutions. Joint Publication of the Office of the United Nations High Commissioner for Human Rights (OHCHR) and the Asia Pacific Forum of National Human Rights Institutions (APF). Available at: www.ohchr.org/Documents/Issues/IPeoples/UNDRIPManualForNHRIs.pdf (last accessed 22 July 2016).

5 UN Declaration on the Rights of Persons Belonging to National or Ethnic, religious and Linguistic Minorities; the Council of Europe Protocol Number 12 to the Convention for the Protection of Human Rights and Fundamental Freedoms, Framework Convention for the Protection of National Minorities; the OSGE Copenhagen Document and the Lund Recommendations on the Effective Participation of National Minorities in Public Life. See later on Section 2.

6 Finnmark Act (Act No. 85 of 17 June 2005 relating to Legal Relations and Management of Land and Natural Resources in the County of Finnmark), published in English on the WIPO official website: www.wipo.int/wipolex/en/details.jsp?id=11129, visited in February 2017.

7 The NDA entered into force on 1 July 2009 can be considered the best example of biodiversity. The act was developed thanks to an intensive consultation process, with all the relevant economic sectors, as well as the Sami Parliament. The major aim was to protect

In other words, the reasons to set up a higher level of protection and preferential rights for indigenous peoples are inherent in the need to provide "a reparation for the lack of understanding with which they were treated in earlier periods", as the International Conference of American State expressly stated in 1938.[8] The acknowledgement of fundamental rights to indigenous peoples is the way to give content to a moral recognition of wrongdoing and lay the foundations of a well-governed system, where self-governance, economic independence and social and cultural autonomy are at the core.

2. PART I

2.1. INDIGENOUS PEOPLES' PARTICIPATORY RIGHTS IN EUROPE

Two peculiar traits connote the legal protection of indigenous peoples in Europe: first, such a protection has been historically focused on minorities, rather than on indigenous groups. As a consequence, the work of the interpreter seems to be quite laborious when trying to apply such guarantees to the specific indigenous groups.[9] Second, it originally focused on those national minorities resulting from the land redistribution after the two World Wars.

Such a preoccupation was addressed mainly to restore the minorities' rights of the peoples of Central and Eastern Europe[10], rather than to provide a wide spectrum of guarantees (substantive and procedural) to the minorities whose rights had been denied and violated. A similar worry was not risen, for example, in the case of indigenous peoples of Northern Scandinavia and the Arctic Peoples of the Russian Federation, as well as the Inuit people of Greenland.[11]

A symptom of such a legal backwardness and gap in protection is recognisable in the wordings of the Permanent Court of International Justice that, in the Eastern Greenland Case, although acknowledging the presence of the Inuit population in the territory in question, did not consider them "as relevant

biological, geological and landscape diversity, as well as the ecological processes through the conservation and sustainable use of natural resources. Lov om forvaltning av naturens mangfold (naturmangfoldloven), available in Norwegian at https://lovdata.no/dokument/NL/lov/2009-06-19-100, visited in February 2017. An translation for information use only is available at https://www.regjeringen.no/en/dokumenter/nature-diversity-act/id570549/, visited in February 2017: Act of 19 June 2009 No. 100 Relating to the Management of Biological, Geological and Landscape Diversity (Nature Diversity Act).

8 Protection of the American Indigenous Population, Res No 11, 8th International Conference of American States, Final Act, 1938, 29.

9 *S. Errico and B.A. Hocking*, (2008), Reparations for Indigenous Peoples in Europe: the Case of the Sami People, in F. Lenzerini (ed. by), Reparations for Indigenous Peoples. International and Comparative Perspectives, Oxford University Press, pp. 363–388.

10 Ibidem, 367.

11 Ibidem, 367.

actors in the case, nor were their wishes taken into consideration".[12] It was only in the late 1990s, that the European Council and the Organization for Security and Cooperation in Europe (CSCE/OSCE) started developing a regulatory framework to protect the indigenous peoples' rights, though still under the qualification of minorities' rights. The achievement in reaching high standards of fundamental rights' protection has been quite remarkable since then, and various international instruments have been consequently approved: among them, it is worth mentioning the UN Declaration on the Rights of Persons Belonging to National or Ethnic, religious and Linguistic Minorities; the Council of Europe Protocol Number 12 to the Convention for the Protection of Human Rights and Fundamental Freedoms, Framework Convention for the Protection of National Minorities[13]; the OSCE Copenhagen Document and the Lund Recommendations on the Effective Participation of National Minorities in Public Life.[14]

It is necessary to add a rider on the application of such provisions to indigenous groups. While the Framework Convention has been applied also to European indigenous peoples[15], this is not the case of Norway, where the Sami continued to hold the view, already stated under the first monitoring cycle of the Framework Convention and then re-expressed and reported in occasion of the Second Opinion of the Advisory Committee, that government policy on national minorities should not be applied to them.[16]

Such a firm stance did not automatically imply that the Framework Convention was without effects in Norway, since the Advisory Committee anyway expressed its satisfaction at the measures taken by the Norwegian institutions to improve the situation of the Sami population, recognised and protected in Norway as indigenous peoples.[17] The Advisory Committee quotes the Finnmark Act No. 85 of June 17, 2005 as the most significant example of cooperation between the

12 Legal Status of Eastern Greenland (*Den v. Nor*), 1933, PCIJ 8ser A/B), No 53.

13 The Framework Convention for the Protection of National Minorities, drawn up within the Council of Europe by Ad Hoc Committee for the Protection of National Minorities (CAHMIN) under the authority of the Committee of Ministers, was adopted by the Committee of Ministers of the Council of Europe on 10 November 1994 and opened for signature by the member States of the Council of Europe on 1 February 1995. See https://rm.coe.int/16800c10cf (accessed June 2nd, 2017).

14 The Lund Recommendations on the Effective Participation of National Minorities in Public Life & Explanatory Note September 1999, Published and disseminated by the OSCE High Commissioner on National Minorities (HCNM) avaiable at: www.osce.org/hcnm/32240?download=true (accessed 7 June 2017).

15 *S. Errico and B.A. Hocking*, (2008), Reparations for Indigenous Peoples in Europe: the Case of the Sami People, in F. Lenzerini cit., p. 367 fn. 22.

16 Second Opinion on Norway adopted on 5 October 2006, ACFC/OP/II (2006)006, 16 November 2006, para 8. See https://www.regjeringen.no/globalassets/upload/aid/temadokumenter/nasjonale_minoriteter/nasjmin_europaradets_tilbakem_norges_andre_rapp_eng.pdf (accessed June 8th, 2017).

17 The Advisory Committee quotes the Finnmark Act No. 85 of 17 June 2005 as the most significant example of cooperation between the National Parliament and the Sami Institutions. See Second Opinion on Norway cit., para 8.

National Parliament and the Sami Institutions, since its approval resulted from the concerted activities of the two Parties and consequently, the content of the Finnmark Act was oriented to enhance the participation of the Sami groups in decisions related to the county of Finnmark. In the opinion of the Advisory Committee, a provision of this kind was certainly encouraged by the favourable climate created by the Framework Convention that significantly contributed to promoting diversity and intercultural dialogue in Norway.[18]

Before analysing in detail the above mentioned legal provisions, it is worth adding a short critical remark to such a conclusion, that gives emphasis on the importance to adopt an inclusive approach when the final purpose of the legal provisions is to provide wider protection to social groups heavily marginalised or at risk of marginalisation. Though the position of the Advisory Committee is largely shareable, it is also true that a legal exception system as the one endorsed by the Sami groups, may risk to cause a gap in the national protection of other minorities – yet not necessarily indigenous to the land they inhabit – that may also suffer of discrimination in the participation to public life.

A more stringent system of guarantees, such as the one set up for the Sami of Norway, should not prevent to implement general provisions protecting all the other minorities living in the territory of the country and entitled to the same participatory rights as the rest of the population.

The inner scope of providing extra protection to minorities is to heal a severe wound in peoples' autonomy and determination, no matter what denomination or category they fall into. It shall not make any difference whether the group in question is qualified as a "minority" or "indigenous". On the contrary, the common ground of protection shall be based on a concerted decision to fully restore the rightful parties: here the need to provide the widest range of guarantees, by extensively interpreting the legal provisions to any group that suffered analogous threats to their identity and environment.

2.2. INTERNATIONAL INSTRUMENTS AND RECOMMENDED REFORMS TO ENHANCE PARTICIPATION OF EUROPEAN MINORITIES

In this paragraph, the legal provisions on minority groups' participation in Europe will be further scrutinised, in connection with the set of reforms that are foreseen as implementing measures. Special attention will be dedicated to the Framework Convention, to the OSGE Copenhagen Document and to the Oslo Recommendations regarding the Linguistic rights of Minorities[19], as well as to

18 Ibidem, para 8.

19 The Oslo Recommendations Regarding the Linguistic Rights of National Minorities & Explanatory Note February 1998, Published and disseminated by the

the Lund Recommendations, that, as said, have been applied to the indigenous groups in Europe and should be extended – in the opinion of the author – to any target groups in need of protection also in those countries that already have a specific set of rules for indigenous groups.

Within the Council of Europe, the Framework Convention for the Protection of National Minorities[20] expressly lists fundamental rights to minority groups and contemplates, among them, the participatory rights to public decision making processes.

In particular, Article 15 of the Framework Convention requires the Parties of the Convention to create an environment conducive to the effective participation to minority groups in any decision that can affect their interests, by stating that "The Parties shall create the conditions necessary for the effective participation of persons belonging to national minorities in cultural, social and economic life and in public affairs, in particular those affecting them".[21]

The objective of such a provision is to encourage and support the implementation of the substantive equality principle between persons belonging to national minorities and those forming part of the majority.[22]

The first reforming steps are probably to be set up at constitutional level, by providing a wide range of measures traditionally associated to participation's enhancements, and namely: 1) free prior consultation to any decision affecting the minorities' rights, by means of their representative institutions; 2) educational programs that can equip the participants with a sound knowledge of the decisions' content; 3) strengthened connections and clear allocation of competences between the central government and the local entities, by following the principles of transparency, decentralisation and subsidiarity; 4) effective involvement of the target groups in the preparation, implementation and assessment of national and regional development plans that are likely to affect them directly.

The activities that enable participation are necessarily linked to the need to take into account the linguistic rights of the minorities: in relation to it, and as a further measure that any State should consider in reforming its guarantees' package, both the Copenhagen Document and Oslo Recommendations regarding the Linguistic Rights of Minorities (1998) make reference respectively to the need of creating a conducive environment to the participation of

---

OSCE High Commissioner on National Minorities (HCNM), at: www.osce.org/hcnm/67531?download=true (accessed 7 June 2017).

20 The Framework Convention for the Protection of National Minorities, cit., https://rm.coe.int/16800c10cf (accessed 2 June 2017).

21 Article 15, Framework Convention for the Protection of National Minorities, drawn up within the Council of Europe by Ad Hoc Committee for the Protection of National Minorities (CAHMIN) cit.

22 Specifically, on the application of the principle of substantive equality to indigenous peoples see the UN Declaration on the Rights of Indigenous Peoples approved 13 September 2007 (A/RES/61/295). Available at: www.un.org/esa/socdev/unpfii/documents/DRIPS_en.pdf (accessed 9 June 2017).

minorities in public affairs in their own language (paragraph 35 Copenhagen Document) and to the duty for public authorities "to enable persons belonging to national minorities to deal with local authorities in their language or to receive civil certificates and attestations in their own language" (Sections 13, 14, 15 Oslo Recommendations).[23]

Such measures offer just few of the many examples of the "conditions" that the States have to establish – as per Article 15 of the Framework Convention – in order to guarantee a substantive equality, by means of a constant participatory relationship and a proactive effort to break down communication barriers in the local political life.

Finally, the Lund Recommendations had the merit to frame the participatory rights within a more comprehensive scenario of "good governance". In particular, the Explanatory Note of Paragraph 6 states that: "The essence of participation is involvement, both in terms of the opportunity to make substantive contributions to decision-making processes and in terms of the effect of those contributions. The notion of good governance includes the premise that simple majoritarian decision-making is not always sufficient. In terms of the structure of the State, various forms of decentralization may be appropriate to assure the maximum relevance and accountability of decision-making processes for those affected, both at the level of the State and at sub-State levels. This may be accomplished through various ways in a unitary State or in federal and confederal systems".[24]

In this case, legal provisions that assure reserved seats to minorities are suggested as implementing measures (by way of quotas, promotions or other measures), as well as the assured membership in relevant committees, with or without voting rights. As a further suggestion to take forward the institutional reforms, the Lund Recommendations endorse the establishment of special bodies supervising on the correct implementation of the substantive equality and accommodate minority concerns.[25]

By the means of its broad scope and consequent measures to ensure good governance, the Lund Recommendations confirm the internationally shared vision on the principal role played by participation in building up the foundations of good governance.[26] Such an achievement is only possible if there is common will to merge top down decisions (legal provisions implementing international instruments, as well as national laws and administrative decisions) and bottom-up approaches (such as implementing measures that enhance participation at all levels and a broader civic engagement, which includes minorities and indigenous peoples). In Part II, some examples of concerted decisions will be mentioned to

---

[23] See Oslo Recommendations above cit.
[24] Second Opinion on Norway adopted on 5 October 2006 cit., Explanatory Note.
[25] See The Lund Recommendations above cit.
[26] Ibidem.

illustrate the importance to grant effective participation since the early stage of the decision making process, in order to enable further participatory guarantees to all the engaged parties.

3. PART II

3.1. INDIGENOUS PEOPLES IN THE ARCTIC REGION AND THEIR PARTICIPATION IN ENVIRONMENTAL DECISIONS

This paragraph will be dedicated to the analysis of the current legal regime applied to indigenous peoples in the Arctic Council (AC).

The analysis will then shift to the further guarantees provided to the indigenous groups in the Arctic, in the legal instruments regarding their engagement in planning activities related to the establishments of protected areas. One milestone in this regard is marked by the above mentioned Finnmark Act (2005), that was actually approved thanks to the concerted efforts of the Norwegian Parliament and the Sami institutions; another important achievement is the approval of the Norwegian Nature Biodiversity Act (NDA, 2009), that envisions as fundamental the role of the Sami in any decisions and actions connected to biodiversity protection.

3.2. ADVANCEMENTS IN THE FULL RECOGNITION OF INDIGENOUS PEOPLES' RIGHTS IN THE ARCTIC

The acknowledgement of the indigenous peoples' status as permanent participants in the Arctic Council is certainly a milestone in the direction of a full recognition of their active role as non-State actors in the Arctic decisions, as well as an enhancement in the recognition of their fundamental right to self-determine themselves, also by means of their active participation in public decisions.

The innovative trait of the AC consists precisely in acknowledging the importance of involving parties other than States in decisions on crucial aspects regarding the protection of the Arctic environment. Such a peculiarity is highlighted in the Introductory Note to the Declaration on the Establishment of the AC ("A key feature of the Council initiative is the involvement of the Arctic region's indigenous peoples")[27] and it continued to be strengthened in the

[27] Canada–Denmark–Finland–Iceland–Norway–Russian Federation–Sweden–United States: Joint Communique and Declaration on the Establishment of the Arctic Council (1996) 35 ILM 1386 with an Introductory note from A. Jenks. Currently, six indigenous organisations have permanent participant status: Aleut International Association, Arctic Athabaskan Council, Gwich'n Council International, Inuit Circumpolar Council, Association of Indigenous Peoples

following legal provisions approved by the Arctic States. As examples, it is worth mentioning the approval of the Arctic Search and Rescue (ASR) Agreement adopted in May 2011, and the Agreement on Cooperation on Marine Oil Pollution Preparedness and Response in the Arctic in 2013.[28] Both the agreements are legally binding instruments negotiated under the auspices of the Arctic Council; and in both occasions the indigenous groups were involved in drawing up their content. As a consequence, their participatory rights in environmental issues were fully recognised in the texts of the documents.

A comparable case of active engagement, followed by the recognition of participatory rights, is the approval of the Finnmark Act, formulated to facilitate the land and natural resources management with a rights-based approach, and in particular aimed to provide "a basis for the Sami culture, reindeer husbandry, use of non-cultivated areas, commercial activity and social life".[29]

The Finnmark Act is a vivid example of concerted activity among central, local and indigenous governments, since the beginning of the preparatory works, when the Ministry of Justice had been in constant contact with the Finnmark County Council and the Sami Parliament. Not coincidentally, the act was approved to restore a procedural injustice committed against the Sami: the act followed the lost battle of the hydro-electric power station on the River Alta, where the Sami's voice had not been heard but their demonstrations and civil disobedience echoed to the point of establishing a Sami Act (1987), a constitutional amendment (1988), the Sami Parliament (1989), and finally the Commissions' report on land rights in Finnmark (1997).[30]

The Finnmark Act in this regard is a clear example of legal provision that offered an effective restoration to a factual injustice, but also of a forward-looking act, with the aim to protect natural diversity by restoring and preserving the land rights of the indigenous peoples living in that land, as well as by establishing a consultation procedure between the National Government and the Sami Parliament.

In line with these achievements, the Norwegian Nature Diversity Act (2009)[31] has foreseen the importance to engage the Sami peoples not only in

---

of North (RAIPON) and the Saami Council in Arctic Council "Permanent Participants" www.arctic-council.org/index.php/en/about-us/permanent-participants accessed 15 July 2016. Observer status in the Arctic Council is open to non-Arctic states, intergovernmental and inter-parliamentary organisations, and non-governmental organisations (NGOs).

28 The text of the 2013 Agreement is available at: https://oaarchive.arctic-council.org/bitstream/handle/11374/529/EDOCS-2067-v1ACMMSE08_KIRUNA_2013_agreement_on_oil_pollution_preparedness_and_response__in_the_arctic_formatted.PDF?sequence¼5&isAllowed¼y (accessed 9 June 2017).

29 Sect. 1, Finnmark Act, Act No. 85 of 17 June 2005 cit.

30 *E.G. Broderstad*, Consultations as a tool. The Finnmark Act –an example to follow?, published in http://munin.uit.no/bitstream/handle/10037/3104/article.pdf?sequence=1 (accessed in February 2017).

31 See fn n. 8.

the consultation process of law-making, but also in planning activities on the conservation and sustainable use of natural resources.

The NDA has welcomed an intrinsic approach to protect biodiversity, by giving to the notion a comprehensive meaning, which includes the protection of the environment, as well as the peoples – with their rights and opinions – whose survival is intrinsically linked to the territory: in this regard, the environment has to provide a basis for human activity, culture, health and well-being, now and in the future, including a basis for Sami culture.

The system is rooted on reciprocal trust between the public and the private parties: on the one hand the widest access to all the relevant information is to be granted to the interested parties, and on the other hand all the interested parties have the duty to inform the relevant authorities of any project that affects protected areas and protected species.

As it emerges from Section 41 of the Act, the cooperation among the parties is the password for a transparent procedure: landowners, interested parties, business operators, representatives of the local communities, including the Sami Parliament and other local authorities have to be informed, heard and consulted when the plan proposal for a protected area is to be submitted and the implementing procedure initiated. Similarly, in Section 43, an ex-post mechanism of transparency is disciplined: the proposal shall be subject to public inspection and consultation, and then submitted to municipal authorities, county authorities, central government agencies, as well as Sami Parliament if the proposal affects Sami interests.

4. CONCLUDING REMARKS

The study has illustrated the diversified range of tools that via international instruments, regional agreements and national legal provisions has been granted to minorities and indigenous groups in Europe and in the Arctic. The analysis of fundamental and procedural rights aimed to describe such guarantees as a *continuum*, rather than as a fragmented and sectoral set of conquests, always bearing in mind their specific target (in some cases only minorities; in other cases indigenous groups; in some others both), as well as their regional or local application (Europe, the Arctic region, Norway).

In this sense, the methodology followed an inclusive approach, as the most ideal tool to restore the longstanding series of injustices committed against minorities and indigenous groups. As such, no distinction is made between rules applicable only to minorities and provisions expressly approved to protect indigenous peoples: the contribution rather encouraged an extensive application of the general recommendations formulated at international level for minorities to all the groups that had to endure severe repression and marginalisation. The underlying criterion refers to the international principle of common minimum necessary standards: its use has been increasingly advocated by human rights law[32], as well as by the European law[33] and it implies that minimum guarantees should be in place to offer legal protection to vulnerable groups.

Such standards are sometimes attacked as being too sectoral and even arbitrary, but the fact that their coverage might in some respects reflect compromise, as in the case minorities' principles applied to indigenous groups, does not mean that they cannot be fair, particularly if they help to cover legal gaps in those systems that do not offer an adequate level of protection to marginalised groups.

32 See, for example, the Declaration of Minimum Humanitarian Standards Adopted by an expert meeting convened by the Institute for Human Rights, Åbo Akademi University, in Turku/Åbo Finland, 2 December 1990, at www.ifrc.org/Docs/idrl/I149EN.pdf (accessed 12 June 2017).

33 *G. Falkner, O. Treib, M. Hartlapp, S. Leiber,* Complying with Europe? The Impact of EU Minimum Harmonisation and Soft Law in the Member States, at www.ihs.ac.at/publications/pol/TreibECPR2004.pdf (accessed 12 June 2017).

NOTIFYING THE PUBLIC AS A PART OF THE PUBLIC PARTICIPATION PROCEDURE IN EU, POLISH AND UKRAINIAN LAW

Viktoriia RACHYNSKA*

ABSTRACT

This article analyses whether EU, Polish, current and planned Ukrainian law are compliant with the Aarhus Convention requirement to public notification during the public participation procedure. This article concerns the personal scope of public notification: the entity responsible for notifying and the entity entitled to get notified. Secondly, it covers the timeliness and effectiveness of public notification. The first one means that the notification shall take place early enough in the public participation procedure as well as in the whole decision-making procedure. The second one is connected to spreading public notification among the entities entitled and willing to participate in the decision making. That could be done via public notice published in printed media, posted at the territory where an activity is planned or at the territory that could be affected by it, disseminated through mass media (TV, radio) or through electronic means, as well as via individual notice.

KEYWORDS

Aarhus Convention; EIA Directive; individual notice; public; public concerned; public notice; public notification; public participation procedure

INTRODUCTION

In accordance with the requirements of international, European and Polish national law when making decisions in environmental matters public authorities should provide the public with an opportunity to participate. Notification on the

* PhD candidate, Opole University.

initiation of the decision-making and of the public participation procedure is the first stage of the public participation procedure.

At international level this stage is mainly regulated in the UNECE Convention *On Access to Information, Public Participation in Decision-making and Access to Justice in Environmental Matters*. It was signed on 25 June 1998 in the Danish city of Aarhus[1] (hereinafter – the Aarhus Convention).

According to Article 6.2 of the Aarhus Convention:

> "The public concerned shall be informed, either by public notice or individually as appropriate, early in an environmental decision-making procedure, and in an adequate, timely and effective manner, inter alia, of:
> (a) The proposed activity and the application on which a decision will be taken;
> (b) The nature of possible decisions or the draft decision;
> (c) The public authority responsible for making the decision;
> (d) The envisaged procedure, including, as and when this information can be provided:
> (i) The commencement of the procedure;
> (ii) The opportunities for the public to participate;
> (iii) The time and venue of any envisaged public hearing;
> (iv) An indication of the public authority from which relevant information can be obtained and where the relevant information has been deposited for examination by the public;
> (v) An indication of the relevant public authority or any other official body to which comments or questions can be submitted and of the time schedule for transmittal of comments or questions; and
> (vi) An indication of what environmental information relevant to the proposed activity is available; and
> (e) The fact that the activity is subject to a national or transboundary environmental impact assessment procedure".

Thus, the Aarhus Convention specifies:
- who shall be informed ("*the public concerned*"),
- when this shall take place ("*early in an environmental decision-making procedure*"),
- in which form this shall take place ("*by public notice or individually*"),
- in which manner this shall take place ("*in an adequate, timely and effective manner*"),
- about what the respective subject shall be informed ("*the proposed activity*" etc.).

To assist the implementation of the Aarhus Convention the Meeting of the Parties to the Convention established the Aarhus Convention Compliance Committee.[2]

---

1 Available at: unece.org/fileadmin/DAM/env/pp/documents/cep43e.pdf.

2 *J. Jendrośka*, Aarhus Convention Compliance Committee: Origins, Status and Activities, JEEPL 2011 (4) p. 301–314.

The Committee consists of nine members, four or five of which are elected at each ordinary session of the Meeting of the Parties. The candidates should be nominated by the Parties, Signatories and NGOs. The Committee's task is to examine compliance issues and make appropriate recommendations.[3] The decisions of the Aarhus Convention Compliance Committee can be considered as a form of case-law, and are used in this article to better understand the provisions of the Aarhus Convention. Furthermore, from time to time the Meeting of the Parties to the Aarhus Convention meets to discuss the implementation of the Convention.[4] The Meeting of the Parties has recently issued *Maastricht Recommendations on Promoting Effective Public Participation in Decision-making in Environmental Matters*[5] (hereinafter – *Maastricht Recommendations*), which is referred to in the article.

As the Aarhus Convention Compliance Committee rightly pointed out, public notification conducted in an appropriate manner is important for the stages of public publication that follow[6]:

- providing the public with access to the documentation of the case,
- submitting comments by the public,
- consideration of the public comments and proposals and taking a decision in the case and
- public notice of the decision made.

Of course, possessing the information on the pending proceedings and on the possibility to participate is a necessary condition of the participation itself. Namely, the entities entitled to participate need to know the subject matter of the proceedings, which is the planned activity. They may be not acquainted with the options of the decisions that could be taken. The necessity to look for this information may complicate the participation in the decision making. Therefore it is the obligation of the public authority to provide the public concerned with the respective data. Apart from the knowledge on the subject matter of the case meaningful participation requires being informed about the necessary procedural frames, such as the time period of the decision making procedure, when and in which forms the public participation can take place, where the additional information could be obtained etc. Other researchers also state that public notification plays a key role in the whole public participation procedure.[7]

---

3 Decision I/7. Report of the first Meeting of the Parties to the Convention on Access to Information, Public Participation in Decision-making and Access to Justice in Environmental Matters ECE/MP.PP/2/Add.8. [www.unece.org/fileadmin/DAM/env/pp/documents/mop1/ece.mp.pp.2.add.8.e.pdf].

4 Article 10 of the Aarhus Convention.

5 Adopted at the Fifth session of the Meeting of the Parties to the Aarhus Convention that took place in Maastricht (the Netherlands) on 30 June and 1 July 2014 (ECE/MP.PP/2014/8).

6 ACCC/C/2004/2 (Kazakhstan), para. 24.

7 *J. Jendrośka & W. Radecki*, Konwencja o dostępie do informacji, udziale społeczeństwa w podejmowaniu decyzji oraz dostępie do sprawiedliwości w sprawach dotyczących środowiska z komentarzem. 1999, p. 87.

The Aarhus Convention also states that "Each Party shall take the necessary legislative, regulatory and other measures, (...) as well as proper enforcement measures, to establish and maintain a clear, transparent and consistent framework to implement the provisions of this Convention".

The EU, Poland and Ukraine are the Parties to the Aarhus Convention, which means that they are obliged to fulfil the above obligations. In order to do that the necessary legislation was adopted.

Namely, in the EU law requirements for public participation in individual decision-making are set in several directives.[8]One of the main ones is the Directive of the European Parliament and of the Council 2011/92/EU of 13 December 2011 *on the assessment of the effects of certain public and private projects on the environment*[9] (hereinafter – the EIA Directive). The respective norms of the Aarhus Convention are implemented also in the IED Directive[10] as well as in the Habitat Directive.[11]

The most important act in the Polish legislation in this area is the Act of 3 October 2008 *on access to environmental information, public participation in environmental protection and on environmental impact assessments*[12] (hereinafter – the Polish EIA Act).

It can be stated that the Polish EIA Act sets some detailed requirements to public notification in comparison with the EIA Directive and the Aarhus Convention. It somehow specifies in which ways the aims outlined in these international documents should be reached. As far as Ukrainian law is concerned, the norms on public notification are rather complicated and quite often not compliant with the Aarhus Convention. It can be said that Poland is rather similar to Ukraine in terms of law, social-political system, historical development and even geographical location. Additionally Poland began its way to European integration earlier than Ukraine. More than 10-year experience of adaptation Polish legislation to European standards can be used while analysing Ukrainian norms on public participation. Polish law can be an inspiration and basis in creating respective Ukrainian norms.

Therefore, this article analyses whether the provisions of the Aarhus Convention, the EIA Directive, the Polish EIA Act and the respective current and proposed Ukrainian legislation are coherent.[13]

---

8 *J. Jendrośka*, Citizen's Rights in European Environmental Law: Stock-Taking of Key Challenges and Current Developments in Relation to Public Access to Information, Participation and Access to Justice, JEEPL 2012 (1) p. 71–90.

9 The Directive of the Council 2011/92/EU on the assessment of the effects of certain public and private projects on the environment, OJ 2012 L 26.

10 The Directive of the European Parliament and of the Council 2010/75/EU on industrial emissions (integrated pollution prevention and control), OJ 2010 L 334.

11 The Directive of the Council 92/43/EEC on the conservation of natural habitats and of wild fauna and flora, OJ 1992 L 206.

12 Official Journal of the Laws of 2008 no. 199, Item 1227.

13 In the quoted above provision of the Aarhus Convention as well as in the EIA Directive (Article 6.2, 6.3.b and 6.5) the word "to inform" is used. Nevertheless, in relation to the said

1. POLISH LAW

The Polish EIA Act requires public authority competent to issue decisions requiring public participation to provide the public with an opportunity to participate in the decision making. The list of decisions requiring public participation is set in the Polish EIA Act as well as in the Environmental Protection Act of 27 April 2001.[14]

One of the main decisions requiring public participation in Poland and in Europe is environmental impact assessment (hereinafter – the EIA).[15] The importance of the EIA conducting was recognized in the principle 17 of the Declaration on Environment and Development (Rio de Janeiro, 3–14 June 1992). The Aarhus Convention also mentions the EIA procedure[16], but it does not include its definition. According to the Espoo Convention the EIA means a national procedure for evaluating the likely impact of a proposed activity on the environment.[17] In Poland the EIA means the procedure for the assessment of the environmental impact of the proposed project, including in particular: the verification of the environmental impact report for the project, the acquisition of the opinions and approvals required by the Polish EIA Act, ensuring the possibility of public participation in the procedure.[18] Within the framework of the EIA, the following should be identified, analysed and assessed: the direct and indirect effects of a given project on the environment, human health and the quality of human life, property, cultural heritage, the interaction between these elements as well as on access to mineral deposits; the possibilities and ways of preventing and reducing the adverse impact of the project on the environment; the required scope of monitoring.[19]

The general framework of public participation is regulated in part III of the Polish EIA Act called "Public participation in environmental protection". This part sets the right of all persons to submit comments and suggestions in the course of a procedure requiring public participation as well the concrete requirements to realization of this right.

institution in the framework of the Convention the term "notification" is more commonly used (*J. Jendrośka*, Instytucja „powiadomienia społeczeństwa" w świetle wymagań prawa wspólnotowego in H. Lisicka (ed.) Prawo ochrony środowiska. Książka jubileuszowa z okazji 40-lecia pracy naukowej, 2008, p. 122). This term is also used in this article.

14 Official Journal of the Laws of 2013, Item 1232.

15 *Aarhus Convention Implementation Guide*, p. 127–128.

16 Article 6.2.*e* of the Aarhus Convention.

17 Article 1vi of the Espoo Convention on Environmental Impact Assessment in a Transboundary Context, February 25, 1991 (entered into force 10 September 1997).

18 Article 3(1.8) of the Polish EIA Act.

19 Article 62 of the Polish EIA Act.

2. UKRAINIAN LAW

Ukrainian legislation on public participation in environmental decision making is more complicated.

Namely, during taking strategic and individual decisions in environmental matters in Ukraine as well as in other countries of Eastern Europe, the Caucasus and Central Asia, a specific combination of state ecological expertise and OVOS procedure has been conducted for a long time.[20]

Generally, these procedures consist of the following. The acronym "OVOS" can be translated as "environmental impact assessment", but it is not the European and American EIA procedure. The OVOS procedure includes preparation of the documentation on the impact of the proposed project on the environment as well as consultations with the public regarding this documentation. Usually a developer is responsible for conduction of OVOS procedure. The OVOS procedure is regulated in a technical regulatory act, which is called "national construction standards".[21] It can be said that setting frames of public consultations on OVOS documentation is strictly connected to the realization of public rights to participate in the decision making. According to the Constitution of Ukraine public rights should be set only in laws, not in technical regulatory acts. Apart from this it has been pointed out in the literature that the public has not been properly notified of these "national construction standards".[22]

The next stage is the state ecological expertise, during which the results of the OVOS are approved by competent authority.[23] This stage is regulated in a separate Law of Ukraine "On Ecological Expertise" of 9 February 1995 no. 45/95-WR[24] (hereinafter the Law of Ukraine "On Ecological Expertise"). It is carried out by public authorities.

Thus, the OVOS procedure is regulated in a technical regulatory act and the state ecological expertise is regulated in the legal act. It should be mentioned that regulating the ecological expertise in the act adopted by the parliament, and the OVOS procedure in an act of lower rank can be called the usual practice in the countries of Eastern Europe, the Caucasus and Central Asia.[25]

---

20 General guidance on enhancing consistency between the Convention and environmental impact assessment within State ecological expertise in countries of Eastern Europe, the Caucasus and Central Asia adopted by Meeting of the Parties to the Convention on Environmental Impact Assessment in a Transboundary Context (Sixth session, Geneva, 2–5 June 2014, ECE/MP.EIA/2014/2), para. 7.

21 DBN A.2.2-1-2003 "The Structure and the Content of the Documents on the Assessment the Expected Impact on the Environment of Buildings" approved by the Order of the State Building Committee 15/12/2003 no. 214.

22 *T. Tretiak*, Pravovi aspekty derzhavnoi ekologicznoi ekspertyzy jak zasobu zabezpecennia provedennia ocinky wplywu na navkolysnie seredowysce u sferi budiwnyctwa, Visnyk Kyiwskogo Nacionalnogo Uniwersytetu im. Tarasa Shewcenka, 92/2012, p. 43.

23 Article 13 of the Law of Ukraine "On Ecological Expertise" 09/02/1995 no. 45/95-BP.

24 Vidomosti Verhovnoi Rady Ukrainy, 21/02/1995 – 1995, no. 8, Article 54.

25 General guidance on enhancing consistency, *supra*, note 14 at para. 13.

The Law of Ukraine "On Ecological Expertise" also foresees so-called public ecological expertise. It may be conducted by the public and its experts. According to Ukrainian legislation the results of this expertise may (not even should) be taken into consideration while taking the decision.[26] Apart from this, it is not a mandatory element of the expertise procedure and it is conducted rather rarely. Therefore, the Aarhus Convention Compliance Committee found that it cannot be considered as a primary form of public participation in environmental decision making referred to in the Aarhus Convention. It may only play an additional role in these terms[27], and therefore is not further explored in this article.

Apart from this, in 2009 in order to facilitate the implementation of the Aarhus Convention in Ukraine an expert group consisted of the members of the Aarhus Convention Compliance Committee and other experts was established. The expert group prepared a draft Decree of the Cabinet of Ministers of Ukraine regarding public participation in environmental decision-making. Ukrainian environmental law lawyers stated that the prepared draft was a high-level document.[28] However, the pressure of a few powerful ministers led to introduction of illegal changes to the prepared document after its adoption by the Cabinet of Ministers of Ukraine.[29] A robust document consisting of 23 pages was reduced to 6 pages of incoherent and contradictory passages.[30] Even though this document is still in force, it is not used in practice.

The next important Act in these terms is the Law of Ukraine "On Urban Development Regulation" dated 17/02/2011 no. 3038-VI.[31] It sets the legal frames of adopting approvals of building projects. This act specifies that a public participation procedure shall be conducted before permitting building projects that are especially dangerous for the environment and projects subject to environmental impact assessment in a transboundary context. Similarly as it is in the case of state ecological expertise the specific requirements for a public participation procedure are set in the above mentioned national construction standards regulating the OVOS stage of the decision-making. Therefore, while

---

26 Articles 16, 42 of the Law of Ukraine "On Ecological Expertise".

27 ECE/MP.PP/2011/11/Add.2, para. 76; ECE/MP.EIA/2014/2, para. 24.

28 EPL's comments on the Committee's draft report dated 10.03.2011, p. 3. [unece.org/fileadmin/DAM/env/pp/compliance/MoP3decisions/Ukraine/correspondence/EPLcomments_CCreport.pdf];
EPL's Report on progress made by Ukraine in the implementation of MOP decisions regarding compliance and on the adopted Action Plan dated 02.11.2010 [www.unece.org/env/pp/compliance/compliancecommittee/ccimpldocsukrainemop3.html].

29 It was adopted by the Decree of the Cabinet of Ministers of Ukraine "On approval of public participation in decision-making in the field of environmental protection" of 29 June 2011 no. 771.

30 For more information see: EPL's position for the forthcoming Aarhus Convention Compliance Committee meeting which is to decide whether the caution imposed on Ukraine be lifted. May 28, 2012. [www.unece.org/fileadmin/DAM/env/pp/compliance/MoP4decisions/Ukraine/Ukraine_IV.9h/frEPL30May12.pdf].

31 Vidomosti Verhovnoi Rady Ukrainy, 2011, no. 34, Article 343.

analysing the current Ukrainian regulations on public participation this article refers to the OVOS stage.

Currently the Ukrainian Parliament has been considering Ukrainian draft EIA Act[32], and approved this draft law on 12.10.2016. However, the President of Ukraine vetoed the draft law and returned it back to the Parliament with some amendments. The Parliamentary Committee contemplated the proposed amendments and the Parliament is going to consider this draft law in the future. According to this draft EIA Act public participation (and respectively the notification stage) takes place twice during the decision-making process. Firstly, at the scoping stage, when the scope of the EIA report is determined. Secondly, at the stage, when the EIA report is discussed. As it is shown below, this Act generally complies with the international and EU legislation.

3. PERSONAL SCOPE OF PUBLIC NOTIFICATION

Public notification in the Aarhus Convention is expressed in an impersonal form ("*the public concerned shall be informed*"). This means that with some exceptions it can be done by different actors.[33] The same provision is in the EIA Directive. The Parties to the Convention and the EU Member States should ensure implementation of this general framework. This foresees the establishment of the subject responsible for public notification. In Poland it is the authority competent to issue the relevant decision.[34]

In Ukraine the whole OVOS stage of decision making (including public notification stage) is conducted by the developer or expert hired by him.[35] National construction standards state that these entities publish the statement of intention in the press as well as conduct notification via local authorities. It is not specified what the latter general statement means. According to Ukrainian draft

---

32 Ukrainian draft EIA Act and all the associated documentation are available at http://w1.c1.rada.gov.ua/pls/zweb2/webproc4_2?pf3516=2009%D0%B0-%D0%B4&skl=9.

33 *J. Ebbesson, H. Gaugitsch, J. Jendrośka, S. Stec, and F. Marshall,* Aarhus Convention Implementation Guide. Second edition. 2013, p. 133. [unece.org/fileadmin/DAM/env/pp/ppdm/Aarhus_Implementation_Guide_second_edition_-_text_only.pdf].
At the same time the Aarhus Convention Compliance Committee expressed doubts whether reliance on the developer in providing for public participation is fully in line with the Convention (ACCC/C/2006/16 (Lithuania), para. 78).
If, according to national law, a third party (e.g., the developer) is entrusted with the obligation to notify the public, that third party should inform the competent public authority who, about what, when and how was notified. That should be done in a timely manner (*Maastricht Recommendations on Promoting Effective Public Participation in Decision-making in Environmental Matters.* Fifth session. Maastricht, the Netherlands, 30 June and 1 July 2014. ECE/MP.PP/2014/8, p. 22).

34 Article 33(1) of the Polish EIA Act.

35 Para. 1(6), 1(9) of the national construction standards.

EIA Act the entities responsible for notifying the public are the developer and sometimes the public authority.[36]

As far as the entities entitled to be informed are concerned, the Aarhus Convention and the EIA Directive clearly identify them. The only difference in the approach used in each of these acts is that in the first act it is the "public concerned", and in the second it is "the public".[37] The reasons for this difference are not known. There may be the following merits for one or another solution. From the point of view of entities obliged to notify (in general it is the public authority) "the public concerned" is a rather narrow group of people. Thus it needs to be clearly defined. The mistake in this regard may mean non-compliance with the Aarhus Convention. At the same time it is easier to notify the clearly defined group of people than to notify "the public", that is absolutely everybody. From the point of view of the public that may be interested in participating in the procedure, it is important to get the right information at the right time.

Determination of the members of the public potentially interested in participating in the proceedings and entitled to get the notification may be based on the following grounds. It should be taken into account that art. 3.2 of the Aarhus Convention requires that its Parties should "*endeavour to ensure that officials and authorities assist and provide guidance to the public in* (...) *facilitating participation in decision-making*". There is a higher probability that subjects entitled to participate will get notified when public notice and individual notification are used simultaneously. Undoubtedly, this involves burdening the public authorities with additional responsibilities. However, this does not seem to be extensive.

Such a solution is accepted in Poland, where two groups of subjects shall be informed about the initiation of the proceedings. The first one is the public concerned. In Poland it is the "parties" to the relevant proceeding and the "entities with the right of a party", which are notified individually. The second one is the public. Interestingly enough, the right to submit comments and suggestions in the public participation procedure belongs to all persons. This concept literally

---

36 Article 4(3) of Ukrainian draft EIA Act.

37 These requirements are set respectively in Article 6(2) of the Aarhus Convention and in Article 6(2) of the EIA directive.
In general, the concepts of "the public" and "the public concerned" are used by these two legal acts. They also were very similarly defined (respectively in Article 2(4) and 2(5) of the Aarhus Convention and in Articles 1(2.d) and 1(2.e) of the EIA Directive and Article 2(1.5) of the Aarhus Convention, Article 1(2.e) of the EIA Directive).
Articles 2(4) and 2(5) of the Aarhus Convention define them in the following way:
"The public" means one or more natural or legal persons, and, in accordance with national legislation or practice, their associations, organizations or groups;
"The public concerned" means the public affected or likely to be affected by, or having an interest in, the environmental decision-making; for the purposes of this definition, non-governmental organizations promoting environmental protection and meeting any requirements under national law shall be deemed to have an interest.

differs a bit from the concept "the public", but the meaning of these two concepts is the same.

According to the Law of Ukraine "On Ecological Expertise" the entity entitled to participation in environmental decision-making is the public.[38] As provided by the national construction standards the entity entitled to participate is the population.[39] Ukrainian law does not include the definition of the public and the population. Ukrainian draft EIA Act states that the entity entitled to be notified is the public, which is defined similarly as in the Aarhus Convention.[40]

4. THE NOTIFICATION MADE IN A TIMELY MANNER

Timely notification should reach the public concerned early enough to be effective.[41] Timeliness of the notification is connected to the time assigned to the public participation procedure as well as to the whole decision-making procedure.

According to Article 6.4 of the Aarhus Convention the possibility to participate should be given to public early enough, "*when all options are open and effective public participation can take place*". This requirement concerns the whole public participation procedure.[42] However, the beginning of the public participation procedure is strictly connected to its first stage, which is the public notification.

The Aarhus Convention Compliance Committee found that the notification is made at the early stage of the decision making procedure if it provides the public concerned with the appropriate amount of time to get notified and to participate. According to Article 6.3 of the Aarhus Convention its Parties should ensure reasonable time-frames for the different phases of the public participation procedures. That means e.g. that the time period set for the following notification stages of public participation procedures cannot begin to run until the notification is effectively made in accordance with the Aarhus Convention. Therefore, timely public notification means ensuring appropriate amount of time for public to become familiar with it. This requirement is not fulfilled, e.g., by giving the public one week to examine the EIA documentation relating to a mining project. Undoubtedly, a week is not enough for the public concerned to get acquainted with "*voluminous documentation of a technical nature and to participate in an effective manner*".[43]

Similarly, Article 6.2 of the EIA Directive requires public notification to take place "*early in the environmental decision-making procedures referred to in*

---

38 Article 11 of the Law of Ukraine "On Ecological Expertise".

39 Para. 1(6), 1(9) of the national construction standards.

40 Article 1(1.2) and Article 4 of Ukrainian draft EIA Act.

41 *Ebbesson, Gaugitsch, Jendrośka, Stec, and Marshall, supra*, note 34 at p. 136.

42 *Maastricht Recommendations*, p. 22.

43 ACCC/C/2009/43 (Armenia), para. 67.

Article 2(2) and, at the latest, as soon as information can reasonably be provided". According to the EIA Directive public participation is a part of a wider procedure (namely the EIA procedure). This means that the above Article of the EIA Directive should be understood in the context of its other provisions, establishing, among others, that "*the public concerned shall be given early and effective opportunities to participate in the environmental decision-making procedures referred to in Article 2(2) and shall, for that purpose, be entitled to express comments and opinions when all options are open to the competent authority or authorities before the decision on the request for development consent is taken*".[44] The notification initiates the public participation procedure, thus its implementation at an early stage of the decision-making process is also important for the effectiveness of the whole public participation procedure.

Polish law seems to be in line with these requirements. Namely, according to the Polish EIA Act the public should be notified prior to the issue and modification of decisions requiring public participation without an undue delay.[45] Till 01.01.2017 Polish law provided for the 21-day deadline for the submission of comments and proposals. This period was considered insufficient and criticised in the literature.[46] However, currently due to the transposition of recent amendments to the EIA Directive public participation period is prolonged to at least 30 days. However, Polish law lacks the guidance as for the precise moment when this period begins. It is not clear, whether it is the moment when the public gets an opportunity to be notified or the moment when it is de facto notified etc. This situation is also criticized and it is suggested that public participation period should begin from effective public notification.[47]

Public authorities should also make the notification and all information attached to it available to the public throughout the full public participation procedure. The representatives of the public, who later joined the procedure may need to get acquainted with all the previous information. Access to the notice is also important in the case of appealing the final decision by the public.

As far as Ukrainian law is concerned, according to annex B to Ukrainian national construction standards the publication of the statement of intention takes place at the very beginning of the OVOS procedure, when only the introductory assessment of the expected impact of buildings on the environment is conducted. It may be told that in Ukraine the notification takes places early enough, "*when all options are open and effective public participation can take place*".

As it was stated above, pursuant to Article 4.3 of Ukrainian draft EIA Act public participation should take place twice in the decision making process. Firstly, at the scoping stage and secondly during assessing the EIA report. The

44 Article 6(4) of the EIA Directive.
45 Article 33(1) of the Polish EIA Act.
46 *Jendrośka, supra*, note 13 at p. 132–133.
47 *Id.*

public is notified about the possibility to participate at these two stages also twice during the decision making. It should be done by the developer and by the relevant public authority. The time period for these two entities to notify the public is three work-days from the moment of submission to the public authority respectively the Notification on the proposed activity subject to the EIA and the Notice on the commencement of public consultations on the EIA Report.[48] Additionally, during the same time period the responsible public authority adds the Notification on the proposed activity subject to the EIA to the Single EIA registry[49] and adds the EIA Report to the same registry.[50]

All the information relevant to the decision making (including the above notification on the planned activity that is subject to EIA and the Notice on the commencement of public consultations on the EIA Report) should be made available for the public.[51] In terms of the Notice on the commencement of public consultations on the EIA Report it is stressed that it should be available for the public during the whole public participation process.[52]

Apart from this, Ukrainian draft EIA Act foresees that the EIA should be conducted before the decision on the planned project is adopted.[53]

It may be told that in the EIA Directive, Polish, current and planned Ukrainian legislation the notification stage takes place early enough in the decision-making process, which is compliant with the Aarhus Convention.

5. THE NOTIFICATION MADE IN AN EFFECTIVE MANNER

According to the Aarhus Convention Compliance Committee the effective notification means that "all those who potentially could be concerned have a reasonable chance to learn about the proposed activity and their possibilities to participate".[54]

This is particularly important for people living in the immediate vicinity of the proposed activity or its environmental effects. Thus, the effectiveness of notification depends on:

- taking into account the size and complexity of the planned activities;
- defining the people, who may be interested in participation (including vulnerable groups);
- adaptation of the notification to the needs and capabilities of these people;

---

48 Article 4(3), 5(5), 8(1) of Ukrainian draft EIA Act.
49 Article 5(6) of Ukrainian draft EIA Act.
50 Article 6(5) of Ukrainian draft EIA Act.
51 Article 4(7) of Ukrainian draft EIA Act.
52 Article 8(3) of Ukrainian draft EIA Act.
53 Article 3(1) of Ukrainian draft EIA Act.
54 ACCC/C/2006/16 (Lithuania), para. 67.

- taking into account external circumstances (such as a large amount of other materials that can hinder reaching notifications to the public concerned).

That means that the methods that will ensure "effective notification" must be determined on a case-by-case basis, taking into account the specificity of each case.[55] For example, if the public concerned do not speak the language in which the documentation is prepared, the documentation should be translated into the language that they understand. This language can be a widely recognized regional *lingua franca* (e.g., English for the EU region, Russian for the countries of Eastern Europe, the Caucasus and Central Asia).[56]

Certain methods of notification are effective in terms of informing the public concerned (which is required by the Aarhus Convention), the other methods are effective in terms of informing the public (which is required by the EIA Directive). This may create some difficulties for the Member States of the European Union, which should apply the requirements of the both acts. But, as it is stated above, Polish legislation combines these requirements. Public concerned is notified individually and the public is informed by special notification.

The Aarhus Convention provides that "*the public concerned shall be informed, either by public notice or individually*". Public notice means the dissemination of information among as many members of the public as possible, making use of the normal means for general and widespread transmission of information.[57] This means that the general public receives sufficient opportunity to get acquainted with the relevant information spread by public notice and can prepare for effective participation in the proceedings. The possibility for the general public to get informed is not ensured when only the public concerned is notified individually. The Parties to the Convention should select one or both of these options.

The EU as the party to the Aarhus Convention selected only public notice. Namely, according to the EIA Directive, the public concerned is entitled to submit comments and proposals during the public participation procedure. In order to make it possible, the public concerned needs to be notified about the decision-making process. At the same time according to the EIA Directive the public and not the public concerned shall be informed of the planned activity. However, the EU Member States are also the Parties to the Aarhus Convention and therefore are obliged not only to fulfil the EIA Directive, but also the Aarhus Convention. The latter refers to notification of the public concerned. In spite of this, the additional requirement of individual notice in the EIA Directive might be useful.

Polish law provides the opportunity for the public and for the public concerned to get notified as it is stated below.

---

55 *Maastricht Recommendations*, para. 59.
56 *Maastricht Recommendations*, para. 65c.
57 *Ebbesson, Gaugitsch, Jendrośka, Stec, and Marshall, supra*, note 34 at p. 133.

Ukrainian national construction standards set that the developer or hired by him expert should publish the statement of intention.[58] It also mentions the necessity to inform the public without specifying, how it should be done.[59] Furthermore, the national construction standards set the list of materials that prove taking public interest into consideration. This list includes the information on publication of the statement of intention in media.[60] However, Ukrainian legislation does not precise what should be done with this list. Namely, it is not stated whether it should be submitted to public authority or published. This shows the lack of sufficient control, whether public notification was published appropriately. Evidently, current Ukrainian legislation lacks more precise norms on the media, in which the statement of intention should be published, their circulation or other aspects of publication important in terms of public participation.

Ukrainian draft EIA Act provides only the possibility of issuing the public (not individual) notice. It should be used twice in the decision-making: when public participation procedure is commenced as well as before assessing the EIA report.[61]

It seems that the EIA Directive, Polish and planned Ukrainian legislation provides for public notification to be spread in an effective manner, but current Ukrainian legislation does not seem to be sufficient in these terms. The specific forms of public notification envisaged at the international, EU and national level (in Poland and in Ukraine) are described below.

6. PUBLIC AND INDIVIDUAL NOTICE

6.1. PUBLICATION IN PRINTED MEDIA

The Aarhus Convention Compliance Committee considered the following example of an ineffective public notice in the press. This is a notice of the planned building a new landfill next to the city Kazokiszki (Lithuania). In the respective locality there were two printed media. The first one was the popular daily local newspaper with the circulation of 1,500 copies. The second one was a weekly official journal with a circulation of 500 copies. Lithuanian legislation did not set any requirements as for in which exactly media public notification should be published. And the developer chose the second one.

Regarding this case the Aarhus Convention Compliance Committee expressed the view that much more effective would be publishing a notice in the popular daily local newspaper than in the official journal published once a week. However,

58 Para. 1(6) of the national construction standards.

59 Paras. 1(6), 1(9) of the national construction standards.

60 Paras. 1(10) of the national construction standards.

61 Articles 4(3), 8(1) of Ukrainian draft EIA Act.

if all local newspapers are issued only once a week, the requirement to ensure an "effective" notification is fulfilled by choosing the one, which has a circulation of 1,500 copies, and not that of the circulation of 500 copies.[62]

The Maastricht Recommendations also indicate that the press where the public notice is placed should correspond to the geographical scope of the potential effects of the planned activities. This press should reach the majority of members of the public who may be affected by a proposed activity or be interested in the decision-making process.[63]

Article 6.5 of the EIA Directive provides for "*publication in local newspapers*".

Article 3.11 of the Polish EIA Act sets that publication in the local press is an additional means of notice if the seat of the competent authority is located in a community other than the community relevant to the subject of the notification.

Current Ukrainian legislation in terms of public notification in printed media was discussed above.

Ukrainian draft EIA Act foresees such obligatory means of notification as two or more printed media with the circulation on the territory that may be affected by the planned activity.[64] Spreading the notification at the territory likely to be affected, not the territory, where the activity is planned, is a condition of an effective notification. However, this planned norm lacks some details regarding the time period during which the notification should appear in the media, as well as regarding the grounds on which the certain media should be chosen (e.g., whether it is a popular one, its circulation).

6.2. BILL POSTING

Maastricht Recommendations suggest using three following places of bill posting:

- "a public place in the immediate vicinity of the proposed activity (e.g., on a prominent fence or signpost on the site of the proposed activity, etc.)"[65];
- places highly frequented by the public concerned and traditionally used for spreading the information (e.g., shops and shopping centres, post office, places of worship (e.g., churches), schools, kindergartens, sports halls, bus stops, meeting places for marginalized groups, sports fields etc.)[66];
- a publicly accessible physical noticeboard of the public authority competent to take the decision.[67]

---

62 ACCC/C/2006/16 (Lithuania), para. 67.

63 *Maastricht Recommendations*, para. 64c.

64 Article 4(2) and Article 4(3) of Ukrainian draft EIA Act.

65 *Maastricht Recommendations*, para. 64a.

66 *Maastricht Recommendations*, para. 64d.

67 *Maastricht Recommendations*, para. 64b.

It should be taken into account that notices at the developer's notice board may only be an additional means.[68]

Article 6.5 of the EIA Directive includes only one example in these terms, which is "bill posting within a certain radius". However, the Directive provides that public notice may also be done by other appropriate means[69], which may mean e.g. putting notice on the noticeboard of the relevant public authority.

The Polish EIA Act follows the above suggestions of Maastricht Recommendations providing the possibility to publish the information in a so-called customary way. That could be done in the vicinity of the proposed project. That may mean placing the information on the notice board at the seat of the authority which is competent in the matter.[70] This means of public notification may be effective in traditional communities, where people set issues personally in the seat of the authority.[71]

The second broad option of public notification to be placed is so-called locality or localities which are relevant in the light of the subject matter of the procedure. It could be an additional method in the cases where the seat of the authority competent in the matter is placed in the area of a commune other than the commune which is relevant in terms of its location in the light of the subject matter of the procedure.

Current Ukrainian legislation does not set any requirements in these terms.

Ukrainian draft EIA Act foresees that the notification should be placed:

- on the notice boards of the local public authority,
- (or) in other public places on the territory whether the activity is planned.[72]

Furthermore, the draft law sets that instead of these two previous ways public may be notified in another way that ensures providing the people living in the city or village where the activity is planned with the information on the activity or other people interested in participating in the decision-making.[73] It should be stressed that attention is paid to spreading the information at the potentially affected territory may be more effective than at the territory where the activity is planned, as it is stated above.

Thus, the possibility to notify the public by bill posting is foreseen in the EU, Polish and planned Ukrainian legislation. It is mainly connected to placing the notification in the public places at the territory where the activity is planned and in the seat of the respective public authority.

68 *Maastricht Recommendations*, para. 68.
69 Article 6(2) of the EIA Directive.
70 Article 3(11) of the Polish EIA Act.
71 *Jendrośka, supra*, note 13 at p. 87–88.
72 Articles 4(2) and 4(3) of Ukrainian draft EIA Act.
73 Article 4(2) of Ukrainian draft EIA Act.

6.3. RADIO, TELEVISION AND SOCIAL MEDIA

Public notice through radio, television and social media (e.g., Facebook, Twitter, blogs), in areas where they are popular forms of communication, may be used as a supplement to, not a replacement of the above forms of notification. Social media may be particularly useful in informing the younger members of society who do not use more traditional media.[74]

Even though the Directive does not mention such ways of notification, as it is stated above, it provides that the public may also be notified by other appropriate means[75], which may mean using radio, television and social media.

According to Polish law notification also may be made in a customary way in the locality or localities which are relevant in the light of the subject matter of the procedure, which may mean the usage of radio, television and social media.

Ukrainian draft EIA Act sets the possibility to notify the public in another way that ensures providing the people living in the city or village where the activity is planned or other people interested in participating in the decision-making with the information on the activity.[76] That may also mean using social media.

The Aarhus Convention Compliance Committee stated that "*journalists' articles commenting on a project in the press, on the Internet or television may be very useful as a supplementary means of informing the public. However, they do not in themselves constitute public notice for the purposes of the Convention and cannot replace it*".[77] Furthermore, nor a small notice in the press among hundreds of advertisements nor a local TV program broadcasted at a time when most of people are at work could not be considered effective.[78]

Thus, radio, television and social media may be used as supplementary means of public notification. It can be said that current Polish and planned Ukrainian law provide for using other appropriate means of public notification, such as radio, television and social media.

6.4. ELECTRONIC MEDIA

The usage of electronic media in appropriate cases is set in the EIA Directive[79], the Aarhus Convention Implementation Guide[80] and the Maastricht Recommendations.[81] The Polish EIA Act refers to placing the information on

74 *Maastricht Recommendations*, para. 65.
75 Article 6(2) of the EIA Directive.
76 Article 4(2) of Ukrainian draft EIA Act.
77 ACCC/C/2009/37 (Belarus), *Maastricht Recommendations*, para. 69.
78 *Ebbesson, Gaugitsch, Jendrośka, Stec, and Marshall, supra*, note 34 at p. 135.
79 Article 6(2) of the EIA Directive.
80 *Ebbesson, Gaugitsch, Jendrośka, Stec, and Marshall, supra*, note 34 at p. 133.
81 *Maastricht Recommendations*, para. 64b.

the Internet homepage of the authority (via a so-called "Public Information Bulletin").[82] According to Ukrainian draft EIA Act public notification should also be done on the Internet site of the competent public authority.[83]

Notification through the website of the project proponents (whether a private or public entity) may only be a supplementary means to notification on website of the public authority competent to take the decision.[84]

Undoubtedly, electronic means are timely and can reach a wide audience in countries where the majority of the population uses the Internet (including people potentially interested in participating in the proceedings).[85] At the other hand, electronic means are ineffective in informing people that do not use the Internet at all or randomly use it.

When selecting the method of notification it is recommended to take into account possible problems that may face people living in remote villages, having low literacy level, or speaking a different language. In these and similar cases additional means of effective notification may be used, for example by contacting relevant NGOs or other bodies that work with those communities.[86]

Therefore, effective public notice must meet certain requirements. Namely, its type, size, location and time should ensure the effectiveness of the notification, which means that the possibly widest amount of people who may be interested in participating in the proceedings is notified.

6.5. INDIVIDUAL NOTICE

According to the Aarhus Convention the public concerned may also be notified individually, which means "*dissemination of information to certain classes of persons individually*".[87]

Such notification is particularly important if the decision may affect the individual interests. Individual notice is also important in terms of non-governmental organizations, which are not located in the immediate vicinity of the planned activity, but which meet the requirements of the public concerned.[88]

One of the ways to ensure that the public concerned is informed by individual notifications is creating mailing lists.[89] Each member of the public should have the possibility to register in advance to receive such notifications. It should be possible to choose geographical regions or topics he or she is interested in. The

---

82 Article 3(11) of the Polish EIA Act.
83 Articles 4(2) and 4(3) of Ukrainian draft EIA Act.
84 *Maastricht Recommendations*, para. 68.
85 *Ebbesson, Gaugitsch, Jendrośka, Stec, and Marshall, supra*, note 34 at p. 141.
86 *Maastricht Recommendations*, para. 67.
87 *Ebbesson, Gaugitsch, Jendrośka, Stec, and Marshall, supra*, note 34 at p. 134.
88 *Id.*
89 ECE/MP.PP/2008/5, para. 56; *Maastricht Recommendations*, para. 70.

list of members of the public who have registered for such notification should be updated from time to time.[90]

According to Polish law, the parties and entities with the right of a party are notified individually in writing (usually – by registered letters) or in the form of an electronic document (at their request or with their consent).[91] The third option of notifying the parties in the Polish law is described above public notice. If such a way of notifying the parties is used, they are considered to be notified after fourteen days from the moment, when the public notice has been made.[92]

Therefore, the individual notice provided for in the Aarhus Convention is specified in the Polish EIA Act. However, it is missed in the EIA Directive, current Ukrainian legislation as well as in Ukrainian draft EIA Act. It should be noted that adding such a possibility to Ukrainian law may be beneficial to the entities entitled to participate in the decision-making.

6.6. GENERAL RECOMMENDATIONS OF THE AARHUS CONVENTION COMPLIANCE COMMITTEE TO NOTIFICATION

The Aarhus Convention Compliance Committee analysing "good practices" in public notification proposes the following:

- to use local authorities as intermediaries between local and central government (responsible for taking the appropriate resolution and for carrying out public participation procedure)[93],
- the simultaneous usage of several notification methods[94],
- to repeat notifications when additional relevant information appeared.[95]

If the various forms of notification are used the information provided by them should be consistent.[96] If there are different forms of written notification of the

90 *Maastricht Recommendations*, para. 70.

91 Article 91(2) of the Administrative Code of 14 June 1960 (Journal of Laws 1960 No. 30, item 168) (hereinafter – the Administrative Code).
Article 391(1) of the Administrative Code provides that the letters may be delivered by means of electronic communication within the meaning of Article 2(5) of the Electronic Services Act of 18 July 2002 (Journal of Laws of 2013, item. 1422).

92 Article 49 of the Administrative Code.
These are a couple cases, when the parties to a proceeding should be notified by public notice. They are the following. The first case in when there is a likelihood that apart from parties to the proceedings that were properly notified there are other parties that are unknown (Article 9(3) of the Administrative Code). Second case is a situation, when the number of parties to the proceeding on issuing decisions on environmental conditions exceeds twenty (Article 74(3) of the Act EIA).

93 ECE/MP.PP/2008/5, para. 56.

94 *Id.*

95 ACCC/C/2009/43 (Armenia), para. 70; *Ebbesson, supra*, note 34 at p. 135.

96 *Maastricht Recommendations*, para. 67.

public concerned, it is recommended that all notifications should be delivered on the same day. If this is not possible, the period of public participation should start to run from the date when the last written notification had effectively reached the public concerned.

Moreover, the form of notification is closely associated with its timeliness. This means that another amount of time is needed to get acquainted, for example, with the notification sent by register mail than with the notification placed in the vicinity of the residence of the relevant person or send by electronic mail.

Maastricht Recommendations list the cases when additional notifications are needed:

- when there is a possibility that not all members of the public concerned have been effectively notified (e.g., some members of the public concerned have not received the original notification due to mail delivery problems, or have not had access to the media through which notification was given, e.g., no access to the Internet);
- when commencement of the proposed activity needs more than one decision requiring public participation under art. 6 of the Aarhus Convention;
- when new significant information appears or the circumstances change in a material way that may require providing the public with a further opportunity to participate;
- if the envisaged public participation procedure has changed in any material way (e.g., the change of time frames of the procedure or of the means of submitting public comments).[97]

7. CONCLUSIONS

Public notification is the first step in the public participation procedure on individual projects.

The Aarhus Convention and the EIA Directive are not precise as to which entity should conduct this step. Polish law states that it should be the public authority responsible for the decision-making. According to current and planned Ukrainian law it is a developer and sometimes the public authority. In the Aarhus Convention the entity entitled to be notified is the public concerned and in the EIA Directive it is the public. Polish and planned Ukrainian law are in line with these requirements; however, current Ukrainian law is not.

According to the Aarhus Convention the notification shall be made in a timely manner, which means that it should reach the public concerned early enough to be effective. This suggests that the public concerned needs appropriate amount of time to read the notification, as well as to participate at the next stages of the public participation procedure. A similar requirement can be found in the EIA

---

97 *Maastricht Recommendations*, para. 62.

Directive, in Polish and in current Ukrainian legislation. According to Ukrainian draft EIA Act that is currently considered by Ukrainian parliament the public participation (and respectively the notification stage) should take place twice during the decision-making process. Firstly, at the scoping stage, when the scope of the EIA report is determined. Secondly, at the stage, when the EIA report is discussed.

The notification should be adapted to its recipient's needs and to the methods by which they usually obtain information. This can be a notice in the press of the proper range, the notification in the vicinity of the planned project, in places frequented by the local community, at the seats of the competent or other local authorities or at a web-page of these authorities as well as via individual notices.

The EU, current and planned Ukrainian legislation provides only for the public notice. The possibility to do that via publication in printed media is foreseen in the EIA Directive, Polish, current and planned Ukrainian legislation. The same (with the exception of current Ukrainian legislation) may be told about bill posting. Apart from this, the EIA Directive provides that the public may also be notified by other appropriate means, which is rather broad. Similarly, Polish and planned Ukrainian legislation foresee that the notification may also be made in a customary way in the relevant locality. This may mean the usage of radio, television and social media. However, this can only be an additional means of notification. The EIA Directive, Polish and planned Ukrainian legislation allow to place notification in electronic media.

Individual notices are mainly done via regular mail or via emails. Only Polish law sets the requirements of such notices.

The drawbacks of separate methods of notifications can be partially amended by the simultaneous usage of several methods of notification. The notification may be repeated if necessary.

The above analysis shows the consistency and coherence of regulation at international, EU and Polish national level of the public notice: its personal scope, making it in timely and effective manner. The current Ukrainian legislation does not meet the international and EU requirements, but Ukrainian draft EIA Act is in line with them. Polish legislation may be used as a basis of developing Ukrainian legislation especially in terms of the territory, where the information on the planned activity should be spread, as well as on using individual notice.

PUBLIC PARTICIPATION RIGHTS ENHANCEMENT WITHIN THE WIND POWER PLANTS LOCATION IN POLAND IN THE CONTEXT OF EU RENEWABLE ENERGY REQUIREMENTS

Kamila SOBIERAJ*

ABSTRACT

A few years old delays in implementation of the Renewable Energy Directive into the Polish legal framework caused that it is likely that Poland may not achieve the national target for share of energy from renewable sources by the year 2020 and indicative trajectories for achieving the national target set out in Renewable Energy Directive (however it is not impossible yet). Additionally, the currently predicted leading role of wind energy sector within renewable energy sources development in Poland (and consequently the possibility of achieving by Poland the national target for share of energy from renewable sources by the year 2020) may be effectively constrained by many public protests regarding wind power plants location in Poland. In order to decline the range of public conflicts regarding wind power plants location, new regulations aiming at public procedural rights enhancement were enacted. The aim of the study is the analysis of possible impact of regulations currently introducing into the Polish legal framework on public conflicts regarding wind power plants declining and consequently the possibility of current and future European Union requirements within renewable energy sources implementation by Poland.

KEYWORDS

European Union requirements; renewable energy sources; wind power plant

* PhD in Law, Assistant Professor at the Environmental Management Law Department, the Faculty of Law, Canon Law and Administration, The John Paul II Catholic University of Lublin.

1. INTRODUCTION

The aim of this article is presenting a possible impact of the currently enacted law on 20 May 2016 regarding investments in wind power plants[1] upon reducing public conflicts connected with the location of wind farms, and in effect the possibility of meeting the current and future EU requirements regarding renewable energy sources. Will the adopted instruments allow to attain both these aims? In view of the fact that the law on wind power investments has been enacted only recently, there are no analyses (publications) in this respect available yet. It must also be emphasized that the subject matter of this article is related to a few collateral issues, which in view of its restricted frame shall only be signalled (a wider discussion might be the subject of a separate study).

2. INCREASING EU REQUIREMENTS REGARDING RENEWABLE ENERGY SOURCES

The current directive 2009/28/EC dated 23 April 2009 concerning promoting the use of energy from renewable sources, amending and consequently abrogating directives 2001/77/EC and 2003/30/EC[2] establishes for the EU member states binding general national targets regarding the share of renewable energy in the final gross consumption of 2020[3] For Poland the share should be equivalent to at least 15%, whereby it must be emphasized this requirement does not concern the installed or available capacity, but the end consumption of energy (consumed energy). The second binding element of the directive is the trajectory of meeting the general national target of 2020. According to Article 3 item 2 of Renewable Energy Directive, during the consecutive two-year periods before 2020, the share of energy from renewable sources ought to equal or exceed the approximate exchange rate designated by Attachment I part B, which has the following relation to the objectives of Poland: 8.76% (2011–2012); 10.14% (2013–2014); 11.31% (2015–2016); 12.87% (2017–2018).[4] Several years' delays in implementing the Renewable Energy Directive resulted that, with a great deal of certainty, Poland may not achieve the general national target in 2020 assigned to our country, as well as to the trajectory of achieving the national target specified in the Renewable Energy Directive (although it is not impossible yet). The rate of renewable sources energy share in the final gross energy consumption in Poland in 2015 amounted to 11.47%

---

1 *Dziennik Ustaw* (English: Journal of Laws) of 2016, item 961, hereinafter referred to as the law on wind power investments.

2 OJ 2009 L 140/16, hereinafter referred to as the Renewable Energy Directive.

3 See Article 3 item 1 of the Renewable Energy Directive in connection with Appendix I part A.

4 *F.M. Elżanowski & M.M. Sokołowski*, Proces inwestycyjny w kontekście pakietu klimatyczno-energetycznego Unii Europejskiej, in M. Cherke, F.M. Elżanowski, M. Swora & K.A. Wąsowski (eds), Energetyka i ochrona środowiska w procesie inwestycyjnym, 2010, pp. 132–133.

and it increased by 4.25 percentage points as compared to the year 2005[5] (this rate is growing relatively slowly then). The lack of stable, complex regulations, in particular concerning the system of support[6] for the manufacturers of electricity from renewable sources of energy, the lack of even predictable shape of new system of support caused by regular changes of the system concept have become the source of market chaos and destabilization, resulting in the entrepreneurs' restraining their decisions to take up investments in renewable energy sources.

Furthermore, in the coming years, a continuing increase of EU requirements as regards the national share of energy from renewable sources in the final energy consumption must be taken into account.[7] At the meeting of the European Council dated 23–24 October 2014, the climate and energy policy Framework until 2030 was adopted. The document initiated a discussion on the frame of new EU binding regulations implementing the climate and energy policy until 2030, which shall impose upon particular Member States inter alia considerably higher national shares of energy from renewable sources in the final consumption of energy. In the content of the quoted document, the main binding aim of EU climate and energy policy until 2030 was designated, which assumes limitation of the internal greenhouse gas emissions until 2030 by at least 40% as compared to the level of 1990. An intermediate target, which has also been adopted, is attaining the share of renewable energy in EU general energy consumption at the level of at least 27%. An efficiently working, reformed EU system of emissions trading shall be the main European instrument applied to achieve 40% of the aim regarding reduction of greenhouse gas emissions. Extensive functional and systemic connections of the EU emissions trading system with the other instruments constituting the so called climate and energy package were also indicated, including regulations concerning renewable energy sources, energy effectiveness, technology of carbon dioxide capture and geological storage. The instruments support effectiveness of the EU emissions trading system within environmental protection, whereby they also contribute to achieving the general aim of greenhouse gases emissions by 40%. In terms of costs, achievement of the effective 40% emissions reduction as compared to 1990 requires therefore also considerable contributions originating among others from the renewable energy sources.

---

5 Central Statistical Office. Energy from renewable sources in 2014, December 2015, p. 47, http://stat.gov.pl/obszary-tematyczne/srodowisko-energia/ accessed 15 September 2016.

6 See more regarding the systems of support e.g *L. Karski*, System wsparcia energetyki odnawialnej. Refleksje na tle postanowień prawa polskiego i unijnego, in M. Rudnicki & K. Sobieraj (eds), Nowe prawo energetyczne, 2013, pp. 51–68; *L. Karski*, Climate Law in Poland, in M. Peeters, M. Stallworthy & J. de Cendra de Larragán (eds), Climate Law in EU Member States: Towards National Legislation for Climate Protection, 2012, pp. 231–258.

7 See more regarding the importance of increasing of renewable energy sources use in the context of strategic objectives of EU energy policy e.g. *A. Gawlikowska-Fyk*, Znaczenie polityki energetycznej w procesie integracji europejskiej, 2011, pp. 173–177.

3. THE PREDICTED LEADING POSITION OF WIND ENERGY WITHIN EU REQUIREMENTS MEETING

The necessity of assuring by Poland the currently binding general national target, which is achieving 15% of renewable resources energy share in the final gross consumption in 2020, and also in the further perspective the considerable increase of EU requirements regarding the level of the national share of renewable energy in the final energy consumption causes that currently there is an urgent need to execute investments regarding the renewably sources energy.[8] Whereby, implementation of investments with respect to wind energy technology will have a considerable influence upon a possibility to meet those objectives. According to the details of the Chief Statistical Office, in the structure of electric energy production from renewable sources in Poland in 2013, wind energy took the second position and amounted to 35.2% (the first position was taken by solid fuels – 46.5%), whereby a considerable increase of energy amount generated by wind farms in 2014 is emphasized (in 2014, the highest increase of power was noted exactly in case of wind farms).[9] The above brings prompts the conclusion that if within the following years wind energy is developing at a similar pace, it will become the primary carrier of renewable energy in Poland. According to the data published by the Energy Regulatory Authority at the end of June 2016, the power of wind farms reached 5.6 GW (out of the total power of renewable energy sources at the level of 8.2 GW).[10]

The predicted leading position ("driving" force function) of wind energy technology in the growth of renewable energy source in Poland (and in effect the possibility of achieving by Poland the general national target of the renewable energy share in the final gross energy consumption in 2020) may be however effectively blocked by numerous public conflicts related to the location of wind power plants. Currently, investments regarding wind energy technology (and exactly location of such undertakings) have become the object of many significant public conflicts in Poland. It effectively inhibits the investment processes, and in many cases results in suspending, and even final discontinuation of such investments' implementation. This, may in turn hinder (and even slow down) this type of investment processes and may contribute to making it impossible for Poland to meet the current and future EU requirements with regard to renewable energy sources. Thus, it is vital to eliminate (and at least curb) these public

---

8 *P. Frączek*, Inwestycje energetyczne w Polsce – wyzwania i perspektywy, in K. Giordano & R. Biskup (eds), Planowanie inwestycji publicznych. Aspekty prawne, ekonomiczne i środowiskowe, 2010, pp. 91–92.

9 *Supra*, note 5, p. 27.

10 Data available at Central Statistical Office Web Site www.ure.gov.pl/pl/rynki-energii/energia-elektryczna/odnawialne-zrodla-ener/potencjal-krajowy-oze/5753,Moc-zainstalowana-MW.html, accessed 15 September 2016.

conflicts not to let them inhibit the development of wind energy technology in Poland. This is the aim of the law in wind power investments enacted.

4. PROTECTION OF THE PUBLIC PARTICIPATION RIGHTS IN THE PROCESS OF WIND FARM LOCATION

According to the conducted research and analyses, the scale of public conflicts accompanying the process of investment location regarding wind farms, as compared to other kinds of investments, often much more oppressive for the public and environment and equally often carried out in Poland, is much wider.[11] "The local community acts against location of wind farms to a higher or lower extent in all regions of Poland".[12] In the recent years "conflicts around locations of wind farms have had the highest share in all location conflicts in the rural areas and in small towns".[13] "(...) as much as 20% of all investments against which protests there have been raised are wind farms".[14] "Wind farms have been definitely the most frequent object of the local protests of village and town communities; more frequent than roads, objects related to waste disposal, biogas plants, factory farms and other investments generating nuisances for the residents".[15] What is more, according to the conducted research and analyses, "in the group of analyzed conflicts about location of wind farms there have been twice more cases in which the investment finally was not implemented rather than cases wherein it was implemented".[16]

What are the main reasons for those conflicts? Analysis of information on the results of inspection carried out by the Supreme Chamber of Control regarding location and building of land wind farms[17] allows to find the reason for this state above all in the insufficient ensuring of public participation in the procedure of wind farms location (lack of wide dissemination of the information on planned investments, lack of identification by public administration authorities and elimination of the potential sources of conflicts at the stage of power plants location, which in turn leads to escalation of conflicts at the later stages of investment process), and also access to justice (in general lack of public interests

---

11 According to the researches conducted and presented in *M. Bednarek-Szczepańska*, Energetyka wiatrowa jako przedmiot konfliktów lokalizacyjnych w Polsce, 1 Polityka energetyczna 2016(1), pp. 53–72.

12 Id., at p. 56.

13 Id., at p. 70.

14 Id., at p. 55.

15 Id.

16 Id., at p. 60.

17 The Supreme Chamber of Control, *Informacja o wynikach kontrolo. Lokalizacja i budowa lądowych farm wiatrowych*, Warsaw 2014, record No. 131/2014/P/13/189/LWR.

securing in the procedure of wind farms' location). On the basis of analysis of the information from the Supreme Chamber of Control inspection's results regarding location and construction of land wind farms, at least three sources of this state of affairs may be pointed out.

Firstly, the source of assuring insufficient public participation in the procedure of wind farms' location, as well as in their access to justice, is the tardiness of the administration authorities in passing the local spatial development plans. According to the legislation in force before the law on wind power investments was enacted, the location of wind power plants could be selected on the grounds of general regulations of the law dated 27 March 2003 on spatial planning and development.[18] According to the content of Article 4 of item 1 of the law on spatial planning, establishing the land use, the layout of public use investments, as well as determination of ways to manage and develop the land are included in the local spatial development plan (the local plan). Whereas, according to the resolutions of item 2 of the aforesaid regulation, in case a local spatial development plan is not available, defining the way of management and conditions of land development takes place through decision on the land development and spatial management (zoning approval).

According to the aforesaid regulations, in the legal framework of Poland the local plan is of primary importance in spatial planning (local plan elaborating should be a principle). In view of the fact, however, that in Poland most communes do not have their local plans (according to statistical data for 31 December 2013 only about 30% of the area of Poland was included in the local plans[19]), in practice also in case of wind farms the principle that investments location is selected on the grounds of the local spatial plan has become an exception.[20] In practice, location of a considerable part of wind farms was selected on the grounds of decision on spatial development and management (zoning approval). During the procedure of drawing up and passing the local plan, it is obligatory to assure the public participation (also in relation to the obligatory strategic assessment of environmental impact, during which the forecast of environmental impact is analysed[21]). On the other hand, in the course of the procedure of zoning

---

18 See Article 59 item 1 of the law dated 27 March 2003 on spatial planning and development, consolidated text *Dziennik Ustaw* (English: Journal of Laws) of 2016, item 778 as amended, hereinafter referred to as the law on spatial planning.

19 The Polish Academy of Sciences, *Analiza stanu uwarunkowań prac planistycznych w gminach w 2013 r.*, Warsaw, 13 February 2015, p. 82.

20 Community is entitled to pass the local spatial plan, however it is not obliged to do it, see more e.g. *H. Nowicki*, Zasady ustawy o planowaniu i zagospodarowaniu przestrzennym, in W. Szwajder (ed.), Aspekty prawne planowania i zagospodarowania przestrzennego, 2013, p. 27; *I. Chojnacka*, Władztwo planistyczne gminy w orzecznictwie sądów administracyjnych i Trybunału konstytucyjnego, Samorząd Terytorialny 2009 (1–2), pp. 72–89.

21 The problem is wide discussed, see more e.g. *A. Fogel*, Prawna uwarunkowania współdziałania organów w strategicznej ocenie oddziaływania na środowisko gminnych aktów planowania przestrzennego, Człowiek i środowisko 2012(1–2), pp. 51–73; *A. Fogel*, Środowiskowe aspekty uprawnień społeczeństwa w sporządzaniu studiów uwarunkowań i planów

approval issuing, a possibility of applying procedural law is vested in case of such investments only to the parties in the proceedings, whereby it must be pointed out that the notion of "the party" and specifically "having a legal interest" is interpreted in judicial decisions quite narrowly (although non-homogenously).[22] The vital meaning has the legal interest that is to be proven by the party concerned. According to the judicature, legal interest based on substantive law regarding establishing conditions for a particular investment (of the public interest and of another type) is vested, in principle, in the owners and perpetual lessees of the property neighbouring with (bordering with) the investment areas, whereas the owners and perpetual lessees of land located farther, depending on the proven range and nuisance of the planned investment's impact upon the land (proving there is a direct connection between the investment and individual legal circumstances of the party concerned).[23] Applying location decisions reduces therefore a chance of the local public to influence the investment process at the initial stage of its implementation. In view of the local community's limited impact upon shaping of that process, protection of the public rights becomes limited.

The second source of assuring the insufficient public participation in the procedure of wind farms location is frequently formal and legal correctness, but inefficiency of the public administration authorities' functioning in the process of elaborating and passing the local plans regarding the information dissemination, identifying by the public administration bodies and eliminating any potential sources of conflicts at the stage of wind farms' location. The information on the results of inspection conducted by the Supreme Chamber of Control regarding location and building of the land wind farms pointed out that in cases where location of wind farms was based on the grounds of local plans, even though the public administration authorities in principle formally meet the legal requirements assuring the public participation at each stage of processing issues related to wind farms' location, they have repeatedly failed to meet their information objectives, conducting actions without due diligence as regards identification,

---

miejscowych, Samorząd Terytorialny 2010(5), pp. 46–61, *A. Fogel*, Partycypacja społeczna w procedurach sporządzania studium uwarunkowań i planu miejscowego – zmiany prawne i problemy faktyczne, Problemy Planistyczne 2009(1), pp. 41–42; *J. Jendrośka & M. Bar*, Oceny oddziaływania na środowisko planów i programów. Praktyczny poradnik prawny, 2009, pp. 33–42, *B. Szulczewska*, Prognoza oddziaływania na środowisko jako narzędzie wspomagające proces planowania przestrzennego, Zeszyty Naukowe Wszechnicy Polskiej 2010(2), p. 67; *Iwona Derucka*, Prawne gwarancje realizacji zadań ochrony środowiska w procedurze planowania przestrzennego, 2013, pp. 105–167.

22 *A. Plicińska-Filipowicz & A. Kosicki*, Strony i sąsiedztwo w sprawach budowlanych, in *A. Plucińska-Filipowicz & M. Wierzbowski* (ed.), Proces inwestycyjno-budowlany. Zagadnienia prawne, 2015, pp. 49–50.

23 See e.g. judgement of Provincial Administrative Court in Rzeszowie dated 24 November 2010, files No II SA/Rz 889/10; judgement of Supreme Administrative Court dated 26 November 2010, files No II OSK 1825/09; judgement of Supreme Administrative Court dated 3 November 2011, files No II OSK 1724/11, http://orzeczenia.nsa.gov.pl accessed 30 November 2016.

and then elimination of a potential source of conflicts.[24] In particular (in the opinion of the Supreme Chamber of Control), there is a necessity to carry out a wide and deliberate information campaign, which is likely to attract the attention of the majority of residents, for example by using diverse forms of passing of the information concerning a planned meeting, inviting independent experts both as regards impact of the investments upon health, as well as acoustics and infrasounds, and also precise presentation of the impact the planned investment may have upon the environment and the inhabitants.[25] Publication of specific information and documents on internet websites in practice is not a sufficient measure.

As the next source of insufficient assurance of the public access to justice, legal loopholes, ambiguities and inconsistencies may be pointed out, as well as the prevailing way of their interpretation by the doctrine and judicature, which leads to a failure in considering the measures of appeal submitted by the parties. Conflicts about location of wind farms, which are not resolved by way of negotiations between the investor and local community shall be resolved by adjudicating of filed appeal against the zoning approval by the public administration authorities and administrative courts and by way of considering a complaint against the zoning approval and against resolutions of county councils by the administrative courts.

Following the content of art. 61 item 1 of the Law on spatial planning, issuing a zoning approval is possible in case the following requirements have been met jointly: 1) at least one neighbouring allotment, accessible from the same public road, has been developed in the way allowing to determine requirements regarding a new development with regard to continuing its function, parameters, features and plot ratios, as well as land development, including dimensions and architectural form of the building objects, building alignment and intensity of the land development; 2) the area has access to a public road; 3) the existing or planned utilities are sufficient for construction project; 4) the area does not require an approval to change the allocation of agricultural land and woodland or it has been included in the approval obtained at the time of drawing up the local plans which lost their validity; 5) the decision conforms to separate regulations. The authority having jurisdiction may not refuse to establish land development conditions if the investment target conforms with the conditions. Zoning approval is a constrained decision, and not discretionary decision.[26] If the zoning application regards an investment whose location conforms to the regulations of the law on spatial planning including the legal regularizations provided for in specific regulations, as well as it meets the formal requirements, the authority

24 *Supra*, note 20, pp. 16 and 27–28.

25 Id., pp. 27–28.

26 *M. Jaśkowska*, Uznanie administracyjne a inne formy władzy dyskrecjonalnej administracji publicznej, in R. Hauser, Z. Niewiadomski & A. Wróbel (eds), System prawa administracyjnego. Instytucje prawa administracyjnego, 2015, pp. 237–276.

having jurisdiction ought to issue a positive decision.[27] Refusing to issue a zoning approval, the issuing authority is obliged to specify a general binding law regulation that opposes issuing the above.[28]

Bearing in mind the above, "Objection of the local residents cannot determine issuing or refusal of a location decision. Regulations of the law on spatial planning do not provide the grounds for refusal to establish a location. Such a decision is an administrative act of constrained type, which means that if a planned investment meets all requirements provided for in the acts of law and does not infringe any separate regulations, it is not permissible to issue a location refusal".[29] The grounds for zoning refusal may not be either the fact that there are no precise test results proving the impact of wind farms upon human health.[30]

Similarly, according to the judicature considering measures of appeal against decisions on spatial conditions and spatial planning (zoning approvals), concerns of the local communities regarding too short distance of the investment from their residences, which poses a threat to their health, in particular in view of the infrasound waves emitted by wind farms, the shadow flicker effect and noise need not be accounted for either. In Poland, the only parameter having an impact onto establishing the distance of a wind farm from the built-up area, especially from those populated ones, is the permissible level of noise emitted by those facilities. However, what was emphasized in the Information on Inspection Results conducted by The Supreme Chamber of Control with respect to location and construction of land wind farms, the law regulating methodology of noise measurement did not guarantee a reliable evaluation of this type of facilities annoyance, since they did not directly cover noise emissions caused by wind turbines.[31] The assumed methodology indicated that measurements must be taken in specific meteorological conditions, above all at the mean speed of wind of up to 5 m/s, whereas in case of wind farms, the highest parameters of noise emissions have been noted at their nominal load at wind velocity of about 10–12 m/s.[32]

Similarly the charges, regarding problems related to wind turbine syndrome or shadow flicker also could not be the grounds for refusal to issue a zoning approval because they were not regulated by law.[33] In view of the fact that in the binding

---

27 See e.g. *T. Bąkowski*, Ustawa o planowaniu i zagospodarowaniu przestrzennym. Komentarz, 2004, pp. 220–222.

28 See Judgement of Provincial Administrative Court in Poznań dated 3 September 2014, files No IV SA/Po 302/14, http://orzeczenia.nsa.gov.pl accessed 30 November 2016.

29 See Judgement of Provincial Administrative Court in Poznań dated 27 January2015, files No II SA/Rz 747/14, http://orzeczenia.nsa.gov.pl accessed 30 November 2016.

30 See Judgement of Provincial Administrative Court in Poznań dated 3 September 2014, files No IV SA/Po 302/14, http://orzeczenia.nsa.gov.pl accessed 30 November 2016.

31 *Supra*, note 20, p. 22.

32 Id.

33 See Judgement of Provincial Administrative Court in Łódź dated 4 June 2014, files No II SA/Łd 201/14, http://orzeczenia.nsa.gov.pl accessed 30 November 2016.

legislation there were no regulations regarding wind farms, defining permissible levels of infrasound noise, or regulations regarding the issue of shadow flicker appearance, there were even no grounds for taking such measurements.[34]

What is more, in the course of wind farm location via a zoning approval, administrative authorities cannot take into consideration aesthetic and landscape values (except for the protected area).[35] According to the judicature, "It is unacceptable to assume that an authority is entitled to evaluate the intended investment through general standards, e.g. protecting the spatial order or architectural and landscape values, and such evaluation might be the grounds for refusal to establish the land development conditions".[36] The authority, issuing a negative decision, ought to base their settling on the grounds of a clear contradiction to an *expressis verbis* restrictive regulation.[37]

According to the Supreme Chamber of Control, in majority of communes subject to inspection (80%), approval issued by the commune's authorities depended on financing the planning scheme documents by investors or providing a donation on behalf of the commune at least equivalent to the costs of changing the arrangements of spatial zoning decision.[38] Consequently, the planning documents passed by the commune accounted for solutions postulated by the investors, which had not always been concurrent with the public interest. According to the regulations of the law on spatial planning, conducting spatial policy of the commune, including passing the study of conditions and directions of spatial planning, as well as the local plan, belongs to the commune's own tasks.[39] One of the supreme principles following from this act is that costs of drawing up the aforesaid documents ought to be incurred by the commune's budget. According to judicature, however, the fact of incurring the cost (at least partially) by another entity (e.g. the investor) is an internal issue of a commune and in the situation wherein planning procedure has been followed, it may not result in the statement of a resolution's invalidity.[40]

---

34 *Supra*, note 20, p. 22.

35 *A. Fogel*, Uwzględnianie wartości przyrodniczych i kulturowych w strategicznej ocenie oddziaływania na środowisko gminnych aktów planistycznych, in Z. Cieślak & A. Fogel (eds), *Wartości w planowaniu przestrzennym*, 2010, p. 103.

36 See, files No IV SA/Po 302/14, judgement of Provincial Administrative Court in Łódź dated 4 June 2014, files No II SA/Łd 201/14, http://orzeczenia.nsa.gov.pl accessed 30 November 2016.

37 See Judgement of Provincial Administrative Court in Poznań dated 3 September 2014, files No IV SA/Po 302/14, Judgement of Provincial Administrative Court in Wrocław dated 28 September 2010, files No II SA/Wr 407/10, http://orzeczenia.nsa.gov.pl accessed 30 November 2016.

38 *Supra*, note 20, pp. 19–20.

39 Id.

40 See judgement of Supreme Administrative Court dated 6 July 2012, files No OSK 996/12; judgement of Supreme Administrative Court dated 7 September 2012, files No OSK 991/11, http://orzeczenia.nsa.gov.pl accessed 30 November 2016.

5. THE IMPACT OF THE WIND FARM INVESTMENTS ACT ON THE INCREASE OF THE PUBLIC PARTICIPATION RIGHTS

According to the resolutions of Article 1 item 1 of the law on wind power investments, the law sets forth the conditions and mode of location as well as construction of wind power plants, and also conditions of wind power plants' location in the vicinity of an existing or planned residential area (although it must be emphasized that the law does not provide for all the issues related to such investments' location). According to the project's initiator, the law is aimed at solving the problem of public conflicts related to wind farm investments, accelerate and improve the procedure of location. The legal act concerned introduces a few provisions, which shall undoubtedly influence the reinforcement of the public participation rights in the process of wind farms location.

The main assumption of the law concerned is excluding the possibility of installing renewable sources energy of over 40 kW capacity on the grounds of a zoning approval and enabling it only on the grounds of the local plans. As provided in Article 3 of the law on wind power investments, location of a wind farm (i.e. the structure according to the construction law regulations, consisting of at least the foundation, tower and technical elements, of capacity higher than capacity of microgeneration according to Article 2 pt 19 of the law dated 20 February 2015 on renewable energy sources[41]) takes places exclusively on the grounds of a local plan. Exclusion of the possibility to construct a renewable energy source of over 40 kW capacity on the grounds of a zoning approval and making it possible exclusively on the grounds of a local plan shall make it possible for the local community (not only for parties in the proceeding) to participate in the proceeding already at the stage of location, which shall allow to identify the legal interests and spatial conflicts existing in the commune so that they could be eliminated at the early stage of investment process.

What is more, the law introduces a minimum distance that the authorities are obliged to maintain while issuing zoning dispositions, as well as the mode of its calculation; whereby the distance may be increased based on the results of environmental impact assessment procedure in case of a particular investment. Following the content of Article 4 item 1 of the law on wind power investments, the distance within which the objects listed below may be located and constructed are: 1) for wind farms – from a residential building or a building including a residential function, as well as 2) a residential building or a building including a residential function – from the wind farm – is equal to or exceeds the tenfold of the wind farm height measured from the ground level to the highest point of the structure, including its technical components, especially the rotor and

41 *Dziennik Ustaw* (English: Journal of Laws) of 2015, item 478 as amended.

the rotor blades atop (total height of the wind farm). Moreover, according to the disposition of item 2 of the above quoted article, such a distance is also required in case of location and construction of wind farms in the vicinity of a national park, a nature reserve, a landscape park or Nature 2000 areas, as well as in case of promotional forest complexes, whereby creating the aforesaid forms of nature conservation and promotional forest complexes shall not require maintaining the distance concerned. In order to guarantee adherence to the requirement concerned, provisions of art. 6 of the law on wind farms impose among others on: 1) the commune's authorities drawing up and passing or amending the study of commune's land use conditions and directions, b) the commune's authorities and voivode (province governor) while drawing up, passing or approving or amendment of the local plan, c) the commune's authorities and voivode (province governor) while issuing the zoning approval, g) the authorities issuing the decision on environmental conditions – the obligation to account for the distance concerned, established according to the aforesaid law requirements. If the local plan provides for location of a wind farm, an architectural and construction administrative authority refuses to issue a building permit, and the authority conducting the proceedings regarding a decision on environmental conditions refuses to approve implementation of the undertaking if the investment does not meet "distance" requirements.[42]

At the stage of drawing up and passing the local plan, the public shall also receive information about the maximum total height of the wind power plants, since according to the content of Article 7 item 1 of the law on wind power investments, such information must be included in the content of the local spatial development plan. It must also be emphasized that location of wind farms (their height) shall be considerably influenced by the regulations issued on the grounds of so called landscape protection law[43], and above all conducting the landscape audit provided therein, which within the motions and recommendations may include guidelines concerning height parameters for building structures.[44] The results and recommendations from the audit concerned consequently ought to be included in the studies and local plans.

In case of the local plans providing for location of wind farms and permitting to exploit a wind farm, the new law on wind power investments grants also to the owners and perpetual lessees of the property located within the obligatory distance the right to lodge an appeal against the local plan at the nearest administrative court.[45] The subject lodging an appeal shall not therefore be obliged to prove their legal interest based on the substantive law regulations or meet other requirements,

---

42 See Article 15 item 3 of the law on wind power investments.

43 Law dated 24 April 2015 on some laws amending in connection with landscape protection instruments enhancing, *Dziennik Ustaw* (English: Journal of Laws) of 2015, item 774, item 1688.

44 *A. Fogel* in A. Fogel (ed.), *Ustawa krajobrazowa. Komentarze praktyczne*, p. 150.

45 See Article 15 item 10 of the law on wind power investments.

which shall on the other hand reduce the issue of too narrow range of subjects considered among other to be parties in the location proceedings.

On the other hand, nonetheless, with regard to the new regulations Poland may not reach the binding general national target of Renewable Energy Sources share in the final gross energy consumption in 2020. In Poland, majority of communes do not have local plans. Wherever those plans are missing, implementation of Renewable Energy Sources exceeding the threshold of 40 kW capacity will be impossible. Local plans are elaborated mainly for the populated areas, but the distance provisions shall limit the amount of space for setting up new wind farms. According to the analyses conducted within The Institute of Environmental Protection, distance limits may cause a reduction of the potential area that might be used to build wind farms by over 27,000 ha throughout Poland.[46]

6. CONCLUSIONS

The previous regulations in force (although they formally provided for the applied protection measures), in practice insufficiently protected the interest of the local community in the process of wind power investments location. The formal guarantee of the public rights in the procedure of wind farms location (in particular by establishing the principle that location of wind farms is based on the local plan, and with the public participation), in order to assure safety to the environment and reduce the nuisance of wind farms to the residents in the neighbourhood, has proven insufficient. Despite the formal existence of the vital legal instruments, in practice mainly the following reasons resulted in absence of securing the public interests in the procedure of wind farms location: the tardiness of authorities in passing the local plans, undue diligence of authorities in actual implementation of procedural rights, legal loopholes, ambiguities and inconsistencies of regulations that have repeatedly influenced rejection of measures of appeal and resulted in public conflicts, whereas their escalation at further stages has often led to suspension of the investment process. Absence (in practice) of the sufficient protection of public interests within the procedure of wind farms location has been leading to public conflicts, which on the other hand have led to suspension, or even final discontinuance of such undertakings' implementation, thereby posing a threat to implementation of the current and future EU requirements by Poland with respect to renewable energy sources.

Adopting the law on wind power investments shall undoubtedly influence the increase of public participation rights in the process of wind farms' location. Exclusion of the opportunity of building renewable energy sources of over 40 kW on the grounds of the zoning approval and making it possible only on the

46 *Z. Cichocki, M. Hajto, M. Bidłasik*, Przestrzenne konsekwencje przyjęcia wybranych kryteriów lokalizacji elektrowni wiatrowych, 2013, p. 5.

grounds of local plans shall enable the public to take part in the proceedings already at the location stage, which as a result shall allow to identify the legal interests and spatial conflicts existing within the commune and eliminate them at the early stage of investment process. The practice of investments location with respect to wind power proves, however, that introducing only the obligation of wind power plants location on the grounds of the local plan may not secure the rights of the local people. Hence, simultaneously the permissible distance of wind farms location from habitats and housing areas has been specified, which shall allow to eliminate (and at least limit) the problem of lack of proper regulations as regards the impact of wind farms upon human health (problems related to tests of community annoyance from location of wind farms in relation to the residential developments and landscape, not accounting for the influence of wind turbine syndrome or shadow flickering upon human health), since the minimum distance shall be guaranteed. The guarantee to all owners and perpetual lessees of property located in the area included in the obligatory distance to be entitled to file an appeal against the local plan to the administrative court shall release those subjects from the obligation of proving a legal interest based on the regulations of substantive law.

On the other hand, nonetheless, with regard to the new regulations Poland may not reach the binding general national target of Renewable Energy Sources share in the final gross energy consumption in 2020. In Poland, majority of communes do not have local plans. Wherever those plans are missing, implementation of Renewable Energy Sources exceeding the threshold of 40 kW capacity will be impossible. Local plans are elaborated mainly for the populated areas, but the distance provisions shall limit the amount of space for setting up new wind farms

Passing the law on wind farm investments shall have a certainly positive impact upon protecting the rights of local community due to the fact it shall decrease the amount of public conflicts related to wind farms location. Provisions of the new law may however negatively impact the chance to fulfil by Poland the current and future EU requirements regarding renewable energy sources. Thus, from the point of view of a feasibility to meet the current and future EU requirements by Poland as regards renewable energy sources, the issue remains unsettled due to the newly introduced regulations of law, only its origin changes (not just public conflicts, but the statutory requirements).

ACCESS TO JUSTICE

ACCESS TO ENVIRONMENTAL JUSTICE IN INDIA: INNOVATION AND CHANGE

Gitanjali Nain GILL*

ABSTRACT

Access to justice is a pillar of democratic governance. It promotes just and equitable outcomes thereby supporting the rule of law. The importance of judicial institutions [courts and specialist tribunals to adjudicate environmental disputes] is widely acknowledged in international instruments. Principle 10 of the Rio Declaration, 1992, strengthens access rights by stating 'effective access to judicial and administrative proceedings, including redress and remedy, shall be provided by states in environmental matters'. In this context, India's commitment to secure environmental justice assumes significant practical importance. This chapter traces and evaluates the role of the Indian judiciary (Supreme Court of India and the National Green Tribunal) in contributing and promoting access to environmental justice. The chapter presents and analyses participatory parity in Indian environmental discourse evolved from the concept of broad and liberal litigant 'standing' in environmental matters facilitated by Supreme Court of India through Public Interest Litigation (PIL) and 'aggrieved party' by the National Green Tribunal (NGT). It reviews appropriate case illustrations in providing victims of environmental degradation with a way to access justice in a participatory manner.

1. INTRODUCTION

A broad understanding of environmental justice involves participation in environmental controversies. Participatory mechanisms can help to meliorate issues of inequality, recognition and the larger question of capabilities and functioning of individuals and communities. 'Parity of participation' comes with the satisfaction of two conditions: 'that institutionalized cultural patterns of

* Professor of Environmental Law, Northumbria Law School, Northumbria University, UK, gita.gill@northumbria.ac.uk.

interpretation and evaluation express equal respect for all participants and ensure equal opportunity…' and 'the resources to enable participation'.[1]

The discourse and understanding of environmental justice has increased and now includes issues of fairness, equity and standing, rights of disadvantaged populations in developing countries and meaningful participation in the decision-making process to promote environmental governance.[2] This chapter focuses on a strong procedural dimension that reflects fair, open, informed and inclusive state institutional processes. In this context, access to justice through an accessible judicial mechanism that offers redress to environmental damage or harm and the protection and enforcement of legitimate interests becomes important.

Access to justice is a pillar of democratic governance. It promotes just and equitable outcomes thereby supporting the rule of law. Courts allow people to hold government, agencies, companies and individuals accountable for the violation of their fundamental rights as enshrined in the constitutional mandate. The UN Development Programme defines access to justice as 'the ability of people to seek and obtain a remedy through formal or informal institutions of justice, and in conformity with human rights standards.[3]

The importance of judicial institutions [courts and specialist tribunals to adjudicate environmental disputes] is widely acknowledged in international instruments. The World Charter for Nature provides 'all persons, in accordance with their national legislation, shall have the opportunity to participate, individually or with others, in the formulation of decisions of direct concern to their environment, and shall have access to means of redress when their environment has suffered damage or degradation.'[4] Additionally, the World Commission on Environment and Development Expert Group on Environmental Law adopted legal principles for environmental protection and sustainable development ensuring 'due process and equal treatment in administrative and judicial proceedings to all persons who are or may be affected by trans-boundary interference with their use of a natural resource or the environment.'[5]

Principle 10 of the Rio Declaration, 1992, strengthens access rights by stating 'effective access to judicial and administrative proceedings, including redress and remedy, shall be provided by states in environmental matters'. Principle

1 *D. Schlosberg*, Defining Environmental Justice, 2007, pp. 25–29.

2 *B. Jessup*, 'The Journey of Environmental Justice through Public and International Law' in B. Jessup and K. Rubenstein (eds.), Environmental Discourses in Public and International Law, 2012, pp. 50–60; *J. Agyeman, R. Bullard and B. Evans*, Just Sustainabilities: Development in an Unequal World, 2003.

3 *R. Jayasundere*, Access to Justice Assessments in the Asia Pacific: A Review of Experiences and Tools from the Region. Bangkok, Thailand: UNDP, 2012, p. 11.

4 Article 23 World Charter for Nature 1982.

5 Article 20 Our Common Future, Annexe 1: Summary of Proposed Legal Principles for Environmental Protection and Sustainable Development Adopted by the WCED Experts Group on Environmental Law.

10 has been recognised as a global framework incorporating elements for good environmental governance. It is characterised as promoting environmental democracy and facilitating the rule of law.[6] The Aarhus Convention[7] promotes Principle 10 and mandates binding environmental obligations that emphasise governmental accountability, transparency and responsiveness thereby bolstering access to justice and the rule of law.

Access to environmental justice is the first step to the achievement of environmental justice goals by articulating in the language of equity the assurance of legal standing for all affected and interested parties; the right of appeal or review; specialised environmental courts and other practical dispute resolution mechanisms.[8] In this context, India's commitment to secure environmental justice assumes significant practical importance. This chapter traces and evaluates the role of the Indian judiciary (Supreme Court of India and the National Green Tribunal) in contributing and promoting access to environmental justice. Accordingly, after this Introduction the chapter is divided into three parts. Part 1 offers an account of the role of specialist environmental judiciary to improve access to justice and environmental governance. Several international declarations and institutions also call for judicial specialisation, envisaging expert courts and trained judges and lawyers in environmental matters. They seek to strengthen capacity building among individuals within the decision-making process at national, regional and global levels. Part 2 presents and analyses participatory parity in Indian environmental discourse evolved from the concept of broad and liberal litigant 'standing' in environmental matters facilitated by Supreme Court of India through Public Interest Litigation (PIL) and 'aggrieved party' by the National Green Tribunal (NGT). It reviews appropriate case illustrations in providing victims of environmental degradation with a way to access justice in a participatory manner. Part 3 is the conclusion.

---

6 Http://web.unep.org/about/majorgroups/partnership/participation-information; See also the 12 Bali Guidelines 2010 that deal with access to justice in environmental matters, demonstrating the importance of the rights-based approach in implementing Principle 10 of the Rio Declaration: guideline 15 (access to review procedures relating to information requests), 16 (access to review procedures relating to public participation); 17 (access to review procedures relating to public or private actors); 18 (liberal standing provisions); 19 (effective procedures for timely review); 20 (access should be not prohibitively expensive and assistance should be available); 21 (prompt, adequate and effective remedies); 22 (timely and effective enforcement); 23 (information provided about access to justice procedures); 24 (decisions to be publicly available); 25 (promoting capacity-building programmes); and 26 (ADR).

7 The UN Economic Commission for Europe Convention on Access to Information, Public Participation in Decision-Making and Access to Justice in Environmental Matters 1998.

8 *G.N. Gill*, The National Green Tribunal of India: A Sustainable Future Through The Principles of International Environmental Law, Environmental Law Review 2014 16(3) p. 183, 184 et seq.

2. ENVIRONMENTAL COURTS AND TRIBUNALS: FACILITATING AND PROMOTING ENVIRONMENTAL JUSTICE

The judiciary plays a 'lead role in shaping the normative interpretation of the legal and regulatory framework'. Justice Weeramantry in the commentary on the Bangalore Principles of Judicial Conduct observed that 'a judiciary of undisputed integrity is the bedrock institution essential for ensuring compliance'.[9] An independent judiciary and the judicial process are vital for the implementation, development and enforcement of environmental law.

There is growing support for judges to play a central role in providing accessible, fair, impartial, timely and responsive dispute resolution mechanisms,. These include developing specialised expertise in environmental adjudication and innovative environmental procedures and remedies. Various international forums and associated documentation have recognised and promoted the role of the judiciary in in vindicating the rights of individuals substantively and in accessing the judicial process.[10] For example, Agenda 21 emphasises the need to provide an effective regulatory framework for improving the legal–institutional capacities of countries to cope with problems of national governance and effective law-making and law-applying in this field.[11] The Johannesburg Principles on the Role of Law and Sustainable Development adopted at the Global Judges Symposium in Johannesburg 2002 state:

> 'We emphasize that the fragile state of the global environment requires the Judiciary as the guardian of the Rule of Law, to boldly and fearlessly implement and enforce applicable international and national laws... We are strongly of the view that there is an urgent need to strengthen the capacity of judges, prosecutors, legislators and all persons who play a critical role at national level in the process of implementation, development and enforcement of environmental law, including multilateral environmental agreements... especially through the judicial process.'[12]

---

9 The Bangalore Principles of Judicial Conduct 2007 highlight seven core values: independence, impartiality, integrity, propriety, equality, competence and diligence. www.unodc.org/documents/corruption/publications_unodc_commentary-e.pdf.

10 For a detailed discussion see *N. A. Robinson*, Ensuring Access to Justice through Environmental Courts Pace Envtl. L. Rev 2012 29, p. 374 et seq.

11 Chapter 8, Agenda 21, paras 8.13, 8.26; www.un.org/esa/sustdev/documents/agenda21/english/Agenda21.pdf.

12 Www.unep.org/delc/judgesprogramme/GlobalJudgesSymposium/tabid/106158/Default. aspx. See also London Bridge Statement 2002 http://weavingaweb.org/pdfdocuments/London%20Bridge%20Statement.pdf; Rome Symposium 2003 http://weavingaweb.org/pdfdocuments/LN290304-Rome%20Statement%20FINAL.pdf; *Justice Paul Stein*, Why judges are essential to the rule of law and environmental protection https://portals.iucn.org/library/efiles/html/EPLP-060/section9.html; *Justice Amedeo Postiglione*, The role of the judiciary in the implementation and enforcement of environmental law www.eufje.org/images/docConf/bud2014/presAP2%20bud2014.pdf.

Also, Klaus Toepfer, UNEP Executive Director, in the 2005 UNEP Global Judges Programme stated:

> 'It is essential to forge a global partnership among all relevant stakeholders for the protection of the environment based on the affirmation of the human values set out in the UN Millennium Declaration: freedom, equality, solidarity, tolerance, respect for nature and shared responsibility. The judiciary plays a key role in weaving these values into the fabric of our societies. The judiciary is also a crucial partner in promoting environmental governance, upholding the rule of law and in ensuring a fair balance between environmental, social and developmental consideration through its judgements and declarations.'[13]

In Europe, the EU Forum of Judges for the Environment (EUFJE) was created in 2004 through which judges exchange information and ideas on the implementation and interpretation of EU legislation and provide training for judges. An aim of the Forum is 'to exchange experiences in the area of training of the judiciary in environmental law, contribute to a better knowledge of environmental law, share experiences with environmental case law and contribute to a more effective enforcement of environmental law.'[14]

In Asia and the Pacific, the Asian Development Bank (ADB) is active in promoting green justice through knowledge-sharing and capacity-building. The ADB is committed to 'strengthen the... legal, regulatory, and enforcement capacities of public institutions on environmental considerations.'[15] In 2010, the ADB organised the Asian Judges Symposium on Environmental Decision-Making, the Rule of Law and Environmental Justice emphasising:

> '... improving environmental and natural resource decision making and adjudication within regional judiciaries, without assuming that any particular form or structure is the best way to achieve effective environmental decision making and adjudication in different country contexts; highlighting environmental specialisation within general courts, as well as exploring work done by specialist environmental courts, boards, and tribunals. Importantly, without drivers for increasing the demand for effective environmental judicial decision-making from the judiciary, environmental judicial specialisations could go unused.'[16]

---

13 UNEP Report UNEP/GC.23/INF/10 (2004), pp. 6, 14–15; also see *D. Kaniaru, L. Kurukulasuriya, and C. Okidi*, UNEP Judicial Symposium on the Role of the Judiciary in Promoting Sustainable Development, Conference Proceedings Fifth International Conference on Environmental Compliance and Enforcement, Monterey, November 1998, p. 22; *M. Decleris*, Strengthening the judiciary for sustainable development (2011) www.unep.org/delc/Portals/119/publications/Speeches/MICHAEL_DECLARIS.pdf.

14 Www.eufje.org/.

15 *J.H. Hovland*, Foreword, Asian Judges Symposium on Environmental Decision Making ADB 2011, p. iv.

16 *Asian Development Bank*, Environmental Governance and the Courts in Asia Law and Policy Reform Brief 2012, p. 1.

Subsequently, the Bhurban Declaration 2012 included a promise for an educated judiciary, specialized courts, countries to improve the development, implementation, enforcement of, and compliance with environmental laws, as well as to make an action plan to achieve the same; strengthen the existing specialized environmental tribunals, as well as train judges and lawyers on environmental law. It included a commitment to establish green benches in courts for dispensation of environmental justice and to make necessary amendments or adjustments to the legal and regulatory structures to foster environmental justice in South Asia.[17]

Further, the ADB approved and supported technical assistance to establish the Asian Judges Network on Environment (AJNE) in 2010. The AJNE is an informal trans-governmental network committed to providing a dynamic forum for judicial capacity-building and multilateral exchanges on environmental adjudication.[18] In this network, the chief justices and judges of the Association of Southeast Asian Nations (ASEAN) and South Asian Association for Regional Cooperation (SAARC) regions have harnessed the collective judicial experience in environmental decision-making in Asia. The AJNE's contribution has been to encourage senior judiciary to recognise a shared professional mission to advance environmental justice beyond their national jurisdiction.

A consequence of these international developments has led many jurisdictions to develop some form of specialised environmental court or tribunal, while embracing a flexible mechanism for dispute resolution. Lord Carnwath, Justice of the Supreme Court of the United Kingdom, in 2012 stated:

> 'There is now widespread acknowledgement of an international 'common law' of the environment based on principles such as sustainability and intergenerational equity. There is now greatly expanded awareness of environmental issues among the judiciary, and the development of specialist courts and tribunals in many countries. ... There has been progress also on public involvement, information and access to justice under Rio Principle 10.'[19]

Chief Justice Brian Preston of the State of New South Wales (NSW), Australia, Land and Environment Court observed:

> 'Increasingly, it is being recognised that a court with special expertise in environmental matters is best placed to play this role in the achievement of ecologically sustainable development... Specialisation [is] not seen to be an end, but rather a means to an end. It [is] envisaged that a specialist court could more ably deliver consistency in decision-making, decrease delays (through its understanding of the characteristics of environmental disputes) and facilitate the development of environmental laws, policies and principles.'[20]

---

17 Www.adb.org/publications/south-asiaconference-environmental-justice.

18 Www.asianjudges.org/about-ajne/.

19 Www.theguardian.com/law/2012/jun/22/judges-environment-lord-carnwath-rio.

20 *B.J. Preston*, Benefits of Judicial specialisation in environmental law: the Land and Environment Court of New South Wales as a Case Study, Pace Environmental LR 2012 29(2), p. 386, 398,403

The finely grained, global 2016 study by George Pring and Catherine Pring on environmental courts and tribunals identifies there were over 1200 ECTs operating in 44 countries, in every major type of legal system (civil law, common law, mixed law, Asian law and Islamic law), at all government levels, from the richest to the poorest nations, with the majority created in the previous 10 years.[21] The exponential growth of ECTs has resulted in the concomitant advantages attached to the specialised forum.[22] These include:

1. specialised expertise in complex legal, scientific and technical matters;
2. freeing the regular courts of significant and steadily increasing workload;
3. uniformity and consistency in decision-making processes;
4. greater dispatch in resolution of environmental controversies and more efficient adjudication;
5. more predictable environmental decision-making;
6. greater governmental accountability in environmental matters;
7. instilling public confidence and trust in the government and judicial system;
8. expanded notion of locus standi for effective public participation and vindication of rights;
9. reduced litigation costs;
10. adoption of flexible rules of procedure;
11. problem-solving approach that moves beyond traditional legal remedies to create innovative solutions resulting in promoting environmental sustainability including protection of human rights; and
12. demonstrating commitment to implement international obligations relating to access to justice, environmental rule of law and environmental sustainability.

Possible disadvantages include[23]:

1. costs to establish and maintain a separate legal system;
2. jurisdictional location of the ECTs to assure convenient access to parties;
3. insufficient caseload;
4. generalist judges not sufficiently trained in environmental matters;
5. tendency of an activist judiciary usurping its power and adopting an unbalanced approach;
6. lack of expertise (judges and lawyers);

---

et seq; also see *A.H. Benjamin*, We, the judges, and the environment, Pace Environmental LR 2012 29 (2), p. 585; *M. Rackemann*, Environmental decision-making, the rule of law and environmental justice, Resource Management Theory and Practice 2011, p. 37 et seq.

21 This part is derivative from the extensive work of *G. Pring, and C. Pring*, The ABCs of the ECTs: A Guide for Policy-Makers for Designing and Operating a Specialised Environmental Court or Tribunal, (UNEP) 2016, p. 1 et seq.

22 *Id.* at p. 13, 14; also see *B.J. Preston*, Characteristics of successful environmental courts and tribunals, Journal of Environmental Law 2014 26(3), pp. 365–393 et seq.

23 *Id.* at p. 15.

7. risk of creating an inferior court below the general courts with less power and status; and
8. scepticism about defining an environmental case and determining the appropriate forum.

Although difficulties exist, the advantages attributed to environmental courts and tribunals are dominant. Specialised judicial forums in environmental matters provide a legitimate forum that helps to access environmental justice by its substantive decisions that protects constitutional, statutory and human rights, and flexible procedural requirements.

Within this context, the role of the Indian judiciary assumes enhanced importance. Access to justice, a pillar of democratic governance, promotes just and equitable outcomes thereby supporting the rule of law. In Fertilizer Kamgar Union v Union of India[24] the Supreme Court stated:

> 'The right of effective access to justice has emerged with the new social rights. Indeed, it is of paramount importance among these new rights since, clearly, the enjoyment of traditional as well as new social rights presupposes mechanisms for their effective protection. Such protection, moreover, is best assured by a workable remedy within the framework of the judicial system. Effective access to justice can thus be seen as the most basic requirement-the most basic 'human right'-of a system which purports to guarantee legal rights.'[25]

The following section reviews the present judicial structures that offer access to environmental justice in India. The initiative presented below has wider international purchase as it is a case study of a growing judicial development.

3. THE INDIAN JUDICIARY: PUBLIC INTEREST LITIGATION AND THE NATIONAL GREEN TRIBUNAL

PUBLIC INTEREST LITIGATION

Public interest litigation (PIL) is the product of realisation of the constitutional obligation of the court aimed at addressing and securing basic violations of human rights at the marginalised sections of society. The traditional adversarial process of 'cause of action', 'person aggrieved', and 'individual litigation' experienced a paradigmatic addition.[26] Social and economic inequality affects millions of

---

24 (1981) 1SCC 568.

25 *Id.* at p. 586.

26 See Report on the National Juridicare: Equal Justice – Social Justice Ministry of Law, Justice and Company Affairs 1977.

people and for these reasons the judiciary adopted the proactive role of providing redress through the innovative process of PIL or as Baxi describes 'social action litigation.'[27] The judiciary made conscious efforts to improve access to the courts for those who were historically and traditionally excluded from the legal process with regard to the protection of their fundamental human rights.[28] The word public interest has been understood as 'interest of a larger section as opposed to an individual interest and has the element of affecting greater section of the society. The expression public interest means act beneficial to general public. It means action necessarily taken for public purpose.'[29]

In Anirudh Kumar v MCD[30] the court stated:

> Our current processual jurisprudence is not of individualistic Anglo-Indian mould. It is broad-based and people-oriented, and envisions access to justice through 'class actions', 'public interest litigation' and 'representative proceedings'. Indeed, Indians in large numbers seeking remedies in courts through collective proceedings, instead of being driven to an expensive plurality of litigations, is an affirmation of participative justice in our democracy. We have no hesitation in holding that the narrow concept of 'cause of action' and 'person aggrieved' and individual litigation is becoming obsolescent in some jurisdictions.[31]

In relation to environmental matters, India's environmental justice discourse resonated from a growing judicial realisation and appreciation of the connection between human rights and environmental protection. The deficiencies in environmental regulation, contradictions and gaps in institutional mechanisms,

27 *U. Baxi*, Taking suffering seriously: social action litigation in the Supreme Court of India Third World Legal Studies 1985 4(1), pp. 107–109. Baxi argued that whereas PIL in the United States has focused on 'civic participation in governmental decision making', the Indian PIL discourse was directed against 'state repression or governmental lawlessness' and was focused primarily to support the rural poor. Also see, *C.D. Cunningham*, Public Interest Litigation in Indian Supreme Court, Journal of Indian Law Institute(1987) 29 p. 494; *P.N. Bhagwati*, Judicial Activism and Public Interest Litigation, Columbia Journal of Transnational Law (1984) 23 p. 561.

28 The development of PIL in India can be traced through three phases. The first phase, or golden era, was in the 1970s and early 1980s when the courts entertained cases concerning the enforcement of the fundamental rights of marginalised and deprived sections of the society. The second phase started in the 1980s when the judiciary through innovative and creative judicial craftsmanship structured to protect ecology and the environment. The third phase saw the expansion of the jurisdictional ambit of PIL to include cases dealing with exposing corruption and maintaining probity and morality in state governance. For a detailed discussion see State of Uttaranchal v Balwant Singh Chaufal (2010) 3 SCC 402; *S. Dam*, Law-making beyond lawmakers: understanding the little right and the great wrong (analysing the legitimacy of the nature of judicial law-making in India's constitutional dynamic), Tulane Journal of International and Comparative Law 2005 13 p. 109, 115–116 et seq; *S. Deva*, Public interest litigation in India: a critical review, Civil Justice Quarterly 2009 28(1) p. 19, 27et seq.

29 *Dighi Koli Samaj Mumbai Rahivasi Sangh v Secretary, Shri Jagannath Ambaji* 2009 SCC OnLine Bom 1034.

30 (2015) 7 SCC 779.

31 *Id.* at p.780.

inefficiencies in administrative enforcement, multi-layered corruption (including political corruption for personal gain) collectively prompted the Supreme Court of India into the de facto role of a caretaker of the environment through PIL.[32] In State of Uttaranchal v B S Chaufal[33] the court observed:

> 'The scale of injustice occurring on the Indian soil is catastrophic. Each day hundreds of thousands of factories are functioning without pollution control devices. Thousands of Indians go to mines and undertake hazardous work without proper safety protection. Everyday millions of litres of untreated raw effluents are dumped into our rivers and millions of tons of hazardous waste are simply dumped on the earth. The environment has become so degraded that instead of nurturing us it is poisoning us. In this scenario, in a large number of cases, the Supreme Court intervened in the matter and issued innumerable directions.'[34]

Such large-scale environmental degradation and adverse effects on public health prompted environmentalists, NGOs and affected citizens to approach the courts, particularly the higher judiciary, for remedial action. Environmental PIL is a product of the higher judiciary's response to the inaction of the state or failures of state agencies to perform their statutory duties that resulted in the endangerment or impairment of people's quality of life as guaranteed by the Constitution of India. In the past two decades the courts have locked together human rights and the environment and entertained PIL petitions from various quarters seeking remedies, including guidelines and directions in the absence of legislation. The use of PIL as a broad-based, people-oriented approach that provides access to justice has become a 'wheel of transformation' for victims of environmental degradation.[35] The 'collaborative approach, procedural flexibility, judicially supervised interim orders and forward-looking relief '[36] by and large received strong public support and acquired social legitimacy.

In this regard, three constitutional provisions, Articles 21, 48 A and 51A (g), have played a significant role in producing a major shift in the environmental landscape of India. Article 21 being a fundamental right guarantees the right to life. The Supreme Court has developed its case law for environmental protection by providing an expansive interpretation of the term 'life' to include the protection and preservation of the environment, ecological balance free from pollution of

---

32 *South Asian Human Rights Documentation Centre*, Human Rights and Humanitarian Law: Developments in Indian and International Law, 2008 p. 423.

33 (2010) 3 SCC 402.

34 *Id.* at p. 437.

35 For details *G.N. Gill*, Human rights and environmental protection in India: a judicial journey from public interest litigation to the National Green Tribunal in A Grear and E Grant (eds), Thought, Law, Rights and Action in an Age of Environmental Crisis, 2015 pp. 123–154; *S.P. Sathe*, Judicial Activism in India 2002 p. 210.

36 *L. Rajamani*, Public interest litigation in India: exploring issues of access, participation, equity, effectiveness and sustainability, (2007) 19(3) *Journal of Environmental Law*, p. 1.

air and water, sanitation, without which life cannot be enjoyed. In Municipal Corporation of Greater Mumbai v Kohinoor CTNL Infrastructure[37] the court stated:

> '... it must be noted that the right to a clean and healthy environment is within the ambit of Article 21, as has been noted in Court on its Own Motion v Union of India reported in 2012 (12) SCALE 307 in the following words: – The scheme under the Indian Constitution unambiguously enshrines in itself the right of a citizen to life under Article 21 of the Constitution. The right to life is a right to live with dignity, safety and in a clean environment.'[38]

Article 48 A, a directive principle of state policy, mandates the state to protect and improve the environment and safeguard forests and wildlife. Article 51A (g) imposes a fundamental duty on every citizen to protect and improve the natural environment including forests, lakes, rivers and wildlife and to have a compassion for living creatures. The social obligation under Article 51A(g) has broadened the scope of 'citizen' to permit public spirited citizens, interested institutions and non-governmental organisations [NGO's] to file and advance PILs for environmental protection. Importantly, the apex court has given effect to Articles 48A, 51A (g) and 21 by citing them as complementary to each other and in appropriate cases have issued necessary directions in environmental cases. In Intellectual Forum, Tirupathi v State of A.P.[39] the Supreme Court observed 'the environmental protection and conservation of natural resources has been given a status of a fundamental right and brought under Article 21 of the Constitution of India. This apart, Articles 48A and 51A (g) are not only fundamental in the governance of the country but also it shall be the duty of the state to apply these principles in making laws and further these two articles are to be kept in mind in understanding the scope and purport of the fundamental rights guaranteed by the Constitution including Article 21.'[40]

The Supreme Court devised new procedures applicable to PIL to provide access to environmental justice to people who otherwise would be denied it. In Mumbai Kamgar Sabha v Abdulbhai Faizullabhai[41] the court, while making a conscious effort to improve judicial access, observed 'procedural prescriptions

---

37 (2014) 4 SCC 538.

38 Id. at p. 556; see also *Delhi Jal Board v National Campaign for Dignity and Rights of Sewerage and Allied Workers* (2011) 8 SCC 574; *M C Mehta v Kamal Nath* (2000) 6 SCC 213; *Narmada Bachao Andolan v Union of India* AIR 2000 SC 3751; *A.P. Pollution Control Board v Prof M.V. Nayudu* AIR 1999 SC 812; *Vellore Citizen Welfare Forum v Union of India* AIR 1996 SC 2715; Virender Gaur v State of Haryana (1995) 2 SCC 57; *Subhash Kumar v State of Bihar* AIR 1991 SC 420; *Chhetriya Pradushan Mukti Sangharsh Samiti v State of Uttar Pradesh* AIR 1990 SC 2060).

39 (2004) 3 SCC 549.

40 *Id.* at p. 576.

41 (1976) 3 SCC 832.

are handmaidens, not mistresses, of justice and failure of fair play is the spirit in which courts must view (processual) deviances.'[42] The relaxation of the rule of *locus standi* constitutes a major procedural innovation. Justice Krishna Iyer, one of the most socially aware and concerned judges, stated:

> '... the truth is that a few profound issues of processional jurisprudence of great strategic significance to our legal system face us. We must zero in on them as they involve problems of access to justice for the people beyond the blinkered rules of 'standing' of the British-India vintage. If the centre of gravity of justice is to shift, as the Preamble of the Constitution mandate, from the traditional individualism oflocus standi to the community orientation of public interest litigation, these interests must be considered.'[43]

Traditional locus standi has been modified in two ways: by representative and citizen standing.[44] Representative standing allows any person, acting bona fide, to advance claims against violations of human rights of victims who because of their poverty, disability or socially or economically disadvantaged position could not approach the Court for judicial enforcement of their fundamental rights. NGO's and environmental activists working on behalf of the poor and tribal people have entered the courts by exercising this procedure. For example, Indian Council for Enviro-Legal Action v Union of India (commonly known as the Bichhri case)[45] was a grass-root initiative by the NGO to take up an industrial pollution issue in rural India and its effect upon the peasant farmers and the local community. In Sterlite Industries v Union of India[46] the Supreme Court observed that voluntary bodies deserve encouragement wherever their actions are found to be in furtherance of public interest, environmental protection and against the mighty and resourceful. The citizen standing provides a platform to seek redress for a public grievance: this affects society as a whole rather than an individual grievance. The cases of Urban and Solid Waste Management[47] and The Taj Mahal[48] were heard as a result of an application through citizen standing,

42 Id. at p. 837.

43 *Municipal Council Ratlam v Vardhichand* (1980) 4 SCC 162, p. 163.

44 *G.N. Gill*, Human rights and the environment in India: access through public interest litigation, Environmental L R (2012) 14 p.201, 203–204 et seq; *M.G. Faure and A.V. Raja*, Effectiveness of environmental public interest litigation in India: determining the key variable, Fordham Environmental L R (2010) 21225; *L. Rajamani*, Public interest litigation in India: exploring issues of access, participation, equity, effectiveness and sustainability, Journal of Environmental Law (2007) 19(3) p. 29; *S. Divan and A. Rosencranz*, Environmental Law and Policy in India, (2001), p. 133; *S. Shankar and P. Mehta*, Courts and socio-economic rights in India in V Gauri and D M Brinks (eds.), Courting Social Justice: Judicial Enforcement of Social and Economic Rights in the Developing World (2008) p. 146–182.

45 AIR 1996 SC 1446; see also *RLEK v. State of Uttar Pradesh and Others* AIR 1985 SC 65; *T. N. Godavarman v. Union of India* AIR 1997 SC 1228.

46 (2013) 4 SCC 575.

47 *Almitra H Patel v Union of India* Writ Petition No 888 of 1996.

48 *M. C. Mehta v Union of India* AIR 1997 SC 734.

whereby public-spirited citizens sought to make the state accountable for its inaction or wrongdoing.

The proactive Supreme Court of India acting as 'amicus environment' through representative and citizen standing has promoted dynamism and capability thereby providing victims of environmental degradation with a way to access justice in a participatory manner. Thus, the liberal interpretation of locus standi has removed traditional procedural shackles in order to enable the hearing of petitions for remedying hardships resulting from a gross violation of fundamental rights and brought by a group or class action, or when basic human rights are invaded, or where complaints of such acts have shocked the judicial conscience. For the purposes of locus standi what is relevant is the substance of breach of law or Constitution complained and not whether the citizen personally suffered little or no harm.[49] The environmental PIL and locus standi introduced a transformative process being polycentric, participatory and democratic in order to meet the challenges of the time.

Although PIL and its associated relaxed procedures have advantages for securing environmental justice they are not without external criticism. The critics see the courts adopting responsibilities traditionally exercised by Parliament and the executive. The widespread jurisprudential question concerning the appropriateness of judicial law making is no better illustrated than in India where the Supreme Court through PIL has been accused of being a hyper active law-making body.[50] The judges are breaching the doctrine of separation of powers by trespassing upon the areas traditionally and properly occupied by the executive and the legislature. For example, Court has issued notices and directives to the central and state governments on multiple environmental issues, such as relocating hazardous industries from the National Capital Region Delhi[51], issuing guidelines for the prevention of noise pollution[52], the conversion of all diesel-powered buses in Delhi to Compressed Natural Gas (CNG)-driven ones to check air pollution.[53] The court, however, has denied any such usurpation. In its pronouncements, it has justified its actions either under a statutory provision or as an aspect of its inherent powers.[54]

---

49 *Bombay Environmental Action Group v State of Maharashtra* (1999) 2 Mah LJ 747.

50 *V. Gauri*, Public Interest Litigation in India: Overreaching or Underachieving? Policy Research Working Paper 5109, The World Bank, (2009) p.4; *A.H. Desai & S. Muralidhar*, Public Interest Litigation: Potential and Problems in B.N. Kirpal, A.H. Desai, G. Subramanium, R. Dhavan & R. Ramachandran (eds), Supreme but not Infallible: Essays in Honour of the Supreme Court of India (2000); *M.P. Jain*, The Supreme Court and Fundamental Rights in S.K. Verma and Kusum (eds), Fifty Years of the Supreme Court of India, (2008) p. 86; *U. Baxi*, How not to judge the judges: notes towards evaluation of the judicial role, Journal of the Indian Law Institute (1983) 25 p. 21.

51 *M. C. Mehta v Union of India* (2004) 12 SCC 18.

52 In re *Noise Pollution* AIR 2005 SC 3136.

53 *M. C. Mehta v Union of India* Order dated 28 July 1998.

54 *G. Sahu*, Implications of Indian Supreme Courts innovation for environmental jurisprudence, Law, Environmental and Development Journal (2008) 4(1) p.3, 17 et seq.

Further, a climate of inconsistency and uncertainty exists with reference to entertaining and rejecting environmental PILs. This has become a serious concern among public-spirited citizens who see the court as the last resort for protecting the environment and citizens' rights. Contrasting judicial decisions reflect environmental bias and inconsistency as:

> 'the right to environmental protection has thus been whimsically applied by individual judges according to their own subjective preferences usually without clear principles guiding them about the circumstances in which the court could issue a mandamus for environmental protection. It appears that when socio-economic rights of the poor come into conflict with environmental protection the court has often subordinated those rights to environmental protection. On the other hand, when environmental protection comes into conflict with what is perceived by the court to be 'development issues' or powerful commercial, vested interests, environmental protection is often sacrificed at the altar of 'development' or similar powerful interests.'[55]

The relaxation of the 'standing rule' has opened the Court to the possibility of 'forum shopping' whereby justice according to law is more personality driven than being institutionalised adjudication. Such judges have become known as 'green judges', 'pro poor', or 'progressive' whilst others seeking media coverage encourage PIL litigation cases in their courtrooms. These judges encourage the cult of individualism that, in turn, reduces the predictability factor associated with the doctrine of precedent. Judgements should be based neither upon the whim of the individual nor the pre-selection of a supportive judge.[56]

The liberal interpretation of locus standi has been criticised because it is promotes litigation within an already litigious society.[57] Cases are lodged within a system that is already groaning under the weight of its case load. What commenced as cost effective and expeditious litigation has become, at times, both expensive and time consuming. For example, in the Delhi Vehicular Pollution case, the original writ was filed in 1985. The case remains active to this day, although many interim orders and directions have been passed.[58]

---

55 *P.R. Bhushan*, Misplaced priorities and class bias of the judiciary, *Economic and Political Weekly*, 2009 44(14), pp. 32–37. Also see *G. Sahu*, Why the underdogs came out ahead: an analysis of the Supreme Court's environmental judgments, 1980–2010, *Economic and Political Weekly*, (2014) 49(4), pp. 52–57; for details see *G. N. Gill*, Environmental Justice in India: The National Green Tribunal, (2017), pp. 50–52; *M. Galanter*, Why the "Haves" Come Out Ahead: Speculations on the Limits of Legal Change, Law and Society Review (1974) 9/1 pp. 95–16; *Banwasi Seva Ashram v State of Uttar Pradesh* AIR 1987 SC 374; *DDA v Rajendra Singh* AIR 2010 SC 2516; *Orissa Mining Corporation v MoEF* (2013) 6 SCC 476.

56 *B. N. Srikrishna*, Judicial Activism-Judges as Social Engineers, Skinning a Cat. SCC Journal 2005 p.8.

57 *S.P. Sathe*, Judicial Activism in India Transgressing Borders and Enforcing Limits, (2002) p. 232; see also *R. Moog*, Delays in Indian Courts, Justice System Journal (1992)16 pp. 19–36.; *M. Galanter*, Law and Society in Modern India, (1989), *Law Commission of India*, Delay and Arrears in Trial Courts, 77th Report (1978).

58 *M C Mehta v Union of India* Writ Petition Civil No. 13029 of 1985.

PIL and locus standi have also been exploited by the usage of bogus litigation that is collusive, profiteering or speculative. Manipulative litigants may seek to damage rivals or competitors through this procedure.[59] In recent years there has grown a feeling that publicity interest litigation has become private interest litigation producing a tendency to being counterproductive. In State of Uttaranchal v Balwant Singh Chaufal[60] the court observed:

> '... unfortunately, of late, it has been noticed that such an important jurisdiction which has been carefully carved out, created and nurtured with great care and caution by the courts, is being blatantly abused by filing some petitions with oblique motives. We think the time has come when genuine and bona fide public interest litigation must be encouraged whereas frivolous public interest litigation should be discouraged...'[61]

Thus, although the environmental PIL both promoted and experienced an expansionist approach from the Supreme Court and resulted in a procedure that allowed indigents and concerned citizens to access the courts via PIL, the process did not prove to be a 'magic bullet'. Within such a restrictive structure PIL could have only a limited impact. Indeed, in 2009 when the Green Tribunal Bill was debated in Parliament figures provided in the federal legislature by Shri Jairam Ramesh, the former Minister of State of the Ministry of Environment and Forests, declared that some 5,600 environmental cases were back logged, awaiting disposal in the High Courts of India.[62] As with all processes it had its weaknesses and limitations. Innovation and change were needed. This occurred through the establishment of the National Green Tribunal (NGT).

THE NATIONAL GREEN TRIBUNAL

The establishment of NGT as a dedicated environmental court was a result of the recommendations of the Law Commission of India in addition to the above-mentioned problems of delay and back logging in PIL.[63] The Indian Parliament

59 *G.N. Gill*, Human rights and the environment in India: access through public interest litigation, Environmental L R (2012) 14 p. 20, 205 et seq; see also *G. Sahu*, Implementation of Environmental Judgments in Context: A Comparative Analysis of Dahanu Thermal Power Plant Pollution Case in Maharashtra and Vellore Leather Industrial Pollution Case in Tamil Nadu, Law, Environment and Development Journal (2010) 6/3 p. 337, 340–341 et. seq.

60 (2010) 3 SCC 402.

61 Id. at pp. 409–410.

62 Lok Sabha Debates http://164.100.47.132/LssNew/psearch/Result15.aspx?dbsl=180.

63 *The Law Commission of India*, One Hundred and Eighty Sixth Report on 'Proposal to Constitute Environment Courts' (2003). The Law Commission of India was influenced by decisions of the Supreme Court of India that in dicta advocated the establishment of environment courts. In *A.P. Pollution Control Board vs. M.V. Nayudu* 1999(2) SCC 718 and 2001(2) SCC 62, *M.C. Mehta vs. Union of India* AIR 1987 SC 965 and *Indian Council for Enviro-Legal Action vs. Union of India* 1996(3) SCC 212 the Supreme Court acknowledged that judges

passed the National Green Tribunal Act in June 2010.[64] It provides for the establishment of a NGT. The Tribunal decides cases relating to environmental protection and conservation of forests and other natural resources including enforcement of any legal right relating to the environment and gives relief and compensation for damages to persons and property. The NGT was established on 18 October 2010 and became operational on 5 May 2011 with New Delhi selected as the site for the Principal Bench.[65] The Ministry of Environment and Forests (MoEF), Government of India, issued a notification, on 17 August 2011, establishing regional benches of the NGT in Bhopal, Pune, Chennai and Kolkata to cover the central, western, southern and eastern zones of India.[66] Additionally, in order to become more accessible to people, especially in remote areas, the NGT follows the circuit procedure of 'courts going to people and not people coming to the courts'.[67] The effect is a reformist approach through a regional and circuit bench development that enables access to environmental justice.

The NGT is a specialised body where the decision-makers hold relevant qualifications and appropriate work experience both in law and technical fields. It is a multi-faceted, multi-skilled body. It produces a coherent and effective institutional mechanism to apply complex laws and principles in a uniform and consistent manner whilst simultaneously reshaping the approach to solve the environmental problem at its source rather than being limited to pre-determined remedies. The combination of legal, scientific and technical expertise has a dynamic impact on the content and development of environmental policies and law.[68]

The NGT, in its commitment to resolve environmental issues, adopts different procedures in order to promote the larger public interest and dramatically expands traditional judicial functions associated with case management and disposal of the individual case. These procedures provide steadfast foundations to guide decision-making in environmental matters that ultimately lead to

face difficulties as a result of lack of scientific knowledge and inadequate exposure and training in environmental matters. Environmental cases involve assessment and evolution of scientific and technical data. It might be desirable to set up environment courts on a regional basis with one professional judge and two experts, keeping in view the expertise required for such adjudication.

64 The National Green Tribunal Act 2010, the Gazette of India Extraordinary (No. 19 of 2010); See for details *G.N. Gill*, A Green Tribunal for India, Journal of Environmental Law (2010) 22(3 pp. 466–468).

65 Ministry of Environment and Forests (MoEF), Government of India, Notification, 5 May 2011, SO 1003 E.

66 MoEF, Government of India, Notification, 17 Aug. 2011, SO 1908 E.

67 Shimla has received circuit benches from Delhi (NGT/PB/157/2013/331 20 December 2013) as has Jodhpur from the central zone (NGT/PB/266/2013/281 2 December 2013), Meghalaya from the eastern zone (NGT/PB/Pr/CB/97/2014/M78) and Kochi from the southern zone (NGT/PB/266/2015/299).

68 For a detailed account see *G.N. Gill*, Environmental justice in India: the National Green Tribunal and Expert Members, Transnational Environmental Law (2016) 5(1) pp. 175–205.

better results based upon a right based approach. For instance, the adoption of an investigative procedure involving the inspection of affected sites by expert members.[69] The purpose of site inspection is to compare and contrast contradictory claims, positions and reports filed by the respective parties. The stakeholder consultative adjudicatory process is the most recent of the NGT's problem-solving procedures.[70] Major issues having a public impact either on public health, environment or ecology can be better handled and resolved when stakeholders are brought together alongside the Tribunal's scientific judges for eliciting the views of all concerned – government, scientists, NGOs, public and the NGT. Stakeholder process evokes a greater element of consent rather than opposition to a judgment.

With the implementation of the NGT Act 2010, 'standing' has been reformulated in terms of an 'aggrieved person' who has access to the Tribunal to seek relief or compensation or settlement of environmental disputes. An aggrieved person has the right to approach the Tribunal under its original[71] or appellate jurisdiction[72], and it is important to note that the 'aggrieved person' in environmental matters has been given a liberal and flexible interpretation. Section 18(2) NGT Act 2010 has wide coverage which also allows any aggrieved person and legal representatives of the various categories to file an application for grant of relief or compensation or settlement of dispute. This includes a person who

a. has sustained an injury;
b. is the owner of the property to which damage has been caused;
c. is the legal representative in the case of death resulting from environmental damage;
d. is a duly authorised agent; e represents a state agency; or
e. is an aggrieved person, including any representative body or organisation

The expression 'person aggrieved' is given a wide connotation and any person directly or indirectly affected or even interested is permitted to ventilate grievance in an application or appeal to address participatory parity. The NGT, in Jan Chetna v MoEF[73] explained the scope and ambit of the term and stated:

> '... the expression aggrieved person cannot be considered in a restricted manner. A liberal construction and flexible interpretation should be adopted. In environmental matters, the damage is not necessarily confined to the local area where the industry is established. The effects of environmental degradation might have far reaching consequences going beyond the local areas. Therefore, an aggrieved person need not

---

69 *K.K. Singh v. National Ganga River Basin Authority*. Judgment 16 October 2014.

70 *Manoj Mishra v. Union of India*, NGT Judgment, 13 January 2015 (now referred to as the Maily se Nirmal Yamuna Revitalization Plan 2017).

71 Section 14, NGT Act 2010.

72 Section 16, NGT Act 2010.

73 Judgment 9 February 2012.

> be a resident of the local area. Any person whether he is a resident of that particular area or not, whether aggrieved or not, can approach this Tribunal. In such a situation, it is necessary to review the credentials of the applicants/appellants as to their true intention or motives.'[74]

The bench, in its liberal interpretation was guided by two reasons: first, the inability of persons living in the area or vicinity of the proposed project to understand the intrinsic scientific details and the effects of the ultimate project and any disaster it may cause and thus the right to any citizen to approach the tribunal regardless of whether he is directly affected by a developmental project or whether a resident of affected area or not; second, the subservience of statutory provisions of National Green Tribunal Act 2010 to the constitutional mandate of Article 51A (g) providing a fundamental duty of every citizen to protect and improve the natural environment. Thus literally, any person can approach the Tribunal and complain of environmental threats or damage as a consequence of the activities of the State or any organization or individual under either original or appellate jurisdiction.[75]

The NGT, for example, allowed an appeal against the Ministry of Environment and Forests for the grant of environmental clearance for expansion of steel and power plant without following the mandatory requirement of a public hearing to the aggrieved party. A public hearing in environmental projects is not just a procedural formality but is meant to ensure that the decision is based on proper assessment, evaluation of the pros and cons including the cost and benefits in general, and takes into account the needs and living conditions of locals. The Tribunal identified a public hearing as a *sine qua non* for not only environmental matters but also in accordance with good governance based on transparency and accountability.

Another judgment that further expands the already liberal definition of an 'aggrieved person' is the case of Betty C. Alvares v State of Goa.[76] The word 'person' was construed to include 'an individual', whether an Indian national or a person who is not a citizen of India. The Tribunal appears to have opened its doors globally to each and every person, including incorporated bodies, who consider themselves 'aggrieved' within the political boundaries of India subject to the enactments specified within Schedule 1 of the NGT Act 2010.[77] The proceedings related to an environmental dispute raised by Betty Alvares (a resident in India but not an Indian citizen) and was held to be maintainable. The Tribunal held

---

74 Id. at paras 21 and 22.

75 See also *Amit Maru v MoEF* Judgment 1 October 2014, *Goa Foundation v. Union of India* Judgment 18 July 2013 and *Vimal Bhai v MoEF* Judgment 14 December 2011.

76 Judgment 14 February 2014.

77 The enactments in Sch. I include the following: Water (Prevention and Control of Pollution) Act 1974; Water (Prevention and Control of Pollution) Cess Act 1977; Forests (Conservation) Act 1980; Air (Prevention and Control of Pollution) Act 1981; Environment (Protection) Act 1986; Public Liability Insurance Act 1981; and Biological Diversity Act 2002.

that it is not necessary that an individual has personally suffered any loss on account of damage caused to the environment by acts of illegal construction and encroachment of the sea beaches thereby violating coastal zone regulations.

Further, the ability both to fast track and to decide cases within six months of application or appeal[78], and the initial filing fee for application or appeal of £10[79], provide access to justice for all potential aggrieved parties. In contrast, the Tribunal has discouraged litigation where some persons with vested interests indulge in meddling with the judicial process either by force of habit or from improper motives. Litigious petitioners will not be entertained by the Tribunal as an 'aggrieved party' and costs will be imposed to deter such people from filing frivolous applications.[80]

Recent work[81] provides evidence that identifies the parties to environmental disputes by analysing some 1130 cases decided by the National Green Tribunal between July 2011 and September 2015. The most frequent plaintiffs are NGOs/ social activists/ public-spirited citizens. They account for 533 plaintiffs (47.2 per cent) of 1130 cases. For example, in Vimal Bhai v. Ministry of Environment and Forests[82] allowed an application by three environmentalists concerning the grant of an environmental clearance for the construction of a dam for hydroelectric power across the river Alakhnanda in Chamoli district of Uttarkhand. The NGT ruled that the three environmentalists were an aggrieved party and that their claim for a public hearing concerning the grant of an environmental clearance was sustainable. The history of PIL and relaxed locus standi (representative and citizen standing)[83] has developed this group as an experienced active body of plaintiffs, hence their regular and successful appearance in all NGT benches. The group success rate in cases they brought stands at 38.3 per cent. This significant number demonstrates both the opportunity to, and the ability for, public-spirited citizens and organisations to use the NGT as a route to seek remedies through collective proceedings instead of being driven into an expensive plurality of litigation, thereby, affirming participative justice.

Affected individuals/communities/residents brought 17.7 per cent of all cases with a success rate of 56 per cent. For example, in R J Koli v State of Maharashtra[84] the Tribunal allowed an application filed and argued in person by traditional fishermen seeking compensation for loss of livelihood due to infrastructural project activities. The relatively low costs of bringing the case coupled with positive

---

78 Section 18(3), NGT Act 2010. This contrasts with the historical and contemporary levels of delay that are, unfortunately, a powerful feature of the Indian court system.

79 Rule 12, National Green Tribunal (Practices and Procedure) Rules 2011.

80 *Rana Sengupta v Union of India*, Judgment 22 March 2013; *Bajinath Prajapathi v Ministry of Environment and Forests*, Judgment 20 January 2012.

81 For a detailed account see *G.N. Gill*, Environmental Justice in India: The National Green Tribunal (2017), pp. 194–195.

82 Judgment 14 December 2011.

83 See above notes 44 and 45.

84 Judgment 27 February 2015.

encouragement by the NGT to litigants in person reflect a conscious effort on the part of the Tribunal to promote access to environmental justice. Indigent and illiterate litigants have been encouraged to speak in their vernacular language (especially at regional benches) to ventilate their grievances and personal and community experiences. Confidence-building in the NGT has and will result in motivating litigation from within these groups who traditionally had little or no access to justice. This reflects a broad-based, people-oriented approach by the NGT.

The locus standi and the liberal interpretation of 'person aggrieved' has opened up access to the Tribunal to promote diffused and meta-individual rights. Nevertheless, with a rapidly increasing workload, delay might become a serious issue for the NGT. On a positive note the transformation sought by the NGT is a metamorphosis of societal environmental interests that encapsulate what is important for the well-being not only of the individual but also the larger public interest. The NGT's legitimacy is grounded in its inclusive participatory mechanisms.

4. CONCLUSION

Green jurisprudence in India reflects the application of an expansive interpretation of the Constitution by a liberal Supreme Court that created a procedure that allowed indigents and concerned citizens to access the courts via PIL and thereafter through the NGT. Principal 10 of the Rio Declaration has been given a radical interpretation and novel application in India. Active, participatory citizenship has been encouraged, particularly by the NGT's decisions, to challenge and bring to account recalcitrant both private and public parties that include the state and para-statal agencies, for their acts of negligence, malfeasance, misfeasance, indifference and indolence regarding their statutory and constitutional responsibilities to protect and maintain the ecology and environment of India.

The NGT has adjudicated according to its enabling statute but has gone much further through judicial activism by producing expansive, innovative judgments based on Article 21 of the Constitution the effects of which go beyond the 'court room' door resulting in far reaching social and economic results. The transformation of public awareness sought by the NGT has helped promote a change in societal attitudes to the environment and related challenges. In essence the Indian judiciary and the NGT have adopted the primary responsibility of environmental protection and promotion.

THE SCOPE OF THE REVIEW IN ENVIRONMENT-RELATED DISPUTES IN THE LIGHT OF THE AARHUS CONVENTION AND EU LAW

Tensions between Effective Judicial Protection and National Procedural Autonomy

Vasiliki (Vicky) Karageorgou*

1. INTRODUCTION

The entitlement of individuals and NGOs to challenge acts or omissions concerning violations of the environmental legislation through effective judicial mechanisms constitutes an important instrument for ensuring the effective implementation of the environmental law.[1] This can be attributed to a major extent to the particularities of the environmental litigation which arise from the specific nature of the environmental interests in the sense that the latter can either relate to the protection of the "commons" and to the damage caused to nature itself, or are diffuse and fragmented by nature, so that they cannot easily be defended by the individual claimants.[2] Furthermore, another particularity of the environmental litigation is that there is a strong imbalance of power among the actors participating in the judicial proceedings.[3] In this context, it seems to be more urgent in environmental law in relation to other fields of law to create an

* Assistant Professor of European Environmental Law, Panteion University of Social and Political Sciences.

1 *J. Ebbesson*, Comparative Introduction in: J. Ebbesson (Ed.), Access to Justice in Environmental Matters in the EU, 2002, p. 4 et seq.

2 *M. Hedemann-Robinson*, EU Implementation of the Aarhus Convention's Third Pillar: Back to the Future over Access to Environmental Justice? Part-1, EEELR 2014 (3), p. 102, 106.

3 *J. Darpö*, Environmental Justice through Environmental Courts? Lessons learned from the Swedish Experience in: J. Ebbesson & Ph. Okowa (Eds.), Environmental Law and Justice in Context, 2009, p. 176.

appropriate framework and to establish the necessary mechanisms, in order to guarantee effective judicial protection for providing just results.

The Aarhus Convention[4] (hereafter AC) has made a significant contribution in terms of enshrining the fundamental procedural right of access to judicial review procedures for challenging the legality of the environment-related decisions, acts and omissions of public authorities or the relevant actions of private persons, blurring thereby the dichotomy between public and individual interests characterizing traditional legal approaches (Article 9). Furthermore, the EU lawmaker revisited certain EU Directives, with the aim of ensuring compliance with the obligations arising from Article 9 of the AC (paras. 1, 2 and 4).

Besides the issues concerning the standing criteria and the remedies provided, another critical issue for ensuring effective judicial protection in environmental disputes relates to what can be contested and the degree to which the courts deal with the arguments brought by the applicants for challenging the relevant acts or omissions ("scope of the review"). Both the relevant provisions of the AC and those of the EU Directives do not contain sufficiently detailed rules on this issue. Subsequently, Member States (hereafter MS) enjoy a certain level of discretion when determining the extent of the judicial review within the framework of the implementation of the AC and the transposition of the relevant provisions of the EU Directives into the national legal systems. Furthermore, the determination of this issue is also heavily influenced by the specific characteristics of the national judicial systems which can also be traced to the relevant legal traditions. In this context, regulative tendencies either in the form of legislative provisions which restrict both the subject and the extent of the judicial control of the environment-related acts or of relevant court practices confining narrowly the scope of review can be observed in quite different legal systems at the EU level. A critical issue which comes to the fore is the inherent conflict between the principle of effective judicial protection, which presupposes rather wide standards of review, and the need to increase the efficiency of the judicial proceedings and observe the principle of legal certainty, which can allow certain types of relevant restrictions.

The main aim of this paper is, thus, to analyse the scope of the review of the environment-related decisions, acts or omissions falling in the scope of Article 9 para. 2 of the AC and the relevant provisions of the EU Directives. Moreover, it will attempt to shed light on how and to which extent the relevant provisions of the AC and the EU law are critical for the determination of the standards of review and the implicit regulation between competing rights, interests and

---

4 Aarhus Convention is a Convention developed within the framework of the United Nations Commission for Europe and constitutes the most prominent and well-developed International Agreement in terms of establishing the framework for participatory environmental democracy. The Convention consists of three pillars: access to environmental information, public participation in environmental decision-making and access to justice in environmental matters. See *M. Pallemaerts* (ed.), The Aarhus Convention at Ten-Interactions and Tensions between Conventional International Law and EU Environmental Law, 2011.

objectives within the framework of the introduction or the modification of the national provisions, taking also the relevant legal traditions into consideration. To this end, the first part of the analysis will focus on the respective provisions of the AC and the EU Directives concerning the scope of the review as well as on the discretion left to MS due to the manner in which they are drafted and the application of the principle of the procedural autonomy (2). Then, the emphasis will be shifted to how the scope of the review is determined in certain different systems of judicial review, with the aim of identifying and analysing the factors to which restrictive approaches concerning the standards of review can be attributed (3). In the next part analysis is devoted to the clarification provided by the relevant Findings of the ACCC and the jurisprudence of the CJEU on this issue (4). The final part of the analysis will concentrate on examining whether the relevant CJEU jurisprudence and the Findings of the ACCC are sufficient for ensuring that either restrictive legal provisions or court practices are avoided or whether other options should be examined (5).

2. THE REGULATORY FRAMEWORK CONCERNING THE SCOPE OF THE REVIEW IN ENVIRONMENT-RELATED JUDICIAL PROCEEDINGS AT SUPRANATIONAL LEVEL

2.1. THE RELEVANT PROVISIONS OF THE AARHUS CONVENTION

The third pillar of the AC, which is laid down in Article 9, concerns access to justice in environmental matters.[5] The aim of the Convention is to ensure wide access to justice by empowering citizens and NGOs to challenge environment-related acts or omissions and to contribute in this way to the effective enforcement of the other two pillars and the environmental legislation in general. In this context, Article 9 stipulates that each Contracting Party has to ensure the legal review of decisions, acts and omissions by a court or an independent body established by law[6] in the following three types of situations: a) the refusal or the inadequate handling of the requests for access to environmental information by the public authorities

5 *L. Lavrysen*, The Aarhus Convention: Between Environmental Protection and Human Rights in: P. Martens et al (eds.), Liber amicorum Michel Melchior, 2010, p. 649, 663 et. seq; *M. Eliantonio*, The Proceduralization of EU Environmental Legislation: International Pressures, Some Victories and Some Way to Go, REALaw, 2015 (1), p. 99, 101–103.

6 The reference to a Court or an Independent Body established by Law is critical in terms of demonstrating that the concept of access to justice established in the AC draws also on the right to fair trial established in International Law (e.g. Article 6 of the European Convention on Human Rights). See *J. Ebbesson*, Access to Justice in Environmental Matters in: The Max Planck Encyclopedia of Public International Law, Vol. I, p. 37, para. 6.

(9(1)) b) the decision-making procedures and the authorization of projects and activities subject to the public participation provisions under Article 6 (9(2)) and c) the violation of provisions of national law relating to the environment by public authorities or private persons that are not covered by the previous two categories (9(3)). Furthermore, Article 9(4) sets minimum standards applicable to the above types of access to justice procedures, namely the provision of adequate and effective remedies, the fairness, the equity and the timeliness of the relevant procedures and the not prohibitively expensive costs.

Besides the differentiation as regards the standing criteria, the scope of the review is also determined differently in the above mentioned three types of situations. In particular, this issue is treated in a more detailed way in the first (para. 1) and the second constellation (para. 2) in relation to the third one (para. 3).[7] The critical provision of Article 9(2) stipulates that the public, subject to having either a sufficient interest or maintaining an impairment of a right where national law requires this as a precondition, including also the NGOs that meet the requirements of the national legislation ("public concerned" – Article 2(5)) should be given access to a judicial review procedure to challenge the substantive and procedural legality of decisions, acts and omissions subject to the public participation requirements of Article 6 of the Convention.[8] Subsequently, the final outcome of the relevant procedures, namely the decisions permitting specific listed activities with a possible significant environmental impact or not (Annex I), and other decisions which in accordance with the national law may have a significant impact on the environment should be subject to a judicial review procedure on the grounds relating to the violation of either substantive norms, procedural norms or even both of them.[9]

In this context, it should be noted that while the term "procedural legality" can be defined quite easily in the sense that it relates mainly to the observance of the public participation provisions as well as the other norms setting the procedure that leads to the final decision, the term "substantive legality" is inherently ambiguous. This can be attributed to the fact that while it is beyond doubt that the above mentioned term covers violations of substantive environmental norms, such as those relating to environmental quality or nature conservation standards and applicable technical standards that have not been sufficiently considered in

---

7 Article 9(3) does not provide any further specification concerning whether either procedural or substantive breaches of national environmental legislation should be subject to judicial review. The systematic and teleological interpretation of this provision, though, leads to the conclusion that all the kinds of violations of the national provisions relating to the environment should be subject to judicial review. See *Aarhus Convention:* An Implementation Guide, 2nd edition, 2014, p. 199; *Hedemann-Robinson, supra*, note 2 at p. 105.

8 *J. Darpö*, Article 9.2 of the Aarhus Convention and EU Law-Some Remarks on CJEUs Case Law on Access to Justice in Environmental Decision-Making, JEEPL 2014 (4), p. 367, 376.

9 Aarhus Convention: An Implementation Guide, *supra*, note 7 at p. 196; *J. Ebbesson*, Access to Justice at the National Level-Impact of the Aarhus Convention and European Union Law in: *M. Pallemaerts* (ed.), *supra*, note 4, p. 247, 259–260; *Lavrysen, supra*, note 5 at p. 664.

the permitting procedure, it is also determined to some extent by the orientation of the relevant judicial systems that place emphasis either on the individual rights protection or on the objective implementation of the legislation.[10] A first conclusion arising from the analysis is that the relevant provision defines the frame concerning the standards of review of decisions permitting activities with significant environmental impact, while it also leaves a significant margin of discretion to the Contracting Parties (hereafter CP) for the specification of this issue. The objective of "ensuring wide access to justice to the public concerned" and the minimum qualitative requirements set in Article 9(4), which are also critical for the determination of the standards of review, nevertheless set certain limits to the discretion of the CP in regulating the issue.

2.2. THE RELEVANT PROVISIONS OF THE EU ENVIRONMENTAL LAW AND THE LIMITS OF DISCRETION OF THE NATIONAL LEGISLATORS

2.2.1. *The incorporation of the third pillar of the AC in the EU legal system concerning national review procedures*

Since the signature of the AC in 1998[11], the EU has adopted certain pieces of legislation in order to comply with the relevant requirements set in the three pillar structured Convention. The requirements concerning the judicial review procedures at the national level were partially incorporated in the EU legal order by the relevant Directives, by which the first and the second pillar of the Convention were implemented at the EU level. The legislative proposal which aimed at the incorporation of the requirements of Article 9(3) of AC by introducing minimum requirements governing the national review procedures in cases of alleged violations of environmental norms whose origins lay in all other areas of the EU environmental law except for those covered by the relevant Directives was, however, never adopted due to the resistance of certain MS on the grounds relating to the principle of subsidiarity.[12] In this context as regards the incorporation of

[10] *J. Darpö*, Effective Justice? Synthesis Report of the Study on the Implementation of Articles 9 (3) and 9 (4) of the Aarhus Convention in Seventeen of the Member States of the European Union in: J.Jans, R. Marcory & A-M. Moreno Molina (Eds.), National Courts and EU Environmental Law, 2013, p. 169, 196.

[11] Aarhus Convention is a mixed agreement signed and ratified both by the EU and all of the MS. The Convention was ratified by the EU through the Council Decision 2005/370, OJ L 124, 17 May 2005. See *J. Jendrośka*, Aarhus Convention and Community Law: the Interplay, JEEPL, 2005 (1), p. 12, 19, 20.

[12] EU Commission, Proposal for a Directive of the European Parliament and of the Council on Access to Justice in Environmental Matters, COM (2003), 624 final, which was withdrawn in 2014 (Withdrawal of obsolete Commission Proposals, OJ 2014 C-153/03). See also *M.*

the access to justice provisions of the AC, the Directive 2003/04[13] introduced minimum standards concerning the national review procedures in the cases of refusal or mishandlings of requests for access to environmental information (Article 6(2)). Furthermore, the Public Participation Directive 2003/35[14], which relates to the public participation in the decision-making procedures for the authorization of projects and activities with significant environmental impact, inserted access to justice provisions both in the EIA Directive (Article 10a) and the then IPPC Directive (Article 15a). The relevant provisions, which have been transferred to the most recent version of the EIA Directive 2011/92/EU[15] (Article 11) and the Industrial Emissions Directive 2010/75/EU[16] (Article 25) without any further changes, are almost identical in terms of content with Article 9 (2 and 4) of the AC.

From a general point of view, the Public Participation Directive and the further relevant legal developments, such as the inclusion of an access to justice provision in the SEVESO III Directive[17] and in the Environmental Liability Directive[18] constitute significant but piecemeal steps towards the

Hedemann-Robinson, EU Implementation of the Aarhus Convention's Third Pillar: Back to the Future over Access to Environmental Justice? Part-2, EEELR 2014 (4), p. 151, 162 et. seq.

13 Directive 2003/4/EC of the European Parliament and of the Council of 28 January 2003 on public access to environmental information and repealing Directive 90/313, OJ L 041, 14.02.2003.

14 Directive 2003/35/EC of the European Parliament and of the Council of 26 May 2003 providing for public participation in respect of the drawing up of certain plans and programmes relating to the environment and amending with regard to public participation and access to justice Council Directives 85/337/EEC and 96/61/EC, OJ L156, 25.06.2003.

15 Directive 2011/92/EU of the European Parliament and of the Council of 13 December 2011 on the assessment of the effects of certain public and private projects on the environment, Text with EEA relevance, OJ L26, 28.01.2012. Directive 2011/92/EU has been amended by Directive 2014/52/EU (OJ L 124, 25.4.2014).

16 Directive 2010/75/EU of the European Parliament and of the Council of 24 November 2010 on industrial emissions (integrated pollution prevention and control) Text with EEA relevance, OJ L 334, 17.12.2010.

17 The provision which was inserted into the SEVESO III Directive (Article 23) and incorporates mainly the provision of Article 9 (2) of the AC stipulates that MS should provide the "public concerned" access to judicial review procedures to challenge the legality not only of individual projects but also of certain plans subject to the public participation provisions of the Directive. Directive 2012/18/EU of the European Parliament and of the Council of 4 July 2012 on the control of major-accident hazards involving dangerous substances, amending and subsequently repealing Council Directive 96/82/EC, Text with EEA relevance, OJ L 197, 24.07.2012.

18 Directive 2004/35/EC on Environmental Liability includes certain procedural provisions which strengthen the enforcement role of the public and the NGOs. In particular, Article 12 provides the right of the public and environmental NGOs, which meet similar standing criteria, as those set in the Public Participation Directive, and of those natural and legal persons affected or likely to be affected by the environmental damage to request the respective competent authority to take action concerning the instances of environmental damage. Article 13 enshrines the right of those private entities entitled to request the competent authority to take action to have access to judicial review procedures, in order to challenge the competent authority's conduct concerning remediation of possible environmental damage. The relevant provisions and especially Article 13 cover thus a field that falls within the scope of Article 9 (3) of the Aarhus Convention. See *Eliantonio, supra,* note 5, p. 99, 114 et seq.

proceduralization of the EU environmental law in terms of introducing norms concerning the enforcement of the relevant norms at the national level. In particular, the fragmented regulatory approach which characterizes the incorporation of the access to justice provisions of the AC in the EU Legal Order as regards national judicial review procedures is underpinned by the fact that significant areas of the EU Environmental Legislation, such those relating to nature (Directive 92/43/EC[19]) or water protection (Directive 2000/60/EC[20]) have been left out.[21]

Furthermore, the relevant shortcomings are exacerbated by the fact that the CJEU did not recognize direct effect on Article 9(3) of the AC in its prominent Ruling in the case *Lesoochranárske zoskupenie VLK v. Ministerstvo životného prostredia Slovenkej republiky*, known in literature as "*Slovak Brown Bear*" *Case* (*LZ I*), on the grounds that the relevant provision is not clear and precise enough to regulate directly the legal position of individuals.[22] From a general point of view, the Ruling is critical for demonstrating that although the Court departed from the relevant case-law (*Merck Genéricos*) and allocated itself the competence to rule on the direct effect of this provision[23], it was still bounded by the judicial prerogatives and its well-established jurisprudence on this issue (e.g. direct effect), so that it could not go so far as to fill the gaps of the relevant EU and national legislation.[24] A relevant positive development in this context is the recent CJEU Ruling in the case *Lesoochranárske zoskupenie VLK v. Obvodný úrad Trenčín* (*LZ II*)[25], which can exert influence on the interpretation of the national procedural rules towards the direction of ensuring wide access to justice in the cases of alleged violations of norms originating from those areas of environmental law for which no specific access to justice provisions are set at the EU level (e.g. water).

---

19 Directive 92/43/EEC of the Council of 21 May 1992 on the conservation of natural habitats and of wild fauna and flora, OJ L206, 22.07.1992.

20 Directive 2000/60/EC of the European Parliament and of the Council of 23 October 2000 establishing a Framework for Community Action in the Field of Water Policy, OJ L 327, 22.12.2000.

21 *C. Poncelet*, Access to Justice in Environmental Matters-Does the European Union Comply with its Obligations?, JEL, 2012, p. 287, 290–291.

22 CJEU Judgment, Case C-240/09, *Slovak Brown Bear*, 2011, I-01255, para. 45. It is worth referring that the Court gave concrete guidelines to the national court as regards how to interpret national procedural requirements consistent with the AC and the principle of the effectiveness of EU Law (paras. 49–51). See *J. Darpö, supra*, note 8, p. 373.

23 The view taken by CJEU concerning its competence to rule on the direct effect of Article 9 (3) was criticized by the legal theory on the grounds that it makes more or less obsolete the Declaration of Competence to the Aarhus Convnention signed by EU. See *J. Jans*, Who is the referee? Access to Justice in a Globalised Legal Order, REALaw, 2011 (1), p. 87, 93.

24 *Poncelet, supra*, note 21, p. 294.

25 CJEU Judgment of 8 November 2016, Case 243/15, *Slovak Brown Bears II* ECLI: EU;C:2016:838. See also Communication from the Commission of 28.4.2017, Commission Notice on Access to Justice in Environmental Matters, Brussels 28.04.2017, C(2017) 2616 final, p.21.

2.2.2. *The determination of the scope of the review and the limits to the national procedural autonomy*

In spite of the fragmentation and the gaps of the current regulatory approach, the contribution of the existing EU law provisions is, as already indicitated, critical for ensuring the effective implementation of significant parts of the environmental legislation through the empowerment of natural persons and the civil society to take legal action. More specifically, this can be attributed to the fact that certain rules, either more or less vaguely formulated, have been introduced and these rules address significant issues of the national procedural law in specific fields of the environmental litigation, such the legal standing, the scope of the review and the costs of the relevant procedures.[26] In this way certain limitations are set to the "autonomous" choice of the means for the implementation of the EU law by the MS (principle of procedural autonomy[27]) as regards the judicial review procedures in concrete areas of the environmental litigation.

In particular, as is the case with the standing criteria[28], the relevant provisions set the frame for the standards of judicial review by introducing the obligation of the national legislators to ensure that the competent courts review the substantive and procedural legality of the decisions taken under the relevant environmental and permitting procedures. In any case, certain room is left to determine the specific depth of the review and the subsequent consequences in cases of violations either of substantive norms, procedural norms or both of them (e.g. annulment or reform of the relevant decisions).

Such an already framed leeway is further limited, as the relevant national rules have to be tested, in any case, against the so-called "Rewe requirements" and mainly against the principle of effectiveness, which presupposes that the relevant rules must not make in practice impossible or excessively difficult the exercise of the rights conferred by the EU law.[29] Furthermore, they have also to be examined with regard to their compatibility with the principle of effective judicial protection as a fundamental principle of EU law, a test which most probably imposes further limitations on the national legislators. This can be at first attributed to the fact that in relation to the principle of effectiveness[30], the principle of effective judicial protection and more specifically in the form of the right enshrined in Article 47

---

26 *Eliantonio, supra*, note 5 at p. 109 et seq.

27 *D-U Galetta*, Procedural Autonomy of EU Member States: Paradise Lost? –A Study on the "Functionalized Procedural Competence" of EU Member States, 2011, p. 7 et seq. and 33 et seq.

28 MS enjoy a certain level of discretion in terms of choosing one of the two basic models (interest-based or right based approach) for determining those entitled to take legal action, but in any case have to recognize a preferential status for NGOs.

29 *J. Jans et al,*, Europeanisation of Public Law, 2007, p. 40 et. seq.

30 *G. Winter*, National Administrative Procedural Law under EU Requirements. With a Focus on Public Participation in: J. Jans, R. Marcory & A-M. Moreno Molina (Eds.), *supra*, note 10, p. 11, 13 arguing that there is a need for further systematic elaboration between the two principles and that possible overlaps can be observed.

of the EUChFR seems to introduce certain specific and positive requirements in cases of the protection of the substantive and procedural rights arising from EU law provisions.[31] In this context, relevant is also the enshrinement of the principle in Article 19 TEU[32], which, in contrast to Article 47 of the EUChFR, is formulated in a "non-right-based" language. Subsequently, the application of this principle also in conjunction with the principle of effectiveness raises the bar even higher concerning the level of judicial protection and more specifically the standards of judicial review in environment-related judicial proceedings, encompassing also cases which concern the objective implementation of the national rules originating from the EU environmental law.[33] In addition, the objective of "ensuring wide access to justice to the public concerned" sets, as it was persuasively argued by the Advocate General Sharpston[34], the parameters within which the discretion of the MS has to be exercised also as regards the determination of the scope of the review in the above-mentioned fields of the environmental litigation.

The ever increasing "limitations" of the national procedural autonomy as regards judicial review procedures in environment-related cases due to the cumulative application of the relevant International (e.g. AC) and EU law provisions and the principle of effective judicial protection are reflected in an illustrative way in the already referred CJEU Ruling in the case *Lesoochranárske zoskupenie VLK v. Obvodný úrad Trenčín* [*LZ II*]. In brief, the Ruling, which is expected to have significant repercussions in the years to come, is critical for the following reasons. The first one is that it demonstrates the significant legal effects of the Aarhus Convention in the EU Legal Order, as the Court interpreted Article 6(3) of the Habitats Directive in the light of Article 6(1)(b) of the AC and recognized in this manner the right of an NGO to participate in an authorization procedure under Article 6(3) (paras. 46–49), which is associated with the right to appeal the relevant decision before the courts. The second reason lies in the fact that having established the participatory right and its implementation under the EU law, the Court finds the jurisdiction to apply Article 47 as a standard in order to assess the compatibility of critical national procedural rules for access to judicial review procedures with its regulatory content (para. 52). Through the interpretation of Article 47 in the light of Article 9(2) and (4) of the Aarhus Convention, the Court established a high standard as regards the effectiveness of the national procedural rules applied to the actions of the NGOs in the field of nature protection legislation, by adopting the position that the right to effective judicial protection presupposes that NGOs can challenge any decision based on Article 6 of the Habitats Directive. Such an approach could be applied by

31 *S. Prechal & R. Widdershoven*, Redefining the Relationship between "Rewe-Effectiveness" and Effective Judicial Protection, REALaw, 2011 (2), p. 31, 38 et seq.

32 This Treaty provision lays down that MS shall provide remedies sufficient to ensure effective legal protection in the fields covered by the EU Law.

33 *Darpö, supra*, note 8 at p. 384.

34 Opinion of Advocate General Sharpston in Case 115/09, *Trianel* [2011], OJ C204/06, para. 70.

analogy to actions concerning alleged violations of provisions in other fields of the environmental legislation.[35] In this way, the Court intervened further in the procedural autonomy of the MS and re-affirmed the view that Article 47 may impose higher standards of judicial protection than the principle of effectiveness.

3. ISSUES ARISING IN DIFFERENT LEGAL SYSTEMS CONCERNING THE SCOPE OF THE REVIEW IN ENVIRONMENT-RELATED JUDICIAL PROCEEDINGS

3.1. INTRODUCTORY REMARKS

The relevant judicial systems for the review of administrative acts and omissions, including also the environment-related ones, can be distinguished mainly into two basic types on the basis of the target setting of the judicial control, which constitutes a critical factor for the determination of both the standing criteria and the scope of the review.[36] The first type of judicial systems is, thus, characterized by its primary aim to guarantee the review of the objective legality of administrative acts or omissions ("system of objective judicial review") and the French system of judicial review can be regarded as the most prominent example of this category.[37] The second type of judicial systems is underpinned by the emphasis placed on the protection of individual rights ("system of subjective judicial review") and the German system can be regarded as the most characteristic model of this category. In the context of the present paper, a comparative analysis of the majority of the judicial systems concerning the scope of the review cannot take place. For the purposes of the analysis, it will be at first examined how the scope of the review is determined in systems of subjective judicial review and in particular in the German system primarily and in the Austrian and Czech systems secondarily, with the aim to shed light on whether the orientation on the individual rights protection may exert influence on the determination of the standards of the judicial scrutiny (3.2.). Then, the emphasis is shifted on how the scope of the

---

35 Commission Notice on Access to Justice, *supra*, note at p. 25; *L. Ankersmit*, Brown Bears II: Aarhus and the Charter show their teeth, European Law Blog (accessed on 20.06.2017); *M.J. van Wolferen*, Case C-243/15 Lesoochranárske zoskupenie VLK v. Obvodný úrad Trenčín, JEEPL 2017(1), p. 136-151.

36 Certain Legal Systems can also be characterized as "mixed systems" in the sense that they include elements of both types of systems of judicial review. See *A. Epiney & K. Sollberger*, Verwaltungsgerichtlicher Rechtsschutz in Umweltangelegenheiten, Rechtsvergleich, europa- und völkerrechtliche Vorgaben und Implikationen für die Schweiz, 2003, p. 106 (concerning the criteria of the classification) and 118 et seq (concerning the mixed systems).

37 *Id* at p. 114 et.seq; *A. Epiney*, Verwaltungsgerichtlicher Rechtsschutz im Umweltrecht im Rechtsvergleich, NVwZ 2014 (8), p.468–469.

review is determined in systems of objective judicial review and especially those that have cassatory procedure in place, such as the Greek system, which is heavily influenced by the French system, with the aim to examine whether a full review of substantive and procedural legality can be ensured (3.3).

3.2. THE SCOPE OF THE REVIEW IN SYSTEMS OF SUBJECTIVE JUDICIAL REVIEW

3.2.1. *The scope of review in the German system of judicial review*

The rights-based approach and the scope of review

The German legal system is underpinned by the rights-based approach, as enshrined in the German Constitution (Article 19(4)) and the Federal Statute on Administrative Judicial Review (*Verwaltungsgerichtsordnung* – hereafter VwGO (Article 42(2)). In this context, any claimant who wants to challenge an administrative decision or an omission before the court has to claim the possible infringement of a norm that protects an individual right under public law ("*Schutznormtheorie*").[38] If such an infringement cannot be claimed, standing is denied and the claim is inadmissible. Departing from the fact that the majority of the environmental norms do not aim at the protection of individual rights under public law ("subjective public rights"), it becomes evident that individuals have faced significant difficulties to receive standing before the courts for challenging environment-related decisions or omissions.[39] The same applied to the environmental NGOs which except for the cases relating to nature protection[40] have been unable to challenge the alleged violations of the environmental legislation for a long time.[41]

Furthermore, the right-based approach exerts influence also on the extent of the judicial control in the sense that the grounds on which legal standing is recognized determine the latter as well. More specifically, in accordance with the relevant provision of VwGO (Article 113 (I)), only complaints that relate to a violation of a rule that establishes a subjective public right of the plaintiff through the contested administrative act, can be claimed admissibly and be considered by

38 *S. Schlacke*, Überindividuelle Rechtsschutz, 2008, p. 54 et seq; *B. Wegener*, Subjective Public Rights: Historical Roots versus European and Democratic Challenges? in: H. Pünder& Ch. Waldhoff (Eds.), Debates in German Pubic Law, 2014, p. 219, 221 et. seq.

39 *Epiney & Sollberger, supra*, note 36 at p. 109; *F. Grashof*, The Different Roads to Judicial Coherence in Public Environmental Law, REALaw 2015 (2), p. 247, 251.

40 *A. Schmidt, C. Schrader & M. Zschiesche*, Die Verbandsklage im Umwelt- und Naturschutzrecht, 2014, p. 20 and 122 et.seq.

41 *German Advisory Council on the Environment*, Access to Justice in Environmental Matters: The Crucial Role of Legal Standing for Non-Governmental Organizations, Statement-February 2005, p. 3.

the court ('substantive rights effect').[42] In this context, the court can review the objective illegality of an administrative act and quash it only insofar as it infringes the legally protected rights of the plaintiff, while certain aspects of legality may fall out of the scope of the trial. Such a limitation of the scope of review, though, raises the issue of whether effective judicial protection can be provided to the members of the multipole relationship that are affected by the relevant decision ("third parties") and moreover of whether such a concept is suitable to ensure the effective protection of collective environmental interests.[43]

The German legal system has also developed a systematic and highly complicated doctrine which consists of certain requirements under which the violation of procedural rules, including the environment-related ones, can be claimed admissibly and the well-foundedness of the relevant pleas can result in the annulment of the relevant decision, and of certain mechanisms for preventing such an annulment.[44] In particular, a critical requirement which has already been mentioned, relates to the violation of a rule through the critical administrative decision, which establishes a subjective public right of the plaintiff. This requirement, though, can be more easily satisfied in cases of alleged violations of substantive rules than of procedural ones, because the relevant procedural norms, including those that establish participation rights in environmental decision-making, are not mainly regarded as establishing individual public rights.[45] Even in the case that the procedural failure can be claimed admissibly and be subject to judicial control, the Court can find recourse to two other provisions that can "save" the critical administrative act from annulment. The first one is the provision of Article 45 of the Administrative Procedure Act (*Verwaltungsvefahrensgesetz* – hereafter VwVfG) which provides the possibility of the rectification of the procedural failure until the decision of the court if certain conditions are met.[46] The second one, which is set in Article 46 of VwVfG and is applied in the case that procedural errors are not corrected, introduces the

42 *K. Gärditz*, Europäisierter Umweltrechtsschutz als Laboratorium des Verwaltungsprozessrechts: Entwicklungspfade zwischen Prozeduralisierung, Objektivierung und Subjektivierung, EurUP 2015 (3), p. 196, 200. A "requirement of connection" was also introduced in 2010 in the Dutch Administrative Law, according to which an administrative decision is not annulled on the grounds of the violation of a rule or a general principle if this rule or principle evidently does not aim at protecting the interest of those who want to rely on it. See *Grashof, supra*, note 39 at p. 255–256.

43 *Darpö, supra*, note 10 at p. 197.

44 *Winter, supra*, note 30 at p. 22 et. seq.

45 *S. Schlacke*, Zur fortschreitenden Europäisierung des (Umwelt-) Rechtsschutzes-Schutznormdoktrin und Verfahrensfehlerlehre erneut under Anpassungsdruck, NVwZ 2014 (1/2), p. 11, 15.

46 *Winter, supra*, note 30 at p. 23–24; *E. Hofmann*, Der Funktionswandel der Verwaltungsgerichtsbarkeit-nur eine Frage des Umweltrechts?, EurUP 2015 (4), p. 266, 267 et.seq. See also Federal Administrative Court (hereafter BVerwG), Judgment of 20 August 2008, Case No4 C11/07, where the Court adopted a rather restrictive approach as regards the rectification of procedural errors relating to the EIA Procedure.

relevance of procedural errors to the final outcome of the contested decision as a precondition for its annulment ("relevance test"). In particular, a procedural failure does not lead to the annulment of the critical decision, if it is evident that it has not influenced its substance.[47] From a systematic point of view, the regulatory concept concerning the significance of the procedural failures on the validity of the administrative decision reflects the notion that underpinned the German administrative law before the increasing influence of the International and EU law provisions, according to which only a secondary importance was attached to the procedural rules, as the procedure was mainly viewed as a means for the implementation of the substantive rules.[48] It is, however, questionable whether this regulatory approach reflected in the above-mentioned provisions is compatible with the fundamental importance attached to the procedural rules and the participatory rights in the EU environmental law. The incompatibility of this regulatory concept with Article 11 of the EIA Directive was to a significant extent certified by the CJEU in its Ruling in the relevant case (C-137/14)[49], which will be analysed at a later point in detail (4.2). Briefly, it should be mentioned that the Court ruled that it is not line with Article 11 to link the possibility of invoking a procedural defect with the requirement that this defect has affected the tenor of the final decision and to refuse the annulment of the contested decision solely on this ground (paras. 55–58).

Furthermore, German law encompasses another feature that leads factually to the restriction of the scope of the judicial review in the administrative-related judicial proceedings. It is the so-called preclusion, which is set both in VwVfG (Article 73(4)) and in certain environmental laws (Article 10(3) lit.e of the Federal Emission Protection Act and Article 2(3) of the Law on Actions in Environmental Matters [*Umwelt-Rechtsbehelfsgesetz* – hereafter UmwRG]). According to the relevant provisions, the comments or objections that could have been put forward in the administrative procedure or in the public consultation procedure but they haven't, cannot be claimed admissibly before the Court.[50] The logic behind the introduction of these provisions lies mainly in the influence that it exerts on the outcome of the decision, the fact that third parties have to submit their comments at an early stage of the procedure and the administration can take them into

---

47 In accordance with the case law of the German Administrative Courts, Article 46 of VwVfG is not applied to the so called "fundamental errors" of procedure. See BVerwG, Judgment of 25.01.1996, Case No 4 C 5/95; BVerwG, Judgment of 13.12.2007, Case No4 C9/06, Rn. 38;Hess VGH, Judgment of 16 September 2009, NuR 2010, p. 438, BVerwG, Judgment of 31 July 2012, Case 4A 7001/11.

48 *H. Pünder*, German administrative procedure in a comparative perspective: Observations on the path to a transnational *jus commune proceduralis* in administrative law, Int J Constitutional Law 2013 (4), p. 940, 942 et. seq.

49 CJEU Judgment of 15 October 2015, Case C-137/14, *Commission v. Germany*, ECLI:EU:C:2015:683.

50 *Hofmann, supra,* note 46 at p. 273–274.

account.[51] Moreover, this feature also serves the observance of the principle of legal certainty and the efficiency of the judicial procedures in the sense that new claims which could delay the process, cannot be claimed admissibly.[52] This feature of the German administrative law was also regarded by the CJEU in the afore-mentioned Judgment in the case *Commission v. Germany* as incompatible with the relevant provision of the EU environmental law (paras. 79–80).

Finally, as regards the depth of the judicial review, it should be mentioned that German Administrative Courts can scrutinize questions of both fact and law, and are equipped with the power of construing the relevant regulatory provisions and applying them to the concrete facts of the case.[53] Subsequently, the interpretation of the vaguely formulated terms set in legislation by the administration as well as the exercise of the administrative discretion can be subject to a full judicial scrutiny.[54]

The possible contribution of a right to a healthy environment in strengthening the procedural right of access to justice

An interesting question that may arise in this context is whether the enshrinement of a right to a healthy environment in the German basic law could be critical in the sense that the violation of a substantive environmental norm would be regarded as a violation of the respective constitutional right, so that it could be challenged and reviewed by the Courts. Before answering this question, it should be mentioned that the establishment of such a right is perceived as the most progressive and simultaneously contested legal development in this field. In particular, proponents of such a right, which can be found in many constitutions, argue that it can contribute to the introduction of stronger environmental laws, to an enhanced enforcement of the environmental legislation also through the reinforcement of the procedural rights and to the recognition of an enhanced status to the protection of the environment when balanced against other constitutionally established rights and objectives.[55] From another point of view, this right-based approach was criticized for certain reasons which relate to the vagueness of the normative content of the relevant right and the difficulties which emerge in the determination of the environmental standards which substantiate

---

51 Federal Constitutional Court (BVerfG), Judgment of 8 July 1982, Entscheidungen des Bundesverfassungsgerichts,61, 82, 114–117; *Winter, supra,* note 30 at p. 19.

52 BVerwG, Judgment of 19.12.1985, Case 7C, Entscheidungen des Bundesverwaltungsgerichts 65, 82 ("Wyhl-II Enstcheidung"); *Hofmann, supra,* note 46 at p. 273.

53 *E. Rehbinder,* Germany in: J. Ebbesson (ed.), *supra,* note 1, p. 231, 243.

54 *Epiney & Sollberger, supra,* note 36 at p. 133. It can be observed, though, that since the famous Wyhl decision of the Federal Administrative Court, the administrative Courts tend to rely, to a considerable degree, on the authority' s appreciation of the relevant risk in cases of complex risk-related decisions. See *Rehbinder, supra,* note 53 at p. 243.

55 *D. Shelton,* Human Rights, Environmental Rights and the Right to the Environment, Stanford Journal of International Law,1991, p 103, 135 et seq; *D. Boyd,* The Environmental Rights Revolution, A Global Study of Constitutions, Human Rights, and the Environment, 2012, p. 29 et seq and 233 et seq.

it by the courts in response to individual claims.[56] Although it is beyond the scope of the current analysis to make an assessment as regards the effectiveness and the utility of such a right, relevant comparative research shows that its impact on the national legal systems which is also reflected in prominent rulings of the national courts, is largely positive.[57]

In the light of the above, the enshrinement of an autonomous environmental right in the German basic law could have a positive impact on strengthening the right of access to justice in environmental matters as regards the "relaxation" of the standing criteria and the extent of the review due to the assumed violation of a substantive constitutional right. In spite of such a positive contribution, such a right based approach was regarded by the majority of legal scholars in the long debate for the constitutionalisation of the environmental protection[58] as a choice, which was not in conformity with the basic structures of the respective legal order for a variety of reasons.[59] Against this background, a constitutional provision (Article 20a) was introduced, according to which environmental protection is recognized as an objective of the State (*Staatszielbestimmung*)[60], while the rather negative perception towards a right to a healthy environment is still dominant.[61] Subsequently, a relevant legal development does not seem possible in the near future, so that the further enhancement of the right of access to justice in environmental matters would mainly be the outcome of pressures arising from the international and EU environmental law.

3.2.2. The scope of the review in other systems of subjective judicial review: the Austrian and the Czech system

The Austrian legal system follows a right-based approach as regards *locus standi* which arises from the orientation of the judicial system to protect subjective public rights.[62] As is the case with the German system of judicial review, the standing

56 *P. Birnie, A.Boyle & C. Redgwell*, International Law and the Environment, 2009, p. 268 et seq.

57 *Boyd, supra*, note 55 at p. 233 et seq.

58 *T-J. Tsai*, Die Verfassungsrechtiche Umweltschutzpflicht des Staates, 1996, p. 48 et seq.

59 The reasons for such a perception, relate, among others, to the regulative context of such a right, which is regarded as incompatible with the concept of rights established in Basic Law (e.g. defensive rights), its weak enforceability, a possible flood of litigation and a threat to democracy due to the shift of power to judges. See *C. Calliess*, Rechtsstaat und Umweltstaat, 2001, p. 421 et.seq; *M. Kloepfer*, Umweltschutz in: Leitgedanken des Rechts, Paul Kirchhof zum 70. Geburtstag, 2013, p. 867, 870 et. seq.

60 *D. Murswiek* in: M. Sachs (Hrsg), Grundgesetz Kommentar, 7ed, 2014, Article 20a, p. 860 et. seq; *A. Voßkuhle*, Umweltschutz und Grundgesetz, NVwZ 2013, p. 1 et.seq.

61 For a different approach *see M. Kotulla*, Verfassungsrechtliche Aspekten im Zusammenhang mit der Einführung eines Umweltgrundrechts in das Grundgesetz, KJ 2000 (1), p. 22–34.

62 This principle is enshrined both in the Act on General Administrative Procedure (Article 8) and in the provisions of Federal and Provincial Environmental Laws, such as the Industrial Code (Article 74). See *U. Giera & K. Lachmayer*, The principle of effective legal protection in Austrian Administrative Law in: Z. Szente& K. Lachmayer (Eds), The Principle of Effective Legal Protection in Administrative Law – A European Comparison, 2016, p. 73, 81–82.

approach is critical for the determination of the scope of the review in the sense that individual plaintiffs cannot put forward claims concerning the violation of rules that do not aim to protect subjective individual rights, so that claims on alleged violations of rules aiming at the protection of the environment in general, (e.g. those relating to the nature protection) fall outside of the scope of the trial.[63]

Only plaintiffs that have wide standing rights, such as the citizen's groups, NGOs and the Ombudsman for the environment (*Umweltanwälte*)[64] can put forward claims as regards the violation of norms, which aim solely at the protection of the environmental interests. Subsequently, if the relevant administrative act is not challenged by this category of claimants, certain violations will not be scrutinized by the courts. In any case if a plaintiff passes the test of the restrictive standing requirements, an intensive review of the substantive and procedural legality of the contested administrative act is provided, which can lead even to its reform. This is due to the fact that Administrative Courts of First Instance, which were established after the major reform of the administrative jurisdiction that came into effect in January 2014, are equipped with reformatory power.[65] The Federal Administrative Court has still the competence to review the relevant EIA Decisions.[66]

In any case, the reformatory power of the Administrative Courts of First Instance raises the delicate issue concerning the determination of the appropriate level of judicial intervention in administrative disputes, including the environment-related ones. At first glance, the power of the administrative judge to conclude the whole proceeding and change the administrative act in compliance with the respective ruling seems to be an appropriate choice in terms of ensuring effective judicial protection also in the environment-related disputes. This can be attributed to the fact that this kind of competence is not only associated with an extensive review of both the substantive and procedural legality of the contested acts, but it also provides the framework for an effective settlement of the disputes, as they are not referred back to the administration. From another point of view though, such a choice raises the difficult issue of the separation of powers between administration and the courts[67], which becomes even more complicated in cases where the administration has discretionary power[68], as it the case with

63 *V. Madner*, Study on the Implementation of Articles 9.3 and 9.4 of the Aarhus-Convention – Austria, 2013, available at: www.ec.europa.eu/environment/aarhus/access_studies.htm, p. 15; *U. Giera & K. Lachmayer, supra*, note 62 at p..81.

64 *Madner, supra*, note 63 at p. 16 et. seq; *U. Giera &K. Lachmayer, supra*, note 62 at p. 85.

65 *Madner, supra*, note 63 at p. 5 et.seq; *K. Pabel*, Die Neuordnung des Rechtsschutzes im Verwaltungsverfahren in Österreich in: Rechtschutz und Verfahren im Vertragspartnerrecht, Schriftenreihe der Universität Passau, 2015, p. 11, 25.

66 *Epiney, supra*, note 37 at p. 466.

67 *J. Därpo, supra*, note 10 at 179.

68 Such an approach is also dominant in the EU Administrative Law, according to which in cases where the administration enjoys a margin of discretion, the judicial control is limited and the relevant act can be annulled only in cases of a "manifest error of assessment". See *Z. Szente*, Conceptualizing the principle of effective legal protection in administrative law in: Z. Szente & K. Lachmayer (Eds), *supra*, note 62, p. 5, 24 et seq.

the issuance of certain environmental permits which involves frequently complex science and risk-related considerations. In conclusion, although the equipment of administrative judges with reformatory power is in conformity with the extensive judicial review provided by the Austrian system and could contribute in ensuring effective judicial protection, it would still be a difficult task for the judges to balance between judicial activism and self-restraint especially in cases where the administration enjoys a wide margin of discretion.

Furthermore, another system of judicial review in which restrictive approaches concerning the scope of the review can be observed, is the Czech system, which is also categorized as a system of subjective judicial review.[69] In particular, the relevant regulatory concept exerts influence on the determination of the standards of review, in the sense that not only the range of claims that can be put forward permissibly by the individual plaintiffs is limited, but also the possibilities of the NGOs to challenge an environment-related administrative act or omission are further restricted. This is due to the fact that in accordance with the interpretation given by the administrative Courts to the relevant legislative provisions, NGOs can claim permissibly only the violation of the rules establishing their procedural rights within the framework of the relevant lawsuits challenging the legality of environment-related acts or omissions.[70]

3.3. THE SCOPE OF REVIEW IN SYSTEMS OF OBJECTIVE JUDICIAL REVIEW: THE CASE OF THE GREEK SYSTEM

The Greek system is heavily influenced by the French administrative law and the relevant system of judicial review[71], and can be, thus, classified as an objective system of judicial review. The foundations for the judicial review of administrative acts and omissions are laid down in the Constitution, while the relevant disputes are categorized either as substantive administrative disputes or as annulment administrative disputes.[72] In the absence of a specific legal provision governing the

---

69 *P. Černý*, Lawsuits of Non-Governmental Organizations in the Czech Legal System-An Efficient Tool of Environmental Protection?, The Common Law Review 2010, p. 13.

70 Supreme Administrative Court, Judgment of 29 July 2004, Case 7 A 139/2001-67; Supreme Administrative Court, Judgment of 30 January 2008, Case No. 8 As 31/2006-78; Supreme Administrative Court, Judgment of 22 July 2009, Case No. 5As 53/2008-243. See also *V Vomacka & I. Jancarova*, Czech Republic in: J. Jans, R. Marcory & A-M. Moreno Molina (Eds.), *supra*, note 10, p. 257, 263–264 referring to the minor changes in the relevant jurisprudence of the Supreme Administrative Court (e.g. Supreme Administrative Court, Judgment of 27 April 2012, Case 7 As 25/2012–21).

71 *J. Schwarze*, European Administrative Law, 2006, p. 169; *P. Dagtoglou*, Administrative Courts Procedure, 2011, p. 33.

72 According to Article 94 of the Constitution the adjudication of substantive administrative disputes belongs to the jurisdiction of the ordinary administrative courts, which scrutinize both the legality of the contested administrative act and the merits of the case. Furthermore,

issue, disputes concerning the alleged violation of the environmental legislation are adjudicated upon a petition for the annulment of the contested administrative act[73] or omission at first and last instance by the Council of State (hereafter CS), which is equipped with the power to quash the critical act or omission (cassatory power).[74]

Due to the influence of the French system, the Greek system is governed by an "interest-based" approach as regards the standing requirements (Article 47 of the Presidential Decree 18/1989), which are even more relaxed in the case of the environment-related disputes.[75] It is also worthy of note that the relevant constitutional provision for the protection of the environment (Article 24) even before the enshrinement of a relevant right, has also contributed, through its dynamic interpretation by the CS, to the recognition of "relaxed" standing criteria in the environment-related disputes.[76] Furthermore, the influence of the French system in conjunction with the constitutional provisions for the review of the administrative acts and the right to judicial protection are critical in the determination of the scope of review, which is defined in a rather broad way in the sense that the claimant can put forward claims concerning the alleged violation of a wide range of norms, so that the CS can scrutinize the objective legality of the contested act or omission.[77]

The critical question which arises is what the exact extent and depth of the judicial scrutiny of the environment-related acts and more specifically of the environment-related permits are, taking into consideration the nature of the

according to Article 95 of the Constitution the annulment of the regulatory and individual administrative acts upon petition belongs to the jurisdiction of the Council of State (e.g. the Supreme Administrative Court) which exercises a strict control of the legality of the contested acts or omissions. See *Dagtoglou*, *supra*, note 71 at p. 19; 120Rn et. seq.; *P. Lazaratos*, Administrative Procedural Law, 2014, p. 11 et.seq.

73 The application of both the EU principle of effective legal protection and the right to a fair trial enshrined in Article 6 ECHR have exerted significant influence on the interpretation of the term of "administrative act" in its broad sense, as only "executing" administrative acts can be challenged admissibly before the CS. This tendency can also be observed in the field of the environment-related jurisprudence (Decision 3059/2009). See *E. Prevedourou*, The Influence of the EU Law on the Judicial Proceedings before the Council of State, 2012, p. 56 et-seq.

74 *G. Siouti & G. Gerapetritis*, Greece in: J. Ebbesson (Ed), *supra*, note 1, p. 261, 263.

75 In accordance with the constant jurisprudence of the CS the legal interest of the applicant must be direct, personal and present. For the standing criteria in the environment-related disputes see *G. Siouti*, Textbook of Environmental Law, 2011, p. 116 et seq.

76 *N. Nikolakis*, The Approach of Procedural Matters in Environment-related Disputes: The contribution of Konstantinos Menoudakos to the Shaping of the Jurisprudence of the Fifth Section of the Council of State in: Hellenic Society for Environmental Law (Ed.), The Judge, the Law and the Environment- Studies in Honour of the H. President of the Council of State Konstantinos Menoudakos, Athens 2016, p. 277, 284, 290.

77 In accordance with Article 48 of the PD 18/1989, the claimant can put forward the following four reasons for the annulment of the critical administrative act or omission: a) incompetence of the administrative organ for the issuance of the critical act b) violation of a substantive formality (type) of the procedure c) substantive violation of a norm provision and d) misuse of power. Although these four reasons for annulment set the frame for the judicial control, they cannot practically limit the extent of the review, because under the third reason the violation of almost all relevant norms can be claimed.

control (legality control). As a starting point, it should be mentioned that the CS reviews the observance of all the relevant procedural rules ("procedural legality"), as it is required by the access to justice provisions of the EU environmental law (e.g. Article 11 of the EIA Directive). Furthermore, the Court reviews the content of EIA as the basis for the relevant permit mainly through the review of its reasoning[78], as it is scrutinized whether the EIA fulfils the requirements of the relevant legislation and its content is sufficient in terms of ensuring that the administration has the necessary information for calibrating and assessing the consequences of the project on the natural environment and examining its compatibility with the relevant EU and national legislation (Plenary Decisions 3478/2000, 613/2002).[79] The Court has also developed certain standards which are critical for the review of the content of the relevant permit and encompass the requirement for the application of a scientific methodology and documentation of the EIA (Decisions 1520/1993, 287/2003 and 2981/2001), the requirement for a holistic assessment (Decisions 2759/1994, 2760/1994, 4033/1998) and that for an in-time assessment (Decisions 2759/1994, 2760/1994, 4498/1998, 26/2014) of the anticipated effects of the project.[80]

The nature of the judicial review, however, determines its limits in the sense that the Court cannot directly scrutinize the assessment of the authority as regards the impact of the project on the environment (Decisions 970/2007, 2636/2009), the choice of the scientific method (Decision 3139/2015) or the relevant technical choices.[81] The Court can review, to some extent the content of the contested act[82], either through the examination of whether the administration erred in facts ("error to the facts")[83], or through the review of the "outer" limits of discretion. In the latter case, the Court scrutinizes on the basis of the file material and the lessons of the common experience whether the administration has committed a

78 *M. Pikramenos*, The Reasoning of Administrative Acts and the Cassatory Judicial Review, 2012, p. 236 et seq.

79 *E. Koutoupa-Rengakos*, Environmental Law, 2008, p. 144.

80 For a comprehensive analysis of the relevant requirements see *E. Koutoupa-Rengakos,* The Contribution of Konstantinos Menoudakos to the jurisprudence of the Council of State as regards the "Institution" of the Environmental Impact Assessment in: Hellenic Society for Environmental Law (Ed.), *supra*, note 76, p. 47, 49 et seq.

81 In the case that permits falling into the scope of the IED Directive are subject to judicial review, the Court mainly scrutinizes whether the administration provided sufficient justification concerning the compliance of the critical technical choices with the relevant legislative requirements (e.g. BATs) or not (Decisions 1492/2013, 550/2015 of the CS).

82 Besides the nature of the judicial control, the Court's approach for a limited review of the assessments of the administration within the framework of the environmental decisions is also based on the principle of the separation of powers (Plenary Decision 217/2016, para. 3).

83 The judicial review of whether the administration erred in facts, is focused on whether the facts and the documentation on which the assessment of the EIA is based, are accurate (Decision 3478/2000, para. 11). If the Court finds out that the administration erred in facts, a substantive violation of an environmental norm is grounded (third reason of annulment). See *Koutoupa*, *supra*, note 80 at p. 71.

"manifest error of assessment" mainly as regards the environmental effects of the project or whether the principle of proportionality was observed or not.[84]

In this context, a specific question which can be raised relates to whether the nature of the control (legality control) provides the appropriate framework for a comprehensive review of the substantive legality of the environment-related decisions, or omissions, as it is required by the access to justice provisions of the EU environmental law. In general terms, the relevant legislative provisions in conjunction with the afore-mentioned jurisprudential standards are critical for ensuring a satisfactory level of scrutiny of the environment-related decisions, acts or omissions. In certain cases, where the EIA decision or the permit under the IED Directive encompasses complex but simultaneously scientifically controversial assessments, it would be critical, though, that the Court can make use of the appropriate means of proof, including the recourse to the opinion of the technical experts, so that it can be scrutinized in an effective manner if the administration had all the necessary and accurate documentation, in order to issue a lawful decision. In this way, the review of the substantive legality of the contested administrative act, also through the review of its reasoning, can, be, thus, realized in a sufficient manner within the prescribed limits.[85] Such an approach would also be useful and appropriate, when the Court will have to scrutinize the fulfilment of the requirement concerning the quality of the EIA Report and the corresponding obligation of the administration to ensure that it has access to sufficient expertise to examine it, which have been introduced by the revised EIA Directive 2014/52/EU (Article 5 (3))[86] and have to be transposed into the national legal order within a set deadline.

Furthermore, another issue relates to the quite recent jurisprudential tendency, according to which the pleas concerning the defaults of the EIA Study both from a procedural and a substantive perspective, and especially those concerning the examination of alternatives which have not been put forward in the public consultation procedures, cannot be claimed admissibly in the judicial proceedings (Decisions 1169/2011, 1943/2012, 4940/2013, 384/2014, 551/2015). This practice which constitutes a form of jurisprudential preclusion[87], and is mainly justified by the need to ensure the efficiency of the judicial proceedings, raises issues of compatibility with the relevant provisions of the Aarhus Convention and EU law, as interpreted by the CJEU (Case C-137/14, *Commission v. Germany*).

---

84 Plenary Decisions 3478/2000, 613/2002, 26/2014, Decision 1675/1999. See also *Koutoupa, supra*, note 79 at p. 145–148.

85 *I. Sarmas*, The Democratic and Social State: The Jurisprudence of the Council of State, 2003, p. 694, 698–699. See also Commission Notice on Access to Justice in Environmental Matters,, *supra*, note 25 at p. 39.

86 *A. Garcia-Ureta*, Directive 2014/52 on the Assessment of Environmental Effects of Projects: New Words or More Stringent Obligations?, Environmental Liability 2014 (6), p. 239, 249–250.

87 *K. Gogos*, Die öffentliche Konsultation im UVP-Vefahren zwischen Artikulation der Öffentlichkeit und Vefahrensbeschleunigung-Parallelwege im griechischen und deutschen Umweltrecht in: E. Hofmann, L. Papadopoulou & K. Gogos (Hrsg), Demokratisch-funktionale Analyse der Öffentlichkeitsbeteiligung im Umwelt-und Infrastrukturrecht, 2016, p. 139, 148–149.

3.4. CRITICAL REMARKS FROM THE COMPARATIVE OVERVIEW

A first critical remark from the overview of the three systems of subjective judicial review is that they do not only have in place restrictive standing requirements, but also confine the scope of the review in a rather restrictive way. Such a determination of the standards of review can result in significant limitations of the judicial scrutiny of the contested decisions or in conjunction with the standing requirements, even in the exclusion of certain decisions from the judicial control. Subsequently, issues of incompatibility with the Aarhus Convention and the EU law are raised, which become subject to the scrutiny of the CJEU, as already mentioned. Furthermore, it seems to be doubtful whether these models of review take sufficiently into consideration the particularities of the environmental litigation as regards the protection of the collective environmental interests. In counterbalance, those systems provide a more intensive scrutiny of the contested administrative acts in the case that the criteria for admissibility and well-foundedness are fulfilled, and remedies, which can even include the reform of the contested act.

A second remark which is derived from the analysis of the Greek system as a system of objective judicial review is that in spite of the nature of the control, a sufficient scrutiny of the substantive legality of the contested environment-related decisions can be ensured in general terms. It should, however, be further discussed how the review can be enhanced through the use of the appropriate means of proof, so that the level of control required by the relevant International and EU standards is in any case met.

A third remark is that a reason which is common in the two categories of judicial systems and to which restrictive approaches in form of both legislative provisions and jurisprudential standards can be attributed, relates to the efficiency of the judicial proceedings.

4. THE DETERMINATION OF THE SCOPE OF THE REVIEW IN THE LIGHT OF THE FINDINGS OF THE ACCC AND THE RELEVANT JURISPRUDENCE OF THE CJEU

4.1. THE RELEVANT FINDINGS OF THE ACCC

The Findings of the ACCC[88] relate to two distinct but inter-related issues concerning the scope of the review in a broader sense and can be thus distinguished

88 The Findings of the ACCC are non-binding, but they can be considered as valid sources of interpretation of the Convention from the perspective of the international law after their

into two categories. In the first category belong the Findings of the ACCC, which relate to the kind of decisions, acts and omissions that are categorized as decisions under Article 6 and are thus subject to review under Article 9(2) of the AC. The relevant Findings are underpinned by the central notion which was expressed quite early[89] that the substantive criterion for the classification of an administrative act or decision as a decision on permitting a specific activity (Article 6) is *its function and effects and not its type*. In this context, the ACCC took the position that the following acts should be classified as decisions under Article 6 and be subsequently scrutinized under the standards of Article 9(2): a) the SEA statements for the "small-scale" Detailed Spatial Plans in the case that they substitute an EIA Decision, because in conjunction with the Plans, they have the legal function of a decision under Article 6[90] b) a town planning permit provided that it is sufficiently precise[91] c) the EIA screening decisions, because their outcome is a determination under Article 6(1)[92] and d) an Act of Parliament adopted further to a hybrid law procedure, because its legal effects (e.g. the authorization of specific activity) amount to a permitting decision.[93] Furthermore, in line with the spirit and the "letter" of the relevant AC provision, the AACC adopted the position that the final permitting decision should be in any case and without additional requirements subject to judicial scrutiny under Article 9 (2) after an appeal by the members of the public concerned, including NGOs.[94]

The second category of Findings relate to the scope of the review *stricto sensu* especially in systems of subjective judicial review. The central line underpinning these Findings is that Parties to the AC should not add further criteria through legislative provisions or court practices that restrict access to judicial review procedures by limiting the arguments that can be put forward by the applicants for challenging a decision. In this context, the ACCC examined, *inter alia*, several provisions of the German, Austrian and Czech legislation in conjunction with the relevant Court practices and came to the following conclusions as regards their compatibility with the critical provision of the Convention: a) the provision of the German Environmental Appeals Act (*Umwelt-Rechtsbehelfsgesetz*, hereafter UmwRG) in the section 2 para. 1.2 and section 2 para. 5 which requires that an NGO must assert that the challenged decision violates provisions "serving the

endorsement by the subsequent Meeting of the CP (*Hedemann-Robinson*, *supra* note 2 at p.105).

89 Belgium ACCC/C/2005/11, ECE/MP.PP/C.1/2006/4/Add.2, para. 29.

90 Bulgaria ACCC/C/2011/58; ECE/ MP.PP/C.1/2013/4, paras. 71, 81.

91 Belgium ACCC/C/2005/11, *supra*, note 89, paras. 32, 33.

92 United Kingdom ACCC/C/2010/45 and ACCC/C/2011/60, ECE/MP.PP/C.1/2013/12, para. 75; Czech Republic, ACCC/C/2010/50, ECE/MP.PP/C.1/2012/11, para. 82.

93 United Kingdom, ACCC/C/2011/60, ECE/MP.PP/C.1/2013/13, para. 53.

94 Bulgaria ACCC/C/2011/58, *supra*, note 90, paras. 79, 80; Czech Republic, ACCC/C/2010/50, *supra*, note 92, para. 78, where the Committee held that the relevant national provision which links the exercise of the participation rights during the EIA procedure with the recognition of *locus standi* to the NGOs for challenging the final decision, is not compatible with Article 9(2).

environment" introduces a limitation, which is not founded on the Convention and therefore contravenes Article 9(2)[95]; b) the requirement of the German UmwRG (section 2 para. 1.1) that an NGO must assert that the allegedly violated provision could be of importance for the challenged decision, which is critical as regards the review of procedural errors, raises doubts as regards whether the German system of judicial review can ensure adequate access for the NGOs to ask the review of the procedural legality of decisions under Article 6. The thesis of the ACCC was grounded on the argument that although the possibility of the national courts to evaluate whether the allegedly infringed provision could be of any importance for the merits of the case is not in general contrary to Article 9(2), the relevant requirement is already considered by the court when deliberating about the admissibility of the action and thereby prevents NGOs from seeking review[96]. c) the "impairment of the right doctrine" of the Czech legal order and its application by the Courts, which results in limiting the right of NGOs to challenge only the procedural legality of the contested decisions, contravenes Article 9(2)[97] and d) the determination of the scope of standing for certain categories of the "public concerned", such as neighbours, in the Austrian legal system, which is also critical for the determination of the range of pleas that can be put forward by them in the sense that it is up to the Courts to accept pleas that go beyond the "impairment of the right" doctrine and relate to general environmental concerns, can raise issues of incompatibility with Article 9(2), if it can be regarded as a general court practice.[98] From a general point of view, it should be mentioned that while the ACCC adopted a quite clear approach concerning the subject of review, the relevant positions concerning the range of the permissible pleas and the extent of the review were more cautious, a fact which can be mainly attributed to the consideration of the different procedural systems and traditions.

4.2. THE RELEVANT JURISPRUDENCE OF THE CJEU

The CJEU has developed a significant body of jurisprudence that deals with the interpretation of the access to justice provisions and covers a wide array of issues ranging from the standing criteria to the costs of the procedure and the scope of the review.[99] The scope of the review in a broader sense has become subject of judicial interpretation and clarification in a series of relevant rulings. In particular, as regards the subject of judicial review the CJEU has made clear in

95 Germany, ACCC/C/2008/31, ECE/MP.PP/C.1/2014/8, paras. 78–80.

96 Id at paras. 87, 88. Furthermore, the ACCC found that the German system does not provide legal clarity as to whether the procedural rights under Article 6 are considered as "fundamental errors" of procedure by the German Courts in the case of their violation (para. 90).

97 Czech Republic, ACCC/C/2010/50, *supra*, note 92, para. 81.

98 Austria, ACCC/C/2010/48, ECE/MP.PP/C.1/2012/4, paras. 63, 66.

99 *Darpö*, *supra*, note 8.

three rulings (*Durgården, Trianel* and *Boxus)* that in any case the members of the "public concerned" should have access to judicial review procedures to challenge the final decision authorizing the project.[100] Moreover, in two Rulings (*Ch. Mellor* and *Gruber*) the Court adopted the position that the "public concerned", which has to be defined in a non-restrictive way, must be able to challenge the screening decisions.[101] It is, thus, critical that the CJEU adopted almost identical positions with those of the ACCC concerning the subject of review on the basis of a teleological interpretation of the critical provisions. Furthermore, the CJEU has dealt with the standards of judicial review in three critical rulings, as will be analysed below.

4.2.1. The ruling in the Trianel case

The first ruling which contained significant clarification not only as regards the *locus standi* but also the standards of review in environment-related judicial proceedings initiated by NGOs was the ruling in the *Trianel* case.[102] The Court's position on the scope of the review was constructed on the basis of the determination of the scope of standing of NGOs[103] and the interpretation of the critical provision of the EIA Directive (Article 10a) in the light of the objective of ensuring wide access to justice. In particular, it took the view that the relevant provision does not provide the basis for limiting the pleas that can

100 CJEU Judgment, Case C-263/08, *Djürgärden*, [2009], ECR I-09967, paras.37–39; CJEU Judgment, Case C-115/09. *Trianel* [2011], ECR I-3673 para. 59; CJEU Judgment, Joined Cases C-128/09 to C-131/09, C-134/09 and C-135/09, *Boxus and Others*, [2011], ECR I-09711, paras. 54–55. In the latter decision the CJEU ruled that national courts have to review the specific legislative act authorizing a project as regards whether the conditions for the application of the exemption from the EIA procedure (Article 1(5) are fulfilled and even in cases where no review procedure in respect of this specific legislative act is provided, any national court before which an act falling in its jurisdiction is brought, has the task of carrying out the review.

101 CJEU Judgment, Case C-75/08, *Christopher Mellor*, [2009], ECR I- 03799, paras. 57–58, where the Court held that interested parties must be able to ensure, if necessary through legal action, compliance with the screening obligation and that this requirement may be met by the possibility of bringing an action directly against the decision not to carry out an EIA. Furthermore, the Court (CJEU Judgment of 15 April 2015, Case C-570/13, *Gruber)* ruled that persons falling into the concept of neighbours may be part of the "public concerned" within the meaning of Article 1 (2) of the EIA Directive and therefore must be able to bring an action against the screening decision or against a subsequent development consent decision (paras. 42–44).

102 The subject of the case was the conformity of a provision of the UmwRG with Article 10a of the EIA Directive. According to the relevant provision (Article 2.1), environmental NGOs could have standing before a court, in an action contesting a decision authorizing an EIA-related project, only in the case that they can show the potential infringement of a rule which confers individual rights.

103 The CJEU ruled that although MS enjoy a significant discretion to determine the conditions for the admissibility of actions and can therefore define the standards for individuals on the basis of subjective public rights, this cannot be applied to NGOs due to their special role for the protection of the common interests (paras. 44–45).

be put forward by the "public concerned" in support of an action challenging the substantive or procedural legality of decisions, acts or omissions covered by that Article (para. 37). Departing from this thesis, the Court came to the conclusion that the NGOs meeting the requirements of the national legislation, must not be refused to put forward pleas relating to the infringement of provisions arising from EU Law, which aim at protecting the environment and not the legal interests of the individuals, in an action against a project approval within the scope of the EIA Directive (para. 50). A critical conclusion that can be inferred from the Court's ruling and was underlined by AG Villalón in his Opinion in the *Alptrip* case[104] is that the finding that a restriction[105] of the right of an NGO to take legal action on the grounds of not demonstrating the impairment of a substantive individual right[106] is incompatible with the relevant provision of the EIA Directive, relates to both the admissibility and the well-foundedness of the relevant action.

4.2.2. *The ruling in the Alptrip case*

The second ruling which clarified to a certain extent the possibility of natural and legal persons (but not NGOs) to seek the annulment of an EIA Decision on the grounds of procedural defaults in systems of subjective judicial review and more specifically in the German one, was the CJEU ruling on the *Alptrip* case.[107] As regards the first issue, the Court developed its position in the line of reasoning adopted in the *Trianel* case, according to which the critical provision (Article 10a of the EIA Directive) does not provide the basis for a limitation of the pleas that can be put forward by the applicants. In this context, the Court held that the relevant rule precludes MS when transposing it[108] from limiting its applicability solely to cases in which the legality of a decision is challenged on the ground that no EIA was carried out, while not extending to cases in which such an EIA was carried out but was irregular (para. 38).

104 Opinion of AG Villalón in Case 72/12, *Alptrip*, delivered on 20 June 2013, para. 80; *Gärditz*, *supra*, note 42 at p. 200.

105 The Federal Republic of Germany took action in response to the Ruling in the Trianel Case by amending UmwRG (Gesetz zur Änderung des Umweltrechtsbehelfsgesetzes und anderer umweltrechtlicher Vorschriften von 21.01.2013).

106 AG Sharpston dismissed the argument of the German Government relating to the intensity of the judicial review that is attributed to the impairment of the right doctrine by claiming persuasively that such a system is of little help if it is totally inaccessible for certain categories of actions. See Opinion of AG Sharpston in Case 115/09, *supra*, note 34, para. 77.

107 CJEU Judgment of 7 November 2013, Case 72/12, *Alptrip*, ECLI:EU:C:2013:712.

108 In accordance with the Court's thesis, the relevant provision of UmwRG (Article 4.1) which provided that the legality of a decision can be challenged without further requirements only on the ground that the necessary EIA or the preliminary assessment was not carried out, is not in conformity with the Article 10a of the EIA Directive.

Furthermore, the Court reviewed one of the two requirements[109] of the German procedural law that have to be cumulatively fulfilled, so that pleas concerning violations of procedural rules, except for the cases covered by Article 4.1 of UmwRG, can be claimed admissibly. As regards the requirement of the so-called causality condition for the purposes of assessing the relevance of procedural errors (Article 46 VwGO), the Court ruled that it is exceptionally permissible under two strict conditions: the first one is that the burden of proof for the relevance of the procedural default is shifted from the applicant to the Court and the competent authority, while the second one relates to the limitation of its application only to procedural errors of minor importance[110] (paras. 52, 53, 54). The justification for the exceptional permissibility of the causality criterion can be found in the importance attached to the effective application of the procedural guarantees for the proper function of the EIA procedure and the exercise of the relevant rights, which seem to have a prerogative in relation to other legitimate objectives, especially in cases of fundamental procedural errors.[111] Furthermore, the views of the CJEU as regards the scrutiny of the procedural errors are also in harmony with its findings in the *Križan* case, where the Court determined that the permissibility and the scope of a possible rectification of a procedural error should be subject to review by the national courts.[112]

4.2.3. The ruling in the Commission v. Germany case

Issues concerning the scope of review in systems of subjective judicial review have been further clarified in the CJEU ruling in the case *Commission v. Germany*, as already mentioned.[113] The first issue which had been previously raised without being reviewed in the Alptrip case related to whether the criterion requiring

---

[109] The other requirement, which was not reviewed by the CJEU on the grounds of the lack of details provided by the national Court, concerns the infringement of a substantive right of the applicant as a precondition for seeking the annulment of the relevant decision (Article 113 VwGO). It is worth mentioning though that AG Villalón examined the relevant requirement in the light of the principle of effectiveness, Article 19 TEU, the importance of the participatory rights and the relevant provisions of the AC. Under this prism, he adopted the reliable thesis, according to which this requirement can be accepted only as an admissibility criterion but not as a criterion relating to the well-foundedness of the action. Opinion of AG Villalón in Case 72/12, *supra*, note 104, paras. 94–99.

[110] The relevant thesis concerning the errors of minor importance is in parallel with the "essential procedural requirement" set in Article 263 TFEU and the jurisprudence as regards the relevance of procedural errors for the annulment of acts of the EU organs. (ECJ Ruling, Case C-117/81, *Geist v. Commission*, [1983], ECR, 2191, para. 7; ECJ Ruling, Case 234/84 *Belgium v. Commission*, [1986], ECR 2263, para. 30). See also Opinion of AG Villalón in Case 72/12 *supra*, note 104, para. 105.

[111] *Gärditz, supra*, note 42 at p. 200 et.seq. The German Legislator responded to the CJEU Ruling in the Alptrip Case with another modification of the UmwRG (BGBl. I 2015, S. 2069).

[112] CJEU Judgment of 15.01.2013, Case C-416/10, *Križan and Others*, ECLI:EU: C:2013:8, paras. 87–91.

[113] CJEU Judgment of 15 October 2015, *supra*, note 49.

an infringement of a subjective public right of the applicant as a precondition for requesting the annulment of the relevant decision (Article 113 VwGO) is in conformity with the access to justice provisions of the EIA (Article 11) and the IED (Article 25) Directives respectively, mainly in the sense of creating an acceptable or not restriction to the scope of the judicial review. In this context and in a substantially divergent view from that of the AG Wathelet[114], the Court ruled that it is within the margin of discretion of the MS provided by the above-mentioned EU law provisions to have in place such a criterion in the case that they have also adopted the "impairment of the right" as a standing criterion (paras. 32–34). Subsequently, the Court adopted the view that this basic feature of the German administrative law does not raise issues of compatibility with the EU law.

The second issue related to the restriction of the situations in which the annulment of administrative decisions falling into the scope of the EIA Directive can be requested on the grounds of procedural defaults. The Court determined that the relevant national provision (Article 4.1 UmwRG)[115] which provides that the right for the annulment of a relevant decision on the grounds of a procedural default can be exercised without further requirements only when an EIA procedure or a preliminary assessment was not carried out, is not in conformity with Article 11 of the EIA Directive, because the regulative context of this provision interpreted in a teleological way precludes from limiting its applicability to certain cases (paras. 47–48). Furthermore, on the basis of the main Finding in the *Alptrip* ruling concerning the exceptional permissibility of conditions restricting the permissible pleas in conjunction with the principle of effectiveness, the Court held that the causality condition (Article 46 VwFG), which has to be satisfied in cases where the annulment of an EIA decision is requested on the grounds of irregularities of the EIA procedure, is not compatible with Article 11 of the EIA Directive to the extent that it places the burden of demonstrating the causality link on the applicant. The contrary position would make the critical provision totally ineffective (paras. 57–62).[116] Furthermore, the Court reiterated its position concerning the compatibility of the provision (Article 113 VwGO) requiring an

114 AG Wathelet adopted the view that the relevant criterion is not in conformity with the EU Law on the grounds that it has the effect of limiting the substantive pleas that can be put forward by the applicants and therefore creates a further restriction for access to justice relating to the scope and the effectiveness of the review which cannot be founded in the relevant provisions. Moreover, in the same line with the Opinion of AG Villalón in the Alptrip Case, AG Wathelet regarded this as a requirement relating to the well-foundedness and not to the admissibility of an action. See Opinion of AG Wathelet in Case 137/14, Commission v. Germany, delivered on 21.05.2015, paras. 57–58.

115 The Court relied on its constant jurisprudence concerning the requirements for the implementation of the provisions of the Directives into the national legal orders (e.g. unquestionable binding force, precision and clarity) to come to the conclusion that these were not fulfilled in the present case, because certain situations were covered by Article 4.1 of UmwRG and others by Article 46 VwFG (para. 51).

116 The ACCC came to the same conclusion as regards the conformity of the causality condition with Article 9(2) of the AC. (Germany, ACCC/C/2008/31, para. 83).

effect on the substantive position of the applicant, which is also a precondition for requesting the annulment of a relevant decision on procedural grounds, with Article 11 of the EIA Directive (para. 63 with reference to paras. 30–34).

Finally, the Court dealt with another feature of the German procedural law, the so-called preclusion, which, as already mentioned, restricts the pleas that can be put forward permissibly before the Court concerning the standing and the scope of the review to those that have been made during the administrative proceedings (Article 2(3) UmwRG and Article 73(4) and (6) VwVfG). Critical for the construction of the Court's thesis was the interpretation of the relevant EU law provisions in the light of the objective of ensuring wide access to justice in the area of the environmental protection and the subsequent need for guaranteeing a sufficient review of the substantive and procedural legality of the relevant decisions or acts, which seem to be of major importance in relation to the effectiveness of the administrative procedures and the principle of legal certainty (paras. 79–80).[117] In this context, the Court ruled that relevant provisions of the German law laying down preclusion are incompatible with the access to justice provisions of the EIA (Article 11) and IED (Article 25) Directives respectively. It is worth referring that the obligation for alignment with the CJEU ruling initiated another modification of UmwRG.[118]

4.2.4. A critical assessment of the three rulings

A first critical remark which arises from the systematic overview of the three rulings is that the CJEU jurisprudence has set significant limits to the margin of discretion left to the national legislators in determining the standards of the review in judicial proceedings relating to acts or omissions falling into the scope of the EIA and the IED Directive, which are initiated by natural and legal persons as well as by NGOs to which a preferential status is recognized.

A second remark is that the central notion which underpins the Rulings and provides the justification for the imposement of limitations to the national legislators, lies in the need to pursue the objective of ensuring wide access to justice to the "public concerned" with a view to protecting and preserving the environment. In particular, it is reflected in a more or less clear way on the content of the relevant decisions that in accordance with the Court's view the relevant EU law provisions give more weight to that objective in relation to other legitimate objectives, such as the effectiveness of the judicial and administrative proceedings and the principle of legal certainty. Such an approach as regards the standards of review should not be viewed "isolated" but in conjunction with the considerable body of the CJEU case-law on access to justice in environmental

---

117 *Hofmann supra*, note 46 at p. 273 with reference to the relevant reasoning of the BVwG.

118 Gesetz zur Anpassung des Umwelt-Rechtsbehelfsgesetzes und anderer Vorschriften an europa- und völkerrechtliche Vorgaben von 29.5.2015 (BGBl. I 2017, I, No32).

matters, which is underpinned by the same "spirit". In this context, restrictive provisions concerning the standards of review especially in those areas covered by the EU law, can hardly pass the "conformity test" of the CJEU.

A third remark relates to the fact that the CJEU recognizes the specific importance of procedural rules in the EU environmental law as means for promoting the implementation of the substantive norms and for empowering citizens to protect the environment, "endorsing" thereby implicitly the increasing trend of proceduralisation in the EU environmental law. This stance was also re-affirmed in a characteristic way in the referred CJEU ruling in the case *Lesoochranárske zoskupenie VLK v. Obvodný úrad Trenčín* (*LZ II*), where the Court recognized through an interpretation of the critical EU Law provision in the light of the relevant provisions of the AC, a participatory right, which can be invoked before the national courts in the case of its alleged violation.

Finally, another observation is that despite the significant contribution of the CJEU Jurisprudence in clarifying significant issues as regards the standards of review, a cautious approach in dealing with "traditional" features of the national procedural systems also emerges. This tendency, as already mentioned, is observed in the ACCC Findings too. In this context, an issue which has not been finally resolved relates to the conformity of the requirement of an impairment of a substantive right with the EU Law. This is due to fact that the Court examined it in relation to the distinctive admissibility criterion and did not deal with its restrictive effects on the scope of the review, its further consequences as regards the non-annulment of certain illegal administrative acts and the conformity issues which may arise in relation to the objective of ensuring wide access to justice in this specific field of law.[119]

5. CONCLUDING REMARKS: RESPONSES FOR ADDRESSING RESTRICTIVE APPROACHES CONCERNING THE SCOPE OF THE REVIEW

The question which arises in this context relates to whether the relevant provisions of the AC and the EU law, as interpreted by the ACCC and the CJEU, have exerted influence on the national legal systems in terms of modifying or setting aside legislative provisions confining restrictively the scope of the review in environment-related judicial proceedings falling into the scope of the critical EU Directives or even further on the respective jurisprudential approaches. For undertaking the effort to answer this question, certain remarks arising from the current analysis should be taken into consideration.

119 *Hofmann, supra*, note 46 at p. 278 et.seq.

A first critical remark relates to the fact that systems of subjective judicial review with the German one being the most prominent example, have undergone significant pressure to modify basic features of their procedural law for ensuring conformity with the international and EU law provisions. Subsequently, the relevant regulatory framework in conjunction with the CJEU jurisprudence primarily and the Findings of the ACCC secondarily have become a major force for inducing reforms of the national rules relating to certain kinds of environment-related judicial proceedings also as regards the standards of review.

A second observation lies in the fact that in spite of this contribution in achieving a minimum level of harmonization as regards the standards of review, significant divergences can be still observed in the different legal systems. These can be attributed to the level of discretion left to the national legislators due to the vaguely formulated provisions in conjunction with the different legal traditions and the structures of the administrative judicial systems. Furthermore, the punctual character of the intervention of the CJEU jurisprudence has to be considered in the sense that MS are in principle not expected to adapt their national legislation in line with the relevant Rulings except for those which have been initiated after requests for preliminary rulings by their national Courts. Furthermore, it should be considered that the induced reforms may also result in situations where different standards of review can apply to cases of violations of norms arising from the EU environmental law in the same national legal system on the basis of the criterion of whether the relevant EU legal instruments have been subject to the proceduralisation process or not.

Within the framework of the consideration of the above remarks, a possible answer to the relevant question could be that the examination of certain options seems to be necessary with the aim to ensure an adequate level of intensity of the review of environment-related acts and omissions as a significant element of the effective judicial protection in the field of the environmental law. These options can be classified in two categories. In the first category can be classified those options which presuppose a legislative intervention at the EU level, while in the second category are classified the less intervening options.

In this context, the most ambitious option of the first category could be the regulation of the scope of review within the framework of a horizontal instrument on access to justice in environmental matters which would encompass a provision stipulating in a clear way that the content of the contested decisions will be scrutinized by the national courts in all the aspects invoked by the applicants.[120] As already mentioned, such an option is not further discussed and pursued after the withdrawal of the Commission Proposal of 2003 for which an agreement could not be found over a decade. Furthermore, another option could be the regulation of this issue in line with the CJEU Findings through the adoption of a Directive which would codify the relevant Jurisprudence on the access to

120 *Darpö, supra,* note 10 at p. 197, 205.

justice in environmental matters.[121] A third option of the first category would be the modification of the existing provisions of the respective Directives in the direction of clarifying further the scope of the trial through the consideration of the jurisprudential standards.

In the second category belong the less intervening choices, such as the Guidelines or other soft-law instruments (e.g. Notices), which are adopted by the European Commission, in order to provide guidance to the national legislators and the courts as regards the content and the application of the relevant provisions concerning the scope of the review and other critical issues, such as standing and remedies.

The discussion of the benefits and the flaws of each option and especially those of the first category is not of practical importance in the current phase of the development of the EU environmental law. This is due to the fact that the Commission decided to address the problems which have been identified in this field by adopting a soft-law instrument and in particular a Notice on Access to Justice in Environmental Matters.[122] The basic aim of this Instrument which has been extensively used in other fields of EU law (e.g. competition) and is mainly based on the relevant CJEU jurisprudence, is to provide clarity as regards the implementation of the critical provisions and to be a useful point of reference for all the actors involved (national administrations, national courts, civil society and the business sector). Against the background of the legislative inaction in this field, this choice seems to be a positive development in terms of providing clarifications concerning the core issues (standing, standards of review, remedies and costs) in a satisfactory manner. It remains, however, to be seen how and to which the extent this Instrument can exert influence on the implementation of the relevant provisions and on the jurisprudence of the national courts towards the direction of ensuring effective judicial protection. Moreover, it does not seem possible that its adoption could put an end to the discussions, which can also be initiated by the dynamic evolution of the CJEU case-law and the disparities of the national procedural systems, about other options which would promote further harmonization and predictability and would guarantee a sufficient level of judicial protection in the field of environmental legislation, taking also into consideration the particularities of the environmental interests.

---

121 *C. Backes, M. Eliantonio & F. Grashof*, To legislate or not legislate:-Rethinking the "effective protection of environmental rights" in the Union: reflections on different methods to improve the system of environmental litigation, Presentation in the 4th EELF Conference, Wroclau 14–16 September 2016, proposing a relevant Directive focusing mainly on the standing criteria.

122 Commission Notice on Access to Justice in Environmental Matters, *supra*, note 25.

IMPLEMENTATION OF THE AARHUS CONVENTION THROUGH *ACTIO POPULARIS*

Article 9(3) of the Aarhus Convention and *Actio Popularis*

Žaneta Mikosa*

ABSTRACT

In the light of topical discussions on the need to broaden the legal standing approach in order to fulfil the requirements of the Aarhus Convention, and thus to facilitate enforcement of environmental law, this article is aimed at discussing the most extensive approach to legal standing (often referred to as an *actio popularis* or open standing). The main focus of the discussion is on Article 9(3) of the Convention, also known as the "enforcement provision," which is claimed to be one of the most challenging provisions with respect to its implementation. Since its adoption there are calls requiring to implement Article 9(3) through an *actio popularis*; however, there are not so many examples in the EU where such an approach to legal standing has been introduced. This article explores how it has been developed through the legislation and court practice in Latvia, addressing also some pros and cons.

The most extensive approach to legal standing is analysed in the context of today's challenges to ensure better enforcement of environmental law, where open standing can be one (if small) response to these challenges.

KEYWORDS

Aarhus Convention; *actio popularis*; legal standing

* PhD cand., Copenhagen University and Riga Graduate School of Law.

1. INTRODUCTION

Environmental protection currently has a prominent place on the international political agenda, with environmental concerns having received special attention since the 1970s. The first global United Nations Conference on the Human Environment in Stockholm in 1972 is often singled out as an important turning point. An impressive amount of environmental legislation has since been adopted; however, scarcity of resources and environmental degradation both pose difficult dilemmas today just as they did in the 1970s. It seems to be true that the situation has even worsened as serious additional environmental challenges have emerged. It is fair to note that "there are some important success stories" in the field of environmental protection[1]; at the same time, "more greenhouse gases than ever are put into the atmosphere, biological diversity is rapidly declining and fish stocks in the oceans are dwindling."[2] As there are "more than 500 international treaties and agreements that relate to the environment,"[3] it is clear that the challenges primarily lie in the implementation and enforcement of already existing commitments and legislation.

Without any doubt, there could be different legal mechanisms and solutions for implementing the requirements needed to ensure environmental protection. Today there seems to be a broad agreement that society needs to be involved in this process more effectively, including through strengthening procedural environmental rights.[4]

In Europe, the Aarhus Convention[5] represents "the most comprehensive effort to establish international legal standards" on environmental procedural rights.[6] The ultimate aim of the Convention is "to increase the openness and democratic legitimacy of government policies on environmental protection" and to ensure an "engaged and critically aware public" as both an "essential player

---

1 *H.C. Bugge*, Twelve fundamental challenges, in C. Voigt (eds), *Rule of Law for Nature*, 2013, p. 3; See also: the European Environmental Agency environmental report of 2015 (SOER 2015), e.g., in the table noting 'positive trends' in area of water and air protection: available <www.eea.europa.eu/soer-2015/synthesis/report/0c-executivesummary>.

2 *C. Voigt*, Preface of Rule of Law for Nature in C. Voigt (eds.), *Rule of Law for Nature*, 2013, p. xiii.

3 UNEP, Global Environmental Outlook 5 (GEO 5), 2012, 464. Available: <www.unep.org/geo/geo5.asp>.

4 See in the Rio Declaration agreed at the UN Conference on Environment and Development (1992), and in particularly Principle 10. The GEO 5 Report referring to Principle 10 has noted that "for the past 20 years regional experience has demonstrated that such rights provide a basis for citizens to participate in safeguarding both human and environmental well-being." *Id.* at p. 459.

5 UNECE Convention on Access to Information, Public Participation in Decision-making and Access to Justice in Environmental Matters (further – Aarhus Convention). United Nations, Treaty Series, vol. 2161, p. 447.

6 *M. Pallemaerts*, 'Introduction' in M. Pallemaerts (ed), *The Aarhus Convention at Ten*, 2011, p. 3.

and partner" in the formulation, as well as in implementation and enforcement of environmental policy.[7] The Convention seeks to achieve these objectives by describing the rights for the public and the duties for states in great detail in terms of three pillars: (i) on access to environmental information; (ii) on public participation in decision-making; and (iii) on access to justice in environmental matters. The third pillar of the Aarhus Convention on 'access to justice' (Article 9), often referred to as "the teeth of the Convention," strives to ensure that the rights provided for the public have "effective judicial mechanisms accessible for the public, including organizations, so that its legitimate interests are protected and the law is enforced."[8] Thus, the Convention is one of the important international legal instruments aiming to promote the implementation of environmental law, especially through its third pillar, which provides for legal mechanisms "to monitor the decisions of public bodies and to take legal action to protect their environment."[9]

The third pillar of the Aarhus Convention contains three different requirements with respect to preconditions on access to justice. This article focuses on the third paragraph: Article 9(3), often emphasised as enforcement provision.[10] This provision can be considered as one of the most important components of incentives responding to challenges on the enforcement of environmental law highlighted above. However, for that the contracting parties of the Convention need to ensure access to "effective remedies" in accordance with the requirements of the Convention where standing for the members of the public plays an important role.

This article firstly discusses the peculiarity of Article 9(3) with respect to the requirements relevant to the rules of legal standing and an *actio popularis* therein. Taking into account that Article 9(3) encompasses the "objective enforcement of law" and thus signalling at rather open standing for the members of the public in the enforcement of law, this article secondly reflects on concerns raised against the most extensive approach to standing in light of separation of powers. In the context of this article, the question discussed is about appropriateness to fear that by granting legal standing to "any" member of the public – thus, "without a particularised injury" to a private applicant – "courts will be displacing executive power" contrary to the traditional role of courts. In this light a question emerged then about whether the legislator is limited to grant standing to "any person" to initiate a lawsuit against an action of a public authority violating environmental law. It is worth noting that the intent of this article is not to discuss in detail

7 Id. at p. 4.

8 Preamble of the Aarhus Convention recital [18].

9 *Supra* note 6, at, p. 4.

10 See e.g. *Hedemann-Robinson*, Enforcement of European Union Environmental Law, (2015), p. 373. See also: *Ebbesson, Gaugitsch, Miklau, Jendrośka, Stec and Marshall*, The Aarhus Convention: An Implementation Guide, 2nd ed., 2014, pp. 197–199 (Further – "Implementation Guide, 2014"). Available: https://www.unece.org/fileadmin/DAM/env/pp/Publications/Aarhus_Implementation_Guide_interactive_eng.pdf.

constitutionality issues on the *trias politica* but rather to reflect on this point more generally to highlight the main concerns and some considerations relevant for further discussion.

Thirdly, *actio popularis*[11] is highlighted as one of three principal approaches to legal standing identified in the European region, pointing out the main differences and the peculiarity of the most extensive approach in the overall conception of legal standing as well as Article 9(3). Finally, this article analyses the development of *actio popularis* through legislation and court practice in Latvia and some *pros* and *cons* of such open standing. It is worth noting that there are not many examples where the most extensive approach to standing authorizing "anyone" have been introduced in the EU Member States. Therefore, it is interesting to reveal why and how it has evolved in Latvia since the 1990s.

2. LEGAL STANDING IN THE AARHUS CONVENTION AND IN ITS "ENFORCEMENT" PROVISION (PECULIARITY OF ARTICLE 9(3))

In order to "take legal action" in "protecting their environment" stipulated by the Aarhus Convention, the rules of legal standing play a decisive role. Accordingly, with the objective to ensure that "effective judicial mechanisms" are accessible to the public, contracting parties of the Aarhus Convention have agreed on some specific rules to be followed in defining legal standing for "Aarhus type" cases, i.e. those that fall under the scope of the Convention. Detailed analysis of those rules is well developed in many other articles[12]; therefore, for the purposes of this article, the focus is on the peculiarity of Article 9(3) and its relation to *actio popularis*.

The third paragraph of Article 9 provides a right to access to justice for "members of the public" without indicating whether it is aimed for the protection of any right encompassed in the Convention.[13] This is in contrast to the first two parts of Article 9, which provide the right to access to justice in the context of

---

11 The term of *actio popularis* is used in this article to refer to a right of '*any person*' to challenge act or omission of a public authority before administrative court, "sanctioned" by the legislator (established by law). However, the question whether it is indeed revival of an ancient concept of *actio popularis* that was developed many centuries ago in Roman law or the legal standing provided for 'any one' in environmental disputes is rather different concept, is under the consideration within author's research study but beyond the scope of this article.

12 See e.g., *M. Pallemaerts (ed.)*, The Aarhus Convention at Ten, 2011; Hedemann-Robinson, Enforcement of European Union Environmental Law, (2015), Part II.

13 Article 9(3) reads as follows: "In addition and without prejudice to the review procedures referred to in paragraphs 1 and 2 above, each Party shall ensure that, where they meet the criteria, if any, laid down in its national law, members of the public have access to administrative or judicial procedures to challenge acts and omissions by private persons and public authorities which contravene provisions of its national law relating to the environment."

a right to information and public participation. Article 9(3) refers to acts and omissions of public authority and private persons that can be challenged if they breach "national law relating to the environment" (further – "environmental law)."[14] It is submitted that Article 9(3) covers both subjective as well as objective context[15], which could be raised through review procedure in order to ensure that "the law is enforced." This scope of Article 9, in turn, affects an approach to legal standing, as "members of the public" have to be enabled to initiate a case against an "act or omission" that breaches environmental law affecting either any "individualized" right or interest or is of a more general nature.[16] It is worth noting that although Article 9(3) also encompasses the right to access to justice to challenge actions of *private persons*, this article further focuses only on actions of *public authority* both due to a limited space of this article as well as rather different legal challenges the two may invoke.

Generally, taking into account the overall objectives of the Convention agreed as part of incentives to improve the enforcement of environmental law based on *inter alia* "straightforward environmental concerns,"[17] *objective law control* with respect to any act or omission breaching environmental law is an understandable solution, as indeed protection of the environment is not necessarily connected with any individual's right or interest but often concerns the interest of the general public in, for example, protecting common resources or limiting pollution in the air we breathe. Hence, Article 9(3) stipulates that "members of the public" have to be entitled to initiate a case also where more general public interests such as these are at stake (further referred to as "public interests"[18]). However, defining under which conditions and when "members of the public" are to be entitled is left to a large extent to contracting parties, providing the possibility of introducing "criteria, if any" that a member of the public has to meet to have standing. Accordingly, it is true that Article 9(3) does not require the establishment of a system of *actio popularis* in domestic laws of contracting parties "with the effect that *anyone* can challenge any decision, act or omission

14 See: *J. Ebbesson*, Access to Justice at the National Level. Impact of the Aarhus Convention and European Union Law. In The Aarhus Convention at Ten, in M. Pallemaerts (ed), 2011, p. 264, noting the difference between "environmental law" and the broader concept embedded in Article 9(3) of the Convention.

15 *N. Sadeleer*, Enforcing EUCHR Principles and Fundamental Rights in Environmental Cases. Nordic Journal of International Law 81, 2012, p. 57.

16 See e.g. case C-240/09 *VLK I*, ECLI:EU:C:2011:125, where the breach of EU nature protection law in relation to protected species (brown bear) was at stake.

17 *J. Ebbesson*, The Notion of Public Participation in International Environmental Law." 8 Yearbook of International Environmental Law, 1998, p. 96.

18 The term "public interest" may encompass a broad range of issues. This article does not aim to define which are "pubic interest" but uses this concept rather to contrast interests that can be personalized (individualized) for legal standing purpose to those which are rather "diffused" as protected by general environmental law.

relating to the environment."[19] At the same time, it has been often emphasised that

> the Parties may not take the clause "where they meet the criteria, if any, laid down in its national law" as an excuse for introducing or maintaining so strict criteria that they effectively bar all or almost all environmental organisations or other members of the public from challenging acts or omissions that contravene national law relating to the environment.[20]

Accordingly, such an interpretation suggests that to ensure "access to a review procedure" for "*all* contraventions of national law relating to the environment"[21] the term "members of the public" under Article 9(3) should include a broader spectrum of the public than only those whose "individual" right or interest is breached.[22] Moreover, they have to be entitled to invoke any breach of environmental law, i.e. either aimed at protecting their "individual" right or of a more general nature, as mentioned above. It is true that those requirements peculiar for the enforcement of environmental law in light of the Aarhus Convention are challenging the "traditional" approach to legal standing and other conceptions.[23] Therefore, it is unsurprising that Article 9(3) of the Convention is one of the most difficult with respect to its implementation for many contracting parties.[24]

There are different approaches to legal standing in the EU Member States. Accordingly there could be different solutions with respect to the implementation of Article 9(3). At the same time, in the context of increasing discussion on the need to liberalise standing rules and challenges in implementing Article 9(3), the approach establishing an *actio popularis* through the legislator "sanctioned" standing to "any" member of the public might be seen as one of the solutions.

However, taking into account that the notion of objective law enforcement or "general legality" check stipulated by Article 9(3) encroaches upon the powers of government or, as some may claim, involves members of the public authorised to represent "public interest" in an area, which according to the traditional separation of powers theory, lies primarily in the competence of executive, this article firstly

19 See findings of the Aarhus Convention Compliance Committee (ACCC) in cases: ACCC/2005/11 Belgium, para 35; ACCC/2006/18 Denmark, para 29; ACCC/2010/48 Austria para 68; ACCC/2008/31; Germany, para 92; ACCC/2008/32 European Union (Part I), para 78, [emphasise added].

20 Id.

21 Case ACCC/C/2008/31 (Germany), para. 94.

22 Implementation Guide, 2014, p. 197, pointing out that paragraph 3 of Art.9 envisages that members of the public may enforce environmental law directly, i.e., by bringing the case to court to have the law enforced "rather than simply to redress personal harm."

23 *J. Ebbesson*, Introduction in Access to Justice in Environmental Matters in the EU, in J. Ebbesson (ed.), 2002, p. 4.

24 Executive Summary Report on access to justice in environmental matters, Inventory Milieu Ltd., 2007, p. 1. Available: http://ec.europa.eu/environment/aarhus/study_access.htm.

reflects on the discussion about legal standing and possible constraints that the most extensive approach to it may invoke in light of separation of powers. What are those concerns raised in relation to legal standing granted by the law to "anyone" without requiring the proof of any personalised "injury" in order to initiate a lawsuit against actions of a public authority when it breaches a particular law? The foregoing suggests that such a broad approach could be taken for the implementation of Article 9(3) of the Convention and indeed has been taken, as discussed later in this article. Therefore, it is worth reflecting on the concerns raised for the purposes of further discussion.

3. LEGAL STANDING AND "THE MOST EXTENSIVE APPROACH" IN LIGHT OF THE PRINCIPLE OF SEPARATION OF POWERS

The discussion highlighted in the question raised in the previous section emerged in the United States in the mid-20th century. It was particularly intense after the US Congress adopted an impressive amount of environmental legislation providing for so-called "citizen suits."[25] Such law as the Endangered Species Act of the US authorised "any person" to initiate a case if a particular environmental law is breached without a need to prove "injury in fact" (further – "ESA-type" citizen suit).[26] It is worth noting that the notion behind Article 9(3) of the Aarhus Convention has been built upon ("modelled on") the US "citizen suit" approach.[27] Therefore, it is worth highlighting the discussion in relation to it and possible limitations in light of the principle fundamental to any western democracy.

The view that legal standing law is to be seen in the light of separation of powers (and through this is to be limited) culminated in the *Lujan* case[28], which

[25] 'Citizen suit' was provided in many of environmental statutes amended between 1970 and 1972, e.g. Clean Water Act of 1976, Noise Control Act of 1972, Clean Air Act, see quite extensive list in: *C.R Sunstein*, What's Standing after Lujan? Michigan Law Review, 1992, (Vol. 91, No. 2), p. 165. Sunstein notes, "Every major environmental statute except FIFRA authorizes a citizen suit."

[26] *R.J. Borchardt*, Lujan v. Defenders of Wildlife: Unwarranted Judicial Interference with Congressional Power and Environmental Protection." Wis. L. Rev. (1993), p. 1361, noting that the citizen suit provision of the ESA "confers automatic standing on any person claiming a violation thereof."

[27] *J. Jendroska*, Access to Justice in environmental matters: key issues. Presentation materials of conference 3 May 2015, Brussels (unpublished), noting that the idea behind drafting of Article 9(3) was to create "a provision equivalent to "citizen suit" in the USA, i.e. to create possibilities to initiate in public interest the enforcement actions against polluters (whether private entities or national authorities) either directly at courts or by forcing public authorities to do so."

[28] Case *Lujan v. Defenders of Wildlife*, 504 U.S. 555 (1992). In this case a dispute was about a decision (regulation as regards application of particular law) establishing that there is no need to organise consultations with the Secretary of Interior and environmental assessment procedure about projects that the US agencies are funding or realizing *outside* the US, contrary

in the words of Magill "bury a long-standing doctrine" of citizen suits with respect at least to "ESA-type" citizen suit as examined in the *Lujan* case.[29] The Supreme Court based its argumentation on two related points seen in light of separation of powers as interpreted by the Court: in particular in relation to the role of courts and power and duties of an executive. The former point is grounded in the presumption of the "traditional role of courts." In *Lujan* the Supreme Court quoted *Marbury v. Madison* (5 U.S., 1803) to point out that "[t]he province of the court is, solely, to decide on the rights of individuals."[30] The Court linking this argument with the principle of separation of powers stressed that "in ignoring the concrete injury requirement described in our cases, they [Congress] would be discarding a principle fundamental to the separate and distinct constitutional role of the Third Branch [judiciary]."[31]

The second argument, i.e. on the executive power, is grounded in the constitutional provisions. Continuing the line of argumentation on the protection of individuals and the "notion of the role of courts," the Supreme Court stressed that the "public interest" (where is no individual "injury-in-fact") is for the other two branches to protect. More specifically it held that "[v]indicating the public interest (including the public interest in Government observance of the Constitution and laws)" is the function of legislator and executive.[32] In *Lujan*, the Supreme Court suggested that an "ESA-type" citizen suit impedes the constitutional power of executive shifting the power of executive to the courts through individuals, which has been authorised to act on behalf of the general interest.[33]

In the context of this article, it is worth discussing whether it is indeed appropriate to fear that "without a particularised injury, courts will be displacing executive power" contrary to the traditional role of courts[34] and thus, the legislator

---

to general requirements of the Endangered Species Act (ESA) that included such obligation. The particular dispute was about two projects that might endanger species in Egypt and Sri Lanka. In the *Lujan case* Justice Scalia was writing for the majority of the US Supreme Court and developed further that concept of linking legal standing with the separation of powers as argued in his renowned article of 1983 See *infra* note 40. In result the Supreme Court invalidated the provision of the ESA establishing so broad access to justice right as for "any person," i.e., "ESA-type" citizen suit. See more detailed discussion on *Lujan* in: *C.R. Sunstein*, What's Standing After Lujan? (1992) Michigan Law Review, Vol. 91, No. 2.

29 *E. Magill*, Standing for the Public: A Lost History. Virginia Law Review, 2009 (Vol. 95, No. 5), p. 1182.

30 Case *Lujan v. Defenders of Wildlife*, 504 U.S., p. 577.

31 Id.

32 Id.

33 According to the Court '[t]o allow [the public] interest to be converted into an individual right by a statute ...and permitting all citizens to sue, regardless of whether they suffered any concrete injury, would authorize Congress to transfer from the President to the courts the Chief Executive's most important constitutional duty, to "take Care that the Laws be faithfully executed."' *Lujan v. Defenders of Wildlife*, 504 U.S., p. 558.

34 This is the main fear associated with the US Supreme Court's reasoning behind its approach in *Lujan* case. See: Sunstein (1992), *supra* note 25, p. 231.

is limited to grant standing to "any person" to initiate a lawsuit against action of a public authority violating environmental law.

At the outset it is worth noting that this *dictum* of the *Lujan* case limiting the legislator "from authorising parties to stand for the public"[35] is heavily criticised by American scholars, who claim that "Lujan's invalidation of a congressional grant of standing is a misinterpretation of the Constitution."[36] Some scholars note it as the "shift from rights-based constitutionalism towards executive-governed," as there would be decisions of government that would escape court control even if somebody discovers a breach of law.[37] However, for others, this possibility of "escape" is in accordance with the division of powers and the so-called "unitary executive theory."[38] According to Scalia's "striking conclusion"[39] in his academic writings, although the statutes may get "lost or misdirected" in the executive branch and thus "unlawfully under-enforced within the bureaucracy," it is a "good thing."[40] Then-judge Justice Scalia saw "the ability to lose or misdirect laws" as "one of prime engines of social change."[41]Thus, Scalia considered "executive non-implementation of statutes as part of a well-functioning democratic process."[42] Others see it rather as a move to an "executive-governed" constitutionalism, as noted above. Nevertheless, Scalia's academic ideas got reflection in the case law of the US Supreme Court, in particular, in such cases as *Lujan*, where Scalia was writing for the majority. At the same time, more recent case law of the US Supreme Court suggests that the *dictum* of the *Lujan* case has not been consistently followed and, more generally, therefore did not have "burying" effect to all other "citizen suits."[43]

In overall, if one looks at the competencies of three branches of government from a nineteenth-century perspective, the fears of the court's interference in the area of the executive branch could be understandable. The structure of judicial review in the nineteenth century was meant to maintain a strict separation between judicial and executive power.[44] Moreover, in the past "courts and commentators doubted the constitutionality of providing judicial review of

35 *Magill*, (2009), *supra* note 29, p. 1182.

36 *Sunstein* (1992), *supra* note 25, p. 166.

37 *L.A. Cisneros*, Standing Doctrine, Judicial Technique, and the Gradual Shift From Right-Based Constitutionalism to Executive-Centred Constitutionalism, 59 Case W.Res. L.Rev, 2009.

38 *H. Krent and E.G. Shenkman*, 'Of Citizen Suit and citizen Sunstain.' 91 Mich. L. Rev. 1992–1993, p. 1810.

39 As labelled by Sunstein in, What's Standing after Lujan? 1992, p. 216.

40 *A. Scalia*, The doctrine of standing as an essential element of the separation of powers. Suffolk UL Rev. 17 1983, p. 897.

41 Id. at p. 897.

42 *Sunstein* (1992), *supra* note 25, p. 216.

43 See: *E. Lloyd*, Citizen Suits and Defenses Against Them. ALI-ABA, June 2012. Washington, D.C., discussing case law and more recent developments with respect to citizen suits in the US.

44 *J.L. Mashaw*, Rethinking Judicial Review of Administrative Action, Cardozo Law Review, 2011 (Vol. 32(6)), p. 2250.

administrative determinations".[45] At the end of the same century recognition emerged that "administrative action must be subject to judicial review."[46] It was certainly different to "the thinking of 1789 when it was thought that the separation of powers deemed to require that the administration's actions be completely free of control or question by the regular judiciary."[47]

In the twenty-first century the judicial competence to review actions of administration (executive acts and even legislation) is not the issue anymore. Thus, one could fairly claim that the role of courts has changed since the development of administrative law and the recognition of competence of courts to review actions of executive. However, whether this competence is designed merely to protect individuals or also include the broader role of the court and society to be involved in "general legality" check depends on a country's particular legal system. At the same time, it seems such international commitments as agreed under the Aarhus Convention are affecting interpretation of contracting parties' national law through broadening the role of the members of the public in direct enforcement of environmental law including with respect to questioning general legality.[48] Accordingly, the recognition of a need to facilitate more effective enforcement of the environmental law in the twenty-first century establishes a strong basis to discuss legal concepts from different perspectives and presumptions.

This trend in reconsidering the interpretation of legal concepts has emerged *inter alia* with respect to the rules of legal standing, which "traditionally was based on a built-in bias unduly favouring economic interests held by individuals and organisations," but which "discriminates against 'diffuse' interests held by the public or large segments of it."[49] Thus, although the concern of the US Court (highlighted in the *Lujan* case) to avoid undue interference with the executive's discretion in enforcing the law is appropriate as government action was challenged. This concern, however, is hardly related to the rules of legal standing at least in European settings.[50] Whether a case is brought by somebody who is

45 Id.

46 See: *L. Jaffe*, Judicial Control of Administrative Action, 1965, pp. 459–546.

47 This 'thinking of 1789' is noted by the US professor Jaffe as "common with nearly all of the Western countries." See: *Jaffe*, *supra* note 46, p. 323, noting French experience as instructive where 'by 1870 had evolved an autonomous court within the administration.' The same is noted by Cappelletti recognising "France as the great pioneer," developing administrative courts (*Conseil d'Etat*) and the system where legal standing "to attack the legality (vires) of administration was conferred upon the private person aggrieved by the challenged action as well as later to "private advocates." See: *M. Cappelletti*, Governmental and Private Advocates for the Public Interest in Civil Litigation: A Comparative Study, Michigan Law Review, 1975, (Vol. 73, No. 5), pp. 875–880.

48 See e.g. Implementation Guide, (2014) p. 199, noting that "the Convention makes it abundantly clear that it is not only the province of environmental authorities and public prosecutors to enforce environmental law, but the public also has an important role to play."

49 *H. Kotz*, Public interest Litigation: A Comparative Survey, in M. Cappelletti et al (eds), Access to Justice and the Welfare State, 1981, p. 102.

50 See *P. Cane*, Controlling Administrative Power. A Historical Comparison, 2016, noting that the US courts uses "another prime purpose" for controlling public power that includes

directly or individually concerned or by somebody who has standing according to a particular law does not lead by itself to interference in the area of executive branch or to a shift of powers.

As a result, one may agree that generous standing for members of the public up to "anyone" if "sanctioned" by the legislator, is "additional scrutiny" of executive and of enforcement of law established by the legislator within its competence rather than interference in exclusive powers of other branches of government.[51]

On the other hand, it is worth noting that whether any approach to the rules of legal standing fits into a country's legal system depends on the constitutional framework of that particular country and its international commitments. Moreover, there is also the interpretation of particular framework changes as intertwined with changing values of the society. One could presume that the values committed to by the contracting parties of the Aarhus Convention affects the interpretation of the public role within the environmental governance that include, *inter alia,* a right to access to justice for members of the public for "all contraventions of environmental law"[52] against which "the public, including organisations," has to have "effective judicial mechanisms" so that "its legitimate interests are protected and the law is enforced."[53]

At the same time, the scope of the term "members of the public" in the context of a right to access to justice of Article 9(3) is to be defined by the contracting parties, as noted above. Thus, whether to authorise "any one" or particular NGOs (as, for example, the approach developed in the so-called Aarhus Regulation, applicable to the EU institutions[54]) is in a sense a political choice of a Party, which shall fit into its constitutional framework.

In relation to the country that is the particular focus of this article, where the legislator has established an *actio popularis* for environmental disputes, the constitutionality of such a broad approach seems to be supported by the Supreme Administrative Court of Latvia when it states that:

> with such an open approach entitling "everyone" to file a lawsuit in cases where environmental law is breached by a public authority: the legislator has stressed important and sensitive areas for society where enhanced legal protection is needed.[55]

"legitimation of the governors" next to "protection of the governed." This arguably may affect also the rules of legal standing.

51 The idea on "additional scrutiny" expressed as contra argument to the approach of the US Supreme Court on 'unconstitutionality' of citizen suit in the form of "ESA-type" actions. See: *R.J. Pushaw,* Justifiability and Separation of Powers, 1995–1996, 81 Cornell L. Rev. 393.

52 *Supra* note 20.

53 Preamble of the Aarhus Convention recital [18].

54 Article 11 of Regulation 1367/2006 on the application of the provisions of the Aarhus Convention [...] to Community institutions and bodies.

55 The Administrative Department of the Supreme Court in judgment of 05.03.2015, case No. SKA-0022/2015, para 13, referring also to previous judgments emphasising the same point, e.g. in case No. SKA-139/2012, para 30.

This in turn fits neatly into the constitutional framework of Article 115 of the Constitution of Latvia, providing obligations to the state to establish "effective systems for environmental protection" to ensure that the right of every person of both present and future generations to a "benevolent environment" is guaranteed.[56]

4. DIFFERENT APPROACHES TO LEGAL STANDING IN EUROPE AND *ACTIO POPULARIS* THEREIN

There are three principal approaches identified in relation to the rules of legal standing of the European Union Member States.[57] Accordingly: (i) the most restrictive approach, according to which a 'subjective' right is required in order to be able to bring action before the court (or as often called a '*rights-based*' approach); (ii) the intermediate approach, which can be characterised by the presence of a requirement that an 'interest' in the subject matter be demonstrated (or as often called an '*interest-based*' approach); and (iii) the most extensive approach, often referred as an *actio popularis,* which may encompass the rules of legal standing authorising "any person" to set the court in motion in order to protect "public interest."

The former two approaches demonstrate a so-called "individualist" (subjective) view that would usually require some "personalised" link to a private applicant to grant standing to challenge an act or omission of a public authority.[58] According to the latter approach (under point (iii)), the requirement to prove a particular "impairment of his individual right" or interest is abandoned. The decisive element is a fact of violation of law, i.e. the entitlement to initiate a case rests on the fact of a breach of environmental law rather than compliance with any "personalised" (subjective) criterion. Therefore, it is primarily about "general legality" and control of law enforcement through judicial means.[59]

---

56 Constitutional Court, Case No. 2002-14-04, para 1, noting the duty of state to establish and maintain such system as part of the right to healthy environment as embedded in Article 115 of the Constitution.

57 See *N. de Sadeleer*, "Access to Justice in Environmental Matters" (final report), 2003, pp. 21–22. See also similar classification in more recent studies on Access to Justice with respect to all EU Member States, e.g. *J. Därpo*, "Effective Justice? Synthesis report" final, 2013-10-11, pp. 11–14. Available: <http://ec.europa.eu/environment/aarhus/studies.htm>.

58 See more details in: *J. Miles*, Standing under the Human Rights Act 1998: theories of Rights Enforcement & the Nature of Public Law Adjudication, Vol. 59 No. 1. The Cambridge Law Journal. 2000, pp. 133–167, analysing two models of the law enforcement: "individualist" and "communitarian" in the context of human rights. See also similar division or *ratio* behind legal standing in: materials of Colloquium of the Supreme Courts of Justice: "The Concept of Interest in Administrative Litigation." (1982).

59 See detailed discussion in: *A. Afilalo*, How Far Francovich?: Effective Judicial Protection and Associational Standing to Litigate Diffuse Interests in the European Union. Harvard Law School, 1998, discussing both approaches "individualist" (subjective) and "general legality."

In general, it is worth noting that today many legal systems are embedding a mixture of these approaches, especially due to the so-called "Europeanisation and internationalisation" of legal requirements in EU Member States that leads to more harmonised rules, including in relation to procedural issues.[60] In addition, an important element for standing is how the court interprets a link (nexus) that a plaintiff has to demonstrate or what would be considered as "personalised harm" for granting standing. The more liberalised interpretation of a link one needs to prove the more the approach can be characterised "along the lines of *actio popularis*."[61]

In fact, an *actio popularis* in Roman law emerged as a phenomenon of a state with "no-police" or any similar enforcement mechanisms.[62] Thus, an *actio popularis* evolved through *ius praetorium*[63] in order to protect "public things" extending in a sense private enforcement mechanism to ensure public order and protect "public things" if threatened by illegal activity.[64] These preconditions of "no-police" for the enforcement of law resembles challenges of today where weak enforcement of environmental law including when general environmental law is breached has led to such international agreements as the Aarhus Convention, embedding a right to access to justice for members of the public to facilitate that "the law is enforced." In this sense, one can agree with Advocate General Sharpston that Article 9(3) of the Convention is "the *actio popularis* provision."[65]

The discretion left in the Aarhus Convention for contracting parties to establish "criteria" as preconditions for standing could be seen as an incentive to allow avoidance from authorising "any" member of the public. However, nothing in the Convention precludes contracting parties from authorising any "member of the public" to play a "watchdog" role in alarming and participating or directly enforcing the law through administrative or judicial mechanisms respectively. There have been quite a number of calls to establish such broad standing rules for the implementation of Article 9(3) since its adoption.[66] However, there are few examples of where the most extensive approach to standing authorising "anyone" have been introduced in relation to environmental disputes covered by

60 See more detailed discussion on this phenomenon in: *S. Prechal*, Europeanisation of National Administrative Law. In J.H. Jans, S. Prechal, and R.J.G.M. Widdershoven (eds) Europeanisation of Public Law, 2015, pp. 39–72.

61 Expression used in: *J. Darpö*, *supra* note 57, characterizing the UK approach to standing. See also case-law e.g. *R v Somerset CC, ex parte Dixon* [1998] 75 P&CR 175; *R v. Inspectorate of Pollution ex p Greenpeace* No 2 [1994] 4 All ER 329.

62 *P. Mercer*, The Citizen's Right to Sue in the Public Interest: The Roman Actio Popularis Revisited. Vol. 21 No. 1. University of Western Ontario Law Review. 1983, p. 103.

63 Id., at p. 97.

64 See detailed discussion in: *J.E. Pfander*, Standing to Sue: Lessons from Scotland's Actio Popularis. Northwestern University School of Law. Public law and Legal Theories Series. No.16–07, (2016).

65 Case C-115/09 *Trianel*, Opinion of AG Sharpston of 16 December 2010, ECLI:EU:C:2010:773, para 42.

66 *Ebbesson* (2002), *supra* note 22.

Article 9(3). Therefore, it is interesting to reveal why and how it has evolved in Latvia over the last two decades.

5. THE EVOLVEMENT OF AN *ACTIO POPULARIS* THROUGH LEGISLATION OF LATVIA

At the outset, it is worth noting that the legal system of the Republic of Latvia had to go through transformation from the Soviet legal system to the Continental Europe where it belonged until the 1940s. During the 1990s, when the country regained independence, it started dismantling the legal system of Soviet times and made huge changes in its constitutional framework including through reviving its Constitution (*Satversme*) of 1922. In relation to the basic structure and concepts as well as the methodology of application of administrative law, Latvia follows other Germanic-based administrative law systems.[67] It is particularly so with respect to administrative procedural law, as several parts of the Latvian Administrative Procedural Law were drafted under the influence of the German Administrative Procedural Law.[68] However, there are also a number of differences and national peculiarities. The rules of legal standing as having evolved through the environmental legislation of Latvia represents one such difference.

In relation to environmental protection, straight after Latvia regained independence, discussions started about the need to develop a new legal framework for environmental protection. As has been noted by some scholars and politicians of that time, some important factors played an essential role in favour of the broader involvement of the society in environmental protection and thus presumably affected decisions to extend their rights through the Law on Environmental Protection of 1991.[69] These factors included: firstly, the fact of the "suddenly" discovered existence of major ecological crises as well as distrust in the executive power that dominated after regained independence and collapse of the Soviet Union.[70] Additionally, some peculiarities or rather "spoiled" notions

67 *K. Vaivods*, Administratīvā procesa tiesā būtība [The essence of the administrative procedures in the court], J. Briede (ed.) Administratīvais process tiesā [Administrative procedure in court], 2008, pp. 23–24.

68 Id.

69 Likums par vides aizsardzību [Law on Environmental Protection]: LR likums. Augstākās Padomes un Valdības Ziņotājs, no. 33, 1991. 29 August, not in force since 2006. It provided, for example, "the public control" of actions of natural and legal persons in observance of environmental law (Art.47).

70 *J. Strautmanis*, Ekoloģisko tiesību pamati [Basics of Law on Ecology], 1997. The reference to 'politicians' are based on discussions through interviews with ex-state minister of the environment and ex-judge of the Constitutional Court who were both leading members of the Parliament for environmental issues in time of the development of the new system for the environmental protection during the 1990s.

of "citizens'" organisations and the public authorities' capability of representing genuine public interest were inherited from a regime dominated by one party, one organisation representing all citizens.[71]

Starting from 1998, the reconsideration of legal standing requirements was also linked with topical discussions about the need to broaden legal standing requirements for environmental disputes following the signature of the Aarhus Convention in 1998 and its ratification in 2002.[72] Already in 2003, a broader notion of the public rights was included in the Law on Environmental Protection of 1991, stating that "any natural or legal person, as well its associations or organisations" has rights *inter alia* to take action on behalf of the public interests in environmental protection to challenge decisions of a state or municipal' institutions relating to environmental protection.[73] The aforementioned "spoiled" notion of "citizen organisations" was presumably behind the reluctance to streamline implementation of the Aarhus Convention through any type of particular citizen's organisations and thus behind the adoption of a very open approach to the concept of "members of the public."

However, these provisions authorising anyone to take action against a breach of environmental law by initiating a lawsuit remained "on paper" for a while. Up to 2005 no cases were reported as being accepted by the courts based on a claim to protect public interest in environmental protection without of involvement of particularised "subjective" rights either of an individual or a member of non-governmental organisation (NGO) that were required to have been "harmed" in legal sense. This in turn meant that illegal action had breached their individual rights, which in the area of environmental protection was rather difficult if possible to prove except for an addressee of an act.

With respect to public-law adjudications more generally, the regulation substantially changed in 2004 when the Administrative Procedural Law (further – APL) came into force.[74] The establishment of specialised courts in accordance to the APL resulted in a remarkable improvement towards more accessible judicial procedures and more transparent work of the public administration.[75]

71 See some details on specificities of the Soviet Union and Eastern Europe to that extent discussed in *Cappelletti*, (1975) *supra* note 47, pp. 868–875.

72 Discussion materials on preparations of amendments of the law on Environmental Protection (2003). The author was participating in those discussions. Materials are available in the Ministry of Environmental Protection, not published.

73 Article 13 of the Law on Environmental Protection (1991) as amended by Law of 15 May 2003. Latvijas Vēstnesis, 82 (2847).

74 Administratīva Procesa Likums [The Administrative Procedural Law] – adopted in 2001, came into force in 2004. Latvijas Vēstnesis, 164 (2551), 14.11.2001.

75 Detailed analysis as regards influence and effect to the administrative procedures in both public institutions and the courts since the introduction of the APL and the establishment of the Administrative courts, see: collection of scholars' and practitioners' articles and opinions of politicians in the special edition of journal Jurista Vārds, 04.02.2014., 5 (807).

Those changes certainly improved general preconditions for the access to justice in environmental matters. However, legal standing requirements were based on a rights-based approach (see explanation above under section 4 point (i)) providing that a private applicant has a right to review procedure in case *his* rights or legal interests are infringed (Article 31(2) of the APL). At the same time, according to the same article there is a possibility for the legislator to establish another approach for legal standing in cases "prescribed by law."[76]

Relatively in parallel of the enactment of the recently adopted APL, work started for drafting a new environmental protection law.[77] During the work of the drafting group, one of the central discussions was about legal standing requirements, including against acts of a public authority violating environmental law. According to *travaux préparatoires*[78], the working group drafting the Environmental Protection Law has discussed a right to access to justice in light of Article 9 of the Aarhus Convention including its requirement that the public has to have "wide access to justice" in environmental disputes. The discussions focused on problems with the "subjective" (individual) rights' concept for the disputes on general breaches of environmental law, as well as on pros and cons of "criteria" to be met to have legal standing in light of the requirements of Article 9(3). In the context of establishing some favourable conditions for particular (environmental) non-governmental organisations to be entitled to act for the environmental protection, some doubts were raised about the adequacy of such an approach as it could lead to a 'monopoly' in an area that "belongs to all of us." At the end of the day, the drafting group proposed the provisions that provided broad rights for the public without criteria in order to "facilitate enforcement of environmental requirements and involvement of the society."[79] Resultantly, the drafted provision stated that "any person, including organisations..." (Article 6 of the draft law) has a right provided under a particular chapter of the law. Article 9 of that draft provided access to justice right where a decision or an omission of a public authority breaches environmental law or threatens the environment. This approach "survived" through discussions in the government approving the draft[80] and through three readings within the

---

76 Article 31(2) reads: "Except for cases prescribed by law, a private person whose rights or legal interests have been infringed or may be infringed may submit an application."

77 The main aim for the drafting of a new law was connected with the need to transpose Directive 2004/35 on environmental liability, the discussions on legal standing for the public was relevant also in the context of this new Directive of 2004.

78 Protocols of working group for the drafting of a new Law on Environmental Protection, No. 2/2005 of 25.03.2005; No. 5/2005 of 02.06.2005. The author of this article was a chair of the working group.

79 Id, Protocol No. 5/2005 of 02.06.2005.

80 Draft submitted from the Government to the Parliament available: http://perseus-2.saeima.lv/L_Saeima8/index.htm.

Parliament. The new law was adopted by 100% of voting parliamentarians supporting it.[81]

The foregoing suggests that the rules of legal standing for environmental disputes covered by the scope of Article 9 of the new Environmental Protection Law entitling anyone to initiate a case against an act or omission of public authority is aimed to be an exception from the general "rights-based" approach "prescribed by law" (further referred as "*environmental exception clause*"). This conclusion is supported by the relatively recent Supreme Administrative Court practice as highlighted below. Moreover, the Supreme Administrative Court has arguably pointed out that "Latvia has chosen a very open approach implementing Article 9 of the Aarhus Convention."[82]

6. *ACTIO POPULARIS* THROUGH COURT PRACTICE IN LATVIA

6.1. THE FIRST CASES TOWARDS *ACTIO POPULARIS*

Notwithstanding the environmental legislation establishing a broad range of rights for society since the 1990s, and in particular, since the new Law on Environmental Protection was adopted in 2006, there has been a trend of limiting a right to access to justice through the application of the so-called "subjective right" conception.[83] The administrative court practice shifted towards recognition of a more open interpretation of the environmental law in 2008. Accordingly, in the first cases of 2008, although the court did not accept these cases as an "environmental disputes," and thus, did not apply "environmental exception clause," the existence of such an exception was noted.[84]

Hence, the jurisprudence of the Supreme Administrative Court has evolved since 2010, with a landmark case applying an "environmental exception clause".[85] In case No SKA-325/2010, the environmental NGO and the political

81 According to the proceedings of the Parliament session of 02.11.2006, dox No. 6461 adopted with 78 (from 100) in favour, nobody – against or abstaining.

82 The Administrative Department of the Supreme Court in the decision of 31.03.2010. case No SKA-325/2010, para 7.

83 *M. Paparinskis*, Piezīmes par vides tiesībām, [Notes on Environmental Rights], Jurista Vārds, 07.11.2006. 44 (447).

84 See, e.g. The Administrative Department of the Supreme Court in the decision of 27.11.2008. case No SKA-477/2008.

85 Case No SKA-325/2010, *supra* note 82. In particular case, environmental NGO (Association established to protecting Jūrmala, resort town) together with the political party (Jaunais laiks) complained to the Supreme Administrative Court after their application challenging a building permit that alleged to be contravening environmental law was rejected at the lower level. After the decision of the Supreme Court on the admissibility of the complaint applying "environmental exception clause", the court of the first instance had rendered judgment in

party were admitted to act through application of the "environmental exception clause," i.e. where they were not required to prove compliance with criteria to demonstrate a breach of their "subjective" right. As a result of the case, the building permit was rendered void as it breached general requirements of environmental law (on protected zones in a coastal area).[86] Thus, the act of public authority was considered to be in breach of the general requirements of "national law relating to the environment;" in other words, the case falling within the scope of Article 9(3) of the Convention. Since then, there have been quite some environmental disputes adjudicated initiated in fact by environmental NGOs in the majority of cases.[87]

Today the court admits that according to Article 31(2) of the APL, a person has to demonstrate that either its subjective right or legal interest is affected or standing is provided by law (as exception), i.e. when a person is entitled to initiate a case protecting other persons or the public interests.[88]

Since the first "case of Article 9(3)" one may note that the jurisprudence of the Supreme Administrative Court has been established indicating that on the one hand, claims from members of the public including environmental NGOs are consistently accepted through applying "environmental exception clause."[89] On the other hand, the trend is emerging to limit possibilities to initiate what the court labels as "trivial" cases where no genuine environmental concerns are at stake.

6.2. ENVIRONMENTAL PROTECTION AS THE "MAIN CONCERN" TO APPLY THE "ENVIRONMENTAL EXCEPTION CLAUSE"

Accordingly, the Administrative Supreme Court has stated that the environmental concerns have to be the main reason for an application to allow such an open approach as *actio popularis* to be applied as an exception to the general rule requiring a breach of a "subjective right." According to the court, an *actio*

favour of the plaintiffs admitting that particular building permit was issued in noncompliance with the law.

86 According to the Law of Protection Zones, there is a mandatory requirement to receive authorisation from the Cabinet of Ministers before any building permit might be issued in a coastal area of the Baltic Sea if forestland needs to be transformed for building purpose.

87 See, e.g. cases of the Administrative Department of the Supreme Court: No SKA-77/2015, SKA-912/2015, SKA-22/2015.

88 Case No SKA-325/2010, para 6, noting that the Law on Environmental Protection provides one of such "exceptions".

89 See *supra* note 87. See also: *S. Meijere*, Tiesu prakses apkopojums teritorijas plānošanas, būvniecības un vides lietās 2008–2012 [The compilation of case law in areas of spatial planning, building and environmental protection 2008–2012.] AT, 2013. Available in the Supreme Court portal: http://at.gov.lv/lv/judikatura/tiesu-prakses-apkopojumi/administrativajas-tiesibas.

popularis should not be admitted in cases where the environmental protection is a minor or a formal element of the complaint, i.e. where the applicant does not appreciably substantiate the threat to the environment.[90] In order to distinguish "real" environmental disputes from "trivial" cases "major importance has to be paid to circumstances an applicant submit substantiating a violation of the public legal interests."[91] Otherwise, according to the court the "environmental exception clause" would "open the door" to the court for "trivial cases" where no serious concerns about the environment are involved.[92]

Thus, the obligation to appreciably substantiate a claim to demonstrate that there are well-founded concerns about a breach of environmental law is an "entrance ticket" to the courtroom instead of "individualised" legal standing criteria required under a "rights-based" approach.

Consequently, a private applicant has legal standing before the administrative court under two types of conditions: a person is entitled to institute a case where his right or legal interest is breached by an act or omission of a public authority (rights-based approach). In addition (as the exception), a person (including NGOs) has a right to initiate a case against an act or omission of a public authority alleged to be contravening environmental law. In the latter case, the applicant needs to substantiate that a claim is aimed at protecting "the public common interests"[93] (thus accepting standing along the lines of *actio popularis*). It is interesting to note that the approach to legal standing for environmental disputes developed by the Administrative Supreme Court reminisces an intention that has been highlighted as was originally behind drafting of Article 9(3) of the Convention aimed to provide "the right to file genuine public interest law-suit."[94]

In the Latvian legal system with two types of possibilities, the court has to decide whether a case has to be qualified as environmental dispute already at the leave stage. This could be challenging, as to a large extent this assessment concerns the individual merits of a case. However, a benefit of such an open approach to legal standing is the broader possibility of avoiding that a substantial breach of environmental law goes "un-redressed"[95] due to the non-existence of an individual having been "harmed" in the legal sense or impossible to proof as in case of a breach of general environmental law. This in turn fits into the

90 The Administrative Department of the Supreme Court judgement of 18.06.2015 case No SKA-912/2015, para 6.

91 Ibid, para 7.

92 Ibid, para 6.

93 The Administrative Department of the Supreme Court judgement of 29.04.2015. case No SKA-77/2015, para 10.4.

94 *J. Jendrośka*, Aarhus Convention and Community Law: The Interplay. JEEPL, 2(1), 2005, p. 18.

95 See similar conclusion with respect to the essence of an *actio popularis* in: *J.E. Pfander*, (2016), *Supra* note 64 sec. I, noting that "the *actio popularis* authorized any person to pursue a claim on behalf of the public in cases where a public delict or wrong might otherwise go unredressed."

notion of Article 9(3) of the Convention to ensure access to justice broader than "simply to redress personal harm."[96] On the other hand, one needs to take into account that in eliminating cases based on the "trivial case" argument, there is a risk of failing to ensure that "access to a review procedure" is "provided for *all* contraventions of national law relating to the environment,"[97] as according to the Aarhus Convention Compliance Committee is required by Article 9(3) of the Convention. However, at this stage when "the trivial case" argument is relatively recent, there is no clear guidance and thus conclusion when the court would deny a case as a "trivial" one and whether that could result in non-compliance with Article 9(3) of the Convention.

Nevertheless, overall the legislation and court practice in Latvia represents a very extended approach to legal standing for environmental matters. Thus, one may presume that it could trigger some practical constraints often associated with such open standing, i.e. the possibility of "flood-gates" and abuse of the court proceedings[98] as well as delays in decision-making. Therefore, this article offers some reflections to that respect in the following concluding remarks section.

7. CONCLUDING REMARKS

It is true that any incentive to liberalise standing, and certainly when extending the rules to *any* person (though in "full age and capacity") to make a public interest application, faces objections that are often of a practical nature, such as on overburdening public administration and courts.[99] In fact, these concerns have equally legitimate aim as those pursued by the Convention on more openness and involvement of the society, including in the enforcement of law, as these practical concerns are connected with the efficiency of governance.

At the same time, as noted by Cane and other scholars, "the floodgates argument" is "unjustified and unrealistic," as concerns have not materialized in "flooding" the courts.[100] One may agree that hitherto there is hardly any

---

96 Implementation Guide, 2014, p. 197.

97 Case ACCC/C/2008/31 (Germany), para. 94.

98 *M. Hedemann-Robinson*, EU Implementation of the Aarhus Convention's Third Pillar – Part 1, EEELR, 2014, p 106; and *B. Hough*, A Re-examination of the Case for a Locus Standi Rule in Public Law, 28 Cambrian L. Rev. 83, p. 93.

99 *P. Cane*, Standing up for the Public. P.L. 1995, Sum, p. 284 noting that approach to open standing for public interest applications is mainly objected due to fears that it would "open the gates to a flood of litigation which would overburden the courts and make public bodies easy targets for the disgruntled and disaffected."

100 Id., See also more general discussion in: *P. Cane*, Controlling Administrative Power. An Historical Comparison. 2016; *P. McClellan*, Access to Justice in Environmental Law – An Australian Perspective. Commonwealth Law Conference, London, 2005. Available: www.austlii.edu.au/au/journals/NSWJSchol/2005/13.html.

evidence that open standing results in floodgates in other countries where broad rights of access to justice have been indicated[101]; and the same can be said about Latvia. In relation to cases before Latvian administrative courts, although there are no official statistics distinguishing environmental disputes from other cases of the administrative court, it has been estimated that cases claiming a breach of environmental law as the main concern (and thus, an environmental exception clause has been applied) account for about 1% of all disputes before the Supreme Administrative Courts each year (it might be twice as much before lower courts, which as well is not a significant amount).[102]

Nevertheless, it is true that in the case of *actio popularis* (or very open standing) there will always be a risk of proceedings from so-called "busybodies", which might delay perfectly lawful government actions.[103] According to Lady Hale, "[d]istinguishing between busybodies and champions is almost as difficult as distinguishing between terrorists and freedom fighters."[104] On the other side, Hale notes that "too close concentration on the particular interest which the claimant may be pursuing risks losing sight of what this is all about-fundamentally," i.e. to avoid from "public wrongs."[105]

In any event, the higher risk of unfounded claims, "trivial" cases or cases from "busybodies" is in a way "the price to pay" for broader possibilities to check actions of public administration facilitating "lawful government."[106] In addition, there is a good reason to believe that a wider possibility to question the legality of an action creates a *preventive* effect stemming from a "judge over the shoulder" attitude.[107] This preventive effect could in turn be one of the important elements in the legal mechanism developed in order to facilitate enforcement of law where illegal actions (or omissions) may easily damage "common good," but could be "difficult if possible to be restored afterwards."[108]

---

101 *P. Cane*, (1995), *Supra* note 99, p. 285; See also studies e.g., referred to in *Supra* note 57, as well as, Milieu Ltd., Summary report on the inventory of EU Member States' measures on access to justice in environmental matters, 2007 and individual country reports. Available: http://ec.europa.eu/environment/aarhus/study_access.htm.

102 Calculations made by the legal adviser of the Administrative Supreme Court in response to the author's inquiry, 13 April, 2016. It confirmed conclusions made during the seminar for judges of the Administrative Court, in Training Centre for Judges of Latvia, 25 September 2013.

103 *Lady Hale*, Who Guards the Guardians? Cambridge Journal of International and Comparative Law, 2014, p. 101.

104 Id. at p. 101.

105 *M. Elliott*, The Constitutional Foundations of Judicial Review, 2001, p. 5, quoted by *Hale*, *supra* note 103 at, p.101.

106 See more detailed discussion on the latter point in: *Miles*, (2000), *Supra* note 58, p. 150.

107 Expression used by Lady Hale in relatively similar context on the developments as regards legal standing, see: *Hale, supra* note 102.

108 *J. Strautmanis*, Vides ētika un vides tiesības, [Environmental Ethic and Environmental law], (2003), pp. 55–56, discussing many 'mistakes' in decisions that concerns the environmental and were irreversible or difficult to correct.

Accordingly, taking into account the discussion above on the development of *actio popularis* in Latvia, one may conclude that possible delays of decision-making within administration and a risk of unfounded cases before the court were the "price" that Latvian society (through Parliamentary representatives) accepted in order to facilitate enforcement of law through opening standing to any member of the public. Moreover, some of the historical preconditions indicated above certainly facilitated the development of such open standing in the area of environmental protection next to the commitments to implement the Aarhus Convention.

In conclusion, the legal mechanism established in one country or another, including the openness to involve a broader range of the society in the enforcement of law, signals how much enforcement the country wants and at what price. For contracting parties of the Convention, there is a certain indication on this "price" that includes opening law enforcement mechanisms to the members of the public in order to address "all contraventions" of environmental law.

Through stipulating the involvement of the society in direct and indirect enforcement of law Article 9(3) aims at supplementing the general enforcement mechanism and not competing with it. In any event, it is up to contracting parties to decide whom to authorise to play the "watchdog" role to contribute to the enforcement of law in accordance with its constitutional framework.

With respect to Latvia and taking into account particular historical preconditions, the *actio popularis* has been introduced through legislation in order to contribute to the then-weak enforcement of environmental law next to the implementation of such international commitments as embedded in the Convention. Since 2008, the most extensive approach to legal standing as the exception to the general rule of standing is acknowledged by the Administrative Supreme Court. Today one may claim that the *actio popularis* was introduced as "additional scrutiny" over enforcement of law, where as noted by the court, the legislator has admitted that "enhanced protection is needed." In light of the twenty-first century perspective and countries international commitments, the role of courts and the society in the enforcement of environmental law is changing.

This is the framework in which it is argued in this article that the most extensive approach to legal standing should not raise concerns highlighted in the discussion on the separation of powers. Although one needs to be aware that the legal mechanism to be introduced for the implementation of Article 9(3) provides for the enforcement of law including possibilities to question "general legality" of actions of public authority that encroaches in the duties of executive; however, whether a lawsuit is initiated by a person "harmed" or by any "member of the public" authorized by law does not by itself shift the powers of the three branches of government. Therefore, concerns raised in light of the separation of powers should not limit the legislator to grant standing to "anyone" if that is "the price" the society is ready to pay for the enforcement of law, especially where "enhanced protection is needed." Certainly the "price" has to fit in the constitutional framework of a particular country, however, for the contracting parties of the Convention it seems it could be contrary to the logic of Article 9(3) if illegal action of authority alleged to be in breach of environmental law may hide behind the rules of legal standing. In this sense, as well as more generally in the context of objective law enforcement embedded in Article 9(3) one has to admit that the *actio popularis* is an approach that neatly fits into such a framework.

PROCEDURAL ENVIRONMENTAL RIGHTS AND NATURE PROTECTION

TOWARDS A LEGALLY ENFORCEABLE DUTY TO RESTORE ENDANGERED SPECIES UNDER EU NATURE CONSERVATION LAW

On Wild Hamsters, the Rule of Law and Species Extinction

Hendrik SCHOUKENS*

ABSTRACT

Over the past two decades ecological restoration has become a major environmental policy objective both at international and EU level. However, the question to what extent such restoration claims can be effectively enforced through legal action before national courts within the context of EU nature conservation law has received little attention so far. In this chapter a case is made for a legally enforceable restoration duty for strictly protected species, such as the Wild hamster, which are listed in Annex IV of the Habitats Directive. Taking into account recent case law developments before the Court of Justice of the EU (CJEU) it is argued that environmental NGOs might step in as effective 'guardians' of endangered species that are in dire need of additional recovery measures in order to stave off imminent extinction. It is demonstrated that the powerful combination of Article 9(3) of the Aarhus Convention and the general principles of EU law is capable of overcoming the traditional procedural obstacles to environmental litigation. Moreover, while the system of strict protection duties contained in Article 12(1) of the Habitats Directive is primarily directed at conserving the 'status quo', the restoration imperative present within the directive can still be used so as to compel Member States to adopt more progressive restoration strategies *vis-à-vis* protected species. The major conclusion is that it is no longer inconceivable to force national and/or regional authorities through court room action to implement more robust restoration programmes aimed at achieving the favourable conservation status of endangered Annex IV species.

* Postdoctoral researcher Ghent University.

1. GENERAL INTRODUCTION

1.1. FROM STATIC PRESERVATION MANAGEMENT TO ECOLOGICAL RESTORATION

> 'Imagine a single survivor, a lonely fugitive at large on mainland Mauritius at the end of the seventeenth century. Imagine this fugitive as a female. She would have been bulky and flightless and befuddled – but resourceful enough to have escaped and endured when other birds didn't. Or else she was lucky. (...) (The dodo) had become rare unto death. But this one flesh-and-blood individual still lived.'[1]

This compelling excerpt from the book The Song of the Dodo, written by David Quammen on the extinction of species in, to quote the author's own words, 'a world that has been hacked to pieces', aptly captures the unenviable fate of the last living survivor of a species that is on the road to extinction. This predicament is currently shared by many other last remaining specimens of endangered species on our Planet. It is widely known that the ecological crisis we are faced with is unprecedented both in terms of scale and scope, with populations of many species on our planet plummeting well below sustainable levels due to increasing human pressure on the ecosystems.[2]

In spite of supranational enforcement present within the EU legal order[3], setting it apart from the international legal system[4], the situation is not substantially different in the European Union (EU). The implementation of the EU Habitats[5] and Birds Directives[6] (EU Nature Directives) has compelled Member States to set up ambitious protection and recovery schemes for a myriad protected habitats and species. Nevertheless, the European biodiversity is still suffering from a continuous decline. Notwithstanding some modest success stories, for example the recovery of large carnivores, such as the Gray wolf (*Canis lupus*), across their

1 *D. Quammen*, The Song of the Dodo, Island Biogeography in an Age of Extinctions, Touchstone, 1996, p. 275.

2 *O. Venter et al.*, Sixteen years of change in the global terrestrial human footprint and implications for biodiversity conservation, Nature Communications 2016, DOI: 10.1038/ncomms12558.

3 See more on this: *H. Schoukens & K. Bastmeijer*, Species protection in the European Union: How strict is strict? In: C.H. Born, A. Cliquet, H. Schoukens, D. Misonne & G. Van Hoorick (eds.), The Habitats Directive in its EU Environmental Law Context: European Nature's Best Hope?, Routledge, 2015, pp. 128–132.

4 In various multilateral environmental agreements non-compliance procedures are provided. However, ensuring full compliance with multilateral environmental agreements remains an important issue of concern. See: *J. Brunnée*, Climate change and compliance and enforcement processes, In: R. Rayfuse & S.V. Scott (eds.), International Law in the Era of Climate Change, Edward Elgar, 2012, pp. 294–300.

5 Council Directive 92/43/EEC on the conservation of natural habitats and of wild fauna and flora, OJ 1992 L 206/7 (further referred to as 'Habitats Directive').

6 Directive 2009/147/EC on the conservation of wild birds, OJ 2010 L 20/7 (further referred to as 'Birds Directive').

former range[7], recent reports reveal that the overall picture for the biodiversity in the EU remains bleak.[8]

The reasons for this lack of immediate results on the ground are manifold, ranging from improper enforcement of protection schemes on the ground to a lack of proper funding. Yet also the lack of a proper recovery focus might be identified as one of the major shortcomings in this regard. Until now, the main policy response to the predicament of many species has consisted of nature conservation laws with a rather static focus on the preservation of the remaining biodiversity in protected sites.[9] However, merely conserving what remains may be illusionary when the populations of an endangered species are close to or below the threshold of extinction and the species' habitat has disappeared throughout its former range.[10] It is therefore not surprising to see the concept of 'ecological restoration' gaining considerable traction among environmental organisations and policy-makers.[11] Instead of exclusively focusing on the maintenance of a static status quo, ecological restoration seeks to return a degraded ecosystem to its 'historical trajectory'.[12] In the Society for Ecological Restoration's 2004 Primer, the concept is further defined as the practice of 'assisting the recovery of an ecosystem that has been degraded, damaged or restored'.[13]

Over recent years, ecological restoration has moreover slowly turned into a global priority. Some authors now speak of an 'emerging age of ecological restoration law'.[14] Explicit restoration policy targets are present both in global and regional biodiversity targets.[15] Within the framework of the 1992 Convention on Biological Diversity[16], the 2010 Aichi Targets set forth the

---

7 *G. Chapron et al.*, Recovery of Large Carnivores in Europe's Modern Human-Dominated Landscapes, Science 2014, 346, p. 1517.

8 *European Environment Agency*, State of nature in the EU Results from reporting under the nature directives 2007–2012, EEA Technical Report, No. 2/2015.

9 See more extensively: *W.R. Jordan III & G.M. Lubeck*, Making Nature Whole. A History of Ecological Restoration, Islandpress, Washington, 2011, pp. 96–100.

10 *B.J. Richardson*, The Emerging Age of Ecological Restoration Law, Journal of European Community & International Environmental Law 2016, 25(3), p. 277.

11 See more extensively: *J. Aronson & S. Alexander*, Ecosystem Restoration is Now a Global Priority: Time to Roll up our Sleeves', Restoration Ecology, 2013, pp. 293–296. See also in a similar vein: *A. Telesetsky, A. Cliquet & A. Akhtar-Khavari*, Ecological Restoration in International Environmental Law, 2017, Routledge, pp. 22–25.

12 *S.K. Allisson*, What do we mean when we talk about ecological restoration? An inquiry into values, Ecological Restoration 2004, 22(4), pp. 281–286.

13 *Society for Ecological Restoration International Science, Policy Working Group*, The SER International Primer on Ecological Restoration, Tucson, Society for Ecological Restoration International, 2004.

14 *Richardson, supra* note 10, p. 277.

15 See more extensively: *A Cliquet, K. Decleer & H. Schoukens*, Restoring nature in the EU: The only way is up? in C.H. Born, A. Cliquet, H. Schoukens, D. Misonne & G. Van Hoorick (eds.), *supra* note 2, pp. 265–284.

16 Convention on Biological Diversity, Rio de Janeiro, 5 June 1992.

goal of restoring at least 15% of degraded ecosystems by 2020.[17] On its turn, the European Commission has embraced ecological restoration in the explicit policy targets that are included in the EU Biodiversity Strategy to 2020.[18] In line with the EU's international obligations, the European Commission adopted an overarching 15% restoration target, along with its commitment to halt the deterioration in the status of all species and habitats covered by EU nature legislation and to achieve a significant and measurable improvement in their conservation status by 2020.[19] Regardless of the lofty and ambitious targets towards ecological or ecosystem restoration, many countries fail to honour their policy pledges in the field and falter in the concrete implementation of the restoration-based principles into national and regional planning policies.[20] For sure, the disappointing results so far can partly be linked to the absence of a clear-cut definition of key concepts, such as 'ecological restoration'[21] and 'degradation', and the lack of a well-defined baseline, which offers a (too?) wide discretion to the EU Member States.[22] Also, one might portend that the targets are impractical and unattainable since it remains unthinkable that 15% of the EU's territory will be restored to a certain historical reference state any time soon.[23] However, while some of this criticism appears to have some merit, it does not alter the fact that ambitious recovery plans remain instrumental in staving off the extinction of several endangered species across the EU and reversing so-called 'tipping points'. So the question is really whether we can still afford to wait for a more consensus-driven approach to emerge in the context of biodiversity management in times of ecological crisis.

1.2. FROM PIECEMEAL LAWSUITS TO MORE ACTIVIST TYPES OF ENVIRONMENTAL LITIGATION

Enter private environmental enforcement. Over the past decades, legal action over the failure to implement comprehensive environmental policies has become an ever more attractive pathway for activist citizens and environmental NGOs.

---

17 CBD, 2010, COP 10 Decision X/2, Strategic Plan for Biodiversity 2011–2020.

18 European Commission, *Communication from the Commission to the European Parliament, the Council, the Economic and Social Committee and the Committee of the Regions, Our life insurance, our natural capital: an EU biodiversity strategy to 2020* (COM(2011) 244 final, 2011).

19 See more extensively: *Cliquet, Decleer & Schoukens, supra* note 15, pp. 268–271.

20 *J. Cortina-Segarra, K. Decleer, J. Kollmann*, Biodiversity: Speed restoration of EU ecosystems, Nature, 2016, 535, p. 231.

21 A distinction is often made between 'restoration', which aims at the recovery of an ecosystem to its original natural state, on the one hand, and 'rehabilitation', which refers to activities that may fall short of returning the ecosystem to its pre-degradation state. See more extensively: *Allison, supra* note 12.

22 *D. Jørgensen*, Ecological restoration as objective, target, and tool in international biodiversity policy, Ecology and Society 2016, 20(4), p. 43.

23 *J.S. Kotiaho*, Target for ecosystem repair is impractical, Nature 2015, 519, p. 33.

Yet as Advocate General Sharpston aptly noted at the hearing in *Trianel* before the Court of Justice of the EU (CJEU)[24], 'the fish cannot go to court', which is but a recent echo of the Christopher Stone's famous words: 'trees have no standing'.[25]

With the extinction crisis continuing unabatedly, the compelling legal question now surfaces as to whether environmental NGOs can sue governments over their apparent negligence or failure to come forward with more ambitious restoration programmes for endangered species before national courts.[26] Instead of focusing on 'reactive' or 'piecemeal' lawsuits, in which the legality of individual hunting derogations or building permits liable to further damage protected species is challenged before administrative bodies or courts, a more activist approach would allow environmental NGOs to tackle the more fundamental shortcomings of nature protection schemes in court. In doing so, they can seek to obtain a mandatory injunction compelling authorities to come forward with more ambitious recovery programmes.

For a long time, though, it was evident to set aside such types of judicial activism as unthinkable, especially within the realm of biodiversity governance, a legal domain characterized by conspicuously vague legal standards. Even so, legal frames are fluid, dependent on societal changes and prone to evolution, amongst others through the course of jurisprudential evolutions. The 2015 ground-breaking *Urgenda* ruling of the District Court of the Hague, in which the Dutch government was ordered to step up its efforts in combatting climate change on the basis of the rather broadly formulated 'duty of care' contained in the Dutch Civil Code, is now often cited as the most recent exponent of this trend towards judicial activism in environmental matters.[27] However, it would be misleading to merely point to the outcome of a single national court case – against which an appeal is lodged – as being instructive for a more comprehensive shift in the appraisal of private environmental enforcement. Interestingly enough, the decision in the Dutch climate case is no longer a standalone ruling but part of a wider jurisprudential trend. In the United States (U.S.) as well, similar climate actions have received a favourable treatment, both in state[28] and federal courts.[29]

---

24 Case C-115/09, *Trianel* [2011] ECR I-3673.

25 *C.D. Stone*, Should Trees Have Standing? – Toward Legal Rights for Natural Objects, 1972, p. 3.

26 For the reasons behind the strategy of some environmental NGOs to increasingly turn to the courts in activist environmental procedures, see: *L. Bergkamp & J.C. Hanekamp*, Climate Change Litigation against States: The Perils of Court-Made Climate Politics', European Environmental and Energy Law Review 2015, pp. 103–105.

27 District Court of The Hague, Stichting Urgenda v. Government of the Netherlands (Ministry of Infrastructure and the Environment), 24 June 2015, C/09/456689/HA ZA 13-1396. See more extensively, amongst others: *K.J. de Graaf & J.H. Jans*, The Urgenda Decision: Netherlands Liable for Role in Causing Dangerous Global Climate Change, Journal of Environmental Law 2015, p. 517.

28 See for instance: *SC Washington (King County), Zoe and Stella Foster and others v. Washington Department of Ecology*, 19 November 2015, no. 14-25295-1 SEA.

29 Most notably, on November 10, 2016 Judge Ann Aiken of the Federal District Court for the District of Oregon issued an order denying the U.S. government and fossil fuel industry's

Most importantly, the progressive case-law evolutions in the context of clean air litigation both before the CJEU and at national level starkly underline the large potential for public interest litigation in matters that are regulated at EU level.[30] And thus, the tentative conclusion might be that it appears no longer unthinkable to bring forward more progressive restoration-based claims in court, especially when framed within the relatively strict statutory framework of the EU Nature Directives.

The idea of suing governments over their biodiversity and restoration commitments is surely thought-provoking in itself. However, given the many procedural as well as substantive complexities that might arise, it merits a closer examination. At the centre of this chapter, a case is made for a legally enforceable restoration duty regarding strictly protected species listed in Annex IV of the Habitats Directive. While the main focus of this chapter is to examine the procedural obstacles regarding judicial activism in the realm of endangered species which are strictly protected under EU law, also the most seminal substantive issues that are inextricably linked to the latter elements are addressed. The research questions that are looked into include the following: on what legal grounds can NGOs claim legal standing for bringing recovery claims regarding endangered species before national courts under EU law?; to what extent is a mandatory injunction against the government to enact more ambitious recovery programmes in line with the separation of powers doctrine?; which substantive criteria can underpin restoration claims in the context of endangered species that go beyond maintaining existing populations in their habitats?

2. THE PLIGHT OF THE WILD HAMSTER IN WESTERN EUROPE: AN APPROPRIATE CONTEXT FOR RESTORATION-BASED CLAIMS?

As noted above, the focus of this chapter is not ecosystem restoration as such. Instead, it is analysed to what extent the omission to adopt adequate recovery programmes for strictly protected species under the EU Nature Directives is challengeable in court. Rather than looking at the myriad procedural and substantive issues to be considered when opting for a more activist type of litigation at national court level through a theoretical lens, the analysis below aims at tackling the most important points through a specific case study of the Wild hamster (*Cricetus cricetus*), also known as the Eurasian hamster, the Black-

procedural motions to dismiss a constitutional climate change lawsuit staged by 21 youth. See: *U.S. District Court For the District of Oregon, Kelsey Cascade Rose Juliana et al. v. The United States of America et al.*, 10 November 2016, Opinion and Order of Judge Aiken.

30 See for instance: Case C-404/13, *ClientEarth* [2014] ECLI:EU:C:2013:805; UK Supreme Court, *R (on the application of ClientEarth) (Appellant) v. Secretary of State for the Environment, Food and Rural Affairs (Respondent)*, 29 April 2015 [2015] *UKSC* 28, [2013] *UKSC* 25.

bellied hamster or the Common hamster. The reason therefore is twofold. First, in spite of its protected status, the Wild hamster has witnessed substantial drops in its populations over the past decades, which underscores the need for robust recovery programmes in order to stave off extinction. Second, the Wild hamster is one of the few endangered species which has featured so prominently in the case-law of the CJEU. And although the causes of decline evidently differ from one species to the other, the more general lessons drawn from this case study will probably be instrumental for other threatened species within the EU.

2.1. FROM AGRICULTURAL PEST TO CRITICALLY ENDANGERED SPECIES IN SEVERAL EU MEMBER STATES?

Until several decades ago, the Wild hamster was regarded as an agricultural pest throughout large parts of Western and Central Europe. Nothing pointed towards its possible extinction in the westernmost part of its range.[31] Yet during the course of the second half of the 20th century the Wild hamster became increasingly rare. The increasingly threatened rodent species, which was already protected under the 1979 Convention on the Conservation of European Wildlife and Natural Habitats (Bern Convention)[32], was listed as a strictly protected species in Annex IV to the Habitats Directive in 1992.[33]

The Wild hamster's presence is almost exclusively connected with human farming practices. Currently, the optimal habitat conditions of the Wild hamster overlap with the most productive agricultural areas, which already hints to the primary causes of its recent demise.[34] Given the sharp reduction in their favourable croplands, the populations of Wild hamsters have seen a decline by more than 99% in Belgium, the Netherlands and the adjacent federal state of North Rhine-Westphalia.[35] The nearby populations present in the Alsace region in France have suffered a similar fate.[36]

The causes of the current predicament of the Wild hamster are easily identifiable. As already alluded to above, there is the substantial change in

---

31 *J.O' Brien*, Saving the common hamster (Cricetus cricetus) from extinction in Alsace (France): potential flagship species conservation or an exercise in futility?, Hystrix, the Italian Journal of Mammalogy 2015, DOI: 404/hystrix 26.2 11230, pp. 89 95.

32 Bern, 19 September 1979, in force 1 June 1982, UKTS No 56 (1982), Cmnd 8738.

33 Except for Hungary, where it is listed in Annex V.

34 *O' Brien, supra* note 31, pp. 89–90.

35 *M.J.J. La Haye, K. Neumann & H.P. Koelewijn*, Strong decline of gene diversity in local populations of the highly endangered Common hamster (Cricetus cricetus) in the western part of its European range, Conservation Genetics 2012, 13, p. 311.

36 *O' Brien, supra* note 31, pp. 89–91; *K. Neuman, H. Jansman, A. Kayser, S. Maak, R. Gatterman*, Multiple bottlenecks in threatened western European populations of the common hamster Cricetus cricetus (L.), Conservation Genetics 2004, 5, pp. 181–193.

agricultural crops since the 1950s, which has significantly reduced the chances of survival of the Wild hamster. The progressive shift towards maize cultivation at the expense of more hamster-friendly crops has been particularly detrimental to the rodent species.[37] The intensification of agriculture has had detrimental effects on the already diminishing population level. In countries like France and Belgium, perennial fodder crops now constitute less than 6% of the arable land, compared with 13–14% in the early 1990s.[38]

The creeping urbanization and fragmentation of the traditional habitats of the Wild hamster have further fragmented the remaining populations of the Wild hamster[39], rendering their survival dependent on *ex situ* protection schemes, including captive breeding and reintroduction efforts.[40] Moreover, recent research suggests that also climate change might cause further compromise the survival chances of the Wild hamster on the long term.[41]

2.2. EXTINCTION THROUGH INACTION?

What makes the plight of the Wild hamster so well-suited for assessing the potential for filing restoration-based lawsuits in the context of EU nature conservation law, is that it is almost exclusively human-induced. It is precisely the lack of effectively implemented and enforced protective schemes that has brought the species to the brink of extinction in several Western-European EU Member States. Even after the entry into force of the Habitats Directive in 1994, which listed the species as a strictly protected Annex IV species and thereby forced EU Member States to ban all detrimental activities to Wild hamsters[42], the policy response in countries such as Belgium (Flemish Region) and France has been notoriously slow. This has led some commentators to speak of 'extermination through inaction'.[43] In the Netherlands, the species was said to be virtually extinct in the beginning of the 21st century, while it is believed that only 30 Wild hamsters remain on the territory

37 See more generally: *K. Ulbrich & A. Kayser*, A risk analysis for the Common hamster (Cricetus cricetus), Biological Conservation, 2004, 117(3), pp. 263–270.

38 *Orbicon, Ecosphère, ATECMA & Ecosystems LTD*, Species report Cricetus cricetus, Wildlife and sustainable farming and the Birds and Habitats Directive 2009, Brussels, Wildlife and Sustainable Farming Initiative.

39 *O' Brien, supra* note 31, pp. 89–91.

40 See more extensively: *M. La Haye, T.E. Reiners, R. Raedts, V. Verbist & H.P. Koelewijn*, Genetic monitoring to evaluate reintroduction attempts of a highly endangered species, Conserv Genet, 2017, DOI 10.1007/s10592-017-0940-z.

41 *M.L. Tissier, Y. Handrich, J.-P. Robin, M. Weitten, P. Pevet, C. Kourkgy & C. Habold*, How maize monoculture and increasing winter rainfall have brought the hibernating European hamster to the verge of extinction, Sci Rep. 2016, 6, p. 25531.

42 See Article 12(1) of the Habitats Directive. See more extensively: Schoukens & Bastmeijer, *supra* note 3, pp. 132–139.

43 Ibid.

of the Flemish Region (Belgium).[44] It must be noted that, over the course of the past decade or so, several conservation and restoration schemes have been set up to support the isolated and fragmented populations in Belgium (Flemish Region), Germany, the Netherlands and France.[45] However, until recently, such efforts have proven to have little effect, partly because they lacked robust repopulation targets, were underfunded and mostly relied upon voluntary conservation efforts by farmers.[46]

The slow and uncoordinated response of the French authorities to drastic population decline is indicative of the inadequate protection efforts elsewhere in the EU.[47] For one, it is striking to note that full legal protection was only accorded to the Wild hamster in France, as late as in 2007, *i.e.* more than 13 years (!) after the entry into force of the Habitats Directive. In other EU Member States a similar non-compliance scenario has emerged.[48] In addition, the French protection rules that had been adopted, were mostly openly ignored throughout planning procedures for infrastructure programmes liable to harm existing or potential habitats for hamsters.[49] This conclusion is not new though. As illustrated by the outcome of the recently concluded Fitness Check of the EU Nature Directives, the protection and conservation rules laid down by those legal instruments often amount to nothing more than a 'paper tiger' and lack robust implementation efforts.[50]

To further underpin the latter findings, one can point to the first generation of French hamster conservation plans, adopted around 2004–2006.[51] Whereas these plans must surely be credited for helping to raise awareness for hamsters among farmers, they were mostly defensive by nature, focusing on the last remaining strongholds of the species, and insufficiently funded to fundamentally reverse the ongoing decline. This was reasserted by the condemnation of France by the CJEU

---

44 See: https://www.natuurpunt.be/nieuws/was-dit-de-laatste-wilde-vlaamse-hamster-20120817 (Accessed 10 April 2017).

45 *La Haye, Neumann & Koelewijn, supra* note 35, pp. 311–312; *H. Schoukens*, Requiem voor de laatste wilde hamster in Vlaanderen: een juridische paradigmashift in the Antropoceen, Tijdschrift voor Omgevingsrecht en -beleid 2016, p. 25.

46 *M.J.J. La Haye, G.J.D.M. Müskens, R.J.M. Van Kats, A.T. Kuiters, H. Siepel*, Agri-environmental schemes for the Common hamster (Cricetus cricetus). Why is the Dutch project successful?', Aspects of Applied Biology 2010, p. 1.

47 See on Belgium more extensively: *Schoukens, supra* note 45, pp. 25–29.

48 Ibid.

49 See for instance with respect to the integration of species protection consideration in spatial planning procedures in the Netherlands: *J.M. Verschuuren*, De laatste wilde hamster in Nederland en de grondslagen van het Europees en internationaal recht, W.E.J. Tjeenk Willink, 2000, Deventer, pp. 20–25.

50 European Commission, Commission Staff Working Document – Fitness Check of the EU Nature Legislation (Birds and Habitats Directive), SWD(2016) 4725 final, available at: http://ec.europa.eu/environment/nature/legislation/fitness_check/index_en.htm (Accessed 10 April 2017).

51 *O' Brien, supra* note 31, pp. 90–92.

in 2011.[52] In order to avoid further infringement proceedings, countries like France have considerably increased the financial means linked to the conservation plans in the past five years. Even so, the current conservation plans are openly challenged by the environmental NGOs for insufficiently guaranteeing the long-term survival of the species in the Alsace.[53] The recent half-hearted protection efforts from other neighbouring countries show remarkable similarities with the French flawed policy response so far.[54] And thus there might still exist a palpable willingness to counter the inadequate policy responses in court.

3. PROCEDURAL OBSTACLES: GRANTING STANDING TO ENVIRONMENTAL NGOS IN ORDER TO ALLOW THEM TO ACT AS GUARDIANS OF THE WILD HAMSTER?

3.1. DIFFERENT ROADS TO THE ENFORCEMENT OF EU ENVIRONMENTAL LAW

Faced with the steep decline and virtual extinction of the local populations of many endangered species, such as the Wild hamster, environmental NGOs might be found increasingly willing to sue their governments over their failure to adopt adequate conservation and recovery schemes. As of today, such actions have not yet been initiated at the national level, also not regarding the Wild hamster. Even so, environmental NGOs have filed complaints with the European Commission – which is the principal 'guardian of the Treaties' – on the inadequate protection of the Wild hamster over the recent years. And indeed, such infringement proceedings could in some cases serve as an effective remedy to enforce EU nature conservation law in the field, as is partly illustrated by the French hamster case. As noted, France was ultimately condemned for its inadequate recovery programmes. Still, the outcome of infringement proceedings can be unpredictable and subject to opaque forms of political decision-making.[55] For instance, in spite of sending Belgium a Reasoned Opinion with regard to the insufficient efforts made to halt the continuous decline of the Wild hamster back in 2005, the European Commission, for reasons unknown, ultimately

---

52 Case C-383/09, *Commission v France* [2011] ECR I-04869.

53 *M. Wintz et al.*, Open letter dated 16 November 2012, www.cricetus-cricetus-cricetus.alsace/les-associations-de-defense-du-cricetus/ (Accessed 10 April 2017).

54 *Schoukens*, *supra* note 45, pp. 53–56.

55 See more extensively: *J. Darpö*, The Commission: A Sheep in Wolf's Clothing? On Infringement Proceedings as a Legal Device for the Enforcement of the EU Law on the Environment, Using Swedish Wolf Management as an Example, Journal of European Environmental & Planning Law 2016, pp. 283–289.

decided not to bring this case before the CJEU.[56] Moreover, even when an actual infringement procedure is launched before the CJEU, the European Commission often struggles with bringing forward the necessary evidence.[57] Rather ironically, the burden of proof will be more easily met when the extinction of a species becomes very likely.[58]

Against this backdrop, environmental enforcement through national court proceedings comes into the picture as an attractive alternative, especially in cases where urgent action is needed to stave off the extinction of protected species. National courts are indeed to be approached as the 'ordinary courts' for implementing and enforcing EU law within the legal systems of the EU Member States.[59] They are competent to scrutinize national decisions or even omissions that might contravene EU law. Until recently, though, more activist types of legal actions in conservation cases had little chance of success in view of the rigid standing rules that often prevailed before the national courts in the context of public interest litigation. Many judges felt reluctant to scrutinize governmental policies in light of environmental standards. By some measures, the rationale used by the U.S. Supreme Court in its 1992 landmark ruling in *Lujan v. Defenders of Wildlife* is still to be cited as one of the more explicit formulations of the 'conservative' approach in this respect.[60] As is known, these proceedings revolved around the standing of environmentalists to challenge agency programmes and are, at least in terms of substance, therefore not that distinct from a potential legal review action in the context of potentially flawed species recovery plans in the EU. When deciding upon the matter, however, the U.S. Supreme Court concluded that *Wildlife Defenders* had failed to meet the Constitutional requirements for individualized injury that would have granted standing under the U.S. *Endangered Species Act*.[61] Most notably, Justice Scalia, who was writing for the majority, dismissed the view that the citizen suit provision of the act amounted to an *actio popularis* clause. He seized the opportunity to reassert that programmatic decisions and rules of general application are not appropriate for judicial review.[62] It is a 'conservative' approach which also many European judges would have concurred with in the mid-1990s.

Going back to the European context, though, it must be noted that the exact scope of the legal standing requirements in environmental cases obviously differs from one jurisdiction to another. Still, it would be all too easy to dismiss Justice

56 *Schoukens, supra* note 45, pp. 28–29.
57 See for instance: Case C-308/08, *Commission v Spain* [2010] ECR-4281.
58 *M. Clement*, What does the obligation of result mean in practice? The European hamster in Alsace, In: C.H. Born, A. Cliquet, H. Schoukens, D. Misonne, G. Van Hoorick (eds.), *supra* note 3, p. 16.
59 Opinion 1/09, Creation of a Unified Patent Litigation System, EU:C:2011:123, para. 80.
60 *U.S. Supreme Court, Lujan v. Defenders of Wildlife*, 504 U.S. 555 (1992).
61 16 USCA §1531 et seq.
62 See more extensively: *K.P. Sheldon, Lujan v. Defenders of Wildlife*: The Supreme Court's Slash and Burn Approach to Environmental Standing, Environmental Law Reporter 1993, p. 10036.

Scalia's approach, which is to be framed within the context of U.S. constitutional law, as exceptional and not transposable to the European context. Generally speaking, the chances that a legal action aimed at a substantive review of recovery efforts would lead to a favourable outcome were indeed also severely restricted within many countries in the EU. Whereas in some EU Member States environmental NGOs enjoyed a relative wide access to justice in environmental cases, sometimes even amounting to an *actio popularis* approach, legal actions launched by environmental NGOs in other EU Member States often clashed with strict standing rules.[63] To give but a few examples, in Germany and Austria the renowned (notorious?) '*Schutznorm*' theory was prevalent, according to which the *locus standi* of natural persons or other persons requires the infringement of an individual, subjective right, which effectively barred environmental NGOs from claiming standing in environmental cases. In Belgium, which opted for an intermediate approach, the Supreme Court cautiously dismissed legal actions launched by environmental NGOs that failed to prove concrete injury.[64] In Sweden, in turn, a reserved approach to public interest litigation, blocking most actions launched by environmental NGOs, persisted until recently.[65]

Also at the level of the European Court of Justice (CJEU), a surprisingly conservative approach to *locus standi* in cases relating to EU protected sites (Natura 2000) was maintained. In 2003, Advocate General Kokott notoriously held in her – in other respects very progressive – Opinion in *Waddenzee* that '(u) nlike in the case of rules on the quality of the atmosphere or water, the protection of common natural heritage is of particular interest but not a right established for the benefit of individuals. The close interest of individuals can be promoted only indirectly, as a reflex so to speak'.[66]

Be that as it may, procedural rules concerning access to justice are not set in stone. The past ten years have seen a remarkable shift in the jurisprudential approach to the traditional standing requirements in environmental cases, which seems to offer more perspective for judicial activism in the realm of ecological restoration. As is widely known, the entry into force of the UNECE Convention on Access to Information, Public Participation in Decision-making and Access to Justice in Environmental Matters[67] within the EU – better known

63 For an overview see: *J. Darpö*, Effective Justice? Synthesis Report of the Study on the Implementation of Articles 9.3 and 9.4 of the Aarhus Convention in the EU Member States of the European Union, 2013, http://ec.europa.eu/environment/aarhus/access_studies.htm (Accessed 10 April 2017).

64 Belgian Supreme Court, 19 November 1982, R.W. 1983–84, p. 2029.

65 See more on this topic: *Y. Epstein & J. Darpö*, The Wild has No Words: Environmental NGOs Empowered to Speak for Protected Species as Swedish Courts Apply EU and International Environmental Law, Journal of European Environmental & Planning Law 2013, 10(3), pp. 250–261.

66 Opinion Advocate General Kokott in Case C-127/02, *Waddenzee* [2004], para. 143.

67 Convention on Access to Information, Public Participation in Decision-making and Access to Justice in Environmental Matters, done at Aarhus, Denmark, 25 July 1998 (further referred to as the 'Aarhus Convention'). The Aarhus Convention entered into force on 1 October 2001.

as the 'Aarhus Convention' – was of great significance for access to justice in environmental cases within the EU. The Aarhus Convention, which has been dubbed a 'driving force for environmental democracy' by some[68], calls for the recognition of a number of procedural rights for individuals and NGOs with regard to the environment.

3.2. ARTICLE 9(3) OF THE AARHUS CONVENTION: A NEW PATHWAY FOR MORE PROGRESSIVE STANDING RULES?

By ratifying the Aarhus Convention in 2005[69], along with its EU Member States, the provisions of that convention have become an integral part of the legal order of the EU pursuant to Article 216(2) of the Treaty on the Functioning of the European Union (TFEU). The objective of the Aarhus Convention, is 'to contribute to the protection of the right of every person of present and future generations to live in an environment adequate to his or her health and well-being'. In spite of its apparent focus on the protection of human health, it also serves as seminal yardstick for ensuring effective legal protection and wide access to justice in biodiversity-related cases. Article 9 of the Aarhus Convention thus serves as an obvious point of departure in the quest for a more liberalized interpretation of national standing rules, a crucial precondition to launch public interest litigation in the context of the imminent extinction of an endangered species, such as the Wild hamster.

However, one should carefully categorize legal actions aimed at reviewing species action programmes within the specific scope of Article 9 of the Aarhus Convention, which distinguishes between different sets of legal standards in terms of possible review action. As such, a possible legal action to force an EU Member State to step up its restoration actions vis-à-vis an EU protected species has to be set apart from a classic administrative lawsuit aimed at reviewing a planning permit for a particular project listed in Annex I to the Aarhus Convention and/or other concrete specific activities that may have a significant effect on the environment. For the latter subject-matter, which encompasses specific activities for which public participation requirements apply, Article 9(2) of the Aarhus Convention grants environmental NGOs with legal standing *de lege*. However, these robust review guarantees are of little use in the context of more activist lawsuits targeting the failure to develop robust recovery programmes for EU

---

68 *J. Watts*, The Aarhus Convention: a Driving Force for Environmental Democracy, Journal of European Environmental & Planning Law 2005, pp. 3–4.

69 Council Decision 2005/370/EC of 17 February 2005 on the conclusion on behalf of the European Community, of the Convention on access to information, public participation in decision-making and access to justice in environmental matters, OJ 2005 L 124/1.

protected species.[70] This equally entails that the specific review procedures provided for in secondary EU legislation, for instance under Article 11 of the Environmental Impact Assessment (EIA) Directive[71], will be ineffective in this respect.

By contrast, Article 9(3) of the Aarhus Convention contains a more generally phrased citizen suit clause which might help environmental NGOs to overcome conservative standing rules in restoration-based lawsuits. Pursuant to Article 9(3) of the Aarhus Convention, Contracting Parties have to ensure that 'members of the public have access to administrative or judicial procedures to challenge acts and omissions by private parties and public authorities which contravene provisions of its national law relating to the environment'. As is widely known, though, the Grand Chamber of the CJEU denied direct effect to Article 9(3) of the Aarhus Convention in its 2011 ruling in *Lesoochranárske Zoskupenie VLK I*[72] since, in its view, this clause did not contain any clear and precise obligation capable of directly regulating the legal position of individuals.[73] Furthermore, whereas the EU legislature introduced an express legal standing right based on the right to participate in secondary EU environmental law, it has so far failed to adopt a new Directive aimed at further implementing Article 9(3).[74] Yet in spite of the above-mentioned reservations, there are several reasons why Article 9(3) of the Aarhus Convention is bound to play an increasingly important role as leverage for environmental NGOs claiming standing in lawsuits revolving around EU protected species.[75]

3.2.1. A high-water mark for procedural obstacles to environmental litigation

Focusing first on the alleged broad wording of Article 9(3) of the Aarhus Convention, it needs to be reiterated that the lack of direct effect of the latter provision has not barred the CJEU from underscoring that the provision, although drafted in broad terms, still aimed to ensure effective environmental protection.[76] In its decision in *Lesoochranárske Zoskupenie VLK I*, the CJEU concluded that 'if the effective protection of EU environmental law is not to

70 In theory, though, it is not excluded to claim judicial review under the terms of Article 9(2) of the Aarhus Convention for plans, programs and regulations, that are, according to national law, subject to participation requirements. See also: *United Nations Economic Commission for Europe*, The Aarhus Convention: An Implementation Guide, 2nd Edition, 2014, p. 193.

71 See Article 11 of Directive 2011/92/EU on the assessment of the effects of certain public and private projects on the environment, OJ 2011 L 21/1 (further referred to as the 'EIA Directive').

72 Case C-240/09, *Lesoochranárske zoskupenie VLK I* [2011] ECR I-01255.

73 Ibid, para. 45.

74 Proposal for a Directive of the European Parliament and of the Council on access to justice in environmental matters, COM(2003)624.

75 See also: *J. Darpö & Y. Epstein*, Thrown to the Wolves – Sweden Once Again Flouts EU Standards on Species Protection and Access to Justice, Nordic Environmental Law Journal 2015, pp. 15–16.

76 *Lesoochranárske zoskupenie VLK I, supra* note 72, para. 46. See more extensively on the EU's implementation of the third pillar of the Aarhus Convention: *M. Hedeman-Robinson*, EU

be undermined, it is inconceivable that Article 9(3) of the Aarhus Convention be interpreted in such a way as to make it in practice impossible or excessively difficult to exercise rights conferred by EU law'[77], thereby implicitly reaffirming the duty of consistent interpretation that rests upon the national courts in this respect. And thus Article 9(3) of the Aarhus Convention could still indirectly be used as interpretation standard when national courts are confronted with ambivalent national procedural rules.

Granted, the 2011 ruling does not as such impose the obligation on national courts to directly set aside or disregard national rules that are contrary to Article 9(3). Nor does Article 9(3) of the Aarhus Convention provide a customised citizen suit right. Either way, national courts are henceforth obliged to interpret national standing criteria and procedural rules, which are often formulated in broad terms, so as to make it possible to challenge decisions or omissions contravening environmental law. Since it can be assumed that most national procedural rules will not expressly bar procedures seeking injunctive relief, Article 9(3) of the Aarhus Convention will probably serve as a useful benchmark against which traditional standing rules are re-interpreted in the specific context of environmental litigation.[78] For one, the default position of the CJEU in *Lesoochranárske zoskupenie VLK I* has already inspired several national courts, such as the Belgian Supreme Court, to reconsider their rigid approach to *locus standi* for environmental NGOs in the context of environmental legislation.[79] All this underlines the strong potential of Article 9(3) of the Aarhus Convention in terms of achieving environmental accountability before national courts, even in the context of restoration-based litigation.

3.2.2. The relatively wide material scope of Article 9(3) of the Aarhus Convention

Subsequently, it needs to be analysed to what extent species recovery plans are reviewable actions pursuant to the Aarhus Convention. As to the flexibility the Contracting Parties enjoy when implementing Article 9(3) of the Aarhus Convention, it is precisely the broad scope of that provision that makes it a highly interesting clause on which more activist types of legal action can be based, such as restoration-based claims in the context of imminent species extinction. Indeed, decisions that fall outside the scope of the first and second pillars of the Aarhus Convention – for instance because they do not relate to the stringent information and public participation rights guaranteed under this framework – should still be open to review under the terms of Article 9(3) of the Aarhus Convention. As is widely known, only decisions enacted by bodies or institutions acting in their

Implementation of the Aarhus Convention's Third Pillar: Back to the Future over Access to Environmental Justice, Part I, European Environmental and Energy Law 2014, 23, pp. 102–114.

77 *Lesoochranárske zoskupenie VLK I, supra* note 72, para. 49.

78 Opinion Advocate General Kokott in Case 243/15, Lesoochranárske zoskupenie VLK [2016], para. 96.

79 Belgian Supreme Court, 11 June 2013.

legislative or judicial capacity can be excluded from judicial review under Article 9 of the Aarhus Convention.[80] Previous findings and recommendations of the Aarhus Compliance Committee have already revealed that acts of a general nature, such as land use plans and other regulations, should be challengeable under Article 9(3) of the Aarhus Convention.[81] Therefore, it would not be a stretch to argue that also species recovery action programmes fall within the substantive scope of Article 9(3) of the Aarhus Convention, even when such programmes often lack direct binding effects.

Moreover, the CJEU has acknowledged that members of the public who are directly affected should be able to challenge relevant plans and programmes (or the failure to adopt such plans) within the scope of EU environmental law.[82] While it remains to be seen whether the latter case-law also is transposable to biodiversity-related proceedings, it can be submitted that also species conservation plans must equally be subject to judicial review under the terms of Article 9(3) of the Aarhus Convention. Likewise, since Article 9(3) of the Aarhus Convention also refers to 'omissions', it is clear that the failure of a government to adopt certain measures, plans or programmes which are obligatory under national or EU environmental law can also be tackled through the lens of Article 9(3) of the Aarhus Convention. It is even not excluded to base such legal actions upon procedural grounds, since such programmes will need to be subjected to prior public participation in some instances. For one, recovery programmes might still qualify as 'plans and programmes' within the meaning of Article 7 of the Aarhus Convention. As a preliminary conclusion, it can therefore be maintained that failure to promulgate adequate recovery measures for EU protected species, such as the Wild hamster, constitutes a reviewable action in view of Article 9(3) of the Aarhus Convention.

3.2.3. *More liberal standing criteria in environmental cases?*

As to the controversial issue of standing in environmental cases, Article 9(3) of the Aarhus Convention forces the parties to the Convention to provide access to the review procedures for 'members of the public' if they meet the criteria, if any, laid down in national law. Admittedly, Article 9(3) of the Aarhus Convention does not refer to 'members of the public concerned' but to 'members of the public'. Therefore, no direct standing *de lege* is granted to environmental NGOs by Article 9(3) of the Aarhus Convention.

---

80 See Article 2(2) d of the Aarhus Convention.

81 See for instance: Communication ACCC/C/2005/11 (Belgium), ECE/MPPP/C.1/2006/4/Add.2, para. 31; Communication ACCC/C/2008/32 (Part I) (European Union), para. 72–74.

82 Joined Cases C-165 to 167/09, *Stichting Natuur en Milieu* [2011] ECRI-04599, para. 100. This case related to programmes that EU Member States were required to adopt according to Article 4 of Directive 2001/82/EC of 23 October 2001 on national emission ceilings for certain atmospheric pollutants (NEC Directive). See also: *L. Squitani & H. van Rijswick*, Improving Legal Certainty and Adaptability in the Programmatic Approach, Journal of Environmental Law 2016, 28, p. 445.

Given the broad definition of the concept of 'the public'[83], though, it can nevertheless be upheld that it effectively covers any natural or legal persons, including environmental organisations. Even so, the referral to 'the criteria, if any, laid down in national law' seems to provide a great deal of freedom to the parties to the Convention in delimiting the scope of the review procedures. Yet these procedural criteria should not be used to the detriment of the legal standing of environmental NGOs.

The question now is whether an environmental NGO might claim standing in a legal proceeding aimed to stave off the extinction of an endangered species. Amongst others, the question arises to what extent the failure to adopt comprehensive species recovery plans can constitute a procedural injury for standing purposes. Again, it might be interesting to briefly turn to the above-mentioned U.S. case law on standing in the context of nature conservation cases. Interestingly, the U.S. Supreme Court was prepared to accept that 'the desire to use or observe an animal species, even for purely aesthetic purposes, is undeniably a cognizable interest for purpose of standing' in its landmark decision in *Lujan v. Defenders of Wildlife*. Even so, the majority still held that the environmental NGO at issue did not succeed in showing either 'that the listed species were in fact being threatened by funded activities abroad' or 'that one or more of (its) members would thereby by 'directly' affected'.[84] Ironically, Justice Kennedy and Justice David Souter held in their concurring opinion that the injury-in-fact requirement would have been complied with if only an airline ticket to the affected geographic areas with endangered species in question had been produced. It is not surprising that one of the lessons environmentalists took home from these rulings was that harm done to the general public or the environment, did not *per se* suffice to claim redress before a court in the U.S. And while the ruling in *Lujan v. Defenders of Wildlife* did not constitute a definite obstacle to more progressive litigation tacts in conservation matters, it still stands out as a striking example of a more conservative approach to standing in environmental cases.

It goes without saying that, if the latter view were to prevail within the context of EU law, this would evidently seriously limit access to justice in the context of species-restoration litigation. However, such approach obiously would be at odds with the rationale underpinning the Aarhus Convention. Indeed, already in one of its first findings on the issue of standing in environmental cases, the Aarhus Compliance Committee underscored that the parties to the Convention cannot use the clause 'if they meet the criteria, if any, laid down in national law' as an excuse for introducing or maintaining criteria that are so strict that they effectively bar all or almost all environmental organisations from challenging acts

[83] See Article 2(4) of the Aarhus Convention which defines the notion as follows: 'one or more natural or legal persons, and, in accordance with national legislation or practice, their associations, organizations or groups'.

[84] *Lujan v. Defenders of Wildlife*, *supra* note 60, p. 563.

or omissions that contravene national law relating to the environment.[85] In other words, access to justice ought to be the rule and not the exception, which seems to hint to a more liberal approach to the admissibility criteria in comparison with the above-mentioned approach of the U.S. Supreme Court.

Moreover, the decisions of the Aarhus Compliance Committee are not a standalone case. A similar rationale is echoed in the CJEU's landmark ruling in *Trianel*. While the latter ruling explicitly related to the former Article 10a of the EIA Directive, implementing Article 9(2) of the Aarhus Convention, the CJEU's holding that national standing rules cannot 'deprive environmental protection organisations (...) of the opportunity of playing the role granted to them both by Directive 85/337 and by the Aarhus Convention', also resonates on a wider level.[86] It bears mentioning that a similar approach is equally to come forward within the context of restoration-based lawsuits that fall within the scope of Article 9(3) of the Aarhus Convention. In particular, since the CJEU was explicitly adamant to reassert in paragraph 46 of the latter judgement that 'it would be contrary to the objective of giving the public concerned wide access to justice and at odds with the principle of effectiveness if such organisations were not allowed to rely on the impairment of rules of EU environment law solely on the ground that those rules protect the public interest'.

In addition, it is to be noted that the beneficial health effects of biodiversity are increasingly conformed by recent scientific studies[87], which might further pave the way for biodiversity-related lawsuits initiated by private individuals. At present, though, recovery-based litigation focussing on the plight of specific species will stand better chance if initiated by environmental NGOs. Thus, in view of Article 9(3) of the Aarhus Convention, environmental NGOs are no longer be required to provide the courts with evidence relating to possible breaches of its property rights or effects upon its research activities in order to be granted standing. In sum, within the framework of restoration-based litigation within the EU, Article 9(3) of the Aarhus Convention appears to grant standing to environmental associations which have the promotion of the conservation of nature and endangered species as their primary statutory objective.

3.2.4. Effective legal remedies, also in restoration-based cases?

Evidently, the prospect of a swift outcome of a national court proceedings will play a crucial role for environmental NGOs when considering the utility of launching legal actions over alleged failures to enact more progressive environmental or conservation plans. In terms of the review procedures that need to be provided

---

85 ACCC Belgium, *supra* note 81, para. 35; Communication ACCC/C/2006/18 (Denmark), ECE/MP/PP/2008/Add. 4, para. 31, 35 and 41.

86 Trianel, *supra* note 24, para. 44.

87 See for instance: *P. ten Brink et al.*, The Health and Social Benefits of Nature and Biodiversity Protection. A report for the European Commission (ENV.B.3/ETU/2014/0039), Institute for European Environmental Policy, London/Brussels, 2016.

for, Article 9 (3) of the Aarhus Convention contains relatively little explicit hints. It merely states that the public should have access to administrative *or* judicial proceedings. Accordingly, Contracting Parties to the Aarhus Convention are not as such required to provide court review procedures to adhere to Article 9(3) of the Aarhus Convention, as long as adequate administrative review procedures are available for environmental NGOs before administrative review bodies. Contracting Parties therefore do not have the primary obligation to provide for review procedures for judicial bodies in order to achieve compliance. It bears reiteration that instruments such as species recovery plans or conservation plans are often poorly regulated in the applicable national or regional laws. In many instances, even the procedures to be followed when drafting up such schemes are not comprehensively laid down itself by legislative or regulatory provisions, let alone that many EU Member States have provided for specific administrative review procedures which allow environmental NGOs to tackle deficiencies in the conservation schemes for endangered species. And even if this were the case, it still needs to be ensured that such proceedings meet the general requirements set out by Article 9(4) and 9(5) of the Aarhus Convention in term of effectiveness. The duties relating to fair and equitable procedures, among others, will therefore be key considerations in this respect.[88]

3.3. A COMPLEMENTARY ROAD TO STANDING: ARTICLE 12(1) OF THE HABITATS DIRECTIVE AND EFFECTIVE JUDICIAL PROTECTION?

Having established that Article 9(3) and (4) of the Aarhus Convention might be seminal to provide environmental NGOs with the necessary legal standing in lawsuits aimed at saving endangered species, it remains worthwhile to contemplate to what extent the general principles of EU law can also not provide for an additional legal basis in this respect. While it is certainly true that the provisions of the Aarhus Convention are to be approached as an integral part of EU law, invoking basic principles of EU law, such as the notion of direct effect, might help to further underpin an activist approach towards environmental litigation. Either way, recent jurisprudential evolutions illustrate that EU law and Article 9(3) and (4) of the Aarhus Convention are mutually reinforcing, especially since they seem to offer environmental NGOs enforceable substantive rights in the context of EU environmental law.[89] Yet legally speaking it remains interesting to analyze

---

88 Aarhus implementation guide, *supra* note 70, pp. 200–202. See also regarding the possibility to seek interim measures: Case C-416/10, Križan [2013] ECLI:EU:C:2013:8, para. 109–110.

89 See also on this topic, albeit in the context of typical administrative review procedures, in which the legality of one or more specific derogations under EU species protection law is challenged: *Darpö & Epstein*, *supra* note 75, pp. 16–19.

the specific articulation between those principles and restoration-based actions in court more into detail.

3.3.1. *Direct effect as a gateway to better legal protection?*

In the context of strictly protection species, reference must first be made to the theory of 'direct effect' and its potential repercussions on the standing of entities invoking possible contraventions of directly applicable provisions of EU law. Admittedly, the CJEU has still to shed light on the question whether the provisions on strict species protection, as included in Article 12(1) of the Habitats Directive, have direct effect. However, in view of the outcome of *Waddenzee*, where the CJEU accepted the direct applicability of Article 6(3) of the Habitats Directive (which lays down the protection duties applicable in the context of EU protected sites (Natura 2000)), it is certainly not unthinkable for the CJEU to reach a similar conclusion with respect to Article 12(1) of the Habitats Directive.[90]

Some national courts, such as the Swedish Supreme Administrative Court, have deduced from the CJEU's ruling in *Waddenzee* that environmental NGOs had the right, in accordance with the Habitats Directive, to enjoy effective protection in national courts.[91] Arguably, one might submit that Article 12(1) of the Habitats Directive in itself leaves distinctively more freedom to the EU Member States than Article 6(3) of the Habitats Directive, which was at issue in *Waddenzee*. Even so, the mere fact that a provision leaves some discretion to the government does not preclude its use of a clear yardstick to assess the adequacy and legality of the substantive review of plans and programmes aimed at the conservation of protected species.[92]

3.3.2. *Effective legal protection as an attractive side-route?*

The above notwithstanding, it remains doubtful whether environmental NGOs are able to claim *locus standi* exclusively from the CJEU's holding in *Waddenzee*, as for instance the Swedish Supreme Administrative Court held in its recent case-law.[93] A more activist types of litigation ought also make reference to the recent jurisprudential evolutions before the CJEU as regards effective legal protection in environmental cases. For one, in its previous case-law relating to air quality, the CJEU had already acknowledged that *individuals* are entitled to take legal action if there is a risk that binding limit values designed to protect, amongst others,

---

90 Case C-127/02, *Waddenzee* [2004] ECR I-7405, para. 66.

91 For exact references, see: *Darpö, supra* note 55, pp. 278–280.

92 See for instance the case-law regarding the direct applicability of the screening rules laid down by Article 4(2) and 4(3) of the EIA Directive: Case C-73/95, *Kraaijeveld* [1995] ECR I-5403, para. 56.

93 *Darpö, supra* note 55, p. 279.

public health may be exceeded.[94] Yet as the EU Habitats Directive does not relate to public health, Advocate General Kokott refused to apply a similar progressive reasoning in relation to the rights that were accorded to the environment by the Habitats Directive back in 2003. In itself, EU environmental law does not seem to grant an enforceable right to resilient biodiversity and species populations either. As alluded to above, this led Advocate General Kokott to conclude that Article 6(3) of the Habitats Directive can only be relied upon before court by environmental NGOs to the extent that avenues of legal redress against measures infringing the abovementioned provisions are already available to them under national law.[95] Furthermore, the CJEU itself did, at the time, not go that far in explicitly granting environmental NGOs new substantive rights or legal remedies in the specific context of Article 6(3) of the Habitats Directive.[96]

Be that as it may, in the meantime a remarkable shift in jurisprudence has been recorded, which leaves ample room for a more progressive understanding of the rights environmental NGOs can derive from possible infringements of the EU Nature Directives. Already back in 2008, Advocate General Sharpston noted that, even in the absence of the provisions on access to justice laid down in Article 9(3) of the Aarhus Convention, the established case-law of the CJEU 'contains numerous statements to the effect that EU Member States cannot lay down procedural rules which render the exercise of rights conferred by Community law impossible'.[97]

The latter line of interpretation constituted a correct understanding of the legal state of affairs in 2008. At the time, it was established case-law that the national procedural rules governing actions aimed at safeguarding rights under EU law must be no less favourable than those governing similar domestic actions (*principle of equivalence*) and must not render it in practice impossible or excessively difficult to exercise rights conferred by EU law (*principle of effectiveness*). It is therefore of little importance that the Habitats Directive lacked explicit provisions on access to justice. For one, in its 2011 ruling in *Lesoochranárske zoskupenie VLK I* the CJEU reinvigorated the link between Article 9(3) of the Aarhus Convention and the principle of effective judicial protection. To be more precise, the CJEU held that, when faced with a potential infringement of the Habitats Directive in respect of strictly protected species (*i.e.* hunting decisions regarding the Brown bear (*Ursus arctos*)), a national court must, in order to ensure effective judicial protection in the fields covered by EU environmental law, interpret national procedural law in line with Article 9(3) of the Aarhus Convention.[98] And thus also more activist

94 E.g. Case C-361/88, *Commission v Germany* [1991] ECR I-2567, para. 16; Case C-59/89, *Commission v Germany* [1991] ECR I-2607, para. 19; Case C-58/89, *Commission v Germany* [1991] ECR I-4983, para. 14; and Case C-298/95, *Commission v Germany* [1996] ECR I-6747, para. 16.

95 Opinion Advocate General Kokott, *supra* note 66, para. 144.

96 *Waddenzee*, *supra* note 90, para. 70.

97 Opinion Advocate-General Sharpston in Case C-263/08, *Djurgården* [2009], para. 80.

98 *Lesoochranárske zoskupenie VLK I*, *supra* note 72, para. 50.

litigation strategies, for instance within the realm of restoration law, are no longer beyond the limit of the law.

By reasserting in its 2014 *ClientEarth* ruling that natural or *legal persons* are entitled to take legal action where there is a risk that limit values designed to protect public health may be exceeded[99], the CJEU implicitly opened the door for an argumentation by which environmental NGOs can claim that an infringement of the EU Nature Directives also comes down to an infringement of their own substantive rights, at least to the extent that they have listed the conservation of endangered species amongst their explicit statutory purposes. It would indeed remain hard to justify why an environmental NGO might claim substantive rights within the framework of EU air quality law while denying such rights within the context of the EU Nature Directives. Such distinction might be defendable in the context of private individuals, since it might be put forward that their health is not directly affected by the loss of a protected species. Yet it makes little sense in the context of environmental NGOs, which are obviously also not directly affected by air pollution either. Admittedly, it would be incorrect to state that the 2014 *Client Earth* ruling constituted the first decision in which the CJEU reasserted the principle of effective legal protection in the context of a lawsuit that was initiated by an environmental NGO. In fact, the CJEU had already done so in its *Janecek* ruling in 2008[100] and also reaffirmed this approach in its *Stichting Natuur en Milieu* decision in 2011.[101] In its decision in *Client Earth*, though, the CJEU explicitly referred to the principle of sincere cooperation, as mentioned in Article 4(3) Treaty on European Union (TEU), and to the duty to provide sufficiently effective legal remedies in the fields covered by EU law, as mentioned in Article 19(1) TEU.[102]

It might therefore be maintained that the latter principles, while ostensibly vague, offer additional support for more activist types of legal actions, for instance in the specific context of the EU Nature Directives. And indeed, if an environmental NGO such as *ClientEarth* can claim standing in cases of infringement of EU air quality norms, why not accept standing to sue for environmental NGOs in restoration-based cases?

As recalled by Advocate General Kokott in her Opinion of 30 June 2016 in *Lesoochranárske zoskupenie VLK II*, the simple fact that the interests of environmental NGOs are explicitly recognized in law entails that they must at least be capable of being concerned by an infringement of directly applicable provisions of EU environmental law, such as Article 12(1) of the Habitats Directive, to an extent sufficient to enable them to rely on those provisions

---

99 *ClientEarth*, *supra* note 30, para. 56.

100 Case C-237/07, *Janecek* [2008] ECR I-6221, para. 42. See also the case-law mentioned *supra* in footnote 94.

101 *Stichting Natuur en Milieu*, *supra* note 82, para. 94.

102 *ClientEarth*, *supra* note 30, para. 52.

before the national courts.[103] As such, the Slovak procedural law at stake in the above-mentioned proceedings related to permitting policies in the context of Article 6(3) of the Habitats Directive, in which an environmental NGO wanted to challenge the legality of a decision to build an enclosure on a Natura 2000 site. In other words, the case did not explicitly relate to judicial review in the context of recovery plans. Still, in its final ruling the CJEU did not hesitate to underline the importance of effective judicial protection in the context of the specific rights inherent in the right of public participation upon which the environmental NGO relied.[104] Accordingly, one might imagine environmental NGOs base more activist lawsuits on a rationale akin to the one used by the CJEU in its recent jurisprudence related to Article 9(3) of the Aarhus Convention. For, even if there is arguably more leeway for EU Member States when implementing the latter provision, the principle of effective legal protection as enshrined in Article 47 of the EU Charter on Fundamental Rights equally seems to urge for a more benevolent approach towards standing in restoration-based proceedings.

3.4. SEPARATION OF POWERS VERSUS MANDATORY INJUNCTION: BEYOND THE TRADITIONAL APPROACH TOWARDS THE *TRIAS POLITICA*

When addressing the effectiveness of legal remedies available under EU environmental law, especially in the context of injunctive relief aimed at forcing the competent authorities to adopt more effective recovery measures for an endangered species, one almost automatically arrives at the point of the *trias politica* doctrine. According to this theory, the powers of government are distributed among three separate branches: the legislative, the executive, and the judiciary branch. In the U.S., which again presents itself as an interesting introductory case-study in this respect, this approach it often coined the 'political question' doctrine' in legal literature.[105] While obviously the exact articulation of the *trias politica* doctrine might differ from one jurisdiction to another – taking into account the distinctive legal traditions – it is fair to say that in many courts a more reluctant approach towards the latter theory has prevailed until recently. Under this so-called traditional view, judges should not hear cases which deal directly with issues that, pursuant to the respective constitutional tradition, should be the sole responsibility of the other branches of government. Judges would thus not have the authority to look behind policy determinations. Therefore, it would not be possible to ask judges to order the government to enact

103 Opinion Advocate General Kokott, *supra* note 78, para. 45–53.

104 Case C-243/15, *Lesoochranárske zoskupenie VLK* [2016] ECLI:EU:C:2016:838, para. 58–63.

105 The political question doctrine was established by the U.S. Supreme Court in its Baker v. Carr ruling. See: U.S. Supreme Court, *Baker v. Carr*, 369 U.S. 186 (1962).

rules or regulations aimed at the recovery of endangered species.[106] Such actions would be non-justiciable. The argument goes that law enforcement is to remain an exclusive competence of the executive branch.[107] It is not surprising, then, to notice that the separation of powers doctrine constituted a formidable barrier for earlier examples of third party enforcement in the context of environmental law. For instance, several first-generation climate cases before U.S. courts were dismissed with reference to the non-justiciability of the political questions that were related to it.[108]

Yet, again some parallels can be drawn to the jurisprudence at the other side of the Atlantic. Also in the Netherlands, the Supreme Court held in its renowned *Waterpakt* case that the *trias politica* would be infringed if a court was asked to order that formal law be created to make up for the fact that the Netherlands had not implemented the EU Nitrates Directive.[109] Similarly, the Belgian Supreme Court declined to uphold a claim in which the Belgian Federal State would have been ordered to alter the current routes used when operating the Belgian national airport.[110] It goes without saying that the separation of powers doctrine will equally have to be faced in the context of restoration-based cases as a possible counterargument, especially when environmental NGO seek a court order requiring the competent authorities to take a specific type of recovery and/or restoration measure.

3.4.1. Towards a more liberal approach of the separation of powers doctrine?

As a first disclaimer, however, it is important to temper the rather traditional understanding of the separation of powers doctrine, which has until recently been a powerful obstacle to more activist forms of environmental litigation. As reiterated by the Dutch District Court in its 2015 climate case ruling, the three traditional branches of government are unmistakably interrelated.[111] This understanding of the *trias politica* doctrine is better known as the well-known system of 'checks and balances'. Consequently, public interest litigation, also in environmental cases revolving around species recovery, could serve as an important correction for an executive branch that misdirects its important legislative purposes.[112] Likewise, one could submit that the question is not so

---

106 This view was amongst others shared by Justice Scalia of the U.S. Supreme Court. See more extensively: *Sheldon, supra* note 62, pp. 10040–10041.

107 See along these lines, albeit in the specific context of the Dutch climate case: *Bergkamp & Hanekamp, supra* note 26, pp. 103–107.

108 See for instance: *Comer et al. v Murphy Oil USA, Inc., et al.*, Civil Action, No. 1:05-CV-436-LG-RHW, Order Granting Defendants' Motion to Dismiss.

109 Dutch Supreme Court, 21 March 2003 ECLI:NL:HR:2003:AE8462, 21/03/2013.

110 Belgian Supreme Court, 3 January 2008, case no. C/06.0322.N/1.

111 Urgenda, *supra* note 27, para. 4.95.

112 *Sheldon, supra* note 62, p. 10040.

much whether a case might have political implications, since such a rigid test would render virtually all legislative and executive actions immune to legal challenges.[113] Rather, the more fundamental issue at stake is whether granting a claim to come forward with more robust restoration measures would require the courts to second-guess political decisions which falls exclusively within the scope of another branch of a government.[114] Put in the specific context of this chapter, it therefore needs to be determined whether the failure to come forward with comprehensive protection and recovery measures can be determined by a national court on the basis of clear-cut rules and science. The answer to the previous questions can be affirmative in the context of EU protected species such as the Wild hamster, the fate of which could be sealed in the absence of further actions. For, indeed, one cannot argue that there is a lack of judicially discoverable and manageable standards to resolve the issue (see *infra*).

On the other hand, one cannot ignore the sharp criticism that has been voiced regarding the compatibility of the Dutch District Court's ruling in the climate case with the separation of powers doctrine. Several authors have questioned whether the court order was fully in line with the *trias politica*, especially since the court order was based on a reputedly vague provision of Dutch tort law.[115] However, it would be wrong to assume that such counterargument would remain confined to climate change-based legal actions. It might also inspire critics of a more activist litigation strategy in restoration-based lawsuits. Yet, whereas this criticism might be particularly attractive to dismiss climate change-related claims based upon tort law[116], it does not necessarily need to lead to the dismissal of restoration-based lawsuits within the context of EU nature conservation law. Indeed, possible future litigation within the context of EU nature conservation law is to be distinguished from tort-based climate litigation. For, while the Dutch court based its injunction in the climate case ruling on the admittedly vague 'duty of care' laid down in Dutch civil law, the EU species protection rules, which are arguably more strictly phrased, can serve as a well-defined standard of review (see also more in detail, *infra*).

That is not to say that restoration-based litigation based upon tort law or more broadly formulated provisions of international or EU law is to be set aside as a senseless strategy for environmental NGOs. However, when explicitly

113 *A. Soete & H. Schoukens*, Klimaatverandering in de rechtbank. De rechter als scherprechter bij een falend milieubeleid?, Nieuw Juridisch Weekblad 2016, pp. 189–191.

114 In her Opinion of 10 November 2016, Judge Ann Aiken of the Federal District Court for the District of Oregon used this rationale when discussing the question as to the compatibility of the climate action with the political question doctrine. See: *Juliana*, *supra* note 29, p. 10.

115 *Bergkamp & Hanekamp*, *supra* note 26, pp. 103–107; *de Graaf & Jans*, *supra* note 27, pp. 223–227.

116 Note that several U.S. courts have already held that climate claims in tort law are nevertheless justiciable and not precluded on the basis of the political question doctrine. See more extensively: *J.R. May*, Political Question Doctrine, In: J.R. May (ed.), Principles of Constitutional Environmental Law, American Bar Association, 2011, pp. 215–241.

framed within the context of EU nature conservation law, which hints at an enforceable duty of EU Member States to conserve and/or restore a species at a favourable conservation status, judges might be less easily accused of 'making new law' instead of merely applying the existing regulations. As a result, national courts might be more inclined to favourably treat restoration claims focusing on a specific species than legal actions aiming for the establishment a more broader, ecosystem-based restoration approach for the wider landscape. Seeing the lack of enforceble landscape-wide restoration duties, the latter type of litigation will most probably face more formidable procedural hurdles, which renders a positive outcome in terms of restoration-based injunctions less likely. This is a paradoxical conclusion, which nevertheless appears inevitable in view of the traditional restraint *vis-à-vis* more activist court room actions.

Evidently, national courts will in any event apply the necessary deference to governmental expertise, the available science and the statutory discretion that is allowed by the applicable rules, especially when they are asked to review existing conservation efforts. Judges, when faced with such cases, will take great care in drafting a legal remedy, with respect for the competent authorities' margin of appreciation when achieving compliance with the EU Nature Directives. For instance, a national court could force a competent authority to take into account more realistic population targets and a specific time-frame within which the plight of an endangered species should be reversed. At the same time, however, it would leave it to the competent authorities to decide upon the precise measures that are needed to reverse the ongoing plight. It should nonetheless be noted that the leeway enjoyed by competent authorities is clearly narrowed when non-compliance with clear-cut rules of EU law could eventually lead to the imminent extinction of the said species, such as is the case with the Wild hamster. The same goes when the extinction of a species is to be approached as the immediate consequence of non-compliance with the protection duties over the previous decades.

Also other recent case-law developments seems to point towards a more activist understanding of the power to judicially review conservation duties in respect of endangered species. A remarkable example thereof can be found in the context of the U.S. 1973 Endangered Species Act. While U.S. courts mostly respect the discretion agencies enjoy when implementing species recovery plans, a different outcome was achieved in the case *Sierra Club v Lujan*. In this case, the court finally decided to sanction the competent agency's failure to implement a recovery plan for more than eight years was jeopardizing several listed species. This ultimately led the court to order the competent agency to take the necessary steps to implement the plan.[117] Whereas this ruling is not to be treated as an

[117] *Sierra Club v Lujan*, 36 Envt. Rep. Cas. (BNA), pp. 1543–1545. See more extensively on the specific role of 'recovery plans' within the context of the U.S. Endangered Species Act: *D.D.*

illustration of a more wide-spread shift towards strict scrutiny in the context of recovery-based litigation in the U.S., it still attests to the potentialities of such strategy in cases of manifest and persisting negligence. In recent legal literature, a more moderate approach towards the political question doctrine is promoted as well, under which the latter theory does not bar legal claims with political ramifications but rather advocates 'an attitude of judicial restraint adopted by the judges when they are asked to review certain categories of sensitive decisions'.[118] In my view, a similar conclusion is in order in the context of more activist legal proceedings within the realm of EU environmental law.

3.4.2. *The re-emergence of Article 9(4) of the Aarhus Convention: effective judicial protection vs the traditionalist approach to the separation of powers theory?*

Regarding the recent shift towards environmental accountability equally reference must be made to Article 9(4) of the Aarhus Convention, which stipulates that trials 'shall provide adequate and effective remedies, including injunctive relief as appropriate, and be fair, equitable, timely and not prohibitively expensive'. This provision, as alluded to above, also applies to restoration-based lawsuits in the context of the EU Nature Directives. Most interestingly, the Aarhus Implementation Guide, which has received considerable attention in the past from the EU courts[119], further elaborates on those adequate and effective remedies. The Guide states that '(w)hen initial or additional damage may still happen and the violation is continuing, or where prior damage can be reversed or mitigated, courts and administrative review bodies must be able to issue an order to stop or to undertake certain action'.[120] Even more so, a stance assuming that indirect political implications arising from a legal action are sufficient to render it 'non-justiciable', would be at odds with the very purpose, and the objective of the Aarhus Convention.

Some portend that, by opening the doors of the courts to more activist types of litigation, concerns about non-compliance should exclusively be raised through the process of democratic elections.[121] In this respect, though, it is perhaps convenient to bear in mind that even in the U.S. Supreme Court's landmark decision in *Baker v Carr*, the Court ultimately concluded that the political question doctrine did not prevent the Court from reaching the merits of a challenge involving district reapportionment, an issue which is political by

Goble, Recovery, In: D.C. Baur & W.R. Irvin (eds.), Endangered Species Act. Law, Policy, and Perspectives, 2010, American Bar Association, pp. 70–104.

118 *P. Daly*, Justiciability and the "political question" doctrine, *Public Law*, 2010, p. 176.

119 See for example: Case T-396/06 *Stichting Milieu Natuur en Milieu and Pesticide Action Network Europe v European Commission* (GC, 14 June 2012), para. 68.

120 *Aarhus implementation guide*, *supra* note 70, p. 200.

121 *Bergkamp & Hanekamp*, *supra* note 26, pp. 102–105.

nature.[122] This fact alone strikingly illustrates the difficulties to be faced when distinguishing between 'apolitical' or 'neutral' and politically charged lawsuits. It is a determination which could also indirectly influence EU judges when appraising more 'activist' types of litigation. For, indeed, the alternative would require judges to indepedently decide upon the degree of "politicalness" applying inherently lose standards.

In view of relatively strict standards regarding the effectiveness of legal remedies, as mentioned in Article 9(4) of the Aarhus Convention, the more 'traditional' approaches to public interest litigation do no longer seem to hold. This is especially the case in a context of past non-compliance with the existing protection schemes. As is demonstrated below, the current predicament of many species is partly linked to underperformance of the existing protection schemes over the past decades. The plight of the Wild hamster constitutes but one of the more notorious examples thereof. And evidently it would be unacceptable to block judicial review in the context of a blatant non-compliance scenario. Even though Article 9(3) of the Aarhus Convention does not explicitly require the courts or administrative review bodies to review both the procedural and substantively legality of decision or omissions, it would be inconsistent to deny a review on the merits within the context of Article 9(3) of the Aarhus Convention merely because of the potential political effects it might generate. Most importantly, the CJEU has recently reasserted that, albeit within the context of Article 9(2) of the Aarhus Convention, the judicial review exercised by national courts cannot be confined to mere procedural defects of decisions yct also has to address potential substantive defects.[123] This all points towards more substantive legal review in the context of EU-related conservation and/or restoration cases.

3.4.3. The principle effective protection of Article 19(1) of the TEU

Within the context of EU law, though, it would be wrong to exclusively focus on Article 9(4) of the Aarhus Convention in order to align the quest for more substantive review of recent recovery actions with the separation of powers doctrine. Also EU law itself appears to urge national courts to reconsider their reluctant approaches to more activist types of environmental legal proceedings. Amongst others, the principle of effective protection, as mentioned in Article 19(1) of the TEU, equally applies within the context of litigation that relates to species that are protected under EU law. According to this provision, which consolidates earlier case-law developments[124], EU Member States shall

122 *Baker, supra* note 105.

123 Case C-72/12, *Gemeinde Altrip* [2013] ECLI:EU:C:2013:712, par. 37.

124 Case C-432/05, *Unibet* [2007] ECR I-2271, para. 65.

provide remedies sufficient to ensure effective legal protection in the fields covered by EU law. The question now arises whether this liberal understanding of the requirement to provide for effective legal remedies is able to trump the more outdated interpretations given to the principle of the separation of powers.

The previous case-law of the CJEU relating to the principle of procedural autonomy is not entirely irrelevant in this regard. Holding that the so-called principle of procedural autonomy is to be subject to the principle of effectiveness, the CJEU held that an action based on a EU law right should be subject to full compensation and that a national system which provided that compensation was subject to statutory limits would not be sufficiently effective.[125] In its landmark ruling in *Factortame I*, for one, the CJEU obliged the House of Lords to set aside a national rule which prevented an interim injunction from being issued against the Crown in order to ensure the full effectiveness of EU law.[126] And while the CJEU has acknowledged that EU law cannot be used to create *new* legal remedies, national courts are bound to interpret national procedural rules, wherever possible, in accordance with the principle of judicial protection.[127]

As demonstrated by the CJEU's recent decision in *Lesoochranárske Zoskupenie VLK II*, in which it was asked to ascertain whether specific Slovak procedural rules concerning the status of an environmental NGO during the course of administrative proceedings were compatible with the requirements of effective judicial protection, laid down in Article 47 of the European Charter on Fundamental rights, among others, national procedural rules need to safeguard rights granted to environmental NGOs by EU law.[128] Interestingly enough, the CJEU's Grand Chamber recognized that the principle of effective judicial protection, as laid down by EU law, and Article 9(4) of the Aarhus Convention are mutually supportive in ensuring effective legal remedies in nature conservation cases.[129] And while the Slovak proceedings at issue explicitly related to more 'traditional' type of administrative review action, it remains hard to see why the CJEU would not let a similar line of interpretation prevail in the context of Article 9(3) of the Aarhus Convention.[130] In addition, the CJEU's remarkably strict jurisprudence regarding the topic of legislative validation of permits within the context of Article 1(4) of the EIA Directive indicates that national courts are bound to scrutinize acts of national parliament whenever necessary to adhere to the requirements of EU environmental law.[131] Whereas scrutinizing acts of

125 Case C-106/77, *Simmenthal* [1978] ECR 629, para. 22–23.
126 Case C-213/89, *Factortame I* [1990] ECR I-3905, para. 20–23.
127 *Unibet*, *supra* note 124, par. 40.
128 *Lesoochranárske zoskupenie VLK II*, *supra* note 104, para. 62–65.
129 *Ibid*, para. 62.
130 Opinion Advocate General Kokott, *supra* note 78, para. 96.
131 Joined cases C-128/09 to C-131/09, C-134/09 and C-135/09, *Boxus and others* [2011] ECR I-9711, para. 53; Case C-182/10, *Solvay* [2012] ECLI:EU:C:2012:82, para. 48.

parliament inevitably encroaches upon the powers of the legislative branch of government, no mention was made in these cases of the separation of powers doctrine as a potential obstacle for the judicial review necessary in order to comply with Article 9(2) of the Aarhus Convention.[132] And while the CJEU might still reassess its stance in this regard against the backdrop of new lines of argumentation based upon the *trias politica* doctrine, it remains doubtful whether the main underpinnings of the above-cited jurisprudence will be altered any time soon.

But there is more. The mere fact that the CJEU itself did not shy away from subjecting the French recovery plans for the Wild hamster in the Alsace to a substantive review in its ruling of 9 June 2011 further proves this point.[133] Likewise, a remarkable parallel can be drawn with the air quality cases that have recently emerged within the scope of the EU Air Quality Directives. In this context, the CJEU has aptly underscored that while under Union law EU Member States have the necessary discretion to determine the content of action plans needed to ensure compliance with the EU's air quality standards, private citizens as well as environmental NGOs have the right to demand a substantive judicial review of such measures.[134] Whereas one could rightfully argue that the Habitats Directives contain less explicitly formulated substantive standards as to obligation to draw up recovery plans needed to ensure the survival and restoration of populations of protected species[135], the prevailing rationale is still similar. In the aftermath of the *ClientEarth* decision of the CJEU, the UK High Court did not see the *trias politica* doctrine as a barrier to check whether the air quality plans, which had been subsequently drawn up by the UK government, were able to achieve compliance with the UK's duties under EU law. Interestingly, the High Court acknowledged that a degree of discretion remains, although the clear-cut EU air quality standards and the continuing non-compliance pushed the Court to carry out a substantive review of the presented air quality plans.[136] Along similar lines, though, it might be claimed that the national courts are thus required to carry out a judicial review of the existing recovery plans for endangered species and, if necessary, order the competent authority to come forward with more robust recovery schemes.

---

132 See more extensively: *H. Schoukens*, Legislative Validation in Times of Environmental Democracy: Going Beyond the Deadlock or a Road to Nowhere? In: B. Vanheusden & L. Squitani (eds.), EU Environmental and Planning Law Aspects of Large-Scale Project, 2015, Intersentia, pp. 85–115.

133 *Commission v France, supra* note 52, para. 27–37.

134 *ClientEarth, supra* note 30, para. 57.

135 Article 23(1) of Directive 208/50/EC of the European Parliament and of the Council of 21 May 2008 explicitly lists the information that needs to be included in 'Air quality plans'.

136 UK High Court, *R (on the application of ClientEarth (No.2) v. Secretary of State for Environment, Food, Rural Affairs* [2016] EWHC 2740, para. 50–54.

4. SUBSTANTIVE ELEMENTS: TOWARDS A CLEAR-CUT RESTORATION DUTY UNDER EU NATURE CONSERVATION LAW FOR STRICTLY PROTECTED SPECIES?

Having established that environmental NGOs have enforceable environmental procedural rights at their disposal under EU and international law, the precise scope of the restoration duties incumbent on EU Member States vis à vis protected species, such as the Wild hamster, now needs to be examined. For, only when plaintiffs can establish the presence of clear-cut standards of review, will a court be found ready to reassess existing, allegedly inadequate conservation strategies. In the above analysis it has already been suggested that the EU Nature Directives might provide for a relatively straightforward benchmark in order to assess whether EU Member States comply with their conservation and recovery duties under the Habitats Directive. Nevertheless, given the novel character of such restoration-based claims, these reassertions merit a more detailed analysis against the backdrop of the most recent jurisprudential evolutions.

4.1. TOWARDS A DUTY TO RESTORE ENDANGERED SPECIES: GOING BEYOND THE STATUS QUO?[137]

4.1.1. A brief contextualisation of Article 12(1) of the Habitats Directive: going beyond 'paper' protection?

It needs little explanation to show that the persuasiveness of restoration-based claim before national courts will at least partly be determined by the strength of the substantive arguments presented. The first substantive topic to be addressed in the context of restoration-based litigation is whether the rules on strict species protection, as included in Article 12(1) of the Habitats Directive, leave any room for restoration-based litigation at all.

In order to find answers to these questions, first a fresh look at the system of strict species protection is in order. For several threatened species, the European legislator laid out strict protection duties, specifically aimed at protecting the actual species itself and the most important parts of their habitats, being the breeding sites and resting places, throughout the whole territory of EU Member States.[138] These species are listed in Annex IV to the Habitats Directive and the

[137] See also: *H. Schoukens*, Saving the Common hamster from extinction through the EU Habitats Directive: A mandatory recovery effort, a remediation of past non-compliance or an exercise in futility?, Nordic Environmental Law Journal 2017, pp. 59–97.

[138] *European Commission*, Guidance document on the strict protection of animal species of Community interest under the Habitats Directive 92/43/EEC, Brussels, 2007, p. 14 (further referred to as 'EC Strict Protection Guidance').

protection scheme associated therewith consists of strict protection measures for species.

The Wild hamster is a typical example of such a species since its habitat, which consists of meadows, grasslands and farm fields, significantly overlaps with agricultural used lands. Under Article 12(1) of the Habitats Directive, EU Member States must take the required measures to establish a system of strict protection for the animal species listed in Annex IV in their natural range, prohibiting deliberate disturbance of these species, particularly during the period of breeding, rearing, hibernation and migration and any deterioration or destruction of breeding sites or resting places.[139]

In view of the subsequent analysis, it is important to point out that the CJEU is particularly determined to safeguard the *effet utile* of the strict protection regime.

For one, the Court has shown itself increasingly stringent when reviewing the EU Member States' implementing regulations. In this respect, it is to be recalled that Article 12(1) of the Habitats Directive relates to individual specimen of the relevant protected species and is not limited to protected sites.[140] To give but one example, in its 2006 decision regarding the German implementation schemes, the CJEU underscored the intention of the EU legislator to give breeding grounds and resting places increased protection against acts causing their deterioration or destruction and denounced more flexible interpretations given to the protection rules.[141]

Moreover, the CJEU does not limit itself to checking whether the national protection rules ensure a full, clear and precise transposition of Article 12(1) of the Habitats Directive. It also investigates whether the EU Member States provide for the application of concrete, coherent and coordinated species protection measures to protect these species in the field, which is not unimportant in the context of restoration-based litigation. This second level of enforcement was adequately illustrated by the Court's landmark ruling as regards species protection in *Caretta caretta*.[142] The referenced case-law is not unimportant in view of the subsequent analysis, either. In the past few years, Ireland has been convicted for not having sufficiently protected several Annex IV bat species[143], while both Cyprus[144] and Greece[145] have been convicted for not having implemented sufficient protection measures for several endangered snake species.[146]

---

139 See also: *Schoukens & Bastmeijer*, *supra* note 3, pp. 132–145.
140 Case C-6/04, *Commission v United Kingdom* [2005] ECR I-9017, para 79.
141 Case C-98/03, *Commission v Germany* [2006] ECR I-53, para. 55.
142 Case C-103/00, *Commission v Greece* [2002] ECR I-1147.
143 Case C-183/05, *Commission v Ireland* [2007] ECR I-137.
144 Case C-340/10, *Commission v Cyprus* [2012] ECLI:EU:C:2012:143.
145 Case C-518/04, *Commission v Greece* [2006] ECR I-42.
146 Case C-504/14, *Commission v Greece* [2016] ECLI:EU:C:2016:105.

Most importantly, however, the CJEU has, as mentioned above, held France responsible for not having implemented sufficient protection measures to preserve the Wild hamster in the Alsace region.[147] While the CJEU has never explicitly stated that Article 12(1) of the Habitats Directive must be interpreted as an 'obligation of result', the strict scrutiny with which it assesses an EU Member State's protection efforts seems to suggest that it clearly goes beyond a traditional best-efforts clause.[148] The French hamster ruling of the CJEU moreover represents the first case in which the CJEU explicitly touched upon the duty of species recovery in the context of Annex IV species.

4.1.2. Beyond conservation, towards recovery: restoring species to a thriving condition?

Against this background, the question now arises whether the above-sketched protection rules, as interpreted in the recent case-law, can also be used to underpin restoration claims for species, such as the Wild hamster, which have been faced with a catastrophic decline in the past decades. Put differently, is an EU Member State allowed to limit its efforts to simply forestalling extinction of Annex IV species such as the Wild hamster or, alternatively, can one infer a positive obligation from the protection duties included in Article 12(1) of the Habitats Directive, requiring the EU Member States to take active steps aimed at the improvement of the conservation status? If the latter question is answered affirmative, restoration-based claims can certainly be filed before national courts in order to force an EU Member State to come up with more robust recovery plans for endangered species.

On the surface, there appears to be limited room to base restoration-inspired claims on the wording of Article 12(1) of the Habitats Directive. In itself, this provision does not refer to 'restoration', nor does it refer to recovery or rehabilitation measures necessary to restore the populations of species that are currently in an unfavourable conservation status. It is therefore not surprising to note that the Habitats Directive is often referred to as a legal instrument which is too concerned with legal bans and restrictions to cause a genuine change in the EU Member States' lax attitude towards sustainable development[149], and, ultimately, facilitate and bolster ecological restoration in the field. The latter conclusion appears to be particularly true for the rules regarding strict species

147 *Commission v France*, *supra* note 52.

148 The mere fact that the CJEU recently seemed to align infringements of Article 6(2) of the Habitats Directive, which is viewed as an obligation of results, with violations of Article 12(1) of the Habitats Directive, seems to point in that direction. See, for instance: *Commission v Greece* 2016, *supra* note 146, para. 157–159.

149 See in this regard, for instance: *F. Kistenkas*, Rethinking European Nature Conservation Legislation: Towards Sustainable Development, Journal of European Environmental & Planning Law 2013, pp. 82–83.

protection, relevant for species such as the Wild hamster. While provisions relating to area protection (Natura 2000), such as Article 6(1) of the Habitats Directive, explicitly urge EU Member States to contemplate conservation measures in order to restore and improve degraded protected sites, Article 12(1) of the Habitats Directive ostensibly remains concerned with passive protection measures, aimed at preventing those activities which might adversely affect the conservation status of a strictly protected species.[150] This led the European Commission to conclude in its 2007 Guidance document that 'Article 12 should not be interpreted as requiring the adoption of pro-active habitat management measures, such as for example the restoration or improvement of habitats for certain species.'[151]

In spite of all the above, a closer look at the wording of the Habitats Directive indicates that the above-mentioned reservation as to the appropriateness of using the protection rules as a legal foundation for restoration-based claims relating to Annex IV species appear to be ill-founded.[152] Indeed, the wording of several core provisions of the Habitats Directive seems to indicate that the latter can, at least partly, serve as an important catalyst for ecological restoration at the EU Member States' level. In article 1, a) of the Habitats Directive, for starters, the notion of 'conservation' is defined as 'a series of measures required to maintain or *restore* the natural habitats and the populations of species of wild fauna and flora at a favourable status'. Hence, when Article 2(1) of the Habitats Directive states that the overall aim of the Habitats Directive is to contribute towards ensuring biodiversity through the conservation of natural habitats and of wild fauna and flora, this also encompasses the restoration measures, if necessary, to achicvc the 'favourable conservation status' for the species listed in its annexes. The objective of the Habitats Directive is defined in positive terms, oriented towards a favourable conservation status and therefore, simply maintaining the status quo might not suffice for species such as the Wild hamster, which find themselves in an unfavourable conservation status in the westernmost parts of their range. It is thus clear that this restoration imperative needs to be taken into consideration when interpreting and applying the specific protection duties, as outlined in Article 12(1) of the Habitats Directive.[153]

This is also in line with the EU's international obligations under the Convention on Biological Diversity.[154] Article 2 of the latter convention defines conservation as '(t)he conservation of ecosystems and natural habitats and the maintenance and

---

150 *Schoukens, supra* note 137; *Cliquet, Decleer & Schoukens, supra* note 15, pp. 272–275.

151 EC Strict Protection Guidance, *supra* note 138, p. 26.

152 See for a more detailed analysis: *Cliquet, Decleer & Schoukens, supra* note 15, pp. 272–275.

153 This has also been explicitly recognised by the European Commission in its Guidance document. See: EC Strict Protection Guidance, *supra* note 138, p. 28.

154 According to the steadfast case-law of the CJEU, provisions of secondary EU law must, in as far as possible, be interpreted in a manner that is consistent with the obligations of the European Union under international law. See amongst others: Case C61/94, *Commission v Germany* [1996]

recovery of viable populations of species in their natural surroundings', whereas Article 8, f) obliges Contracting Parties to '*(r)ehabilitate* and *restore* degraded ecosystems and *promote* the recovery of threatened species, inter alia, through the development and implementation of plans or other management strategies' (emphasis added).[155] In turn, Article 9, which includes specific obligations as to *ex situ* conservation, underlines that such actions should be predominantly complementing *in situ*-measures and targeting 'the *recovery* and *rehabilitation* of threatened species and (...) the reintroduction into their natural habitats under appropriate conditions' (emphasis added). It is not farfetched to use the previous international commitments as interpretation yardstick when applying protection duties included in EU environmental directives.

This preliminary conclusion seems to be endorsed by the outcome of the French hamster case, in which the European Commission accused France of not having taken adequate and sufficient measures to secure the continued existence of the Wild hamster population in the Alsace region. Admittedly, while many of the above-mentioned jurisprudence of the CJEU focused on cases of inadequate application of the protection rules for strict protected species, the recovery rationale underpinning the submissions in the French hamster case is unequivocal. For instance, when taking a closer look at the criticism expressed by the European Commission regarding the French conservation measures pertaining to the Wild hamster, it cannot be ignored that the proceedings at least partly revolved around the precise extent of the duty of an EU Member States to take necessary restoration measures in order to allow the recovery of an Annex IV species which is currently at an unfavourable conservation. In her Opinion in the French hamster case, Advocate-General Kokott explicitly touched upon the apparent dichotomy between the wording of Article 12(1) of the Habitats Directive and the explicit restoration rationale upon which the Commission's claims were based. While not stating that Article 12(1) of the Habitats Directive has to be interpreted as an obligation of result, simply 'striving' to effectively protect threatened Annex IV species will in her view not suffice to comply with the latter provision.

In addition, the Advocate General firmly rejected the French claim that the aim of creating viable populations in the long term goes beyond what is required by Article 12(1)(d) of the Habitats Directive. In paragraph 83, Advocate General Kokott decisively concluded that '(...) if, as in the present case, the populations of the species are so small that they may die out because of natural fluctuations in numbers, an effective system of protection must aim to achieve a sufficient

ECR I3989, para. 52; Case C341/95, *Bettati* [1998] ECR I4355, para. 20; Case C286/02, *Bellio F.lli* [2004] ECR I3465, para. 33.

155 See more extensively: *Schoukens*, *supra* note 137; *Telesetsky, Cliquet & Akhtar-Khavari*, *supra* note 11, pp. 111–115.

increase in stocks'.[156] This all points towards an unmistakably robust recovery duty for EU Member States, at least for Annex IV species such as the Wild hamster, which are currently in an unfavourable conservation status.

4.2. THE FAVOURABLE CONSERVATION STATUS AS BASELINE: A REVIEWABLE STANDARD FOR RESTORATION-BASED LITIGATION?

Assuming that the recovery rationale underpinning the Habitats Directive covers Annex IV species, the more pragmatic question as to the exact number of hamsters that is needed on the territory of an EU Member State to comply with the Habitats Directives is to be analyzed. In theory, the Habitats Directive puts forward a clear-cut reference scenario to be used as a benchmark when drafting conservation plans, *i.e.* the so-called 'favourable conservation status'. This is a legal concept explicitly defined by Article 1(i) of the Habitats Directive.[157] Pursuant to the latter provision, the conservation status of a species encompasses 'the sum of the influences acting on the species concerned that may affect the long-term distribution and abundance of its populations within the territory referred to in Article 2'. In addition, the conservation status of a species will be regarded as 'favourable' according to the Habitats Directive when population dynamics of the species concerned indicate that it is maintaining itself on a long-term basis as a viable component of its natural habitat, the natural range of the species is neither being reduced nor is likely to be reduced for the foreseeable future and there is, and will probably continue to be, a sufficiently large habitat to maintain its populations on a long-term basis.

Little explanation is needed to understand that this concept still leaves considerable freedom to the EU Member States, which might affect the chances of success linked to restoration-based litigation considerably. In their recent review of the concept of 'favourable conservation status' in the context of large carnivores, *Trouwborst et al.* concluded that 'legal uncertainty persists' and, in view of clear-cut rulings by the CJEU, 'conclusive statements' regarding the exact implication of the concept of 'favourable conservation status' are not warranted in the current context.[158] This is conclusion is not illogical seeing that the CJEU

---

156 Opinion Advocate General Kokott in Case C-383/09, *Commission v France* [2011], para. 84.

157 See more extensively: *Y. Epstein, J.V. Lopez-Bao & G. Chapron*, A Legal-Ecological Understanding of the Favorable Conservation Status for Species in Europe, Conservation Letters 2015, 9, pp. 81–88; *Y. Epstein*, Favourable Conservation Status for Species: Examining the Habitats Directive's Key Concept Through a Case Study of the Swedish Wolf, Journal of Environmental Law 2016, 28, pp. 221–244; *A. Trouwborst, L. Boitani & J.D.C. Linnell*, Interpreting 'favourable conservation status' for large carnivores: how many are needed and how many are wanted?, Biodiversity and Conservation 2016, pp. 37–58.

158 *Trouwborst, Boitani & Linnell, supra* note 157, pp. 55–57.

has not yet handed down an extensive decision in which it has come forward with more substantial guidance regarding the concrete interpretation of the latter concept.

Over the past few years, however, the European Commission has produced several guidance documents in which the concept of favourable conservation status is further clarified to the EU Member States. While these guidance documents are not binding in legal terms[159], they nevertheless contain important clues as to the concrete application of the concept of favourable conservation status, as is demonstrated below. Next to the 2007 Guidance document regarding species protection, the 2011 Guidelines (2011 FCS Guidelines), which clarify how EU Member States should report the favourable conservation status in the context of the obligation to report under Article 17 of the Habitats Directive, also provide us with important clues in this respect.[160]

4.2.1. At what territorial level is the favourable conservation status to be achieved?

A first crucial question to be pondered pertains to the geographical scale at which the conservation status of a species needs to be measured. Evidently, relatively small and urbanized EU Member States, such as Belgium and the Netherlands, would benefit from an approach whereby the favourable conservation status of the Wild hamster is to be achieved at European level or at *supra*-national or population level, for instance taking into account all remaining populations of the Wild hamster in Western Europe and possibly beyond. However, if the latter viewpoint were to prevail this would probably constitute a significant obstacle to restoration-based litigation initiated before national courts. Amongst others, it could require environmental NGOs to summon other neighbouring states, which are also partly responsible for the management of transboundary populations. This might give rise to procedural complications linked to, amongst others, state immunity. It is thus reasonable to conclude that merely assessing the favourable conservation status at European level would further complicate a swift outcome of restoration-based types of litigation before national courts.

Be that as it may, a supranational approach appears to be in line with the wording of the Habitats Directive, which pursuant to Article 2(1) aims to 'contribute towards ensuring bio-diversity through the conservation of natural habitats and of wild fauna and flora in the European territory of the EU Member States to which the Treaty applies'.[161] On the other hand, using a *supra*-national

159 *Epstein, supra* note 157, p. 227.

160 *D. Evans & M. Arvela*, Assessment and Reporting under Article 17 of the Habitats Directive: Explanatory Notes, Guidelines for the Period 2007–2012, 2011 (further referred to as '2011 FCS Guidelines').

161 *Schoukens, supra* note 137, pp. 72–77.

benchmark could set a bad precedent for some EU Member States since it could enable them to hide behind the performance of others.[162] In the context of strict species protection, though, the prevailing view is that the national level, when combined with a population approach, is the appropriate benchmark to be used in this perspective.[163] Accordingly, while the European Commission does not necessarily require the EU Member States to achieve a favourable conservation status for each Annex IV species within its own borders, it is particularly keen on assessing whether the national conservation efforts allow the populations concerned to effectively contribute to the maintenance of the species at biogeographical level.[164]

The French hamster case equally seems to point in that direction since the CJEU only took into consideration the conservation status of the Wild hamster in the French Alsace region and did not take into account other populations in neighbouring countries.[165] Also in other infringement proceedings that had been initiated by the European Commission on the inadequate protection of the Wild hamsters the focus was put exclusively on the territory of the said EU Member State.[166] Taking the plight of the Wild hamster as an concrete example, it can be maintained that even small EU Member States such as the Netherlands and Belgium have enough space to achieve the favourable conservation status at national level, at least if robust habitat restoration is considered. Thus, one cannot simply state that it would be unreasonable to hold EU Member States like Belgium or the Netherlands accountable for not achieving the favourable conservation status at national level.[167]

4.2.2. *How to establish a precise and easily reviewable baseline: uncertain science vs discoverable standards?*

In order to scrupulously review government actions, judges require clear-cut legal standards and/or criteria. Evidently, assessing a government's compliance with the EU air quality standards – which include fixed numerical limit values to be achieved in certain parts of the territory with explicitly defined room for exceedances – is easier than reviewing compliance with relatively vague and surprisingly flexible standards, such as the concept of 'favourable conservation status' put forward by the Habitats Directive. In the former hypothesis, one simply

162 *Trouwborst, Boitani & Linnell, supra* note 157, pp. 48–50.
163 Ibid, p. 49; *Epstein, supra* note 157, pp. 242–243.
164 See amongst others: *European Commission*, Additional Reasoned Opinion in Infringement Proceeding 2010/5200 (Swedish) 19 June 2015, para. 44–51. See more extensively: *Epstein, supra* note 157, pp. 222–225.
165 *Commission v France, supra* note 52, para. 24.
166 *European Commission*, Reasoned Opinion in Infringement Proceeding 2001/4984 (Dutch) 13 July 2005.
167 See also: *Trouwborst, Boitani & Linnell, supra* note 157, p. 50.

needs to compare the monitoring data with the applicable standards, whereas the latter involves a further understanding of the notion 'favourable conservation status'. This ecological concept can (and should) be further operationalized in terms of specific population numbers and habitat acreages at national and regional level, which will require further study. In some cases it may even involve best expert judgment.

As adequately illustrated by the recent quarrels between Sweden and the European Commission with regard to the exact number of wolves necessary in order to achieve the favourable conservation status for this protected species in Sweden, the establishment of population numbers for protected species can, given the possible repercussions on economic and social interests, give rise to tensions and conflicts between different stakeholders.[168] The same can be said about the return of the Wild hamster to agricultural lands, which might entail important economic repercussions for farmers. Paradoxically, it is precisely the absence of objective, numerical population targets at EU level that may give rise to more restraint at court level. Opponents of more activists types of environmental litigation often refer to the difficulties of using 'inconclusive' environmental science in legal proceedings. For instance, in their appraisal of recent trends in climate change litigation within the Netherlands, *Bergkamp* and *Hanekamp* concluded that '(m)aking decisions under conditions of substantial uncertainty and contingency necessarily involves highly subjective, value judgments'.[169]

When it comes to the specific population targets that need to be set when considering recovery strategies for Annex IV species, similar reservations, albeit on a smaller scale, might be in order. For, how to assess whether the population targets or habitat acreages used in national or regional recovery strategies are in line with the available scientific consensus, when scientists quarrel among themselves about how to establish viable population targets? To give but one example, at present there is a majority of scientists who believe that in order to be genetically viable, a population of any given species must at least consist of 500 'effective individuals', which requires a total population threshold of about 5,000 individuals.[170] However, some scientists still maintain that a total population of 500 to 1,000 individuals is sufficient to retain the 'evolutionary potential' of a population.[171] The recent discord in the available scientific literature about the suitability of a 'carrying capacity approach' as an alternative to the well-founded consensus that a favourable conservation status must be based on a deviation

168 *Commission v France*, *supra* note 52, para. 24.
169 *Bergkamp & Hanekamp*, *supra* note 26, p. 108.
170 *L.W. Traill, B.W. Brook, R.R. Frankham & C.J.A. Bradshaw*, Pragmatic population viability targets in a rapidly changing world, Biological Conservation 2010, 143, p. 29.
171 *I.R. Franklin & R. Frankham*, How large must populations be to retain evolutionary potential?, Animal Conservation, 1998, 1, pp. 69–73.

from extinction can be cited as another glaring example of how a lack of legally discoverable standards could impede a swift handling of restoration-based litigation in a national court.[172]

While the above-mentioned concerns related to the lack of comprehensive standards of review are understandable to a certain extent, a situation of conflicting scientific views on a certain environmental topic is not exclusively limited to the specific context of restoration-based litigation. It is indeed common for many types of environmental litigation, where each party tries to rely on its own experts to prove their respective points before court. It is no longer uncommon to notice that the substantive conclusions of an Environmental Impact Assessment (EIA) are subsequently contradicted by other 'independent' reports, drafted by other scientists and/or submitted by opponents of the project development concerned. Even so, this fact alone does no longer sway judges to dismiss claims pertaining to the substantive underpinnings of ecological evaluations altogether, as is evidenced by case-law regarding Article 6(3) of the Habitats Directive.[173] Furthermore, with reference to Article 11 of the EIA Directive, the CJEU has already concluded that a judicial review in the context of an EIA should not be limited to cases in which the legality of a decision is challenged on the ground that no EIA has been carried out. The scope of a judicial review should also go beyond reviewing procedural legality issues and equally allow national courts to assess whether an EIA is vitiated by defects, possibly in light of contradictory reports submitted by NGOs.[174] Thus, while scientific information evidently needs to be approached with the necessary caution, further scientific disagreement about the exact threshold to be used when setting population targets could not serve as an excuse to opt for goals that clearly stand at odds with the available science. This is especially the case when the available evidence unequivocally points to a risk of impending extinction.

A certain level of unpredictability is inherent to any ecological system, especially in times of climate change. It is indeed widely accepted that adaptation-oriented conservation strategies are needed to deal with the anthropocentric impacts on the current distribution of species.[175] In some instances, rapid climate change might even call into question the effectiveness of restoration strategies simply aimed at the restoration of environments to historic baselines or action aimed at the recovery of one single species, such as the Wild hamster. Either way, the necessity of proactive actions such as habitat restoration or reintroduction

172 See: *Epstein, Lopez-Bao & Chapron*, *supra* note 157, p. 85. However, *Trouwborst et al.* dismissed the approach as unworkable as a general rule in the context of large carnivore management. See: *Trouwborst, Boitani & Linnell*, *supra* note 157, pp. 53–54.

173 See for instance: Case C-404/09, *Commission v Spain* [2011] ECR I-11853, par. 92–93.

174 Gemeinde Altrip, *supra* note 123, para. 37. See also: Case C-137/14 *Commission v Germany* [2015] ECLI:EU:C:2015:683, para. 37.

175 See for instance: *J. McDonald et al.*, Rethinking legal objectives for climate-adaptive conservation', Ecology and Society 2016, 21(2), pp. 25–34.

aimed at the recovery of viable populations will be undisputed in many extinction scenarios.[176] In such instances, an approach whereby a government would establish conservation targets that are contrary to the available scientific consensus on what is required to bring a species back to a favourable conservation status would be manifestly contrary to the strict application of the precautionary principle.[177]

Even the fact that there would exist no general consensus among scientists as to the exact number of a species in order to achieve long-term survival cannot serve as a justification to delay the establishment of a robust recovery programme. And although the precautionary principle is one of the most debated concepts of current environmental law, a fact that is further underscored by the many definitions it has[178], it is widely accepted that it consists of three common elements, *i.e.* a threat of harm, uncertainty, and action.[179] Generally speaking, the precautionary principle, which is further detailed in Article 191 of the TFEU, aims at ensuring a higher level of environmental protection through a preventative decision-making process in the case of risk. Accordingly, given the possible lack of scientific consensus (for instance, with respect to the exact population threshold), proof of the fact that establishing lower thresholds is *not* harmful for the long-term survival of the species must be provided by those taking that action.[180]

In a context where the population of an endangered species finds itself at a tipping point, it can easily be maintained that there is a risk of significant harm, which requires immediate and comprehensive conservation action by the competent authorities. In addition, in its case-law regarding the appropriate assessment referred to in Article 6(3) of the Habitats Directive, the CJEU underlined that ecological assessments are to be based on the best available scientific knowledge in the field.[181] Along similar lines it can be submitted that Article 12(1) of the Habitats Directive prevents competent authorities from setting population targets that might risk not to effectively avoid extinction scenarios for the said species.

---

176 See also: *P.J. Seddon*, From reintroduction to assisted colonization: moving along the conservation translocation spectrum, Restoration Ecology 2010, 18(6), pp. 796–802.

177 See more extensively in this respect: *R. Frins & H. Schoukens*, Balancing Wind Energy and Nature Protection: From Policy Conflicts Towards Genuine Sustainable Development, In: L. Squitani, H. Vedder & B. Vanheusden (eds.), Sustainable Energy United in Diversity – Challenges and Approaches in Energy Transition in the European Union, 2014, pp. 84–115.

178 See more extensively: *A. Trouwborst*, Precautionary Rights and Duties of States, 2006, pp. 21–35.

179 Ibid, p. 30.

180 See along similar lines: *European Commission*, Communication from the Commission on the Precautionary Principle, COM(00) 1 final.

181 See, by analogy, in the context of Article 6(3) of the Habitats Directive: Waddenzee, *supra* note 90, para. 59 and 61.

4.2.3. Additional ways to operationalize the recovery rationale: favourable reference range and population targets?

While the definition of 'favourable conservation status' for a species included in Article 1(i) of the Habitats Directive remains conspicuously opaque, it still contains the necessary standards allowing judicial review. For instance, pursuant to the latter definition, the 'favourable conservation status' requires among other things that '*the natural range of the species is neither being reduced nor is likely to be reduced for the foreseeable future, and *there is, and will probably continue to be, a sufficiently large habitat to maintain its populations on a long-term basis'. To further illustrate this point, the specific context of the Wild hamster needs to be taken into consideration. Here, the available science is conclusive on the fact that over the past decades the habitat of the species has experienced a substantial decline, which has brought the species to the verge of extinction. In order to define the favourable conservation status of an endangered species, reference needs to be made to the above-mentioned 2011 FCS Guidelines, which contain several clear reference value concepts to be used in order to evaluate whether the actual range or population of a species is sufficiently large to come to the conclusion that it has reached a 'favourable conservation status' in an EU Member State.[182] These standards, which should be exclusively based on ecological considerations according to the European Commission, are useful reference criteria when reviewing conservation efforts in national courts. In particular, concepts like 'favourable reference population' and 'favourable reference range' turn out to be instrumental to further delineate the conservation and restoration duties by the Habitats Directive.

Critics might submit that a concept such as 'favourable reference population' (FRP) leaves too much leeway in order to be used as a clear-cut yardstick by judges in restoration-based types of litigation. Granted, the definition contained in the 2011 FCS Guidelines seems to confirm this conclusion. It reads as follows: 'Population in a given biogeographical region considered the minimum necessary to ensure the long-term viability of the species; favourable reference value must be at least the size of the population when the Directive came into force; information on historic distribution/population may be found useful when defining the favourable reference population: 'best expert judgement' may be used to define it in absence of other data'.[183] Opponents might quickly point to the fact that the definition seems to explicitly recognize its incomplete nature with the explicit reference to 'expert judgment'.

To a certain extent, the latter criticism could be overcome by putting forward the use of the concept of 'minimum viable population' (MVP), *i.e.* the

---

182 2011 FCS Guidelines, *supra* note 160.

183 Ibid, pp. 17–18.

smallest number of individuals required for a population to have a specified probability of persisting in its natural environment.[184] The latter concept is not explicitly put forward by the Habitats Directive. Yet as noted above, the notion of 'viable population' is mentioned in the definition of 'in situ conservation', laid down by the Convention on Biological Diversity. To further complicate matters, though, MVPs can be determined in numerous ways. This might again indicate that it represents an ill-suited benchmark for judges to review an EU Member State's recovery efforts in light of Article 12(1) of the Habitats Directive. A method to estimate MVPs consists in determining the minimum area that a population needs to inhabit in order to escape environmental catastrophes. In recent years, though, a relatively large amount of attention has been paid to the evolutionary potential of a population (evolutionary MVP), *i.e.* the population size required at equilibrium to balance the loss of quantitative genetic variation with the gain from mutation.[185] However, one of the most prominent methods in this respect are the so-called population viability analyses (PVA), which use demographic and environmental information to project future population dynamics.[186] And while some discussion remains concerning the exact size of populations, there is currently a general consensus that MVPs should consist of thousands of individuals in order to ensure viable populations of endangered species.[187]

In the light of the above, MVPs could therefore be used as *de minimis* yardstick by national courts when reviewing an EU Member States' compliance with their recovery duties within the framework of Article 12(1) of the Habitats Directive. Support for this thesis can be found in the case-law of the CJEU itself. For instance, the CJEU noted in the French hamster case that 'there were no populations of the (Wild hamster) (…) which reached its minimum viable population threshold, which is estimated at 1,500 individuals spread over an area of contiguous suitable land of 600 hectares'.[188] To be more precise, the French recovery policy consisted in at least achieving three pockets of populations measuring around 1,500 individuals in the Alsace region. This approach was based on the scientific work regarding MVPs within the context of the Wild hamster[189] and is also applied in other EU Member States.[190]

---

184 *Schoukens, supra* note 137. On the concept 'minimum viable population', see amongst others: *M. Shaffer*, Minimum Population Sizes for Species Conservation, Bio Sci 1981, 31, pp. 131–134.

185 See among others: *Franklin & Frankham, supra* note 171, pp. 69–73.

186 *Traill et al., supra* note 170, p. 29.

187 *Traill et al., supra* note 170, p.33; *J.M. Reed & E.D. McCoy*, Relation of Minimum Viable Population Size to Biology, Time Frame, and Objective, Conservation Biology 2014, 28, p. 867.

188 *Commission v France, supra* note 52, para. 24.

189 See: *A. Kayser*, Contemplation about minimum viable population size in common hamsters, In: I. Losinger (ed.), The Common hamster Cricetus cricetus, L 1758. Hamster biology and ecology, policy and management of hamsters and their biotope. Proc. 12th Inter2. Hamsterworkgroup, 16–18 October 2004, Strasbourg, Paris.

190 *Schoukens, supra* note 137, pp. 83–88.

In spite of the above, it is not completely unthinkable to base restoration-based claims partly on the broader concept of 'favourable reference population' (FRP), which is put forward in the 2011 FCS Guidelines. While this concept refers to a similar minimum viability threshold as the MVP, it is generally agreed that the former should be set at a higher level than the MVP.[191] Along those lines, one can thus argue that a recovery programme for an Annex IV species needs to include comprehensive population targets which allow the species to maintain itself on a long-term basis, possibly even going beyond MVP. For now, though, the CJEU still has to pronounce itself on the exact application of the MVP when determining the favourable conservation status of a said species. Furthermore, at EU Member States' level, different approaches are currently applied.[192] In the ongoing infringement proceedings against Sweden concerning its wolf population, the Commission stated that the Swedish population target, which was based on a population viability analysis aimed at determining the minimum population of wolves that would have a less than 10% chance of extinction after 100 years, was not capable of guaranteeing viability.[193] This all hints at a higher level of scrutiny, especially in cases where species are at risk of imminent extinction. The strict line of interpretation might be reinforced in cases when there is a significant risk of inbreeding, which is for instance the case for the few remaining and fragmented populations of Wild hamsters.[194]

On a more general note, *Traill et al.* concluded that '(c)urrent evidence from integrated work on population dynamics shows that setting conservation thresholds at a few hundred individuals only is a subjective and non-scientific decision, not an evidence-based biological one which properly accounts for the synergistic impacts of deterministic threats'.[195] This led them to conclude that conservation efforts are ideally aimed at managing 'biologically relevant MVPs', which cover at least 5,000 adult individuals. Evidently, such general statements will need to be supplemented in legal proceedings by dedicated scientific research which focuses on the specific threats that the species concerned is facing, in order to convince judges to review national or regional recovery efforts that might fail to ensure the long-term survival of the said species.

---

191 *Epstein, supra* note 157, pp. 229–231.

192 *A.J. McConville & G.M. Tucker*, Review of the Favourable Conservation Status and Birds Directive Article 2 interpretation within the European Union, Natural England Commissioned Reports, pp. 19–20.

193 *European Commission, supra* note 164, para. 44–51. See also: *Epstein, supra* note 157, pp. 222–225.

194 *Schoukens, supra* note 137, pp. 87–88; *La Haye, Neumann & Koelewijn, supra* note 35, pp. 319–321.

195 Ibid, p. 32. See also: *B.W. Brook, N.S. Sodhi & C.J.A. Brashaw*, Synergies among extinction drivers under global change, Trends in Ecology and Evolution, 23, pp. 453–460.

4.3. AN ALTERNATE ROUTE FOR RESTORATION CLAIMS: REMEDYING PAST NON-COMPLIANCE AND UNLAWFUL DAMAGE TO SPECIES?

As aptly demonstrated by *Epstein et al.*, the preparatory work of the Habitats Directive attests to the fact that it has never been the explicit objective of the European legislator to increase a species population to its historical level.[196] After having extensively reviewed the legislative process leading to the Habitats Directive, it is concluded that 'the legislators intentionally rejected requiring that species populations approach historical levels'.[197] However, the latter findings do not take away that environmental NGOs can also try to obtain an injunctive relief against competent authorities by framing such legal actions as instruments to address the unlawful damage to a species caused by decades of poor enforcement of the species protection rules. Accordingly, going back in time could provide for another alternative route to force national or regional authorities to come forward with more ambitious recovery plans.[198] As such, historical distribution and potential range are recommended by the European Commission in its 2011 FCS Guidelines as explicit criteria when determining the favourable conservation status. For instance, when defining the notion of FRP, it is stated that the 'favourable reference value must be at least of the size of the population when the Directive entered into force'.[199] In that respect, it is noteworthy that several EU Member States, including the Netherlands, Ireland, Belgium (Flemish Region) and Germany, explicitly use the populations levels or range at the time of the entry into force of the Habitats Directive as reference scenario when setting conservation targets.[200]

Tackling the imminent extinction of a protected species as a case of remediation of unlawful harm to biodiversity presents itself as another attractive option for formulating restoration-based claims, without possibly needing to take a more troublesome detour via the concept of 'favourable conservation status'. Especially in cases where Annex IV species are now in an unfavourable conservation status due to earlier non-compliance with the strict protection duties, as is for instance the case for the Wild hamster, one could state that an EU Member State has the legal obligation to restore the populations of such species at least to the level on the date of entry into force of the Habitats Directive (1994 for EU Member States such as France, Belgium, Germany and the Netherlands). In the French hamster case, Advocate General Kokott did note that the European Commission could not claim an obligation to restore hamster populations to a previously existing level,

196 *Epstein, Lopez-Bao, Chapron, supra* note 157, p. 85.

197 *Esptein, supra* note 157, p. 239.

198 *Schoukens, supra* note 137, pp. 87–88.

199 2011 FCS Guidelines, *supra* note 163 pp. 16–17.

200 In the absence of detailed research data, these levels are estimated on the basis of more recent data.

on the grounds that France may not have given sufficient protection to the Wild hamster in the past.[201] However, implicitly she indicated that such a restoration claim is not unthinkable by acknowledging that '(it) is true that, as early as 1994, a system of strict protection had to be introduced for the Wild hamster, and it is possible that past omissions may give rise to an obligation on the part of EU Member States to provide for restoration'.[202]

Although the CJEU has not explicitly shed light on this thought-provoking stance regarding species recovery as remediation action in its decision in the French hamster case, the comprehensive examination of the French conservation plans, which also included habitat restoration and repopulation measures, seems to point towards more scrutiny in cases of non-compliance. Moreover, back in 2000, the CJEU had already ruled that an EU Member State cannot derive an advantage from its failure to adhere to its obligations.[203] A more lenient stance might have the effect of encouraging EU Member States to forego a strict application of the protection schemes, as has been the case for the Wild hamster in many countries. It is moreover settled case-law of the CJEU that EU Member States are principally obliged to remedy non-compliance with EU environmental law.[204]

As recently as in 2014, the CJEU reinforced this stance in *Cascina Tre Pini* by explicitly ruling that an EU Member State's failure to fulfil the obligation to grant protection to a degraded Natura 2000 site does not warrant the withdrawal of the protected status. EU Member States should rather take the necessary measures to restore sites that have been degraded due to non-observance of the protection rules when issuing unlawful permits for new developments, for instance.[205] Likewise, in *Grüne Liga Sachsen*, which revolved around the compatibility of an already completed bridge with the protection rules tied to Natura 2000 sites, the CJEU suggested EU Member States are obliged to adequately assess the negative effects of this construction if this had not been done in the context of the decision-making procedure prior to the construction. In doing so, even the hypothesis of complete demolition of the bridge needed to be evaluated.[206] This seems to reinforce the view that, at a very minimum, national courts can instruct EU Member States to remedy a protected species to its baseline on the date of entry into force of the Habitats Directive by adopting more robust

---

201 Opinion Advocate General Kokott, *supra* note 156, para. 51.

202 In her Opinion of 18 February 2016 in the case C-504/14 *Commission v Greece*, Advocate General Kokott expressly put emphasis on the temporal application of the protection schemes for sea turtles (Caretta caretta). See: Opinion Advocate General Kokott in Case C-504/14, *Commission v Greece* [2016] para. 125.

203 Case C-347/98, *Commission v France* [2000] ECR I-10799, para. 50.

204 Case C- 348/15, *Stadt Wiener Neustadt* [2016] ECLI:EU:C:2016:882, paras. 48–47; Case C201/02, *Wells* [2004] ECR I- I-00723, para. 68.

205 Case C-301/12, *Cascina Tre Pini s.s.* [2014] ECLI:EU:C:2014:214, para. 50.

206 Case C-399/14, *Grüne Liga Sachsen eV* [2016] ECLI:EU:C:2016:10, paras. 74–75.

recovery programmes. Especially in cases where the population levels of an endangered species at the time of the entry into force of the Habitats Directive surpass the conservation objectives established in order to achieve a favourable conservation, this 'remediation approach' might present itself as an interesting alternative argumentation-line in restoration-based litigation. In such cases, one might force the EU Member State in question to point its recovery strategy to re-establish former population levels of an endangered species.

The Environmental Liability Directive (Directive 2004/35/CE)[207], which also includes damage by operators to protected Annex IV species under the broader notion of ecological damage, might serve as additional source of inspiration here.[208] Admittedly, the set of preventative and remedial duties the Environmental Liability Directive puts forward is not aimed at addressing generic shortcomings in the enforcement of protection and conservation duties by governmental bodies.[209] However, the Environmental Liability Directive explicitly reinforces the 'polluter pays principle', also mentioned in Article 191(2) of the TFEU.[210] In this regard, it is interesting to note that the concept of 'baseline condition' is further defined by the Environmental Liability Directive as 'the condition at the time of the damage to the natural resources and services that would have existed had the environmental damage not occurred, estimated on the basis of the best information available'.[211] Annex I to the Environmental Liability Directive defines more detailed criteria on how to determine whether significant adverse changes to the baseline condition have occurred.[212] Amongst others, the species' capacity, after damage has occurred, to recover within a short time, without any intervention other than increased protection measures, is mentioned as one of the criteria to be taken into account. In view of the approach set out by the Environmental Liability Directive, one might thus argue that recovery strategies must at least focus on re-establishing baseline conditions for endangered species. Whereas minor fluctuations in population levels do not require short term actions, general recovery policies should first and foremost aim to restore the species to resilient population levels. Achieving the baseline conditions is to be the default position in this regard and could therefore be used as an alternate standard of review in restoration-based litigation.

207 Directive 2004/35/CE of the European Parliament and of the Council of 21 April 2004 on environmental liability with regard to the prevention and remedying of Environmental Liability, OJ 2004 L 143/56 (further referred to as 'Environmental Liability Directive').
208 Article 3(1)(b) of the Environmental Liability Directive.
209 *V. Fogleman*, The threshold for liability for ecological damage in the EU, C.H. Born, A. Cliquet, H. Schoukens, D. Misonne & G. Van Hoorick (eds.), *supra* note 2, pp. 193–195.
210 See for instance, consideration 2 in the preamble to the Environmental Liability Directive.
211 Article 2, 14 of the Environmental Liability Directive.
212 Article 2(1) and Annex I of the Environmental Liability Directive.

4.4. WHICH CONCRETE MEASURES ARE OBLIGATORY TO FOSTER RECOVERY FOR ENDANGERED SPECIES?

From the above analysis, it can be deduced that for species currently not in an unfavourable conservation status, such as the Wild hamster in many EU Member States, a continued improvement in status is needed.[213] As a penultimate step in our analysis, it now needs to be ascertained what type of measures EU Member States are legally required to take under Article 12(1) of the Habitats Directive. For only such measures will be enforceable through legal action before national courts.

As a preliminary remark, it is to be underlined that Article 12(1) of the Habitats Directive does not lay out the specific measures an EU Member State needs to take in order to be in line with its obligations under the Habitats Directive. For one, the latter provision does not explicitly compel EU Member States to draft species action plans in order to adhere to their obligations under Article 12(1) of the Habitats Directives. Still, in its 2007 Guidance document the European Commission explicitly put forward so-called 'species actions plans' as a good practice for the EU Member States when implementing their duties under Article 12(1) of the Habitats Directive.[214] Moreover, Article 8(f) of the Convention on Biological Diversity explicitly obliges Contracting Parties to achieve restoration and rehabilitation through the development and implementation of plans or other management strategies. In its 2007 decision on the Irish implementation regime, the CJEU also held Ireland liable for not having adopted such plans for the majority of the Annex IV species that are present on its territory.[215] Although it would probably be too far-fetched to deduce a general duty to establish species action plans for every single Annex IV species from the latter ruling, it still becomes apparent that such instruments are highly valued by the CJEU when reviewing the EU Member States' compliance with Article 12(1) of the Habitats Directive. In line with the above, such species action plans might take the form of transboundary population management plans if deemed necessary in view of the interlinkages between several transboundary subpopulations of the Wild hamster.[216]

Yet going beyond the formal name-tag to be given to recovery measures, it remained unclear whether, legally speaking, EU Member States had the obligation to implement repopulation, reintroduction and habitat restoration measures in order to comply with their obligations under Article 12(1) of the

---

213 See more extensively: *H. Schoukens*, Going beyond the Status Quo: Towards a Duty for Species Restoration under EU Law?, In V. Sancin & M.K. Dine (eds.) *International law: contemporary concerns and challenges in 2014. GV Založba, Ljubljana*, Slovenia, pp. 352–354.

214 EC Strict Protection Guidance, *supra* note 138, p. 29.

215 *Commission v Ireland*, *supra* note 143, paras 14–15.

216 See also regarding large carnivores: *Trouwborst, Boitani & Linnell*, *supra* note 157, pp. 51–52.

Habitats Directive. Above, it has been noted that a recovery rationale should underpin the establishment of conservation targets within the context of endangered species that are in an unfavourable conservation status. Admittedly, while prohibitions are in general of a defensive nature, they can help to restore or improve habitats in so far as they enable positive natural developments to take place.[217] In times of ecological change and degradation, though, it is widely accepted that more proactive conservation actions, such as reintroduction aimed at re-establishing a viable population of a focal species within its historic range, are crucial to avoid further losses.[218] However, in view of the content of the 2007 Guidance document on strict species protection it still remains dubious whether Article 12(1) of the Habitats Directive can be relied upon in order to force a competent authority to consider more far-reaching recovery measures, such as reintroduction/captive breeding an habitat restoration programmes.[219] The European Commission is of the opinion that proactive restoration measures, such as comprehensive repopulation efforts and/or habitat restoration, are not covered by Article 12(1) of the Habitats Directive. Applying the latter narrative in the context of species such as the Wild hamster would probably exacerbate the current predicament. This is acknowledged by recent ecological research, which underscores that both reintroduction efforts and habitat restoration are key to avoid extinction of the Wild hamster in the westernmost parts of its habitat.[220]

Nevertheless, Advocate General Kokott held that France was not required to take restoration or repopulation measures in areas that are currently not occupied by the Wild hamster.[221] In its decision of 9 June 2011, though, the CJEU ostensibly was not hindered by the Advocate General's detailed observations as to the scope of the recovery measures that were required. When studied more into detail, the CJEU focused on the sharp decline of the hamster populations between 2001 and 2007, a time when France had to implement and effectively enforce the strict preventative measures that have been outlined above.[222] The EU judges implicitly seemed to approach the repopulation and habitat restoration measures as remediation measures, needed to amend the non-compliance caused by the insufficient enforcement of the preventative measures. Ultimately, CJEU did require France to come up with sufficient remedial measures which are able to reverse the negative trend. And such measures seem to include the establishment of repopulation areas, which cover a large part of the hamster's historical range

217 Opinion Advocate General Kokott, *supra* note 156, para. 45.

218 *IUCN/Species Survival Commission (SSC)*, Guidelines for reintroduction and other conservation translocations: version 1.0, IUCN/SSC, 2013, p. 1.

219 EC Strict Protection Guidance, *supra* note 138, p. 26.

220 *M. La Haye, V. Verbist & H.P. Koelewijn*, Behoud van Vlaamse en Nederlandse hamsters: Genetisch herstel en akkerbeheer gaan hand in hand, Natuur.focus 2010, pp. 159–166.

221 Opinion Advocate General Kokott, *supra* note 156, para. 69.

222 *Commission v France, supra* note 52, para. 27.

and in which stricter rules on the development of maize crops and urbanization projects are applicable.[223]

Therefore, seeking redress for past losses of protected species might also require an EU Member State to consider proactive restoration measures. Interestingly so, the Environmental Liability Directive provides a workable definition of 'remedial measures', which might also be useful in the present context. Pursuant to Article 2, 11° of the Environmental Liability Directive such measures should be interpreted so as to cover 'any action, or combination of actions, including mitigating or interim measures to restore, rehabilitate or replace damaged natural resources and/or impaired services, or to provide an equivalent alternative to those resources or services as foreseen in Annex II'. In Annex II a further distinction is made between 'primary'[224], 'complementary'[225] and 'compensatory remediation'.[226] In the specific context of the Environmental Liability Directive, which focuses on incidents and accidents leading to ecological damage and it as such not targeting non-compliance scenarios initiated by national authorities, preference must be given to primary remediation over complementary remediation. Both these concepts seem to encompass habitat restoration actions as well as reintroduction efforts. It is thus clear that reintroduction and habitat restoration measures are to be regarded as 'common' remediation measures, also within the context of the EU Nature Directives.

That said, national judges, when faced with restoration-based claims, might feel inclined to issue more open injunctions, which focus on certain minimum population levels to be achieved. Mandatory injunctions ordering competent authorities to adopt one particular recovery measure, such as species reintroduction, will probably remain exceptional. Even though it has been established that also reintroduction schemes and habitat restoration can be tagged as mandatory efforts to further implement the recovery duties pursuant to Article 12(1) of the Habitats Directive, especially for species on the verge of disappearance due to earlier non-compliance. In situations where only a few individual of an endangered species remain, national judges might therefore still be found ready to instruct national authorities to consider specific reintroduction measures in order to reverse the current predicament, especially when such actions are already recommended by the available scientific reports. The plight of the Wild hamster in Western-Europe might be one of the cases in which these conditions are met.

---

223 *Schoukens*, *supra* note 213, pp. 352–354.

224 Pursuant to Annex II, 1(a) 'primary' remediation is any remedial measure which returns the damaged natural resources and/or impaired services to, or towards, baseline condition.

225 Pursuant to Annex II, 1(b) 'complementary' remediation is any remedial measure taken in relation to natural resources and/or services to compensate for the fact that primary remediation does not result in fully restoring the damaged natural resources and/or services.

226 Pursuant to Annex II, 1(c) 'compensatory' remediation is any action taken to compensate for interim losses of natural resources and/or services that occur from the date of damage occurring until primary remediation has achieved its full effect.

4.5. ECONOMIC CONSIDERATIONS AS ADDITIONAL OBSTACLES TO JUDICIAL REVIEW?

Saving species in decline, such as the Wild hamster, can turn out to be very costly. To put things in perspective, the French government assigned 10.3 million EUR to the latest set of measures aimed at conserving and restoring its hamster populations in the Alsace region[227], whereas the Flemish government allocated 623,500 EUR to the implementation of the recently adopted hamster species protection programme.[228] Needless to say, the question can be raised whether such amounts of money for species on the brink of extinction is still allowed in times of budgetary austerity. For many politicians, investing large sums of money in a so-called 'no-hoper'-species, which will almost certainly go extinct, is to be dismissed as an example of unsound governmental management, especially whenever such actions might have important repercussions for other economic stakeholders and more ecosystem-based restoration actions are more attractive. Also in restoration-based litigation such elements will probably come to surface at some point, for instance as an argument to call for additional deference when crafting a precise remedy or injunction to address the imminent extinction.

When approached from the angle of the Habitats Directive, though, reference can be made to Article 2(3), which states that conservation and restoration measures taken pursuant to the Habitats Directive are to take economic, social and cultural requirements into account, as well as local characteristics. Also case-law concerning programmes of measures that need to be adopted within the scope of the EU Air Quality Directive seems to acknowledge that, at least in this specific context, economic considerations can play a role when establishing a programme to reduce exceedance of air quality standards.[229] However, economic interests cannot undermine the aim of achieving a favourable conservation status for Annex IV species.[230] As such, the lack of a clear-cut deadline as to achieving the favourable conservation status grants some leeway to the EU Member States. It might also render it less evident for judges to issue concrete instruction to competent authorities. Yet in *Grüne Liga Sachsen*, the CJEU ruled that'(s)o far as concerns the economic cost of the steps that may be considered in the review of alternatives, including the demolition of the works already completed, as relied on by the referring court, it must be stated (...) that that is not of equal importance to the objective of conserving natural habitats and wild fauna and flora pursued by the Habitats Directive'.[231] *A fortiori* EU Member States should

227 *O' Brien*, *supra* note 31, pp. 93–95.
228 See: www.vilt.be/623500-euro-voor-redden-van-wilde-hamster (Accessed 10 April 2017).
229 Janecek, *supra* note 100, para. 47.
230 Opinion Advocate General Kokott, *supra* note 156, para. 85.
231 *Grüne Liga Sachsen*, *supra* note 206, para. 77.

the result of earlier non-compliance.[232] Therefore a mere referral to the costs should also not bar a national court from ordering an EU member State to adopt specific recovery measures.

Interestingly, the CJEU held in its 2014 ruling in *ClientEarth* that, while EU Member States have a degree of discretion in deciding which precise measures to adopt under the EU Air Quality Directive, 'those measures must, in any event, ensure that the period during which the limit values are exceeded is as short as possible'.[233] And it is exactly this what should be reviewable through legal action before national court, also in the context of a strictly protected species which finds itself on the verge of extinction due to previous non-compliance.

5. CONCLUSION

Ecological restoration has gradually come to the fore as one of the global policy priorities in the battle against ongoing biodiversity decline. However, the actual recovery measures at national level often lag behind the ambitious pledges made at international or European fora. The plight of the Wild hamster serves as an adequate illustration of how a lack of coordinated and comprehensive recovery efforts could actually lead to the local extinction of a species within just a few decades. Yet given the extent of the current biodiversity crisis in this era, which is by some aptly referred to as a 'sixth extinction wave' in view of the palpable character of the loss of biodiversity[234], we no longer have the luxury of standing idle and waiting for comprehensive governmental action to save species on the brink of extinction.

In contrast to recent evolutions in New Zealand, where national parks and rivers have recently been granted legal personhood, protected nature within the EU currently lacks such explicit legal recognition.[235] As a result, endangered species like the Wild hamster cannot go to court themselves or be directly represented by a 'guardian' in order to force governments to come forward with more effective recovery schemes. And although the Habitats Directive implicitly prompts EU Member States to implement restoration efforts for endangered

---

232 *Schoukens*, *supra* note 137, pp. 94–95.

233 *ClientEarth*, *supra* note 30, para. 57.

234 *A.D. Barnosky, N. Matzke, S. Tomiva, G.O.U. Wogan, B. Swartz, T.B. Quental, C. Marshall, J.L. McGuire, B. Mersey & E.A. Ferrer*, Has the Earth's sixth mass extinction already arrived?, Nature 2011, 471, pp. 51–58.

235 In March 2017, the New Zeeland Parliament adopted a law that granted a river the full legal rights of a person. This law recognized the elevated legal status of the 90-mile Whanganui River, whose interests will now be represented in court by two guardians from the indigenous community. See: www.economist.com/news/asia/21719409-odd-legal-status-intended-help-prevent-pollution-and-other-abuses-new-zealand-declares (Accessed 10 April 2017). Back in 2014, Te Urewera, an area of forested hills in the north-east that used to be a national park, became a person for legal purposes in 2014.

species, it is apparently lacking an explicit enforceable 'right of restoration', as for instance explicitly provided for in the Constitution of Ecuador.[236]

This chapter has revealed that within the context of EU nature conservation law, environmental NGOs might still step in as indirect guardians of endangered species in order to force national and regional authorities through legal actions to make more coordinated efforts to recover species that are in an unfavourable conservation status. While such forms of judicial activism would probably be dismissed as 'unthinkable' until recently, the past years have witnessed a steady rise of ground-breaking rulings relating to private enforcement in environmental cases. And thus also restoration-based litigation is no longer off chart, especially not when focused on species that are facing imminent extinction.

To be more precise, the powerful combination of Article 9(3) of the Aarhus Convention and the general principles of EU law seems trite in order to overcome traditional procedural obstacles to environmental restoration-based, also in the context of biodiversity-related cases. As the law stands today, bedrock principles such as the separation of powers or a limited standing approach can no longer be tagged as insurmountable procedural hurdles for more activists types of restoration-based litigation. Moreover, as aptly illustrated by the French hamster case, there is not necessarily a blatant lack of clearly identifiable criteria and legal standards to be used as benchmarks by judges when reviewing national conservation strategies. The leeway left for the competent authorities will be significantly reduced if the said biodiversity is already in a degraded state and the available science clearly points to a limited set of recovery actions. At a very minimum, this analysis has indicated that it is no longer inconceivable to sue governments with respect to their ineffective conservation policies and to ask for comprehensive remediation of the past losses in respect of strictly EU protected species. Whereas conflicting views on what is to constitute a 'viable population levels' could compromise the launching of effective lawsuits, the apparent predicament of many species, such as the Wild hamster, will probably render judges more prepared to substantively review existing recovery strategies.

Yet it would be a mistake to think that the judiciary is a panacea for all ills. The ongoing species decline is multifactorial and therefore legal actions will often not suffice to avert extinction. In addition, an exclusive focus on high-intervention strategies for listed, threatened species will not suffice to address the more general decline of more common species and biodiversity. Indeed, it is probably ironic to note that, from a legal perspective, restoration-based lawsuits have a higher success rate when focused on strictly protected species. While such species might function as flagship species for more landscape-wide restoration efforts, this will not always be the case. It is moreover this author's opinion that effective

236 Article 72 explicitly recognizes that '(n)ature has the right to restoration'. See: https://therightsofnature.org/wp-content/uploads/pdfs/Rights-for-Nature-Articles-in-Ecuadors-Constitution.pdf (Accessed 10 April 2017).

restoration programmes are evidently contingent on intensive, prior deliberations with all relevant stakeholders in order to ensure adequate implementation in the field. Obviously, a more activist approach towards public interest litigation before national courts, seeking injunctive relief to impose the implementation of more comprehensive restoration schemes, is but one of the many pathways to ensure an effective implementation of the restoration commitments. If overly used, it might even create a backlash for environmental governance, since it paradoxically could urge the legislator to include more vague and therefore less enforceable terminology in future environmental agreements.

Even so, in view of the recent surge in environmental activism and the inability of the Commission to address all complaints brought before it, public interest litigation at national level can serve as useful leverage to force the EU Member States through mandatory injunctions to take their restoration commitments more seriously. If anything, such restoration-based lawsuits can urge an authority to take action in the face of imminent extinction dangers. For, as the phrase goes, *extinction means forever...*

RECOGNITION OF RIGHTS OF NATURE, AS A SUBJECT OF LAW, IN THE INTERNATIONAL ENVIRONMENTAL LAW FRAMEWORK

Santiago Vallejo Galárraga*

ABSTRACT

The present article aims to analyse the foremost theoretical foundations that support the recognition of Nature, as a subject of international law and a holder of rights, as a legitimate, independent, representative and more enforcing mechanism to stop the environmental depletion. It will also tackle a brief description about the initial conditions to acknowledge the legal intervention of Mother Earth as an actor within the international community.

KEYWORDS

Holder of rights; Legal standing; Mother Earth; Nature; Subject of international law

1. INTRODUCTION

One of the most remarkable achievements attained during the last Conference of the Parties on the Framework Convention on Climate Change – carried out from 30 November to 11 December 2015 – was the commitment of '[h]*olding the increase in the global average temperature to well below 2 °C above pre-industrial levels and to pursue efforts to limit the temperature increase to 1.5 °C* […]', as an explicit objective of the 'Paris Agreement'.[1]

---

* PhD candidate, University of Szeged.

1 Paris Agreement to the United Nations Framework Convention on Climate Change, Paris, 12 Dec. 2015. Annex to UN Doc. FCCC/CP/2015/L.9, 12 December 2015. Article 2(a).

Certainly, it was not the first time that nations had subscribed these kinds of commitments, given they already agreed to achieve '[...] *stabilization of greenhouse gas concentrations in the atmosphere at a level that would prevent dangerous anthropogenic interference with the climate system*'[2], by means of the subscription of the original Framework Convention on Climate Change in 1992. Likewise, through the Kyoto Protocol of 1997, they agreed to '[...] *ensure that their aggregate anthropogenic carbon dioxide equivalent emissions of the greenhouse gases* [...] *do not exceed their assigned amounts, calculated pursuant to their quantified emission limitation and reduction commitments* [...]'[3]

Nevertheless, it seems that these legal mechanisms have not been sufficiently effective to achieve the expected results, above all if one notices that '[m]*ost of the warming occurred in the past 35 years, with 16 of the 17 warmest years on record occurring since 2001*', according to the National Aeronautics and Space Administration (NASA)[4], which is due to the fact that '[...] *recent anthropogenic emissions of greenhouse gases are the highest in history*[5], inter alia. Therefore, it is curious how difficult it has been to enforce international law, despite the widely known environmental repercussions of global warming on air temperature, precipitation, sea level, water and carbon cycles, and associated ecosystems, among other worldwide threats.

Given its important weight in terms of emissions, likely one of the most common explanations one can find in environmental law refers to the notorious lack of commitment from United States of America (USA), whose refusal to ratify the Kyoto Protocol, and other international environmental instruments[6], is extensive. However, another no less remarkable reason includes the inefficient, or even somehow missing, system of sanctions to address breaches. Indeed, for instance, the parties of the Paris Agreement decided not to adopt a procedure to claim and to punish potential non-compliances. Besides, it is important to question what the actual legal effect of international agreements is in practice, considering that at least three of the highest greenhouse gas emitting countries –

2 United Nations Framework Convention on Climate Change, New York, 9 May 1992, in force 21 Mar. 1994, UN Document No. 30822, United Nations Treaty Series, vol. 1771, p. 107, Article 2.

3 Kyoto Protocol to the United Nations Framework Convention on Climate Change, Kyoto, 11 December 1997, in force 16 February 2005, UN Document No. 30822, United Nations Treaty Series, vol. 2303, p. 162, Article 3.

4 *National Aeronautics and Space Administration*, NASA, NOAA Data Show 2016 Warmest Year on Record (GISS, 18 January 2017) <https://www.giss.nasa.gov/research/news/20170118/> accessed 28 March 2017.

5 *Intergovernmental Panel on Climate Change*, IPCC, Climate Change 2014: Synthesis Report, Contribution of Working Groups I, II and III to the Fifth Assessment Report of the IPCC, 2014.

6 For example, the United States of America has not ratified the Basel Convention on the Control of Transboundary Movements of Hazardous Wastes and their Disposal of 1989, the Convention on Biological Diversity of 1992, or the Stockholm Convention on Persistent Organic Pollutants of 2001, among others.

China[7], the USA[8] and the Russian Federation[9] – are members of the permanent Security Council of United Nations (UN), the most decisive political body, along with the General Assembly. Moreover, it is widely known that several countries have postponed achieving their emissions reduction goals, mostly pleading potential injuries to their economic systems. Under these circumstances, it seems challenging to believe states could be penalized by the UN because of any breach of duties, which implies a paradox, especially if one considers – even if only in a rhetorical manner – the UN is the main entity responsible to ensure the fulfilment of international law. At the end of the day, the polluters will also be the same protectors of nature, meaning the country members of UN would somehow act as judges and juries.

At the national level, similar conditions occur, except there are different actors playing their own roles. For example, states are usually seen as the guardians of nature given their powers to enact and enforce laws, and punish harmful actions. In contrast, individuals and companies are often considered as contaminators. Nevertheless, according to the results of a quantitative analysis looking at historic records of fossil fuel and cement production worldwide, from 1854 to 2010, published by Richard Heede in 2013, '[...] *nearly two-thirds of historic carbon dioxide and methane emissions can be attributed to 90 entities*' at a global scale, 44% of which are State-owned.[10] As in the previous case, the consequence will also be an inadequate confusion of interests, between the polluter and the entity responsible for the environmental care and control.

In this setting, one may wonder if states, individually or as a part of the UN, are able to represent pure environmental interests in practice, in a completely independent manner, without influencing global or national measures of public policy toward other different ends than conservation or protection of natural resources. Evidence of climate change would seem to demonstrate that economic development and progress have usually prevailed over environmental issues and that they continue doing so.

---

7 According to its projections, China reported an engagement to reduce the emissions of carbon dioxide by 2020, between 40% and 45% per unit of the Gross Domestic Product (GDP) below the 2005 level. China's Intended Nationally Determined Contributions (INDC) submitted on 30 June 2015, at p. 3. Available at: www4.unfccc.int/Submissions/INDC/Published%20 Documents/China/1/China's%20INDC%20-%20on%2030%20June%202015.pdf.

8 In the case of the United States of America by 2020, it has foreseen to achieve a reduction of about 17% below the 2005 level of emissions of carbon dioxide. U.S. Cover Note, INDC and Accompanying Information submitted on 31 March 2015, at p. 1. Available at: www4.unfccc.int/Submissions/INDC/Published%20Documents/United%20States%20of%20America/1/U.S.%20Cover%20Note%20INDC%20and%20Accompanying%20Information.pdf.

9 The Russian Federation has proposed a reduction of greenhouse gas emissions of around 25–30% from 1990 levels by 2030. Intended nationally determined contribution (INDC) and clarifying information submitted on 1 April 2015, at p. 3. Available at: www4.unfccc.int/Submissions/INDC/Submission%20Pages/submissions.aspx.

10 *R. Heede*, Tracing anthropogenic carbon dioxide and methane emissions to fossil fuel and cement producers, 1854–2010, Climate Accountability Institute, 2014, (122), pp. 229, 238.

In contrast, an alternative current of thought has emerged, based on biocentrist approaches, that promotes the recognition of nature as a subject of law, endowed of certain rights, like a mechanism '[...] *to transform structures and systems that cause climate change and other threats* [...]'. In this sense, the idea of a 'Universal Declaration of Rights of Mother Earth', proposed during the World People's Conference on Climate Change and the Rights of Mother Earth, carried out in Cochabamba, Bolivia, on 22 April 2010[11], is quite probably very well framed into the notion of legitimate representation of natural interests, not only before the international community, but also before other national actors. Besides, it could help to enshrine key aspects, such as independence to enact and enforce international environmental law.

Consequently, this essay is mainly aimed at analysing the most important theories that support the acknowledgement of nature as a holder of rights in the international legal framework, as a legitimate, independent, representative and more enforcing mechanism to protect the planet from pollution and overexploitation of its natural resources, which will include a critical approach important to the draft Universal Declaration of Rights of Mother Earth. By the end, it will also tackle a brief description about how the recognition of a new subject of law could operate in the international legal arena.

2. CHRISTOPHER STONE AND OTHER PROMOTERS OF LEGAL STANDING OF NATURE

In general terms, thinking about Nature as a holder of rights, and consequently as a subject of law, is not fairly recent. Indeed, one of the first references dates from 1971, when Earl Finbar Murphy asserted that '*there seem*[ed] *to be forming out of nature a kind of entelechy implying a term to all things*', in the context of the relationship between the urban civilization's demands, the rural environment's needs and their correlative effects.[12]

In 1972, Christopher Stone explicitly wrote that he was quite seriously proposing '[...] *to give legal rights to forest, oceans, rivers and other so-called "natural objects" in the environment – indeed, to the natural environment as a whole*'.[13] His reasoning was intensely supported on the extension of certain rights towards 'natural life', as it had historically happened with new bearers before law, such as children, women, blacks, Indians, foetuses, among others. As recognized

11 Universal Declaration of Rights of Mother Earth. Cochabamba (Bolivia), 22 April 2010. World People's Conference on Climate Change and the Rights of Mother Earth. Available at: http://therightsofnature.org/wp-content/uploads/FINAL-UNIVERSAL-DECLARATION-OF-THE-RIGHTS-OF-MOTHER-EARTH-APRIL-22-2010.pdf.

12 *E. Murphy*, Has Nature Any Right to Life? The Hastings Law Journal 1971 (22) p. 482.

13 *C. Stone*, Should Trees Have Standing? – Toward Legal Rights for Natural Objects. Southern California Law Review 1972 (45.2) p. 456.

by Stone himself, granting legal standing to the 'natural environment' occurred to him on the merits of the famous case: Sierra Club v. Morton[14], as a means to back up the claimant's allegation against that of the defendant's, relative to lack of right to sue, while it was pending appeal before the U.S. Supreme Court.[15]

While the case's roots could be found in 1965, the controversy actually started in 1969, when the U.S. Forest Service granted a 30-year permit to Walt Disney Productions, Inc. to construct a complex and a ski-resort on eighty acres of Mineral King Valley, located in the Sierra Nevada Mountains, adjacent to Sequoia National Park. The whole project comprised installations for lodging, food, swimming, parking, and transportation, among other facilities. In addition, a 20-mile high speed road and a 66-kilovolt power line were expected to be built, approvals for which had to be issued by the Department of the Interior.[16]

Initially, the suit filed by Sierra Club[17] was successful, given that the Federal District Court granted a preliminary injunction grounded on possible '[…] *excess of statutory authority, sufficiently substantial and serious to justify* […]' it, and rejected the respondents' allegation with regard to the club's right to sue.[18] Nevertheless, the Ninth Circuit Court of Appeals reversed the previous judgment, reasoning that Sierra Club was not the proper plaintiff because their members did not allege any affectation, which somehow could financially harm or jeopardize them. Besides, the tribunal argued that the general interest in conservation was not enough '*…to challenge the exercise of responsibilities on behalf of all citizens by two cabinet level officials of the government acting under Congressional and Constitutional authority*'.[19]

Finally, the U.S. Supreme Court upheld the Ninth Circuit's judgment in April 1972, affirming that a mere 'interest in a problem' by itself cannot be invoked as the starting point of litigation, because the Court would not be able to refuse future law suits, brought purely on basis of good faith and a 'special interest'.[20]

Despite this adverse decision, the whole process has always been seen as positive by Sierra Club members[21], maybe not only due to the fact that the project

---

14 U.S. Supreme Court: Case 70-34, *Sierra Club v. Morton, Secretary of the Interior,* et al. [1972] 405 U.S. 727.

15 *C. Stone,* Should Trees Have Standing? Revisited: How far will Law and Morals Reach? A Pluralist Perspective. Southern California Law Review 1985 (59.1) p. 2.

16 U.S. Supreme Court, *supra,* note 14 at p. 729.

17 The Sierra Club is a non-profit organization, founded by conservationist John Muir in 1892 (Sierra Club, 2016, available at www.sierraclub.org/about), that sued arguing '[…] *a special interest in the conservation and the sound maintenance of the national parks, game refuges and forests of the country,*[…]' (U.S. Supreme Court, *supra,* note 14 at p. 730).

18 U.S. Supreme Court, *supra,* note 14 at p. 731.

19 U.S. Court of Appeals, Ninth Circuit: Case F.2d 24 *Sierra Club v. Hickel, Secretary of the Interior, et al.* [1970] 9th Cir. 433.

20 U.S. Supreme Court, *supra,* note 14 at p. 739.

21 *L. Hartog,* Sierra Long Live the King. Sierra Club, 2009, available at: http://vault.sierraclub.org/sierra/200907/mineralking.aspx.

was never built, but essentially because Mineral King Valley was annexed into Sequoia National Park in 1978.[22]

Within the Court's reasoning in Sierra Club v. Morton, there are two key issues to address: representation and economic sense of nature's rights as requirements to legal standing.

2.1. IS THE LEGAL REPRESENTATION OF NATURE POSSIBLE?

Professor Stone profoundly analysed the legal obstacles to represent natural objects, and especially wilderness areas, before courts, being aware of the importance of legal actions to promote their conservation. The author suggested that guardianship be handled in the same way it is used to represent incompetent people or corporations in their lawful businesses, even with regard to estates; namely through appointing a guardian (could be '*ad litem*'), a conservator or a committee, as appropriate.[23] '[I]*f standing were the barrier, why not designate Mineral King, the wilderness area itself, as the plaintiff "suffering legal wrong,* [...]' allowing the club to be the legal representative, he continued stating twelve years later[24], and perhaps he would continue doing so nowadays, because it still seems to be the standard of the U.S. Courts. Indeed, last year in Conservation Law Foundation Inc. v. Continental Paving, Inc., the Court's main reasoning to deny the defendant's motion was that '[t]*he "relevant showing for purposes of Article III standing* [...] ***is not injury to the environment but injury to the plaintiff.*** *"* [...] *Therefore, some individualized specificity is required'.* In other words, the claimants were successful in Conservation Law Foundation Inc. v. Continental Paving, Inc. but failed in Sierra Club v. Morton for the same reason. While, the former were able to prove an 'actual injury' concerning their activities of swimming, canoeing, hunting, hiking and kayaking, given the pollution of the Soucook and Merrimack Rivers[25], the latter could not do the same. In conclusion, '[...] *the "injury in fact" test requires more than an injury to a cognizable interest. It requires that the party seeking review be himself among the injured.*[26]

Another relevant opinion came from Justice William O. Douglas, one of the Supreme Court members who took part in Sierra Club v. Morton. His dissent became an historic milestone among the promoters of nature's rights, because he compared the environmental issues with the role played by 'inanimate objects',

---

22 Sec. 314, Public Law # 95-625, Appendix B, Addition of Mineral King Valley to Sequoia National Park, 10 November 1978.

23 *C. Stone*, *supra*, note 13 at p. 464.

24 *C. Stone*, *supra*, note 15 at p. 2.

25 U.S. Court of District of New Hampshire: Case 2016 DNH 220 *Conservation Law Foundation, Inc. v. Continental Paving Inc. D/B/A Concord Sand & Gravel* [2016] D.N.H. 2016.

26 U.S. Supreme Court, *supra*, note 14 at p. 734–5.

such as ships or corporations, whose legal personality was wide enough not only to be considered as legitimate adversaries before courts, but also to accomplish maritime or other business ends. In a certain way, legal standing would allow 'environmental objects' to sue for their own preservation and look after their interests, through legal representation. He even suggested the shift of the case label to 'Mineral King v. Morton'.[27]

By the end, both authors share the opinion about enacting a law to promote representation. Douglas, for example, thought in a federal rule to allow litigating in the name of natural things '[...] *about to be despoiled, defaced, or invaded by roads and bulldozers and where injury is the subject of public outrage*'[28], just as Stone had done it by affirming that '[t]*he rights of the environment could be enlarged by borrowing yet another page* [...]' from the law.[29] It meant a future vision of at least thirty-five years concerning the course of certain legislation about this acknowledgement, as it ensued with the Ecuadorian Constitution of 2008[30] or the Bolivian Rights of Mother Earth Act of 2010[31], whose contents are strongly related.

Other authors have tackled the question of standing from diverse outlooks. One of those voices corresponded to Professor Godofredo Stutzin, who suggested to stop thinking about the environment as a human right, such as it was conceived in the Stockholm Declaration[32], and asked if one had not '[...] *discovered the rights of a new legal entity called Nature (or the Environment) by admitting that the natural environment has to be protected against human activity*'.[33]

Shortly after, during the First National Congress of Environmental Law at the Catholic University of Valparaiso (Chile), carried out in 1977, Stutzin stated that recognition of nature as a juristic person was not only lawfully possible but imperative, '[...] *a genuine "sine qua non" condition to structure authentic Ecological Law, able to cease the accelerated process of Biosphere's destruction*'. Under similar reasoning as Justice Douglas', Stutzin focused on the feasibility of using the category of juristic person in nature, as though it would be a corporation, as a means to accomplish the ends of justice and public welfare. Indeed, he supported the idea that nature is not a fictitious entity, since it counts on worthier and higher interests to be protected, such as a real (natural) existence, an unmatched setting

27 Id. at pp. 742–3.
28 Id. at p. 741.
29 Of course, Stone was referring specifically to the Environmental Protection Act and not to the law in a general sense (see: *C. Stone*, *supra*, note 13 at p. 484).
30 Constitución de la República del Ecuador, publicada en el Registro Oficial # 40, de 20 de octubre de 2008.
31 Ley de Derechos de la Madre Tierra, Ley # 71, Gaceta oficial de Bolivia, 21 de diciembre de 2010.
32 Declaration of the United Nations Conference on the Human Environment in Report of the United Nations Conference on the Human Environment, [1972] U.N. Doc. A/CONF.48/14Rev.1.
33 *G. Stutzin*, Should We Recognize Nature's Claim to Legal Rights? Environmental Policy and Law, 1976 (2) p. 129.

of organization, stability, vitality, autonomy, and a performance of vital functions that enables human existence.[34]

2.2. IS THERE AN ALTERNATIVE VIEW TO THE ECONOMIC SENSE OF ENVIRONMENTAL RIGHTS?

When one critically analyses the final decision of the U.S. Supreme Court in Sierra Club v. Morton, it can be observed that it was not enough only to be part of the injured, because the general consensus on damages encompassed a very well-defined economic sense: '[...] *the fact of economic injury is what gives a person standing to seek judicial review* [...], *but once review is properly invoked, that person may argue the public interest in support of his claim* [...]'.[35] Therefore, one could even conclude that its members did not understand the Club's interest over Mineral King Valley because it was not clear how to calculate the potential cost of injure.

In his dissenting opinion, Justice Douglas posited that it is not necessary to count on only economically valuable damages in order to protect environmental rights before courts, because there are other values to emphasize their importance, such as spiritual, aesthetic, recreational or ecological ones, inter alia. For instance, he quotes the case of the river, as '[...] *the living symbol of all the life it sustains or nourishes – fish, aquatic insects, water ouzels, otter, fisher, deer, elk, bear, and all other animals, including man, who are dependent on it or who enjoy it for its sight, its sound, or its life*'.[36] Then, one may wonder: What are those rights? What are their contents?

At first glance, Christopher Stone had a clue: the 'doctrine of irreparable injury'. It is worth to reflect on the existence of a certain kind of rights that '[...] *might be deemed "absolute," at least to the extent of, say, Free Speech*' for humans, given that several environmental impacts perhaps may yield irreversible damages to ecosystems, such as the loss of endangered species. Unfortunately, it has been (indeed 'is still' in much legislation) commonly difficult to define the term 'irreparable' in practice, even as 'irreversible', which has provoked as a result that sometimes '[...] *the marginal costs of abating the damage seem too clearly to exceed the marginal benefits,* [...]'. Even when it is about the example of extinction, its monetary assessment would be impossible and consequently it could not be compensated by means of a redress. Stone knew the situation very well and was already pretty aware that there were also political pressures that avoided the effective utilization of the irreparable harms doctrine, but it has been always an

---

34 *G. Stutzin,* Un imperativo ecológico: reconocer los derechos de la naturaleza. Ambiente y Desarrollo, 1984 (1.1) pp. 97, 104.

35 U.S. Supreme Court, *supra,* note 14 at p. 737.

36 Id. at p. 743.

alternative at least in the environmental field. Indeed, despite the high uncertainty to determine what the expression 'irreparable' means, it is lawfully indispensable to count on an accurate framework to set its limits, because otherwise it would entail an uncontrolled devastation of ecosystems.[37]

In this vein, when certain species stop existing, it is quite difficult – or even impossible – to assess the loss in an economic sense. For this reason, the right to respect the existence of nature could be included in the 'absolute rights' category, formulated by Professor Stone. Besides, it is worth it to mention that although the relationship between existence and life could be seen as pretty obvious, in practice it is very important to mark off the limits of respect for nature, given that all of life depends on it. If the scope is too wide or too tight, survival of humans and nonhumans would be jeopardized.

Paul Taylor intends to somehow delimit the scope of the term 'existence' of an individual nonhuman to '[...] *the full development of its biological powers*', which means a guarantee of its life and the involved natural cycles. However, he does not speak from the standpoint of nature's rights, but he does from a human's duties to nature, since it is sufficient, to him, when legal protection is granted to plants and animals. He states that it already means a '[...] *public recognition to their inherent worth*'.[38]

However, his argumentations are remarkable because his view has been incorporated in current legislation in force, as it appears both in the Ecuadorian Constitution and Bolivian law. Indeed, in the Ecuadorian Constitution it is explicitly provided that: '*Nature, or Pacha Mama*[39]*, where life is reproduced and occurs, has the right to integral respect for its existence and for the maintenance and regeneration of its life cycles, structure, functions and evolutionary processes*'.[40] Likewise, according to Bolivian law, Mother Earth is entitled to live, i.e. to maintain the integrity of life systems and natural process to support them, as well as its capacities and conditions for its regeneration.[41]

Back to the topic of economic assessment, if the right to respect the existence of nature is priceless, the question will be how states are going to protect ecosystems by means of law, but without a monetary estimation. Perhaps the response is currently centred around the 'Precautionary Principle'.

The Precautionary Principle may turn out to be very useful, given its effectiveness not only to reduce environmental risks, but also to avoid potential harms, to the extent that the protective measures are valid when there is no

---

37 Cf. *C. Stone*, *supra*, note 13 at p. 485–6.

38 *P. Taylor*, The Ethics of Respect for Nature, Environmental Ethics 1981 (3) pp. 199, 218.

39 Pacha Mama is the indigenous term used to name 'Mother Earth'. The expression is in the official Kichwa language.

40 Georgetown University & Center for Latin American Studies Program, Translation of the Constitution of the Republic of Ecuador, Political Database of the Americas, 2011, Available at: http://pdba.georgetown.edu/Constitutions/Ecuador/english08.html Article 71.

41 Ley de Derechos de la Madre Tierra, *supra*, note 31, Article 7.

scientific certainty of harm, which frequently cannot be monetarily assessed. Probably due to these reasons, the preliminary injunction, requested by the Sierra Club, was the self-explanatory legal action at the time and would be it again nowadays. Besides, it is usually supported in practice that an injunction is precisely the judicial instrument to elude or lessen irreparable harm, '[...] *a type of injury for which no remedy at law suffices,* [...]' that may seriously threaten ecosystems.[42]

In effect, it is not strange that some authors used to examine the concept of irreparable harms closely to the implementation of the Precautionary Principle in legal research[43], as a mechanism of environmental protection, not only due to the impossibility to obtain economic value to seek a reparation, but also as a response to those more complicated cases in which there is not any scientific evidence of the potential ecological injury. In this sense, one contemporary example in legal practice could be identified in the Article 396 of the Ecuadorian Constitution, in which it is provided that in case of doubt about the existence of an environmental impact, although there were '[...] *no scientific evidence of the damage, the State shall adopt effective and timely measures of protection*'.[44]

Unfortunately, it must be said that in current practice experts continue using the cost-benefit analysis, as a method to evaluate environmental degradation. In some way, this form of seeing the natural world arises from traditional Western philosophy in which ecosystems have been deemed as mere things, or 'goods' from a legal perspective. Things or goods are always valuable in monetary terms, and there are several methods and tools[45] to carry the process out. Nowadays, this way of thinking is still in full force all around the world. For instance, it is enough to look at the current British guidance on environmental impact assessment to realize it. In fact, the purpose of the document is: '[...] *to provide guidance and supporting material to enable departments to understand and quantify,* ***where possible in monetary terms,*** *the wider environmental consequences of their proposals*'.[46]

---

42 *S. Gifis*, Law Dictionary, Barron's, 2003, p. 271.

43 See: *C. Sustein*, Two Concepts of Irreversible Environmental Harm, University of Chicago Public Law & Legal Theory, 2008. Working Paper 218.

44 Georgetown University & Center for Latin American Studies Program, *supra*, note 37, at Article 396.

45 Among the most known ones, it can be mentioned: the Revealed Preference Methods (Market-price, Production function, Travel cost and Hedonic pricing), the Stated or Expressed Willingness-to-pay Methods (Contingent Valuation, Choice Experiments and Benefits Transfer), and Costs of Conserving Natural Resources (Management costs, Opportunity costs of conservation and External costs). See: *J. Mburu (ed.)*, Economic Valuation and Environmental Assessment: Training Manual. German Ministry of Education and Research (BMBF), BIOTA-East Africa Project, Center for Development Research (ZEF) and The World Conservation Union-Eastern Africa Regional Office (IUCN-EARO), 2005, pp. 36 et seq.

46 U.K. Department for Environment, Food & Rural Affairs, Assessing environmental impact: guidance. 9 April 2013. Available at https://www.gov.uk/guidance/assessing-environmental-impact-guidance.

In contrast, a different view concerns the concept of the incommensurability of environment elements as the foundation of the so-called 'strong sustainability', a notion from Ecological Economics which has even inspired innovative forms to analyse environmental issues, such as 'Multi-criterial Evaluation', as a response to the restrictions of the cost-benefit mechanisms, whose approach is unidimensional and exclusively directed to the economic concern. The idea consists of combining a series of different elements (social, environmental, cultural and even also economic, among others) to obtain a descriptive matrix – with several options – which can be seen from multiple dimensions (compromise-solutions), and not only from a mere economic value.[47]

Consequently, based on mechanisms like Multi-criterial Evaluation or other similar ones, decision makers, and even judges, would authorize or settle the human intervention over the environment with tools that could be used beyond the strict economic interest. However, not even this shift of perspective would be necessary, if nature would be considered as a subject of law, because under this circumstance its economic assessment would make no sense.

3. THOMAS BERRY AND THE THEORY OF EARTH JURISPRUDENCE

In 1999, the historian Thomas Berry wrote that the main cause of the planet's destruction could be found in a 'mode of consciousness' that had bestowed all rights only to humans to the detriment of non-humans, especially from the standpoint of the industrial-commercial world, emphasizing that the very existence of nature is aimed at human possession and use. Taking into account that American jurisprudence is oriented directly to personal human rights, Berry believed that '[...] *there can be no sustainable future, even for the modern industrial world, unless these inherent rights of the natural world are recognized as having legal status*'.[48]

At this point, with regard to Berry's argument about the close relationship between possession and the existence of nature, a profound economic significance reappears in its treatment, specifically referring to the judicial and administrative processes of environmental protection, derived mostly from the concept of non-human living things like mere objects and not as subjects of law. Consequently, living non-human beings are seen as goods, as it was mentioned, according to several laws and thus incapable to exercise any kind of rights. Meanwhile, humans are holders of rights over those goods, such as possession or use, but often also as property rights, as it has been pointed out by Susana Borràs, for whom

---

47 In deep, see: *J. Martínez-Alier, G. Munda & J. O'Neill*, Weak comparability of values as a foundation for ecological economics. Ecological Economics, 1998 (26), pp. 277–86.

48 *T. Berry*, The Great Work: Our Way into the Future. Bell Tower, 1999 pp. 4, 60, 61.

'[t]*he consequence has been that environmental laws and regulations, despite their preventive approach, have developed so as to legalize and legitimate environmental harm*'.[49]

In this context, Berry's approach is aimed at encouraging a proportional distribution of the planet's great commons (land, water, air) among all the members of the Earth community, depending on their particular needs, where a human being is not the centre, but only one more element within the processes of life. For that purpose, it is desirable to count on a 'new jurisprudence', as an alternative mechanism to enhance the human-earth relationship, through the articulation of adequate conditions for the integral functioning of those life processes.[50]

Berry's call for a 'new jurisprudence' became crucial to lay the groundwork of 'Earth Jurisprudence', a relatively new '[...] *emerging legal theory based on the premise that rethinking law and governance is necessary for the well-being of Earth and all of its inhabitants*', '[...] *recognizes a kinship with the field of environmental ethics* [...]' and '[...] *embraces the connection between Earth justice and social justice*'.[51] The initial and premature grounds of Earth Jurisprudence, included its own denomination, were originally agreed on by a group of philosophers who gathered with Berry in 2001, during a conference organized by GAIA Foundation in northern Virginia, USA.[52]

The most important theoretical contribution, elaborated by Thomas Berry, was to match the whole elements of Earth at the same level, by proposing a group of three fundamental rights: to be, to dwell, and to fulfil its role in the ever-renewing processes of the Earth community.[53] However, they are specific to every species, according to their own roles: humans have human rights, birds have bird rights, rivers have river rights, and so on.[54]

From an ethical perspective, the conditions of equality proposed by Berry, can only be understood by focusing on the role of each element of nature as an intrinsic value, in contrast to the traditional belief of classic Aristotelian philosophy, where natural elements are seen as mere instrumental values that are subordinated to higher ends.[55] Thus, the difference between standard principles

---

49 *S. Borràs,* New Transitions from Human Rights to the Environment to the Rights of Nature. Transnational Environmental Law. Cambridge University Press, 2016 (5:1) pp. 113–4.

50 *T. Berry, supra*, note 48, at p. 61.

51 *J. Koons,* Key Principles to Transform Law for the Health of the Planet, in P. Burdon (ed.) Exploring Wild Law: The Philosophy of Earth Jurisprudence, 2011, p. 45.

52 *M. Bell,* Thomas Berry and an Earth Jurisprudence: An Exploratory Essay, Trumpeter: Journal of Ecosophy, 2003 (19.1), p. 70.

53 It is important to notice the parallelism between Berry's proposal mainly with the right of 'respect for the existence of nature'.

54 *T. Berry,* Evening Thoughts, in B. Filgueira & I. Mason, Wild Law: Is there any evidence of earth jurisprudence in existing law and practice? UK Environmental Law Association & Gaia Foundation, 2009 (Appendix Three), p. 56.

55 For further analysis, see: *D. Keller,* Environmental Ethics: the big questions, Blackwell Publishing, 2010, pp. 5–6.

and those of Earth Jurisprudence becomes substantial, given that no benefit is any more important than another.

Furthermore, to guarantee the accurate condition of Earth's existence, property rights flexibility should be necessary, given that they would not have more value than other rights. In case of conflict, it would be quite probable that existence rights prevail over property. Berry is rather precise in affirming that '[h]*uman rights do not cancel out the rights of other modes of being to exist in their natural state*'.[56] The criticism to private property and its functions in the market is much more severe from this current of thought.

Another important proponent of 'Earth Jurisprudence' is Cormac Cullinan, who drew international attention, through the publication of his book: 'Wild Law: A Manifesto for Earth Justice' in 2002. His work became relevant, due to his attempts to search for an explanation of the Earth Jurisprudence theory from a legal angle. To this author, the reference to the Wild Law is not contradictory as could be thought, given that the term 'wild' – in common parlance – is usually close in meaning to other expressions, such as 'unkempt', 'barbarous', 'uncivilized', 'unrestrained', 'irregular' or 'out of control', among others; while 'Law' is an explicit reference to 'bind', 'constrain', 'regularize' or 'civilize', and so on. Wild Law should be understood more like a forthcoming to 'human governance' than a classic branch of law. In other words, it is about '[...] *laws that regulate humans in a manner that creates the freedom for all the members of the Earth Community to play a role in the continuing co-evolution of the planet*'.[57]

In the core of Cullinan's proposal is support for a change of the governance systems and philosophies as necessary to correct the disturbed relationship between Earth and mankind, inasmuch as old traditional systems have not been able to avoid, prevent or reduce the loss of biodiversity, pollution, deforestation, climate change and other contemporary environmental problems. In his own words, it is '[...] *needed to guide the realignment of human governance systems with the fundamental principles of how the universe functions* [...]', and it is what the author calls: 'Great Jurisprudence'.[58]

According to Filgueira and Mason, an accurate interpretation of Cullinan's opinion about why the old systems do not work out efficiently to protect the planet is fully in harmony with the previous arguments on the concept of natural world; ergo, legal systems treat Earth as a 'resource' and '[...] *value it only as such when in fact it is the organism that sustains all forms of life*'.[59] Hence, again the response is a change in the concept of nature, from object to subject of law, to a holder of rights.

56 *T. Berry*, *supra*, note 54, at. p. 56.

57 *C. Cullinan*, Wild Law: A Manifesto for Earth Justice (Extract), in Center for Earth Jurisprudence. An Introduction to Earth Jurisprudence: Guiding Principles and Wild Law Possibilities, 2011, p. 8.

58 Id., at p. 6.

59 *B. Filgueira & I. Mason*, Wild Law: Is there any evidence of earth jurisprudence in existing law and practice? UK Environmental Law Association & Gaia Foundation, 2009, p. 3.

4. THE RIGHTS OF MOTHER EARTH

As it was previously mentioned, the draft Universal Declaration of the Rights of Mother Earth was debated and written during the World People's Conference on Climate Change and the Rights of Mother Earth in 2010. Its importance mainly lies in being the first attempt to regulate and promote the respect for nature's rights at a global level, although there is a no less remarkable and explicit recognition of nature as a subject of law, through a quite suggestive phrase: *'Mother Earth is a living being'*[60], which sums up the entire proposal and its key issue.

In general terms, the proposal seems to be inspired by Paul Taylor and the principles of his Egalitarian Biocentrism, which has arisen as an alternative view to anthropocentric approaches. It can be noticed from the draft's preamble, whose first paragraph leaves no room for anthropocentrism: '[...] *considering that we are all part of Mother Earth, an indivisible, living community of interrelated and interdependent beings with a common destiny*'.[61]

Essentially, anthropocentrism represents a traditional Western philosophy where humans are seen in a better hierarchical position than other living beings, because the former are endowed with intrinsic values, meanwhile the latter are only instrumental and valuable if they are useful to humans. It is a human-centred outlook to understand the interrelation between mankind and nature. Instead, biocentrism is a life-centred philosophical theory, where intrinsic values are granted to all kinds of life, without exception. It is ruled by four fundamental principles shown below.

Even though it is an interesting proposal that sets aside the world prevailing theories concerning to legal standing, it does not stop being a mere statement of good purposes; namely a list of rights and duties. One can say it is a good start, but it is still not possible to pose a potential solution to the key questions: representation and economic assessment. There is only a faint reference to promote friendly economic systems with nature.[62]

The principles of biocentrism[63] are as follows:

4.1. HUMANS ARE MEMBERS OF THE EARTH'S COMMUNITY

Taylor asserts that human beings are members of the Earth's Community of Life, certainly not the most important ones, but they occupy the same place as other living species. A brief association between this principle and the draft could be

---

60 Declaration of Rights of Mother Earth, *supra*, note 11, at Article 1[1].

61 Id. at Preamble 1.

62 Id. at Article 3(i).

63 *P. Taylor*, Respect for Nature: A theory of Environmental Ethics. Princeton University Press, 2011 (Twenty-fifth anniversary edition), pp. 99 et seq.

supported on the aforementioned first statement and also on the fifth, where it is set as a requirement to the recognition of human rights, at least a concomitant acknowledgment of rights of nature, i.e. *"affirming that to guarantee human rights it is necessary to recognize and defend the rights of Mother Earth and all beings in her and that there are existing cultures, practices and laws that do so"*.[64]

4.2. NATURE IS A SYSTEM OF INTERDEPENDENCE

The natural world is described as a web by Taylor, where every living being is interconnected to and depends on others. Indeed, the very definition of 'being', individually seen, is linked to its relationships as an integral part of Mother Earth.[65]

Any change experienced by the system of interdependence, either in populations or in environments may cause potential adjustments in the whole mesh. Even though this principle explicitly appears also in the first statement, the fourth is perhaps clearer: '*convinced that in an interdependent living community it is not possible to recognize the rights of only human beings without causing an imbalance within Mother Earth*'.[66]

4.3. ORGANISMS AS TELEOLOGICAL CENTERS OF LIFE

To Taylor, individual organisms should be seen as teleological centres of life, which entails that living entities are always looking for their own welfare through their own means. Basically, the moral ends are closely related to survival in order to maintain biological operations and get adapted to potential environmental modifications. In his words, a teleological centre of life is '[...] *unified, coherently ordered system of goal-oriented activities that has a constant tendency to protect and maintain the organism's existence"*.[67] This tenet is reproduced almost exactly in the draft: '*Mother Earth is a unique, indivisible, self-regulating community of interrelated beings that sustains, contains and reproduces all beings*'.[68]

4.4. DENIAL OF HUMAN SUPERIORITY

The denial of human superiority is the most important precept for Taylor and his theory, because it is the explanation about how the assignment of intrinsic values to all kinds of life works out. There is not a hierarchical organization on it,

---

64 Declaration of Rights of Mother Earth, *supra*, note 11, at Preamble 5.
65 Id., at Article 1[3].
66 Id., at Preamble 4.
67 *P. Taylor*, *supra*, note 62, at p. 122.
68 Declaration of Rights of Mother Earth, *supra*, note 11, at Article 1[2].

although there are specificities. For example, while humans are endowed of free will, birds can fly, certain mammals can run faster or autotrophs (plants) can produce their own food (photosynthesis).[69]

5. RIGHTS OF NATURE IN THE INTERNATIONAL LAW FRAMEWORK

The international acceptance of State sovereignty over its natural resources implies, in certain a sense, they can be exploited with some freedom, of course except when it concerns transboundary resources, as in Hungary v. Slovakia.[70] In fact, in Article # 3 of the Convention on Biological Biodiversity it is provided that '[s]*tates have* [...] *the sovereign right to exploit their own resources pursuant to their own environmental policies*, [...]', in concordance to Article # 15, where can be found an explicit recognition of the sovereign rights of states over their natural and genetic resources.[71] Likewise, in the Covenant on Civil and Political Rights one can identify a similar example: '*All peoples may, for their own ends, freely dispose of their natural wealth and resources* [...]'.[72]

Consequently, states have been extracting and exploiting their natural resources, either themselves or by granting environmental permits to the private sector, which is not really a problem *per se*, but denotes certain implications about their legitimacy and independence to promote conservation and control pollution, according to their national regulations in force. Moreover, environmental issues become crucial if one takes into account that the current legal framework has not been totally effective at a local or international level.

5.1. LEGITIMACY AND INDEPENDENCE OF STATES

As it was mentioned, Richard Heede concluded that almost two-thirds of historic emissions (1854–2010) of the most important greenhouse gases could be

---

69 *P. Taylor*, *supra*, note 62, p. 130.

70 The case '*Gabcikovo-Nagymaros Project*' consisted of binational Treaty agreed to between Slovakia (ex-Czechoslovakia) and Hungary to construct a set of dams along the Danube River in 1977. Hungary abandoned the works in 1989 while Slovakia made adjustments to its part of the project in 1991. Then, Hungary claimed its right to terminate the agreement, alleging environmental concerns, due to execution of unilateral measures by Slovakia, which provoked the diversion of the river. At the end, the Court rejected Hungary's claim (International Court of Justice, ICJ REP 1997 7).

71 Convention on Biological Biodiversity, in Chapter XXVII. Environment, Vol-2, Rio de Janeiro, 5 June 1992, U.N. Doc. Ch_XXVII_8.

72 International Covenant on Civil and Political Rights, 16 Dec. 1966, in force 23 March 1976. Annex to the Resolution adopted by the General Assembly. UN Doc. A/RES/21/2200. Article 1(2).

attributed to only ninety companies worldwide, with half of them emitted from 1986; i.e. the exact period when the main agreements about climate change and other environmental concerns had been agreed to. Besides, forty of these entities were State-owned (44%).[73]

Certainly, these research outputs were quite controversial, and maybe even debatable, as it could be seen in a blog post made by Severin Borenstein, who criticized the argument suggesting that responsibility for the greater part of global warming lies only in the fossil fuel industry, solely through the 90 largest companies around the world. In a sarcastic tone, he questioned: '*Really? If those evil fossil fuel companies would just stop producing their energy poison, the problem would be solved?*' He considered that the main challenge is not located in the offer, but in the demand, i.e. the consumers and government agencies, who are usually more interested in energy prices than other economic actors.[74]

In any event, being true or not that just 90 enterprises are to blame for climate change or pollutant emissions, the truth is that almost half of them are State-owned, which entails a remarkable consequence in terms of environmental public policy. Indeed, knowing beforehand that aforementioned states own potential polluting industries, as part of their assets, one may wonder if it is a rightful matter that they also control and promote environmental policy. Are not there contradictory interests? How can one fight against global warming and discharge hazardous emissions at the same time? Perhaps there is not a rational response to these questions or it is not easy elaborate it, given that there is often a lack of legitimacy and independence in state actions with regard to environmental measures that authorities are obligated to take. In addition, the processes of environmental impact assessments are often criticized because the potential pollutant activities under control are reviewed by the very promoters, i.e. states. This ensues with all 'strategic projects', according to the national interests: electricity generation, construction of roads, mining, oil and gas extraction, among others. The question about legitimacy and independence stays as a strong dilemma under these circumstances.

Going back briefly to the introduction of this article, the situation turns out similar to the close relationship between the UN and their important members, such as China, U.S.A., Russia, France, United Kingdom, inter alia. At some point, institutional bodies become judge and jury, and this is exactly what happens with states when they are agents of development. They have to promote potentially harmful projects and protect the environment at the same time. There is a controversial conflict of interests.

---

73 *R. Heede*, *supra*, note 10, at pp. 229, 238.

74 *S. Borenstein*, Is demonizing "big carbon" a strategy or a copout? Energy Institute at HAAS School of Business, University of California Berkeley, 16 December 2013. Available at: https://energyathaas.wordpress.com/2013/12/16/is-demonizing-big-carbon-a-strategy-or-a-copout/?utm_source=Blog+Dec+16%2C+2013&utm_campaign=blog49&utm_medium=email.

In context, if states are not completely able to guarantee enough legitimacy and independence in their actions to protect ecosystems, then it is necessary to count on a new institutional actor in order to accomplish this objective. Nevertheless, in practice there is not another entity capable to replace the State functions, because each one represents different interests in the local and even transnational spheres. Neither non-governmental organizations nor associations of consumers or producers, nor environmentalists can fulfil the state role because they do not have power of enforcing the law, and due to their lack of representation.

In this framework, pertaining to Dixon & McCorquodale, it is worthwhile to agree that '[t]*he global nature of environmental issues means that national action by itself, while important, may be insufficient, and that significant international cooperation is required*'.[75] In this sense, the recognition of nature as a subject of international law, independent from any particular State, could be an alternative to ensure the necessary legitimacy to fight against environmental depletion.

5.2. NATURE AS A NEW ACTOR ON THE INTERNATIONAL SCENE

It is widely known that states have been the main actors in the international context, even to the point of being deemed as the only ones, from the perspective of the orthodox positivist doctrine. In a certain sense, as Hersch Lauterpacht explains, the overriding opinion had been to ascribe subjective rights to states in an exclusive way; meanwhile human beings were regarded solely as objects of those protections, given their condition of nationals at issue.[76]

Nevertheless, despite the textual allusions to the orthodox positivist assertion, according to Professor Malcom Shaw, nowadays one is not really able to argue that kind of 'dogmatism', because institutional entities – either religious, political or even commercial – have gradually acquired the condition of 'international persons', entailing an increasingly complicated scene of global interactions.[77]

This progressive recognition of new subjects, such as insurgents, international organizations and even individuals, did not take place overnight. On the contrary, it has been a slow process that has taken a lot of time, and has also implied abundant doctrinal debate and arduous political negotiations. To Antonio Cassese, there are several reasons to justify the inclusion of new members in the international community, such as national liberation movements and individuals for instance, in whose cases the ideological factor played a remarkable role, given the popularization of the human rights doctrine, mainly in the Western democracies

---

75 *M. Dixon & R. McCorquodale*, Cases & Materials on International Law, Oxford University Press, 2003, p.454.

76 *H. Lauterpacht*, International Law: Collected Papers. Vol. 2 (Cambridge University Press, 1975), at p. 489.

77 *M. Shaw*, International Law. Cambridge University Press, 2003, p. 177.

since mid-twentieth century.[78] For this reason, suggesting that Nature could be a new participant, lawfully legitimized, in the international sphere is definitely not an easy task.

5.3. NATURE, FROM A COMMODITY TO A BEARER OF RIGHTS

The concept of nature in the legal parlance has been profoundly human-centred, especially with regard to international, legally binding instruments. In fact, the most generalized idea refers to environmental issues as part of the human right to a healthy environment. For example, one can take explicit quotations from the International Covenant on Economic, Social and Cultural Rights (1966), the International Covenant on Civil and Political Rights (1966), the Convention on International Trade in Endangered Species of Wild Fauna and Flora (1973), the U.N. Framework Convention on Climate Change (1992), the Convention on Biological Diversity (1992), the U.N. Convention to combat desertification in those countries experiencing serious drought and/or desertification, particularly in Africa (1994), among others.

In addition, this notion is extensively reinforced by several of the most remarkable instruments of environmental policy, starting by the Stockholm Declaration of 1972, in whose first principle has been declared that people can exercise their rights in an 'environment of quality'.[79] Similarly, in the first principle of the Rio Declaration of 1992, one can read that '[h]*uman beings are at the centre of concerns for sustainable development*'.[80]

Therefore, the recognition of nature as a subject of law, and subsequently as a holder of rights entails a complete shift of structure. It is about leaving the idea of natural resources seen as commodities, goods or mere things, and entering to a new sphere where there is a new actor endowed of certain privileges as others.

In this framework, this change of structure implies thinking about nature as a juristic person, whose main characteristic consists of being a 'holder of rights and duties', as it has been asserted over time. Georg Schwarzenberger[81] and Jean Salmon[82] are a couple of examples in the international law field. Besides, it will be necessary to include the right to sue before any tribunal as the best manifestation of the exercise of its international personality. The question concerning 'representation' is also part of it.

---

78 *A. Cassese*, International Law (Oxford University Press, 2001), at. pp. 69–70.

79 Stockholm Declaration, *supra*, note 32, at Principle 1.

80 Rio Declaration on Environmental and Development, in Report of the United Nations Conference on Environment and Development, [1992] U.N. Doc. A/CONF.151/26 (Vol. I).

81 *G. Schwarzenberger*, A Manual of International Law, Vol. I. Stevens & Sons Limited, 1960, p. 47.

82 *J. Salmon (ed)*, Dictionnaire de Droit International Public. Bruylant, Bruxelles, 2001, p. 1062.

However, the aforementioned peculiarities are not enough because a subject of customary law could also possess them and be a legal person without necessity of any recognition, as it is stated by Ian Brownlie. To him, it is crucial that legal personality can denote certain additional capacities, such as '[…] *to make claims in respect of breaches of international law, […] to make treaties and agreements valid on the international plane, and the enjoyment of privileges and immunities from national jurisdictions*'.[83]

Unfortunately, only states can possess the legal powers listed by Brownlie. Because of that, some authors divide the subjects of international law between original or principal ones[84] (states) and derivative or secondary ones (international organizations, national liberation movements and individuals).[85] In this sense, since it is quite clear that nature cannot be considered a state, hereinafter the main question will be if it is possible or not to address its legal recognition from the standpoint of secondary subjects, although it can be an entirely new topic of study.

In any case, it is worthwhile to mention that secondary subjects of law are also called 'derivative ones' since they are created by a derivation from the state will. For instance, international organizations were founded by means of the subscription of international treaties or agreements, which usually corresponds to necessities of cooperation[86] or any other ends, as it was pointed out by Cassese.[87] This legal structure could be useful for nature.

To conclude, what states and the other subjects of law share in common is the idea of recognition. Despite the fact that '*there is not a procedure in international law for the ascertainment, declaration or registration of a new State*', as it is held by Perrin de Brichambaut et al.[88], it is one the most addressed topics in the legal studies about personality. Without any kind of recognition (unilateral declarations, treaties, agreements, U.N. sessions, and so on), there is not any subject. Therefore, in the case of Nature, an explicit recognition by the international community would be a previous condition.

6. CONCLUSIONS

1. Legal standing of nature is not a constructed theory, but a concept in continuous transformation. The ethical development of the grounds have to

83 *I. Brownlie*, Principles of Public International Law. Oxford University Press, 1963, pp. 52–3.

84 Certain authors, such as Cassese, consider that insurgents are also traditional subjects of international law. Insurgents are parties of a military dissidence, armed conflict or rebels succeeding in controlling a section of territory, within a sovereign state, that claims international recognition. See: *A. Cassese, supra*, note 78, at p. 66.

85 *L. Aledo*, Le Droit International Public Dalloz, 2005, pp. 23.

86 Id., at p. 39.

87 *A. Cassese, supra*, note 78, at. pp. 69–70.

88 *M. Perrin de Brichambaut, J. Dobelle & M. d'Haussy*, Leçons de droit international public, Presses de Sciences PO et Dalloz, 2002, p. 52.

be debated in wider spaces in order to reach a better diffusion and improve its contents.

2. Through the recognition of rights of nature, it would be possible to maintain more legitimacy and independence from the states and their interests in branches like environmental management, public policy, among others.

3. A realistic representation of Nature as a holder of rights is only possible from the perspective of International Law. If it is not at a global level, the result will be that polluters and judges will be the same moral entities in every single country.

4. The proposal of a Universal Declaration could be considered as a good beginning but it still requires a much deeper analysis, above all considering its implications about legal enforcement and the potential limitation to its exercise.

5. Given that it is a theory under construction, there are a lot of topics for future research. For instance: The implications of rights of property, the shift from Human Rights towards Rights of Nature, or the derivative personality of Nature.

STRENGTHENING CONSERVATION THROUGH PARTICIPATION: PROCEDURAL ENVIRONMENTAL RIGHTS OF LOCAL COMMUNITIES IN TRANSBOUNDARY PROTECTED AREAS

Emma Mitrotta*

ABSTRACT

Procedural environmental rights can be applied across state borders by way of the non-discrimination principle. This 'transboundary' or 'extraterritorial' dimension is first explored in the framework of regional organisations, such as the European Union and the Southern African Development Community (SADC), that can facilitate the emergence of higher participatory standards and, based on those standards, foster legislative harmonisation among the member states. The regional framework influences the dynamics of interstate cooperation in all fields, including for the conservation of shared natural resources. In the context of cross-border conservation initiatives, like transboundary protected areas (TBPAs), the extraterritorial application of procedural environmental rights can strengthen public participation of local communities. These communities are entitled to procedural environmental rights as 'public concerned' towards all partner countries since the creation of a TBPA can impinge on their survival and livelihoods. Indeed, local communities have a primary role in the sustainable management of natural resources, and their participation is crucial for the long-term success of cross-border conservation. Transfrontier Conservation Areas (TFCAs) have been established to frame cross-border conservation efforts in the SADC region; therefore, the Kavango Zambezi Transfrontier Conservation Area is used to exemplify the extraterritorial dimension of procedural environmental rights of local communities in the context of TBPAs.

* PhD Candidate, School of International Studies, University of Trento (Italy).

KEYWORDS

Biodiversity conservation; Community participation; EU; Good governance; KAZA TFCA; Local communities; Procedural environmental rights; SADC; Transboundary protected areas.

1. INTRODUCTION

Biodiversity is borderless: rivers often flow through political boundaries, ecosystems stretch over countries, and wild animals do not respect frontiers. Nevertheless, international borders have fragmented natural spaces, and divided territories and people: in most of the cases, such demarcations were drawn artificially disregarding not only ecological considerations, but also socio-cultural and language aspects.

In these contexts, transboundary protected areas (TBPAs)[1] can be used as effective tools to frame cross-border conservation efforts as well as to reconnect communities divided by externally imposed boundaries. The effective participation of such communities[2] to the protection and management of these

---

1 The term TBPA is used by the International Union for the Conservation of Nature (IUCN) to identify transboundary conservation initiatives, thus encompassing a wide variety of approaches and arrangements adopted to this end. In this essay, the concept of TBPAs is used in a broad sense to identify any type of transfrontier conservation effort. See *B. Lausche*, Guidelines for Protected Areas Legislation, 2011, pp. 268–269.

2 In this essay, the concept of 'local communities' is used in general terms to identify the inhabitants of a circumscribed area that share their living space, have access to a common pool of natural resources, and interact with each other. The composition of local communities is context-specific and can include indigenous peoples. The identification of local communities is contended in international law, for an in-depth discussion on this topic, see *A. Bessa*, Traditional local communities in international law (Doctoral Dissertation, European University Institute) 2013. Defining 'indigenous peoples' goes beyond the scope of my essay, however, it is important to acknowledge that this concept has been extensively debated in international law. A comprehensive definition of 'indigenous peoples' in international law is missing, not only for the historical and cultural differences among the various groups, but also because indigenous peoples have been refusing externally imposed solutions and preferring a self-identification approach. In addition, a few distinctive criteria have been elaborated at the international level in order to assess the applicability of indigenous rights. For further details refer to the work of the Working Group on Indigenous Populations (a subsidiary organ of the Sub-Commission on the Promotion and Protection of Human Rights operating since 1982), the Permanent Forum on Indigenous Issues, and the UN Special Rapporteur on the Rights of Indigenous Peoples; refer, in particular, to *E.-I. Daes* (Special Rapporteur of the Sub-Commission on Prevention of Discrimination and Protection of Minorities and Chairperson of the Working Group on Indigenous Populations), Study on the protection of the cultural and intellectual property of indigenous people, U.N. Doc. E/CN.4/Sub.2/1993/28 (1993); see also *A. Fodella*, International Law and the Diversity of Indigenous Peoples, Vermont Law Review 2006 (30) 3 p. 565; *P. Thornberry*, Indigenous Peoples and Human Rights, 2002. Moreover, Cittadino provides a useful analysis of the jurisprudence of human rights bodies contributing to the recognition of indigenous peoples' participatory rights in environmental decision-making and identifies four main trends: (1) political rights,

transboundary natural spaces and the biodiversity resources included therein is essential to ensure good governance. However, the recognition of procedural environmental rights to local communities in TBPAs cannot be taken for granted.

In this essay, I explore the application of procedural environmental rights across state borders and their recognition to local communities in TBPAs. In the first section, I explain that the principle of non-discrimination and equal access enables the transboundary or 'extraterritorial' dimension of public participation, especially in the framework of regional organisations, such as the European Union (EU) and the Southern African Development Community (SADC). This extraterritorial dimension is equally applicable in TBPAs. In the second section, I discuss why local communities can be considered as 'public concerned': these communities have a privileged connection to natural resources and play a primary role for their conservation and sustainable management, including when conservation-dedicated initiatives are in place. Hence, I explore the recognition of procedural environmental rights to local communities in national protected areas (PAs). In the third section, I discuss the entitlement of local communities to exercise the same participatory rights in a transboundary context; for this purpose, I use the Kavango Zambezi Transfrontier Conservation Area as a case study.

2. THE EXTRATERRITORIAL DIMENSION OF PUBLIC PARTICIPATION

The idea of and concerns for public participation is not relegated to the environmental sphere, but has its roots in the very concept of democracy and builds on existing human rights concepts. For instance, in its Article 21(1), the 1948 Universal Declaration of Human Rights states that 'Everyone has the right to take part in the government of his country, directly or through freely chosen representatives'.[3] Its application to environmental matters was anticipated

---

(2) formal standards of participation, (3) the paradigm of effective participation, and (4) the prior informed consent of communities. See *F. Cittadino*, Public Interest to Environmental Protection and Indigenous Peoples' Rights: Procedural Rights to Participation and Substantive Guarantees, in E.J. Lohse & M. Poto (eds) in cooperation with G. Parola, Participatory Rights in the Environmental Decision-Making Process and the Implementation of the Aarhus Convention: A Comparative Perspective, 2015, pp. 75–90. On the role of the international jurisprudence for the protection of indigenous peoples rights in the environmental field see *A. Fodella*, Indigenous Peoples, the Environment, and International Jurisprudence, in N. Boschiero, T. Scovazzi, C. Pitea & C. Ragni (eds.), International Courts and the Development of International Law, 2013, pp. 349–364.

3 U.N. GAOR, 3RD Session, Res. 217A (III), UN Doc A/810 (1948). The connection between participatory rights in environmental matters and human rights regimes is acknowledged and mentioned several times throughout this essay, but it falls outside its scope of analysis. For a brief overview refer to *J. Ebbesson*, Principle 10: Public Participation, in J. E. Viñuales (ed.), The Rio Declaration on environment and development: A commentary, 2015, p. 297 et

under the guise of environmental education in Principle 19 of the Stockholm Declaration[4] and affirmed more clearly in Principle 23 of the World Charter for Nature and Principle 10 of the Rio Declaration.[5] Public participation has been codified at national level and included in several international conventions; its maximum expression is reflected in the 1998 UNECE Convention on Access to Information, Public Participation in Decision-making and Access to Justice in Environmental Matters[6] which represents a milestone in international law.

Public participation is complex both in its conceptual structure and in its practice. It is composed of three distinct pillars: (1) access to information, (2) participation in decision-making, and (3) access to administrative and judicial remedies. They are strongly interlinked and mutually reinforcing: while accessing appropriate information is essential to satisfy the right to know[7] and to participate meaningfully in decision-making, accessing remedies provides the opportunity to both redress unjust outcomes[8] (including the refusal to access information and the use of inappropriate decision-making procedures) and directly enforce environmental law provisions, thus reinforcing the application and respect, on the part of the state and other relevant actors, of the other two pillars and of environmental law in general. It is understandable that there are several degrees of public participation since its practical application depends on the jurisdictional system considered, for example in terms of participatory mechanisms provided by national provisions, and on the conditions on the grounds, like the availability and collection of environmental information, the capability of responsible authorities/actors to share such information, and the competence of the public to contribute to decision-making processes.

In addition to the three aforementioned pillars, there is a forth and cross-cutting component that is the principle of 'non-discrimination' and equal access in environmental matters. This principle defines the 'extraterritorial' dimension of participatory rights since it enables their application across borders.[9] Ebbesson

seq. See also *P. Birnie, A. Boyle & C. Redgwell,* International Law and the Environment 3rd ed., 2009, pp. 288–289.

4 See UN Conference on the Human Environment, Stockholm, 5–16 June 1972.

5 See UN Conference on Environment and Development, Rio de Janeiro, 3–14 June 1992.

6 Convention on Access to Information, Public Participation in Decision-Making and Access to Justice in Environmental Matters, Aarhus, 28 June 1998 – in force 30 October 2001, 2161 UNTS 447. Hereinafter, Aarhus Convention. Given the importance of this Convention, it is used as a reference point in this essay, for example to define key terms as 'public concerned'.

7 For example, to know the environment we are living in, to know potential risks that would affect the environment surrounding us, to know how certain activities could affect environmental conservation. The right to know is also functional to exercise the right to live in a healthy environment, thus reinforcing the human rights to life, to health, and to family.

8 *J. Ebbesson*, Access to Justice in Environmental Matters, in R. Wolfrum (ed.), Max Plank Encyclopedia of Public International Law (online ed.), para. 2.

9 This principle is also called 'national treatment' and, according to Nanda and Pring, has both a substantive and procedural character. In its substantive stance, it requires states to treat environmental harms caused to other states as seriously as they would do for harms occurred to their own territory or citizens. As such, it is asserted in the 1974 OECD Principles

explains that it allows 'members of the public to participate in decision-making and trigger judicial and administrative procedures in environmental matters across state borders'[10] and that it 'matters also for access to information in transboundary contexts'.[11] The non-discrimination and equal access principle is widely accepted: for instance, Article 3(9) of the Aarhus Convention reiterates its application to the three public participation pillars,[12] while other instruments focus only on one of them.[13] This wide acceptance is said to indicate that the principle of non-discrimination and equal access in environmental matters has achieved the status of general international law.[14]

Ebbesson highlights that non-discrimination does not impose international minimum standards for public participation, rather it extends the application of national participatory standards to persons across state borders – i.e. extraterritorially – in order to provide non-nationals with '*no less effective opportunities* to make use of remedies and procedures *for the protection of health and the environment* in the state of the harmful activity or installation [emphasis added]'.[15] The rationale behind Ebbesson's reasoning should not be limited to environmental damages as a consequence of harmful activities or installations,

Concerning Transfrontier Pollution (Title C), Principle 13 of the UNEP Draft Principles on Shared Natural Resources, Article 13 of the WCED Legal Principles for Environmental Protection and Sustainable Development, and Principle 14 of the Rio Declaration. Moreover, on the substantive level, non-discrimination derives from good neighbourliness, equity, and fairness, but, is also motivated by the fact that 'equal access to justice is yet imperfectly available, so that a state's environmental harms in other states may leave those victims without a practical remedy'. From a procedural point of view, it demands that a state, proposing or carrying out an activity with transboundary environmental effects, grants non-nationals that are going to (or are likely to) be affected by such activity equal access to information, participation, and remedies as it provides to its own citizens. *V. P. Nanda & G. W. Pring*, International Environmental Law and Policy in the 21st Century, 2013, p. 59.

10 *J. Ebbesson*, Public Participation in Environmental Matters, in R. Wolfrum (ed.), Max Plank Encyclopedia of Public International Law (online ed.), para. 7.

11 *J. Ebbesson*, Access to Information on Environmental Matters, in R. Wolfrum (ed.), Max Plank Encyclopedia of Public International Law (online ed.), para. 6. See also, *J. Ebbesson*, The Notion of Public Participation in International Environmental Law, Y.B. Int'l Envtl. L. 1998 (8), p. 51, 82.

12 This is also the case of Art. 9 of the Convention on the Transboundary Effects of Industrial Accidents, Helsinki, 17 March 1992 – in force 19 April 2000, 2015 UNTS 457.

13 For example, transboundary access to information and participation in decision-making are expressly foreseen by Art. 3(8) of the Espoo, Convention on Environmental Impact Assessment in Transboundary Context, Espoo, 25 February 1991 – in force 10 September 1997, 1989 UNTS 309. The equal access to administrative and judicial remedies is widely embedded in international environmental law instruments; for instance, it is foreseen in Article 3 of the Nordic Environment Protection Convention, which predates the Rio Declaration. On this point, see *G. (Rock) Pring & S. Y. Noé*, The Emerging International Law of Public Participation Affecting Global Mining, Energy, and Resources Development, in D. M. Zillman, A. Lucas, & G. (Rock) Pring (eds), Human Rights in Natural Resource Development: Public Participation in the Sustainable Development of Mining and Energy Resources, 2002, p. 44 et seq.

14 *J. Ebbesson*, Access to information, *supra*, note 11 at para. 6, and Access to Justice, *supra*, note 8 at para 7.

15 *J. Ebbesson*, Access to Justice, *supra*, note 8 at para. 7.

but should be applied to environmental protection in general, in line with the preventive approach that has evolved in international environmental law over the years.[16] Prevention can be interpreted in extensive terms as encompassing environmental protection and conservation, thus including integrated ecological planning and management in a long-term perspective, preservation of biodiversity, and sustainable development.[17]

The extraterritorial application of participatory rights is crucial in the context of regional organisations since higher participatory standards in one country can boost improvements towards this direction in the other partner countries. This result is facilitated by the presence of an appropriate regional legal framework, as in the case of the EU, where law harmonisation has been consistently and expressly pursued, including in the field of participatory rights. The EU is a party to the Aarhus Convention and has put in place several measures to ensure its implementation at community level as well as in the member states.[18] Far from imposing complete uniformity, EU secondary law has created a common ground for the recognition of participatory rights in all EU countries and is fostering changes in those countries that do not as yet fulfil the existing obligations, especially in relation to access to remedies. Hence, European citizens can access remedies in any member state different from the one of their nationality to seek redress in environmental matters on the basis of non-discrimination and equal access.[19] In the context of judicial procedures, the claimant can also rely on EU provisions on public participation that are precise, clear and unconditional, but have not been applied in the state of the trial,[20] thus strengthening both

---

16 On this point, Kiss and Shelton explain that most of the international environmental treaties adopt a preventive logic rather than a responsive logic: '[T]he objective of almost all international environmental instruments is to prevent environmental deterioration (...). Only a few international instruments rely on other approaches, such as the traditional principle of state responsibility for harm already caused or direct compensation of the victims by the originator of the pollution'. *A. Kiss & C. Shelton*, Guide to International Environmental Law, 2007, p. 92. In addition, Sands highlights that 'the preventive principle seeks to minimise environmental damages as an object in itself' and that it is applicable to transboundary contexts as demonstrated by international jurisprudence such as the Trail Smelter Arbitration, the Lac Lanoux Arbitration, and the Nuclear Tests case. *P. Sands*, Principles of International Environmental Law, 2003, p. 246 et seq.

17 *A. Kiss & C. Shelton*, *supra* note 16 at p. 92 et seq.

18 For further details see the draft report prepared by the Commission as the basis of the 4th EU Aarhus Implementation Report and currently open for consultation at http://ec.europa eu/environment/aarhus/pdf/EU_aarhus_implementation_report_2017.pdf [accessed 29 December 2016].

19 Also Article 18 of the Lisbon Treaty introduces the principle of non-discrimination based on nationality. Treay of Lisbon Amending the Treaty of European Union and the Treaty Establishing the European Community, Lisbon, 13 December 2017 – in force 1 December 2009.

20 The European Court of Justice has actively strengthened the primacy of EU law over national laws especially through the theory of direct effect introduced in the Van Gend en Loos judgement (Case 26–62), while the supremacy doctrine was developed in the decision of the Costa/ENEL (Case 6–64). The Treaty of Lisbon explicitly recognises the primacy of EU law over the law of the member states (Declaration n. 17).

the application of participatory rights in a transboundary context and of EU law. Therefore, the presence of a regional legal framework with effective participatory provisions strengthens public participation in both its national and extraterritorial dimensions.

The Southern African Development Community (SADC),[21] instead, does not have any common provision on participatory rights,[22] but such rights are recognised in some member states more than others. For instance, public participation is entrenched in the South African legal framework: Section 24 of the Constitution establishes the environmental rights of South Africa's citizens and, in its paragraph (b), foresees a proactive attitude of the government which, according to A. Du Plessis, 'implies a need for public participation in environmental decision-making at all levels'.[23] Such a need is further exemplified in other constitutional provisions that encourage the involvement of the public, especially at local level,[24] and it is conceived as a principle governing public administration.[25] Participation in decision-making is complemented by the right to access to information[26] and the right to just administrative action;[27] therefore, the South African Constitution integrates the three pillars of public participation. This constitutional framework is supplemented by secondary legislation[28] that emphasises the importance

---

21 SADC is an international organisation (Art. 3 of the founding Treaty) aiming to achieve economic development, peace and security, growth, poverty alleviation, higher standard and quality of life of the peoples of Southern Africa through regional integration based on democratic principles, and equitable and sustainable development. It is composed of Southern African Countries, namely Angola, Botswana, Democratic Republic of Congo, Lesotho, Madagascar, Malawi, Mauritius, Mozambique, Namibia, Seychelles, South Africa, Swaziland, United Republic of Tanzania, Zambia, and Zimbabwe. Regional cooperation is functional to achieve the objectives established in Art. 5 of the SADC Treaty, therefore, it has a multi-sectoral character as exemplified in Art. 21 of the same Treaty. Declaration and Treaty of the Southern African Development Community, Windhoek 17 August 1992. Hereinafter, SADC Treaty.

22 In this regard, Ebbesson highlights that the development of participatory rights has mostly occurred at regional level through both their inclusion in environmental agreements and the jurisprudence of human rights bodies. Nevertheless, he notices remarkable geographical asymmetries: Europe and Central Asia are the most supportive to participatory rights, the Americas and Africa also promote these rights to a significant degree, while Asia and the Pacific are the weakest in this sense. See *J. Ebbesson*, Principle 10, *supra*, note 3 at p. 293, 298 et seq. In Ebbesson's analysis emerges that several provisions of the 1981 African Charter on Human and Peoples' Rights (Nairobi, 27 June 1981 – in force 21 October 1986) are relevant for the promotion of participatory rights in Africa (*id.* at 302). Notwithstanding the gap of participatory provisions at SADC level, those included in the African Charter bind SADC countries that are all parties to it. Moreover, by virtue of Article 19(3), the Aarhus Convention is open to all the member states of the United Nations, therefore, any SADC state could accede to the aforementioned Convention upon approval by the Meeting of the Parties.

23 *A. Du Plessis*, Public Participation, Good Environmental Governance and Fulfilment of Environmental Rights, PER 2008 (2), p. 14.

24 Constitution of the Republic of South Africa (1996), Section 152(1)(e).

25 Constitution of the Republic of South Africa (1996), Section 195 (e).

26 Constitution of the Republic of South Africa (1996), Section 32.

27 Constitution of the Republic of South Africa (1996), Section 33.

28 For further details on South African secondary legislation including participatory provisions, see *A. Du Plessis*, Public Participation, *supra* note 23 at p. 15 et seq.

of participation in environmental matters also as a means of personal and community growth – by understanding and being aware of environmental issues – and of inclusion of all interested and affected parties. Nevertheless, the favour that public participation finds with the South African legal framework is exceptional in the context of the SADC region, where participatory mechanisms are sometimes foreseen in national laws, but are not operational in many countries, especially those under authoritarian regimes, or recently pacified and undergoing a democratic transition. Despite the fact that participatory rights are missing in the SADC legal framework, this regional organisation could provide the platform for legal harmonisation among its member states and, in this context, South African participatory standards could guide the harmonisation process. Although legal harmonisation is not specifically foreseen by the SADC Treaty, it can be considered as both functional to achieve its objectives and connected to policy harmonisation that is required in Article 5(1)(a). Therefore, despite the absence of effective regional participatory standards, the presence of a regional organisation not only can foster a legal harmonisation process that enables the development of public participation at national level in its member states, but also favours its extraterritorial dimension in a successive phase.

The extraterritorial dimension of participatory rights can also be conceived in the context of cross-border conservation initiatives, like SADC transfrontier conservation areas (TFCAs). The Protocol on Wildlife and Law Enforcement[29] has established TFCAs[30] to frame cooperation among SADC states over transboundary natural resources.[31] In the framework of TFCAs, partner countries are adapting

29 Adopted in Maputo, Mozambique, 18 August 1999. Hereinafter, SADC Wildlife Protocol.

30 SADC Wildlife Protocol, Article 4(2)(f). Article 1 of the same Protocol defines a Transfrontier conservation area as 'the area or the component of a large ecological region that straddles the boundaries of two or more countries, encompassing one or more protected areas, as well as multiple resources use areas'; therefore, TFCAs can be seen as a declination of TBPAs and are meant to encompass both core conservation areas and buffer zones. Currently, there are eighteen TFCAs in the SADC region and they are categorised depending on their legal status and development stage: Category A – Established TFCAs include those established through a Treaty or any other form of legal agreement between the partner countries; Category B – Emerging TFCAs are based on a memorandum of understanding that formally initiates the cooperative process; and Category C – Conceptual TFCAs are those proposed by SADC member states as potential TFCAs, but without an official mandate from the partner countries. For further information refer to the dedicated page www.sadc.int/themes/natural-resources/transfrontier-conservation-areas/ [accessed 08 April 2017].

31 Defining shared or transboundary natural resources is a difficult task since they can be interpreted as embracing diverse terrestrial and aquatic ecosystem units (e.g., wetland, forest, lagoon, coral reef) as well as terrestrial and marine species that move across boundaries. I conceive them in a broad sense, thus including any element coming from nature that can be used by people and is shared by two or more countries for geographical or ecological reasons. Usually, the possibility to both utilise a resource and benefit from it is a strong engine for cooperation which is traditionally conceived in terms of intergovernmental cooperation. Nevertheless, sub-national authorities and local communities have an important role to play due to their direct connection with the natural resources. Transboundary natural resources are usually shared by a limited number of countries and can be effectively governed through

their legislation and policy on key issues in order to move closer to each other and achieve precise cooperative objectives. For example, in the Great Limpopo TFCA,[32] Mozambique has been improving biodiversity conservation standards over the last years inspired by South African legislation. For this purpose, in 2014, it signed an *ad hoc* Memorandum of Understanding (MOU) with the Republic of South Africa and increased penalties for wildlife crimes, including poaching of endangered species, in the bill on conservation areas. Arguably, a TFCA can foster a similar harmonisation process in relation to public participation: for instance, a transboundary conservation or development project may require the consultation and involvement of communities across the borders, thus creating the need to frame their participation and replicate, at the TFCA level, participatory mechanisms existing in partner countries. Potentially, such a process would lead to several results: first, the development of national legislation on public participation and appropriate participatory mechanisms in the partner state(s) that are not endowed with them; second, the design of participatory mechanisms that can be used in a transboundary context, for example that of the TFCA; and third, the overall strengthening of public participation both at national and TFCA levels. Moreover, the harmonisation process initiated at the TFCA level can have positive repercussion at regional/SADC level by advancing the participatory standards of other SADC member states and, eventually, leading to the adoption of regional instruments[33] dedicated to public participation. Therefore, in addition to their importance for conserving biodiversity, TFCAs or similar cooperative frameworks can be valued for their role in advancing public participation and empowering local communities that, in this context, can be defined as 'public concerned'.

3. PARTICIPATION OF LOCAL COMMUNITIES AS 'PUBLIC CONCERNED' IN PROTECTED AREAS

In the context of public participation, it is possible to distinguish the public and the 'public concerned'. The former includes all actors outside the governmental administration – namely, individuals, groups, civil society organisations, indigenous people, and local communities –,[34] while the latter refers to a more

collective actions. See *E. Benvenisti*, Sharing Transboundary Resources: International Law and Optimal Resource Use, 2004, p. 33.

32 The Great Limpopo TFCA (GLTFCA) has developed as the second phase of cooperation between Mozambique, South Africa, and Zimbabwe that signed an agreement in 2002 to create the Great Limpopo Transfrontier Park (GLTP). For further information see www.greatlimpopo.org/ [accessed 29 December 2016].

33 These could range from policy guidelines to a Protocol on public participation, thus having different degrees of legal force.

34 Article 2(4) of the Aarhus Convention defines 'the public' as 'one or more natural or legal persons, and, in accordance with national legislation or practice, their associations, organizations, or groups'.

restricted group of subjects that are 'affected or likely to be affected by, or have an interest in, the environmental decision-making'.[35] The Aarhus Convention reiterates these conditions in several provisions[36] and, in Article 9(2), clearly demands the access to administrative and judicial review procedures for members of the concerned public. Therefore, depending on the context considered, it is necessary to identify who is concerned in order to ensure effective participatory mechanisms to these subjects. For instance, in the case of protected areas, local communities can be identified as public concerned due to the repercussions that these areas have on their survival and subsistence.

In fact, these communities have often developed physical and cultural connections with their surrounding environment over time.[37] Aware of the significance of natural resources and the surrounding natural space for their survival and concerned with their preservation, these communities conceived conservation regimes long before national governments created protected areas.[38] Most of the times, the latter have privileged pure conservation objectives leading to the displacement of local communities that had inhabited or used certain territories for centuries.[39] Nevertheless, the perception of protected areas has evolved over time and benefitted from the innovative approaches developed since the 1972 Stockholm Conference and even more in 1992 in Rio. Since then, biodiversity conservation has to be pursued together with the sustainable use of natural resources, the preservation of ecosystem services, and the realisation of socio-economic developmental objectives. This evolution was guided by lessons learned in the field

---

[35] According to Article 2(5) of the Aarhus Convention, this definition extends to 'non-governmental organizations promoting environmental protection and meeting any requirements under national law [that] shall be deemed to have an interest'.

[36] The conditions are: '(a) having a sufficient interest or, alternatively, (b) maintaining impairment of a right, where the administrative procedural law of a Party requires this as a precondition'.

[37] Local communities could be permanently settled or mobile, they usually 'have extended residence in a given environment, a rich tradition in their relationship with the land and the natural resources, well-established customary tenure and use practices, effective management institutions and a direct dependence on the resources for their livelihoods and cultural identity. They too claim "rights" to their land and natural resources' *G. Borrini-Feyerabend et al*, Indigenous and Local Communities and Protected Areas: Towards Equity and Enhanced Conservation, 2004, p. 8.

[38] *G. Borrini-Feyerabend*, Indigenous and local communities and protected areas: rethinking the relationship, Parks 2002 (12), p. 5. It is worth noticing that traditional practices might not be in line with international environmental standards, as in the case of hunting protected or threatened species. Moreover, the access of local communities/indigenous peoples to natural resources could be restricted for preserving biodiversity, as in the case of some protected areas. There is an emerging literature on reconciling indigenous rights and biodiversity conservation, see *E. Desmet*, Indigenous Rights Entwined with Nature Conservation, 2011. See also *F. Cittadino*, Indigenous Rights and the Protection of Biodiversity: A Study of Conflict and Reconciliation in International Law (Doctoral Dissertation, University of Trento), 2017.

[39] The history of conservation has also been a history of exclusion in South Africa; see *J. Carruthers*, National Parks in South Africa, in H. Suich, B. Child and A. Spenceley (eds), Evolution and Innovation in Wildlife Conservation: Parks and Game Ranches to Transfrontier Conservation Areas, 2009, pp. 35–49.

that demonstrated the need to both integrate the specific protected territory and resources in the surrounding context, and engage with indigenous peoples and local communities in order to establish successful conservation regimes.[40]

The connection between local communities and natural resources is entrenched in international environmental law. The Rio Declaration includes public participation in its Principle 10[41] and specifically acknowledges the role of local communities and their strong connection with nature in Principle 22.[42] In line with these principles, the primary role of indigenous people and local communities in the conservation and management of natural resources was recognised by several international conventions or acknowledged by their governing bodies. For instance, Articles 6 and 15 of the 1989 ILO Convention Concerning Indigenous and Tribal Peoples in Independent Countries[43] require state parties to ensure the participation of these people through consultation or other appropriate means to enable their involvement in decision-making as well as in the use, management and conservation of natural resources. In its Resolution VII.8 on Local Communities and Indigenous People,[44] the Conference of the Parties to the Ramsar Convention[45] reiterates the traditional rights, values, knowledge, and institutions of these communities related to the management of wetlands; it also includes a set of guidelines aimed to ensure their participation in the management of wetlands. The Convention on Biological Diversity[46] not only highlights the importance of 'indigenous and local communities embodying traditional lifestyle relevant for the conservation and sustainable use of biological diversity' in its Article 8(j), but also recognises the strong link between conservation and sustainable use by including both of them among its goals together with compelling a fair sharing of benefits deriving from the utilisation of genetic resources.[47] Therefore, sustainable use and conservation are not alternative objectives; rather, sustainable use through

40 G. *Borrini-Feyerabend et al.*, *supra*, note 37 at p. 8.

41 Principle 10 starts by affirming that 'environmental issues are best handled with the participation of all concerned citizens, at the relevant level' and follows by mentioning the three pillars of public participation at the national level.

42 Principle 22 reads as follows: 'Indigenous people and their communities, and other local communities, have a vital role in environmental management and development because of their knowledge and traditional practices. States should recognize and duly support their identity, culture and interests and enable their effective participation in the achievement of sustainable development'.

43 ILO Concerning Indigenous and Tribal Peoples in Independent Countries (No. 169), Geneva, 27 June 1989 – in force 5 September 1991, 1650 UNTS 383.

44 Ramsar, COP 7 Resolution VII.8 'Guidelines for establishing and strengthening local communities' and indigenous people's participation in the management of wetlands'.

45 Convention on Wetlands of International Importance especially as Waterfowl Habitat, Ramsar, 2 February 1971 – in force 21 December 1975, 996 UNTS 245. Hereinafter, Ramsar Convention.

46 Convention on Biological Diversity, Rio de Janeiro, 5 June 1992 – in force 29 December 1993, 1760 UNTS 79. Hereinafter CBD.

47 CBD, Article 1.

appropriate management can be instrumental to conservation. In addition, Ebbesson highlights that the 2010 Nagoya Protocol on Access Benefit-Sharing[48] does not only foresee the participation and involvement of indigenous and local communities through procedures of prior informed consent and approval for accessing genetic resources, but directly 'addresses participatory processes across state borders: [hence,] the parties must cooperate in transboundary contexts with the involvement of indigenous and local communities concerned'.[49] All the more reason for ensuring the preferential relation between communities and natural resources in the context of protected areas, as exemplified in Goal 2.2 of the CBD Programme of Work on Protected Areas.[50]

The role of communities in these areas has been enhanced by international organisations, such as the International Union for Conservation of Nature (IUCN), which advanced the conceptual development and practice of protected areas. With the aim to help standardise descriptions of existing conservation experiences, IUCN developed, at first, a PA categories system, that reflects the main management objectives of the areas, and then, identified the different governance approaches for PAs indicating who owns, controls, and has responsibility for their management.[51] These two elements have been integrated in the so called IUCN protected areas matrix that is a classification system comprising both management categories and governance types. For instance, Category V 'Protected Landscape/ Seascape' identifies 'a protected area where *the interaction of people and nature* over time has produced an area of distinct character with significant ecological, biological, cultural and scenic value: and where *safeguarding the integrity of this interaction is vital* to protecting and sustaining the areas and its associated nature conservation and other values [emphasis added]'.[52] This Category focuses on the connection between nature and people and aims to preserve it since it is vital for both community livelihood and nature conservation. Hence, whoever is responsible for decision-making and management in PAs belonging to Category

48 Nagoya Protocol on Access to Genetic Resources and the Fair and Equitable Sharing of Benefits Arising from Their Utilization to the Convention on Biological Diversity (Nagoya, 29 October 2010 – in force 12 October 2014), in CBD Decision 10/1, 'Access to genetic resources and the fair and equitable sharing of benefits arising from their utilization' U.N. Doc. UNEP/CBD/ COP/10/27 (2011). In particular, see Articles 6 and 21.

49 *J. Ebbesson*, Principle 10, *supra*, note 3 at pp. 296-297.

50 The CBD Programme of Work on Protected Areas was adopted by the Conference of the Parties to the CBD Convention and included in COP Decision VII.28. Hereinafter, CBD PoWPA. Goal 2.2 requires 'to enhance and secure involvement of indigenous and local communities and relevant stakeholders' and poses as its target 'the full and effective participation by 2008, of indigenous and local communities, in full respect of their rights and recognition of their responsibilities, consistent with national law and applicable international obligations, and the participation of relevant stakeholders, in the management of existing, and the establishment of new protected areas'. UN Doc UNEP/CBD/COP/DEC/VII/28 (2004).

51 For an exploratory review of IUCN work on protected areas see *B. Lausche*, *supra*, note 1; *N. Dudley* (ed.), Guidelines for Applying Protected Areas Management Categories, 2008.

52 *N. Dudley*, *supra*, note 51 at p. 20.

V has to take into consideration the need of people inhabiting the area and involve them actively in its management. To this end, management authorities have to foresee mechanisms for the meaningful participation of communities. Therefore, communities can be considered as public concerned, and procedural environmental rights apply to them with a reinforced character.[53]

Moreover, among IUCN governance approaches, Type D corresponds to 'Governance by indigenous people and local communities', which represents a step forward in empowering communities in the framework of conservation since, in these PAs, 'the management authority and responsibility rest with indigenous people and/or local communities through various forms of customary or legal, formal or informal, institutions and rule'.[54] In this case, procedural environmental rights should find their maximum expression in terms of decision-making and direct participation in managing natural resources; nevertheless, access to information and access to justice might still be hindered since they imply the involvement of other actors, and depend on the legislative framework applicable in the relevant jurisdiction. When other governance approaches apply – i.e., Type (A) governance by government, Type (B) shared governance, or Type (C) Private Governance[55] – procedural environmental rights have to be recognised to local communities to ensure good governance.

There is no single definition of governance nor of 'good governance'.[56] Generally speaking governance refers to how society defines and achieves its goals and priorities: the processes used to take decision and implement them, the actors involved, and the structures set in place to this end. Governance embraces multiple aspects and public participation is one of them since it contributes to evaluate its quality – i.e., how one governs – in a specific context. Good governance is strongly linked to human rights principles and is essential for sustainable development, including in the context of protected areas.[57] Meaningful involvement of the (concerned) public in environmental matters represents a manifestation of good governance and Lausche confirms that the Aarhus Convention is 'the leading international instrument for defining and elaborating a good governance framework of principles for governments'.[58] In protected areas, local communities

53 Ebbesson explains 'by providing for participation for the public concerned, a broader range of burdens and benefits may be taken into account'. *J. Ebbesson*, Public Participation, *supra*, note 10 at para. 11.

54 *N. Dudley, supra*, note 51 at p. 26.

55 *Id.* at pp. 26–27.

56 For IUCN it consists in 'the interaction among political and social structures, processes and traditions that determine how power and responsibilities are exercised, how decision are taken, and how citizens or other stakeholders have their say'. *B. Lausche, supra*, note 1 at p. 40. See also the different definitions of governance used by international organisations and collected by Lausche, *id.* at p. 41.

57 See Element 2 of the CBD PoWPA, and, in particular, activities 2.1.3 and 2.1.5 as well as Goal 2.2 and the connected activities. *Supra*, note 50.

58 *B. Lausche, supra* note 1 at p. 44.

embody the notion of public concerned, hence, their meaningful involvement in PA-related decision-making and management contributes to good governance.

Moreover, public participation contributes to the fulfilment of citizens' environmental rights that are human rights illustrating 'the integrated interrelationship between humans and the environment and the claim of people to an environment of a particular quality'.[59] Protected areas are purposely established to conserve valuable natural resources and, under certain circumstances, allow for their sustainable use – i.e., to maintain an environment of a particular quality – thus motivating public participation in this context. Nevertheless, these areas are experiencing several threats generated inside, such as inappropriate management and poaching, and outside their boundaries, like off-site pollution and climate change-related events,[60] with serious repercussion on biodiversity conservation.

It has been argued that the provisions of the Aarhus Convention apply to all projects supported by state parties in other countries, including financial and technical assistance for the development of (transboundary) PAs.[61] Moreover, although the Aarhus Convention has been negotiated and adopted in the framework of the United Nations Economic Commission for Europe, it is open to all UN Member States upon approval by the Meeting of the Parties by virtue of Article 19(3); therefore, virtually any States can become party to this Convention. In the context of PAs, the three participatory pillars acquire a specific connotation:

(1) The right of the public to access environmental information implies two types of duties on the government: a proactive duty and a reactive duty.[62] In the first case, government agencies collect, compile, and actively disseminate information without request. In relation to PAs, the relevant information to be made public include draft and final PA system plans, proposals to declare an area as protected, draft and final management plans as well as monitoring, evaluation, and financial reports to detail the expenditure of public money. Furthermore, PA legislation has to identify the government agencies or other bodies responsible for providing access and distribution of relevant information, where and how this can be accessed, and the process and timeframe for commenting.[63] The reactive duty of the government consists in the obligation to provide information upon request of the public. Again, PA legislation will define the details on how to obtain the information, the agencies responsible, timeframe, etc., as well as clarify the conditions to respect when information is refused.[64] The sound application of this right results, on the one hand, in enhanced transparency, legitimacy,

---

59 *A. Du Plessis, supra*, note 23 at pp. 3–4.
60 *B. Lausche, supra*, note 1 at p. 1.
61 *B. Lausche, supra*, note 1 at p. 44.
62 *G. (Rock) Pring & S. Y. Noé, supra*, note 13 at p. 29–30.
63 *B. Lausche, supra*, note 1 at p. 44.
64 *B. Lausche, supra*, note 1 at p. 45.

and accountability of governmental actions and PA authorities, on the other hand, in an increased environmental education of the public (Principle 19 of the Stockholm Declaration) and strengthens their capacity to exercise the other two participatory rights.

According to Verschuuren, the government has a proactive duty of information in relation to the public concerned, while it exercises a reactive duty towards the general public.[65]

(2) Public participation in decision-making consists in contributing to important decisions by providing written comments or participating to meetings and expressing opinions in these contexts. In order to be appropriate and well-informed, such a contribution presupposes the access to accurate, relevant, and clear information. Nevertheless, competent agencies need to take into consideration people's comments accurately, otherwise the effort of the public would be vain. In the case of PAs, crucial decisions relate to the spatial delineation of a protected area, the identification of management authorities, the development of management plans as well as strategies for a PA system or an MPA network, the revision of draft environmental and social impact assessment of proposed actions.[66]

(3) Accessing administrative and judicial remedies has several applications: to appeal the refusal of access to information, to gain review of decisions made by PA authorities under the law, to seek redress for inappropriate environmental governance in the context of PAs, to seek damages for environmentally harmful activities carried out within the protected space as well as to prevent such activities, and to directly enforce protected areas law and environmental law more generally.[67] Rules and procedures for accessing justice and appealing administrative decisions authorised by law have to be foreseen in PA legislation if are not already provided at national level. Hence, access to justice is a means to reinforce the exercise of the other two participatory rights; moreover, it gives people the power to monitor the action of PA authorities, thus making these authorities accountable to people.

National PAs legislation has to encompass all the aforementioned provisions or complement existing laws that are adequate for participation purposes.

When people hold or claim rights over existing or proposed protected areas as well as place spiritual and cultural values on these areas or natural features located therein,[68] they can be identified as public concerned. It is often the case

---

65 *J. Verschuuren*, Public Participation regarding the Elaboration and Approval of Projects in the EU after the Aarhus Convention, in T.F.M. Etty & H. Somsen (eds.), Yearbook of European Environmental Law, 2004, pp. 29–48.

66 *B. Lausche, supra*, note 1 at p. 44.

67 *V.P. Nanda & G.W. Pring, supra*, note 9 at p. 56.

68 The linkages between local communities, especially indigenous people, and nature or natural elements can be related to religious beliefs and traditional practices like in the case of sacred sites. Their importance can be appreciated also by people with a different value system, and

that local communities live within or adjacent to PAs,[69] hence, they are always entitled to procedural environmental rights as public concerned since they are 'affected or likely to be affected by, or having and interest in, the environmental decision-making'[70] related to these PAs. Such a situation requires a proactive attitude of PA authorities and governments towards local communities.

4. COMMUNITY PARTICIPATION IN TRANSBOUNDARY PROTECTED AREAS

When ecological and political boundaries do not coincide, cross-border conservation efforts can be conceived and implemented through the creation of a TBPA, which can be established in several ways, the most common and simple to visualise being the linkage of two or more contiguous PAs across a national boundary. The creation of TBPAs responds to the recent trend of expanding conservation areas and integrating them with the surrounding environment since they often encompass intervening land or operate as a means to foster sympathetic sustainable use across the borders.

The effective governance of transboundary natural resources is a key issue in international environmental law. To this end, international environmental regimes support a stronger development of TBPAs: for instance, Goal 1.3 of the CBD PoWPA is specifically dedicated to it. Also the World Heritage Convention foresees the possibility to recognise world heritage sites that cross national boundaries,[71] and the Ramsar Convention demands consultation and coordination between relevant parties for the designation and management of transboundary wetlands.[72] In the context of TBPAs, the role of local communities is as important as it is in the national context.[73] Besides, it would be illogical to think that the conditions for good governance and the procedural environmental rights applicable to local communities in a PA – hence, within domestic jurisdiction – fade out in the context of a TBPA. Moreover, the principle of non-discrimination and equal access allows for the extraterritorial application of procedural environmental rights, including in the context of TBPAs, in line with

transcend biodiversity and ecological considerations. These 'cultural heritages' can benefit from transboundary conservation. On this point see *M. Vasilijević et al.*, Transboundary Conservation: A Systematic and Integrated Approach, 2015, p. 29 et seq.

69 *Id.*

70 Aarhus Convention, Article 2(5).

71 UNESCO Convention Concerning the Protection of the World Cultural and Natural Heritage (Paris, 16 November 1972 – in force 17 December 1975) 11 ILM 1358 (1972). Hereinafter, WHC.For more information on transboundary world heritage sites see http://whc.unesco.org/en/list/?&_dc=1512409712217&transboundary=1 [accessed 4 December 2017].

72 Article 5 of the Ramsar Convention and Ramsar COP 1999 Resolution VII.19, paragraph 2.1.1.

73 In this regard see *M. Vasilijević et al.*, *supra* note 68 at p. 26 et seq.; and *T. Sandwith et al.*, Transboundary Protected Areas for Peace and Co-operation, 2001, p. 19 et seq.

the expanded application of participatory rights at multiple governance levels as foreseen in the Rio+20 outcome document The Future We Want.[74]

In TBPAs, cross-border cooperation is meaningful in ecological as well as social terms. Among the key management principles that guide the design and management of a TBPA, two confirm the relevance for participatory rights: (1) bring communities together across political boundaries; and (2) involve and benefit local communities in policy formation, PA planning and management.[75] Moreover, Article 3(7) of the Aarhus Convention requires contracting parties to apply procedural environmental rights in international environmental decision-making processes and within the framework of international organisations in matters relating to the environment. Regardless of being a party to the Aarhus Convention, the rationale behind this article can be extended to the application of participatory rights in TBPAs. In fact, TBPAs can be conceived within a broader cooperative framework such as an international organisation, as is the case of TFCAs in the SADC region, or are international organisations themselves.[76] Furthermore, the design, management and, more generally, governance of a TBPA result from international environmental decision-making processes, hence, the states or authorities involved in these processes have to respect participatory rights at all levels.

Partner states have established cross-border conservation initiatives, like SADC TFCAs, in order to conserve and manage shared natural resources as a unit and, for this purpose, joint management institutions are usually created. The cooperative process automatically qualifies local communities as concerned public since they are both affected by the creation of the cross-border cooperative framework and interested in the conservation and management of the shared natural spaces and resources included therein. Therefore, mechanisms for their participation have to be foreseen in the context of TBPAs, as it is happening in the case of the Kavango Zambezi Transfrontier Conservation Area (KAZA TFCA).[77]

This is the world's largest TFCA, spanning approximately 520,000 km^2, and the only one having a Secretariat with coordinating functions.[78] The application of procedural environmental rights can be directly and indirectly derived from the provisions of its founding Treaty. Among the principles guiding the Partner States in pursuing the cooperation objectives, Article 5(1)(g) requires to 'create forums and facilitate consultation and *effective participation of Stakeholders in decision making* with respect to the development of policies and strategies related

74 UN General Assembly, 'The Future We Want', U.N. Doc. A/RES/66/288 (2012), para. 99. On this point see *J. Ebbesson*, Principle 10, *supra*, note 3 at p. 294.

75 *B. Lausche, supra*, note 1 at p. 271.

76 For instance, the KAZA TFCA is an international organisation according to Article 3 of its founding Treaty.

77 The Treaty on the Establishment of the Kavango Zambezi Transfrontier Conservation Area TFCA has been signed in Luanda (Angola) on 18 August 2011 by Angola, Botswana, Namibia, Zambia, and Zimbabwe. Hereinafter KAZA TFCA Treaty.

78 KAZA TFCA Treaty, Article 14.

to the management and development of the KAZA TFCA [emphasis added]'. The definition of 'Stakeholders' in Article 1[79] includes individual or group of individuals with a stake in the development and management of the KAZA TFCA and arguably encompasses 'Local Communities' that are defined in the same article as 'groups of people living in and adjacent to the area of Kavango Zambezi TFCA bound by cultural, social and economic relations based on shared interests and transboundary resources'.[80] Therefore, the Treaty recognises the multiple links between people across borders for cultural, social, and economic reasons as well as their connection to transboundary resources. Since local communities have a stake in the development and management of the KAZA TFCA, they can be defined as public concerned. Hence, the 'forums' mentioned in Article 5(1)(g) are participatory mechanisms operating at a transboundary level for the involvement of local communities that are public concerned.

The participation of local communities is also in line with one of the objectives of the KAZA TFCA acknowledging that the improved livelihood of local communities and poverty reduction pass through an improved governance of shared natural and cultural resources.[81] The idea that public participation and environmental protection are mutually reinforcing derives from the connection traced between human rights and the environment.[82] Furthermore, Article 8(1)(c) calls on states to ensure community participation[83] and this explicit obligation can be widely interpreted to encompass all the three participatory pillars. Moreover, partner countries have to ensure the respect of the rights of communities and other stakeholders provided in their domestic laws,[84] arguably, Article 8(1)(e) applies to participatory rights foreseen in national provisions and determines

---

79 According to Article 1 of the KAZA TFCA Treaty: '"Stakeholders" means individuals or groups of individuals or representative institution with a stake, direct or indirect interest in the development and management of the KAZA TFCA or a right recognized under the laws of the partner states in the areas comprising the KAZA TFCA'.

80 KAZA TFCA Treaty, Article 1.

81 Article 6(1)(e) requires to 'develop and implement programmes that shall enhance the Sustainable Use of Natural Resources and Cultural Heritage Resources to improve the livelihoods of Local Communities within and around the KAZA TFCA and thus contribute towards poverty reduction'.

82 In describing the reciprocal relationship between human rights and the environment, Pring and Noé note that 'when the environment suffers, people suffer and when people suffer, the environment suffers. Another connection that has been observed is that governments that fail to respect and uphold human rights are also likely to fail to protect the environment. It is increasingly recognized that in order for the people to protect the environment, they must have political rights, inducting the right of public participation'. *G. (Rock) Pring & S.Y. Noé, supra*, note 13 at p. 51. Ebbesson explains that participatory rights have been identified in human rights global and regional instruments and embodied in human rights jurisprudence, especially in Europe, the Americas, and Africa. See *J. Ebbesson*, Principle 10, *supra*, note 3, at p. 297 et seq.

83 According to Art. 8(1)(e) of the KAZA TFCA Treaty, partner states have the obligation to 'ensure stakeholder engagement at the national and local level with the involvement governmental authorities, communities, Non-Governmental Organization and Private Sector'.

84 KAZA TFCA Treaty, Article 8(1)(e).

their extraterritorial dimensions by requiring their respect in the context of the TFCA. Therefore, in so far as (community) participatory rights are foreseen in the legislation of KAZA partner states, they are extraterritorially applicable in the context of the TFCA.

In addition to state obligations, the Treaty requires the KAZA Secretariat to engage with relevant stakeholders in the process of drafting and implementing the KAZA TFCA action plan.[85] Although this provision seems to be limited to the decision-making processes resulting in the TFCA action plan, its scope is expanded by the expression 'full participation of relevant stakeholders' that arguably refers to the effectiveness of participatory processes. Participation is effective when the community, which can arguably be embraced within the notion of relevant stakeholders, is able to influence the outcome of the decisional process;[86] for this purpose, participation needs to be informed and culturally appropriate.[87] Therefore, Article 14(4)(c) can be interpreted as establishing the proactive duty of the Secretariat to provide culturally appropriate information to local communities for their full participation in decision-making processes.[88]

While community rights to access information and participate in decision-making easily emerge from the text of the Treaty, access to remedies is needed to ensure the respect of the other two rights and make their implementation

---

85 KAZA TFCA Treaty, Article 14(4)(c).

86 The Endorois case offers guidance on what 'effective participation' means. For a brief summary of the case, refer to para 1 'The complaint is filed by the Centre for Minority Rights Development (CEMIRIDE) and Minority Rights Group International (MRG), on behalf of the Endorois Community. (...)The Complainants allege violations resulting from the displacement of the Endorois community, an indigenous community, from their ancestral lands, the failure to adequately compensate them for the loss of their property, the disruption of the community's pastoral enterprise and violations of the right to practise their religion and culture, as well as the overall process of development of the Endorois people'. In paragraph 281, the African Commission maintained that informing the affected community of an impending project as a *fait accompli* does not leave any space for the community to influence the outcome. Illiteracy and a different understanding of property use and ownership affected the position of the Endorois community that failed to grasp the impact of permanent eviction from their land and behaved accordingly. The community attitude demonstrates the inadequacy of the consultation undertaken by the Kenyan State. According to paragraph 282, 'it was incumbent upon the Respondent State to conduct the consultation process in such a manner that allowed the representatives to be fully informed of the agreement, and participate in developing parts crucial to the life of the community'. 276/2003 – Centre for Minority Rights Development (Kenya) and Minority Rights Group International on behalf of Endorois Welfare Council v Kenya.

87 For instance, Cittadino discusses the proactive role of human rights bodies in crafting legal criteria for the effective participation of indigenous people in environmental matters: informed participation and cultural appropriateness are key requirements in this sense. *F. Cittadino*, Public Interest to Environmental Protection, *supra*, note 2 at p. 82 et seq.

88 As already said, meaningful participation in decision-making is based on sound knowledge of the environmental issues at stake: since local communities are public concerned, relevant authorities, both KAZA institutions and national authorities, have the proactive duty to provide communities with information useful to take informed decisions.

effective.[89] When explaining the difference between principles and rights, Verschuuren affirms that 'rights can be invoked in court, whereas principles can only play a role in combination with a legal rule';[90] since the Treaty prescribes community participation in decision-making, which in turn presupposes access to information, local communities should have access to remedies to uphold their participatory rights against a non-compliant partner state or the KAZA TFCA itself. It has been argued that such accountability can be based on Article 3 of the founding Treaty that recognises the KAZA TFCA as an international organisation with legal personality, and consequently with the capacity to sue and be sued.[91]

Moreover, although stakeholders' participation in decision-making is said to be a guiding principle in Article 5(1)(g), the three pillars of participation can be conceived as rights in the framework of the KAZA TFCA Treaty because of their connection with the objectives contained in Article 6(1)(a) and (e): biodiversity conservation purposes and improved communities' livelihoods. Indeed, community participation is essential for the realisation of the substantive right to environmental protection.

Therefore, the application of participatory rights stems from the KAZA TFCA Treaty regardless of their inclusion in the legislation of KAZA partner states. Hence, it can be argued that national legislative discrepancies are overcome by the supranational/TFCA framework since the Treaty imposes participation for the achievement of its cooperative obligations. In addition, since the development of this TFCA relies strongly on external funds coming from Aarhus member states (for example the German KfW[92]), it can also be argued that the Aarhus Convention is applicable in this context,[93] and even more so by means of its Article 3(7) since the KAZA TFCA is specifically defined as an international organisation.[94]

Hence, local communities, regardless of their nationality, are entitled to participatory rights in the context of the KAZA TFCA. These communities can exercise such rights towards any of the partner states – whether national legislation

89 In this regard, Ebbesson stresses that the three components are closely-related and all crucial for effective public participation in environmental matters. In particular, 'access to justice is a means to having decisions and decision-making process reviewed'. See *J. Ebbesson*, Principle 10, *supra*, note 3 at p. 291.

90 *J. Verschuuren*, *supra*, note 65 at p. 2.

91 *W. D. Lubbe*, Straddling Border and Legal Regimes: A Legal Framework for Transfrontier Biodiversity Conservation in SADC (Doctoral Dissertation, North-West University) 2015, p. 231.

92 The KfW Development Bank provides financial and technical resources in developing and transition countries on behalf of the German Federal Ministry for Economic Cooperation and Development (BMZ).

93 Lausche argues that the provisions of the Aarhus Convention 'are fully applicable to all projects supported by the Convention Parties in other countries. This has implications for protected areas by bilateral and multilateral aid from countries which have ratified the Convention'. *B. Lausche*, *supra* note 1, p. 44.

94 KAZA TFCA Treaty, Article 3.

includes participatory mechanisms or not – and the KAZA TFCA itself, on behalf of the Secretariat, for their failure in both effective community engagement and the achievement of transboundary biodiversity conservation.

5. CONCLUSIONS

Community participation in environmental matters in general and PAs in particular is based on several grounds. From a human right perspective, it is a form of political participation[95] and a manifestation of the freedom of opinion and expression,[96] and it is foreseen by international law concerning indigenous people.[97] It is included in relevant environmental regimes and conservation initiatives: not only the aforementioned CBD, Ramsar, and WHC, but also the UNESCO MAB Programme[98] and other instruments relating to marine protected areas.[99] It is reasonable in ecological terms since communities inhabiting valuable natural spaces for long time have developed traditional knowledge and management practices that preserved the surrounding environment and natural resources therein. It is in line with the principles for good governance in the context of PAs.[100] Although these areas were initially created as conservation fortresses, their understanding – in terms of conservation objectives – changed significantly with the introduction of the concept of sustainable development, thus adopting a more people-oriented focus. Moreover, it has been acknowledged that the fate of conservation initiatives strongly depends on the involvement of local communities.[101] Participatory rights are a powerful tool to ensure the involvement of local communities in conservation efforts, including in a transboundary context.

---

95 See, for instance, article 21 of the UN Declaration of Human Rights, *supra*, note 3; article 25 of the International Covenant on Civil and Political Rights, U.N. GAOR, 21ST Sess., Supp. No. 16, at 52, UN Doc. A/6316 (1966), as well as other regional conventions. *J. Ebbesson*, Public Participation, *supra*, note 10 at para. 30.

96 Art. 19 of the UN Declaration of Human Rights, *supra* note 3.

97 Articles 6 and 15 of the ILO Convention No. 69, *supra*, note 43.

98 The Man and the Biosphere Programme (MAB) was launched by UNESCO in 1971 as an Intergovernmental Scientific Programme dedicated to improve the relationship between people and their environments through the adoption of an interdisciplinary approach. Further information available at www.unesco.org/new/en/natural-sciences/environment/ecological-sciences/man-and-biosphere-programme/ [accessed 29 December 2016].

99 *A. Gillespie*, Protected Areas and International Environmental Law, 2007, pp. 171–172.

100 Dudley identifies nine principles to this end: legitimacy and voice, subsidiarity, fairness, do no harm, direction, performance, accountability, transparency, human rights. *N. Dudley*, *supra*, note 51 at p. 28.

101 See *A. Gillespie*, *supra*, note 99 at p. 168; *B. Lausche*, *supra*, note 1 at p. 16; and *G. Borrini-Feyerabend*, *supra*, note 38. That public participation is crucial for the success of governmental decisions on environmental issues or development projects has been highlighted by several authors, see Verschuuren referring to Lee & Abbot, *supra* note 65, pp. 2–3. See also *G. (Rock) Pring & S.Y. Noé*, *supra*, note 13 at p. 25.

Local communities can be identified as public concerned when located within or in the vicinity of a TBPA, especially for their direct connection to natural resources and the impact that such a cooperative mechanism may have on their life and subsistence, and the surrounding environment. A meaningful participation of local communities in TBPAs is beneficial under serval points of view. First, it advances the democratisation of environmental processes; second, it contributes to the long-term success of TBPAs; third, it empowers communities and reinforces good governance of shared natural spaces; fourth, it helps preserving biodiversity at local level – as to say, within the TBPA and the cooperative space – as well as at global level since it contributes to conservation efforts implemented worldwide.

The extraterritorial dimension of participatory rights is guaranteed by the principle of non-discrimination and equal access, hence, states are required to ensure cross-border participation of the public (concerned) regardless of its nationality. The extraterritorial application of participatory rights is particularly beneficial when regional organisations are in place since they facilitate the emergence of higher participatory standards at national and supranational level. In fact, in order to achieve cooperative objectives, partner states are motivated or required (as in the case of the EU) to harmonise their national law in specific fields. In the case of public participation, more advanced participatory standards in one partner country can arguably guide the harmonisation process and be replicated in the other partner countries. The same dynamics exist in cross-border cooperative mechanisms that, at times, are established in the framework of regional organisations, as in the case of SADC TFCAs. These two cooperative frameworks – namely, SADC as a regional organisation and the TFCAs as cross-border mechanisms for cooperation over shared natural resources – interact with and can influence each other. On the one hand, the regional legal and policy framework can demand harmonisation of national systems and influences cooperation also in the context of TFCAs; on the other hand, specific TFCA objectives can lead partner states to harmonise their legislations and policies in a specific field and scale this harmonisation process up to the regional level. This reasoning can be applied to public participation in the context of SADC TFCAs: a stronger SADC framework on public participation would arguably reinforce participatory standards in SADC member states and in the context of TFCAs. Conversely, the enhancement of participatory standards at SADC level could derive from harmonisation processes initiated within TFCAs that foresee public participation in their founding Treaties, as in the case of the KAZA TFCA. Interestingly, cooperative dynamics can lead to fill up normative or policy gaps in member states, hence resulting in the development of national participatory standards.

Despite being considered a regional instrument, the Aarhus Convention has a global vocation by way of its Article 19(3). Moreover, its provisions are not only meant to guide participation in a national context, but apply also to international environmental decision-making processes and within the framework of international organisations,[102] thus being relevant for TBPAs. In the case of the KAZA TFCA, in addition to the numerous participatory provisions included in the Treaty and despite the fact that KAZA partner countries are not members of the Aarhus Convention, it can be argued that this Convention finds application through the technical and financial support provided by Aarhus-partner countries. Therefore, the entitlement of local communities as public concerned and the extraterritorial dimension of their rights can be both derived from the KAZA Treaty and the Aarhus Convention.

In conclusion, cross-border conservation initiatives, like TBPAs, should be valued not only for their contribution in terms of biodiversity conservation, but also as functional to empower local communities by strengthening their participatory rights across borders with repercussions in terms of good environmental governance.

102 Aarhus Convention, Article 3(7).

PROCEDURAL ENVIRONMENTAL RIGHTS AND EIA

PUBLIC PARTICIPATION AND EIA IN THE MULTI-STAGE DECISION-MAKING PROCESS: THE CZECH EXAMPLE

Petra Humlíčková* and Vojtěch Vomáčka**

ABSTRACT

In Czechia, the EIA procedure is the very first step in a long chain of permitting procedures. This chapter focuses on such multi-stage decision-making process from the perspective of public participation, and provides several examples from the Czech case law and administrative practice. The authors conclude that the quantity of various specific regimes itself has a huge impact on effectiveness of public participation and the narrow scope of various proceedings seems restrictive, pushing the public to carefully select its arguments or employ a "carpet bombing" tactics instead. Moreover, multiple decision-making generates costs on all sides, including investors and administrative bodies.

KEYWORDS

Czech Republic; EIA; infrastructure development; public participation

1. INTRODUCTION

The separate environmental impact assessment (EIA) usually forms a part of a multi-stage decision making process which, at first glance, brings additional requirements as regards coordination of the official authorities and their statements or decisions.

Furthermore, a multi-stage decision making process might create problems which are not obvious *per se* but may present substantial threat to effective public participation.

---

* Assistant professor at Charles University, Prague; legal attorney.
** Assistant professor at Masaryk University, Brno; legal advisor at the Supreme Administrative Court of the Czech Republic.

In our contribution, we will discuss these issues on example of the legal regulation in Czechia and its recent changes. We focus on the advantages and disadvantages of the EIA as a part of the multi-stage decision making process from the perspective of public participation, and provide several examples from the Czech case law and administrative practice to answer the question whether the public participation can be an effective and under which conditions.

2. QUEST FOR COMPLIANCE

First of all, some introductory remarks should be made as regards a long struggle of the Czech legislator to fulfil the criteria of the EIA Directive.[1] While most of the Member States opt for the EIA procedure integrated into the existing procedures for development consent to projects, some countries, including Czechia, use the second option offered by Article 2.2 of the EIA Directive[2] and establish a specific, separate procedure to comply with the aims of the Directive.[3]

2.1. HISTORICAL DEVELOPMENT

The EIA procedure was introduced in the Czech legal system more than two decades ago, in 1992.[4] Current legislation was adopted in 2001 and has been amended several times since then.[5] In 2006, the European Commission had opened a case against Czechia, and although it amended its legislation in 2009, the case was brought to the Court of Justice.[6] Problems were identified with several aspects of the access to justice provisions and insufficient temporal effects of the new legislation which applied only to the projects for which the environmental impact assessment began after the amendment entered into force. In 2013, another infringement procedure was initiated with much broader scope, threatening to stop the EU subsidies if additional amendments were not made.[7]

---

1 Directive 2011/92/EU of the European Parliament and of the Council of 13 December 2011 on the Assessment of the Effects of Certain Public and Private Projects on the Environment, OJ L 26, 28.1.2012, p. 1.

2 Article 2.2 of the EIA Directive: "*The environmental impact assessment may be integrated into the existing procedures for development consent to projects in the Member States, or, failing this, into other procedures or into procedures to be established to comply with the aims of this Directive.*"

3 See *P. Černý & J. Jendroška*, Transposition and Implementation of EIA Directive in some EU Member States (with special emphasis on transport infrastructure cases), ELNI Review 2007 (1), pp. 18–19.

4 See Act no. 244/1992 Coll. on Environmental Impact Assessment.

5 See Act no. 100/2011 Coll. on Environmental Impact Assessment.

6 See CJEU Judgment: Case C-378/09, *Commission v Czech Republic*, ECLI:EU:C:2010:337.

7 Infringement action no. 2013/2048 against the Czech Republic due to incorrect transposition of the Art. 1, 2, 3, 4, 5, 6, 7, 8, 9, 11 and 13 and Annexes I, II, III and IV of the EIA Directive in the Czech law.

The main concerns were identified as the non-binding nature of the EIA opinion in Czechia, insufficient influence of the public and the NGOs over the building authorization procedures and the impossibility to challenge the substance of the EIA opinion before court. In combination, these shortcomings had enabled changes of projects during the subsequent permitting procedures rendering the result of the EIA completely ineffective, without a proper remedy available to the public concerned.

The deficiencies were remedied by another amendment adopted in 2015[8] which created a specific regime for the procedures for development consent subsequent to the EIA procedure.[9] There is also a new specific-to-specific regime which was introduced in 2016.[10] It deals exclusively with selected, most important TEN-T projects and aims to use the outdated EIA statements based on the law from 1992 for requests concerning EU co-funding, without all the EIA procedures necessarily redone. This approach has been presented nation-wide as a complete exemption from the EU law, which is not correct[11], and the actual regulation leaves much to be desired as regards description of the new specific regime including public participation. Its flexible and vague procedural provisions may in practice turn counterproductive.[12]

Last but not least, Czech authorities and courts still ignore some conclusions of the Aarhus Convention Compliance Committee (ACCC) regarding public participation in Czechia. The case that reached the ACCC[13] is of a particular importance for the issue of the EIA in the multi-stage decision-making process.[14] The Committee considered that the Czech legal framework did not ensure that in the permitting decision due account was taken of the outcome of public

8 See Act no. 39/2015 Coll. Amending Act no. 100/2011 Coll. on Environmental Impact Assessment and Some Other Acts.

9 See *P. Humlíčková, V. Vomáčka & V. Zahumenská*, Novela procesu EIA – více otázek než odpovědí, České právo životního prostředí, 2015 (37), pp. 7–36.

10 See Act no. 265/2016 Coll. Amending Act no. 100/2011 Coll. on Environmental Impact Assessment and Some Other Acts.

11 See for example answer given by Mr. Vella on behalf of the Commission, 30 August 2016, P-006000/2016: *"Act approved by the Czech Government on 15 June 2016 would apply only to the EIA statements of ten specific projects and that the building permits would be issued according to the new Czech EIA legislation. This means that requirements regarding protection of the environment and public health, including public participation in permit procedures and access to judicial review will apply."*

12 See *V. Vomáčka & L. Buhýľová*, Zvláštní režim procesu EIA pro vybrané prioritní stavby (k novele č. 256/2016 Sb.), České právo životního prostředí, 2016 (41), pp. 45–52. Or *M. Franková*, Malé zamyšlení nad „rychlonovelou" zákona o posuzování vlivů na životní prostředí, České právo životního prostředí, 2016 (41), pp. 53–56.

13 See U.N. Econ. & Soc. Council [ECOSOC], Sub-Comm'n Economic Comm'n for Europe, Compliance Comm., Findings and Recommendations with Regard to Communication ACC/C/2010/50 Concerning Compliance by the Czech Republic. Prepared by the Compliance Committee and adopted on 29 June 2012.

14 See *H. Müllerová & P. Humlíčková*, Nové přístupy k implementaci Aarhuské úmluvy v ČR, 2014, pp. 19–23.

participation.[15] This changed in 2015 when the EIA statement became binding for the subsequent proceedings (see below). However, the Committee also rightly noted that while the EIA procedure is an open participatory process, *"participation in the decision-making for the subsequent phases is limited to those members of the public that are recognized by law as "parties" to the land-use and building proceedings; that, consequently, members of the public concerned during the EIA procedure are not the same as the members of the public in the subsequent land-use and building permitting procedures; that NGOs have limited rights to participate after the conclusion of the EIA procedure; and that tenants, while they may be able to participate in the EIA procedure, are not able to participate in the subsequent stages, because the law does not recognize them as "parties" to those procedures, but usually limits parties to natural persons whose in rem rights are affected or likely to be affected."*[16]

This discrepancy in public participation stems from the restrictive interpretation of the concept of impairment of rights which omits other property rights than ownership contrary to article 6, paragraph 3, of the Convention. Especially tenants are not considered public concerned, even though they have been or will be tenants for a long period of time. Nevertheless, and this will be evident from the next sub-chapter, the list of the participants and conditions for their participation differ notably among the permitting procedures subsequent to the EIA procedure without any valid reason.

The Committee further criticised the Czech legislator for limiting the rights of the NGOs to access review procedures regarding the final decisions permitting proposed activities, such as building permits.[17] While this issue has been considerably improved towards the NGOs, because the EIA Act now clearly states that the NGOs are entitled to challenge the development consent[18], other members of the public concerned must rely on the *ad hoc* interpretation of the "directly affected rights". Direct applicability of the EIA Directive[19] as regards public participation has been confirmed by the Czech administrative courts[20], but has been rarely applied in practice and has not helped to solve the problem of restrictive scope of participants and requirements of *locus standi*. This is partly because of the obvious lack of will of the judiciary, partly because it was not called upon in proper manners or by a proper subject (for example a tenant).

---

15 Id., para. 71.

16 Id., para. 68.

17 Id., para. 78.

18 See Act no. 100/2011 Coll. on Environmental Impact Assessment, §9d.

19 See *J. Jendroška*, Public Participation in Environmental Decision-Making. Interactions Between the Convention and EU Law and Other Key Legal Issues in its Implementation in the Light of the Opinions of the Aarhus Convention Compliance Committee, in: M. Pallemaerts (ed.), The Aarhus Convention at Ten, 2011, pp. 111–112.

20 Most notably in judgment of the Supreme Administrative Court of 22 July 2011, No. 7 As 26/2011 - 175.

Tomoszková correctly observes that the main reasons for struggling with the duty to implement the EIA Directive "result from its postcommunist culture that creates: (1) a disrespect for law and overly critical attitude towards the European Union; (2) diminishing value of civil society and treating the active citizens as a irreconcilable opposition, not a partner; and (3) a lack of constructive communication among politicians, administrative authorities, and all stakeholders (citizens, businesses, etc.)."[21] To be more specific, it is important to emphasize three points of a crucial role in practical application of the frequently amended regulation. Firstly, and that is obvious from the previous summary, there are some elements of the effective EIA procedure the Czech legislator has been continuously struggling to address properly, especially with the binding character of the EIA statement and public participation. Secondly, during the course of time, the Czech legislator has employed a minimalistic approach to the legislative changes requested by the Commission, abstaining from anything that is not urgent and necessary. This means that merely the implementing law is amended, but the remaining legislation is not adjusted accordingly. Thirdly, there is a very sophisticated and complicated system of multi-stage decision making process in Czechia, with multiple authorities responsible for particular procedures. Czech administrative courts continuously deal with questions concerning relationship and hierarchy of certain procedures within a wider chain of building permitting. For example, it is still not clear whether the permit to fell wood species is a precondition for the building permit or vice versa. Nor is it clear whether the exception to the protection of endangered species must be obtained before the land use permit, the building permit or the operating permit.

2.2. CHAIN OF PROCEDURES

As a result, we may witness many variations within the complex system of the permitting procedures which is ruled partially by the EU-related legislation and partly by the fragmented national legislation. Because of the minimal harmonization, there is a specific EIA regime that applies to the procedures for development consent following the EIA procedure. In general, this is not contrary to the EIA Directive and stems rather naturally from the fact that the EIA Directive does not cover all the permitting procedures. The "*development consent*" defined in Article 1.2(c) of the EIA Directive has been interpreted restrictively by the Court of Justice (CJEU) as covering only the decisions that allow for placing or execution of the project, not all possible decisions needed for

21 *V. Tomoszková*, Implementation of the EU Directive on Environmental Impact Assessment in the Czech Republic: How Long Can the Wolf Be Tricked?, 6 Wash. & Lee J. Energy, Climate & Env't. 451 (2015), pp. 457–458.

execution and operation of the project.[22] This, in effect, restricts the scope of the Directive. However, if the differences between the EIA regime and the non-EIA regime are significant, some concerns may arise.

Currently, the outcome of the EIA process in Czechia is either a negative result of the screening procedure in the form of administrative decision, or a binding EIA statement. The EIA procedure is not a standard, full proceeding with participants. It is a process of preparation and adoption of a binding statement which is used in the subsequent permitting proceedings. Therefore the EIA statement is used in the procedures for development consent and these procedures are governed by the aforementioned EIA regime. There are very often other procedures before the final permit is issued. In these procedures, the EIA statement applies only as a background, non-binding material for the decision. This renders some confusion as regards the dual status of the EIA statement. Moreover, some additional requirements of the EIA Directive are fulfilled exclusively in the procedures for development consent, leaving the other procedures in the realm of the old, non-EIA regulation. For example, to keep the permitting procedures consistent, in the EIA regime each assessed project obtains a so-called coherence stamp which serves for verification that the project has not been changed after the EIA procedure. In the non-EIA regime, there is no such verification of the project. Further on, we will analyse these specifics from the perspective of the public participation.

2.3. THE SPECIFIC REGIME AND THE SPECIFIC-TO-SPECIFIC REGIME

The public concerned may participate in a large variety of the permitting proceedings. Nevertheless, this does not mean that there is a coherent regulation of the public participation in the Czech legal system. Currently, we may notice stipulations on public participation in various legal acts: in Act no. 114/1992 Coll. on the Conservation of Nature and Landscape[23], Act no. 254/2001 Coll. on Water and Amendments to Some Acts (The Water Act)[24], Act no. 76/2002

---

22 See, in particular, CJEU Judgments: C-2/07, *Abraham and Others*, ECLI:EU:C:2008:133, para. 20; C-215/06, *Commission v Ireland*, ECLI:EU:C:2008:380, para. 51; C-121/11, *Pro-Braine and Others*, ECLI:EU:C:2012:225, para. 38.

23 See §70 of the Act on the Conservation of Nature and Landscape according to which a locally appurtenant organizational unit of a civic association, the main purpose of which is the conservation of nature, is entitled to participate in administrative proceedings in respect of protection of nature and landscape, with exception of the procedures for development consent for the purposes of the EIA procedure.

24 See §115(7) of the Water Act according to which civic associations the purpose of which is environmental protection according to their statute are entitled to become the position of party to the proceeding held under this Act, with exception of permission for a water management structure construction and permissions considered development consent for the purposes of the EIA procedure.

Coll. on Integrated Pollution Prevention and Control, on the Integrated Pollution Register and Amendments to Some Acts.[25] Generally, these acts list the NGOs among the participants of the particular proceeding. The only exception is the Act. No. 114/1992 Coll. which opens all proceedings with influence on nature and landscape for public participation. In these acts, conditions for public participation are not stringent, but the participation is limited, mainly to the issues linked to protection of nature and landscape.

In the EIA regime, the regulation seems to work in the opposite manner. The NGOs may participate in any procedure for development consent following the EIA and are entitled to any objections relevant to the EIA procedure. However, the NGOs are only deemed to have interest in the environmental decision-making procedures if active for 3 years or supported by at least 200 signatures. There are some additional indirect obstacles to the effective participation in the EIA regime that alter common rules for administrative proceedings. For example, delivery of documents and notices is simplified in the EIA regime and the participants, despite their actual number, are notified merely by a public notice.

Furthermore, the legislator has not clearly stated, which procedures should be deemed procedures for development consent and fall under the EIA regime. For this reason, the NGOs and other subjects including the official authorities wait for the jurisprudence to confirm or refute their assumptions in this respect which may take years. Though the CJEU provides guidance upon the definition of the "*development consent*"[26], it is not clear whether the definition covers various permits issued according to the Czech Building Code[27] or other acts including the controversial Atomic Act[28] which expressly excludes any participants to the proceedings other than the applicant. Moreover, Czech legislator decided to adopt a definition of the "*subsequent proceeding*" which slightly differs from the concept embodied in the EIA Directive. It covers "*any proceeding according to specific acts in which a permission for placement or execution of the project is issued*"[29], but the legislator has listed the particular acts in a footnote and the list includes for example Act on Integrated Pollution Prevention and Control even though the "*integrated permit*" allows for operation and not the execution of the project.

Furthermore, the specific public participation in the EIA regime might be modified by the specific overlapping regime for infrastructure development which for example sets different time limits. And it might be modified even further in case of the selected most important TEN-T projects.

---

25 See §7 of the Act on Integrated Pollution Prevention and Control according to which civic associations or public benefit societies whose sphere of business consists in enforcing public interests pursuant to special regulations, may participate in the proceedings.

26 *Supra*, note 22.

27 Act. no. 183/2006 Coll. on Town and Country Planning and Building Code (Building Act).

28 Act no. 263/2016 Coll., Atomic Act.

29 See §3 g) of Act no. 100/2011 Coll. on Environmental Impact Assessment.

2.4. TOO MANY VARIABLES

Subsequent to the EIA procedure, the decision making process consists of the development consents (issued in the specific EIA regime) and other permits (issued in the non-EIA regime). For example, to build an average wastewater treatment plant, the investor must obtain six or seven decisions in the separate administrative procedures. All of these procedures are governed by common rules, yet differ in their scope, the range of participants and the competent authority. Specific rules for these procedures are spread among a huge amount of legislative pieces dealing with land use and building, protection of nature, water management, waste treatment etc. If the EIA for the project has been carried out, then the first subsequent procedure in which the land use permit is granted, the planning permission proceedings, falls within the EIA regime. The public concerned may expect a notice of commencement of the proceedings delivered to their address, but the specific regime of delivery applies and no individual notice is served. Therefore, the public concerned has to check regularly the official notice boards whether there is a new proceeding to participate in. The NGOs may participate in the proceedings if active for 3 years or supported by 200 persons.

In the subsequent proceedings, the waste treatment permit, the water treatment permit or permit to fell wood species is issued. These proceedings do not fall within the EIA regime. The NGOs may participate in these proceedings as regards nature and landscape protection and on different conditions, provided that they submit request to be informed, in advance, of all the intended interventions and initiated administrative proceedings that could involve the nature and landscape protection under a specific Act. They may further participate as regards of water protection, but again under different conditions. If the integrated permit under the IPPC national regulation (Act. 76/2002 Coll.) is required instead of the separate permits, the EIA regime applies. The next proceeding is usually the building permit proceeding which falls under the specific EIA regime. After that, the test operation permit is issued in a separate proceeding which falls under the non-EIA regime. Once again, the NGOs may participate in this proceeding only as regards nature and landscape protection and on different conditions then in the EIA regime.

The system becomes even more confusing when we look at the particular remedies available to the NGOs. In the non-EIA regime, the NGOs may challenge the particular decision and appeal to a higher administrative instance, but are usually restricted to nature and landscape protection and have to participate in the proceedings first. In the EIA regime, the NGOs may even appeal to the land use permit or other development permit without prior participation in the proceedings.[30]

---

[30] See *L. Dvořák*, Zákon o posuzování vlivů na životní prostředí. Komentář, 2016, pp. 67–70; *L. Bahýľová, T. Kocourek & V. Vomáčka*, Zákon o posuzování vlivů na životní prostředí. Komentář, 2015, pp. 101–107.

As far as the judicial protection is concerned, the plaintiffs including the NGOs and other members of the public concerned have to meet criteria of *locus standi*. Conditions for legal standing in administrative and judicial proceedings are similar, yet not the same. The administrative courts consider impairment of rights independently on the participation in administrative proceedings, although in theory, both proceedings match each other and form related phases of effective public participation. For a long time, judicial interpretation restricted the NGOs to point at only procedural aspects of the administrative decision because legal entities enjoyed no substantive rights in connection to environmental harm. Under the threat of the European Commission, minor changes have been introduced and the NGOs in the EIA regime may now challenge the outcome of the subsequent proceedings in court from both substantive and procedural aspects. Nevertheless, the Constitutional Court stepped into the game in 2014, overturned its settled case law and concluded the NGOs may claim violation of the right to favourable environment should they demonstrate a close relationship to the issue at question.[31] As a consequence, the administrative courts have developed a set of conditions of impairment of rights, most notably a local activity of the NGO, which is independent on participation in the administrative proceedings and applies to all environmental cases, in both EIA and non-EIA regimes. Some NGOs may hence easily obtain 200 supporters and participate in the administrative proceedings subsequent to the EIA procedure, but still fail to qualify for access to justice. In practice, this disparity contributes to the lack of transparency in the system of the public participation.

The time limit provided for the judicial decision in the EIA regime is shortened and the judges have to consider suspensive effect of the legal action *ex officio*, unlike the non-EIA regime in which they fully rely on the proposals of the parties. Moreover, the specific overlapping regime for infrastructure development slightly changes judicial review procedure of in both EIA and non-EIA regimes which is confusing especially for the judges as they can hardly see from the text of the action filed, whether it falls within the EIA regime, a non-EIA regime or another, specific regime to the general rules of the Code of Administrative Justice.[32] These specific regimes have not been embodied in the codes of administrative proceedings or of administrative justice but remain diffused among narrowly focused norms of environmental or building law.

If we take a look at the other members of the public concerned, they are in a difficult position, too. The affected neighbours, for example, also have to pay attention to the official boards. They may challenge the land use permit, but cannot appeal the test operation permit because they do not even belong among the participants of the proceedings. However, they may challenge the operation permit at the court as the *locus standi* is considered separately from the regulation

31 Judgment of the Czech Constitutional Court of 30 May 2014, no. I. ÚS 59/14.

32 Act no. 150/2002 Coll., Code of Administrative Justice.

of the proceedings. In some cases, there is only a one-level administrative proceedings and no administrative review is possible. And there is also limited standing in some cases. For example a negative screening conclusion that the project is not subject to the EIA might be challenged only by the investor and the public concerned. And, as it was already mentioned, Czech authorities and courts still ignore conclusions of the Aarhus Convention compliance Committee and interpret the concept of impairment of rights restrictively, omitting other property rights than ownership.

2.5. MANY STEPS TO STUMBLE OVER

The efforts of the government to simplify and streamline the permitting procedures continuously fail for several reasons which are similar but exceed the abovementioned unwillingness towards both international and EU law. Major proposals focus on amending the Building Act[33] and pay little attention to the environmental legislation and the permitting process at whole. The law-making seems to suffer from the division of the power among the competent ministries and pressure of the business lobby. Due to generally high number of unexplained legislative changes, the adopted amendments often differ substantially from the original proposals. As regards public participation, the main discussion during the legislative process is running round in circles for decades, targeting the NGOs as public enemies.

As for the investors, stringent time limits and set of preconditions of the public participation can hardly balance the fact that the whole procedure consists of six, seven, or even more decisions that are subject to administrative and judicial review which may postpone the project. This alone renders a great difference in profitability between complying with the law and making use of legal loopholes such as retrospective permitting in case of unauthorized construction or operation. On the other side, public participation may easily turn into extortion.

3. CASE STUDIES

The following part of the paper builds on the above analysis of the environmental impact assessment in Czechia and demonstrates the most fundamental disadvantages and limitations of the Czech approach on four specific cases, in particular, the EIA procedure as a specific, separate procedure, and a very complicated multi-level decision making. The following issues that are specific to a separate EIA process will be described:

---

33 Act no. 183/2006 Coll. on Town and Country Planning and Building Code (Building Act).

- EIA statement with no consequent permits
- Outdated facts in environmental impact assessment
- Implementation of a different project than has been considered in EIA
- (Ab)use of data from EIA

3.1. EIA STATEMENT WITH NO CONSEQUENT PERMITS

The first example concerns changes in case of the new type use of the long-term existing buildings. The relevant production hall is situated in the middle of family houses in the historic town of circa 15 thousand inhabitants. Since the mid-fifties of the 20th century, special automatic machines for screw and wire mills had been produced here. Two decades later on, the production switched to the wire-drawing machines for steel cord inserts for vehicle tires. During this period, the manufacturing operations did not bother the surroundings. Since 2010, an investor began to consider the use of existing buildings for the surface treatment of the galvanized sheet metal. This would fundamentally change the influence of the operation on the environment and living conditions of the local residents, especially by odour and air pollution.

The investor has implemented the plan in already existing buildings. Therefore he deemed sufficient to obtain the EIA, since the construction project matched the wording of paragraph 4.4, Category I of Annex no. 1 of the EIA Act (surface treatment of metals or plastic materials, including paint shops, with a capacity of over 500 thousand square meters/year of total surface treatments).[34] The investor also requested for an integrated permit, which was issued in 2014 by the regional authority.

None of the residents in the area has intervened in the EIA process or the integrated permitting, despite the fact that the notification was published on the official notice board and information about the EIA documentation was published online. The regional authority received no dissenting opinion, and therefore refrained from holding the public hearing concerning the EIA documentation and the EIA assessment.[35] The project was subsequently given a favourable EIA statement. The non-existent public participation was not a result of the acceptance of the project, but rather of ignorance and lack of public awareness.[36] This can probably be ascribed to the previous non-disturbing industrial production in the area and also to the official designation of the project which did not indicate how annoying the planned production would be.

---

34 Act no. 100/2001 Coll. on Environmental Impact Assessment.

35 See the EIA statement No. 59296/ENV/13. Available online: http://portal.cenia.cz/eiasea/detail/EIA_OV1130. [cit. 7.2.2017].

36 See the articles in local press, e.g. Nymburský deník. 18 March 2014. Available online: http://nymbursky.denik.cz/zpravy_region/zinkovna-nymburk.html. [cit. 7.2.2017].

The investor completely omitted any application for a permit under the Building Act and carried on with the reconstruction of the production halls merely on the basis of the integrated permit which serves for production activities. After the citizen initiative, the building authority started proceedings for the building removal due to the non-existent land use and building permit. The investor therefore requested an additional building permit and numerous objections and comments of the public concerned had been raised. Despite of these comments, an additional building permit was issued and authorized the investor to the minor building changes of the production halls.[37] Without detailed and convincing justification, the building authority rejected the conditions of the EIA statement relating to the implementation phase of the construction project, and stated: "Because the building is already done, it is not possible to set these conditions in the operative part of the decision – the phase of construction has already been completed."[38]

However, the investor and the building authority completely neglected the fact that according to § 81(2) of the Building Act, the decision on alteration of the building structure is required for changes in use of the building, which were subject to the EIA. Therefore, apart from the additional building permit, the land use permit should have been issued. Its absence led to the situation that it was not possible to examine the EIA procedure which is commonly reviewed in the context of the land use procedures.

The additional building permit was annulled after a few years of the court dispute[39] and a new building permit has not been issued at the time of this publication. The investor still operates the facility on the basis of the permanent building use permit issued five decades ago for an entirely different purpose. Both the investor and the building authorities refuse to provide the permanent building use permit to the public and stop (ban) operation of the factory because of the lack of land use and building permits.

The above-described case shows the first disadvantage of the separate EIA and a multi-stage system of interconnected decisions. It is not clear which specific permission is necessary for the location of the building, the construction and use of the building. Even the administrative authorities with their limited or narrow competences orient themselves in this complex system with great difficulty. Additionally, in case of obtaining "advanced permission" (e.g. permanent building use permit), prior authorization is not examined or required (e.g. building permit). In this case, the role of the environmental impact assessment is considerably

37 See the additional building permit – 13 October 2014, No. 110/13467/2014. Available online: www.mesto-nymburk.cz/index. php?sekce=2 & zobraz=uredni-deska-archiv & detail=5.

38 See the EIA statement No. 59296/ENV/13. Available online: http://portal.cenia.cz/eiasea/detail/EIA_OV1130. [cit. 7.2.2017].

39 See the judgement of Regional court in Prague, June 30, 2015, No. 47 A 6/2015 – 100; the judgement of Supreme Administrative Court, December 11, 2015, No. 5 As 150/2015 – 81. Available online: www.nssoud.cz. [cit. 7.2.2017].

weakened, because the EIA statement is not reviewable independently in Czechia, but only in the context of the subsequent decisions.

Take for example the following excerpt from the EIA statement: "The possible spread of odours from the plan under consideration will be minimized by the guidance of air equipment to capture emissions. Specifically, in the case of emissions from the dryer line and emissions from the spray booths (repair defectively painted parts) will be routed through the afterburner unit. In case of the dryer exhaust jointing lines, the air should be conducted through an activated charcoal filter. Towing acid vapours will be routed through alkaline absorption. The obligation to operate these devices will be embedded in the operating rules. Given the above, change from the perspective of a possible odour cannot be expected compared with the current situation."[40] The manufacturing procedures do not comply to the above procedure, filters and afterburner units do not have sufficient capacity and odours from the operation normally escape through windows, open doors or other vents. As a consequence, the conditions of the EIA statement easily become unenforceable, such as this one: "In the case of odour nuisance prepare and perform effective measures to eliminate odour in cooperation with the competent authorities."[41] This condition is not complied with for more than 3 years. Although the neighbours have complained about smell, there has been no effective action.

3.2. OUTDATED FACTS IN ENVIRONMENTAL IMPACT ASSESSMENT

The EIA was introduced in the Czech legal system in 1992 as a separate procedure.[42] The validity of the EIA statement was not limited until 2001 when the new EIA Act was adopted.[43] As a result, some EIA statements which were 15 years old or even older, had been deemed valid. The new EIA Act did not solve this problem completely. Although the validity of the EIA statements is limited to 5 years now, this period may be extended repeatedly.

Due to the independence of the EIA procedure, the investors often apply for an assessment in advance. This is further supported by fear of new legislation, which can turn less favourable to them. As a result, the EIA does not meet the aims and objectives of the EIA Directive because it does not deal with sufficient and current data on the authorized project. Some of the problems, which are described in closer detail in the following subchapters, include transfer of information from

40 See the EIA report No. 59296/ENV/13, p. 22. Available online: http://portal.cenia.cz/eiasea/detail/EIA_OV1130. [cit. 7.2.2017].

41 See the EIA statement No. 59296/ENV/13, condition no. 31. Available online: http://portal.cenia.cz/eiasea/detail/EIA_OV1130. [cit. 7.2.2017].

42 See Act no. 244/1992 Coll. on Environmental Impact Assessment.

43 See Act no. 100/2001 Coll. on Environmental Impact Assessment.

the EIA procedure to the strategic assessment of planned projects or changes of the project which has been assessed and carried out. Jendrośka correctly recalls that *"(a)s far as the application of this obligation to individual procedures is concerned, the major issue is its application to environmental impact assessment procedures (whether EIA or SEA), in particular in relation to so-called scoping stage of such procedures when the scope of analysis and studies in the assessment documentation is determined including quite often also the scope of alternatives to be examined."*[44] Carrying out the EIA too soon contradicts even the crucial requirement of the Aarhus convention of early public participation.

The main problems of a premature EIA turn out later on in the subsequent proceedings – the obsolescence of the information obtained, changes in legal regulations, new scientific and technical knowledge or changes of the location in which the particular project is to be implemented. Nowadays, these problems are solved by two specific instruments in Czechia, which we will discuss in detail below, and draw attention to their shortcomings.

The outdated EIA statements following the "old" EIA Act from 1992 cannot obviously meet the requirements of the EIA Directive and have to be reconsidered based on the recent amendment to the "new" EIA Act[45] which introduced a new obligation of the project developer (investor) to acquire a verification of the EIA statement. The verification of the EIA statement is issued by the EIA authority in a form of binding statement. It verifies that the content of the EIA statements issued before April 2015 is in compliance with the requirements of the legislation implementing the EIA Directive – i.e. the EIA Act from 2001 in the current version.[46]

Almost all projects assessed under the old EIA Act have been already built or have already obtained all the necessary permits. The EIA verification does not affect them. The situation is different in the case of about 100 transportation projects that have not been built and are in various stages of preparation. After negotiations with the European Commission, these transport projects have been divided into two groups. The vast majority of them (about 90) have been left in the current regime. These projects will need a new EIA procedure because of the obsolete EIA statements.

One of the aforementioned projects is the section of the Prague bypass which shall link several highways in the southeast part of the city. The bypass section is a highway with a length of 12.5 km with three lanes in each direction and the expected traffic of about 125.000 vehicles per day. The corresponding EIA

44 *J. Jendrośka*, Public Participation under Article 6 of the Aarhus Convention. Role in Tiered Decision-Making and Scope of Application, in: G. Bándi, Environmental Democracy and Law. Public Participation in Europe, p. 119.

45 See Act no. 39/2015 Coll. Amending Act no. 100/2011 Coll. on Environmental Impact Assessment and Some Other Acts.

46 See *D. Židek*, Posuzování vlivů na životní prostředí po novele č. 39/2015 Sb. – základní přehled, in: V. Vomáčka & D. Židek, Posuzování vlivů záměrů a koncepcí na životní prostředí, 2016, pp. 14–29.

statement is only a few pages long. It was issued in 2002 and has not yet been published on the internet. Nevertheless, the Czech Republic and the investor argued that such EIA statement is valid and can be used as a basis for the bypass construction. If allowed, the project would be permitted on the basis of incomplete and outdated information that had been obtained without sufficient public involvement.

A specific amendment was adopted for the remaining dozen of projects with the obsolete EIA statements (TEN-T projects). The amendment introduced a specific procedure for issuing a binding opinion which updates the old statement without a completely new EIA. The amendment should allow continuity in the planning and permitting process of the most prepared and most important structures in the framework of the planned transport network.[47] The new "quasi EIA procedure" eliminates the use of specific provisions on notification of procedure, screening procedure, documentation and assessment. Basically, the opinion is issued at the request of the investor complemented with a brief document containing a description of the current technical solution of the project and its impact on the environment and public health. The amendment established virtually no procedural or substantive requirements for the procedure, the application, public participation or the assessment itself.

The situation is similar in the case of extending validity of the EIA statements issued according to the new EIA Act. The validity of the statement is 5 years and this period is interrupted provided that the follow-up proceedings have been initiated, i.e. if the investor submits a request for the land-use permit or if the project is built. However, if the investor does not act at all for five years, the validity of EIA statement can still be extended by 5 years, even repeatedly, if the investor proves that there have been no substantial changes in the project, in the conditions in the affected areas or any new knowledge related to the documentation and development of the new technologies applicable to the project. Once again, the vague and brief stipulations have established virtually no procedural or substantive requirements for the procedure of extending validity of the EIA statement, the application, public participation or the assessment itself.

In practice, for example, the validity of the EIA statement for the construction of the second runway of the largest Czech airport was extended, even though the project had been significantly altered: number of projected take-offs and landings changed and one of the existing runways was excluded from use. The competent authority nevertheless held that there had been no substantial change in the project implementation.[48]

This clearly demonstrates one of the major disadvantages of the separate EIA procedure. It can be performed more than 10 years before obtaining land use

---

47 See art. 23a Act no. 100/2001 Coll. on Environmental Impact Assessment.

48 See the EIA statement, 25 May 2011, No. 68161/ENV/11. Available online: http://portal.cenia.cz/eiasea/detail/EIA_MZP090. [cit. 7.2.2017].

permits and thus more than 15 – 20 years before the actual construction and operation of the project. The main problem is then obsolescence of the information obtained, changes in legal regulations, new scientific and technical knowledge or changes in the location in which the projects are to be implemented. Czechia started to address this shortcoming, especially under pressure from the European Union. However, the solution is only formal due to the lack of specific regulation which makes the whole process even more complicated as it does not lead to the update of information, leaving the aims and purpose of the EIA Directive aside.

3.3. IMPLEMENTATION OF A DIFFERENT PROJECT THAN HAS BEEN CONSIDERED IN THE EIA

Any multi-stage decision making process has to cope with major changes of the project which come at different phases of permitting. Due to the he separate and often premature EIA procedure, the assessed projects are often very different from the projects that are actually implemented. Before the EIA Act amendment in 2015[49], the EIA statement was obligatory, but non-binding. Therefore the conditions of the EIA statements had not to be necessarily taken over to the subsequent decisions and there was no procedure to ensure coherence between the assessed project and the authorized project.

In practice, this caused serious problems which are evident from permitting of another section of the Prague bypass, this time the southern one, a 9 km long highway. The EIA was carried out in 2002[50], the bypass was put into operation in 2010. The assessed and the implemented construction differed in numerous characteristics. First change is the road surface. The original asphalt surface was replaced by concrete, which, although more durable, is also significantly noisier. The acoustic studies modelling the noise were based on the lower maximum speed limit (90 km/h compared to 130 km/h). The increased maximum speed resulted again in a negative effect on the actual noise levels. The traffic volume study for the EIA was based on the total number of 28.300 vehicles per day. The real volume of traffic exceeds 50.000 of vehicles per day with a very high proportion of cargo (around 15.000 trucks per day). This passage shows that the EIA was significantly undervalued in terms of transport volume. The result of all these changes is that according to the environmental impact assessment the noise at night should range from 30.3 to 37.9 db. In fact, the noise level at night is about 50 dB which is about ten times higher than was originally estimated in the EIA.

The part of the EIA Act amendment from 2015 is an instrument called a "coherence stamp" which stipulates that the identity of the assessed project

---

49 See Act no. 39/2015 Coll. Amending Act no. 100/2011 Coll. on Environmental Impact Assessment and Some Other Acts.

50 See the EIA statement, 18 January 2002, No. NM700/38/52/OPVŽP/02RP.

is checked and validated through the verification binding opinion. At the beginning of the follow-up procedure for development consent (typically land-use or building permit procedure), the investor must submit documentation including a full description of any changes compared to the assessed project. The EIA authority confirms that there have been no changes with significant negative impact on the environment between the present authorized project and project assessed. Otherwise, in case of any change with significant negative impact on the environment, particularly the increase of its capacity or the change its technology, operations management or manner of operation, it is obliged to initiate a reassessment.

The coherence stamp should contribute to a higher compliance with the EIA conclusions and hence with a more effective protection of the public concerned. In fact, some sort of verification mechanism seems essential for any multi-stage decision making process. However, in the Czech case, the legislator has not clearly stated, which procedures should be deemed procedures for development consent and demand the coherence stamp (see sub-chapter 2.3.). For this reason, the NGOs and other subjects including the official authorities wait for the jurisprudence to confirm or refute their assumptions in this respect which may take years.

3.4. (AB)USE OF DATA FROM EIA

The separate EIA procedure demands the investors to assess the impacts of the particular project as soon as possible, in advance of the necessary development consent. This may well result in a case when the EIA is carried out even before the strategic environmental assessment (SEA), which forms an integral part of the land use plan preparation. Such situation is inconsistent with the logical sequence of the land use planning and the building permitting. First, the project should be defined by the planning documentation (including an environmental impact assessment of this plan) and later on, assessed as such. The failure to follow this procedure leads to a very specific assessment of each individual aspects of the project without considering the complex influence on a wider territory and the public interest.

The preparation of the land use plan of Prague provides a nice example, once again concerning the Prague ring road and expansion of Prague's airport for the second runway.

The project to complete the ring road around Prague was assessed in 2002.[51] The land use plan of Prague was approved at 2014.[52] During the land use plan preparations, the Ministry of Environment requested that "... *all the major*

51 See the EIA opinion from 30 April 2002, Ref.: NM700 / 1327/2020 / OPVŽP/02.

52 See Land use plan of Prague. Available online: www.iprpraha.cz/clanek/46/zasady-uzemniho-rozvoje [cit. 7.2.2017].

investment plans in … traffic …, will be rigorously assessed for their environmental impact (SEA, EIA), the conclusions and recommendations of which will be taken over administrative proceedings and administrative decisions about their placement and authorization. "[53] The EIA statement regarding the missing part of the Prague ring road prefers the so-called regional variant, which runs north from the city centre. The southern variant, which runs closer to the city centre, might be permitted only as a backup solution: "*based on the conclusions of the report it can be said that in terms of environmental impact implementation of both variants is acceptable, the other options were excluded. In terms of environmental impact, we recommend realization of the regional variant, which we consider more appropriate in the long term. The southern variant is an extreme solution, the implementation of which may be allowed if the land use plan of Prague excludes the possibility of the regional variant.*"[54]

Despite the EIA statement, the land use plan relies on the southern variant without properly excluding the possibility to follow the regional variant. The land use plan is binding and the administrative authorities are thus obliged to comply with an option which is contrary to the EIA statement which is now also binding. Even though it has not yet been indicated which part of the EIA statement is legally binding in this particular case or whether the EIA procedure has to be repeated, the problem seems to be evident.

The same land use plan works quite differently with the results of assessment for the Prague airport. It respects them to the smallest details. This, however, causes problems because of use of outdated information. The EIA process was launched in 2004 by notification, the EIA documentation had been revised in 2009 and the process was completed in 2011 by issuing a statement. The parameters and predicted number of take-offs and landings for 2020 as well as data on population, the status of the territory and the needs of the airport are therefore based on data from 2006. The land use plan was approved in 2014 and contributes to the false predictions that already in 2020, the airport will suffer from lack of capacity. Current data from 2017 render such forecast completely unrealistic.

The EIA statement contains very specific information (such as the distribution of aircraft movements at individual runways, the number of take-offs and landings at various times of day etc.). By simply taking this data from EIA statement, the city of Prague has resigned to assess the needs and possibilities of transport of the area. The whole assessment is based solely on the EIA project and requirements of the airport owner which is naturally only interested in the airport development.

The environmental impact assessment answers whether the investor's project can be realized, under which conditions and what would be its impacts, while the

---

53 See Land use plan of Prague. Available online: www.iprpraha.cz/uploads/assets/dokumenty/zur/2014/Piloha_odvodnni__2a.pdf. [cit. 7.2.2017].

54 See the EIA opinion from 30 April 2002, Ref.: NM700 / 1327/2020 / OPVŽP/02.

land use plan should answer whether the positive benefits of the project outweigh the negative effects and the society intends to implement the project. Those are two different categories that should not be mixed up. The environmental impact assessment does not address the project form the wider perspective including other options, needs and public interests, and only considers one particular project within a specific territory. If such project is not properly debated and anchored in the land use planning documentation, it is presented in the form proposed by the investor with a strong emphasis on the investor's interests. These general considerations and limitations of investor's plan cannot be replaced by overtaking the results of environmental impact assessment of the project to the land use plan.

4. CONCLUSIONS

Neither the EIA Directive nor the IPPC Directive seems to prevent multiple permit decisions in the Member States[55] and the national legislator has certain discretion as to which range of options is to be discussed at each stage of the decision-making. Such stages may involve various individual decisions authorizing the basic parameters and location of a specific activity, its technical design, and finally its technological details related to specific environmental standards.[56] Nevertheless, as this chapter clearly demonstrates, the separate EIA procedure results in a complicated multi-level decision making process which is far from being transparent and user friendly. Even though this approach should employ more opportunities for the public to participate, which should be considered as a major advantage, in practice, these opportunities are limited as the public concerned must follow and fulfil numerous procedural conditions in order to raise its objections. It seems that the quantity of various specific regimes itself has a huge impact on effectiveness of public participation. Moreover, the narrow scope of various proceedings seems restrictive, pushing the public to carefully select its arguments or choose a "carpet bombing" tactics instead. Individuals may only participate if their property rights are directly affected. This means that individuals who do not have any property rights, but may be affected by the decision, are simply excluded from the proceedings and judicial protection.

Multiple decision-making does not only affect public participation, but generates costs on all sides, including investors and administrative bodies. The investor, in particular, can hardly rely on any specific time schedule to start and finish the project, carrying the risk of further assessment of changes of the projects or changes in the area affected. Furthermore, the investor is not provided

---

55 See European Community ACCC/C/2006/17; ECE/MP.PP/2008/5/Add.10, 2 May 2008, para. 45.

56 See Czech Republic ACCC/C/2010/50; ECE/MP.PP/C.1/2012/11, 2 October 2012, para. 69.

substantive space for negotiations due to narrow scope of the proceedings which applies to the official authorities as well. This undermines the concept of partnership among investor, authorities and public concerned – and supports fertile ground not even for multiple defects of administrative decisions, but also for bribery and blackmailing.

To be fair, there are some advantages of the separate EIA procedure. For the investor, it is much easier to assess and transfer the project in a specific phase of its permitting procedure. The EIA statement sets binding conditions applicable in all procedures for development consent and may force the investor to reconsider the project and start again with a new EIA. In such case, the environmental decision-making is not limited to the conduct of an EIA procedure, but extends to any subsequent phases of the decision-making, such as land-use and building permitting procedures, as long as the planned activity has an impact on the environment. Provided the subsequent procedures are swift and transparent, they present valid opportunities for the public to participate and put less pressure on administrative bodies which only deal with limited aspects of the project. All the permitting procedures must be however based on strict time limits, or rules for updating the assessment based on principles of interconnection and conditionality of the procedures. Any major changes in the project should be subject to strict and precise rules, following the project based approach. The same applies to the EIA statement itself, which should be used only for a limited time, or, provided it is necessary for the project, updated with regards to the changes in legal regulations, new scientific and technical knowledge or changes in the location affected.

USE OF THE BOUNDING CONDITIONS ENVELOPE CONCEPT IN THE POLISH SYSTEM OF ENVIRONMENTAL IMPACT ASSESSMENTS

Mariusz Wójcik*, Paweł Grabowski**, Maciej Stryjecki*** and Dominik Gajewski****

ABSTRACT

The subject of the publication is an analysis of legal and procedural conditions for the use of the Bounding Conditions Envelope ("BCE") concept in the system of environmental impact assessments ("EIA") of projects in Poland. The publication presents key aspects constituting the essence of the impact assessment procedure (screening, scoping, variant analysis, public participation, optimal content of decision on environmental conditions ("environmental decision") and relationship between the primary EIA and reassessment at the construction permit stage) in the context of applicability of the BCE. Although this topic has not yet been assessed in terms of adaptation to the Polish legal system, the BCE has already been applied in an environmental decision for the first offshore wind farm project and to a scoping decision for the first Polish nuclear power plant project; both are briefly described. The article is divided into two main sections. The first one presents the results of an analysis of using the BCE under the Polish legal system and its influence on public participation. The second part presents methodological principles and practical application of the BCE in EIA of projects.

KEYWORDS

bounding conditions envelope; EIA; Environmental Impact Assessment; offshore wind energy; Poland; project

* Project manager, Foundation for Sustainable Energy.

** PhD, Faculty of Law and Administration, University of Lodz.

*** President of the board SMDI Doradztwo Inwestycyjne sp. z o.o.

**** Legal Advisor / Infrastucture, Energy and Environmental Expert at LEWIATAN Confederation and Partner at the Legal Advisors' Office Otawski, Dziura Jędrzejewski and Partners.

1. INTRODUCTION

The subject of the publication is an analysis of legal and procedural conditions for the use of the Bounding Conditions Envelope ("BCE") concept in the system of environmental impact assessments ("EIA") of projects in Poland. The BCE allows the investor to perform EIA using maximal project parameters without having to specify e.g. specific technology or the final number of units. This topic has not yet been assessed in terms of adaptation to the Polish legal system.

The article is divided into two main sections. The first one presents the results of an analysis of using the BCE under the Polish legal system and its influence on public participation. The second part presents methodological principles and practical application of the BCE in EIA of projects.

The aim of the article is to analyse the effectiveness of procedural modalities determining the application of the BCE in the Polish system of individual EIAs. The publication presents the key aspects constituting the essence of the impact assessment procedure (screening, scoping, variant analysis, public participation, optimal content of a decision on environmental conditions ("environmental decision") and relationship between the primary EIA and reassessment at construction permit stage) in the context of applicability of the BCE. Its aim is also to answer the following questions: how does the BCE ensure optimum quality of the EIA procedure; is the BCE providing the public with sufficient information regarding the scope of the project, its impacts and the results of EIA while at the same time maintaining the flexibility of defining the final solutions; does it guarantee the fulfilment of statutory obligations by specialized environmental authorities? Emphasis is laid on the role of secondary EIA as a key instrument allowing for verification of the project's impacts on the environment in its final form.

The development of projects that are likely to have significant effects on the environment, especially in the energy sector, requires optimization and a rational balance of the environmental surveys and analyses (in terms of cost, investment risk and ensuring fulfilment of legal and environmental requirements). It is strictly linked with the need to establish the bounding conditions of the project, including key parameters and technical solutions ("project envelope") in the early stage of the investment process. It should allow to identify the scope and extent of environmental surveys and subsequent analyses for the purpose of EIA. This applies mainly to those location and technical parameters that may have significant effects on the environment. In practice identification of the final set of characteristics describing the investment may become problematic at the EIA stage. It is particularly noticeable in the fields that are characterized by a rapid technological development (e.g. offshore wind energy) or a long period between the environmental decision and the construction permit (e.g. nuclear energy). It should be stressed that many of the parameters that form the project envelope are linked to the environmental conditions, established in EIA, which often influence the choice of technological solutions incorporated and described in detail in the final design. The BCE is therefore a tool allowing flexible interpretation of the investor's intentions in the initial stages of the investment while at the same time binding the project development process with the results of EIA. Such approach has already become a practice abroad, as indicated, among others, by the International Atomic Energy Agency ("plant parameter envelope")[1] and the UK's Infrastructure Planning Commission ("Rochdale Envelope").[2]

In July 2016 the first decision on environmental conditions fully based on the BCE concept was issued for the first offshore wind farm project in Poland. The decision does not determine a specific technology or final project parameter values; it does, however, determine bounding project parameters which are crucial in terms of impact on the environment such as:

- maximum number of turbines;
- maximum turbine height;
- maximum clearance between turbine rotor and sea surface;
- four alternative foundation solutions.

What is important, the decision imposes on the investor the obligation to perform supplementary EIA at the construction permit stage, which is the final development consent. At that stage the final project design will be verified against BCE used in the first EIA procedure.

The BCE concept has also been used in the scoping stage of the procedure for the issuing of the environmental decision for the first Polish nuclear power plant. At the initial stage of investment the investor was unable to specify the exact nuclear technology; therefore, a BCE approach was used in the project information sheet. The scoping decision based on the project information sheet was issued in May 2016 and allows to perform EIA without specifying the concrete nuclear technology. Instead, project characteristics in the EIA report should include maximum parameters "project envelope" from all technologies considered.

2. CONDITIONS AND PROCEDURAL SAFEGUARDS IN THE APPLICATION OF THE BOUNDING CONDITIONS ENVELOPE IN EIA OF PROJECTS

2.1. RATIONALE FOR USING BCE UNDER THE POLISH SYSTEM OF EIA OF PROJECTS

The examination of conditions and safeguards of legal and procedural application of the BCE in EIA of projects under the existing Polish legal order is burdened with

1 International Atomic Energy Agency, Managing Environmental Impact Assessment for Construction and Operation in New Nuclear Power Programmes, Nuclear Energy Series No. NG-T-3.11, 2014, pp. 8.

2 Infrastructure Planning Commission, Using the 'Rochdale Envelope', 2011.

the novelty of this topic and its broadness. In fact, it is the first time in Poland that the BCE is the subject of any scientific study. The framework of this article allows only for a general indication of the research matter related to administrative and legal aspects of using the BCE in EIA of projects.

Within this article only a small fraction of the current Polish legal system related to EIA has been subject to research.[3] The analysis is limited to the individual environmental impact assessment system (EIA of projects). The emphasis was put on identifying legal norms allowing for the use of the BCE approach and on showing the main conditions as well as procedural and legal safeguards in the application of the envelope method (such as the place and role of EIA in the investment process, procedural safeguards for the participants of the procedures).

The subject of the analysis were the legal provisions of the Act of 3 October 2008 on the provision of information on the environment and its protection, public participation in environmental protection and environmental impact assessments ("EIA Act"), including provisions which will be in force as of January 1st, 2017.

Ensuring adequate tools in the impact assessments of projects which strengthen the potential of conciliating the interests of investors and other parties (other participants of administrative procedures, e.g. local communities) has an immense legal meaning. In terms of environmental protection law a clash of two interests can be observed: one to exploit the environment and one to protect it. It should be noted that one of the objectives of the European Union is sustainable development with a high level of environmental protection.[4]

Based on the provisions of the European Parliament and Council Directive 2011/92/EU on the assessment of the effects of certain public and private projects on the environment ("EIA Directive")[5] it is necessary for projects likely to have significant effects on the environment[6] to undergo EIA prior to a decision directly authorizing the commencement of this project ("development consent"). In the Polish legal system the development consent is comprised of a number of administrative decisions. In this perspective, one should observe the placement of the environmental impact assessment procedures in the Polish system, which has a sequential character. There are two basic sequences of legal actions[7] which are shown in Figure 1.

---

3 Act of 3 October 2008 on the provision of information on the environment and its protection, public participation in environmental protection and environmental impact assessments (Journal of Laws 2016, item 353, as amended) and Regulation of the Council of Ministers of 9 November 2010 on projects likely to have significant effects on the environment (Journal of Laws of 2016, item 71).

4 Article 191 paragraph 1 and 2 of the Treaty on the Functioning of the EU (OJ 2010 C 83/13) requires EU Member States to ensure the highest level of environmental protection.

5 OJ 2012 L 26/1.

6 Projects listed in annex I and II of the EIA Directive – in Poland those projects are collectively referred to as projects that may have significant effect on the environment.

7 *I. Weiss*, Strings of legal actions in building processes, Monitor Prawniczy 1995 (5) pp.151.

Figure 1. Types of sequences of legal actions in the investment process of projects likely to have a significant impact on the environment

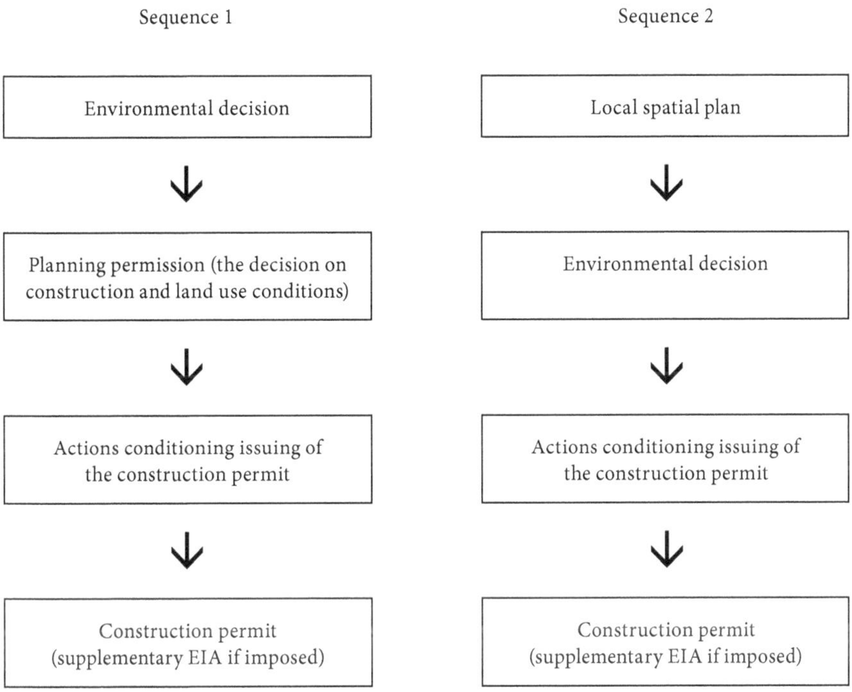

The choice of sequence is determined by the presence of the spatial development plan. In case such a plan has not been passed by the municipal council for the investment area, the investor is obliged to obtain the planning permission following the decision on environmental conditions. If such a spatial development plan is in place, sequence 2 applies and within the procedure for issuance of the decision on environmental conditions compliance with the plan is verified. When looking at the sequences of actions it should be noted that the environmental decision has primacy over selection of location. What is more, according to Article 61 paragraph 1 point 1 of the EIA Act the basic EIA is performed within the procedure for issuing of the environmental decision (one of the first steps in the investment process sequence). This is in accordance with Article 6 paragraph 4 of the EIA Directive, which states that such assessment should begin when all options of the project are open. In principle, the assessment should be carried out as soon as possible to identify and assess all impacts on the environment and to adjust the project (avoid or mitigate impacts). Hence, during the first EIA it should be possible to choose project options in order to allow environmental management of the investment (e.g. in order to provide safeguards of procedural rights for other parties). Such an assessment should cover not only the effects of the works envisaged but above all, the location and effects (externalities) of the project.

A drawback of such placement of EIA in the investment process (including screening and scoping process which precede preparation of the EIA report) is a requirement to provide a description of the proposed project and its impact on the environment at a very early stage of the process. Changes to the EIA Directive introduced with the Directive of the European Parliament and of the Council 2014/52/EU of 16 April 2014[8] further expand the obligations of investors to characterize the investment and its impacts. It is also apparent in the amendments to Polish legal system. An example, among others, is the newly introduced Article 62a of the EIA Act indicating wider requirement as to the contents of the project information sheet which is submitted at the scoping stage.[9] Prior to the aforementioned amendment, lack of proper quality information about the planned investment was often very problematic.[10] In consequence the requirement to perform EIA (which is facultative for investments that can potentially have significant impact on the environment and which depends on decision of the appropriate authority based on the project information sheet) can be a result of insufficient information about the project rather than the aim to balance the relations between using and protecting the environment.[11]

The precise definition of the investor's intentions is on one hand crucial for the procedure and on the other hand is subject to uncertainty (risk). To improve and provide flexibility to specification of the scope of the planned investment boundary criteria should be utilized – bounding conditions envelope based on the maximum foreseen scenario.

A set of bounding parameters related to a planned investment would constitute the basis for parametrization of the investor's intentions while initiating the procedure for issuing of the environmental decision. What is important, Article 73 paragraph 1 of the EIA Act[12] confirms that it is the investor who shapes the subject of the procedure (the project) and the possible content of a decision. The public administration body conducting the administrative proceedings is bound by the application of the investor.[13]

---

8 OJ 2014 L 124/1.

9 Commentary of B. Opaliński to Article 62a of the EIA Act in publication "Act of 3 October 2008 on the provision of information on the environment and its protection, public participation in environmental protection and environmental impact assessments. Commentary", C.H.Beck 2016, pp. 148–150; increasing requirements extends also to the EIA report.

10 Existing deficiencies e.g. in project information sheet include fragments regarding the balance of materials, resources and fuels which often point solely on the kind of natural resources that will be necessary for the implementation of the project, without providing quantitative data ("small amounts of water") and technical data. In fragments related environmental protection solutions authors often put project justification instead.

11 *M. Płoszka*, Projects likely to have significant effects on the environment, Decyzje Środowiskowe, Wolters Kluwer S.A., 2015 pp. 23–24.

12 The procedure to issue a decision on the environmental conditions shall be instituted at the request of the party who plans to undertake the project.

13 *Z. Bukowski*, Administrative proceedings in matters relating to environmental impact assessments, Przemysł chemiczny a ochrona środowiska, 2010 (5), pp. 148–151.

2.2. FLEXIBILITY IN THE POLISH SYSTEM OF EIA

The EIA process should allow such level of flexibility within the assessment that guarantees procedural capabilities to shape the final option for which the environmental decision will be issued. The participants to EIA (including the formal public consultation after submission of the EIA report) should therefore assume openness of different options. This allows for fulfilment of Article 81 paragraph 1 of the EIA Act, which gives the public authority responsible for issuing the environmental decision to indicate, in consultation with the investor, other option of the project than the one proposed by the investor.

It should be emphasized that the envelope, describing the maximum parameters of the investment (i.e. those parameters which have the greatest impact on individual elements of the environment) should allow for the assessment of the most important environmental factors and externalities of the project considered by an investor in EIA.

The conclusions of EIA conducted in such a way would indicate the thresholds of environmental sensitivity for individual types of impacts. Based on that approach public authority responsible for the issuance of the environmental decision would determine acceptable individual parameters, emissions and/or levels of disturbances that the proposed project may have on the assessed location(s). Parameterization based on bounding conditions would then provide a real possibility of shaping the project in the environmental sense.

It should be noted that the environmental decision is one of the first decisions in the investment process. Content of the decision, together with the project description attached to it must be specific, however the possibility to clearly define the project and the environmental conditions depends on, among others, specifics of the sector, methodology used, legal determinants, available knowledge, technological achievements (available technologies). In this light it is not desirable to have an excessively detailed project description (which does not allow the possibility of correcting those parameters which are irrelevant from an environmental point of view), nor is it desirable to have it too general (i.e. in such a way that it is not possible at a later stage to verify whether it is still the same project as referred to in the environmental decision). Both the overly generalized and excessively detailed project characteristics may be replaced by a rational designation of BCE, thus making the process more effective.

2.3. PUBLIC PARTICIPATION AND PROCEDURAL SAFEGUARDS IN BCE APPROACH

When analyzing public participation in EIAs where BCE is used it is worth looking into the procedural safeguards of the parties of the proceedings (including members of the public) when using BCE.

Firstly, public authorities have responsibility to control the type and level of detail of information characterizing the investment. In that sense the public should be presented with confirmed, verified and sufficient information. This control should include formal as well as substantive criteria. The sufficiency of the project description should be assessed in view of the ability to compare the description formed for the purpose of screening/scoping/environmental impact assessment with the description developed in subsequent proceedings related to the project (including construction permit).

Secondly, the public authority responsible for issuing of the environmental decision has the obligation to make the information about submission of an application for issuing of an environmental decision public and post the information in publicly accessible records. This obligation also applies to other stages of the procedure i.e. the decision concerning the need to perform EIA (if EIA is facultative) and decision on the scope of the EIA report (if applicable).

Thirdly and perhaps most importantly, according to Article 68 paragraph 2 of the EIA Act "In defining the scope of the report, the authority may – considering the location, character and magnitude of the environmental impact of the project:

[...]

2) indicate:
   a) the types of alternative options which need to be examined,
   b) the types of impacts and the elements of the environment which require detailed analysis,
   c) the scope and methods for the assessment."

This provision confirms that a public authority responsible for issuing the environmental decision should authorize the admissibility and sufficiency of the use of the BCE approach.

As of 1 January 2017 apart from the competence to indicate the types of options, impacts and environmental elements that require detailed analysis, a public authority may also define the scope of project description and the detail of the data submitted. Article 68 paragraph 2 is part of the scoping process and the use of BCE approach at this stage is not only admissible but can be advisable in certain cases. In fact, project description characterized using BCE would allow for gradual clarification of the project itself and EIA based on the environmental data gathered from surveys, analyses performed and consultation conducted.

Importantly, it is possible for the investor, prior to submitting the application for issuing of the environmental decision to open a dialogue with the local communities and other stakeholder in order to consult the boundary conditions of the investment or the scope of environmental surveys (this should not be confused with the obligation of the authority responsible for issuing the environmental decision to provide public participation following submission of the EIA report). This increases the efficiency of the BCE approach and procedural safeguards for the participants of the subsequent EIA procedure.

2.4. SUPPLEMENTARY EIA AND BCE

Decision on the environmental conditions is one of the first steps of an investment process and is also first stage in a multistep environmental impact assessments procedure. The environmental decision is in principle an initial decision as it affects other decisions issued in the process. The environmental decision binds the authorities issuing subsequent decisions e.g. construction permit (according to the Article 86 of the EIA Act) guaranteeing observance of the environmental conditions in the final project design. It has to be noted however that the project characterized with the use of BCE in the environmental decision can be more clearly defined and even changed to some extent further along the process. A key tool in this respect is the so-called supplementary EIA carried out within the procedure for issuing the construction permit (or other equivalent development consent).[14]

To put it in context, according to the EIA Directive Article 8a paragraph 1 the environmental conditions for a project should be defined in the decision allowing realization of the investment i.e. a development consent (in Polish law it is equivalent to a construction permit or an analogous decision replacing that permit). In the Polish system environmental conditions are primarily set in the environmental decision which can have place in a fairly large time interval from the development consent. The environmental decision is not a development consent, its role is to establish condition for safe environmentally-wise development of the investment which are further transferred to, for example, a construction permit. Large time interval and a series of legal as well as investment processes along the way will lead to a more defined project design which can be assessed in environmental terms in the supplementary EIA conducted within the procedure for issuing of the construction permit. It is important to emphasize that supplementary EIA is not obligatory for all investments and such obligation can be imposed on the investor in the environmental decision.

In the context of the BCE approach, the supplementary EIA should be seen as a procedural safeguard for the participants of EIA. On one hand the investor has the right to apply changes to the project characterized by BCE. On the other hand if the conditions set in the environmental decision are changed a supplementary EIA will have to be conducted. In such case, prior to obtaining a development consent, an EIA report supplemented with new and/or updated information has to be provided. What is important at the supplementary EIA it is not possible to change the location of the investment, but only to clarify the environmental conditions due to the preparation of a detailed project documentation.

In conclusion BCE allows to provide the participants of the EIA proceedings with: the scope of the project, its impacts and results of the assessment, it

14 According to provisions of section V chapter 4 titled "Supplementary environmental impact assessment" of the EIA Act.

also allows to influence the shape of the investments, while at the same time maintaining investor's flexibility to define final solutions. For that reasons institutionalizing the use of BCE in the Polish law or at least increasing its effectiveness by appropriate provisions would be beneficial to the investor and other stakeholders of investment projects alike.

3. METHODOLOGICAL PRINCIPLES OF EIAs USING BCE

In order to understand BCE it is important to explain the methodology of using this approach in EIAs. The methodology can be broken down into several steps, each of which is shortly described.

3.1. IDENTIFICATION OF POTENTIAL OPTIONS

Within this step all potential solutions and options are identified. According to the Article 66 paragraph 1 point 5) it is obligatory to provide in the EIA report a description of the options analysed, including: the option proposed by the proponent, a reasonable alternative, and the option which is most favourable for the environment, along with reasons for their choice. Therefore it is important to distinguish between project options and solutions which will form BCE and which are not considered as project options. This distinction will significantly affect further steps. As an example, in case of the First Polish Nuclear Power Plant project BCE included all potential reactor technologies because at the stage of the environmental decision it was not possible to choose any of them as the preferred option. Decision on the chosen reactor technology will be made at a later stage in the investment process, after the environmental decision is issued. In the same case, project options included among others potential locations and cooling system technologies, both of which can be identified at this stage of the project.

3.2. IDENTIFICATION OF KEY IMPACTS OF THE PROJECT ON THE ENVIRONMENT

In this stage all the key impacts associated with the project are identified and those that might be significant for the environment are chosen for further analysis. This stage is done prior to any environmental surveys and is based on the overall understanding of the technology and the processes involved. All potential solutions and options of the project including technological, organization and location options are considered. The significance of the impacts is revised after the environmental surveys and relevant analyses are performed.

3.3. IDENTIFICATION OF PROJECT PARAMETERS AFFECTING THE SCALE OF IMPACTS (E.G. HEIGHT, POWER OUTPUT, NOISE EMISSION)

Based on the identified key impacts a list of parameters is identified which may directly or indirectly affect the scale and significance of project impacts. The set of parameters depend on the technological as well as environmental conditions. Examples of such parameters can be: power output of a power plant which directly affects the water usage for cooling, height and rotor diameter of a wind turbine which affect the migration routes of birds, or number of foundations in offshore wind farms which directly lead to seabed degradation.

It is practical to create a matrix showing relations between: 1) the type of emission or disturbance caused by the project, 2) the source of the emission or disturbance (activity or part of the project which causes emissions or disturbance), 3) the impact caused by the emission or disturbance, 4) the type of parameter which affects the scale of emission or disturbance. An example of such chain of relations can be noise emission. In this case the source of the emission is e.g. generator, pumping station etc. The noise emission may cause the following impacts: deterioration of living conditions, loss of habitats for noise sensitive fauna etc. The parameters directly related to the scale of the impact can be: noise emission parameters of emitters, number of units generating noise, presence of natural or artificial noise screens etc. The matrix should enable to create a list of key parameters significant in relation to the impacts caused by the project.

3.4. ESTABLISHING THE INITIAL BCE

Following identification of key parameter maximum values are assigned to those parameters. The values should express the intentions of the investor as to the maximum size, power output etc. of the potential investment. This way BCE will include the worst possible scenario impact-wise. In practice BCE is established by setting together all potential solutions (e.g. different technologies) which are to be included in BCE and their parameters. Next, for each parameter a maximum value is identified, this means the value which causes the maximum impact. This way a set of parameters is brought together forming the initial envelope of the project (initial BCE) which describe its characteristics. It is possible to have different BCE for different project options e.g. different location options would allow for different solutions and in consequence, different BCE. All those conditions have to be clearly described in the EIA report.

Within this step a maximum range of potential impacts is also identified. Based on that information the environmental survey programme is conducted. Since the exact scale of impacts is not know at this stage a margin of error should be included.

It is important to note that the final BCE is in major part dependent on the environmental conditions and the capacity and sensitivity of the receptors which become known after the environmental surveys and subsequent analyses are finished. In the following steps the initial BCE might be changed if analyses prove that some of the project parameters cause significant impacts (e.g. excessive use of water which cannot be minimized or compensated) and have to be limited.

3.5. PERFORMING EIA FOR BCE AND ESTABLISHING THE FINAL BCE

The EIA process using BCE is conducted similarly to an ordinary EIA when all project details are already known. The difference is that a project is described with the use of BCE instead of constant precise project parameters.

In the process of EIA the maximum extent of the project is analysed and mitigation solutions are proposed taking into account the data on the environment and results of analytical process. In case certain impacts are impossible to mitigate BCE is revised and a lower value of parameter is set. This way final BCE is developed based on the sensitivity of receptors.

Such approach allows to assess the most pessimistic scenario in terms of impact on the environment. This way the investor has the flexibility in project design and can alter it as long as maximum values are not exceeded.

3.6. ISSUING OF THE ENVIRONMENTAL DECISION

Although issuing of the environmental decision is the responsibility of the relevant authority in order for BCE to be effective the decision should also be based on the BCE approach. This means that the conditions set in the decision should be formulated by indicating maximum project parameters instead of precise and constant values. Earlier in the article an example of a decision based on BCE approach for the first offshore wind farm project in Poland was described. In the decision the following design conditions were set for the investor:

- maximum number of turbines
- maximum turbine height
- maximum clearance between turbine rotor and sea surface
- four alternative foundation solutions.

This proves that such an approach is feasible under the Polish legislation.

3.7. VERIFICATION OF BCE

The final project design requires verification in terms of compliance with BCE set in the environmental decision. This means an assessment should be made if the impacts caused by the final project design do not exceed those assessed with the use of bounding conditions. In order to that the Polish legal system equips the environmental authorities with certain set of tools:

1. **Obligation to meet conditions set in environmental decision** – the project design has to comply with the conditions set in the environmental decision
2. **Supplementary EIA** – as described earlier in the article the authorities can impose on the investor the obligation to perform a supplementary EIA within the procedure for the issuance of the construction permit. At this stage the final project design is known and can be verified against BCE. It is important to note that public participation is obligatory at the supplementary EIA which guarantees involvement of the public in the development of the final project.
3. **Environmental monitoring** – the environmental authorities can oblige the investor to carry out environmental monitoring throughout the construction and operation stage and also to perform post-construction environmental analysis.

3.8. CHALLENGES IN USING BCE

BCE approach may have certain drawbacks, mainly due to its novel character. BCE may cause confusion among the public and other parties involved due to the fact that the project description does not include the final solution. Instead it includes a set of bounding parameters which are much harder to visualize. It is therefore very important to properly present the project description, especially in the non-technical summary which is intended for the general public.

Although the BCE approach gives flexibility to the investor it may create an overly pessimistic perception of the projects. The role of BCE is to describe the project with the set of maximum (most pessimistic) parameters even though the final project design might me much less intensive. This in turn may lead to a negative attitude of local communicates towards the investment.

Conservative approach using BCE may also lead to a negative environmental decision due to significant cumulative impacts. It is theoretically possible that several projects in the vicinity use the BCE approach in the environmental procedures. In such case the environmental authority has to take into account the maximum impacts of the two projects which may lead to a negative decisions.

BCE approach may tempt the investor to provide too little information on the project arguing that it is at a very early stage of development and there are insufficient data available. This in turn may cause the authorities to issue a negative environmental decision due to insufficient information about the project. It is important to emphasize that BCE approach is not an excuse not to provide detailed information about the project. In fact BCE requires much more effort than an ordinary approach because all potential scenarios, options and solutions should be described in detail.

4. CONCLUSIONS

Environmental impact assessment of projects with the use of BCE has only recently been tested against the Polish legal system therefore it is not directly reflected in Polish acts. Nevertheless, it has been proven in theory and in practice that the Polish legal system does enable procedural and legal effectiveness of EIAs for projects based on the BCE approach, guaranteeing at the same time procedural rights of the public involved.

BCE allows for flexible interpretation of the investor's intentions in the initial stages of the investment while at the same time binding the project development process with the results of EIA. It is mainly dedicated to projects which are characterized by long investment development process, in sectors with rapid technological development and when there is uncertainty of final investment parameters.

One of the key elements of the Polish legal system that enables the use of BCE is the multistage character of EIAs, thanks to which BCE, if needed, can be verified at the development consent stage, within the supplementary EIA.

It is worth highlighting the operational assurance of rights of the public i.e. participants in the EIA (resulting, inter alia, from the Aarhus Convention of 25 June 1998 on access to information, public participation in decision-making and access to justice in environmental matters) through the use of BCE. Firstly, the envelope approach makes the public more effective in shaping the investment and implementing the right of access to administrative procedures. In particular, this is done through an interactive negotiating system of the project's envelope with participants in the EIA (taking into account local priorities / local preferences).

Secondly, a wider range of open options allows for more efficient variant analysis. Bearing in mind that leaving the open options15 in the EIA process before the final decision[16] is one of the most important rights of the public (participants

---

[15] Article 6(4) Aarhus Convention of 25 June 1998 on access to information, public participation in decision-making and access to justice in environmental matters; *M. Micińska*, Public participation in environmental protection. Administrative and legal instruments, Publishing house Adam Marszałek, Toruń 2011 pp. 46; provisions of the European Parliament and Council Directive 2011/92/EU.

[16] *J. Jendrośka, W. Radecki*, on access to information, public participation in decision-making and access to justice in environmental matters with commentary, Centrum Prawa Ekologicznego Biuro Informacji i Porad o Prawie Ekologicznym, Wrocław 1999, pp. 24, 86–88.

to the procedure), the BCE appears to be an effective tool assuring this right. The envelope approach gives the participants the opportunity to influence the final shape of the investment, ensuring a fairly wide openness of options (Article 6 of the Aarhus Convention) in the variant analysis.

Thirdly, it should be noted that the EIA is based on a system of relations between the fields of environmental impacts, the planned project, the environment itself, and the sphere of decision and social control. Thanks to the BCE, the information flow regarding the envelope framework of the project allows gradual optimization of the latter with effective implementation of the rights of the public (resulting, inter alia, from the Aarhus).

In summary BCE can enable more effective public involvement in the investment process.

BCE does, however, pose certain challenges due to lack of final solutions in the project description and a conservative approach which comes from presenting the maximum possible impacts which might lead to an overly negative perception of the project by the public. In order to mitigate that risk it is important to provide in the EIA report sufficient details and clear explanation of the investment process.

SPECIAL PROVISIONS ON THE ISSUANCE OF ENVIRONMENTAL DECISIONS IN SECTORAL LEGISLATION IN POLAND

Sergiusz Urban*

1. INTRODUCTION

There are two important features of the Polish system of issuance of development consent for projects requiring the Environmental Impact Assessment that need mentioning for the purpose of this article: the first one is the multi-stage nature of the development consent in Poland and the other is that the first stage thereof is the "environmental decision", summarizing the findings of the Environmental Impact Assessment. The latter is regulated by the Act of 3 October 2008 on the access to environmental information, public participation and the Environmental Impact Assessment (OJ 2016 item 353 text codified as amended[1], further referred to as EIA Act).[2]

At the same time, the Polish legal system provides for several sectoral Acts that derogate the general rules of the issuance of environmental decisions and replace them with separate provisions that are more favourable for the investors and at the same time lowering the safeguards for the environment. Those changes encompass the elements as mentioned:

- restrictions imposed on the proceedings of the issuance of the environmental decisions,
- automatic assignment of the immediate enforceability to the environmental decisions,
- stricter rules of challenging the environmental decisions,

* PhD, Head of Environmental Law Practice at WKB Wiercinski Kwiecinski Baehr Law Firm.

1 Http://isap.sejm.gov.pl/DetailsServlet?id=WDU20081991227 (in Polish).

2 For more in-depth insight into Environmental Impact Assessment system in Poland see *M. Bar, J. Jendrośka*, Decyzja o środowiskowych uwarunkowaniach i inne wymagania prawne ochrony środowiska w procesie inwestycyjnym. Praktyczny poradnik prawny, Wrocław 2011; *A. Lipiński*, Prawne podstawy ochrony środowiska, Kraków 2004, p. 58–62.

- prohibition of the quashing of the administrative decisions issued at the last stage of the development process.

The following reservation has to be made: while it is true that the environmental decisions are in many cases preceded by the Environmental Impact Assessment, it is not a prerequisite for their issuance; even if a project in the course of so-called screening procedure (see Article 4 of Directive 2011/92/EU of the European Parliament and of the Council of 13 December 2011 on the assessment of the effects of certain public and private projects on the environment as amended, OJ L 26, 28 January 2012[3]) was found to be of non-EIA nature, the environmental decision is still required. However, for the sake of the clarity of this dissertation, it is focused solely on the environmental decisions issued for the projects requiring the Environmental Impact Assessment.

While the subject matter of following considerations appears to be of substantial importance, it has not been previously discussed in the domestic nor international literature and remained unexplored until now; this is the first attempt to the comprehensive approach to these issues which might seem quite surprising given their significance and impact on the environmental protection.

2. THE EXEMPTIONS FROM THE GENERAL RULES APPLICABLE TO THE ENVIRONMENTAL DECISIONS

As already indicated, the issuance of environmental decision, being the first stage of the development consent in Poland, is regulated by the Act of 3 October 2008 on the access to environmental information, public participation and Environmental Impact Assessment.

At the same time, there are a number of separate Acts (*lex specialis*) in the Polish legal system that regulate certain aspects relating to the Environmental Impact Assessment and the subsequent environmental decisions in a different manner. The reasoning for the adoption of these Acts is always the necessity of assuring swift implementation of projects (and/or categories thereof) that are deemed of particular importance for State economy or safety[4,5]. The number of Acts of this nature is growing with time.

What is important to understand is that they do not provide for a comprehensive, stand-alone set of rules relating to the environmental decisions but tend to replace only certain elements of the general framework. However,

3 Http://eur-lex.europa.eu/legal-content/EN/TXT/?uri=CELEX:32011L0092.
4 E.g. "Spec-Act will facilitate development of energy projects" www.rp.pl/Nieruchomosci/307239973-Specustawa-ulatwi-inwestycje-energetyczne.html.
5 E.g. "Spec-Act will facilitate development of transmission lines" https://www.teraz-srodowisko.pl/aktualnosci/Nowa-specustawa-ma-ulatwic-inwestycje-w-sieci-przesylowe-1278.html.

these amendments are significant since they have a serious impact on both procedural and material safeguards serving the purpose of assuring the adequate quality of the EIA such as the time necessary for the environmental assessment or the right to appeal.

These sectoral acts are uniformly less favourable for the environment from this perspective. It is due to the fact that the changes they provide for impose substantial restrictions on the general rules of issuance of environmental decisions and they are officially declared to serve the purpose of streamlining the development process ("radically"[6]).[7] As a matter of fact the "regular" administrative procedures in Poland are burdensome and tend to be lengthy indeed, therefore anything that extends their duration, e.g. the possibility to appeal from the environmental decision, is considered as an obstacle that requires overcoming. When taking into account the fact that it is not uncommon among the investors to perceive the environmental legislation solely as the unnecessary administrative burden, it is no surprise that these Acts, also called "Spec-Acts", are warmly welcomed, both by the developers and the authorities, as a way to "facilitating the process of assessment of environmental impact of projects" and "streamline their implementation".[8] While this aim seems legitimate, the facilitation is in practice achieved by restrictions imposed on the procedural and material rights, especially on the possibility of appeal from the administrative decisions, as this legal tool is relatively often used when major projects are at stake, attracting public attention and, quite naturally, raising opposition.[9]

Mentioned underneath are the most imminent examples of this kind of legislation:

- the Act of 10 April 2003 on the special rules of preparation and development of public roads (OJ 2015 item 2031 text codified)[10],
- The Act of 7 September 2007 on the preparation for the finals of 2012 UEFA European Football Championships (OJ 2010 No 26 item 133 text codified)[11],

---

6 The reasoning of the project of Act on the special rules of preparation and development of the public utility airports, item 1148 dated 17 September 2009, pp. 20–23 http://ww2.senat.pl/k7/dok/sejm/026/1148.pdf.

7 See for example the reasoning of the project altering the Act on the special rules of preparation and development of public roads, item 3575 dated 19 June 2015, p. 12 www.sejm.gov.pl/Sejm7.nsf/druk.xsp?nr=3575 and the same grounds provided for by the Higher Chamber of the Polish Parliament: www.senat.gov.pl/aktualnosci/art,8062,78-posiedzenie-senatu.html (in Polish).

8 See e.g. "Railway Spec-Act will facilitate upgrade of railway tracks and save billions" www.portalsamorzadowy.pl/artykuly/,79397.html.

9 A good example is the project of huge coal power plant to be located in clean environment of Pomerania (northern Poland). The Environmental Impact Assessment for this project was successfully questioned twice by non-governmental organizations, more at www.pl.clientearth.org/sukces-spoleczenstwa-obywatelskiego-na-pomorzu-elektrownia-polnoc-juz-po-raz-drugi-nie-otrzymuje-zgody-na-budowe/ and http://stopep.org/en (in English).

10 Http://isap.sejm.gov.pl/DetailsServlet?id=WDU20030800721 (in Polish).

11 Http://isap.sejm.gov.pl/DetailsServlet?id=WDU20071731219 (in Polish).

- the Act dated 12 February 2009 on the special rules of preparation and development of the public utility airports (OJ 2015 item 2143 text codified)[12],
- the Act of 24 April 2009 on the liquid petroleum gas terminal in Świnoujście (OJ 2016 item 1731 text codified)[13],
- the Act dated 8 July 2010 on the special rules of preparation and development of projects serving the purpose of flood protection (OJ 2015 item 966 text codified)[14],
- the Act of 29 June 2011 on the preparation and development of investments in nuclear energy as well as supporting projects (OJ 2011 No 135 item 789 text codified)[15],
- the Act of 24 July 2015 on the preparation and development of strategic projects relating to the transmission lines (OJ 2016 item 1812 text codified).[16]

As one can see, the Spec-Acts regulate the implementation of various infrastructural projects such as the construction of public roads, construction of the liquid petroleum gas terminal in Świnoujście (please note that under this title a lot of other sub-projects are hidden, dispersed throughout Poland), construction of airports, investment in nuclear energy infrastructure and construction of transmission lines. Other acts of similar nature are in the course of preparation or planned.

2.1. RESTRICTIONS IMPOSED ON THE PROCEEDINGS OF THE ISSUANCE OF THE ENVIRONMENTAL DECISIONS

The discussion of specific aspects in which the general system of administrative "checks and balances" relating to the environmental decisions is being altered shall start with the restrictions imposed on the duration of proceedings on the issuance of the environmental decisions.

Several Spec-Acts are very strict in this regard, obliging the authority to issue the environmental decisions in a given, usually very short, period of time. In many cases the deadline is set at 45 days or even as few as 30 days. Otherwise, they might find themselves punished with financial penalties for a delay equal 500 PLN (approximately 120 EUR) per day.[17] This might of course rise reasoned concern whether the authority will be able to correctly and fully assess the environmental impacts of the project or it would focus is efforts on meeting the

12 Http://isap.sejm.gov.pl/DetailsServlet?id=WDU20090420340 (in Polish).
13 Http://isap.sejm.gov.pl/DetailsServlet?id=WDU20090840700 (in Polish).
14 Http://isap.sejm.gov.pl/DetailsServlet?id=WDU20101430963 (in Polish).
15 Http://isap.sejm.gov.pl/DetailsServlet?id=WDU20111350789 (in Polish).
16 Http://isap.sejm.gov.pl/DetailsServlet?id=WDU20150001265 (in Polish).
17 See e.g. Articles 20 and 35 of the Act of 29 June 2011 on the preparation and development of investments in nuclear energy as well as supporting projects.

deadline and avoiding the penalty instead. The assumption can be made that the adequate quality of the assessment would not always be the main focus of the authority hosting the proceeding.

Furthermore, certain limitations have been imposed on the participation of ecological NGOs in the environmental proceedings: the only organizations entitled to participate are those functioning for over a year[18].[19] It is worth mentioning that these provisions were subsequently adopted by the general rules and nowadays the EIA Act provides for the same requirement while originally no similar restriction was included there.[20]

2.2. AUTOMATIC ASSIGNMENT OF THE IMMEDIATE ENFORCEABILITY TO THE ENVIRONMENTAL DECISIONS AND THE CONSEQUENCES FOR THE CHALLENGING OF THESE DECISIONS

The common characteristic of all special Acts is that they attribute the environmental decisions with the feature of immediate enforceability.[21] This means that these decisions can directly serve as the basis for the issuance of subsequent administrative decisions during the process of the development of the project, even in case they are challenged. Normally, such feature may be granted in the course of case-by-case screening and furthermore, several court judgements stated that the "regular" environmental decisions cannot be enforced directly as their very nature does not allow for it since they do not serve as stand-alone basis for the execution of the projects[22].[23]

18 See e.g. Articles 20 and 35 of the Act of 29 June 2011 on the preparation and development of investments in nuclear energy as well as supporting projects.

19 See also *J. Sommer*, Prawo udziału organizacji społecznych w sprawach dotyczących ochrony środowiska, [in:] Ochrona Środowiska. Prawo i Polityka, No 4(34)/2003, p. 24, *M. Bar, J. Jendrośka, K. Tarnacka*, Prawo do sadu w ochronie środowiska, Wrocław 2002, pp. 91–94, *J. Jendrośka, M. Bar*, Zmiany w regulacji prawnej udziału społeczeństwa w ochronie środowiska, [w:] Prawo i środowisko No 3(43)/2005, p. 79, *M. Micińska*, Udział społeczeństwa w planowaniu przestrzennym i procesie budowlanym, [w:] Ochrona środowiska. Prawo i Polityka, No 1(39)/2005, p. 50,, J. Jendrośka, M. Bar, Prawo ochrony środowiska. Podręcznik, Wrocław 200, p. 128–129, *M. Kopeć*, Formy udziału społeczeństwa w postępowaniach administracyjnych dotyczących ochrony środowiska, energetyka i ochrona środowiska w procesie inwestycyjnym, red. M. Cherka, F. M. Elżanowskl, M. Swora, K.A. Wasowskl, Warszawa 2010, pp. 145–153.

20 The relevant modification of Article 44 para 1 of EIA Act was introduced at the beginning of 2015.

21 See e.g. Article 25 para 1 of the Act of 24 July 2015 on the preparation and development of strategic projects relating to the transmission lines.

22 See e.g. the judgement of Supreme Administrative Court dated 6 July 2010, sign. II OZ 658/10 http://orzeczenia.nsa.gov.pl/doc/2AA72FB6D0 and the judgement of Voivodship Administrative Court in Cracow dated 22 February 2011, sign. II SA/Kr 880/10, http://orzeczenia.nsa.gov.pl/doc/E3D0F1383A.

23 See also *A. Kosieradzka-Federczyk*, Decisions on the environmental conditions and their executability. Legal analysis, [in:] Przegląd Prawa Ochrony Środowiska, No 2/2013, p. 47–67.

When enforced directly though, the environmental decision might allow the developer to obtain the subsequent part of the "development consent" even if it is challenged. Taking into account the fact that the appeal procedure is lengthy and it can take several months up to a year, to finalize it with a decisive conclusion, the subsequent decision might be on its way or even already be issued. In the latter case, the possibility to challenge it on the grounds that it was based on the environmental decision that was found defective, might be not possible (please refer to the discussion under point 4), as opposed to the general rules set by the Administrative Code of Conduct.[24]

2.3. SPECIAL RULES OF CHALLENGING THE ENVIRONMENTAL DECISIONS

The challenging of the environmental decisions regulated by the sectoral Acts might also be more difficult than when general rules apply. This is due to the fact that most of the special Acts impose a number of limitations on the access to the appeal, especially by shortening the time-limit for filing the appeal by half (7 days instead of 14 days assured by the general rules of administrative proceedings)[25] and by obliging the authorities to decide on the appeal in the like-limited period of time (14 days instead of 30 days).[26]

The changes might affect the very nature of the appeal as well since some of these Acts provide for the obligatory elements of the appeal from the environmental decision and require to explain precisely the allegations along with evidence to support them.[27] This is a serious derogation from the general rules of Administrative Code of Conduct which are far more lenient and do not require any of that.

It shall be also noted that these Acts prohibit the quashing of the environmental decisions after 14 days of their issuance provided the construction process was initiated, even when gross violation of law has been identified by the court.[28] There is no need to mention that the general rules of administrative proceedings do not provide for similar restraints.[29, 30]

---

24 OJ 2016 item 23 text codified http://isap.sejm.gov.pl/DetailsServlet?id=WDU19600300168 See its Article 145 para 1 point 8.

25 See e.g. Article 25 of the Act of 24 July 2015 on the preparation and development of strategic projects relating to the transmission lines.

26 See e.g. Article 34 of the Act of 24 April 2009 on the liquid petroleum gas terminal in Świnoujście.

27 See e.g. Article 25 para 2 of the Act of 24 July 2015 on the preparation and development of strategic projects relating to the transmission lines.

28 See e.g. Article 13 of the Act dated 12 February 2009 on the special rules of preparation and development of the public utility airports.

29 See *Z. Bukowski*, Postępowanie administracyjne w sprawach z zakresu ocen oddziaływania na środowisko, Toruń-Włocławek 2010, pp. 40–41, 209–220.

30 Furthermore, the conformity of these provisions with international legislation might be questioned as well. See also *K. Gruszecki*, Ustawa o udostępnianiu informacji o środowisku i

2.4. PROHIBITION OF THE QUASHING OF THE ADMINISTRATIVE DECISIONS ISSUED AT THE LAST STAGE OF THE DEVELOPMENT PROCESS IN THE CONTEXT OF THE (COMPLEMENTARY) ENVIRONMENTAL IMPACT ASSESSMENT CONDUCTED AS A PART THEREOF

As already indicated, the "development consent" in Poland is composed of more than one decision in most cases, e.g. the environmental decision and the construction permit. Since there are certain aspects of the environmental impact of the projects that might be correctly identified and assessed only at this late stage of the development of the project, the legislation allows for the complementary Environmental Impact Assessment to be conducted in conjunction with the proceeding of issuance of the administrative decision finalizing the development process.[31]

Just as in the case of environmental decisions, some special Acts do not allow for revoking of these subsequent administrative decisions after 14 days of their issuance provided the actual construction of the project has been initiated[32]; this applies also when gross violation of law has been identified by the court. In such case the court is entitled only to articulate the grounds for which it finds that the law has been breached but the identification of such infringement does not lead to the quashing of this decision.[33] Again, the general rules of Administrative Code of Conduct do not provide for similar provisions.[34]

Provided the possibility of challenging such decision is seriously limited, even if the court finds is seriously defective due to the breach of regulations relating to the EIA, the access to effective judicial appeal procedure might become ineffective and illusory.[35]

---

jego ochrony, udziale społeczeństwa w ochronie środowiska oraz o ocenach oddziaływania na środowiska, Wrocław 2009, p. 117–128.

31 Article 88 of the EIA Act.

32 See e.g. Article 27 of the Act of 24 July 2015 on the preparation and development of strategic projects relating to the transmission lines.

33 See e.g. Article 13 of the Act dated 12 February 2009 on the special rules of preparation and development of the public utility airports.

34 See *J. Goździewicz-Biechońska*, Wadliwość decyzji administracyjnych w procesie inwestycyjno-budowlanym, Warszawa 2011, pp. 237–279, 282–306.

35 See see *M. Bar, J. Jendrośka*, Decyzja o środowiskowych uwarunkowaniach i inne wymagania prawne ochrony środowiska w procesie inwestycyjnym. Praktyczny poradnik prawny, Wrocław 2011, p. 101–102, 139–140.

3. CONCLUSIONS

The conformity of the special provisions discussed in this article with the general rules set by the international legal conventions and European Union law might be questioned.

Please note in that respect that according to the Principle X of the Rio Declaration "(...) each individual shall have (...) the opportunity to participate in decision-making processes. States shall facilitate and encourage public awareness and participation by making information widely available. Effective access to judicial and administrative proceedings, including redress and remedy, shall be provided". Similarly, Article 1 of the Aarhus Convention states that "In order to contribute to protection of the right of every person (...) to live in an environment adequate to his or her health and well-being, each Party shall guarantee the rights of access to information, public participation in decision making, and access to justice in environmental matters (...)"[36],[37]

It is doubtful whether the special Acts reflect correctly the aim, which is full and effective public participation in the decision-making process, access to effective legal procedures and the ability to challenge the decisions that might result in the impact on the environment.

Unfortunately, it might be observed that the care for the environment has at least partially been sacrificed in the pursuit of streamlining the development process. While this goal sometimes is legitimate, it should always be well justified and the results should always be monitored if the measures taken are really adequate. None of the above could be observed in this case.

For this reason the question shall be asked whether the proper balance between the efficiency of the development process and the protection of the environment is maintained. In that respect, it could be argued that the special legislation does not assure that equilibrium, especially when taking into account the fact that the concrete projects prepared under these special Acts are far too often random, developed slowly and with significant delays. A good example of the latter was the plan continued as late as in 2015 to build a hotel on the basis of the Act of 2007 relating to the EURO 2012 tournament.[38] This question is not just a rhetorical – please note that also the European Commission had doubts whether this approach is acceptable. After serious consideration it has initiated the formal proceeding against Poland on 29 April 2016. The Commission complained before the Court of Justice of the European Union about the inconformity of the

---

36 Convention on Access to Information, Public Participation in Decision-Making and Access to Justice in Environmental Matters, 25 June 1998.

37 See *G. Bandi, O. Csapo, L. Kovacs-Vegh, B. Stagel, S. Szilagyi*, The environmental jurisprudence of the European Court of Justice, Budapest 2008, pp. 191–195.

38 Http://poznan.naszemiasto.pl/artykul/nad-malta-moze-powstac-wiezowiec,3180281,art,t,id,tm.html (in Polish).

restrictions imposed by the above-mentioned Special Acts with the Article 11 of the EIA Directive on the grounds of limited access of the interested parties to the judicial review (infringement 2016/2046).[39]

Furthermore, one shall also consider the fact that even if any of these derogations were not significant when assessed alone, altogether they shall raise serious concerns. What might also be worrying is that these special Acts serve the legislator as the blueprint ready to be copied and pasted in new pieces of legislation or even replace the general rules relating to the environmental decisions. As to the latter, similar attempts have already taken place[40], even if the government is denying that fact.[41]

---

39 More on that proceeding and the allegations in the letter of Polish Minister of Foreign Affairs dated 14 October 2016, point 2, p. 2–3 http://legislacja.rcl.gov.pl/docs/2/12290463/12382112/12382115/dokument250412.pdf (in Polish).

40 Www.greenpeace.org/poland/pl/wydarzenia/polska/Koniec-ochrony-polskiej-przyrody/.

41 See the official statement of the Ministry for the Environment dated 9 December 2016 https://www.mos.gov.pl/kalendarz/szczegoly/news/oswiadczenie-ministerstwa-srodowiska/.

PROCEDURAL ENVIRONMENTAL RIGHTS AND CLIMATE CHANGE

(UN)COMFORTABLY NUMB: THE ROLE OF NATIONAL COURTS FOR ACCESS TO JUSTICE IN CLIMATE MATTERS

Esmeralda Colombo*

"A Karachi lawyer (...), questioned about access to environmental justice, dryly remarked that in the city there was no environment, no justice and no access to either."
Martin Lau, Access to Environmental Justice: Karachi's Urban Poor and the Law, 2007, p. 178.[1]

ABSTRACT

Principle 10 of the Rio Declaration brought about the proceduralisation of environmental rights, but did not warrant the fulfillment of the right to access justice in environmental matters. Such void is all the more perceived at a time when the pressing nature of climate change is prompting individuals and NGOs to take action in courts. Albeit absent from the international climate change treaty regime, access to justice now appears to be emerging in national climate change cases.

In light of a new strand of cases decided as of 2015, I argue that domestic courts are increasingly applying international norms in order to allow individuals and NGOs to access justice in climate change matters. I conclusively hold that such a mechanism not only adheres to Principle 10 of the Rio Declaration, but it may also boost the enforcement of international law and its legitimacy, notwithstanding a number of challenges.

* Esmeralda Colombo is a research fellow at the University of Bergen in Norway. The author wishes to thank the organizing committee of and participants to the European Environmental Law Forum held in Wrocław, Poland, in September 2016. The author extends her sincere thanks to the editorial committee and an anonymous reviewer. The author may be contacted at ec3104@columbia.edu.

1 *M. Lau*, Access to Environmental Justice: Karachi's Urban Poor and the Law, in: A. Harding (ed.), Access to Environmental Justice: A Comparative Study, 2007, p. 177, 178.

KEYWORDS

Climate litigation; Enforcement; Legitimacy; Paris Agreement; Principle 10 Rio Declaration

1. INTRODUCTION

Given the almost universal consensus on the Paris Agreement, as well as its entry into force[2], implementation has now become the most pressing legal challenge in addressing the threats and opportunities of climate change. Civil society organizations have consistently taken part in climate change negotiations ever since the 1992 UN Conference on Environment and Development (also called 'Earth Summit'), yet a novel tactic of mounting pressure has lately appeared at an unprecedented rate. Namely, climate change litigation, by which individuals and NGOs require national adjudicating bodies to hold governments accountable for damages and/or mounting threats to individuals, the climate and the environment at large.[3] The limelight seems to have expanded from public participation in the ambit of Conferences of the Parties and informal meetings to national courts and national human rights bodies compelling governments to abide by their obligations.

Besides public participation, a further element of climate change matters is worth considering. The decisive conundrum of enforcement is still relevant. The Paris Agreement grew out of the United Nations Framework Convention on Climate Change ('Framework Convention' or 'UNFCCC'), the same Convention leading to a somewhat scorned international instrument such as the Kyoto Protocol.[4] Such a scorn was not immediate, but it rather came about as a sediment of prolonged political battles, lack of perceived legitimacy, as well as enforcement

---

2 The Paris Agreement entered into force on 4 November 2016. 2015 Paris Agreement on Climate Change, FCCC/CP/2015/L.9/Rev.1 ('Paris Agreement').

3 For the purposes of the present contribution, the type of climate litigation under consideration consists of legal actions taken by individuals and NGOs against their own government and/or private companies before national courts. The novel strand of litigation analysed in light of Rio Principle 10 and for the prospective enforcement of the Paris Agreement is one seeking the application of international law, along with national law, for the disposition of the case in terms of climate protection.

4 On Canada withdrawal from the Kyoto Protocol, see *J.M. Glen & J. Otero*, Canada and the Kyoto Protocol: An Aesop Fable, in: E.J. Hollo, K. Kulovesi & M. Mehling (eds), Climate Change and the Law, 2013, p. 489. On Japan and Russia declaration not to sign for a Second Commitment Period, see *H. Kimura*, Climate Change and Policy in Japan, in: E.J. Hollo, K. Kulovesi & M. Mehling (eds), *supra*, note 5, p. 585, 593. *Y. Yamineva*, Climate Law and Policy in Russia: A Peasant Needs Thunder to Cross Himself and Wonder, in: E.J. Hollo, K. Kulovesi & M. Mehling (eds), *supra*, note 5, p. 551, 562.

shortcomings within the Protocol.[5] In the face of political stalemate, individuals and NGOs resorted to national courts, but in the country featuring the largest percentage of climate change litigation, namely the United States, "most direct impacts thus far have occurred through courts interpreting statutory law in a way that includes climate change considerations,"[6] without reference to international norms and instruments.

National judges, however, have recently become uncomfortably numb with this sort of self-restraint on the use of international norms and are increasingly applying the latter for allowing individuals and NGOs to access courts and bring forward demands of climate justice, on both the procedural and substantive planes.

I will solely consider the mechanism known as the indirect application of international law, also called the consistent interpretation of national law with international law, namely one of the three avenues of enforcement of international law by national courts, the other two being the direct application of international law in national courts and the award of damages upon the violation of international law on the part of the state's political branches. By indirect application or consistent interpretation, I mean "the interpretation of domestic law in conformity with international obligations."[7]

The question is, why are national judges increasingly interpreting national law in conformity with international climate change instruments and principles? National judiciaries might have initially posited that wide leeway was commendable for States to wield in such a sensitive area as climate change, rife with hazardous risks and prospective remodelling of economic policies. Notwithstanding, judges

5 Political battles might be attributed to the way the principle of Common But Differentiated Responsibilities and Capabilities ('CBDRs') was spelled out in the Kyoto Protocol, making it largely obsolete. See *P-M. Dupuy and J.E. Viñuales*, International Environmental Law, 2015, pp. 149–150. Lack of legitimacy might be traced back to both the perceived unfairness of the system as well as to the lack of transparency in information sharing, see *M. Doelle*, Compliance and Enforcement in the Climate Change Regime, in: E.J. Hollo, K. Kulovesi & M. Mehling (eds), *supra*, note 5, p. 165, 168. On the enforcement shortcomings, see the few powers of the two branches, namely the facilitative and enforcing branches, of the Compliance Committee of the Kyoto Protocol, in *Dupuy and Viñuales, supra*, note 6 at p. 45, and the account given by *Doelle, supra*, note 6 at p. 184.

6 *J. Peel and H.M. Osofsky*, Climate Change Litigation. Regulatory Pathways to Cleaner Energy, 2015, p. 38.

7 *A. Nollkaemper*, National Courts and the International Rule of Law, 2011, p. 139. The three techniques enabling courts to give effect to an international obligation are direct effect, consistent interpretation and reparation see *id.* at pp. 117–213. On the potential of national courts for the enforcement of international law see, *inter alia*, *A. Cassese*, International Law, 2005, pp. 307–310 and *G. Scelle*, Précis de droit des gens: principes et systématique – Pt.2, 1934, pp. 10–12. National courts usually prefer to undertake procedural reviews through the indirect application of international law. See *Nollkaemper, supra*, note 8 at p. 165. The specific mechanism of consistent interpretation is also poised to set aside the controversy on monist/dualist/hybrid systems. See *A. Tzanakopoulos*, Domestic Courts as the 'Natural Judge' of International Law: A Change in Physiognomy, in J. Crawford & S. Nouwen (eds), Select Proceedings of the European Society of International law, vol 3, 2011, p. 155, 161–165.

are currently realizing that it may take a long time for an unchecked political process to fulfil legal obligations and societal expectations. Climate hazards are still a Damocles' sword, yet one national judges are apparently willing to handle by allowing individuals and NGOs to sue their respective governments through reliance on international law.

I begin by seizing the legacy of Principle 10 of the Rio Declaration[8] and related instruments. I maintain that such instruments support the use of international law for access to justice purposes in national courts. I later review the most prominent cases where, albeit in its infancy, a new strand of litigation appears to promote access to justice in climate matters by applying international law along with domestic norms. The Paris Agreement might also lend itself to being the object of domestic litigation and I overview it in this light. I conclude this contribution by holding that the indirect application of international law in domestic courts appears to advance individuals and NGOs' access to justice in climate matters, also contributing to the enforcement and legitimacy of the relevant international law, notwithstanding a number of limitations.

2. A NORMATIVE FRAMEWORK. RELOADING PRINCIPLE 10 OF THE RIO DECLARATION

In the present paragraph, I put forward a synthetic framework related to the normative character of Principle 10 of the Rio Declaration and related international instruments. I evaluate whether the legacy of Principle 10 of the Rio Declaration in terms of access to justice implications upholds the consistent interpretation of national law with some of the provisions and principles enshrined in the climate change regime. When applied in national courts, such provisions would allow individuals and NGOs to access justice and request that national governments account for climate change inaction or ineffective action.[9] I eventually argue that, by relying on international law, national courts can interpret either constitutional or other domestic provisions in order to allow the widest possible access to justice for individuals and NGOs in climate matters. In the absence of a universal instrument on access to justice in environmental matters, such a mechanism is poised to carry out the rationale underlying Principle 10 of the Rio Declaration in terms of access to justice obligations on the part of States and fulfil rights, especially procedural environmental rights, granted at the domestic level.

---

8 Rio Declaration on Environment and Development, UN Doc. A/CONF.151/26 (vol. I); 31 ILM 874 (1992).

9 The access to justice prong of Principle 10 of the Rio Declaration recites as follows: "Effective access to judicial and administrative proceedings, including redress and remedy, shall be provided."

I do not specifically address the access to justice component of regional instruments, most notably the Aarhus Convention, in an effort to canvass the normative framework applicable onto access to justice at international law. Moreover, as a methodological caveat, I refer to access to justice with no further conceptual clarifications. In respect of the term 'access to justice,' the latter usually refers to solely environmental matters, whereas the expression often mentioned when relating to a commensurate right in other matters is the right to an effective remedy.[10] In respect of the meaning of access to justice, I herein relate to both its procedural and substantive profiles, given the recognition among commentators that something more than access to courts is implied in access to justice.[11]

Access to justice in environmental matters was first enshrined in Principle 10 of the Rio Declaration, which resulted from the widely participated 1992 Earth Conference.[12] Among all three access rights warranted by Principle 10 of the Rio

10 For the use of access to justice in a non-environmental field, see *F. Francioni*, Access to Justice as a Human Right, 2007 and *F. Francioni*, Access to Justice, Denial of Justice and International Investment Law, EJIL 2009 (20) p. 729. On the term "access to justice," which does not appertain to the lexicon of most international human rights treaties, see *F. Francioni*, The Right of Access to Justice under Customary International Law in: F. Francioni (ed.), Access to Justice as a Human Right, 2007, p. 24. For the use of the "rights to remedy" in environmental matters, see Human Rights Council, Report of the Independent Expert on the Issue of Human Rights Obligations Relating to the Enjoyment of a Safe, Clean, Healthy and Sustainable Environment, John H. Knox (UN Doc A/HRC/22/43 (Dec 24, 2012)), p. 12.

11 On the instrumentality of access to justice for attaining substantive outcomes, see, *inter alia*, *R. MacDonald*, Access to Justice and Law Reform, Windsor YB Access Just 2001 (19), p. 317, 319–320, questioning whether access is conflated with justice. *M. Pallemaerts*, Proceduralizing Environmental Rights: the Aarhus Convention on Access to Information, Public Participation in Decision-Making and Access to Justice in Environmental Matters in a Human Rights Context, Human Rights and the Environment. Proceedings of Geneva Environment Network roundtable, United Nations Environment Program, 2004, p. 18, where the author highlights that the right to a healthy environment has been expressly recognized in the Aarhus Convention. On the inclusion of more than solely standing within the concept of access to justice, see *J. Darpö*, Effective Justice? Synthesis Report of the Study on the Implementation of Articles 9(3) and 9(4) of the Aarhus Convention in Seventeen of the Member States of the European Union in: J.H. Jans, R. Macrory & A-M. Moreno Molina (eds), National Courts and EU Environmental Law, 2013, p. 169, 179. *J. Ebbesson*, Comparative Introduction in: J. Ebbesson (ed.), Access to Justice in Environmental Matters in the EU – Accès à la justice en matière d'environnement dans l'UE, 2002, p. 1, 13. Council of Europe, Manual on Human Rights and the Environment, 2nd edition, 2012, 12.

12 The first international instrument on public participation in environmental matters is probably the 1972 Stockholm Action Plan for the Human Environment. See Declaration of the United Nations Conference on the Human Environment, Stockholm, 16 June 1972, UN Doc A/CONF 48/14/Rev.1. The 1982 World Charter for Nature more clearly provided on access to justice and prescribed that all persons must have the opportunity to participate in environmental decision-making and have "access to means of redress when their environment has suffered damage or degradation." See UN General Assembly, World Charter for Nature, 28 October 1982, A/RES/37/7, availabel at www.refworld.org/docid/3b00f22a10.html, last access: 6 April 2017, point 23. The IUCN's Draft International Covenant on Environment and Development laid down provisions mandating States to ensure that all persons have a right to information, participation in decision-making and access to justice. IUCN & ICEL, Draft International Covenant on Environment and Development, 4th ed., 2010, Article 14(5). See *M. Soveroski*,

Declaration, access to justice is especially impactful. First, it bolsters the other two rights, namely access to information and public participation in decision-making.[13] Secondly, given the absence of a general instrument on access to justice in environmental matters, access to justice prompts the deployment of human rights litigation techniques and is expected to be secured through a greater interaction between human rights and environmental law.[14] Short of imposing legal obligations on States, the Rio Declaration soon appeared "instrumental for the development of national laws as well as international law on public participation in environmental matters."[15]

The Rio Declaration was intended to be read along the lines of Agenda 21, namely another offspring of the Earth Summit crafted as the "blueprint for the future implementation of sustainable development."[16] Even though Agenda 21 contains no reference to access to justice or the application of international law by national judiciaries, access to justice through international law would indirectly comport with the rationale of Agenda 21, whose basic point was "action at national level."[17]

Besides some further initiatives on implementation[18], the Earth Summit anniversary held in Johannesburg in 2002 was expressly intended to advance

Environment Rights versus Environmental Wrongs: Forum over Substance?, Review of European Community & International Environmental Law 2007 (16), p. 261, 270.

13 *C. Redgwell*, Access to Environmental Justice, in: F. Francioni (ed.), *supra*, note 11, p. 153, 167. See also the Implementation Guide on the Bali Guidelines: *Stephen Stec for and on behalf of the World Resources Institute and UNEP*, Putting Rio Principle 10 Into Action: An Implementation Guide, 2015, p. 98.

14 *Redgwell, supra*, note 14 at p. 155. See also *A. Boyle*, The Role of International Human Rights Law in the Protection of the Environment in: A. Boyle & M.A. Anderson (eds), Human Rights Approaches to Environmental Protection, 1996, p. 43. *P. Lawrence*, An Atmospheric Trust to Protect the Environment for Future Generations? Reform Options for Human Rights Law, in: G. Bose & M. Düwell (eds), Human Rights and Sustainability. Moral Responsibilities for the Future, 2016, p. 25, 32.

15 *J. Ebbesson*, Public Participation and Privatisation in Environmental Matters: An Assessment of the Aarhus Convention, Erasmus Law Review 2011 (4), p. 71, 72. *J. Ebbesson*, Principle 10. Public Participation in: J.E. Viñuales (ed.), The Rio Declaration on Environment and Development: A Commentary, 2015, p. 287, 293, expounding the rise of treaties enshrining the right to information and participation in decision-making after the UNCED.

16 *D. Hunter, J. Salzman & D. Zaelke*, International Environmental Law and Policy, 5th ed., 2015, p. 166. Agenda 21, which was adopted at the Earth Summit, limited its mandate to the sole recognition of public participation in decision-making concerning the environment. See *Ebbesson, supra*, note 16 at 289. Agenda 21, U.N. GAOR, 46th Sess., Agenda Item 21, UN Doc A/Conf.151/26 (1992), I.B (5.17 and 5.45). Some further provisions stresses the role of women in participatory decision-making.

17 *J.C. Dernbach*, Sustainable Development as a Framework for National Governance, Case Western Reserve Law Review 1998 (49), p. 1, 5. On the exiguous access rights content of Agenda 21, see *Ebbesson, supra*, note 16 at 289.

18 See, for instance, instruments concerning the UN Environment Program, namely the UNEP Governing Council (1997) Nairobi Declaration on the Role and Mandate of UNEP, held in Nairobi from 27 January – 7 February 1997, 19th Session, UNEP/GC19/1/1997 and the UNEP Governing Council, Programme for the Development and Periodic Review of Environmental Law for the First Decade of the Twenty-first Century ('Montevideo Programme III'), Decision

the cause of "implementation, accountability and of partnership,"[19] yet neither the Johannesburg Declaration nor its Plan of Implementation mentions access to justice as a prospective means for the implementation of sustainable development.[20]

Conversely, that same year members of national judiciaries from all over the world assembled in Johannesburg and carved out the "Johannesburg Principles on the Role of Law and Sustainable Development" ('Global Judges' Symposium') through which the convened judges vehemently reiterated the call for national judges to apply not only national law, but also international law.[21] The Principles championed at the Global Judges' Symposium were later noted with appreciation by the UNEP Governing Council in 2003[22], which called on the UNEP Executive Director to mobilize "the full potential of the judiciaries around the world for the implementation and enforcement of environmental law, promoting access to justice for the settlement of environmental disputes, public participation in environmental decision-making, the protection and advancement of environmental rights and public access to relevant information."[23] In the absence of a specification of whether the applicable law be either national or international, it appears that the UNEP Governing Council encourages national judiciaries to apply the whole of the relevant law, be it domestic law or international law, which conforms to the rule of law.

21/23 (adopted 9 February 2001), available at http://web.unep.org/divisions/delc/montevideo-programme, last access: 6 April 2017. The latter mentions access to justice as a means for preventing and mitigating environmental damage for victims and potential victims of environmentally harmful activities, see *id.*, para. 1(3)(d)(i).

19 UNEP Executive Director Klaus Töpfer in his speech at the WSSD Opening Plenary of 26 August 2002 as referred to in *A. Rest*, Enhanced Implementation of International Environmental Treaties by Judiciary – Access to Justice in International Environmental Law for Individuals and NGOs: Efficacious Enforcement by the Permanent Court of Arbitration, Macquarie Journal of International and Comparative Environmental Law 2004 (1), p. 1, 2.

20 The Johannesburg Declaration, UN Doc A/CONF1999/L6/Rev3 (4 September 2002). Brief reference to the Aarhus Convention was made under Chapter IX of the Johannesburg Plan of Implementation, UN DocA/CONF199/L1 (4 September 2002). See also *Rest*, *supra*, note 20 at p. 2, commenting on the lack of a thorough recognition of the role of non-state actors. Access to justice was mentioned in the 2002 Johannesburg's Plan of Implementation, see United Nations Report of the World Summit on Sustainable Development, para. 128.

21 See, for instance, the Johannesburg Principles on the Role of Law and Sustainable Development (Johannesburg Global Judges Symposium, 18–20 August 2002), available at https://www.eufje.org/images/DocDivers/Johannesburg%20Principles.pdf, last access: 6 April 2017, p. 1: "We affirm that an independent Judiciary and judicial process is vital for the implementation, development and enforcement of environmental law, and that members of the Judiciary, as well as those contributing to the judicial process at the national, regional and global levels, are crucial partners for promoting compliance with, and the implementation and enforcement of, international and national environmental law."

22 UNEP Governing Council, Decision Decision 22/17 on Governance and Law (7 February 2003), available at www.unep.org/GC/GC22/REPORTS/K0360710English.pdf, last access: 6 April 2017, p. 65.

23 *Id.* at p. 66.

In 2010 the UNEP Governing Council gave new impetus to Principle 10 by adopting the UNEP Bali Guidelines for the Development of National Legislation on Access to Information, Public Participation and Access to Justice in Environmental Matters ('Bali Guidelines'), which promote the effective implementation of States' "commitments to Principle 10 of the 1992 Rio Declaration on Environment and Development within the framework of their national legislation and processes."[24]

The Bali Guidelines make access to justice central by devoting to the latter 11 out of 26 Guidelines. Guideline 18 specifically addresses what is still the most pressing issue in terms of access to justice, namely standing[25], by stressing that "States should provide broad interpretation of standing in proceedings concerned with environmental matters with a view to achieving effective access to justice."[26] Therefore, the process of relaxing domestic standing requirements through the indirect application of international law would appear in line with Bali Guideline 18.[27] Even more broadly, Guideline 17 appears to address both procedural and substantive rights by spearheading an *actio popularis*-type of standing[28] as well as the enforceability of environmental substantive rights on the part of the public. The somehow utopian view on both prongs, procedural and substantive, gives rise to the sober consideration by which the Rio Declaration and the instruments ensuing therefrom pertain to soft law and the only legally binding instrument in the field is the Aarhus Convention.[29]

---

24 UNEP, *Guidelines for the Development of National Legislation on Access to Information, Public Participation and Access to Justice in Environmental Matters ("Bali Guidelines")* (Adopted by the Governing Council of the United Nations Environment Programme in decision SSXI/5, part A of 26 February 2010, 2010), p. 4. Access to justice was also recalled and expanded to non-national contexts within the outcome of the 2012 Rio Conference on Sustainable Development ('Rio+20'), *The Future We Want*. See Report of the United Nations Conference on Sustainable Development, Rio de Janeiro, 20–2 June 2012, UN Doc A/CONF.216/16, para. 99.

25 *Redgwell, supra*, note 14 at p. 161. On the difficulties of attaining standing even in the liberal jurisdictions of England and Wales, see *M. Adebowale*, Using the Law: Access to Environmental Justice Barriers and Opportunities. A paper, 2004, p. 39.

26 On the official comment to Guideline 18, see UNEP, *supra*, note 25 at p. 107.

27 An earlier case to this regard is the *Minors Oposa* case by which a Filipino court relied on intergenerational equity for granting broad standing rights, as cited *id.* at p. 108. See also *infra*, para. 4. On the reference to the Bali Guidelines for constructing the provisions for access to justice, see *Ebbesson, supra*, note 16 at 297.

28 See UNEP, *supra*, note 25 at pp. 105–107.

29 Convention on Access to Information, Public Participation in Decision-Making and Access to Justice in Environmental Matters (Aarhus Convention) 2161 UNTS 447; 38 ILM 517 (1999). See also Almaty Guidelines on promoting the application of the principles of the Aarhus Convention, UN Doc. ECE/MP.PP/2005/2/Add.5 of 20 June 2005 available at www.unece.org/fileadmin/DAM/env/documents/2005/pp/ece/ece.mp.pp.2005.2.add.5.e.pdf, last access: 12 April 2017. Short of a comprehensive bibliography on access to justice, as it is enshrined in the Aarhus Convention, see *J. Maurici*, Aarhus and Access to Justice, Judicial Review 2011 (16), p. 253; Y. Epstein, Access to Justice: Remedies: Article 9.4 of the Aarhus Convention and the Requirement for Adequate and Effective Remedies, Including Injunctive Relief, 2011, available at http://uu.diva-portal.org/smash/get/diva2:874844/FULLTEXT01.pdf, last access: 12 April 2017; *Ebbesson, supra*, note 16. *P. Oliver*, Access to Information and to Justice in EU Environmental Law: The Aarhus Convention (Symposium on EU Law. Developments

Indeed, the access to justice component of Principle 10 is rarely litigated.[30] Besides its soft-law character, at least three limitations to its fulfilment stand out. Firstly, it is procedural in kind but also calls upon States to provide domestic remedies based on the legal process, differently from the other two access rights.[31] Secondly, both at international law and within the specific regime established by the Aarhus Convention, States enjoy great flexibility to determine the standing requirements and types of redress, thus having the possibility to make procedural norms of domestic law a hurdle, rather than the means, for furthering justice.[32] Thirdly, States enjoy enough leeway to pass substantive norms that are not always consistent with obligations undertaken at the international level. Such an enforcement conundrum is all the more urgent in climate matters, where procedural interests are not easily amenable to individual petitioners and substantive rights may depend on and yield to political discretion.

Lastly and with specific reference to climate-related issues, access to justice – albeit absent at the level of general treaties – could have been specifically encapsulated within the climate change regime, but this has not yet occurred.

The Framework Convention is silent on access to justice, limiting its precepts to the two other pillars, as recalled in Article 6 UNFCCC.[33] Such pillars were tackled within a country-driven work program adopted in 2002 with the view

in Honor of Judge Konrad Schiemann), Fordham Int'l LJ 2013 (36), p. 1423; *G. Garçon*, The Rights of Access to Justice in Environmental Matters in the EU – The Third Pillar of the Aarhus Convention: Validity and Scope of the Review Procedures under Regulation (EC) No 1367/2006, EFFL 2013 (8), p. 78; *L. Lavrysen*, Access to Justice in Environmental Matters: Perspective from the European Union Forum of Judges for the Environment, 2014, available at https://aarhusclearinghouse.unece.org/resources/access-to-justice-environmental-matters-perspectives-from-european-union-forum-of-judges, last access: 12 April 2017; *O.W. Pedersen*, The Price is Right: Aarhus and Access to Justice, CJQ 2014 (33), p. 13; *B. Pirker*, Access to Justice in Environmental Matters and the Aarhus Convention's Effects in the EU Legal Order: No Room for Nuanced Self-executing Effect? RECIEL 2016 (25), p. 81. On the unique compliance mechanism provided by the Compliance Committee, see *J. Jendrośka*, Aarhus Convention Compliance Committee: Origins, Status and Activities, JEEPL 2011 (8), p. 301; *S. Marsden*, Direct Public Access to EU Courts: Upholding Public International Law via the Aarhus Convention Compliance Committee, NordJInt'l L 2012 (81), p. 175. In relation to the ECtHR, see *C. Schall*, Public Interest Litigation Concerning Environmental Matters before Human Rights Courts: A Promising Future Concept?, JEL 2008 (20), p. 417.

30 UNEP, *supra*, note 25 at p. 98.

31 *Id.* at p. 95.

32 *Redgwell*, *supra*, note 14 at pp. 169–170. Besides standing, injunctive reliefs are often unavailable/ineffective even within the very successful regime created by the Aarhus Convention. See UNECE, The Aarhus Convention: An Implementation Guide, 2nd ed, 2014, 200–201. On the discretionary leeway allowed under the Aarhus Convention, see *L. Squintani & E.J.H. Plambeck*, Judicial Protection Against Plans and Programmes Affecting the Environment: A Backdoor Solution to Get an Answer from Luxembourg, JEEPL 2016 (13), available at https://www.ris.uu.nl/ws/files/24801621/JEEPL_13_3_4_pre_print.pdf, last access: 27 October 2017, 6.

33 1992 United Nations Framework Convention on Climate Change, 1771 UNTS 107, Article 6(a)(ii)(iii). See also *J.R. May & E. Daly*, Global Environmental Constitutionalism, 2014, pp. 238–239.

of facilitating the implementation of Article 6 UNFCCC, but nothing appears to have ensued from this preparatory document.[34] Similarly, the Kyoto Protocol does not refer to access to justice and neglects the UNFCCC-protected right to participate in decision-making, thus limiting its express recognition to the right to access information.[35] In the same mould of the UNFCCC, the Paris Agreement restrains itself to public participation and public access to information, skipping any reference to access to justice.[36]

Notwithstanding, access to justice before national courts may also be achieved by relying on environmental procedural, rather than substantive, rights as granted in national legal systems. Principle 10 gave rise to the proceduralisation of environmental rights, probably as a substitute for the contentious recognition of any substantive right to environment.[37] In what has been portrayed as a "global environmental constitutionalism," the constitutions of more than sixty countries presently recognize or promote procedural rights[38], and the constitutions of about three dozen countries specifically grant procedural rights in environmental matters.[39] Moreover, provisions on access rights are more generally retrievable in domestic statutes and regulations. Procedural rights may provide a turning point in climate change litigation in that they empower courts with wider discretion in comparison to substantive rights[40], which are liable to propel debates on the allegedly political character of judicial decision-making.

Further domestic sources such as environmental law, tort law and again constitutional law, could also inform interpretive techniques facilitating access to justice in environmental matters at the substantive level.[41]

Both procedural and substantive provisions of domestic law can additionally be enhanced in their access to justice significance when interpreted in light of international law norms. By relying on the international law principle of inter-generational equity, for instance, courts may relax national requirements of *locus*

---

34 Decision 11/CP.8, New Delhi Work Programme on Article 6 of the Convention, UN Doc. FCCC/CP/2002/7/Add.1, 28 March 2003.

35 Kyoto Protocol to the United Nations Framework Convention on Climate Change UN Doc FCCC/CP/1997/7/Add.1, Dec. 10, 1997; 37 ILM 22 (1998), Article 10(e). Procedural rights are also included under the Clean Development Mechanism (CDM), *T. Koivurova, S. Duyck & Leena Heinämäki*, Climate Change and Human Rights, in: E.J. Hollo, K. Kulovesi & M. Mehling (eds), *supra*, note 5, p. 287, 315 et seq.

36 Article 12 Paris Agreement.

37 *Pallemaerts, supra*, note 12 at 14. On the recognition of the right to a healthy environment, see, *inter alia, D.R. Boyd*, The Environmental Rights Revolution. A Global Study of Constitutions, Human Rights, and the Environment, 2011. *Soveroski, supra*, note 13 at 270–271.

38 *May & Daly, supra*, note 34 at 241.

39 *Id.* at p. 243.

40 *H. McLeod-Kilmurray*, Lowering Barriers to Judicial Enforcement: Civil Procedure and Environmental Ethics, in: L.R. Paddock et al. (eds), Compliance and Enforcement in Environmental Law, 2011, p. 289.

41 See the influential Oslo Principles on Global Climate Change Obligations, http://globaljustice.macmillan.yale.edu/news/oslo-principles-global-climate-change-obligations (last visit: 12 April 2017).

standi, thus allowing the widest possible access to justice for individuals and NGOs in climate matters within an interpretation that is still *secundum legem*.[42]

Access to justice can still be hindered by obstacles relating to standing, justiciability, remedies, and enforcement.[43] Yet, Rio Principle 10 is poised to be reloaded through a variety of instruments, among which constitutional provisions, environmental law, tort law, and procedural rights, along with international law norms.

According to a commentator, the mechanism by which national courts apply international environmental law "reflects Principle 10 of the Rio Declaration and the goals which have been implemented in the meantime by the Århus Convention on Access to Information, Public Participation in Decision-Making and Access to Justice in Environmental Matters."[44]

The indirect application of international law for access to justice reasons, however, does not go without risk and has been questioned in terms of enforcement and legitimacy. To these latter points I now attend.

3. ENFORCEMENT, LEGITIMACY AND LIMITATIONS

By sketching the legacy of Principle 10 of the Rio Declaration, I have tentatively evaluated whether access to justice in environmental matters can be enhanced by the consistent interpretation of domestic law with international law norms. Having responded in the affirmative, I herein offer a brief assessment of consistent interpretation with reference to effective enforcement and legitimacy. In fact, within a circular approach, international norms are poised to advance access to justice in national courts, but are also advanced through the participation of the public in courts, leading to the judicial enforcement of international law in national courts through consistent interpretation.[45] Yet, enforcement has been understood as being conditional on the perceived legitimacy of the international norms to be applied. I thus here consider enforcement as entwined with legitimacy. At the end of this paragraph, I conclusively hold that the consistent interpretation of domestic norms with international law appears to be beneficial to the effective enforcement and legitimacy of international law, but some limitations are notably outstanding.

Besides its intrinsic value as a right in itself, access to justice has also been credited for ensuring "the effective enforcement of environmental law in domestic forums".[46] By mounting the tide of especially global environmental

42 Cases overviewed under para. 4 attest to this assertion.

43 *May & Daly, supra*, note 34 at p. 243.

44 *Rest, supra*, note 20 at 4.

45 See *Redgwell, supra*, note 14 at 165 on access to justice as a means for the effectiveness of both domestic law and international environmental law.

46 *Redgwell, supra*, note 14 at 159. *Ebbesson, supra*, note 16 at 289–290. *J. Ebbesson*, Compatibility of International and National Environmental Law, 1996, p. 219. *J. Razzaque*, Information,

constitutionalism and the proceduralisation of environmental rights at the national level, such non-state actors as individuals and NGOs are in the position to invoke international law norms in order to advance both procedural and substantive claims, thus contributing to a more likely application of international law norms through the activity of national courts.[47]

With respect to legitimacy, the international environmental norms considered more legitimate have been characterized to be the ones that courts will more likely apply. Therefore, the legitimacy of the norm is apt to allow for its effective enforcement.[48] In a circular spiral, however, the judicial incorporation of norms of international law is also going to contribute to the increased legitimacy of the norms applied[49], as well as to the emergence of customary rules at international law.[50]

Public Participation and Access to Justice in Environmental Matters in: S. Alam & others (eds), Routledge Handbook of International Environmental Law, 2013, p. 137, 138. *Redgwell*, *supra*, note 14 at 165 on access to justice as a hinge for the effectiveness of both domestic and international environmental law and 168 with specific reference to the absence of "supranational forums for the direct enforcement of international environmental law." UNEP, *supra*, note 25 at 96: "From the perspective of the public, an individual's access to environmental information, to procedures for participation in decision-making that may affect him or her, and to redress and remedy to enforce relevant rules and procedures, are a means of ensuring a high level of environmental quality." See also *D. Estrin*, Limiting Dangerous Climate Change: The Critical Role of Citizen Suits and Domestic Courts – Despite the Paris Agreement, CIGI Papers Series 2016 (101), available at https://www.cigionline.org/sites/default/files/paper_no.101.pdf, last access: 6 April 2017, 25. Generally on the attainment of international law goals through national implementation, see *Ebbesson, supra*, note 47, 52 and 55. But see *A. Harding*, Access to Environmental Justice: Some Introductory Perspectives in: A. Harding (ed.), *supra*, note 1, p. 1, 3: "although it is commonly asserted that enhanced citizen participation results in better environmental policy and improved enforcement of environmental standards, this hypothesis has rarely been subject to testing on a comparative basis."

47 *Ebbesson, supra*, note 47, 55.

48 This statement can be fully grasped if couched within one of the applicable theories of enforcement, namely the framework portrayed by the late Professor Thomas Franck, according to whom compliance derives from the compliance-pull of a norm, resulting from its legitimacy. *T.M. Franck*, The Power of Legitimacy Among Nations, 1990, p. 24: "Legitimacy is a property of a rule or rulemaking institution which itself exerts a pull toward compliance on those addressed normatively because those addressed believe that the rule or institution has come into being and operates in accordance with generally accepted principles of right process." The contributing factors are a norm's historical pedigree, the norm's determinacy, its coherence and its adherence. See *id.* at pp. 38 and 49. See also *S.R. Ratner*, Persuading to Comply On the Deployment and Avoidance of Legal Argumentation, in: J.L. Dunoff & M.A. Pollack (eds), Interdisciplinary Perspectives on International Law and International Relations: The State of the Art, 2013, p. 568, 569–570. For a similar interlinkage between legitimacy and enforcement, see *Ebbesson, supra*, note 47, 42. On the "cycles" of legitimacy the UNFCCC has recurrently gained, see *C. Bausch and M. Mehling*, Alternative Venues of Climate Cooperation: An Institutional Perspective, in: E.J. Hollo, K. Kulovesi & M. Mehling (eds), *supra*, note 5, p. 111, 138.

49 On the role of domestic institutions in internalising international law norms and promoting compliance therewith, see *H.H. Koh*, Why Do Nations Obey International Law?, The Yale Law Journal, 1997 (106), p. 2599, *H.H. Koh*, The 1998 Frankel Lecture: Bringing International Law Home, Houston Law Review, 1998 (35), p. 623 and *B.A. Simmons*, Mobilizing for Human Rights: International Law in Domestic Politics, 2009, p. 130.

50 International Court of Justice, Arrest Warrant of 11 April 2000 (*Dem Rep Congo v Belg*), 2002 ICJ REP 3, paras. 56–58. See *E. Benvenisti*, Reclaiming Democracy: The Strategic Uses of Foreign and International Law by National Courts, American Journal of International

Yet, some limitations to this form of judicial enforcement loom on the horizon. The indirect application of international law cannot replace the role that national institutions different from national judiciaries have in the incorporation, transformation and policy-making related to international law.[51] Furthermore, some specific shortcomings of the envisaged mechanism for enhancing access to justice and enforcing international law are quite notable.

Firstly, there might be a need for "communitarian" judges, namely judges supporting "the idea of representative democracy" and those that are able to understand "principles of sustainable development."[52] In fact, the legal culture of each national system is still overtly impactful on the indirect application of international law on the part of national courts.[53] Moreover, courts' attitude may change over time.[54]

Secondly, strained relationships between the executive and the judiciary might ensue if the judiciary is perceived to overstep its boundaries in violation of the principle of separation of powers.[55]

Law 2008 (102), p. 241, 248. In a broader conceptualization of access to justice, the category of legitimacy extends beyond norms to encompass accountability, as well as "ideas about participation and the democratization of knowledge," which are also "ultimately linked to the continued legitimacy of the legal system," see *J.A. Leitch*, Looking for Quality: The Empirical Debate in Access to Justice Research, Windsor Y B Access Just 2013 (31), p. 229, 230–231.

51 *Ebbesson, supra*, note 47, 220.

52 *Adebowale, supra*, note 26 at p. 14. *D. Robinson*, Public Interest Environmental Law – Commentary and Analysis, in: D. Robinson & J. Dunkley (eds), Public Interest Perspectives in Environmental Law, 1995, 294 at p. 313. Cf. the concept of communitarian judges with that of transnationalist judges in the US, *D. Sloss*, United States, in: D. Sloss (ed.), The Role of Domestic Courts in Treaty Enforcement. A Comparative Study, 2009, p. 504 et seq.

53 The Netherlands, for example, is considered open to international law. See *A. Nollkaemper*, The Netherlands, in D. Sloss (ed.), *supra*, note 55, p. 326, 369: "The open nature of the constitution means the Netherlands has given up safety valves that most other states still have in their possession." See also *Simmons, supra*, note 51 at p. 130.

54 *Nollkaemper, supra*, note 56 at p. 369 with reference to the role of international human rights treaties in Dutch courts.

55 See *F. Du Bois*, Social Justice and the Judicial Enforcement of Environmental Rights and Duties, in: A. Boyle & M.R. Anderson, Human Rights Approaches to Environmental Protection, p. 153, 174, who delimits the judicial implementation of environmental rights, but generally upholds it: "so defined, the judicial implementation of environmental rights would not amount to the usurpation of legislative or executive roles. Nor would it force a court invariably to give in to the demands of environmental special-interest groups, allowing itself to be captured by them. It would certainly expand the role of the judiciary beyond the limits set by those who seek to restrict it to consideration of the procedural rationality of decisions or to policy implementation rather than formulation. But it would do so within limits derived from the specific place in the network of governmental bodies which courts occupy by virtue of their institutional attributes." See also *id.*, pp. 159–162, 169 and 172. *H.H. Koh*, Transnational Public Law Litigation, Yale LJ 1991 (100), p. 2347, 2357. With reference to the US case-law, Koh hammers out three exceptions: the comity exception, the separation-of-power and related political question doctrines, and the judicial incompetence exception. See *id.* See also *Nollkaemper, supra*, note 8 at 161 and 164. *K.J. de Graaf and J.H. Jans*, The Urgenda Decision: Netherlands Liable for Role in Causing Dangerous Global Climate Change, Journal of Environmental Law 2015 (27), p. 517, 523, referring to the critique voiced after the rendering of *Urgenda*. See also *Squintani & Plambeck, supra*, note 33 at 15 and relevant literature. See *infra* para. 4.

Thirdly, even communitarian judges crafting their decisions as not to violate the principle of separation of powers would sometimes be at pains in applying international environmental treaties in that the latter may not appear to lay down rules but rather encourage the attainment of goals.[56]

Fourthly, litigation might not be an effective mode of enforcement in that litigation in national courts may be costly and time-consuming. Even advocates of this method of enforcement underline that there is a number of alternatives to litigation, such as the development of a loss and damage mechanism within the climate negotiations.[57]

Lastly, national decisions ensuing from the application of the envisaged mechanism may restrain States' leeway in international relations, especially at a time when States are still negotiating in order to consolidate the Paris architecture.

A possible cure for such drawbacks may rest on the joint application of Principle 10 Rio Declaration, as well as related international and domestic instruments, with Principle 13 Rio Declaration, which provides that States shall develop national law regarding liability and compensation for the victims of pollution and other environmental damage.[58] Notwithstanding, such a mode of making access to justice conditional on the characterization of individuals and NGOs as victims may lead to restricted access to courts, especially for NGOs. Moreover, there is no binding obligation on governments to pass such legislation given the soft law character of the Rio Declaration.

It does not appear, however, that the mechanism under consideration is to be constrained to *national* environmental issues.[59] I am now to overview recent case-law that, albeit non-final, is carrying out the rationale entailed in the indirect application of international law for such a *transnational* environmental issue as climate change.

4. A NEW STRAND OF CLIMATE CHANGE LITIGATION

As emerged in the foregoing, recent litigation in national courts, however, has made wide use of climate change law and international environmental

56 *M. Francheteau-Laronze*, L'application du droit international de l'environnement par le juge national: éléments d'analyse comparative, in: S. Maljean-Dubois & L. Rajamani (eds), La mise en œuvre du droit international de l'environnement / Implementation of International Environmental Law, 2011, p. 607, 620. Moreover, even when international norms are sufficiently clear also on the means for achieving the purported goals, they may fall short of offering an adequate protection to the environment. See *Ebbesson, supra*, note 47 at 38–9.

57 *K. Boom, J-A. Richards and S. Leonard*, Climate Justice: The International Momentum Towards Climate Litigation, 2016, p. 61.

58 *Ebbesson, supra*, note 16 at 308.

59 Cf. *Rest, supra*, note 20 at 4.

principles allowing individuals to access justice and have the whole of the law, be it domestic or international, enforced both procedurally and substantially.[60] After overviewing this new strand of climate change litigation, I conclude by highlighting the similarities in the interpretive techniques applied by the relevant judiciaries and commenting on the inter-judicial dialogue among courts, which mirrors the inter-plaintiff dialogue among claimants.[61]

I would chronologically tackle three cases, which have been decided in the Netherlands, Pakistan and the United States. None of these decisions are final, yet it appears sensible to review them in consideration of their novelty, import on Principle 10 of the Rio Declaration as well as the ripple effect on other jurisdictions.

The *Urgenda* case is an action in tort, which was brought to the District Court of The Hague by the *Urgenda* Foundation, namely a Dutch NGO striving for a "more sustainable society," with a primary – albeit not exclusive – focus on the Netherlands.[62] In June 2015, the three-judge panel found the State liable of hazardous negligence and enjoined it to increase the emission reduction target from approximately 17% to at least 25% by 2020 compared to 1990. The ruling is now on appeal.

It appears that the court in *Urgenda* granted rights, both procedurally and substantively, by indirectly applying international law and EU law. No similar application of international law had ever been made within a national climate change case.

With respect to standing, the court interpreted *Urgenda*'s bylaws in light of international law principles and treaty norms: sustainable development as articulated in the Brundtland Report, especially in its global and intergenerational dimension; Article 2 of the UN Framework Convention on Climate Change ('UNFCCC'), which sets forth the objective of the UNFCCC and Articles 2 and 8 of the European Convention on Human Rights ('ECHR'). Such an application resulted in *Urgenda*'s standing even on behalf of non-Dutch individuals and future generations.[63]

---

60 In the case decided in the United States, the relevant judge has considered the substantive plane of the controversy solely as related to two motions to dismiss and a motion to strike.

61 The possibility for national courts to protect the global commons by an interpretation pursuant to public international law has already been foreshadowed by some commentators, among whom *Rest, supra*, note 20 at 8.

62 *Urgenda v The Netherlands*, The Hague District Court (June 24, 2015) ECLI:NL:RBDHA:2015:7196 (original language: ECLI:NL:RBDHA:2015:7145), para. 2.2. An excerpt of Article 2 of Urgenda's bylaws reads as follows: "1. The purpose of the Foundation is to stimulate and accelerate the transition processes to a more sustainable society, beginning in the Netherlands." Urgenda filed the case on its own behalf, as well as on the behalf of 886 individuals.

63 *Urgenda v The Netherlands, supra*, note 66 at para. 4.8, applying Article 3:305a of the Dutch Civil Code. According to some commentators, civil law procedures available at Dutch law are not effective for challenging plans and programs. See *Squintani & Plambeck, supra*, note 33 at 15. Specifically on standing, even the joint combination of Articles 6:162 and 3:305a of the Dutch Civil Code would not allow for standing in defence of a general interest, according to *id.*

On the substantive plane, the claim was adjudicated under the theory of unlawful hazardous negligence (Book 6, Section 162 of the Dutch Civil Code) and the court materialized the standard herein assumed by perusing not only Dutch tort law and constitutional law, but also international law and EU law.[64]

A duty of care for environmental protection is imposed on the Dutch executive by Article 21 of the Dutch Constitution. The latter was read in light of international law and EU law in order to curb the executive's discretion. When it comes to international law, the Court made principles binding: the no-harm principle as well as the principles of the international climate policy, and specifically, the protection of the climate system, for the benefit of current and future generations, on the ground of "fairness," the precautionary principle, and the principle of sustainable development.[65] With respect to EU law, the Court dwelled on Article 191(1) of the Treaty on the Functioning of the European Union ('TFEU')[66], and specifically the principle of a high level of protection for the environment, the precautionary principle, and the prevention principle.

---

at 16–17. On the changes in Dutch legislation, presently allowing standing in administrative courts under a *Schutznormtheorie*, see *J. Darpö*, *supra*, note 12 at 176 and *J.H. Jans*, The Netherlands in: J.H. Jans, R. Macrory and A-M. Moreno Molina (eds), *supra*, note 12, p. 323, 342–345. Be that as it may, it should be borne in mind that the case under consideration is not a challenge to plans and programs, nor a case brought before administrative courts.

64 Urgenda brought the action under Book 6, Section 162, of the Dutch Civil Code whether or not in combination with Book 5, Section 37, of the Dutch Civil Code, the later spelling off the discipline of private nuisance. The Court maintained that it was not necessary to examine the claim under the prong provided by the theory of private nuisance.

65 Such principles are retrieved from Articles 2 and 3 of the UNFCCC, *Urgenda v The Netherlands, supra*, note 66 at para 4.56.

66 *Urgenda v The Netherlands, supra,* note 66 at paras. 4.60–4.62. Treaty on the Functioning of the European Union (2009), Official Journal C 326, 26/10/2012 P. 0001 – 0390. Given the methodological choice of appraising the case law from an international law perspective, I do not consider whether access to justice could have been derived by either EU law or the Aarhus Convention. On standing see, however, AG Sharpston's interpretation of standing under the Aarhus Convention, *Case C-263/08 Djurgården-Lilla Värtans Miljöskyddsförening ECLI:EU:C:2009:421, Opinion of AG Sharpston* para. 63; *Case C-240/09 Lesoochranárske zoskupenie VLK ECLI:EU:C:2011:125*, para. 52; *Case C243/15 Lesoochranárske zoskupenie VLK ECLI:EU:C:2016:838*, paras. 45 and 65. Moreover, I do not consider whether the case could have been brought as a challenge to plans or programs drafted by the Dutch government in climate matters. Such a possibility is hinted at by *Squintani & Plambeck*, *supra*, note 33 at 16. It is worthwhile to note, however, the absence of EU instruments requiring access to justice in the context of plans and programs, *Squintani & Plambeck*, *supra*, note 33 at 4. According to the authors, such an absence pose both the European Union and its Member States in non-compliance with the Aarhus Convention. See *id.* Notwithstanding, one treaty provision and three principles would allow for access to justice in the context of plans and programs, most notably Article 19(1) of the Treaty on European Union ('TEU'), the principle of equivalence, the principle of effectiveness, and the principle of effective judicial protection. See *id.*, at 4. The absence of more precise secondary EU instruments to allow for access to justice in the context of plans and programs is apparently at odds with the Aarhus Convention. See, *id.* On the sweeping character of Article 7 of the Aarhus Convention, as requiring access to justice in the context of plans and programs devised by public authorities through regulatory decisions, see *J. Jendrośka*, Public Participation in Environmental Decision-Making. Interactions Between

Articles 2 and 3 of the UNFCCC intersperse the whole decision. While Article 2 carves out the Framework Convention's objectives, Article 3 is deployed by the court in order to remark two different obligations. Firstly, the imperative for industrialized countries to take the lead as a component of the principle of Common but Differentiated Responsibilities and Respective capabilities ('CBDR/RC'). Not until this decision did the significance of the CBDR/RC principle dawn upon national judiciaries.[67] Secondly, the obligation of all Parties to the Framework Convention not to postpone measures for lack of scientific certainty, which is a component of the precautionary principle.

Once the court assessed the existence of a legally binding duty of care on the executive relating to climate change mitigation measures, it pursued its analysis by hammering out the minimum degree of care that the Dutch State is expected to secure towards Urgenda and its constituency. The causal nexus between Dutch emissions and climate change was established on the basis of previous case-law on joint liability, as well as by virtue of the very nature of climate change, where even relatively low emissions contribute to climate change. Moreover, the court adduced that Dutch *per capita* emissions are some of the highest worldwide. On the basis of ECtHR case-law on Articles 2 and 8 ECHR, the court concluded that the Netherlands ought to fulfill positive obligations of environmental protection. The Court concluded by asserting that the executive is liable for the level of care that is capable of dispelling the high risk of hazardous climate change.[68] In order to reach quantitative terms, the court did not rely on principles but rather on climate change science, specifically the Intergovernmental Panel on Climate Change ('IPCC') latest reports, as well as on the obligation binding the Netherlands as a Signatory Party to the UN Climate Change Convention and the Kyoto Protocol. A higher mitigation target, the court held, is in line with the principles of inter-generational equity, precaution and prevention.[69] The Court advanced an economic analysis of the costs of compliance and considered the effectiveness of mitigation measures over adaptation measures.[70]

---

the Convention and EU Law and Other Key Legal Issues in its Implementation in the Light of the Opinions of the Aarhus Convention Compliance Committee in: M. Pallemaerts (ed.), The Aarhus Convention at Ten, 2011, p. 93, 122–123.

67 *P. Galvão Ferreira*, 'Common But Differentiated Responsibilities' in the National Courts: Lessons from *Urgenda v. The Netherlands*, Transnational Environmental Law 2016 (5), p. 329, 331. On the operationalization of the CBDRs principle, see *Dupuy and Viñuales, supra*, note 6 at pp. 74–75. On the interpretive function of Article 3 of the UNFCCC, see *id.* at 53: "The preambles of the Kyoto Protocol as well as certain decisions adopted by the Conference of the Parties ('COP') to the UN Framework Convention on Climate Change or by the Meeting of the Parties ('CMP') to the Kyoto Protocol refer to the principles enshrined in Article 3 of the UNFCCC as a guide to interpretation. The 'interpretive function' also operates beyond the direct application of these environmental norms and instruments, in particular when the application of other international law norms is likely to have an impact on the environment."

68 See *Urgenda v The Netherlands, supra,* note 66 at paras. 4.65–4.66.

69 *Urgenda v The Netherlands, supra*, note 66 at para. 4.76.

70 *Urgenda v The Netherlands, supra*, note 66 at para. 4.76.

In light of the foregoing, the court compelled the government to reach an emission reduction target of at least 25% instead of approximately 17%, which was the emission reduction target set under the EU Emission Trading Scheme ('ETS') Directive, in comparison to 1990 levels.[71] Efforts exceeding the ETS targets were deemed compatible with EU law in light of Article 193 TFEU on the possibilities for EU Member States to maintain or introduce more stringent protective measures than EU measures.[72]

The second case that I am to overview was decided by a Pakistani court. *Leghari* falls within a constitutional type of litigation that a lawyer from a farming family of Lahore brought against the Pakistani government. With an order issued in September 2015, the Lahore's Green Bench ordered the establishment of a Climate Change Commission ('CCC') tasked with implementing Pakistan's Climate Change Policy and Framework for the effective enforcement of the people of Punjab's fundamental rights.[73] The relevant legislation was already in place for the period 2014 – 2030, yet it was admittedly lacking implementation. The so-called climate change orders are still being issued by Justice Syed Mansoor Ali Shah.

As for *Urgenda*, the court in *Leghari* granted rights, both procedurally and substantively, by indirectly applying international law.

In light of the fundamental-right type of litigation, Judge Shah established the court's jurisdiction.[74] The Court granted standing on the ground of the public interest type of litigation pursued by petitioner, without a requirement on plaintiff to show a specific interest in the matters. On the substantive plane, the relevant Judge found that the Pakistani central government had violated a number of constitutionally protected fundamental rights. An infringement was found of the right to life (Article 9), which implicitly includes the right to a healthy and clean environment, the right to human dignity (Article 14), to property (Article 23) and the right to information (Article 19A). The Green Bench read the provisions in light of sustainable development, the precautionary principle, the principle of

71 Directive 2003/87/EC of the European Parliament and of the Council of 13 October 2003 establishing a scheme for greenhouse gas emission allowance trading within the Community and amending Council Directive 96/61/EC (Text with EEA relevance), OJ L 275, 25.10.2003, p. 32–46. On the modes the Court expanded the existing doctrine of danger creation, see *M. Quené*, Report on Urgenda Foundation v The State of the Netherlands, ILDC 2456 (NL 2015) (2015), A1-A3. The Court affirmed that Urgenda could not directly rely on international norms on the ground of Article 93 of the Dutch Constitution, which makes binding on all persons *by virtue of their contents* provisions of treaties and of resolutions by international institutions (emphasis added) (para 4.42). Still those norms were deployed by the Court itself to flesh out the content of the duty of care in climate change matters, as well as the limits applicable to the executive's discretion in the field.

72 See *Urgenda v The Netherlands, supra*, note 66 at paras. 2.55 and 4.82.

73 *Leghari v Federation of Pakistan and others*, Lahore High Court, WP No 25501/2015 (Sept 14, 2015).

74 Article 199 of the Constitution of Pakistan, relating to the jurisdiction of High Court to issue orders ('writ jurisdiction').

environmental impact assessment (EIA), inter and intra-generational equity, as well as the public trust doctrine.[75]

The legacy of this decision for climate change law is notable. With striking similarities to the Dutch case, the judiciary required the executive branch to enforce climate change policies. Judge Shah intervened not only on the objectives to be reached[76], but also on the coordination between ministries and governmental bodies. Notwithstanding the lack of reference to either the IPCC or the UNFCCC, the Pakistani judge wielded a wide array of principles of international environmental law as interpretive standards in the reading of the Pakistani Constitution.

The third and last case I will broach is *Juliana v United States*, whereby a group of young people and a guardian for future generations have sued the United States and other governmental officials for failure to take measures to decrease greenhouse gas emissions under the theory that defendants are violating substantive due process rights (5th Amendment), specifically life and liberty. The case has broken new ground in Oregon, where it is under adjudication in the U.S. District Court for the District of Oregon (Eugene Division).

A Magistrate Judge was asked to evaluate the interveners' and government's motions to dismiss, as well as the government's motion to strike.[77] In the words of Magistrate Judge Coffin, plaintiffs asserted "a novel theory somewhere between a civil rights action and NEPA/Clean Air Act/Clean Water Act suit to force the government to take action to reduce harmful pollution".[78] The relevant Magistrate Judge recommended granting standing on the ground of an "alleged concrete injury of a constitutional magnitude"[79] as well as a substantive right granted by the Due Process Clause under the Public Trust Doctrine.[80]

Federal Judge Aiken fully adopted the Magistrate Judge's recommendations by ruling out the alleged non-justiciable nature of the claim[81] and recognising "the right to a climate system capable of sustaining human life" within the province of Due Process Claims, which in turns triggers strict scrutiny on the part of the judiciary.[82] The Federal Judge upheld the reading of the claim also

---

75 *Leghari v Federation of Pakistan and others*, Lahore High Court, W.P. No. 25501/2015 (Sept 4, 2015), para. 7.

76 *Leghari v Federation of Pakistan and others*, Lahore High Court, WP No 25501/2015 (Jan 18, 2016), paras. 3–4.

77 On the role of the Magistrate Judge in federal courts, see Fed. R. Civ. P. 72(b).

78 *Kelsey Cascade Rose Juliana et al v the United States of America et al*, 6:15-cv-1517-TC (Thomas M Coffin, Magistrate Judge, Findings and Recommendations to the District Court for the District of Oregon, 8 April 2016), available at http://ourchildrenstrust.org/sites/default/files/16.04.08.OrderDenyingMTD.pdf, last access: 6 April 2017, p. 3.

79 *Id.* at p. 7. The Magistrate cited *US v Students Challenging Regulatory Agency Procedures*, 412 US 669 (1973), p. 687.

80 *Kelsey Cascade Rose Juliana et al v the United States of America et al.*, *supra*, note 78 at 17–23.

81 *Kelsey Cascade Rose Juliana et al v the United States of America et al*, 6:15-cv-1517-TC (Judge Aiken, Opinion and Order, District of Oregon, 10 November 2016), available at https://static1.squarespace.com/static/571d109b04426270152febe0/t/5824e85e6a49638292ddd1c9/1478813795912/Order+MTD.Aiken.pdf, last access: 6 April 2017, pp. 16–17.

82 *Id.* at p. 32.

in light of the public trust doctrine[83], as the Magistrate recommended.[84] Rather than addressing "the standing of future generations or the merits of plaintiffs' argument that youth and posterity are suspect classifications," the relevant judge expressed its awareness of the "intergenerational dimensions of the public trust doctrine."[85]

Notwithstanding some notable differences, the domestication of international law sources – and especially principles – appears strikingly similar in all three cases under consideration. All three courts made use of the indirect application of international norms. By construing national law in light of international norms or constitutionally recognized human rights, courts relaxed standing requirements and achieved – or are poised to achieve[86] – substantive outcomes for the protection of the environment. Such outcomes either go beyond existing domestic legislation, as in the Dutch and US cases, or are meant to streamline the effective enforcement of existing domestic policies and laws on climate change, as in the Pakistani case.

The *Urgenda* court appeared to make the most extensive use of international sources, especially with reference to the no-harm principle and Articles 2 and 3 UNFCCC. Moreover, it deployed the principle of inter-generational equity on both the procedural prong and substantive prong of the ruling.

On the ground of their common law systems, the Pakistani and US judges made use of the public trust doctrine. Even though the argumentation on the dispositive effect played by this doctrine is still scant, judges in both countries succeeded in conjuring up the 'ghost' of public interest litigation and its powerful techniques. Moreover, specific international environmental principles have been developed within the public trust doctrine, most notably the principle of inter-

---

83 *Id.*

84 The public trust doctrine was already considered applicable in an early case filed by young petitioners with the support of the same NGO, Our Children Trust, even though the relevant judge did not rule in favour of the youth. *Foster v Washington Department of Ecology*, No 14-2-25295-1Fo (Wash Super Ct, 19 November 2015), available at ourchildrenstrust.org/sites/default/files/15.11.19.Order_FosterV.Ecology.pdf, last access: 6 April 2017. The relevant judge denied the petition to review brought by the youth in that the agency whose conduct was under examination had already started a rulemaking process as directed by the Governor. The Court, however, asserted the constitutional character of the claim as well as the application of the public trust doctrine to the case. The Court later vacated portions of the November order under the extraordinary circumstances ground. The new order mandated that "a rule be issued by the end of calendar year 2016 and that a recommendation to the legislature be made during the 2017 session," Judge Hollis Hill, *Foster v Washington Department of Ecology*, No 14-2-25295-1, transcript at 18-20 (Wash Super Ct, 29 April 2016) (oral ruling), available at http://westernlaw.org/sites/default/files/2016.04.29-WA%20ATL%20Final%20Decision%20Bench%20Ruling%20Transcript.pdf, last visit: 12 April 2017, p. 20.

85 *Kelsey Cascade Rose Juliana et al v the United States of America et a*, *supra*, note 26 at p. 50. See also *id.* at p. 50, where Judge Aiken illustrates the influence that intergenerational considerations played on the Founding Fathers, especially in the reading of substantive due process rights.

86 The US case has still not been adjudicated on the merits.

generational equity, which was invoked and recognized in both *Leghari* as well as within the procedural account of *Juliana v United States.*[87]

Even though this new strand of litigation is still at its inception, it already appears a novel one for at least two reasons. Firstly, as it was tentatively shown, the interpretive techniques are innovative in the field of climate change law for the extensive use courts made of international sources. Secondly, it appears that courts have started to engage in an inter-judicial dialogue whereby they cite, or at least they refer to, one another.[88]

Whilst it is still premature to refer to a global community of courts willing to indirectly apply climate change law and international environmental law principles[89], it may be safe to hold that an inter-plaintiff community is fast rising. Further lawsuits are being brought in different continents and plaintiffs often trace their resolution to sue to previous successful – albeit non-final – decisions, such as *Urgenda.*[90] NGOs also appear to close ranks and cooperate for diffusing litigation

87 See, *inter alia*, *E. Brown Weiss*, The Planetary Trust: Conservation and Intergenerational Equality, Ecology LQ 1984 (11), p. 495 and *C. Redgwell*, Intergenerational Trusts and Environmental Protection, 1999.

88 Quite explicitly Magistrate Judge Coffin cited *Urgenda* in its review of the redressability prong of standing, *supra*, note 78 at 11.

89 On the concept of a 'global community of courts' and related scholarship, see *A-M. Slaughter*, A Global Community of Courts, Harvard International Law Journal 2003 (44), p. 191; *A-M. Slaughter*, A Typology of Transjudicial Communication, University of Richmond Law Review 1994 (29), p. 99; *A-M. Slaughter*, Judicial Globalization, Virginia Journal of International Law 2000 (40), p. 1103. Cf. *Benvenisti, supra*, note 52, p. 241 and *E. de Wet et al.*, Transnational Legal Dialogue, a Human Rights-Based Hierarchy, and the Creation of Norms, American Society of International Law Proceedings of the Annual Meeting 2010, p. 453.

90 See *Thomson v Minister for Climate Change Issues* (10 November 2015), No CIV-2015- (HC, New Zealand), available at web.law.columbia.edu/sites/default/files/microsites/climate-change/files/Resources/Non-US-Climate-Change-Litigation-Chart/nz_case_statement_of_claim.pdf, last visit: 12 April 2017. Plaintiff refers to the *Urgenda* decision as inspiring for her to bring the climate lawsuit based on national law and international law against New Zealand, see *J. Schwartz*, In Novel Tactic on Climate Change, Citizens Sue Their Governments, *The New York Times*, May 10, 2016, available at www.nytimes.com/2016/05/11/science/climate-change-citizen-lawsuits.html?_r=0, last access: 6 April 2017. See also a recent Norwegian case, based on both international law and national law, *Greenpeace Nordic Ass'n and Nature & Youth v Norway Ministry of Petroleum and Energy* (Oslo District Court, petitioned filed 18 October 2016), available at http://wordpress2.ei.columbia.edu/climate-change-litigation/files/non-us-casedocuments/2016/20161018_3593_petition.pdf, last visit: 12 April 2017. The petition cites Urgenda, see ibid, 4. Moreover, one of the NGOs representatives cites both *Urgenda* and the climate litigation brought by the NGO promoting *Juliana v United States* in *A. Melli et al.*, Norway's Dash for Arctic Oil Violates its Own Constitution, *The Ecologist*, October 16, 2015, available www.theecologist.org/News/news_analysis/2985911/norways_dash_for_arctic_oil_violates_its_own_constitution.html, last access: 6 April 2017. See an Indian case based upon international law and national law where petitioner cited the decision of Judge Aiken in *Juliana v United States, Pandey v. India Original* Application No: -- of 2017 (25 March 2017) (National Green Tribunal) at para 45.

strategies,[91] while some further cases involving the application of international law are presently pending before bodies different from national courts.[92]

Some questions are, however, still looming on the horizon. For instance, the court in *Urgenda* stopped short of analysing the Netherlands' obligations under international law vis-à-vis its obligation under EU law, which had been set at an emission reduction target of approximately 17% in comparison to 1990 values. The court did not clarify whether the legality of the target under EU law could play as either a 'defence' or an 'attenuating factor' of the breach of both domestic and international obligations.[93] By the same token, what is the main strength of the *Leghari* decision, namely the recursive orders issued by the relevant judge, may turn out to be fairly impractical in legal systems different from the Pakistani one. With reference to *Our Children's Trust*, the decision denying the motions to dismiss and to strike is highly promising for the use of the principle of intergenerational equity in the reading of the public trust doctrine. Notwithstanding, the use of further applicable international principles and treaty-based norms is quite exiguous.

Be that as it may, the main objection to this strand of cases is the alleged violation of the separation of powers principle, which has come to be a ground for

---

91 The NGO Urgenda reports a Belgian case, *VZW Klimaatzaak v Kingdom of Belgium et al* (Brussels' Court of First Instance, Belgium, 2015), in its website: http://www.urgenda.nl/en/climate-case/international.php, last visit: 26 October 2017. A further Pakistani case has been grounded on both national law and international law. It has been brought by a minor, whose father is supported by Our Children's Trust, the NGO organizing plaintiffs in *Juliana v. United States*. See *Ali v Federation of Pakistan* (1 April 2016), Constitutional Petition (Supreme Court of Pakistan, Islamabad), available at http://climatecasechart.com/non-us-case/ali-v-federation-of-pakistan-2/, last visit: 16 August 2017. See ELAW Bulletin, 'Children Making the Case for the Climate' 29 July 2016, available at http://www.elaw.org/children-making-case-climate>, last visit: 16 August 2017.

92 Commission on Human Rights of the Philippines, Case No CHR-NI-2016-0001, Petition Requesting an Investigation of the Responsibility of the Carbon Majors for Human Rights Violations or Threats of Violations Resulting from the Impacts of Climate Change, Submission in Support of Petitioners, submitted by: The Sabin Center for Climate Change Law (16 December 2016), available at http://columbiaclimatelaw.com/files/2016/12/Wentz-and-Burger-2016-12-Submission-Case-No.-CHR-NI-2016-0001.pdf, last access: 6 April 2017.

93 On different argumentations on the same point, see *M. Peeters*, Urgenda Foundation and 886 Individuals v. The State of the Netherlands: The Dilemma of More Ambitious Greenhouse Gas Reduction Action by EU Member States RECIEL 2016 (25), p. 123, 125-126. Yet, it does not appear that a preliminary reference to the Court of Justice of the European Union was necessitated by the mixed agreement *character* of the UNFCCC and the Kyoto Protocol. In fact, the *Urgenda* court applied the UNFCCC and other pieces of international law through the mechanism of consistent interpretation, and not direct effect. Moreover, the court does not appear to rule on the legality of EU measures. In fact, further emissions reduction is mandated on the part of the court as an objective for the Dutch State to attain. It will be the government's responsibility to deploy the means toward such end without derogating from EU law and through effective measures. If further emissions reduction is not allowed within the ETS, the Dutch States would thus need to consider emissions reduction outside ETS-sectors. All in all, it does not appear that the Dutch Government, defendant in this case, asked for such a preliminary reference.

challenging the legitimacy of the *Urgenda* decision, most notably.[94] It appears that the Urgenda court replied to such objection by asserting that "it is an essential feature of the rule of law that the actions of (independent, democratic, legitimised and controlled) political bodies, such as the government and parliament can – and sometimes must – be assessed by an independent court."

All in all, individuals' increased reliance on the judiciary in order to vindicate their environmental rights relating to climate protection appears to be paid off by rising judicial engagement. Characterizing such instances as scattered examples of judicial activism, or even as "outcome-oriented aberrations"[95] 'chill' legal analysis on the implications of this type of decisions and may bring about impactful consequences, especially to the detriment of governments and corporations. Governments would risk being compelled to step up their climate mitigation and adaptation efforts within a timeframe and processes influenced by courts. By the same token, corporations might be exposed to unexpected litigation risk on the ground of not only domestic law but also international law.

Yet, the prospective availability of the mechanism for the effective enforcement of the Paris Agreement is still to be assessed. I will do so in the next paragraph.

5. ACCESS TO JUSTICE AT PLAY WITHIN THE PARIS AGREEMENT

In the present paragraph, I briefly consider whether the Paris Agreement can lend itself to the purported mechanism by which national judges indirectly apply international law and allow for the enhanced access to justice of individuals and NGOs in climate change matters. After considering whether it is possible to characterise the Paris Agreement as a binding instrument, I turn to the possibility for individuals and NGOs to invoke some of its provisions in national courts in order to have their respective governments compelled to abide by it. I argue that the Paris Agreement lends itself to the envisaged mechanism of the consistent interpretation of domestic law with international law. Nevertheless, it is possible to achieve some of the objectives set forth in the Paris Agreement also by hinging on conventions and instruments different from the Paris Agreement, as well as by relying on international environmental principles.

Even before the withdrawal of the United States from the Paris Agreement, the latter had already been characterized as a non binding-agreement by the Obama Administration. Even though there might have been strategic reasons for the Obama Administration not to consider the Paris Agreement a binding

94 *Urgenda v The Netherlands, supra*, note 66 at para. 4.95. On the separation of powers principle, see *supra* fn. 58.

95 *C. Bruch*, Is International Environmental Law Really "Law"? An Analysis of Application in Domestic Courts, Pace Environmental Law Review 2006 (23), p. 423, 425 and 463.

instrument at international law[96], there is some truth in holding the agreement fairly different from clearly binding treaties.

The Paris architecture features a bottom-up approach, which might be more effective than the top-down streamline of the Kyoto Protocol but still testifies to the absence of a centralized compliance body evaluating governments' enforcing measures.

The Agreement's new governing body coincides with the so-called CMA[97], while multiple bodies act as facilitators.[98] Yet, the CMA1 will have time to complete decisions on the procedures for implementing the Paris Agreement until 2018. What appears to be clear is the duty for States to communicate Nationally Determined Contributions ('NDC') towards achieving the objective of the Convention as set out in its Article 2 every five years.[99] Even though "parties shall account for their nationally determined contributions,"[100] the Paris Agreement does not encompass an enforcing branch but rather a transparency framework "to promote effective implementation"[101] by way of national communications, international assessments, biennial reports, as well as international consultation[102], facilitated by an expert-based and non-punitive committee.[103] The transparency framework should comprise a built-in flexibility mechanism.[104] Furthermore, the Conference of the Parties is entrusted with a global stocktake to undertake in 2023 and every five years[105], yet the latter will be preceded by an early stocktake through a facilitative dialogue in 2018.

Two circumstances may turn to be hurdles to the effective enforcement of the Paris Agreement. Firstly, the "built-in flexibility"[106] envisioned by the Paris architecture within the Transparency Framework can turn into a possible stalling point in that it ought to take into account "Parties' different capacities" and build upon "collective experience," without a real understanding of whether flexibility is especially meant for developing countries with limited capacities. Secondly, the

---

96 Cf. *L.L. Martin*, The President and International Commitments: Treaties as Signaling Devices, Presidential Studies Quarterly 2005 (35), p. 440, 441.

97 "CMA" means the Conference of the Parties serving as the meeting of the Parties to this Agreement.

98 For example, the Ad Hoc Working Group on the Paris Agreement ('APA') develops recommendations and procedures allowing for the implementation of the agreement. Further bodies are the Ad Hoc Working Group on the Paris Agreement Subsidiary Body for Scientific and Technological Advice ('SBSTA') and the Subsidiary Body for Implementation ('SBI'). The procedural wrinkle of the Agreement was addressed head-on at the first CMA ('CMA 1') when COP22 met in Marrakesh in November 2016 and will be completed "at the latest" when CMA 1 resumes at COP24 in 2018.

99 Article 3 Paris Agreement.

100 Article 4(13) Paris Agreement.

101 Article 13(1) Paris Agreement.

102 Article 13(3) and (4) Paris Agreement. See also 13(13) Paris Agreement.

103 Article 15(2) Paris Agreement.

104 Article 13(1) Paris Agreement.

105 Article 14 Paris Agreement.

106 *Supra* fn. 107.

expert-based committee aimed at facilitating implementation of and promoting compliance with the Agreement shall elect "a manner that is transparent, non-adversarial and non-punitive."[107] In the absence of implementing decisions, the significance of this statement cannot be grasped yet.

In light of the foregoing, it appears in order to assess whether the purported mechanism of enforcement of international environmental law through domestic climate change litigation could be applied also for the enforcement of the Paris Agreement. Furthermore, such an analysis could be of guidance for predicting whether national judiciaries are likely to interpret the agreement as devoid of binding effects.

According to some commentators, the inherent structure of the Paris Agreement calls for some kind of enforcement through domestic courts.[108] The interstice where the Agreement is situated springs from the combination of both general wording and specific obligations. In light of the first, national judiciaries might consider the Paris Agreement either arduously enforceable at the political level or requiring an excessive amount of time for achieving climate mitigation goals and the protection of human rights. Accordingly, domestic judges could turn to the few specific obligations laid down in the Agreement in order to apply them indirectly through the mechanism of consistent interpretation. In light of existing specific obligations, national courts may be able to hold the *forum* State accountable.[109]

For instance, Article 4 Paris Agreement pertains to the achievement of a "balance between anthropogenic emissions by sources and removals by sinks of greenhouse gases in the second half of this century."[110] Such a provision might

---

107 Article 15(2) Paris Agreement.

108 The Status of Climate Change Litigation. A Global Review, UNEP-Sabin Center for Climate Change (May 2017), available at http://columbiaclimatelaw.com/files/2017/05/Burger-Gundlach-2017-05-UN-Envt-CC-Litigation.pdf, last visit: 14 June 2017, p. 17. *S. Stefanini*, Next Stop for Paris Climate Deal: the Courts, *Politico*, January 11, 2016, *Politico*, available at www.politico.eu/article/paris-climate-urgenda-courts-lawsuits-cop21/, last access: 6 April 2017; *M. Wilder et al.*, The Paris Agreement: Putting the First Universal Climate Change Treaty in Context, Baker & McKenzie, January 11, 2016, www.bakermckenzie.com/en/insight/publications/2016/01/the-paris-agreement--putting-the-first-universal /, last access: 6 April 2017, p. 24. *Estrin*, *supra*, note 71 at p. 25. *Boom, Richards & Leonard*, *supra*, note 60 at 3.

109 For the term 'forum' State, see *Nollkaemper*, *supra*, note 8 at p. 15. Cf. *Francioni*, The Right of Access to Justice under Customary International Law, *supra* note 11 at 8: "the individual right of access to justice must primarily be ensured within the domestic legal system where the violation of human rights has occurred."

110 Article 4(1) Paris Agreement. Parties should achieve such balance "on the basis of equity, and in the context of sustainable development and efforts to eradicate poverty." The article mentions the use of "best available science," as well as the differential treatment to the benefit of developing countries. The whole paragraph reads as follows: "In order to achieve the long-term temperature goal set out in Article 2, Parties aim to reach global peaking of greenhouse gas emissions as soon as possible, recognizing that peaking will take longer for developing country Parties, and to undertake rapid reductions thereafter in accordance with best available science, so as to achieve a balance between anthropogenic emissions by sources and removals by sinks of greenhouse gases in the second half of this century, on the basis of equity, and in the context of sustainable development and efforts to eradicate poverty."

serve judges in the prospective interpretation of energy plans that are being reviewed in national courts, all the more so in light of the obligation for States to "pursue domestic mitigation measures with the aim of achieving the objectives" of nationally determined contributions.[111] In order to expound the potential of Article 4, it would also be sensible to rely on the obligation for developed countries to take the lead "by undertaking economy-wide absolute emission reduction targets"[112] in a progressive way.[113]

Besides the Paris Agreement, climate protection might ensue from the application of other conventions or international environmental principles in national courts, which cannot be here overviewed due to the limited purpose of this work.[114]

Be that as it may, the Paris Agreement has already started its trajectory in courts. Child Rabab Ali filed a petition with Pakistan's Supreme Court alleging violations of constitutionally protected Fundamental Rights, the Public Trust Doctrine, and a series of environmental principles[115], conventions and instruments.[116] Among the latter, feature notably the Framework Convention, the Kyoto Protocol, the Rio Declaration and the Paris Agreement. Among a range of specific acts or omissions by Pakistan's government, the petitioner contested the approval of a plan to develop coal, which is anticipated to commensurately increase greenhouse gas emissions and displace residents in that region, besides direct and indirect environmental degradation. For the time being, no court has adjudicated the issue yet.

In conclusion, it appears that the Paris Agreement lends itself to the envisaged mechanism of enforcing international law and enhancing access to justice for individuals and NGOs. This quality has been recognized also by some practitioners negatively assessing the impact of a prospective judicial enforcement. They recognize the possibility for the Paris Agreement to be enforced in national courts since, in their view, the Paris Agreement improperly builds on the concessions by the Signatory Parties that their hitherto efforts so far have been inadequate.

---

111 Article 4(2) Paris Agreement.

112 Article 4(4) Paris Agreement.

113 Article 4(3) Paris Agreement. See also *B. Walsh et al.*, Pathways for Balancing CO2 Emissions and Sinks, Nature Communications 2017 (8), p. 1.

114 On UNCLOS and climate change, see, inter alia, *L.F. Damrosch & S.D. Murphy*, International Law: Cases and Materials, 2014, p. 1368.

115 *Ali v Federation of Pakistan*, Constitutional Petition No ___ / I of 2016 (1 April 2016). Petitioner alleged the violation of the principle of sustainable development, the precautionary principle, the obligation to undertake an environmental impact assessment as well as the principle of inter-generational equity.

116 Petitioner cites Principle 15 Rio Declaration, the 1971 Ramsar Convention, the 1972 Convention on Protection of World Cultural and Natural Heritage, the 1979 Convention on the Conservation of Migratory Species of Wild Animals, the 1985 Convention on the Protection of the Ozone Layer, the 1992 United Nations Convention on Biological Diversity, the 1992 United Nations Framework Convention on Climate Change, the 1997 Kyoto Protocol, as well as the 2015 Paris Agreement.

According to these commentators, however, the judicial enforcement of the Paris Agreement would be "an unconstitutional usurpation of power by activist groups and unelected and unaccountable judges that could undermine legislative power and the role of positive law in deciding legal disputes."[117]

Time appears now ripe for pulling some threads on the discussion concerning the role of national courts for access to justice in climate matters.

6. CONCLUSIONS

An effective, legitimate and fair legal system should not be a given. Rather, its actual construction highly depends on the interface of at least three levels of government, namely the international, regional and national levels.

By centring on the latter level, I contend that the indirect application of international environmental norms, along with constitutional, environmental, tort and procedural law at the domestic level, is poised to advance two different goals. Firstly, it enhances access to justice for individuals and NGOs in climate change matters. Secondly, it clearly allows for the domestication and enforcement of international law through national courts. By achieving both goals, it also contributes to the perceived legitimacy of international law. Such a mode of enforcement of international law can find legitimation in a possible reading of Principle 10 of the Rio Declaration and related instruments.

Furthermore, some recent case-law initiated before the adoption of the Paris Agreement carries out the prediction that national courts are increasingly applying international norms along with national law for the adjudication of climate change cases and controversies. I positively evaluate the availability of such application for the purpose of enforcing some of the provisions enshrined in the Paris Agreement as well.

Notwithstanding a number of limitations, I hold national courts' engagement with international climate law to be not only required in order to shore up the democratic principle of access to justice in climate matters, but also to be beneficial for the upholding of the international and domestic rule of law.[118] As it was aptly noted, "once in front of a tribunal, a claimant can argue all legal bases – international environmental law, national environmental law, or even pursue legal actions (where these are available) such as nuisance, tort, or other civil law."[119]

---

117 *L. Bergkamp and S.J. Stone*, The Trojan Horse of the Paris Agreement on Climate Change: How Multi-Level, Non-Hierarchical Governance Poses a Threat to Constitutional Government, 2015, available at https://ssrn.com/abstract=2715145, last visit: 12 April 2017, p. 3.

118 One should not view the two levels in isolation. On the misleading distinction between a rule of law at the international level and a rule of law at the national level, see *Nollkaemper, supra*, note 8 at pp. 2–3.

119 *Soveroski, supra*, note 13 at 272.

Nonetheless, such a mode of enforcement appears to be non-exhaustive and solely complementary to other modes of enforcement. Prospective litigation is expected to ensue especially if States Party to the Paris Agreement were not to devise effective enforcement mechanisms within the Paris Agreement itself, thus falling short of existing societal expectations.

ACCESS TO INFORMATION, THE HIDDEN HUMAN RIGHTS TOUCH OF THE PARIS AGREEMENT?

Delphine MISONNE*

KEYWORDS

Access to information; Climate change; Paris Agreement; Procedural rights

INTRODUCTION

In a conference on the importance of procedural environmental rights, aimed at collecting and comparing experience gained with the adoption and implementation of these rights under various legal instruments, our contribution explores how the Paris Agreement on Climate Change echoes Principle 10 of the Rio Declaration, as far as the 'access to information' pillar is concerned.

> 'Parties shall cooperate in taking measures, as appropriate, to enhance climate change education, training, public awareness, public participation and public access to information, recognizing the importance of these steps with respect to enhancing actions under this Agreement[1]'.

This is what Article 12 of the Paris Agreement stipulates, a provision that did not reach the headlines in Paris during COP21 in December 2015, and the formulation of which did not raise heated debates at that very moment. However, the explicit mention of the importance of public access to information with respect to enhancing actions in the Paris Agreement on Climate Change deserves notice and explanation for at least two reasons: firstly, due to the scope and status of the Paris Agreement; secondly, due to the specific nature of procedural rights.

* Prof. Delphine Misonne, Université Saint-Louis Bruxelles, FNRS Research Associate.

1 Article 12 of the Paris Agreement on Climate Change.

Scope and status. The 2015 Paris Agreement on Climate Change is a worldwide agreement, negotiated within the framework of the United Nations, and a legally binding treaty within the meaning of the Vienna Convention on the Law of Treaties.[2] By contrast, the 1998 Aarhus Convention on Access to Information, Public Participation in Decision-Making and Access to Justice in Environmental Matters[3], which decisively pushes the right for everyone to obtain access to environmental information held by public authorities, is only a regional treaty – it was negotiated within the framework of the UN Economic Commission for Europe –, even if its sphere of influence is actually much broader than the territory of its 47 Parties.[4] As far as Principle 10 of the 1992 Rio Declaration[5] is concerned, the Declaration only pertains to the category of 'soft law', a classification revealing its strong inspirational effect but lack of formal bindingness, even if this did not prevent it from gaining a major jurisprudential relevance.[6] Due to the fact the Paris Agreement is both, formally, a 'hard law' and 'worldwide' instrument, the mention of the importance of public access to information on the environment opens interesting perspectives. Negotiated under the framework of the United Nations and directly linked to the 1992 Framework Convention on Climate Change, the Paris Agreement has the potential to gather together a large number of Parties, far beyond the relatively modest number of Parties which gather for the Aarhus Convention[7], and far beyond the sole legal orders where public access to information on the environment is already firmly established. Considering this context, one can legitimately ask whether, due to Article 12 of the Paris Agreement in particular, the international community is now set on the path towards globalising some of the democratic requirements that are inherent to Principle 10 of the Rio Declaration. Could the Paris Agreement serve as a vehicle for consolidating fundamental democratic values across the globe?

---

2 *D. Wirth*, Cracking the American Climate Negotiators' Hidden Code: United States and the Paris Agreement, Climate Law, Vol. 6, No. 1–2, p. 152–170, 2016/Boston College Law School Legal Studies Research Paper No. 393, March 24, 2016, p.3; *S. Maljean-Dubois, M.Wemaere*, The Paris Agreement, a starting point towards achieving climate neutrality?, Carbon & Climate Law Review, 2016, pp.1–4.

3 Convention on Access to Information, Public Participation in Decision-making and Access to Justice in Environmental Matters (Aarhus, 25 June 1998; in force 30 October 2001) ('Aarhus Convention').

4 *M. Pallemaerts (Ed.)*, The Aarhus Convention at Ten, Europa Law Publishing, 2011, 440 p.; *J. Ebbesson*, Public Participation and Privatisation in Environmental Matters: An Assessment of the Aarhus Convention, Erasmus Law Review (2011), 71–89.

5 Rio Declaration on Environment and Development, Report of the UN Conference on Environment and Development (UN Doc. A/CONF.151/26/Rev.1 (Vol. I), 14 June 1992), Annex ('Rio Declaration'), Principle 10.

6 *J. Viñuales* (Ed.), The Rio Declaration on Environment and Development: a Commentary, Oxford, OUP, 2015, p.34.

7 Such as Canada and United States, Members of the UNECE, but not signatories to the Aarhus Convention.

Procedural rights. The second reason explaining the interest Article 12 of the Paris Agreement could raise stems from the debate on human rights. As the reader may know, no mention of the wording 'human rights' could be made explicitly in the final main part of the Paris Agreement, despite fierce plaidoyers and long-prepared negotiations dealing with that aspect.[8] Except for an acknowledgement in the preamble and an implicit reference in Article 2, via the expression '*in a manner that does not threaten food production*'[9], human rights are often, to the dismay of many, said to have been fully wiped out.[10] But are human rights really out of the game in the new climate regime? When one knows the crucial importance of procedural human rights[11] with particular respect to enhancing environmental protection[12], could we not consider that Article 12 is the hidden human rights touch of the Paris Agreement, that could potentially evolve towards something much more substantial in the mid-term future?

---

8 See, inter alia: *D. Bodansky*, Climate change and human rights, unpacking the issues, Georgia Journal of International and Comparative Law, 38, 2010, pp. 511–524.

9 Article 2, §1, b.

10 As recalled by *D. Magraw, A. Rosemberg, D. Padmanabhan, Deepika*, Human Rights, Labour and the Paris Agreement on Climate Change, Environmental Policy and Law; 46.5 (October 2016), 313–320: "In terms of human rights, as well as labour issues, an unprecedented coalition bringing together a variety of constituency groups, including human rights and environmental NGOs, trade unions, women and gender-based groups, indigenous peoples, youth and peasants pushed strongly for robust language in the authoritative parts of the agreement; the demand was for placement of this text in the Preamble as well as in the operative Article 2 of Section C. As one of the last compromises made in Paris, however, language on these was restricted to the Preamble alone".

11 *UNEP* report on Climate change and Human rights, 2015, 43 p.; *J. Knox*, Mapping Human Rights Obligations Relating to the Enjoyment of a Safe, Clean, Healthy and Sustainable Environment, Focus report on human rights and climate change, Report of the Special Rapporteur on the issue of Human Rights, June 2014; *J. Knox*, Human Rights Principles and Climate Change (July 9, 2014), Oxford Handbook of International Climate Change Law, Cinnamon Carlarne, Kevin R. Gray, and Richard Tarasofsky eds., 2015; Wake Forest Univ. Legal Studies Paper No. 2523599. Available at SSRN: https://ssrn.com/abstract=2523599; *J. Knox*, Climate Change and Human Rights Law, 50 VA. J. INT'L L., 2009,163; *OHCHR*, Report on the Relationship Between Climate Change and Human Rights, UN Doc 2009, A./HRC/10/61.

12 "In recent years, international human rights tribunals and other bodies have identified ways that environmental harm can interfere with the enjoyment of human rights, and have clarified that States have obligations to protect human rights against such interference. For example, States have duties to provide access to environmental information, to protect rights of free expression and association in relation to environmental issues, and to provide for participation in environmental decision-making"; "Human rights law imposes procedural obligations on states, including duties to assess environmental impacts on human rights and to make environmental information public, to facilitate public participation in environmental decision-making, and to provide access to effective legal remedies for environmental harm to the enjoyment of human rights. Closely related to the right to participate in environmental decision-making are the rights of freedom of expression and of association", as recalled by *J.Knox*, Human Rights, Environmental Protection and The Sustainable Development Goals, 24 Washington International Law Journal 517 (2015), pp. 1–3; *M. Dellinger*, Ten Years of the Aarhus Convention: How Procedural Democracy is Paving the Way for Substantive Change in National and International Environmental Law, 18:1 Colorado Journal of International Environmental Law and Policy Law (2009), 311–364.

Our contribution to the present volume, which, as presented at the EELF Wroclaw conference in September 2016, was only exploratory, is built around three questions:

- Does the mention of the importance of public access to information in the Paris Agreement confirm previous discourse or, on the contrary, reveal a breakthrough as far as provisions of multilateral treaties on climate change are concerned?
- Does this interest in public access to information become crystallised in the nationally determined contributions[13] – those spontaneous pledges that are a new central feature in the climate regime – as submitted by states from all over the world in preparation and implementation – of the Paris Agreement?
- More crucially, what might the follow-up of Article 12 involve, both for Parties and for existing institutions? Could, for instance, the crucial and specific focus on transparency, which is also at the very heart of the Paris Agreement, be inspired or even moulded by procedural rights to access to information?

But before proposing to answer these three questions and in order to better contextualise their relevance, it is necessary to provide a short description of the Paris Agreement.

1. THE PARIS AGREEMENT ON CLIMATE CHANGE

1.1. A TREATY

The Paris Agreement on Climate Change is a new treaty, legally binding under the international law of treaties.[14] It was finalized in Paris in December 2015 and it entered into force on 4 November 2016, an unprecedented speed with respect to multilateral environmental agreements. The normative density of the Agreement is weak but its strengths lay in the new collaborative processes it entails. The Treaty holds the international community together around the reaffirmation of a same concern and, more importantly, reboots the global 'commoning process' towards the achievement of a very demanding, but shared, project. That project is to hold the increase in the global average temperature to well below 2 °C above

13 As described under Article 3 of the Paris Agreement, "As nationally determined contributions to the global response to climate change, all Parties are to undertake and communicate ambitious efforts as defined in Articles 4, 7, 9, 10, 11 and 13 with the view to achieving the purpose of this Agreement as set out in Article 2. The efforts of all parties will represent a progression over time, while recognizing the need to support developing country Parties for the effective implementation of this Agreement."

14 As governed by the Vienna Conventions on the Law of Treaties. See note 2 here above. The agreement that was reached in Paris, in 2015, is actually made of two parts: a Treaty (the binding Paris Agreement) and an accompanying Decision (non-binding, but that shall be an element of the context helping to interpret the Treaty), Decision 1/CP21.

pre-industrial levels and pursue efforts to limit the temperature increase to 1.5 °C above pre-industrial levels, recognizing that this would significantly reduce the risks and impacts of climate change.[15]

1.2. NOT A TREATY FOR ALL

The treaty is binding upon the parties but the density of the normative content is weak. That very weakness was actually one of the conditions of its adoption. This must be explained in the light of various factors. Among them is the trick that has been used in the hope to guarantee its swift entry into force, a trick that indeed kept its promises. Due to the specificities of American politics, it appeared necessary to mould the new proposed instrument under the form of an 'executive agreement', that could be adopted by the sole President without passing through Congress. A Congress, with its republican majority, which is definitely not keen to adopt very prescriptive new regimes.[16] The purpose of such a by-pass was to guarantee that the United States could effectively and rapidly become Party to this new Agreement – a difficult issue when one remembers that the United States did not join the Kyoto Protocol. It was also necessary in order to meet the threshold of 55% of the global emissions that was fixed for the entry into force of the new Agreement. However, this arrangement had to be genuine and, as a consequence, it did drastically impact the content of the new Agreement: no assigned substantive reduction targets nor possibilities to impose any kind of sanctions at an international level etc. In short, the content had to be smooth and lenient enough to allow for it to be viewed as the mere execution of a previously adopted legal base, such as a treaty on Climate Change – not the 1997 Kyoto Protocol but the 1992 United Nations Framework Convention on Climate Change (UNFCCC).

1.3. A LONG-AWAITED TREATY

Besides that issue, Paris cannot be properly understood without taking the measure of other difficulties encountered in the past[17], while negotiating the follow-up of the Kyoto Protocol and its fatal deadline of 2012. A difficulty that culminated with the setback of the Copenhagen Conference of the Parties, in 2009, nearly putting

---

15 Article 2, a, Paris Agreement.

16 *D. Wirth*, The International and Domestic Law of Climate Change: A Binding International Agreement Without the Senate or Congress?", Harvard Environmental Law Review, Vol. 39 Iss. 2; 2015, p. 522; *L. Rajamani*, The Devilish Details: Key Legal Issues in the 2015 Climate Negotiations, 2015, 78 MLR 826.

17 See among others: *L. Rajamani*, The 2015 Paris Agreement: Interplay Between Hard, Soft and Non-Obligations, Journal of Environmental Law, 2016, 28, 337–358; *S. Lavallée & S. Maljean-Dubois*, L'Accord de Paris: fin de la crise du multilatéralisme climatique ou évolution en clair-obscur?, RJE, 2016, 41, 19–36.

a final point to the common project. A project that formally started some decades ago, in 1992, with the adoption of the United Nations Framework Convention on Climate Change (UNFCCC) and soon became more sophisticated in 1997 with the adoption of the Kyoto Protocol. The Kyoto Protocol, praised on the European scene and despised on the other side of the Atlantic, directed the international community towards more severe commitments: it assigned quantified reductions of greenhouse gases with fixed deadlines. But these more severe commitments rested only on the Parties listed in Annex I to the Framework Convention – a list of developed countries, according to the categorization of the early nineties, with no consideration of the fact that new economic competitors on the worldwide scene had already emerged. Parties that were not on the list were not submitted to any quantified restrictions, but were still engaged in the continuation of promises to do their best in assessing their own emissions and pay further attention to the climate change problematic with the possible help, precisely, of Annex I countries. That bipolarity was one of the building blocks of the whole climate regime when it all started, as its very existence is constructed upon a principle of 'common but differentiated responsibilities'. An asymmetry in duties and obligations, in full consideration of the respective responsibilities[18], capacities but also needs of each part of the world, but reduced to a binary configuration. With, on the one hand, a list of debtors (the historic polluters) and, on the other hand, non-Annex I countries which rather adopted a posture of creditor that they will not easily be prepared to surrender.

1.4. A BRAND NEW TYPE OF TREATY

So, writing the next chapter of the common battle against greenhouses gases was certainly no trifling matter and the Paris agreement was, in that sense, an immense diplomatic success. A success forged on a bet and a change of paradigm. The daring was to ask Parties to spontaneously propose what they were ready for, instead of continuing to try, desperately, to mutually agree upon the adoption of assigned commitments. The change of paradigm was to allow trust to be built around shared but global objectives, via a specific rhythm of procedural obligations, while parties hold control on what they agree to be committed to. The bet was that the compilation of all 'intended nationally determined contributions' could effectively lead to the transition the world needed in an acute and urgent climate change crisis.

18 Climate change is linked to anthropic greenhouse gases. A large part of them comes from the combustion of fossil fuels – a combustion that started, on a very large scale, with the industrial revolution in Northern Countries two centuries ago. This allows for an understanding of their role as 'historic polluter' that justified, in 1992, post-developed countries to install at the forefront of the combat against climate change, including on financial transfer issues.

Self-commitments. Under that configuration, various concepts are essential. Among them, the 'nationally determined contribution'[19],. 'Each Party shall prepare, communicate and maintain successive nationally determined contributions *that it intends to achieve*.' The binding force of the substantial part of these contributions will depend upon the specifications of their own content which is, so far, not standardized. Still, the Treaty specifies in the same Article 4.1. that 'Parties *shall* pursue domestic mitigation measures, with the aim of *achieving* the objectives of such contributions[20]'. This sounds rather like an obligation to reach a result (would a result be mentioned in there). Moreover, those national contributions shall not remain static. They are submitted to an obligation to be changed every five years. Those frequent changes must 'represent a progression beyond the Party's then current nationally determined contribution and reflect its highest possible ambition, reflecting its common but differentiated responsibilities and respective capabilities, in the light of different national circumstances[21]'.

Transparency. Another key concept is 'transparency', as governed under Article 13 which establishes 'an enhanced transparency framework for action and support, with built-in flexibility which takes into account Parties' different capacities and builds upon collective experience', this 'in order to build mutual trust and confidence and to promote effective implementation'. On that aspect, the Treaty is very detailed as regards the purpose of such a transparency framework: '*The purpose of the framework for transparency of action is to provide a clear understanding of climate change action in the light of the objective of the Convention as set out in its Article 2, including clarity and tracking of progress towards achieving Parties' individual nationally determined contributions, etc.*[22]'. There is less detail on what shall happen with the submitted information, except that it shall undergo a technical expert review[23], which shall consist of a consideration of the Party's support provided, as relevant, and the implementation and achievement of its nationally determined contribution.[24] The review shall also identify areas of improvement for the Party, and include a review of the consistency of the information, taking into account the flexibility accorded to the Party in the light of their capacities. But how shall the review be connected to the necessity to expose the results of that exercise to the public at large, is not yet specified. A lack of precision that might be more than an oversight. Regarding the broader issue of

19 For which no definition is provided.
20 Emphasis added.
21 Article 4, §3. All these terms would of course need further developments.
22 Article 13, §5. And, according to §4: '*The transparency arrangements under the Convention, including national communications, biennial reports and biennial update reports, international assessment and review and international consultation and analysis, shall form part of the experience drawn upon for the development of the modalities, procedures and guidelines*'
23 Article 13, §11.
24 Article 13, §12.

public participation in the new transparency processes, S. Duyck already pointed out, at the time the new Agreement was still at an early stage of negotiation, that 'in Cancun, governments elaborated a new MRV[25] process, abandoning the existing institutional framework providing positive and negative incentives to promote the implementation of the convention. Doing so, negotiators endorsed the view that respect for commitments can be meaningfully promoted through reliance on reputational costs associated with non-compliance. At the same time the procedures adopted by parties restrict the opportunities for an engagement of civil society in this process. The states-centric nature of the MRV process thus ignores the crucial role that NGOs could play in providing public exposure with regards to the successes and failures of governments to respect their mitigation commitments'.[26]

This being explained, we shall now turn back to our three questions regarding the relevance and possible impact of Article 12 of the Paris Agreement, as far as the public access to information dimension is concerned.

2. ACCESS TO INFORMATION IN INTERNATIONAL AGREEMENTS ON CLIMATE CHANGE

2.1. PREVIOUS AGREEMENTS ON CLIMATE CHANGE

The mention of access to information in the Paris Agreement is, as such, not new to international agreements on climate change. Both the 1992 Framework Convention on Climate Change and the 1997 Kyoto Protocol contain provisions on access to information. According to Article. 6, UNFCCC, Parties shall '*promote and facilitate at the national and, as appropriate, sub-regional and regional levels, and in accordance with national laws and regulations, and within their respective capacities: (…) (ii) public access to information on climate change and its effects.* According to Article 10, e, of the Kyoto Protocol, '*All Parties shall facilitate at the national level public awareness of, and public access to information on, climate change.*'

But the wording in Article 12 ('Parties shall cooperate in taking measures, as appropriate, to enhance climate change education, training, public awareness, public participation and public access to information, recognizing the importance of these steps with respect to enhancing actions under this Agreement) is not a copy-and-paste of either of those provisions. It is not the mere repetition of what

25 Measurement, Reporting and Verification Framework.

26 *S. Duyck*, MRV in the 2015 Climate Agreement: Promoting Compliance Through Transparency and the Participation of NGOs (January 10, 2015). Carbon and Climate Law Review, 2014/3, 175–187, Available at SSRN: https://ssrn.com/abstract=2557175, p.21.

can be found in the framework Convention to which it is embedded.[27] There are interesting differences which deserve to be enhanced.

First, the core of Article 12 is the reference to a necessity to cooperate: Parties shall cooperate[28] – a cooperation between Parties on Public Access to Information. That wording sets Article 12 apart from the wording of the two other Treaties (Article 6 UNFCCC; Article 10 Kyoto Protocol) but also of Principle 10 of the Rio Declaration, all specifically focused on the national dimension, a domestic promise that is not always highlighted: 'although the Rio Declaration has an international dimension, Principle 10 is actually domestic in scope.'[29]

What is more, Paris insists on '*the importance of these steps with respect to enhancing actions under this Agreement.*' The statement can be tracked back to a jargon that has been used for some years now in various meetings and decisions related to the implementation of Article 6 of the UNFCCC.

Article 6 UNFCCC led to an intense diplomatic activity, culminating in the creation of a 'Dialogue on Action for Climate Empowerment'[30], with a Doha programme that heavily insisted on the 'country-driven approach' to the implementation of Article 6 of the Convention but also explicitly admitted that 'international cooperation can enhance the collective ability of Parties to implement the Convention', identifying the need to establish a network of national focal points and to facilitate a regular exchange of views in order to build or strengthen existing skills and capacities.[31] The focus is on the facilitation of public access to information, by providing the information that is needed, taking into account factors such as quality of internet access, literacy and language issues. Rights are not explicitly mentioned in that Doha programme but, beyond the appearance of keeping the issue of access to information to something rather technical, its operationalisation also discusses possible linkage to the issue of rights and obligations, as under the Aarhus Convention model.[32] In Lima, at COP20 in 2014, a Ministerial Declaration explicitly stressed 'that education, training, public awareness, public participation, public access to information,

---

27 The Paris Agreement complements the 1992 Framework Convention on Climate Change (UNFCC); all its Parties must be Parties to the framework Convention; all definitions on the framework Convention are applicable to the Paris Agreement; The Paris Agreement enhance the implementation of the Framework Convention; The Conference of the Parties of the framework Convention shall serve as the meeting of the Parties to the Paris Agreement.

28 The obligation 'shall' and not the potestative 'should'.

29 *E. Dannemaeir*, A European Commitment to Environmental Citizenship: Article 3.7 of the Aarhus Convention and Public Participation in International Forums, Oxford Yearbook of International Environmental Law, Vol. 18, 2007, pp. 32–64.

30 Decision 15/CP18. a participatory platform acting as a regular forum to Parties to share their experiences in the implementation of Article 6 of UNFCCC, launched in 2012 at COP18 (Doha) with a 'Doha Work Programme on Article 6 of the Convention', a new step in the continuation of other programmes.

31 FCCC/SBI/2016/6, May 2016 Report on the Progress made under that Doha Programme, p.11.

32 Idem.

knowledge and international cooperation *play a fundamental role in meeting the ultimate objective of the Convention and in promoting climate-resilient sustainable development*'.[33]

As a consequence, it appears that Article 12 of the Paris Agreement cannot be approached, in any way, as a breaking point. It is rather the outcome of a slow maturation, bringing added value in comparison with pre-existing provisions.

2.2. AARHUS' IMPACT

One can also wonder whether the surge of such a provision in the Paris Agreement could also be rooted in the external dimension of the Aarhus Convention, emerging from its Article 3.7, according to which '*Each Party shall promote the application of the principles of this Convention in international environmental decision-making processes and within the framework of international organizations in matters relating to the environment*'. This requirement is known as having actually contributed to the diffusion of an Aarhus-type participatory model within international negotiations, and inside the Conference of the Parties, especially within the UN Climate Change regime.[34] It opened doors to non-state actors and transformed the composition of national delegations, exactly as is expanded upon in the Almaty Guidelines on Promoting the Application of the Principles of the Aarhus Convention in International Forums.[35] As observed by E. Dannemaeir, Article 3.7 of the Aarhus Convention has normative and methodological implications and participates in the construction of some form of global environmental citizenship.[36] One step further, one can ask whether the spilling-over effect might also impact the content of new treaties, and not only the negotiation processes, as we see happening with Article 12 of the Paris Agreement.

---

33 Decision 19/CP20. Emphasis added.

34 *S. Duyck*, Promoting the Principles of the Aarhus Convention in International Forums: The Case of the UN Climate Change Regime, RECIEL 22 (4) 2015, pp. 123–138. The author mentions that 'Governments that are parties to both legal instruments have relied on three main approaches to promote the Aarhus principles in the UNFCCC: (i) involvement of domestic stakeholders when preparing contributions to the negotiation process; (ii) promotion of public participation in the negotiation process itself; and (iii) support for UNFCCC outputs that uphold public participation in the implementation of climate policies and projects', while noticing that the third option was only very modestly activated.

35 Almaty Guidelines on Promoting the Application of the Principles of the Aarhus Convention in International Forums ('Almaty Guidelines'), in: Aarhus Convention, Decision II/4, Promoting the Application of the Principles of the Aarhus Convention in International Forums (UN Doc. ECE/MP.PP/2005/2/Add.5, 20 June 2005); *U. Beyerlin*, Aligning international environmental governance with the 'Aarhus principles' and participatory human rights, in *A. Grear and L. Kotze*, Research Handbook on Human Rights and the Environment, EE, 2015, pp.333–352.

36 *E. Dannemaeir*, op.cit., pp.49–50.

2.3. A SPECIAL PLACE IN THE PARIS AGREEMENT

Article 12 of the Paris Agreement is short and does not contain any detail, in contrast to most other articles of the Paris Agreement which present the particularity to be rather 'overinflated'. It fits between an Article 11 devoted to capacity-building and an Article 13 devoted to Transparency.

The draft version of that provision cannot be traced back any earlier than the version of 23rd October 2015[37], under a new 'Article 8 Bis' that managed to squeeze in the pre-existing structure with a choice to be made between two similar options, containing only two brackets ('shall', 'should'). That choice was quickly settled in favour of the prescriptive 'shall', as can be inferred from the 5th December version, on the eve of the COP21, under its current wording, confirming it did not raise much discussion in the crucial last round in Paris.

The real challenge was actually not 'if' but 'where'.[38] Mention in an isolated article has already proved to be a winning strategy for attracting attention and insisting on the importance of the issue, with regard to all actions that shall take place under the Paris Agreement. Attracting attention also means financing and the possible promotion of a specific working group and process, in the continuity of UNFCCC's Article 6 Dialogue on Empowerment.

The accompanying decision of the Conference of the Parties[39] keeps the legacy of that discussion. It only addresses the 'public access to information' discussion into its section on 'capacity building'[40], which is a bit confusing. But what it stipulates is worth noticing, as the Decision is, in itself, an important part of what was agreed upon in Paris and it will play a role in the interpretation of the formal Agreement:

> The Conference of the Parties '§83. Calls upon all Parties to ensure that education, training and public awareness, as reflected in Article 6 of the Convention and in Article 12 of the Agreement are adequately considered in their contribution to capacity-building';
>
> '84. Invites the Conference of the Parties serving as the meeting of the Parties to the Paris Agreement at its first session to explore ways of enhancing the implementation of training, public awareness, public participation and public access to information so as to enhance actions under the Agreement'.

37 Draft agreement and draft decision on workstreams 1 and 2 of the Ad Hoc Working Group on the Durban Platform for Enhanced Action, Work of the ADP contact group, Version of 23 October 2015, 23:30hrs.

38 According to our contacts within the Belgian Delegation to the COP21.

39 Decision 1/CP21, FCCC/CP/2015/10/Add.1.

40 At its §§83 & 84.

3. THE CONTENT OF NATIONALLY DETERMINED CONTRIBUTIONS

The content of the nationally determined contributions is not standardized. Each future Party had to determine what it wanted to pledge and submit, as it wished, in preparation for COP21.[41] The content of these proposals has not been formally integrated to the Paris Agreement, but they are made accessible online. Since the entry into force of the Agreement, it is an obligation resting on the secretariat to record nationally determined contributions communicated by Parties in a public registry.

Among those contributions are very few that pay attention to the issue of access to environmental information, besides their main provisions on emissions mitigation and adaptation to climate change.

The contribution of Costa Rica insists on the adoption of an 'Open Government policy', strengthening accountability mechanisms, information access and availability, and citizen participation.[42] Less to the point, but still relevant, Mexico's contribution includes a specific focus on early warning systems that could protect the population and increase its adaptive capacity. China expresses the wish to strengthen the role of public supervision and participation in low-carbon development.

Many contributions insist, on the other hand, on the fact that they were elaborated through a genuinely participatory process.[43]

According to the data produced in a May 2016 report on the progress made in implementing the Doha work programme on Article 6 of the 1992 Framework Convention on Climate Change, 'around 134 Parties mentioned at least one of the six elements covered by Article 6 of the Convention[44] in their intended nationally determined contributions. Several Parties reported that they involved

---

41 There proposals when then called INDC's (intended nationally determined contributions).

42 It provides details on a National Environmental Information System (SINIA) that was created under the National Geo-Environmental Information Center (CENIGA) at the Ministry of Environment and Energy, and foresees promoting an open data policy for all relevant climate information available for any citizen, announcing the creation of two open participation councils, one technical-scientific and one multi-stakeholder platform which will accompany the government's climate planning and management.

43 All contributions are available on a NDC registry, available at www4.unfccc.int/ndcregistry/Pages/Home.aspx.

44 Besides access to information, Article 6 UNFCCC mentions education, raising awareness, public participation, training of professionals and ... international cooperation (understood as follows: International cooperation and exchange can play a major role in strengthening national activities on climate change education, training and public awareness. Many governments need access to expertise and financial and technical resources so that they can develop their own climate change programmes. And all countries can benefit from sharing success stories, exchanging personnel and strengthening institutional capacity. This section features links to experts and organizations that are committed to promoting international cooperation in this field), as synthetized on the UNFCCC portal.

civil society, the private sector, academia, NGOs, multilateral organizations and other relevant stakeholders in the design of their INDCs. Some Parties indicated that public participation would be enhanced for coordinating and implementing their INDCs. Parties also stressed the key role that international cooperation will play in enhancing the implementation of their INDC's".[45]

4. THE FOLLOW-UP OF ARTICLE 12

4.1. BEYOND CAPACITY-BUILDING: AN INTEGRATION CLAUSE

Article 12 conveys an important message but it remains to be seen how far it could impact the Paris process itself, beyond a multiplication of international encounters aiming at 'sharing experiences' and 'drawing lessons', in the continuation of capacity-building essentials.

Due to the special nature of the Paris Agreement, the involvement of the public in the follow-up of measures to be effectively adopted by Parties shall be crucial in its success. The care governments will take of this follow-up will be definitively dependant on and responsive to what the respective public opinion requests.

Public access to information, however, is not proposed as a cross-over dimension under the Paris Agreement. Unless we consider it to be, under Article 12 – more precisely if it is interpreted as a possible integration clause.

There is a need, for instance, to draw clearer links between the implementation of Article 12 and the work that shall be done on Article 13, dedicated to transparency, that is broadly acclaimed as being one of the main innovations – if not the most important, indeed the true backbone[46] – of the Paris Agreement. As already mentioned, Paris does not directly contain strict and explicit reduction targets as far as greenhouse gas emissions are concerned, but creates virtuous circles inviting Parties to constantly work on their ambition, in a collective effort to reach global goals. In that regard, Article 13 is central, for it fixes the essentials of the reporting process and organises a review of the information that shall be transmitted by all parties. The review is announced to be a very difficult exercise, due to a kind of bias which places sophisticated greenhouse gas accounting at the core centre of the verification processes. The review is described as being 'technical'[47], and experts will be the main operators. If, as mentioned

45 FCCC/SBI/2016/6, §71, p.13. The Parties are not named.

46 C. *Martini*, Transparency: The Backbone of the Paris Agreement, Yale Center for Environmental Law & Policy, policy paper, May 29, 2016, available at http://envirocenter.yale.edu/transparency-the-backbone-of-the-Paris-Agreement.

47 Article 13, §11.

by J. Vinuales[48], one of the novelties in Article 13 is precisely that it 'relies on public pressure (perhaps a form of 'naming and shaming') to nudge States into taking action', we might ask if the current guarantees (yet to be expanded) are solid enough to make sure that the huge amount of information collected under Article 13 shall be available to all, and understandable to the general public. Quoting A.S. Tabeau, it might also be recalled that 'global governance has created a new level of political opacity that requires rebalancing though the adoption of transparency measures'.[49] An opacity that, if not taken care of, could prevent the public from exercising its constructive pressure.

How they are to be performed and what is to become of these technical reviews is still to be decided at the conference of the Parties, which received the mandate to adopt common modalities, procedures and guidelines, as appropriate for the transparency of action and support.[50] It could be useful to take hold of Article 12 to request *inter alia*, under Article 13, a need to provide for non-technical summaries and a public access, in due time, to the conclusions of the reviews.

Idem under Article 14 and its periodical global stocktakes the outcome of which 'shall inform Parties in updating and enhancing, in a nationally determined manner, their actions and support in accordance with the relevant provisions of this Agreement, as well as in enhancing international cooperation for climate action'.

4.2. TOWARDS A COOPERATION ON CREATING NEW RIGHTS

Many steps down the line, one can also ask whether that call for a better international cooperation in relation to public access to information might create new opportunities to improve the issue of 'public access' across the world to information on climate change (and related policies), through the adoption of new collaborative implementing instruments.

There might be a very long way to go between stating the importance of public access to environmental information in enhancing actions under the Paris Agreement and the recognition of a subjective right to such access to information. Still, when one knows that 'at least half of the nations of the globe have adopted comprehensive legislation aimed at guaranteeing access to environmental information, whether through general, cross-cutting information laws, or through laws dealing specifically with environmental information[51]',

---

48 *J. Vinuales,* The Paris Climate Agreement: An Initial Examination, February 2016, available at https://www.ejiltalk.org.

49 *A.S. Tabeau*, Evaluation of the Paris Climate Agreement According to a Global Standard of Transparency, CCLR, 1, 2016, p.24.

50 Article 13, §13.

51 As mentioned in UNEP, Putting Rio Principle 10 into Action, 2015.

one might think that, for the other half, Article 12 could still usefully act as a seed tray.

Procedural dimensions – and associated rights – are a sort of detour that has proved to be an excellent manner to pave the way towards the recognition or affirmation of more substantial rights. Not only an interesting trigger factor, but also a crucial one in boosting the follow-up of environmental issues by the public at large.[52] The right of access to information is also a prerequisite to the exercise of other procedural rights relating to public participation and access to justice.[53]

Public access to information on climate change science and policies is not yet guaranteed as a right under all national constitutions or national legislations across the world and there is certainly a need to consolidate that dimension where it already exists, *de iure* or *de facto*, passively or actively.[54]

4.3. A NECESSARY PART OF FUTURE NATIONALLY DETERMINED CONTRIBUTIONS

The importance of public access to information 'with respect to enhancing actions under this Agreement' might suggest that such a dimension should also be integrated in nationally determined contributions, would Parties happen to reach an agreement, in the future, on a common template.

Of course, Article 12 is not mentioned in Article 3, which invites Parties to undertake and communicate ambitious efforts 'as defined in Articles 4, 7, 9, 10, 11 and 13 with the view to achieving the purpose of this Agreement as set out in Article 2. The efforts of all Parties will represent a progression over time, while recognizing the need to support developing country Parties for the effective implementation of this Agreement'. But either on the basis of the integrative dimension we propose, or due the fact the accompanying Decision demonstrates, as already explained, that the mention of Article 11 actually also encompasses the dimensions embraced under Article 12, this would certainly fit with the purpose of the instrument, the 'NDCs'.

An insertion in all national contributions would entail a submission to the non-regression requisite that shall characterize these self-made commitments, as they are supposed to represent 'a progression beyond the Party's then current nationally determined contribution' and reflect 'its highest possible ambition', whatever that idealistic-sounding request may mean.[55]

---

52 *A. Boyle*, 'Human Rights and the Environment: Where Next?', The European Journal of International Law, vol.23, 3, 613–642.

53 UNEP report on Climate change and Human rights, 2015, p.16. Cfr Report of the Special Rapporteur on the issue of Human Rights, 2016.

54 *New York Times online*, January 20, 2017, 'With Trump in Charge, Climate Change References Purged From Website', by C. Davenport.

55 Article 4, §3.

5. CONCLUSION

A bit too far-fetched for a 'non-issue'? There might indeed be something in Article 12 of the Paris Agreement that needs to be highlighted, in relation to Principle 10 of the Rio Declaration in theory and practice.

Article 12 is a potential crucible for a renewal of the dynamics, at worldwide level, on how to improve concerted action in relation to access to environmental information, in direct relation to climate change facts and policies – or even more generally, especially in countries where the Aarhus Convention does not apply. Such discussions do actually already take place under Article 6 of the UNFCCC but they could find in Article 12 a new impetus and a new motivation, beyond the mere continuation of capacity-building essentials, in order to move the discussion on public access to information to the explicit field of procedural rights.

Article 12 could also act in an interesting way as a horizontal integration clause, that might condition the content of the nationally determined contribution, or even give more flesh to the notion of 'transparency', as currently understood under the Paris Agreement. There cannot be true transparency without broad and guaranteed public access to environmental information. If 'the obligation to endure gives us the right to know'[56], so does the obligation to trust the sugary promises made under the Paris Agreement. In that regard, Article 12 could provide one of the impetuses the international community still needs to consolidate that right to know, in relation with the achievement of the global objectives the Agreement proposes.

[56] *R. Carson*, Silent Spring, Houghton Mifflin, New York, 1962, Chapter 2.

ACCESS TO JUSTICE IN CLIMATE CHANGE LITIGATION FROM A TRANSNATIONAL PERSPECTIVE: PRIVATE PARTY STANDING IN RECENT CLIMATE CASES

Samvel VARVAŠTIAN*

ABSTRACT

Climate change litigation has grown intensively in recent years, becoming an important feature of climate governance in the US and a growing trend in some other jurisdictions. However, climate plaintiffs have traditionally encountered many procedural hurdles, including standing, which has often barred access to justice. To have standing, a party must be able to show some kind of interest in the outcome of the case, which usually stipulates the presence of a concrete injury emanating from an identifiable entity or the existing law. In case of climate change litigation, plaintiffs must thus assert actual injury from industry or state action/inaction with regard to GHG emissions and the resulting climate change, which may still be somewhat difficult from a scientific point of view. This chapter seeks to explore the current trends in private party standing in the US, Australian and European climate cases.

KEYWORDS

Access to justice; Australia; climate change; Europe; litigation; private parties; standing; United States

* Legal researcher working on climate change, air quality, public health and related human rights (Mykolas Romeris University).

1. INTRODUCTION

Over the last three decades, the global problem of climate change has been widely discussed and recognized at the highest international level through state participation in various mechanisms, including the much anticipated Paris Agreement adopted at the end of 2015.[1] Within the scientific circles, the consequences of climate change are commonly considered as potentially devastating and, taken at their worst, even deadly for many ecosystems and human communities alike.[2] However, despite the growing international consensus on the necessity of abating climate change, primarily by gradually curbing the global greenhouse gas (GHG) emissions – the result of massive use of fossil fuels and the key driver for global warming – the lack of political will to address the problem in a decisive way has continued to pose a critical challenge to the objective of stabilizing the planet's climate.[3]

The persisting inconsistencies in the regulatory response led to the rise in litigation. To date, defining climate change litigation may still be somewhat difficult, as the latter has taken many forms, including the lawsuits challenging agency permits and rules, lawsuits against governmental inaction with regard to GHG emissions, lawsuits exploring the legal avenues offered by common law and many more.[4] It is true though that despite the constantly growing number of such cases, their jurisdictional distribution has been very uneven, and so far only a few jurisdictions – predominantly pertaining to the common law legal system, most notably the US and Australia – have established a body of relevant case-law.[5] In those jurisdictions climate cases have already become a common feature of climate governance[6]; furthermore, the judiciary itself has been increasingly

---

1 Paris Agreement under the United Nations Framework Convention on Climate Change, CFCCC/CP/2015/L.9/Rev.1. See also *L. Rajamani*, The 2015 Paris Agreement: Interplay Between Hard, Soft and Non-Obligations, Journal of Environmental Law 2016(28), pp. 337–358.

2 See, in general, the Intergovernmental Panel on Climate Change (IPCC), 2014: Climate Change 2014: Synthesis Report. Contribution of Working Groups I, II and III to the Fifth Assessment Report of the Intergovernmental Panel on Climate Change [Core Writing Team, R.K. Pachauri and L.A. Meyer (eds.)]. IPCC, Geneva, Switzerland, 151 pp.

3 See *R. Lazarus*, Super Wicked Problems and Climate Change: Restraining the Present to Liberate the Future, Cornell Law Review 2009(94), pp. 1153–1233.

4 For a discussion on the definition of climate change litigation, see *D. Markell & J.B. Ruhl*, An Empirical Assessment of Climate Change in the Courts: A New Jurisprudence or Business as Usual?, Florida Law Review 2012(64), pp. 26–27; *J. Peel & H.M. Osofsky*, Climate Change Litigation's Regulatory Pathways: A Comparative Analysis of the United States and Australia, Law & Policy 2013(35), pp. 152–153.

5 See *J. Peel & H.M. Osofsky*, Climate Change Litigation: Regulatory Pathways to Cleaner Energy, 2015, pp. 16–18. See also *M. Wilensky*, Climate Change in the Courts: An Assessment of Non-US Climate Litigation, Duke Environmental Law & Policy Forum 2015(26), p. 131.

6 *Peel & Osofsky*, *supra*, note 4 at p. 175.

identified as an important actor in tackling climate change.[7] And yet, the process of bringing climate cases before the courts has usually been all but smooth, as plaintiffs have traditionally encountered many procedural hurdles in bringing forward their claims.[8] Among those hurdles, standing has established a notorious reputation, particularly for its role in barring many private parties[9] in the US access to justice.

In general terms, to have standing, a party must be able to show some kind of interest in the outcome of the case.[10] The purpose of standing, therefore, includes determining the persons that could seek judicial review, ensuring that only those directly concerned are able to litigate the questions at issue.[11] On the other hand, the over-strict application of the standing doctrine can significantly limit the access to justice, particularly in cases of public interest litigation.[12] As with the other procedural challenges, the problems related to plaintiffs' standing are not unique to climate change litigation, nor to environmental litigation as a whole. However, the application of the standing doctrine itself may differ across different jurisdictions.[13]

This chapter seeks to explore the current trends in private party standing in climate cases within three different jurisdictions – the US, Australia and Europe. The next part of the chapter will focus on the US, as the jurisdiction most prolific in terms of relevant jurisprudence, and will be divided into three sections, each discussing a particular group of cases: 1) cases concerning climate change impact assessment; 2) cases concerning the regulation of GHG emissions and air quality; 3) common law cases. The third part will discuss standing in Australian climate cases and the last one will address the revolutionary Dutch *Urgenda* case in Europe.

2. STANDING IN THE US

In assessing standing in contemporary environmental litigation, the US federal courts have commonly relied on the renown Supreme Court's case *Lujan v.*

---

7 See e.g. *B.J. Preston*, The Contribution of the Courts in Tackling Climate Change, Journal of Environmental Law 2016(28), pp. 11–17.

8 See *Peel & Osofsky*, *supra*, note 5 at pp. 266–267.

9 In this chapter, the term 'private parties' refers to individuals and NGOs.

10 Sierra Club v. Morton, 405 U.S. 727, 731–732 (1972). See also *A. Scalia*, The Doctrine of Standing as an Essential Element of the Separation of Powers, Suffolk University Law Review 1983(17), p. 882.

11 *W. Fletcher*, The Structure of Standing, Yale Law Journal 1988(98), p. 222.

12 On public interest litigation in the context of climate change see e.g. *J. Lin*, Litigating Climate Change in Asia, Climate Law 2014(4), pp. 140–149.

13 See e.g. *J. Hammons*, Public Interest Standing and Judicial Review of Environmental Matters: A Comparative Approach, Columbia Journal of Environmental Law 2016(41), p. 515.

Defenders of Wildlife[14], which revolved around the compliance of the US government's activities abroad with the federal endangered species legislation, and resulted in a restrictive approach to environmental plaintiffs' standing.[15] In that case, the Supreme Court articulated a three-element 'irreducible constitutional minimum of standing' (the *Lujan* test): 1) an injury in fact (that is, an invasion of a legally protected interest) – which is *(a)* concrete and particularized and *(b)* actual or imminent and not conjectural or hypothetical; (2) a causal connection between the injury and the conduct complained of – that is, the injury has to be fairly traceable to the challenged action of the defendant, and not the result of the independent action of some third party; and (3) a likelihood that the injury will be redressed by a favourable decision.[16] The Supreme Court has since held that in environmental cases, the injury within this meaning should not be interpreted as injury to the environment itself, but rather as injury to the plaintiff[17], hence environmental plaintiffs must be able to demonstrate their use of the affected area to adequately allege injury in fact.[18]

As shall be discussed below, in terms of climate change litigation, the application of the *Lujan* test has been quite problematic, because of the complex scientific background to the global problem of climate change itself.[19] Fortunately enough, though, the issue of climate science has not proven to be an insurmountable obstacle in the way of standing, as demonstrated by the Supreme Court's position in its first and, perhaps, most renown climate case, *Massachusetts v. EPA*.[20] In this case, the plaintiffs, including the state of Massachusetts, other states, local governments and private organisations, alleged that the US Environmental Protection Agency (EPA) has abdicated its responsibility under the federal air quality legislation – the Clean Air Act (CAA) – to regulate automobile GHG emissions.[21] The Supreme Court recognized at the highest level the causal link between GHG emissions and climate change, and the impact of climate change on the environment and stated that the widely shared nature of such an injury does not diminish the interest of the concrete party.[22] Moreover, the Court held that the fact that there are other major GHG emitters like China and India,

---

14 *Lujan v. Defenders of Wildlife*, 504 U.S. 555 (1992).

15 See, in general, *C.R. Sunstein*, What's Standing After Lujan? Of Citizen Suits, "Injuries," and Article III, Michigan Law Review 1992(91), pp. 163–236.

16 *Lujan*, at 560–561.

17 *Friends of the Earth, Inc. v. Laidlaw Environmental Services (toc), Inc.*, 528 U.S. 167, 181 (2000).

18 *Id.*, at 183 (quoting the earlier Supreme Court case *Sierra Club v. Morton*, at 735).

19 It is worth mentioning that in some climate cases, the judiciary explicitly distanced itself from this issue by alluding, *inter alia*, to the lack of scientific and, accordingly, regulatory competence to deal with climate change, thus simply 'bouncing' the problem back to the traditional decision-making bodies. Thus, in *AEP v. Connecticut*, the Supreme Court stressed that 'judges lack the scientific, economic, and technological resources an agency can utilize in coping with issues of this order' (*American Elec. Power Co., Inc. v. Connecticut*, 564 U.S. 410, 428 (2011)).

20 *Massachusetts v. E.P.A* 549 U.S. 497 (2007).

21 *Id.*, at 505.

22 *Id.*, at 499, 553–555.

should not preclude the US agency from its regulatory duty, even if the latter by itself is unable to solve the global problem, since '[a] reduction in domestic emissions would slow the pace of global emissions increases, no matter what happens elsewhere.'[23] However, although this case arguably facilitated standing for state plaintiffs, with the Supreme Court holding that the injury to the state of Massachusetts lawmaking and regulatory capabilities required relaxed standing, it did not provide an answer with regard to standing of private parties.[24] This part will now turn to examine the relevant cases in detail.

2.1. CASES CONCERNING CLIMATE CHANGE IMPACT ASSESSMENT

This category of cases, revolving around the question whether climate change should be considered in environmental impact assessment, is by far the oldest in the context of climate change litigation, dating back to its dawn in the early 1990s[25]; throughout the years, private plaintiffs faced the challenges to standing with mixed success.

In a number of earlier cases, courts denied standing because the alleged failure to consider the impact of climate change arguably could not be traced to plaintiff's injury. This was the court's line of reasoning in case *Center for Biological Diversity v. U.S. Department of the Interior*, where environmental NGOs challenged a leasing plan for oil and gas development in the outer continental shelf off the coast of Alaska, claiming that the leasing programme violated the National Environmental Policy Act (NEPA), because the agency failed to take into consideration the effects of climate change.[26] Relying on the *Lujan* test, the Court of Appeals for the District of Columbia Circuit stressed that the 'standing analysis does not examine whether the environment in general has suffered an injury', but rather whether a party has suffered an injury that affects it in a 'personal and individual way'.[27] With regard to the latter, the court held that the plaintiffs averred that any significant adverse effects of climate change 'may' occur at some point in the future, but this does not amount to the actual, imminent, or 'certainly impending' injury required to establish standing.[28] Furthermore, the court held that climate change is a harm that is shared by humanity at large, and the redress that plaintiffs seek – to prevent an increase in global temperature – is not focused any more on the plaintiffs than it is on the remainder of the world's

23 *Id.*, at 499–500.
24 See *D.S. Green*, Massachusetts v. EPA Without Massachusetts: Private Party Standing in Climate Change Litigation, Environs: Environmental Law & Policy Journal 2012(36), pp. 35–63.
25 See *City of Los Angeles v. National Highway Traffic Safety Admin.* 912 F.2d 478 (D.C. Cir. 1990).
26 *Center for Biological Diversity v. U.S. Dept. of Interior*, 563 F.3d 466 (D.C. Cir. 2009).
27 *Id.*, at 478.
28 *Id.*

population[29], thus the alleged injury is too generalized to establish standing.[30] A fairly similar conclusion was reached in some other earlier climate cases falling into this category.[31]

On the other hand, private parties in some other earlier climate cases arising under NEPA were successful in terms of standing. In the 2011 case *WildEarth Guardians v. US Forest Service*, for instance, an environmental NGO challenged the environmental impact statement issued by the agency with regard to coal mining operation on National Forest land, claiming that the agency failed to identify reasonable alternatives for reducing methane levels within mines and the respective impact on climate change.[32] In support of its standing, the organization presented a declaration from one of its members, who described the various ways that climate change injured his interests, namely, how it negatively affected his habitual outdoor activities.[33] The District Court for Colorado stressed that an association has standing if: '(a) its members would otherwise have standing to sue in their own right; (b) the interests it seeks to protect are germane to the organization's purpose; and (c) neither the claim asserted nor the relief requested requires the participation of individual members in the lawsuit.'[34] In the present case, the court agreed with the plaintiff NGO that the contested decision would cause injury to its members' enjoyment of the lands at issue and the injury was not conjectural or hypothetical and was traceable to the action of the defendants, thus standing was granted.[35]

In recent years, the tradition of granting standing to private parties in such cases has been upheld. A notable example of this is the case *WildEarth Guardians v. Jewell*[36], where environmental organizations claimed that the Bureau of Land Management failed to adequately consider several environmental concerns, including the increase in local pollution and global climate change caused by future mining, before authorizing the leasing of the tracts of federal land.[37] The plaintiff NGOs stated that the agency's decision harmed the interests of their members, who had aesthetic interests in the land surrounding the tracts concerned and planned to visit the area regularly for recreational purposes.[38] Although the District Court for Columbia was persuaded that the increase in local air, water and land pollution from mining on the above-mentioned tracts injured the plaintiffs' members, it denied standing because arguably they could not demonstrate a link

---

29 *Id.*

30 *Id.*

31 See *Amigos Bravos v. U.S. Bureau of Land Management*, 816 F.Supp.2d 1118, 1123 (D.N.M. 2011).

32 *WildEarth Guardians v. US Forest Service*, 828 F.Supp.2d 1223, 1233–1234 (D. Colo. 2011).

33 *Id.*

34 *Id.*, at 1234–1235.

35 *Id.*

36 *WildEarth Guardians v. Jewell*, 738 F.3d 298 (D.C. Cir. 2013).

37 *Id.*, at 305.

38 *Id.*, at 305–306.

between their members' recreational and aesthetic interests, 'which are uniformly local, and the diffuse and unpredictable effects of GHG emissions.'[39] However, according to the Court of Appeals for the District of Columbia Circuit, such an approach 'sliced the salami too thin'.[40] Although the D.C. Circuit still considered that the respective environmental groups 'cannot establish standing based on the effects of global climate change', it stressed that they have established 'a separate injury in fact not caused by climate change – the harm to their members' recreational and aesthetic interests from *local* pollution' and concluded that the 'aesthetic injury follows from an inadequate [environmental impact assessment] whether or not the inadequacy concerns the same environmental issue that causes their injury'.[41] Most importantly, the court agreed that 'if the [agency was] required to adequately consider each environmental concern, it could change its mind about authorizing the lease offering'.[42] This line of reasoning found support in some other recent cases.[43]

It may be observed that in these cases the issue of harm from local pollution prevailed over the alleged global impact of climate change, although the consideration of the latter was held important in preventing the above-mentioned harm. The situation was somewhat different in the 2015 case *WildEarth Guardians v. US Forest Service*[44], where, similarly, environmental NGOs challenged agency decisions approving coal leases that would expand coal mines in area partially within national grassland, which was a unit of national forest system, claiming that the agency did not take a hard look at direct, indirect and cumulative local air quality impacts as well as climate impacts resulting from coal mining and combustion.[45] The plaintiff NGOs relied on the declarations from their members, who provided numerous examples of how local air pollution – including haze, dust clouds, particulate matter emissions – and/or climate change-related weather events negatively impacted their lives.[46] Notably, with regard to climate change, it is important to notice that these declarations were made by the respective NGOs' members from different and, often, geographically not proximate states, including Colorado, Florida, New Jersey, Texas, California and Wyoming.[47] The District Court for Wyoming, referring to the two above-mentioned decisions, rejected the argument that 'petitioners lack standing when they assert that coal leasing in the areas of concern would impact global climate change and would

39 *Id.*, at 306–307.
40 *Id.*, at 307.
41 *Id.*
42 *Id.*, at 306.
43 See *High Country Conservation Advocates v. United States Forest Service*, 52 F.Supp.3d 1174, 1187 (D. Colo. 2014); *Montana Environmental Information Center v. U.S. Bureau of Land Management* 615 Fed.Appx. 431 (9th Cir. Mem. 2015).
44 *WildEarth Guardians v. US Forest Service* 120 F.Supp.3d 1237 (D. Wyo. 2015).
45 *Id.*, at 1246.
46 *Id.*, at 1250–1255.
47 *Id.*

in turn threaten their members' enjoyment of the at-issue areas' and concluded that 'petitioners have standing to challenge the [decision] even if their argument that [this decision] failed to adequately analyze climate change impacts has no common nexus with the concrete injury to recreational interests'.[48]

In contrast, the issue of analysing the impact of climate change was central in the recent case concerning biodiversity and endangered species, *Oceana v. Pritzker*, where the plaintiff – an environmental group – had to demonstrate its standing on behalf of its members in a lawsuit, challenging the opinion of National Marine Fisheries Service with regard to loggerhead sea turtles.[49] The contested opinion, *inter alia*, allegedly failed to explain the connection between evidence of present and short-term effects caused by climate change and led the agency to the conclusion that climate change would not result in any significant impact on the species.[50] The District Court for Columbia stressed that an organizational plaintiff, such as Oceana, 'may have standing to sue on its own behalf to vindicate whatever rights and immunities the association itself may enjoy or, under proper conditions, to sue on behalf of its members asserting the members' individual rights.'[51] The court acknowledged that Oceana had standing to challenge the agency's decision on behalf of its members because it proffered declarations from five of them, who stated that they enjoyed observing and/or studying loggerheads and had plans to continue doing so.[52] Since the agency's decision permitted an unlawfully excessive amount of harm to loggerheads, which threatened the enjoyment and study of those animals by those members, vacating this decision would redress the above-mentioned injury.[53] The court thus concluded that Oceana's members had standing to sue in their own right and while their interests were germane to Oceana's purpose as an ocean conservation group, and their individual participation was not required either by the nature of Oceana's claims or by the relief that it requested, Oceana had organisational standing to sue on their behalf.[54]

The situation, though, was different with regard to organisational standing in case *Kunaknana v. US Army Corps of Engineers*[55], where an environmental NGO and residents of a town in Alaska challenged the decision to issue a permit to a company to fill certain wetlands in the National Petroleum Reserve in order to develop a drill site.[56] The plaintiffs claimed, *inter alia*, that the issuance of the permit violated NEPA because the defendant relied on outdated environmental

48 *Id.*, at 1257.
49 *Oceana, Inc. v. Pritzker*, 125 F.Supp.3d 232 (D.D.C. 2015).
50 *Id.*, at 250–252.
51 *Id.*, at 240.
52 *Id.*, at 241.
53 *Id.*
54 *Id.*
55 *Kunaknana v. U.S. Army Corps of Engineers* 23 F.Supp.3d 1063 (D. Alaska 2014).
56 *Id.*, at 1067–1068.

impact assessment and failed to carry out supplemental analysis in light of new information about the impact of climate change.[57] The District Court for Alaska granted standing to residents, holding that their habitual activities within the vicinity of the project's area, namely 'aesthetic, spiritual, cultural, religious, and recreational enjoyment' of the land, could be directly harmed by the project, traceable to the defendant's actions and redressable by a favourable court decision.[58] However, the court denied standing to the NGO, holding that none of its members' declarations indicated any past activities in the project area or concrete plans to visit it in the future, while their general interest in certain animal species was insufficient to confer standing to challenge a single project affecting some portion of those species with which they had no specific connection.[59]

2.2. CASES CONCERNING THE REGULATION OF GHG EMISSIONS AND AIR QUALITY

Another established trend in climate change litigation has seen the exploration of the avenues offered by legislation concerning GHG emissions and air quality, namely the CAA; the general picture of private party standing in these cases, though, was fairly similar to that in the cases described in the category above.

Thus, in an early case *Northwest Environmental Defense Center v. Owens Corning Corp.*, where environmental groups brought action alleging that manufacturer was constructing facility without having obtained preconstruction permit required under the CAA, the District Court for Oregon noted that the challenged future GHG emissions sources were local and members of the plaintiff organizations resided, worked, and recreated near the partially-completed facility.[60] The court, therefore, agreed that 'those individuals would suffer some direct impact from emissions entering into the atmosphere from defendant's facility, as would the local ecosystem with which these individuals constantly interact.'[61] With regard to those emissions impact on global warming and the subsequent harm to the plaintiff, the court observed the indirect nature of such a link; yet it stressed that the adverse effects alleged in plaintiffs' complaint would be felt by them in the place of their residence, which was also the place of defendant's emissions sources.[62] The court, therefore, stated that while the adverse effects from the emissions would not necessarily be limited to that geographical place, the 'plaintiffs' injuries are not diminished by the mere fact that other persons

57 *Id.*, at 1093.
58 *Id.*, at 1085.
59 *Id.*, at 1078–1084.
60 *Northwest Environmental Defense Center v. Owens Corning Corp.* 434 F.Supp.2d 957, 965 (D.Or. 2006).
61 *Id.*
62 *Id.*

may also be injured by the defendant's conduct'.[63] Furthermore, even though the defendant was not the only entity allegedly 'discharging pollutants into the atmosphere that may adversely impact the plaintiffs,' the court held that the traceability element 'does not require that a plaintiff show to a scientific certainty that the defendant's emissions, and only the defendant's emissions, are the source of the threatened harm.'[64] Finally, with regard to redressability, the court concluded that 'in environmental and land use cases, the challenged harm often results from the cumulative effects of many separate actions that, taken together, threaten the plaintiff's interests', thus 'the relief sought in the complaint need not promise to solve the entire problem'.[65]

Strangely enough, the considerations on standing in this case, though subsequently endorsed by the Supreme Court in *Massachusetts v. EPA*, did not find much support in courts in the following years. An example of this is the recent case *Washington Environmental Council v. Bellon*, where environmental organisations sought to compel the Washington State Department of Environmental Quality and other agencies to regulate GHG emissions from the state's five oil refineries, by claiming that the agencies failed to define the emission limits and apply those limits to the oil refineries in question in violation of the CAA.[66] Although the defendants admitted that in Washington, GHGs have caused climate-related changes, such as 'rising sea levels, coastal flooding, acidification of marine waters, declines in shellfish production, impacts to snow pack and water supplies, agricultural impacts on the east side of the Cascades, and changes in forest fires' and did not dispute the fact that the oil refineries in question emit GHGs[67], they contended that the case must be dismissed for lack of standing.[68] In support of their standing, members of the plaintiff NGOs submitted affidavits attesting to their current and future recreational, aesthetic, economic, and health injuries resulting from elevated levels of GHGs, including their impeded ability to enjoy habitual outdoor activities, damage to their property caused by flooding and wildfires as well as respiratory health problems in their families.[69]

The Court of Appeals for the Ninth Circuit agreed that the above-mentioned facts satisfied the injury in fact requirement of the Lujan test[70]; however, it held that plaintiffs did not meet their burden in satisfying the 'irreducible constitutional minimum' requirements under either the causality or redressability prong.[71] With regard to causality, the court delved into a lengthy discussion on how the

63 *Id.*
64 *Id.*, at 967.
65 *Id.*, at 968.
66 *Washington Environmental Council v. Bellon*, 732 F.3d 1131, 1135 (9th Cir. 2013).
67 *Id.*, at 1136.
68 *Id.*, at 1138–1139.
69 *Id.*, at 1139–1141.
70 *Id.*, at 1141.
71 *Id.*, at 1147.

plaintiffs' position was compromised by the global scale and nature of climate change, its drivers and effects. Thus it held that plaintiffs offered only 'vague, conclusory statements' that the agencies' failure to set the standards at the oil refineries contributed to GHG emissions, which in turn, contributed to climate change that resulted in their purported injuries.[72] Specifically, the court held that plaintiffs' causal chain from the lack of the above-mentioned standards to their personal injuries consisted of 'a series of links strung together by conclusory, generalized statements of contribution, without any plausible scientific or other evidentiary basis that the refineries' emissions are the source of their injuries.'[73] The court concluded that 'attempting to establish a causal nexus in this case may be a particularly challenging task' due to the 'natural disjunction between plaintiffs' localized injuries and the greenhouse effect,' as GHGs, 'once emitted from a specific source, quickly mix and disperse in the global atmosphere and have a long atmospheric lifetime' and there is 'limited scientific capability in assessing, detecting, or measuring the relationship between a certain GHG emission source and localized climate impacts in a given region.'[74]

Furthermore, the court stressed that 'there are numerous independent sources of GHG emissions, both within and outside the [US], which together contribute to the greenhouse effect', while the above-mentioned oil refineries in Washington are responsible for 5.9% of GHG emissions in Washington, which renders the effect of this emission on global climate change 'scientifically indiscernible'.[75] In court's view, in contrast to the situation in *Massachusetts v. EPA*, where the Supreme Court held that the GHG emission levels from motor vehicles were a 'meaningful contribution' to global GHG concentrations, given the fact that the US automobile sector accounted for 6% of world-wide carbon dioxide, the GHG emissions contribution in the present case was not meaningful from a global perspective.[76] Similarly, with regard to redressability, the court stated that as the effect of collective emissions from the oil refineries on global climate change is 'scientifically indiscernible,' and plaintiffs' injuries were likely to continue unabated even if the oil refineries were subject to the requested standards.[77]

A somewhat similar decision was reached in another recent case, *Communities for a Better Environment v. EPA*, where three environmental NGOs challenged EPA's decision not to alter primary national ambient air quality standards for carbon monoxide (CO) and not to adopt secondary standards.[78] According to the CAA, the EPA had to establish the latter standards for six common air pollutants, including CO; the primary standards had to be set at a level 'requisite to protect the

---

72 *Id.*, at 1142.
73 *Id.*
74 *Id.*, at 1143.
75 *Id.*, at 1143–1144.
76 *Id.*, at 1145–1146.
77 *Id.*, at 1147.
78 *Communities for a Better Environment v. E.P.A.*, 748 F.3d 333 (D.C. Cir. 2014).

public health,' which encompassed human health, while the secondary standards had to be set at a level 'requisite to protect the public welfare,' which encompassed, *inter alia*, the welfare of animals, the environment and climate.[79] Specifically with regard to climate change, it is worth noting that since 1985 EPA has found that a secondary standard for CO was not needed to protect the public welfare, and the five-year review of the above-mentioned standards initiated by the EPA in 2007 focused on CO effect on climate, as the only element of public welfare known to be affected by it.[80] In 2011, the EPA concluded that the link between CO and climate change was tenuous, thus it could not determine whether any secondary standard would reduce climate change.[81] Plaintiffs, accordingly, challenged the lack of a secondary standard, contending that CO 'will worsen global warming and in turn displace birds that one of petitioners' members observes for recreational purposes'.[82]

The Court of Appeals for the District of Columbia Circuit, however, held that plaintiffs have failed to establish the causation element of standing, because they 'have not presented a sufficient showing that [CO] emissions in the [US] – at the level allowed by EPA – will worsen global warming as compared to what would happen if EPA set the secondary standards in accordance with the law as petitioners see it'.[83] The court was persuaded by the EPA's findings that CO effects on climate change involved 'significant uncertainties', thus it was impossible to anticipate how any secondary standard that would limit its ambient concentrations in the US would in turn affect climate and thus any associated welfare effects, and concluded that plaintiffs' theory of causation was 'a bridge too far'.[84]

2.3. COMMON LAW CASES

Among the US climate cases falling under the common law category, the one extremely interesting, in terms of private party standing, is the renowned *Comer v. Murphy Oil*.[85] According to the plaintiffs – the property owners in Mississippi – the defendants, including a number of fossil fuel producing companies, caused the emission of GHGs that contributed to global warming and, accordingly, to a rise in sea levels, which added to the ferocity of Hurricane Katrina, ultimately destroying plaintiffs' property.[86] Unlike cases in other categories, this lawsuit was directed not against the regulating bodies, but against the actual polluters

79 *Id.*, at 334.
80 *Id.*, at 335.
81 *Id.*
82 *Id.*, at 338.
83 *Id.*
84 *Id.*
85 *Comer v. Murphy Oil USA*, 585 F.3d 855 (5th Cir. 2009).
86 *Id.*, at 859.

themselves, with plaintiffs asserting claims for compensatory and punitive damages based on, *inter alia*, state common law actions of public and private nuisance.[87] The Court of Appeals for the Fifth Circuit granted plaintiffs standing, holding that all three elements – that is injury, causation and redressability – were satisfied. In particular, the court reiterated the Supreme Court's position in *Massachusetts v. EPA* with regard to causal chain between GHG emissions, global warming, extreme weather events (namely the severity of flooding and hurricanes) and, consequently, the related damage to private property.[88] Similarly, the court rejected allegations that GHG emissions from the defendants' activities were too negligible to consider, holding that the 'fairly traceable' test should not be used as an inquiry into whether a defendant's pollutants are the sole cause of an injury but rather whether 'the pollutant causes or *contributes to* the kinds of injuries alleged by the plaintiffs', while the claimed monetary damages accounted for redressability.[89]

The case, though, was ultimately dismissed, and on refile, the District Court for the Southern District of Mississippi held that the plaintiffs lacked standing because their claims were not fairly traceable to the companies' conduct.[90] According to the court, '[a]t most, the plaintiffs can argue that the types of emissions released by the defendants, when combined with similar emissions released over an extended period of time by innumerable manmade and naturally-occurring sources encompassing the entire planet, may have contributed to global warming, which caused sea temperatures to rise, which in turn caused glaciers and icebergs to melt, which caused sea levels to rise, which may have strengthened Hurricane Katrina, which damaged the plaintiffs' property.'[91] Most interestingly, the court availed itself of what might be described as a scientifically-impossible test to plaintiffs' standing, put forward by the defendants: '(1) what would the strength of Hurricane Katrina have been absent global warming; (2) how much of each Plaintiff's damages would have been attributable to Hurricane Katrina if it had come ashore at a lower strength; and (3) how much of each Plaintiff's damages was attributable to failures by others, [for example] governmental agencies, to prevent additional injury.'[92] It does seem, though, that such a narrow interpretation of traceability represents a rather radical approach, which, in case of general acceptance, would most probably render climate change litigation impossible. Fortunately, however, many courts have been unwilling to introduce such draconian measures to test plaintiffs' standing.

An example of a much more positive approach may be observed in another very interesting line of common law climate cases, the so-called atmospheric

87 *Id.*
88 *Id.*, at 861–864.
89 *Id.*, at 866–867.
90 *Comer v. Murphy Oil USA, Inc.*, 839 F.Supp.2d 849 (S.D. Miss. 2012).
91 *Id.*, at 861.
92 *Id.*, at 862.

trust litigation. These cases, involving children plaintiffs, is the result of a nationwide legal campaign initiated in 2011 in every state in the US. In such cases, the plaintiffs recourse not to the 'conventional' statutory provisions on air quality or impact assessment, but to the common law public trust doctrine – an ancient doctrine requiring government to hold vital natural resources in trust for the public beneficiaries, thus protecting those resources from monopolization or destruction by private interests[93] – which is explicitly enshrined in some state constitutions and grants environmental human rights.[94] Although so far the success rate of such cases has been rather low, they have shown an interesting and quite promising trend with regard to liberalization of the standing requirements.

For example, in *Kanuk v. Alaska*, the plaintiffs – a group of Alaskan children, acting through their guardians – requested the Superior Court of Alaska to, *inter alia*, declare the atmosphere a public trust resource under the state's Constitution, and that the state has an affirmative fiduciary obligation to protect and preserve it for present and future generations of Alaskans, by reducing the CO_2 emissions by at least 6% per year from 2013 through at least 2050 and preparing and maintaining a full and accurate annual accounting of Alaska's CO_2 emissions.[95] The plaintiffs supported their claims by alleging that they had been specifically and personally affected by climate change in the form of erosion from ice melt and flooding from increased temperatures, decline of animal life and receding glaciers, which negatively impact the ability to enjoy and pass on local traditions, and culture.[96]

Although the superior court did not go into details of the case and dismissed it as non-justiciable[97], on the appeal, the Supreme Court of Alaska approached the case more diligently. With regard to standing, the court agreed with the plaintiffs that the alleged injuries from climate change were both specific and personal.[98] The court concluded that the complaint showed direct injury to a range of recognizable interests, especially in light of the court's broad interpretation of standing and the policy of promoting citizen access to justice, thus the plaintiffs' allegations were sufficient to establish standing.[99] Furthermore, the court was not persuaded by the argument that climate change affects the humanity at large and does not distinguish the plaintiffs from any other person in Alaska.[100] The court stressed the individual nature of the harm to the plaintiffs and further contended

93 *M.C. Wood & C.W. Woodward IV*, Atmospheric Trust Litigation and the Constitutional Right to a Healthy Climate System: Judicial Recognition at Last, *Washington Journal of Environmental Law & Policy* 2016 (6), pp. 647–648.

94 *A.B. Klass*, The Public Trust Doctrine in the Shadow of State Environmental Rights Laws: A Case Study, *Environmental Law* 2015 (45), pp. 439–440.

95 *Kanuk ex rel. Kanuk v. State, Dept. of Natural Resources*, 335 P.3d 1088, 1091 (Alaska 2014).

96 *Id.*, at 1092–1093.

97 *Id.*, at 1091.

98 *Id.*, at 1092–1093.

99 *Id.*, at 1093.

100 *Id.*

that denying injured persons standing on grounds that others are also injured would effectively prevent judicial redress for the most widespread injury solely because it is widespread, which would perverse the public policy.[101] The court also agreed with the plaintiffs that according to this line of reasoning, no lawsuit could ever be filed concerning any matter of public interest, thus most environmental litigation would be prohibited.[102] This case, though, was decided by a state court; however a fairly identical position on plaintiffs' standing was reached in two other similar public trust climate cases by another state court and federal court respectively.[103]

3. STANDING IN AUSTRALIA

In a general sense, climate change litigation in Australia followed a pattern fairly similar to its US counterpart, focussing on challenges to administrative decisions or conduct related to approval of developing coal-fired power plants, coal mines, etc.[104] At the same time, in Australia, the procedural barriers related to standing have been less of a hurdle due to open standing provisions in most environmental and planning laws.[105] In such cases, the emphasis is usually made on the injury to the environment itself, rather than injury to any particular plaintiff.[106] Of course, the focus on environmental injury may still be a problem in case of climate change. Thus, for example, in an early case *Wildlife Whitsunday*, where environmental conservation groups challenged the administrative decisions concerning the development of two new coal mines, contending that the resulting GHG emissions would contribute to global warming and thus cause harm to important and vulnerable ecosystems, including the Great Barrier Reef World Heritage Area, the Federal Court of Australia refused to acknowledge the contested projects' detrimental effect to the environment and dismissed the case.[107] Specifically, the court stated that the connection between the burning of coal at some particular place in the world, the resulting GHG emissions, their contribution to global warming and the latter's impact on the environment, was far from obvious.[108]

---

101 *Id.*, at 1094.

102 *Id.*

103 See *Funk v. Wolf*, 144 A.3d 228 (Pa. Cmwlth. 2016); *Juliana v. United States*, 217 F.Supp.3d, 1224 (D. Or. 2016).

104 See *B.J. Preston*, The Influence of Climate Change Litigation on Governments and the Private Sector, *Climate Law* 2011(2), p. 486.

105 *Peel & Osofsky*, *supra*, note 5 at p. 275.

106 *E.D. Kassman*, How Local Courts Address Global Problems: The Case Of Climate Change, *Duke Journal of Comparative & International Law* 2013 (24), p. 215.

107 *Wildlife Preservation Society of Queensland Proserpine/Whitsunday Branch Inc v. Minister for the Environment & Heritage & Ors* [2006] FCA 736.

108 *Id.*, para. 72.

Meantime, in those cases where the question of standing did emerge, Australian courts followed the common law 'special interest' test, which requires more than intellectual or emotional concern of individuals in the protection of the environment, yet holds that formal representation in a consultative process, government's recognition and/or funding, or a nexus with protection of a particular segment of the environment may be sufficient to establish organisational standing.[109] In *Haughton v. Minister for Department of Planning and Ors*, for instance, the Land and Environment Court of New South Wales upheld the standing of an individual, who challenged the Minister's for Planning approvals for two new coal-fired power stations, claiming, *inter alia*, that the Minister failed to consider the principles of ecologically sustainable development and the impact of those projects on climate change as the elements of the public interest.[110] In support of his standing, the applicant presented numerous arguments, affirming his interest in the matter, including commitments to environmental activism and campaigns, active membership in an NGO focussing on combating climate change, which contributed to the related public engagement, as well as the fact that he himself lived in an area, susceptible to severe weather events that could be worsened due to climate change.[111] The court was persuaded by these arguments and held that 'there can be no doubt as to the significant interest and concern held by [the plaintiff] in the anthropogenic effects of climate change brought about by the combustion of fossil fuels, particularly in the use of coal as the source of energy for the production of electricity.'[112] The court also recognized that 'that interest and concern extends beyond that which may be held by many members of the public', as indicated by the plaintiff's environmental activities[113], even despite the fact that his concerns and views 'are not unique'.[114]

To a similar effect was the Victorian Civil and Administrative Tribunal's decision in case *Dual Gas*, where three environmental NGOs and an individual challenged a works approval for a new power station, which was supposed to introduce new power generation technology using brown coal and natural gas.[115] According to the project developers, the new plant was to produce power with a lower GHG emissions intensity than conventional coal-fired power plants, thus effectively becoming a 'part of the solution' to global climate change; however, the project's opponents argued that it actually was a 'part of the problem', as it still contributed to substantial GHG emissions in Victoria.[116] These were essentially the arguments of the private parties who opposed the project's approval in the

---

109 *Dual Gas Pty Ltd & Ors v Environment Protection Authority* [2012] VCAT 308, para. 116.
110 *Haughton v Minister for Planning and Macquarie Generation* [2011] 185 LGERA 373, para. 9.
111 *Id.*, para. 82.
112 *Id.*, para. 93.
113 *Id.*
114 *Id.*, para, 94.
115 *Dual Gas*, paras. 1–2.
116 *Id.*, paras. 3–5.

present case, by claiming that the project will result in a discharge of GHG emissions and other air pollutants, including sulphur dioxide, nitrogen oxides and particulates, that is inconsistent with the air quality management.[117]

The court delved into a quite thorough discussion on the matter of affected person's interests and, accordingly, standing under the relevant legislation. It concluded that the latter granted a more liberal test for standing in environmental matters than the 'special interest' test applied at common law; yet the court remained unconvinced that the relevant provisions gave open standing to any person, thus some kind of interest must still have been demonstrated.[118] This interest, in court's view, had to be demonstrated through a 'material connection with the subject matter of the decision under review' and might have emanated from 'a genuinely held and articulated intellectual or aesthetic concern [...], as opposed to a broader environmental concern generally.'[119] The difficulty, however, once again lay in determining the 'point beyond which the affectation of a person's interests by a decision should be regarded as too remote or too general to support standing', even where there is very wide, albeit not unlimited standing.[120] The court held that in such cases, certain principles may apply in order to overcome the above-mentioned difficulties, including 'the nature of the particular proposal for the works approval, the materiality or breadth of its potential environmental impact, and the involvement of the person in the works approval application process.'[121]

In the present case, the court deemed relevant that the potentially global impact of GHG emissions rendered wider standing appropriate, even in cases 'where a person may not have a direct connection to the location of the works approval', as opposed to situations where localised emissions of air pollutants was contested and where, accordingly a greater connection should be established.[122] However, even with regard to GHGs, the court considered important the materiality threshold in relation to 'the type or size of the works or emissions that is relevant to whether a person's interests are genuinely affected' as well as to 'the connection of the person to the particular subject matter of the decision under review'.[123] With regard to the two latter criteria, the court held that the significant contribution of GHG emissions in this specific case 'raises potential issues of material interest or concern to all Victorians, and creates an almost unique level of "affected interests" and standing compared to the more usual sort of works approval matters', while 'participation in the process or some genuine connection with the proposal may be a relevant factor in demonstrating more than a general

117 *Id.*, para. 8.
118 *Id.*, paras. 116–118.
119 *Id.*, para. 129.
120 *Id.*, para. 132.
121 *Id.*, para. 133.
122 *Id.*, para. 134.
123 *Id.*

environmental concern, and something that amounts to an affected interest.'[124] Applying these two principles to the parties objecting the project in the present case, the court, therefore, concluded that all four of them demonstrated genuine connection with GHG emissions and climate change; however, only three of them were able to provide evidence of their involvement in the present works approval process, thus satisfying the standing requirements.[125]

4. STANDING IN EUROPE: THE DUTCH URGENDA CASE

As already mentioned, climate change litigation has been largely a US and, to a lesser extent, Australian phenomenon; meanwhile, the bulk of climate-related European cases has traditionally revolved around the established EU emissions trading scheme (EU ETS) before the EU courts and under the provisions of the EU law.[126] Such cases have not been driven by NGOs, but almost exclusively by the EU Member States and European Commission, while cases brought by the industry have been commonly dismissed due to the restrictive approach to private party standing in the EU law.[127] At the same time, along with its Member States, the EU itself is a member of the Aarhus Convention[128], an international legal instrument, presenting a rights-oriented approach to environmental protection[129], and described as a key driver for environmental rights in Europe[130], with the public access to justice in environmental matters being one of the Convention's three pillars.[131] Although the provisions of the Convention have been applied in the EU law, the ambiguity surrounding the access to justice of private parties

124 *Id.*

125 *Id.*, para. 135–138.

126 See *Wilensky, supra*, note 5.

127 See *J. van Zeben*, Implementation Challenges for Emission Trading Schemes: The Role of Litigation, in S.E. Weishaar (ed.) Research Handbook on Emissions Trading, 2016, pp. 232–256. For an insight into public access to EU courts in environmental matters see *S. Marsden*, Direct Public Access to EU Courts: Upholding Public International Law via the Aarhus Convention Compliance Committee, Nordic Journal of International Law 2012(81), pp. 175–204.

128 Convention on Access to Information, Public Participation in Decision-Making and Access to Justice in Environmental Matters, adopted on 25 June 1998, entered into force on 30 October 2001. Available in English at www.unece.org/env/pp/treatytext.html. See also *J. Jendrośka*, Aarhus Convention and Community Law: the Interplay, Journal for European Environmental & Planning Law 2005(2), pp. 12–21.

129 See *M. Fitzmaurice*, Note on the Participation of Civil Society in Environmental Matters. Case Study: The 1998 Aarhus Convention on Access to Information, Public Participation in Decision-Making and Access to Justice in Environmental Matters, Human Rights & International Legal Discourse 2010(4), pp. 47–65.

130 *J. Jendrośka*, Citizen's Rights in European Environmental Law: Stock-Taking of Key Challenges and Current Developments in Relation to Public Access to Information, Participation and Access to Justice, Journal for European Environmental & Planning Law 2012(9), p. 73.

131 See Article 9 of the Convention.

in environmental matters at the EU level has persisted[132], never mind the fact that at the national level, standing of environmental NGOs is acknowledged everywhere in Europe.[133] Still, even though the Aarhus Convention has been invoked in several climate-related European cases, including the EU ETS case-law, so far it has been applied with regard to the access to information and public participation[134] and its potential application from the access to justice perspective in future climate cases remains to be seen.

This last part will thus focus only on one but very significant recent national case *Urgenda v. the Netherlands.*[135] The case concerned the Dutch NGO Urgenda request to have the Hague District Court order the government to take more action to mitigate climate change, principally by reducing the GHG emissions in the Netherlands by at least 25%, compared to 1990, by the end of 2020.[136] The case was based on a complex synthesis of Dutch constitutional and civil law, international climate and human rights law, EU law and the scientific data provided by the IPCC, and attracted enormous attention of legal scholars.[137]

---

132 See, for example, *C. Poncelet*, Access to Justice in Environmental Matters – Does the European Union Comply with its Obligations?, Journal of Environmental Law 2012(24), pp. 287–309; *H. Schoukens*, Articles 9(3) and 9(4) of the Aarhus Convention and Access to Justice before EU Courts in Environmental Cases: Balancing On or Over the Edge of Non-Compliance?, European Energy and Environmental Law Review 2016(25), pp. 178–195.

133 *S. Benvenuti*, Access to Justice in Environmental Matters. Which Role for the European Networks of Judges?, Journal for European Environmental & Planning Law 2014(11), p. 172.

134 See, for example, *Greenpeace Ltd v Secretary of State for Trade and Industry* (Queen's Bench Division, Administrative Court, 2007, EWHC 311 (Admin)) (concerning a challenge to the decision with respect to public consultations on the UK Government's energy policy); *Environment-People-Law v Ministry of Environmental Protection of Ukraine* (Lviv Administrative Court of Appeal, 2010, available at http://epl.org.ua/en/law-posts/violation-of-the-legislation-on-the-right-to-information-and-public-participation-in-climate-change-issues-by-the-ministry-of-environmental-protection-in-ukraine/) (concerning a request for information on the development of climate change policy in Ukraine); Case C-524/09 *Ville de Lyon v Caisse des dépôts et consignations* [2010] ECR I-14115 (concerning a request for information on the GHG emission allowances sold in France); Case 204/09 *Flachglas Torgau GmbH v Bundesrepublik Deutschland* [2012] ECLI:EU:C:2012:71 (concerning a request for access to information relating to the Law on the national allocation plan for GHG emission licences in Germany).

135 *Urgenda Foundation v. The State of the Netherlands*, C/09/456689 / HA ZA 13–1396 (2015) (Hague District Court, the Netherlands) (available in English at www.urgenda.nl/documents/VerdictDistrictCourt-UrgendavStaat-24.06.2015.pdf) (last visited 29 December 2016).

136 *Id.*, para. 3.1.

137 These are just some publications in English: *J. Lin*, The First Successful Climate Negligence Case: A Comment on Urgenda Foundation v. The State of the Netherlands (Ministry of Infrastructure and the Environment), Climate Law 2015(5), pp. 65–81; *K.J. de Graaf & J.H. Jans*, The Urgenda Decision: Netherlands Liable for Role in Causing Dangerous Global Climate Change, Journal of Environmental Law 2015(27), pp. 517–527; *L. Bergkamp & J.C. Hanekamp*, Climate Change Litigation against States: The Perils of Court-made Climate Policies, European Energy and Environmental Law Review 2015(24), pp. 102–114; *J. van Zeben*, Establishing a Governmental Duty of Care for Climate Change Mitigation: Will Urgenda Turn the Tide?, Transnational Environmental Law 2015(4), pp. 339–357; *A.S. Tabau & C. Cournil*, New Perspectives for Climate Justice: District Court of The Hague, 24 June 2015, Urgenda

With regard to its nature, the Urgenda case stands closest to the US common law public trust cases, but with one important exception: in it, the plaintiff NGO claimed that it represented the interests of not only Dutch citizens but also foreigners and future generations.[138] The defendant – the state of the Netherlands – accepting Urgenda's standing with regard to its representation of Dutch citizens, challenged the international and intergenerational dimensions of Urgenda's claim.[139] Furthermore, the state defendant contended that it could not be held liable for climate change, since its emissions formed but a tiny fraction of the global totals and many other parties contribute to climate change with their emissions.[140] As might be easily perceived, this argument was used in some of the cases discussed above; however, in case of Urgenda, it was used not to challenge the plaintiff's standing, but on the merits. And although analysing the latter is not within the scope of this chapter, it is worth noting that the court dismissed such arguments on the grounds of shared global responsibility for climate change and issued the requested order.[141]

In assessing Urgenda's standing to represent the interests of foreign citizens, the court referred to the Dutch Civil Code, according to which individuals or legal persons are only entitled to bring an action to the civil court if they have a sufficient personal interest in the claim.[142] With regard to NGOs, the Civil Code stipulates that 'a foundation or association with full legal capacity may also bring an action to the court pertaining to the protection of general interests or the collective interests of other persons, in so far as the foundation or association represents these general or collective interests based on the objectives formulated in its by-laws'.[143] At the same time, legal persons can only bring their action to the court if they have made sufficient prior efforts to enter into a dialogue with the defending party to achieve the requirements set forward.[144]

The court noted that Urgenda's claims against the state belonged to the group of claims that national legislature foresaw and wanted to make possible, by setting

Foundation versus the Netherlands, Journal for European Environmental & Planning Law 2015(12), pp. 221–240; *J. Lambrecht & C. Ituarte-Lima*, Legal Innovation in National Courts for Planetary Challenges: Urgenda v State of the Netherlands, Environmental Law Review 2016(18), pp. 57–64; *M. Peeters*, Urgenda Foundation and 886 Individuals v. The State of the Netherlands: The Dilemma of More Ambitious Greenhouse Gas Reduction Action by EU Member States, Review of European, Comparative & International Environmental Law 2016(25), pp. 123–129; *S. Roy & E. Woerdman*, Situating Urgenda v the Netherlands within Comparative Climate Change Litigation, Journal of Energy & Natural Resources Law 2016(34), pp. 165–189.

138 *Urgenda*, para. 4.5.

139 *Id.*

140 *Id.*, para. 4.78.

141 *Id.*, paras. 4.79 and 5.1.

142 *Id.*, para. 4.4.

143 *Id.*

144 *Id.* The court acknowledged that Urgenda has met this requirement, making sufficient efforts to attain its claim by entering into consultations with the state.

out that an environmental organisation's environmental protection claims without an identifiable group of persons needing protection, were allowable.[145] The court further stressed that Urgenda's by-laws stipulated that it strived for a more sustainable society, 'beginning in the Netherlands'.[146] It should be observed, that with regard to the term 'sustainable society', Urgenda specifically referred to the definition of 'sustainable development' in the 1987 report of the World Commission on Environment and Development of the United Nations (the Brundtland Report), which provided the following definition: 'Sustainable development is development that meets the needs of the present without compromising the ability of future generations to meet their own needs.'[147]

The court agreed with the plaintiff that the formulation of Urgenda's by-laws demonstrated prioritisation, but not limitation, to Dutch territory – hence the interests that Urgenda wanted to defend concerned primarily, but not solely, the territory of the Netherlands.[148] In other words, the court recognized that the term 'sustainable society' had an inherent international (and global) dimension; therefore, by defending the interests of a 'sustainable society', Urgenda was actually protecting interests that crossed national borders.[149] Consequently, the court was persuaded that Urgenda could partially base its claims on the fact that emissions in the Netherlands also had consequences for persons outside the Dutch national borders, since Urgenda's claims were directed at such emissions. The court also agreed that the term 'sustainable society' has a clear intergenerational dimension, which was expressed in the above-mentioned definition of 'sustainability' in the Brundtland Report; therefore, in defending the right of not just the current but also the future generations to availability of natural resources and a safe and healthy living environment, Urgenda also strived for the interest of a sustainable society.[150]

5. CONCLUDING REMARKS

It may be quite difficult to draw any concrete parallels between the discussed climate cases, given the extremely uneven distribution of them among the above-mentioned jurisdictions and the different nature of the respective national legal systems as well as numerous other limitations. Nevertheless, the discussed case-law certainly enables us to have a broader picture of the relevant issues as they unwind on a macro level.

145 *Id.*, para. 4.6.
146 *Id.*, para. 4.7.
147 *Id.*, para. 2.3.
148 *Id.*, para. 4.7.
149 *Id.*
150 *Id.*, para. 4.8.

Thus, it is clear that in the US, private plaintiffs have faced the challenges to standing with mixed success, which seems to have depended strongly on the judiciary's approach to the scientific side of the problem. As a result, courts' views on standing may not necessarily be consistent and differ on a case-by-case basis. Private parties have often been granted standing in cases concerning climate change impact assessment; however, in many of such cases, the decisive role in establishing standing was played by the issue of local pollution and not global climate change. For the same reason plaintiffs have been denied standing in cases concerning the regulation of GHG emissions, as courts were unwilling to accept the fact that local emission sources or air quality standards had any palpable impact on climate change. At the same time, this does not seem to extend to the emerging atmospheric trust litigation, where, on the contrary, the contested emissions are state- or nation-wide and where plaintiffs rely on common law and constitutional provisions.

From a transnational perspective, it may be observed that in case of NGOs the most important issue is the active involvement of the organisation in the related action; however, the scope of the latter varies between jurisdictions, from representation of its affected members' interests, organisational legal background to governmental recognition and participation in specific projects.

In the end, it may be easy to argue that courts were never meant to be the proper arena for climate change in the first place. But then, if persons suffering injuries from climate change are denied access to justice simply because of the application of various legalistic mechanisms, the judiciary's ability to protect those interests from the most insidious and far-reaching challenges that humanity faces literally goes up in smoke. For this reason, standing in climate change litigation should not be used as a tool to simply discard cases raising 'inconvenient' global issues, which may someday, in a most devastating way, affect everyone on the planet.

www.ingramcontent.com/pod-product-compliance
Ingram Content Group UK Ltd.
Pitfield, Milton Keynes, MK11 3LW, UK
UKHW051918100926
8556IPUK00021B/1241

9 781780 686103